Thomas G. Wong

Introduction to Classical and Quantum Computing

ISBN: 979-8-9855931-0-5 (Paperback)
ISBN: 979-8-9855931-1-2 (Hardcover)

Library of Congress Control Number: 2022900358

Book design by Thomas Wong

www.thomaswong.net

Published by Rooted Grove, Omaha, Nebraska

www.rootedgrove.com

4 5 6 7 8 9 10

For my students.

Preface

Dear Reader,

This textbook for newcomers who are interested in quantum computing as a potential career, but who may not be ready for advanced books or courses. The only prerequisite for this book is trigonometry, also called pre-calculus. You are not expected to have taken advanced math beyond that, and you are not expected to have experience with programming. So, if you are an advanced high school student or a beginning university student, this textbook is for you.

That said, this book is not merely a conceptual overview of quantum computing. I will teach the math and programming skills that may be missing. Since you are interested in quantum computing as a potential career, I want to equip you with the skills you will need for more advanced topics.

If you are more advanced, and especially if you have already studied linear algebra, then you may find this textbook too elementary. For a more mathematically rigorous introduction to quantum information science, I refer you to *Quantum Computation and Quantum Information* by Michael Nielsen and Isaac Chuang, affectionately called "Mike and Ike," like the chewy, fruit candy with the same name. It is the standard advanced text, and for good reason.

I hope this textbook will help you realize that you can do it, that you can understand quantum computing. I hope it will inspire you to study quantum computing more deeply, and I hope that some of you might even choose quantum computing as a career. If so, I look forward to calling you colleagues and learning from your discoveries.

This textbook stemmed from an introductory special-topics course that I taught at Creighton University, and I thank each class of students for sharing the journey of developing and refining the course content. I must also thank those who have taught me quantum computing in both formal and informal roles. I could not have done it without you.

Tom Wong

Contents

Chapter 1
Classical Information and Computation

Computers have come a long way. The first computers were people, not machines, who performed calculations. Indeed, the term "computer" dates as far back as the early 1600's, centuries before the digital age. Human computers persisted into modern history, with NASA, for example employing people to compute launch trajectories for the space program and other scientific endeavors through the 1960's. Of course, mechanical and then electronic computers have since taken over, evolving from massive machines that filled entire rooms, to personal computers on our desktops, to smaller and smaller devices. Now, nearly everyone has a electronic computer in their pocket—a smartphone—that is more powerful than the computers that landed people on the moon. Computers have become so polished that we can use and even program them without understanding how they work at a fundamental level. That's not a bad thing. It has allowed computers to become tools for more and more people. My physics students can perform numerical computations and solve scientific problems without needing to understand bits and bytes.

One day, quantum computing will get to this point of accessibility, where we can use and program them without worrying about their details. But we are not quite there, yet. In their development, quantum computers are where classical computers were decades ago. Their inner working still matter, and to understand these inner workings, it is helpful to understand the inner workings of regular, classical computers. So, in this chapter, we will look at the basics of classical computing. If you have studied the fundamentals of classical computing or electrical engineering, this may be review for you. Even so, the topics may be worth seeing again because they have been carefully selected for their quantum analogues in later chapters.

Furthermore, quantum computing is not developing in isolation of classical computing. Many of the design decisions for quantum computers stem out of what is done with classical computers. Without knowing classical computing, some aspect of quantum computing may seem arbitrary. A rudimentary understanding classical computing makes it easier to understand quantum computing.

The following table lists many of the concepts we will be covering in this book.

Concept	Classical	Quantum
Fundamental Unit	Bit	Qubit
Gates	Logic Gates	Unitary Gates
Gates Reversible	Sometimes	Always
Universal Gate Set (Example)	{NAND}	$\{H, T, \text{CNOT}\}$
Programming Language (Example)	Verilog	OpenQASM
Algebra	Boolean	Linear
Error Correcting Code (Example)	Repetition Code	Shor Code
Complexity Class	P	BQP
Strong Church-Turing Thesis	Supports	Possibly Violates

In this chapter, we will cover the "Classical" column, beginning with bits. Then, we will perform computation on these bits using logic gates and include discussions about universal and reversible logic gates. The math of classical computing is boolean algebra, and we can program classical circuits using hardware description languages. We will then look at classes of problems that are easy or hard for computers, and we will end this chapter with the prospect that quantum computers may be significantly faster than classical computers at some tasks. In the rest of the book, we will cover the quantum computing column of the table.

1.1 Bits

The term *bits* has become fairly commonplace, where many people will state that bits are zeros and ones. Whether you already knew that does not matter. The point is, have we taken a moment to consider what bits really are? Are they just numbers? Why are they important for computers? Let us begin our journey by exploring bits deeply.

1.1.1 Coins

Consider a coin, such as the United States one-cent penny from 2016, which features former President Abraham Lincoln as "heads" and the Union shield as "tails."

Assuming that coins do not balance on their edges, a single coin lying on a flat surface either has heads facing up or tails facing up. Let us call these two possible conditions, or *states*, heads (H) and tails (T).

If we have two coins, there are four possible states: Both coins can be heads (HH), the first can be heads and the second can be tails (HT), the first can be tails and the second can be heads (TH), or both can be tails (TT). That is, the possible states are:

HH, HT, TH, TT.

Since the first coin has two possible states (heads or tails), and the second coin has two possible states (heads or tails), there are $2 \times 2 = 2^2 = 4$ possible states for the two coins.

Adding a third coin, there are now eight possible states. They could all be heads, some mixture of heads and tails, or all tails. Listing all the permutations, the possible states are now

HHH, HHT, HTH, HTT, THH, THT, TTH, TTT.

Since each of the three coins has two possible states, there are $2 \times 2 \times 2 = 2^3 = 8$ possible states for three coins.

Generalizing this, if we have n coins, the possible states range from all heads, through a mixture of heads and tails, to all tails:

H ... HH, H ... HT, ..., T ... TT.

With n coins, there are 2^n possible states.

Exercise 1.1. How many possible states do (a) four coins have? (b) five coins? You do not need to list the states, just how many there are.

1.1.2 Dice

In contrast, consider a standard six-sided die.

It has six possible outcomes, the numbers 1 through 6. So, the possible states of a die are

$1, 2, 3, 4, 5, 6.$

Next, say we have two dice. Each die can take the values 1 through 6, so both could be 1, the first could be 1 and the second could be 2, and so forth. If the first die is 3 and the second is 5, let us write the configuration as $(3, 5)$. Then, listing all of these, the possible states of two dice are

$$(1,1),(1,2),(1,3),(1,4),(1,5),(1,6),$$
$$(2,1),(2,2),(2,3),(2,4),(2,5),(2,6),$$
$$(3,1),(3,2),(3,3),(3,4),(3,5),(3,6),$$
$$(4,1),(4,2),(4,3),(4,4),(4,5),(4,6),$$
$$(5,1),(5,2),(5,3),(5,4),(5,5),(5,6),$$
$$(6,1),(6,2),(6,3),(6,4),(6,5),(6,6).$$

Since each die has six possible states, there are $6 \times 6 = 6^2 = 36$ possible states for the two dice.

Following the pattern, with three dice, there are $6^3 = 216$ possible states. Listing these would take too much space. Generalizing, with n dice, there are 6^n possible states.

Exercise 1.2. How many possible states do (a) four dice have? (b) five dice? You do not need to list the states, just how many there are. A calculator may be useful.

1.1.3 Encoding Information

Now, how much *information* can coins and dice carry? Say I am trying to communicate the colors of the rainbow, which in the United States are typically listed as red, orange, yellow, green, blue, indigo, and violet.[1] These seven colors can be represented, or *encoded*, by the possible configurations of three coins or two dice:

Color	Coins	Dice
Red	HHH	(1,1)
Orange	HHT	(1,2)
Yellow	HTH	(1,3)
Green	HTT	(1,4)
Blue	THH	(1,5)
Indigo	THT	(1,6)
Violet	TTH	(2,1)

So, if I give you three coins, first heads then tails and then tails again, you can *decode* it and determine the color green. Alternatively, I can give you two dice, the first 1 and the second 4, to indicate the color green. In this example, the rest of the configurations (TTT for the coin, and (2,2) through (6,6) for the dice) are unused and do not mean anything, or they can be assigned to the same colors so that multiple states can encode green, for example.

We see that a coin carries less information than a die; it takes three coins to distinguish the seven colors of the rainbow, compared to two dice. This is because a

---

[1] In American elementary schools, many students memorize this by taking the first letter of each color and combining them into the acronym ROY G. BIV.

coin can only distinguish between two states (heads and tails), while a die is able to distinguish between six states (1 through 6). Since two states is the fewest number of states that can be distinguished, a coin carries the smallest amount of information possible. This leads us the following idea:

> Something with two states carries the
> smallest amount of information possible.

Exercise 1.3. Some board games use a twenty-sided die. How many twenty-sided dice does it take to encode the seven colors of the rainbow?

Exercise 1.4. How many (a) coins and (b) six-sided dice would it take to represent the 26 letters of the English alphabet? Ignore upper and lowercase, spaces, punctuation, etc., so there's only 26 letters total.

1.1.4 Physical Bits

Many physical systems only have two states. We already discussed coins, which can be heads or tails. Another example is a light switch, which can be "off" or "on." As another example, information is stored on optical discs (e.g., CDs, DVDs, and Blu-ray discs) using a laser that burns holes into the disc, called "pits." For example, one of my students took a zoomed-in picture of a DVD using an atomic force microscope, shown below:

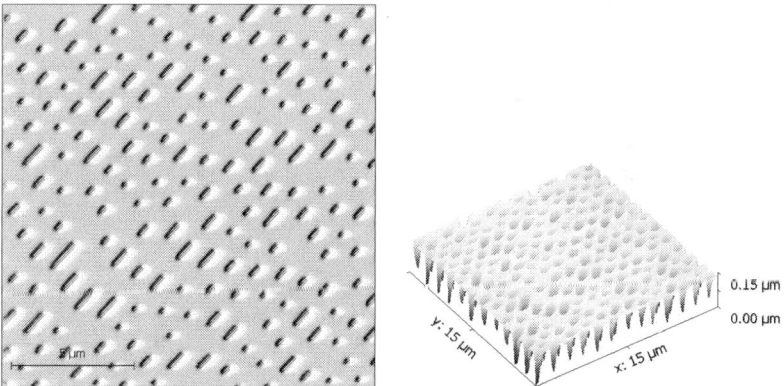

Image credit: Jeffrey Y. Wong, Creighton University, taken August 24, 2018

The picture shows microscopic holes and trenches burned into the disc, i.e., the pits. Where there is no hole is called a "land." So, the two states are whether there is a pit or a land, and to read the disc, a laser shines on the disc and detects whether there is a pit or a land.

Physical systems with more than two possible states can be treated as only having two if we simply ignore the rest of the possible states. For example, if I have an electronic circuit, then many different voltage levels are possible.[2] In conventional computers, however, we typically only use two values, 0 volts and 5 volts, so we effectively only have two states.

All of these examples have, or effectively have, just two states, called by different names: heads/tails, off/on, pits/lands, and 0 V / 5 V. Rather than using so many different names, it is often easier to use generic names for the two states so that we can describe the state without regard for the underlying physical system. Mathematically, it is convenient to use the binary digits 0 and 1. This is summarized in the table below

Physical System	States	
Coin	Heads	Tails
Switch	Off	On
Disc	Pit	Land
Voltage	0 V	5 V
Binary Digit	0	1

With this convention, regardless of the physical system, we can just refer to the two possible states as 0 and 1, the binary digits.

Since binary digits are used so much in computing, an abbreviation for *b*inary di*git* was invented: the *bit*. So, a bit is just a binary digit, which can be 0 or 1, which represent the states of any physical system with two states. Since systems with two states carry the smallest amount of information possible, a bit carries the smallest amount of information possible:

A bit is the smallest unit of classical information.

1.1.5 Binary

Previously, when we had three coins, we wrote the eight possible states as

HHH, HHT, HTH, HTT, THH, THT, TTH, TTT.

Now, replacing heads and tails with the bits 0 and 1, the eight possible states are now written as

000, 001, 010, 011, 100, 101, 110, 111.

In other words, we can write the state in terms of numbers, and numbers are useful because we can use math to describe and manipulate them.

---

[2] Voltage is the amount of electrical pressure pushing charges in the circuit, but you do not need to know this.

What kind of numbers are these states? They are *binary numbers*, or *base 2 numbers*. These are also called *binary strings* or *bit strings*. For example, if we have five bits, one possible state is

$$11010 \quad \text{or} \quad 11010_2,$$

where the subscript of 2 can be included to clarify that it is a binary (base-2) number. We pronounce this as "one one zero one zero," and optionally say "base 2" afterward. It is *not* pronounced "eleven-thousand ten" because it is not a regular, decimal (base-10) number. Actually, what decimal number does it correspond to?

To figure this out, let us first remind ourselves how normal decimal numbers work. Consider the number "six-thousand one-hundred seventy-four" (6174). It has a six in the thousands place, literally meaning there are six thousands, a one in the hundreds place, meaning one hundred, a seven in the tens place, meaning seven tens, and a four in the ones place, meaning four ones. That is,

$$\begin{aligned} 6174 &= 6 \cdot 1000 + 1 \cdot 100 + 7 \cdot 10 + 4 \cdot 1 \\ &= 6 \cdot 10^3 + 1 \cdot 10^2 + 7 \cdot 10^1 + 4 \cdot 10^0. \end{aligned}$$

So, each digit represents how many of each power of 10 we have.

For binary numbers, each digit similarly denotes how many of each power of 2 we have. Back to our question from a couple paragraphs ago, we can find what decimal number that 11010_2 corresponds to:

$$\begin{aligned} 11010_2 &= 1 \cdot 2^4 + 1 \cdot 2^3 + 0 \cdot 2^2 + 1 \cdot 2^1 + 0 \cdot 2^0 \\ &= 1 \cdot 16 + 1 \cdot 8 + 0 \cdot 4 + 1 \cdot 2 + 0 \cdot 1 \\ &= 26. \end{aligned}$$

So, we have one in the sixteens place, one in the eights place, zero in the fours place, one in the twos place, and zero in the ones place, and the binary number 11010 corresponds to the decimal number 26 twenty-six.

In the example 11010_2, the leftmost bit contributes 16 to the number, the most of any bit. For this reason, the leftmost bit is called the *most significant bit*. Similarly, the rightmost bit can only contribute 1 to the number, and for this reason, the rightmost bit is called the *least significant bit*.

We can also count in binary. To understand how, let us think about how we normally count from zero to one-hundred. For clarity, we write the leading zeros. To begin, the rightmost digit increments from 0 to 9:

$$000, 001, 002, 003, 004, 005, 006, 007, 008, 009, \ldots$$

The rightmost digit has reached its maximum value, so for the next number, it rolls over from 9 to 0, and the middle digit increments by 1, yielding 010. Continuing,

$$010, 011, 012, 013, 014, 015, 016, 017, 018, 019, \ldots$$

Again, the rightmost digit has reached its maximum value, so for the next number, it rolls over from 9 to 0, and the middle digit increments by 1, yielding 020. Continuing,

$$020,021,022,023,\ldots,098,099,\ldots$$

The rightmost digit has again reached its maximum value, so for the next number, it rolls over from 9 to 0, and the middle digit needs to increment by 1. But it has also reached its maximum value, so it also rolls over from 9 to 0, and the left digit is incremented, yielding 100.

We can apply the same procedure to count in binary. Say we have a bit string of length 3. It starts with 000, and we increment the rightmost digit, yielding 001. Incrementing again, the rightmost bit has reached its maximum value (since a bit can only be 0 or 1), so it rolls over from 1 to 0, and the middle bit is incremented, yielding 010. Incrementing again, we have 011. Incrementing again, the rightmost bit rolls over from 1 to 0, the middle bit also rolls over from 1 to 0, and the leftmost bit increments from 0 to 1, yielding 100. Continuing this procedure, we can count from 000 to 111, which is counting in decimal from 0 to 7:

Binary (Base 2)	Decimal (Base 10)
000	0
001	1
010	2
011	3
100	4
101	5
110	6
111	7

Exercise 1.5. Convert the following binary numbers (base 2) to decimal numbers (base 10):
(a) 10111_2.
(b) 11001010_2.

Exercise 1.6. Convert the following decimal numbers (base 10) to binary numbers (base 2):
(a) 42.
(b) 495.

Exercise 1.7. Base-16, commonly called *hexadecimal*, is another frequently used number system in computing. The sixteen digits are 0, 1, 2, 3, 4, 5, 6, 7, 8, 9, A, B, C, D, E, F. So the letter A is ten in decimal, B is eleven in decimal, ..., and F is fifteen in decimal. For example, converting the hexadecimal number F2A to decimal,

$$F2A = 16^2 \cdot F + 16^1 \cdot 2 + 16^0 \cdot A$$
$$= 256 \cdot 15 + 16 \cdot 2 + 1 \cdot 10$$
$$= 3840 + 32 + 10$$
$$= 3882.$$

(a) Convert the hexadecimal number 3B7C to a decimal (base 10) number.

(b) Convert the hexadecimal number FF to a binary (base 2) number. (So two hexadecimal numbers can represent eight bits.)

(c) HTML uses hexadecimal to encode colors using the *RGB color model*. RGB stands for the (additive) primary colors red, green, and blue, and by adding together different amounts of their light, the other colors can be produced. [From painting, you may be familiar with the (subtractive) primary colors, red, yellow, and blue.] The amount of red, green, and blue ranges from 0 to 255, with 0 being none of the color, and 255 being the full amount of the color. This range of 0 to 255 corresponds to the hexadecimal numbers 00 through FF. An HTML color code uses six hexadecimal numbers, like FA10E4, with the left two digits (FA) corresponding to the amount of red, the middle two digits (10) corresponding to the amount of green, and the right two digits (E4) corresponding to the amount of blue. This particular mix of colors results in a bright pink. Convert the hexadecimal numbers FA, 10, and E4 to decimal.

Exercise 1.8. Negative numbers can be encoded in binary using *two's complement*, where the most significant bit is negative, while the remaining bits are positive. For example, in two's complement,

$$11010_2 = 1 \cdot (-2^4) + 1 \cdot 2^3 + 0 \cdot 2^2 + 1 \cdot 2^1 + 0 \cdot 2^0$$
$$= 1 \cdot (-16) + 1 \cdot 8 + 0 \cdot 4 + 1 \cdot 2 + 0 \cdot 1$$
$$= -6.$$

Convert each of the following two's complement numbers to decimal:

Binary (Two's Complement)	Decimal (Base 10)
000	?
001	?
010	?
011	?
100	?
101	?
110	?
111	?

1.1.6 ASCII

Computers store information using bits (0's and 1's), but in our world, we often store information and communicate using text (letters, punctuation, etc.). How do we bridge this divide? How do we encode text using bits?

Historically, computers encoded letters, numbers, symbols, and special commands (like carriage return or newline) using the American Standard Code for Information Interchange, commonly abbreviated as ASCII (pronounced ass-key). ASCII uses 7 bits, so they have $2^7 = 128$ possible states from 0000000 through 1111111. Of these, ninety-five of the bit strings encode printable characters, and they are shown in Table 1.1. The remaining thirty-three bit strings encode non-printable characters, like the "escape" key.

For example, the following binary string encodes the text "Tom."

Table 1.1: Printable ASCII characters (glyphs) and their binary and decimal encodings.

Binary	Decimal	Glyph	Binary	Decimal	Glyph	Binary	Decimal	Glyph
0100000	32	space	1000000	64	@	1100000	96	`
0100001	33	!	1000001	65	A	1100001	97	a
0100010	34	"	1000010	66	B	1100010	98	b
0100011	35	#	1000011	67	C	1100011	99	c
0100100	36	$	1000100	68	D	1100100	100	d
0100101	37	%	1000101	69	E	1100101	101	e
0100110	38	&	1000110	70	F	1100110	102	f
0100111	39	'	1000111	71	G	1100111	103	g
0101000	40	(	1001000	72	H	1101000	104	h
0101001	41	)	1001001	73	I	1101001	105	i
0101010	42	*	1001010	74	J	1101010	106	j
0101011	43	+	1001011	75	K	1101011	107	k
0101100	44	,	1001100	76	L	1101100	108	l
0101101	45	-	1001101	77	M	1101101	109	m
0101110	46	.	1001110	78	N	1101110	110	n
0101111	47	/	1001111	79	O	1101111	111	o
0110000	48	0	1010000	80	P	1110000	112	p
0110001	49	1	1010001	81	Q	1110001	113	q
0110010	50	2	1010010	82	R	1110010	114	r
0110011	51	3	1010011	83	S	1110011	115	s
0110100	52	4	1010100	84	T	1110100	116	t
0110101	53	5	1010101	85	U	1110101	117	u
0110110	54	6	1010110	86	V	1110110	118	v
0110111	55	7	1010111	87	W	1110111	119	w
0111000	56	8	1011000	88	X	1111000	120	x
0111001	57	9	1011001	89	Y	1111001	121	y
0111010	58	:	1011010	90	Z	1111010	122	z
0111011	59	;	1011011	91	[	1111011	123	{
0111100	50	<	1011100	92	\	1111100	124		
0111101	61	=	1011101	93	]	1111101	125	}
0111110	62	>	1011110	94	^	1111110	126	~
0111111	63	?	1011111	95	_			

$$\underbrace{1010100}_{T}\underbrace{1101111}_{o}\underbrace{1101101}_{m} = \text{Tom}$$

So, if I want to send you my name, I can just send you these twenty-one bits. Once you have the bits, you decode it into the text "Tom."

In modern times, there are many more characters to encode. There are other languages with different alphabets or characters, plus emojis and other symbols. So, more than 7 bits are needed to encode all of them. The most common modern standard is UTF-8, or the Unicode Transformation Format, and it uses up to 32 bits (for $2^{32} = 4\,294\,967\,296$ states). The first 128 bit strings in UTF-8 are the ASCII characters.

Exercise 1.9. Write your first name as an ASCII bit string.

Exercise 1.10. Decode the following ASCII characters:

1010001 1110101 1100001 1101110 1110100 1110101 1101101

1.2 Logic Gates

In the previous section, we introduced bits, the fundamental unit of classical information. We can encode whatever information we would like using bits, such as words, characters, and even pictures. In this section, we explore how to manipulate bits so that we can compute using them.

We manipulate bits using *logic gates*, which take one or more bits as inputs and, depending on the input, outputs one or more bits. Let us explore the simplest examples of logic gates next, which manipulate a single bit. Then, we will learn about logic gates that act on two bits. Following this, we will discuss what logic gates are physically and explain how they can perform all computations.

1.2.1 Single-Bit Gates

The simplest logic gates take one bit as input and then outputs one bit, which we can draw as a *circuit diagram*:

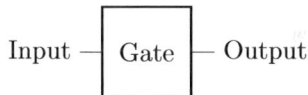

Input — | Gate | — Output

This circuit is read left to right. The input bit on the left travels along the line or *wire* into the gate, which we have drawn as a generic box. A bit comes out of the gate on the right, traveling along the line, and it is the output.

Since the input is a single bit, it can only be a zero or a one. We can list these two possibilities in a table called a *truth table*:

Input	Output
0	?
1	?

Depending on which gate we have, the outputs will be different, so we have used question marks as placeholders for now. How many possible outputs are there? Well, there are two outputs, and each output can be 0 or 1, so there are $2 \times 2 = 4$ possible outputs. Hence, there are four possible single-bit gates, which we describe now.

- The *identity gate* does nothing to the bit: 0 remains 0, and 1 remains 1. The identity gate is sometimes depicted by a triangle:

$$A \quad \triangleright \quad A \qquad \begin{array}{c|c} A & A \\ \hline 0 & 0 \\ 1 & 1 \end{array}$$

In our circuit diagram, we have labeled the input bit as A. Since it goes through the identity gate (the triangle) unchanged, the output on the other side is also A. Or as a wire, A comes in, nothing happens, and A comes out. Above, we also filled in the truth table so that the input and output are both simply A. The first row of the truth table indicates that if the input is 0, the output is 0. The second row indicates that if the input is 1, the output is 1.

Since the identity gate does nothing, we often omit the triangle and just draw a longer wire:

$$A \text{ ——— } A$$

Again, this is read left-to-right, so the input bit A moves through the wire and comes out the other side as the output, unchanged.

The identity gate is sometimes called the *buffer gate*.

- The *NOT gate* flips a bit from 0 to 1, or 1 to 0. Its circuit diagram is a triangle with a small circle:

$$A \quad \triangleright\!\circ \quad \overline{A} \qquad \begin{array}{c|c} A & \overline{A} \\ \hline 0 & 1 \\ 1 & 0 \end{array}$$

The input bit A goes through the NOT gate from the left, and the resulting output is $\overline{A}$, where the overline denotes negation (i.e., the flipped or opposite bit). The behavior of this circuit is completely described by the above truth table, and it shows that when 0 is the input, 1 is the output, and vice versa.

In many texts, $\overline{A}$ is also denoted $\neg A$, where $\neg$ means negation. The NOT gate is sometimes called the *inverter gate*.

- The *always 0 gate* always outputs 0, regardless of the input. It does not have a standard circuit diagram since it is not commonly used, but its truth table is

$$\begin{array}{c|c} A & 0 \\ \hline 0 & 0 \\ 1 & 0 \end{array}$$

The first line of the truth table indicates that when the input is 0, the output is 0. The second line indicates that when the input is 1, the output is 0.

- The *always 1 gate* always outputs 1, regardless of the input. It does not have a standard circuit diagram since it is not commonly used, but its truth table is

$$\begin{array}{c|c} A & 1 \\ \hline 0 & 1 \\ 1 & 1 \end{array}$$

The first line of the truth table indicates that when the input is 0, the output is 1. The second line indicates that when the input is 1, the output is 1.

These are all four possible logic gates with a single input and a single output.

1.2.2 Two-Bit Gates

A two-bit logic gate takes two bits as input, say A and B. Although a two-bit logic gate can have multiple outputs, the simplest case just has one output. So, its circuit diagram and truth table would look like

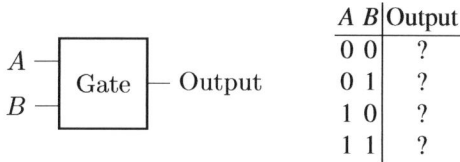

A B	Output
0 0	?
0 1	?
1 0	?
1 1	?

This truth table has four rows because there are four possible inputs: A and B can both be 0, A can be 0 and B can be 1, A can be 1 and B can be 0, or both can be 1. Note we listed these in numerical order, since 00, 01, 10, and 11 are the decimal numbers 0, 1, 2, and 3. Writing them in numerical order is the convention.

Depending on the gate, the outputs will be different, so they have question marks in the above truth table for now. Since each of the four outputs can be 0 or 1, there are $2^4 = 16$ possible two-bit gates. Next, we discuss five of the most important ones.

- The *AND gate* outputs 1 only when both input bits are 1. Its circuit diagram and truth table are

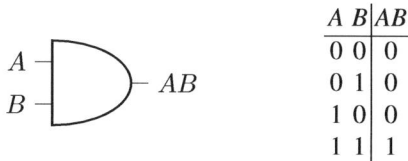

A B	AB
0 0	0
0 1	0
1 0	0
1 1	1

In this circuit diagram, two bits A and B go through the AND gate, resulting in AB. Note that standard multiplication works here: $0 \cdot 0 = 0$, $0 \cdot 1 = 0$, $1 \cdot 0 = 0$, and $1 \cdot 1 = 1$. In many texts, AB is also denoted $A \wedge B$. This is called the AND gate because it outputs 1 when A and B are 1. Or, in the language of logic, if we take 0 to be false and 1 to be true, then AB is true when A and B are both true.

- The *OR gate*, which outputs 1 if either input (or both) is 1. Its circuit diagram and truth table are

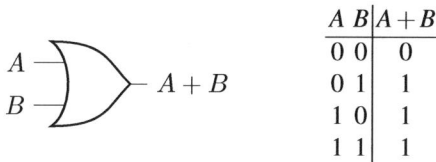

A B	A + B
0 0	0
0 1	1
1 0	1
1 1	1

Following many texts, we denote the OR of A and B as $A + B$, although this is not actually addition since $1 + 1 = 1$. In some texts, it is also denoted $A \vee B$.

- The *Exclusive OR (XOR) gate*, which outputs 1 when only one input is one, but not both. Its circuit diagram and truth table are

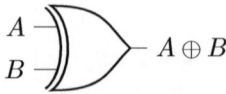

A B	$A \oplus B$
0 0	0
0 1	1
1 0	1
1 1	0

We write the XOR of A and B as $A \oplus B$, i.e., a plus sign with a circle around it. Mathematically, $\oplus$ is addition modulo 2, meaning we take the remainder after dividing by 2. You are probably familiar with modulo in other contexts, like a circle has $360°$, so $370°$ is equivalent to $10°$. Mathematically, we would write this as $370° = 10°$ mod $360°$, meaning when you divide $370°$ by $360°$, you get a remainder of $10°$. With $\oplus$ we take the remainder after dividing by 2, so we have

$$0 = 0 \text{ mod } 2,$$
$$1 = 1 \text{ mod } 2,$$
$$2 = 0 \text{ mod } 2,$$
$$3 = 1 \text{ mod } 2,$$
$$4 = 0 \text{ mod } 2,$$
$$5 = 1 \text{ mod } 2,$$
$$\vdots$$

Hence, the last line of the truth table for $A \oplus B$ is $1 \oplus 1 = 2$ mod $2 = 0$ mod 2.

• The *NAND gate*, which stands for NOT of AND, and which outputs the NOT of the AND of the bits. Its circuit diagram and truth table are

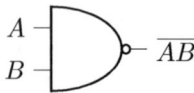

A B	$\overline{AB}$
0 0	1
0 1	1
1 0	1
1 1	0

Note the circuit diagram is a regular AND gate, with a small circle to indicate a NOT. We denote NAND by negating an AND, so it is written as $\overline{AB}$.

• The *NOR gate*, which stands for NOT of OR, and which outputs the NOT of the OR of the bits. Its circuit diagram and truth table are

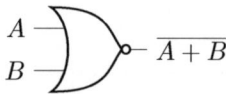

A B	$\overline{A+B}$
0 0	1
0 1	0
1 0	0
1 1	0

Note the circuit diagram is a regular OR gate, with a small circle to indicate a NOT. We denote NOR by negating an OR, so it is $\overline{A+B}$.

Exercise 1.11. Consider the following gate that inverts the inputs before passing them into an OR gate, sometimes called a *negative-OR gate*:

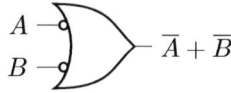

$$A \quad \overline{A} + \overline{B}$$

$$B$$

(a) Write the truth table for this circuit.
(b) What logic gate is this equivalent to?

Exercise 1.12. Consider the following gate that inverts the inputs before passing them into an AND gate, sometimes called a *negative-AND gate*:

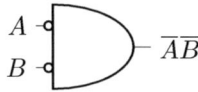

$$A \quad \overline{AB}$$

$$B$$

(a) Write the truth table for this circuit.
(b) What logic gate is this equivalent to?

1.2.3 Logic Gates as Physical Circuits

So far, we have discussed what logic gates *do*, but we have not discussed what logic gates *are*. Let us address that here. While there are many different ways to make logic gates, but the most common way is using electric circuits. I do not assume that you know circuits, so we will start slowly.

To begin, here is a drawing of a circuit that consists of a battery, two switches, a light bulb, and some wires to connect them:

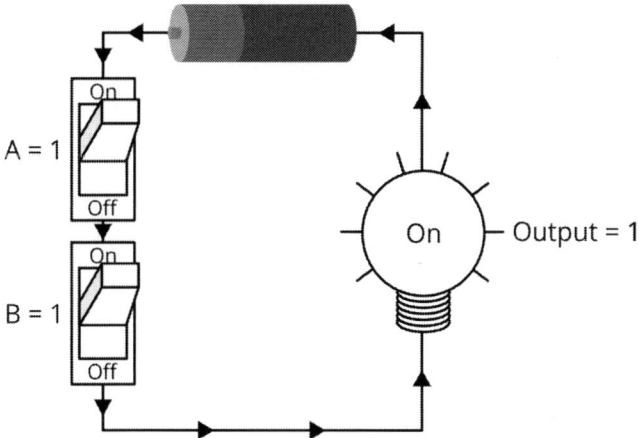

In the above drawing, the two switches correspond to inputs *A* and *B*. They are both in the "on" position, so both inputs are 1. In this case, electricity is able to flow through the circuit, coming out from the left side of the battery (the side of the

battery with the bump, or the *positive* side), down through the switches, right across
the bottom wire, up through the light bulb, and back into the right side of the battery
(the flat side of the battery, or the *negative* side). Electricity flows from the positive
side of the battery to the negative side, and this counter-clockwise flow is indicated
by arrows on the wires. Since electricity is flowing through the light bulb, it turns
on. The light bulb is the output, and so the output is 1 when both inputs A and B are
1.

Next, let us turn off only the first switch while keeping the second switch on, so
$A = 0$ and $B = 1$:

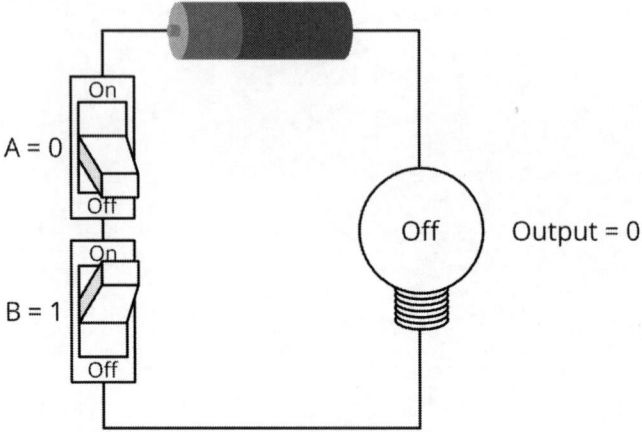

In the above drawing, the electricity is unable to flow in the circuit because the first
switch is turned off. This disconnects the connections, so the electricity does not
have a path to flow. It does not matter that switch B is still on. So, the light bulb is
off, and the output is 0.

Let us try the opposite. We turn on switch A and turn off switch B, so $A = 1$ and
$B = 0$:

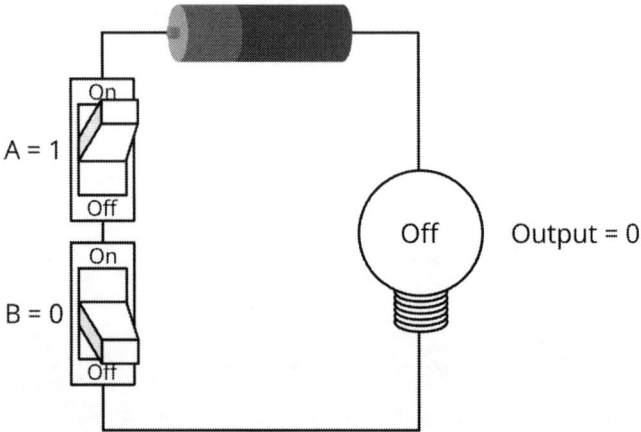

In the above drawing, electricity again is unable to flow. It does not matter that electricity can get through switch A, it cannot get through switch B. So, the light bulb is off, and the output is 0.

Finally, let us turn off both switches, so $A = 0$ and $B = 0$:

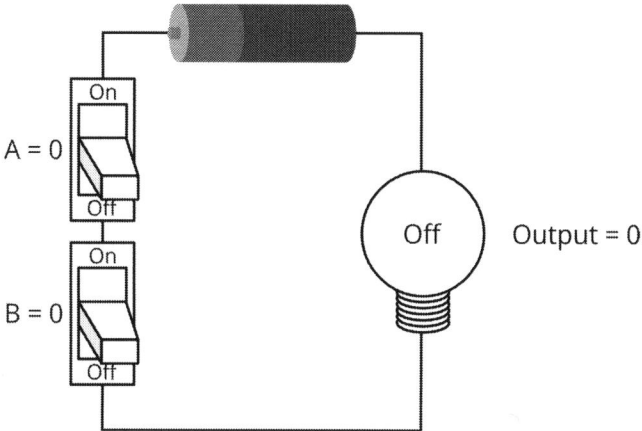

Reordering these results so that the inputs are in numerical order, the truth table for this circuit is

A B	Output
0 0	0
0 1	0
1 0	0
1 1	1

This is the truth table for the AND gate, so the circuit we have been examining is an AND gate. The light bulb only lights up with switch A and switch B are both on. This is an example of how to create a logic gate using an electrical circuit.

Let us look at another circuit, this time consisting of one switch (input) and one light bulb (output):

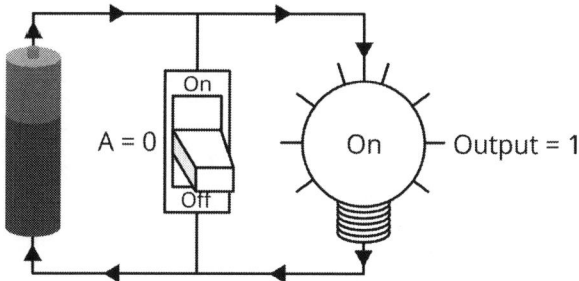

In the above picture, current flows out from the top of the battery (the positive side, which has a bump). It cannot pass through the switch because the switch is off, so it travels through the light bulb and returns into the bottom of the battery. So, when $A = 0$, the output is 1.

Now, let us flip on the switch:

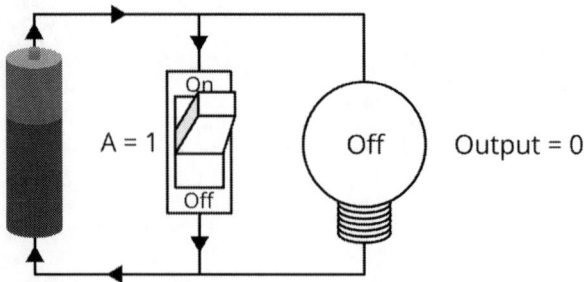

Current again flows out from the top of the battery. Since the switch is on, the current can flow through either the switch or the light bulb. It turns out that given this option, electricity will simply flow through the switch only and not the light bulb. This is because it takes practically no effort to flow through the switch, but it takes considerable effort to flow through the light bulb. Since no electricity is flowing through the light bulb, it remains off. Thus, when $A = 1$, the output is 0.

Summarizing these results in a truth table,

A	Output
0	1
1	0

This is the truth table for a NOT gate, so the circuit in this example is a NOT gate.

Similarly, we can create simple electrical circuits that implement each of the other logic gates.

Exercise 1.13. Consider the following electrical circuit:

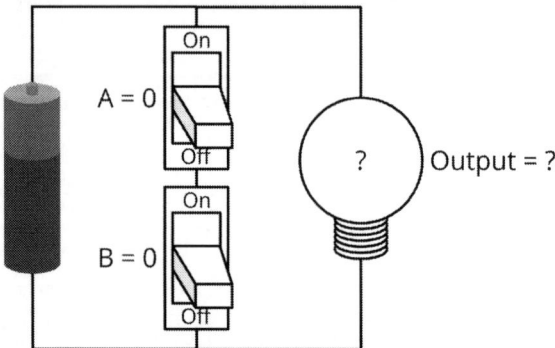

Answer the following questions.

(a) Say $A = 0$ and $B = 0$. Sketch the circuit and draw arrows indicating the path through which the electricity is flowing. Is the light bulb off or on?

(b) Say $A = 0$ and $B = 1$. Sketch the circuit and draw arrows indicating the path through which the electricity is flowing. Is the light bulb off or on?

(c) Say $A = 1$ and $B = 0$. Sketch the circuit and draw arrows indicating the path through which the electricity is flowing. Is the light bulb off or on?

(d) Say $A = 1$ and $B = 1$. Sketch the circuit and draw arrows indicating the path through which the electricity is flowing. Is the light bulb off or on?

(e) What logic gate does the circuit correspond to?

Exercise 1.14. Consider the following electrical circuit:

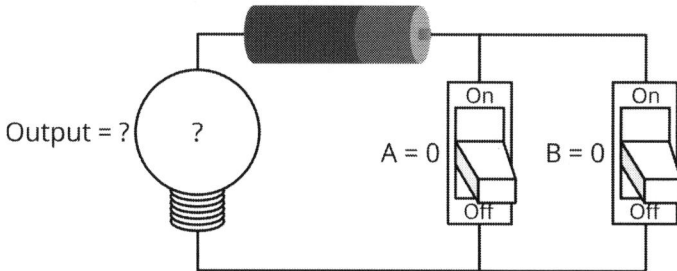

Answer the following questions.

(a) Say $A = 0$ and $B = 0$. Sketch the circuit and draw arrows indicating the path through which the electricity is flowing. Is the light bulb off or on?

(b) Say $A = 0$ and $B = 1$. Sketch the circuit and draw arrows indicating the path through which the electricity is flowing. Is the light bulb off or on?

(c) Say $A = 1$ and $B = 0$. Sketch the circuit and draw arrows indicating the path through which the electricity is flowing. Is the light bulb off or on?

(d) Say $A = 1$ and $B = 1$. Sketch the circuit and draw arrows indicating the path through which the electricity is flowing. Is the light bulb off or on?

(e) What logic gate does the circuit correspond to?

Exercise 1.15. Consider the following electrical circuit:

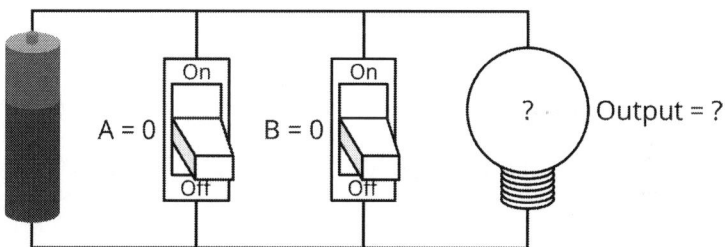

Answer the following questions.

(a) Say $A = 0$ and $B = 0$. Sketch the circuit and draw arrows indicating the path through which the electricity is flowing. Is the light bulb off or on?

(b) Say $A = 0$ and $B = 1$. Sketch the circuit and draw arrows indicating the path through which the electricity is flowing. Is the light bulb off or on?

(c) Say $A = 1$ and $B = 0$. Sketch the circuit and draw arrows indicating the path through which the electricity is flowing. Is the light bulb off or on?

(d) Say $A = 1$ and $B = 1$. Sketch the circuit and draw arrows indicating the path through which the electricity is flowing. Is the light bulb off or on?

(e) What logic gate does the circuit correspond to?

Exercise 1.16. In some homes in the United States, special switches are used so that two switches control a single light. Often, these switches are located at opposite ends of a stairway or a hallway, and either switch can be used to turn the light on or off. A traditional switch enables or disables the flow of electricity through a single wire. In contrast, these special switches, called *three pole switches*, choose between two different wires. The following electrical circuit gives an example:

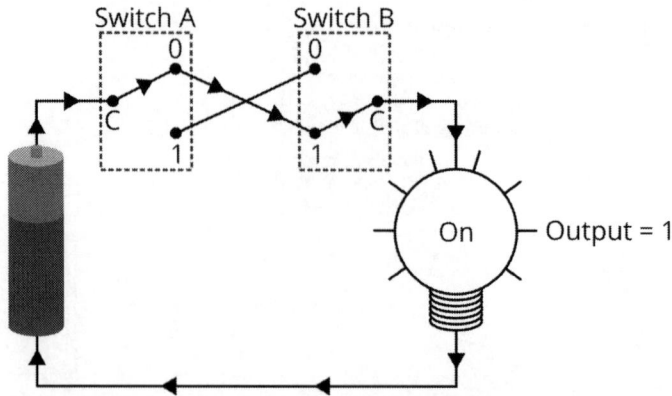

Each switch has three poles, labeled C, 0, and 1. Switch A is current flipped up, which connects C and 0. Switch B is currently flipped down, which connects C and 1. In this configuration, there is a complete path for the electricity to flow. It comes out of the positive end of the battery, through Switch A along $A = 0$, then down to $B = 1$, then through Switch B, then down through the light bulb, left through the bottom wire, and up to the negative end of the battery. So, the light bulb is on when $A = 0$ and $B = 1$.

(a) Say $A = 0$ and $B = 0$. Sketch the circuit and draw arrows indicating the path through which the electricity is flowing. Is the light bulb off or on?

(b) Say $A = 1$ and $B = 0$. Sketch the circuit and draw arrows indicating the path through which the electricity is flowing. Is the light bulb off or on?

(c) Say $A = 1$ and $B = 1$. Sketch the circuit and draw arrows indicating the path through which the electricity is flowing. Is the light bulb off or on?

(d) What logic gate does the circuit correspond to?

We have seen that electrical circuits can be used to create logic gates by connecting switches in various ways. The switches themselves have changed over time, however. Early electrical computers used *relays* or *vacuum tubes* as the switches. A relay is a switch that uses an electrically controlled magnet (i.e., an "electromagnet") to turn on and off the switch. In a *vacuum tube* (also called a vacuum valve), one can turn on and off the flow of electricity between two pieces of metal, one called an anode, and other called a cathode, that is heated. For example, in the 1940's, during World War II, the British built a now-famous computer called Colossus to help break German codes. The first generation Colossus computer had roughly 1,600 vacuum tubes, and the second generation had about 2,400. Vacuum tubes often failed, however, and needed replacement.

Nowadays, computers use *transistors* as the switches. They are typically made of silicon, a common semiconductor, with some other elements to control how easily electricity flows through certain areas. Transistors have several benefits. They have no moving parts (i.e., they are "solid-state" devices), so they are more reliable. They are smaller, which allows computers to be smaller, and they are also faster. Currently, a single computer processor can have tens of billions of transistors, which is a huge improvement over Colossus's 2,400 vacuum tubes.

Exercise 1.17. Visit the website https://en.wikipedia.org/wiki/Transistor_count.

(a) Pick an older computer processor. Which one did you pick, what year was it introduced, and how many transistors did it have?

(b) Pick a newer computer processor. Which one did you pick, what year was it introduced, and how many transistors did it have?

1.2.4 Multiple Gates

We can combine logic gates to create more interesting operations. For example, say we nest two AND gates together:

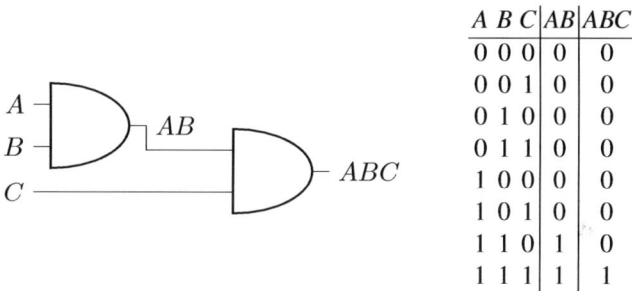

A B C	AB	ABC
0 0 0	0	0
0 0 1	0	0
0 1 0	0	0
0 1 1	0	0
1 0 0	0	0
1 0 1	0	0
1 1 0	1	0
1 1 1	1	1

To find the above truth table, we can first calculate AB, which is the output of the first AND gate. Then, to get the final output, we can take the AND of AB with C, and we see that this is precisely ABC, the AND of all three bits, because the output is 1 only when all three inputs are 1. Then, for simplicity, we often draw this as a single AND gate, but with three inputs:

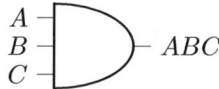

With more inputs, additional AND gates can be nested, or more input lines can be drawn on a single AND gate.

As a more complicated example, consider the following circuit, which contains an XOR gate, NOT gate, and AND gate:

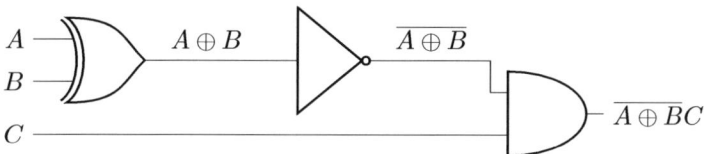

The truth table for this, including its intermediate steps, is shown below:

A B C	$A \oplus B$	$\overline{A \oplus B}$	$\overline{A \oplus B}C$
0 0 0	0	1	0
0 0 1	0	1	1
0 1 0	1	0	0
0 1 1	1	0	0
1 0 0	1	0	0
1 0 1	1	0	0
1 1 0	0	1	0
1 1 1	0	1	1

This resulting behavior does not have a standard, nice name, unlike the first example of the three-bit AND gate. To write it as a single gate, we can just give it whatever name we would like and draw it as a generic box:

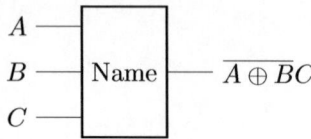

Exercise 1.18. Consider the XOR of three bits A, B, and C, which can either be two two-bit XOR gates strung together, or a single three-bit XOR gate:

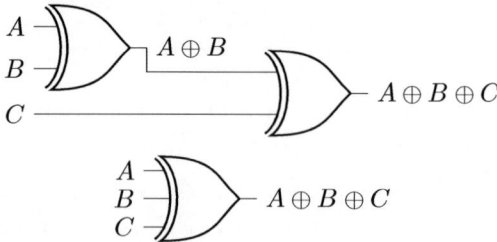

(a) What is the truth table for this circuit?
(b) When there is an even number of 1's in the input (we call this *even parity*), what is the output?
(c) When there is an odd number of 1's in the input (we call this *odd parity*), what is the output?

Exercise 1.19. What is the truth table for the following circuit diagram?

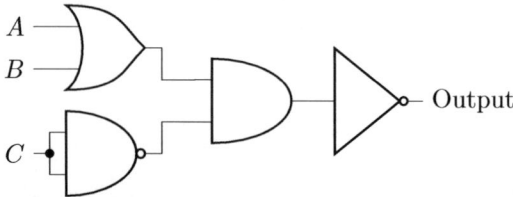

Note the solid dot simply means that the wires are connected there. Then, C is both inputs of the NAND gate, so the gate takes the NAND of C with itself.

Exercise 1.20. Answer the following questions:
(a) How many possible one-bit logic gates are there?
(b) How many possible two-bit logic gates are there?
(c) How many possible three-bit logic gates are there?
(d) How many possible four-bit logic gates are there?
(e) How many possible n-bit logic gates are there?

1.2.5 Universal Gates

Previously, we described five of the sixteen possible two-bit gates (AND, OR, XOR, NAND, and NOR). But what about the other eleven? To make matters worse, for a three-bit gate, the truth table has eight entries, and each output can be 0 or 1, meaning there are $2^8 = 256$ possible three-bit gates. Do we need to list all of them, too?

Thankfully, the answer is no. We do not need separate gates for all of these possibilities because we can reproduce all of them using just a few type of gates. We call a set of gates that can perform all possible logic operations a *universal gate set*, and here are some examples:

- {NOT, AND, OR} is a universal gate set. Given *any* truth table, we can implement it using only NOT, AND, and OR gates. For example, consider the following truth table for a circuit with three inputs, A, B, and C:

A B C	Output
0 0 0	1
0 0 1	1
0 1 0	0
0 1 1	0
1 0 0	1
1 0 1	0
1 1 0	1
1 1 1	0

We can create a circuit composed of NOTs, ANDs, and ORs with this truth table by looking at every case where the output is 1, then combining them all together using ORs. Beginning with the first line of the truth table, the output is 1 when $A = 0$, $B = 0$, and $C = 0$. This is $\overline{A}\,\overline{B}\,\overline{C}$. Next, the output is 1 when $A = 0$, $B = 0$, and $C = 1$. This is $\overline{A}\,\overline{B}C$. Jumping to the fifth line of the truth table, the output is 1 when $A = 1$, $B = 0$, and $C = 0$, which is $A\overline{B}\,\overline{C}$. Finally, from the seventh line of the truth table, the output is 1 when $A = 1$, $B = 1$, and $C = 0$, which is $AB\overline{C}$. The output is 1 whenever any of these are true, so the circuit is $\overline{A}\,\overline{B}\,\overline{C} + \overline{A}\,\overline{B}C + A\overline{B}\,\overline{C} + AB\overline{C}$. As a circuit diagram, it is:

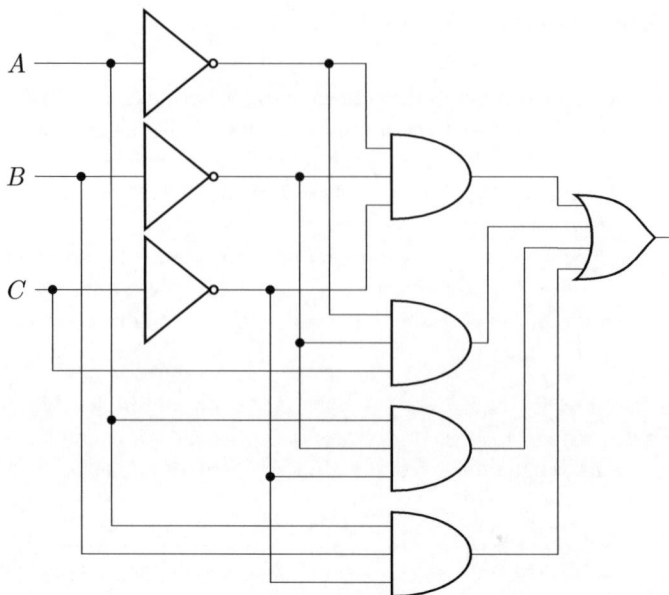

This is a rather complicated circuit, and later in this chapter, we will learn an algebraic way to simplify such circuits (it simplifies to $\overline{A+B} + A\overline{C}$). But for now, the important point is that we can always use NOT, AND, and OR gates in this manner to implement any truth table.

Exercise 1.21. Draw a circuit diagram using only NOT, AND, and OR gates that implements the XOR gate.

Exercise 1.22. Draw a circuit diagram using only NOT, AND, and OR gates that corresponds to the following truth table with input bits A, B, and C:

A B C	Output
0 0 0	0
0 0 1	1
0 1 0	1
0 1 1	0
1 0 0	0
1 0 1	1
1 1 0	0
1 1 1	1

- {NOT, AND} is a universal gate set. To prove this, note the following circuit of NOTs and ANDs calculates the OR of bits A and B:

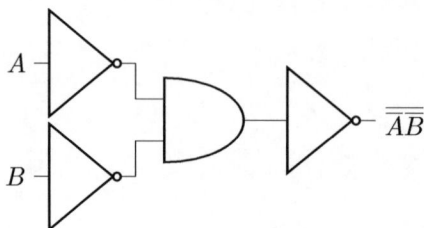

A B	$\overline{A}$ $\overline{B}$	$\overline{A}\,\overline{B}$	$\overline{\overline{A}\,\overline{B}}$
0 0	1 1	1	0
0 1	1 0	0	1
1 0	0 1	0	1
1 1	0 0	0	1

First, the inputs A and B go through NOT gates, resulting in $\bar{A}$ and $\bar{B}$. Then, those become the inputs into an AND gate, resulting in $\overline{A}\overline{B}$. Finally, this is inverted, yielding $\overline{\overline{A}\overline{B}}$. This is the exact same truth table as $A + B$, so this circuit, which only contains NOTs and an AND, implements the OR gate. Then, since $\{\text{NOT}, \text{AND}, \text{OR}\}$ is a universal gate set, just $\{\text{NOT}, \text{AND}\}$ is also a universal gate set.

Exercise 1.23. Draw a circuit diagram using only NOT and AND gates that corresponds to the following truth table with input bits A, B, and C:

A B C	Output
0 0 0	0
0 0 1	0
0 1 0	1
0 1 1	0
1 0 0	0
1 0 1	1
1 1 0	0
1 1 1	0

- $\{\text{NAND}\}$ is a universal gate set, so we say that NAND is a *universal gate*. So, with only NAND gates, one can construct all logic gates. To prove this, let us show that NAND gates can produce the NOT and AND gates, since we already know that $\{\text{NOT}, \text{AND}\}$ is universal.
  First, we can get a NOT gate from NAND by connecting a bit to both inputs:

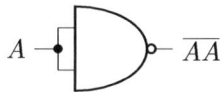

A	AA	$\overline{AA}$
0	0	1
1	1	0

Next, to get AND, note that NAND followed by NOT is simply AND. That is, if we apply NOT twice, they cancel out, leaving AND:

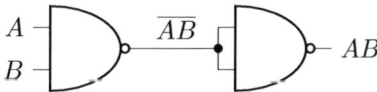

A B	$\overline{AB}$	$\overline{\overline{AB}}$
0 0	1	0
0 1	1	0
1 0	1	0
1 1	0	1

Since $\{\text{NOT}, \text{AND}\}$ is a universal set of gates, and NAND can reproduce both of them, NAND is a universal gate.

Exercise 1.24. Draw a circuit diagram using only NAND gates that implements the OR gate.

Exercise 1.25. Draw a circuit diagram using only NAND gates that implements the following truth table:

A B	Output
0 0	1
0 1	0
1 0	0
1 1	1

Exercise 1.26. Draw a circuit diagram using only NAND gates that corresponds to the following truth table with input bits A, B, and C:

A B C	Output
0 0 0	1
0 0 1	0
0 1 0	1
0 1 1	0
1 0 0	1
1 0 1	0
1 1 0	1
1 1 1	1

Hint: You could create a circuit using {NOT, AND, OR}, then replace the ORs with NOTs and ANDs so that only {NOT, AND} are used, and then replace the NOTs and ANDs with NANDs. This would be a lot of NAND gates, however! To save you from this tedium, I will tell you that this truth table can be created with just two NAND gates.

- {NOT, OR} is a universal gate set. See Exercise 1.27.

Exercise 1.27. In this problem, we will prove that {NOT, OR} is universal. To do this, we already know that {NOT, AND, OR} is universal, so we simply need to show that AND gates can be constructed using {NOT, OR}.

Write the truth table for the following circuit, and verify that it corresponds to the AND gate.

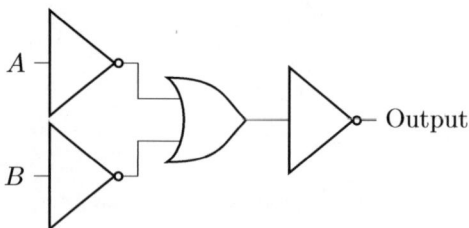

- {NOR} is a universal gate set, so NOR is a universal gate. See Exercise 1.28.

Exercise 1.28. In this problem, we will prove that NOR is a universal gate. To do this, we know from Exercise 1.27 that {NOT, OR} is universal, so we simply need to show that NOT and OR can be constructed using NOR gates.

(a) Write the truth table for the following circuit, and verify that it corresponds to the NOT gate.

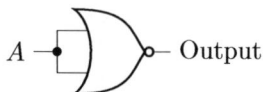

(b) Write the truth table for the following circuit, and verify that it corresponds to the OR gate.

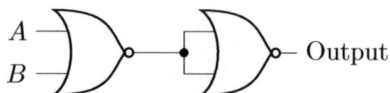

1.3 Adders and Verilog

As an application of the logic gates we have introduced, let us create a logic circuit that adds two binary numbers. First, we will give an overview of how to manually add binary numbers. Then, we will construct different circuits for adding the various parts of a binary number, and we will code these circuits using Verilog, a hardware description language. Finally, we will assemble these circuits into a full circuit that adds binary numbers. In doing so, we will see that logic circuits can be used to compute things, like adding numbers, and indeed everything that a computer does is based on logic circuits.

1.3.1 Adding Binary Numbers by Hand

Say we want to add two binary numbers, like 1011 "+" 1110, where "+" denotes normal addition, not OR. So we want to find

$$1011$$
$$\text{"+" } 1110$$

Let us work through each column of bits, from right to left.

Starting with the rightmost bits, 1 plus 0 is 1. Nothing carries to the next column, so we write a small zero above the next column.

(carry)	0
	1011
"+"	1110
(sum)	1

Now for the second bits (from the right), we have the carry of zero plus one plus one. In decimal, $0 + 1 + 1 = 2$, but in binary, it is 10. So, the sum at the bottom is 0, and 1 carries to the next column.

(carry)	10
	1011
"+"	1110
(sum)	01

For the third bits (from the right), we have $1 + 0 + 1$, which again is 2 in decimal or 10 in binary, so the sum at the bottom is 0, and 1 carries out to the next column.

(carry)	110
	1011
"+"	1110
(sum)	001

Finally, for the leftmost bits, we have $1 + 1 + 1$, which is 3   (carry) 1 1 1 0
in decimal or 11 in binary. So, the sum at the bottom is 1,   1011
and 1 carries to the next column. This final carry becomes
a fifth digit of the sum.   "+" 1110

                                                                     (sum) 11001

Thus, 1011 "+" $1110 = 11001$. Converting this from binary to decimal, $11 + 14 = 25$, as it should be.

In general, to add two 4-bit numbers $A_3A_2A_1A_0$ and $B_3B_2B_1B_0$, we need to carry four numbers C_4, C_3, C_2, C_1, and we get a five-bit sum $S_4S_3S_2S_1S_0$:

$$
\begin{array}{cl}
\text{(carry)} & C_4\,C_3\,C_2\,C_1 \\
 & A_3A_2A_1A_0 \\
\text{"+"} & B_3B_2B_1B_0 \\
\hline
\text{(sum)} & S_4S_3\,S_2\,S_1\,S_0
\end{array}
$$

Since the leftmost carry is the leftmost digit of the sum, $S_4 = C_4$.

In the next several sections, we will create a circuit to perform this addition process. To add the rightmost column, we need a circuit that adds two bits and outputs a carry and a bit of the sum. This is called a *half adder*. For the remaining columns, we need a circuit that adds *three* bits (a carry into the sum and the two bits we want to add) and outputs a carry and a bit of a sum. This is called a *full adder*. By stringing together a half adder and several full adders into a circuit called a *ripple-carry adder*, we can add binary numbers.

1.3.2 Half Adder

Let us begin by creating a circuit that adds two bits. In general, there are four possibilities for these two bits:

(carry) 0	(carry) 0	(carry) 0	(carry) 1
0	0	1	1
"+" 0	"+" 1	"+" 0	"+" 1
(sum) 0	(sum) 1	(sum) 1	(sum) 0

Let us call the input bits A and B, the sum S, and the carry bit C. Then the truth table is

A	B	S	C
0	0	0	0
0	1	1	0
1	0	1	0
1	1	0	1

From this, we see that the sum is the XOR of A and B, and the carry is the AND of A and B. Thus,

$$S = A \oplus B, \quad C = AB.$$

As a circuit diagram, it is

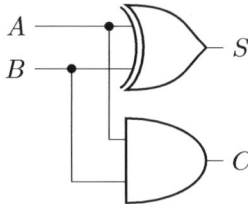

This is called a *half adder*.

Rather than manually wiring this circuit, we can code it using a *hardware description language* (HDL), which describes the structure and behavior of computer hardware, in this case, digital logic circuits. HDLs can be used to program a field-programmable gate array (FPGA), which is an integrated circuit whose logic gates can be configured in software.

The two most common HDLs for logic design are Verilog and VHDL, and here we will focus on Verilog. Although the following Verilog code can be used for actual hardware, we will use an online Verilog simulator at `https://tutorialspoint.com/compile_verilog_online.php`. Here is the website when it is first loaded:

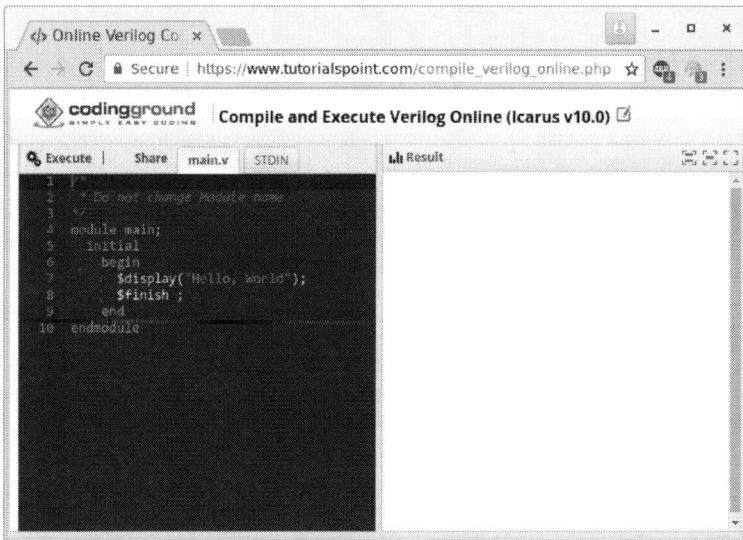

If you click the Execute button in the top-left corner of the webpage, the following appears in the Result section of the webpage:

In the first and second lines, $ indicates that a command is being given. In the first line, the command is `iverilog`, which is the compiler. The option `-o main` specifies that the output (`-o`) should be a file called `main`, so after this command is run, we should get an executable file called `main`. Continuing, the first line, `*.v` denotes all files with the extension `.v`, so we are compiling all files with that extension. Notice from the left pane that our code is in a file called main.v, so this will be compiled. Now, in the second line, `vvp` is the simulator, and the executable we are simulating is called `main`. Our program outputs `Hello, World` to the third line.

Now, in the left panel, we can replace the code with the Verilog code for the half adder:

```verilog
module main;
    reg A,B;
    wire S,C;

    xor xor1(S,A,B);
    and and1(C,A,B);

    initial
        begin
            A=0;
            B=1;
            #5; // Wait 5 time units.
            $display("Sum = ",S);
            $display("Carry = ",C);
        end
endmodule
```

In the main module, we define two *registers* A and B. Each register allows the assignment and storage of a bit, which we will later do in the initialization block. We also define two wires S and C. A wire takes some value depending on the circuit, and we cannot simply define it to take some value. Next, we create the circuit by creating an instance of the XOR gate which we call xor1, and an instance of the AND gate which we call and1. For both of these, the first argument is the output, and the remaining arguments are the inputs. For example, `xor xor1(S,A,B)` computes the XOR of *A* and *B*, and the result is *S*. Now for the initial block, we assign the registers A and B the values 0 and 1, respectively. After this assignment has been made, we wait 5 of the simulation's time units so that the circuit has had a chance to respond to our inputs. Then, we print the values of the carry and sum. Executing this, we get

As expected, when we add 0 and 1, we get 1 with a carry of 0.

To make the half adder more easily reusable, we can replace it by a single circuit symbol, which we label HA for half adder:

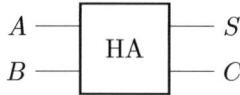

In Verilog, we do this by creating a module (or function) for the half adder:

```
module halfadd(S,C,A,B);
    input A,B;
    output S,C;

    xor xor1(S,A,B);
    and and1(C,A,B);
endmodule

module main;
    reg A,B;
    wire S,C;

    halfadd half1(S,C,A,B);

    initial
        begin
            A=0;
            B=1;
            #5; // Wait 5 time units.
            $display("Sum = ",S);
            $display("Carry = ",C);
        end
endmodule
```

Here, the name of the module is halfadd, and it takes four parameters (S,C,A,B), which we specify as inputs and outputs. The half adder contains an instance of the AND gate and an instance of the XOR gate. In the main module, we instantiate the half adder, and the instance is named half1. Executing this, we get

```
ılı Result

$iverilog -o main *.v
$vvp main
Sum = 1
Carry = 0
```

This is the exact same result as before, which is expected because we did not change anything except move the half adder into a module.

Exercise 1.29. Code the following circuit in Verilog.

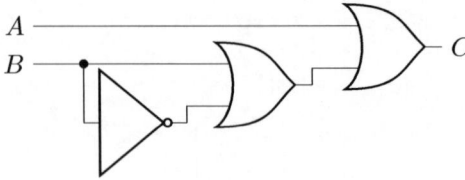

Using your Verilog code, try all possible inputs for A and B and fill in the outputs in the following truth table:

A	B	C
0	0	?
0	1	?
1	0	?
1	1	?

Do your results make sense?

1.3.3 Full Adder

After adding the first two bits, the remaining bits need to be added along with whatever was carried in. Since this includes a carry bit, it is called a *full adder*. Let us call the bits we are adding A and B, and let us call the bit we carry in C_{in}. The outputs are the sum S and carry out C_{out}. Here is a truth table for what the addition should do:

A	B	C_{in}	S	C_{out}
0	0	0	0	0
0	0	1	1	0
0	1	0	1	0
0	1	1	0	1
1	0	0	1	0
1	0	1	0	1
1	1	0	0	1
1	1	1	1	1

From the truth table, we see that the sum S is 1 whenever one of the inputs A, B, or C_{in} are 1, or when all three of them are 1. This is equivalent to the XOR of all three bits:

$$S = A \oplus B \oplus C_{in}.$$

From this truth table, we also see that the carry out is 1 when A and B are both 1, or when $C_{in} = 1$ and $A \oplus B = 1$:

$$C_{out} = AB + C_{in}(A \oplus B).$$

Putting these together, the logic circuit is

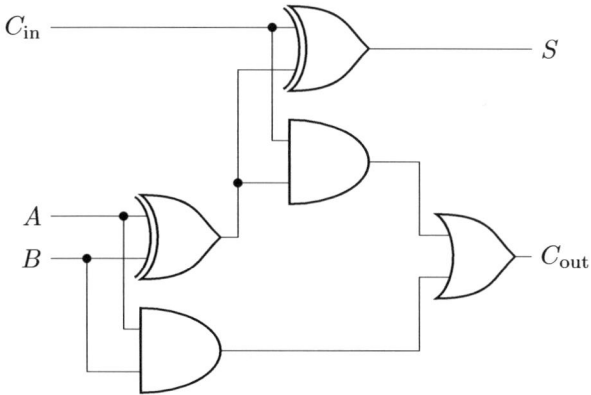

Note that there are two groups containing an AND and an XOR:

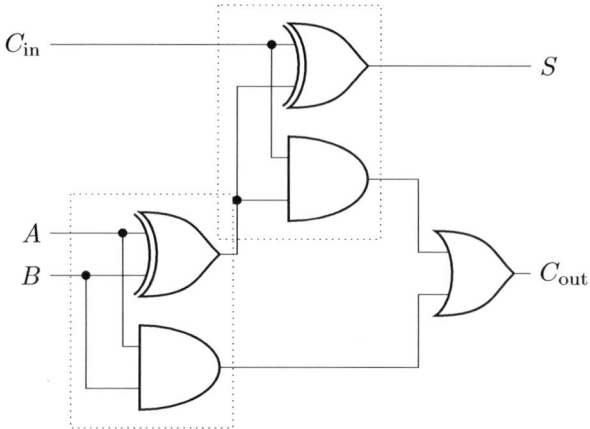

Each of these is a half adder! So the full adder is equivalent to

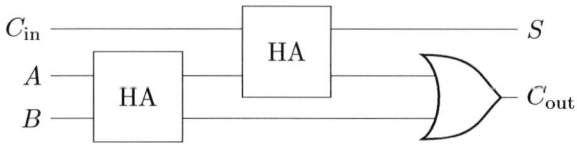

To make the full adder more easily reusable, we can replace it by a single circuit symbol, which we label FA for full adder:

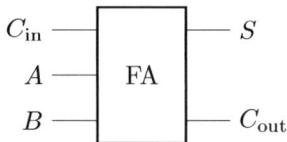

In Verilog, we can code a module for the full adder:

```
module halfadd(S,C,A,B);
```

```
      input A,B;
      output S,C;

      xor xor1(S,A,B);
      and and1(C,A,B);
  endmodule

module fulladd(S,Cout,Cin,A,B);
      input Cin,A,B;
      output S,Cout;
      wire w1,w2,w3;

      halfadd half1(w1,w2,A,B);
      halfadd half2(S,w3,Cin,w1);
      or or1(Cout,w3,w2);
  endmodule

module main;
      reg Cin,A,B;
      wire S,Cout;

      fulladd full1(S,Cout,Cin,A,B);

      initial
          begin
              Cin=1;
              A=0;
              B=1;
              #5; // Wait 5 time units.
              $display("Sum = ",S);
              $display("Carry = ",Cout);
          end
  endmodule
```

Executing this, we get

```
ıı. Result
$iverilog -o main *.v
$vvp main
Sum = 0
Carry = 1
```

As expected, $1 + 0 + 1$ results in 0 with a carry out of 1.

Exercise 1.30. The full adder from class contains two XOR gates, two AND gates, and one OR gate. Replace the OR gate with an XOR gate. What is the truth table of this new circuit? How does it compare to the truth table of the full adder from class?

1.3.4 Ripple-Carry Adder

Using these adders, we can assemble them to add binary numbers. Let us denote the bits of the binary numbers $A_3A_2A_1A_0$ and $B_3B_2B_1B_0$. We can use a half adder to add bits A_0 and B_0, then carry the bit into a full adder to add bits A_1 and B_1, then continue adding the successive bits using full adders:

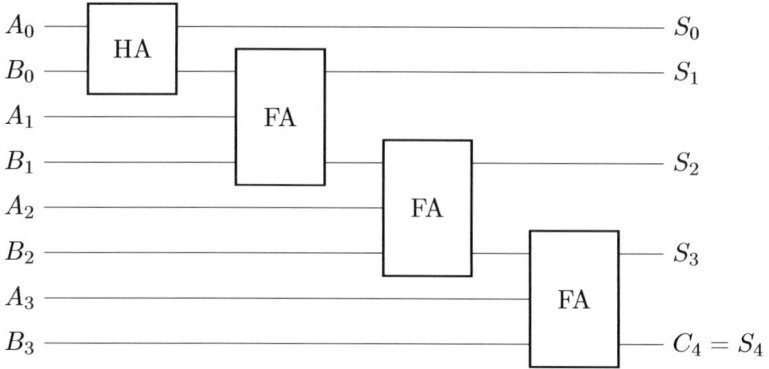

This is called a *ripple-carry adder*, since the carry from one addition ripples to the next addition. Let us code it in Verilog:

```
module halfadd(S,C,A,B);
    input A,B;
    output S,C;

    xor xor1(S,A,B);
    and and1(C,A,B);
endmodule

module fulladd(S,Cout,Cin,A,B);
    input Cin,A,B;
    output S,Cout;
    wire w1,w2,w3;

    halfadd half1(w1,w2,A,B);
    halfadd half2(S,w3,Cin,w1);
    or or1(Cout,w3,w2);
endmodule

module rippleadd(S,A,B);
    input [3:0] A,B;
    output [4:0] S;
    output Cout;
    wire [3:1] C;

    halfadd half1(S[0],C[1],A[0],B[0]);
    fulladd full1(S[1],C[2],C[1],A[1],B[1]);
    fulladd full2(S[2],C[3],C[2],A[2],B[2]);
    fulladd full3(S[3],S[4],C[3],A[3],B[3]);
endmodule

module main;
    reg [3:0] A,B;
    wire [4:0] S;
    wire Cout;
```

```
      rippleadd ripple1(S,A,B);

   initial
      begin
          A=4'b1011;
          B=4'b0011;
          #5; // Wait 5 time units.
          $display(A,"+",B,"=",S);
          $display("%b",A,"+%b",B,"=%b",S);
      end
endmodule
```

To explain this code, in the `rippleadd` module, the line `input [3:0] A,B;` defines
A and B to each have four inputs indexed from 3 to 0. That is, $A = A_3A_2A_1A_0$, and
the way we write each of these bits in Verilog is $A[3]$, $A[2]$, $A[1]$, and $A[0]$. The same
holds for B. In the next line, we similarly define $S = S_4S_3S_2S_1S_0$. A couple lines
later, we define $C[3]$, $C[2]$, and $C[1]$ as the three carry bits, and we did not define
$C[4]$ because this final carry out is exactly $S[4]$. In the initial block, A and B now
binary numbers of length 4. We assign their values in binary using `4'b` followed by
the binary number. By default, displaying A and B prints them as decimal numbers,
so we use the `%b` format code to print them in binary instead.

⊪ Result

```
$iverilog -o main *.v
$vvp main
11+ 3=14
1011+0011=01110
```

Exercise 1.31. Using the 4-bit adder that we coded in Verilog, what is 1001 plus 0111?

Exercise 1.32. Code an 8-bit adder in Verilog. Use it to add 10101101 and 00111001.

1.3.5 Ripple-Carry with Full Adders

For simplicity, one may prefer to only have full adders in the circuit. To do this, we
can replace the first half adder with a full adder with a carry-in of 0.

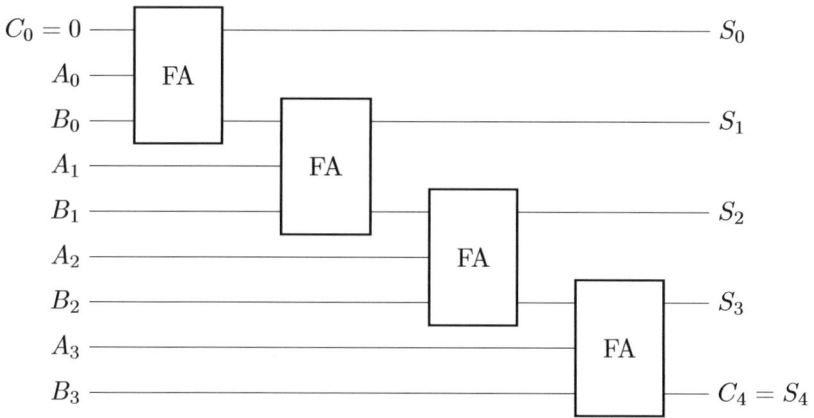

In other words, we are adding

$$\begin{array}{r} \text{(carry) } C_4\,C_3\,C_2\,C_1\,C_0 \\ A_3A_2A_1A_0 \\ \text{``+''}\quad B_3B_2B_1B_0 \\ \hline \text{(sum) } S_4S_3\,S_2\,S_1\,S_0 \end{array}$$

but fixing $C_0 = 0$.

Exercise 1.33. Using Verilog, code the 4-bit ripple-carry adder that only uses full adders, no half adder. Use it to add 0110 and 1110.

1.3.6 Circuit Complexity

If the ripple-carry adder consists entirely of full adders, then adding two n-bit numbers requires n full adders. Each full adder uses five logic gates, for a total of $5n$ logic gates.

Of course, since the first full adder has a carry-in of zero, it can be replaced with a half adder. This reduces the number of gates by three, so the number of logic gates is $5n - 3$.

1.4 Circuit Simplification and Boolean Algebra

Previously, we learned that $\{\text{NOT}, \text{AND}, \text{OR}\}$ is a universal gate set. We demonstrated this by creating a circuit that implemented a given truth table. The circuit was $\overline{A}\overline{B}\overline{C} + \overline{A}\overline{B}C + A\overline{B}\overline{C} + AB\overline{C}$, and we claimed that it could be simplified to $\overline{A} + \overline{B} + A\overline{C}$. Now, we are going to prove this. One way is to show that their truth tables are the

same. But, it would be nice to have an algebraic way to show that their outputs are
equal, i.e.,

$$\overline{ABC} + \overline{A}\overline{B}C + A\overline{B}\overline{C} + AB\overline{C} = \overline{A+B} + A\overline{C}.$$

In this section, we will learn how to do this using the rules of algebra for bits, called
boolean algebra. These rules will allow us to simplify complicated circuits in a
systematic, algebraic manner.

1.4.1 Order of Operations

First, we need to learn how to read boolean expressions. Consider the following
expression on three inputs A, B, and C, which contains one OR and one AND:

$$A + BC.$$

When implementing this, do we do the OR first, i.e., $(A + B)C$, or the AND first,
i.e., $A + (BC)$? Does it even matter? To see, let us work out the truth table for each
option:

A B C	$(A+B)C$	$A+(BC)$
0 0 0	0	0
0 0 1	0	0
0 1 0	0	0
0 1 1	1	1
1 0 0	0	1
1 0 1	1	1
1 1 0	0	1
1 1 1	1	1

So the order in which we do the operations matters. Just like in regular math, where
we multiply (and divide) before adding (and subtracting), the convention in boolean
algebra is that AND is done first, then OR. Thus,

$$A + BC = A + (BC).$$

1.4.2 Association, Commutativity, and Distribution

AND and OR also follow several familiar properties from elementary algebra. First,
they are associative:

- $ABC = (AB)C = A(BC)$
- $A + B + C = (A + B) + C = A + (B + C)$

AND and OR are also commutative:

- $AB = BA$
- $A + B = B + A$

Finally, both are distributive, meaning AND distributes into OR, and OR distributes into AND:

- $A(B+C) = AB + AC$
- $A + (BC) = (A+B)(A+C)$

The last point is likely the most foreign. It is *not* true when adding and multiplying numbers (e.g., $2 + 3 \cdot 4 \neq (2+3)(2+4)$, since the left-hand side evaluates to 14, and the right-hand side evaluates to 30), but it is true of AND/OR with bits!

1.4.3 Identities Involving Zero and One

Our first identities involve 0 and 1. They can be proved by writing out their truth tables, or by the arguments given below.

- $A0 = 0$, since A and 0 are never both 1.
- $A1 = A$, since A and 1 are both 1 when A is 1.
- $A + 0 = A$, since 0 is never 1, so A or 0 is whatever A is.
- $A + 1 = 1$, since A or 1 is always 1.

The first three are consistent with elementary algebra: multiplying by 0 yields 0, multiplying by 1 does nothing, and adding 0 does nothing. The last point, however, is different. In boolean algebra, "adding" 1 yields 1 because it is the OR operator, not addition.

1.4.4 Single-Variable Identities

There are several identities involving logic gates on only a single bit A and its inverse $\overline{A}$. They can be proved by writing out their truth tables, or by the arguments given below.

- $A = \overline{\overline{A}}$, since inverting twice results in the original bit.
- $AA = A$, since A and itself is just A.
- $A\overline{A} = 0$, since A and $\overline{A}$ are inverses, they are never both 1.
- $A + A = A$, since A or itself is just A.
- $A + \overline{A} = 1$, since A and $\overline{A}$ are inverses, one of them is always 1.

These identities now differ substantially from adding and multiplying numbers, e.g., $3 \cdot 3 = 3^2$.

1.4.5 Two-Variable Identities and De Morgan's Laws

There are some important identities involving two bits A and B. They can be proved by writing out their truth tables, or since they are less obvious, we also provide algebraic proofs for each.

- $A + AB = A$. Regardless of B, when $A = 0$, $A + AB = 0$, and when $A = 1$, $A + AB = 1$, so the result is entirely dependent on A. As an algebraic proof,

$$A + AB = A1 + AB = A(1 + B) = A1 = A.$$

- $A + \bar{A}B = A + B$. When $A = 1$, $A + \bar{A}B$ is clearly 1. When $A = 0$, then $\bar{A} = 1$, so $\bar{A}B = B$. As an algebraic proof,

$$A + \bar{A}B = A + (\bar{A}B) = (A + \bar{A})(A + B) = (1)(A + B) = A + B.$$

The next two points are called *De Morgan's Laws*, which states that the NOT of an AND is the OR of the NOTs, and the NOT of an OR is the AND of the NOTs.

- $\overline{AB} = \bar{A} + \bar{B}$. For $\overline{AB}$ to be 1, AB must be 0. Thus, A and B are not both 1. At least one of them must be 0, which is $\bar{A} + \bar{B}$. In Exercise 1.11, this statement that NAND and negative-OR are equivalent was proved using truth tables. The following algebraic proof is more complicated, so consider it optional.

Proof. We begin by showing that if X and Y satisfy $X + Y = 1$ and $XY = 0$, then they are inverses, i.e., $Y = \bar{X}$:

$$\bar{X} = \bar{X}1 = \bar{X}(X + Y) = \bar{X}X + \bar{X}Y = 0 + \bar{X}Y$$
$$= XY + \bar{X}Y = (\bar{X} + X)Y = 1Y = Y.$$

In the second equality, we used $X + Y = 1$, and in the fifth equality, we used $XY = 0$. With these two assumptions, we found that $\bar{X} = Y$, so the inverse of X is Y. It must also be true that the inverse of Y is X, which we can prove by inverting both sides of $\bar{X} = Y$, resulting in $\bar{\bar{X}} = \bar{Y}$, which simplifies to $X = \bar{Y}$, so the inverse of Y is X.

Now, assigning $X = AB$ and $Y = \bar{A} + \bar{B}$, let us show that $X + Y = 1$ and $XY = 0$. First,

$$
\begin{aligned}
X + Y &= AB + (\bar{A} + \bar{B}) &&\text{Substitution}\\
&= AB + (\bar{A} + \bar{B})(1) &&A1 = A\\
&= AB + (\bar{A} + \bar{B})(A + \bar{A}) &&A + \bar{A} = 1\\
&= AB + \bar{A}A + \bar{A}\bar{A} + \bar{B}A + \bar{B}\bar{A} &&\text{Distributive Property}\\
&= AB + 0 + \bar{A} + A\bar{B} + \bar{B}\bar{A} &&\bar{A}A = 0, \bar{A}\bar{A} = \bar{A}, \text{Commutative Prop}\\
&= A(B + \bar{B}) + \bar{A} + \bar{B}\bar{A} &&\text{Distributive Property}\\
&= A(1) + \bar{A} + \bar{B}\bar{A} &&B + \bar{B} = 1
\end{aligned}
$$

$$= 1 + \overline{B}\overline{A} \qquad\qquad A1 = A, A + \overline{A} = 1$$
$$= 1. \qquad\qquad\qquad 1 + A = 1$$

Next,

$$XY = AB(\overline{A} + \overline{B}) \qquad\qquad \textit{Substitution}$$
$$= AB\overline{A} + AB\overline{B} \qquad\qquad \text{Distributive Property}$$
$$= A\overline{A}B + AB\overline{B} \qquad\qquad \text{Commutative Property}$$
$$= 0\overline{B} + \overline{A}0 \qquad\qquad A\overline{A} = 0$$
$$= 0 + 0 \qquad\qquad\qquad A0 = 0$$
$$= 0.$$

Since $X + Y = 1$ and $XY = 0$, $\overline{X} = Y$, and so $\overline{AB} = \overline{A} + \overline{B}$, which is De Morgan's Law. □
(The square symbol signals the end of a proof.)

- $\overline{A + B} = \overline{A}\overline{B}$. The left-hand side is 1 when the OR of A and B is 0, which only occurs when A and B are both 0. The right-hand side is 1 only when A and B are both 0. So, the two sides are equal. Logically, this says that A or B is false, since it is false that neither A or B are true, both A and B must be false. In Exercise 1.12, this statement that NOR and negative-AND are equivalent was proved using truth tables. As with the previous point, the following algebraic proof is more complicated, so consider it optional.

Proof. The proof is very similar to the previous one, but we take $X = A + B$ and $Y = \overline{A}\overline{B}$. First, we show that $X + Y = 1$:

$$X + Y = (A + B) + \overline{A}\overline{B} = (A + B)(A + \overline{A}) + \overline{A}\overline{B} = AA + A\overline{A} + BA + B\overline{A} + \overline{A}\overline{B}$$
$$= (A + BA) + \overline{A}(B + \overline{B}) = A + \overline{A} = 1.$$

Next, we show that $XY = 0$:

$$XY = (A + B)\overline{A}\overline{B} = A\overline{A}\overline{B} + B\overline{A}\overline{B} = 0\overline{B} + \overline{A}0 = 0.$$

Since $X + Y = 1$ and $XY = 0$, $\overline{X} = Y$, and so $\overline{A + B} = \overline{A}\overline{B}$, which is De Morgan's Law. □

Symbolically, breaking the NOT overline bar into two can be done at the expense of changing AND to OR, or vice versa. A useful mnemonic for it is, "Break the line, change the sign!"

In our previous discussion of universal gates, we showed that the NOT of A could be implemented by making A both inputs of a NAND gate. We can now prove this algebraically using De Morgan's Law. Starting with the NAND of A with itself,

$$\overline{AA} = \overline{A} + \overline{A} = \overline{A}.$$

We also showed that the OR gate, $A+B$, could be implemented using three NOTs and one AND, $\overline{\overline{A}\overline{B}}$. We proved this by writing the truth table, but now we can also prove it algebraically using De Morgan's theorem:

$$\overline{\overline{A}\overline{B}} = \overline{\overline{A}} + \overline{\overline{B}} = A + B.$$

Similarly, we showed in Exercise 1.27 using a truth table that the AND gate, AB, could be implemented using three NOTs and one OR, $\overline{\overline{A}+\overline{B}}$. Using De Morgan's theorem,

$$\overline{\overline{A}+\overline{B}} = \overline{\overline{A}}\,\overline{\overline{B}} = AB.$$

1.4.6 Circuit Simplification

Using these boolean identities, let us go through three examples of simplifying circuits using boolean algebra, beginning with the example from the beginning of the section.

1. Back to the example that started this section, let us show that $\overline{A}\overline{B}C + \overline{A}BC + A\overline{B}\overline{C} + AB\overline{C} = \overline{A+B} + A\overline{C}$ using boolean algebra:

$$
\begin{aligned}
\overline{A}\overline{B}C + \overline{A}BC + A\overline{B}\overline{C} + AB\overline{C} &= \overline{A}\overline{B}(\overline{C}+C) + A(B+\overline{B})\overline{C} && \text{Distributive Property} \\
&= \overline{A}\overline{B}1 + A1\overline{C} && A+\overline{A}=1 \\
&= \overline{A}\overline{B} + A\overline{C} && A1 = A \\
&= \overline{A+B} + A\overline{C}. && \text{De Morgan's Law}
\end{aligned}
$$

Note the second-to-last line uses three NOT gates, two AND gates, and one OR gate, whereas the last line uses two NOT gates, one AND gate, and two OR gates, so it uses one fewer gate.

2. As another example, consider the following circuit with seven gates:

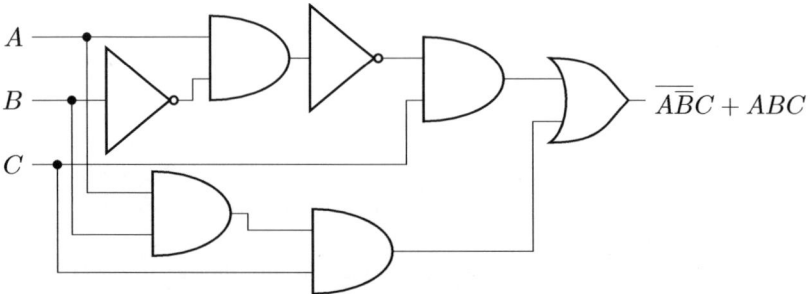

This circuit implements $\overline{A}\overline{B}C + ABC$. Let us use boolean algebra to simplify it:

$$\overline{A\overline{B}}C + ABC = (\overline{A} + \overline{\overline{B}})C + ABC \qquad \text{De Morgan's Law}$$
$$= (\overline{A} + B)C + ABC \qquad \overline{\overline{B}} = B$$
$$= \overline{A}C + BC + ABC \qquad \text{Distributive Property}$$
$$= \overline{A}C + (1+A)BC \qquad \text{Distributive Property}$$
$$= \overline{A}C + 1BC \qquad 1+A = 1$$
$$= \overline{A}C + BC \qquad 1B = B$$
$$= (\overline{A} + B)C. \qquad \text{Distributive Property}$$

This complicated circuit is equivalent to $(\overline{A} + B)C$, which only has three gates:

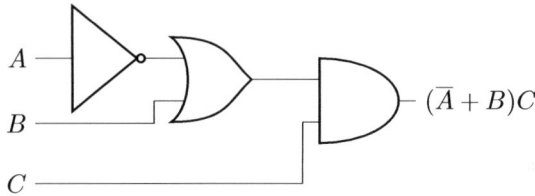

3. For our third example, we have $(A+B)(\overline{A}+B+C)\overline{C}$:

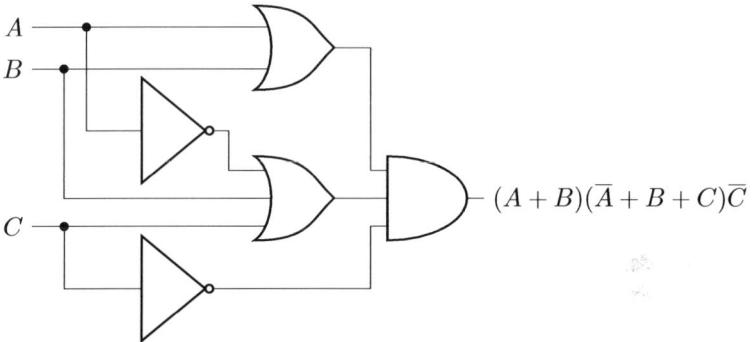

As drawn, it has five gates. Two of the gates, however, have three inputs, and if we were to replace each of them with two two-bit gates, we would have seven gates total. Simplifying it,

$$(A+B)(\overline{A}+B+C)\overline{C}$$
$$= A\overline{A}\overline{C} + AB\overline{C} + AC\overline{C} + B\overline{A}\overline{C} + BB\overline{C} + BC\overline{C} \qquad \text{Distributive Property}$$
$$= 0\overline{C} + AB\overline{C} + A0 + B\overline{A}\overline{C} + B\overline{C} + B0 \qquad A\overline{A} = 0, BB = B$$
$$= AB\overline{C} + B\overline{A}\overline{C} + B\overline{C} \qquad A0 = 0, A+0 = A$$
$$= (A+\overline{A}+1)B\overline{C} \qquad \text{Distributive Property}$$
$$= (1)B\overline{C} \qquad A+1 = 1$$
$$= B\overline{C}. \qquad 1A - A$$

So, the output of the circuit is only dependent on B and C, not A. It only needs one NOT gate and one AND gate.

Exercise 1.34. Simplify $\overline{A}(\overline{A+B})$. Hint: Your final result should be a single logic gate.

Exercise 1.35. Simplify $(A+\overline{B})(A+B+\overline{C})$. Hint: Your final result should have one NOT gate and two OR gates.

Exercise 1.36. Simplify the following circuit:

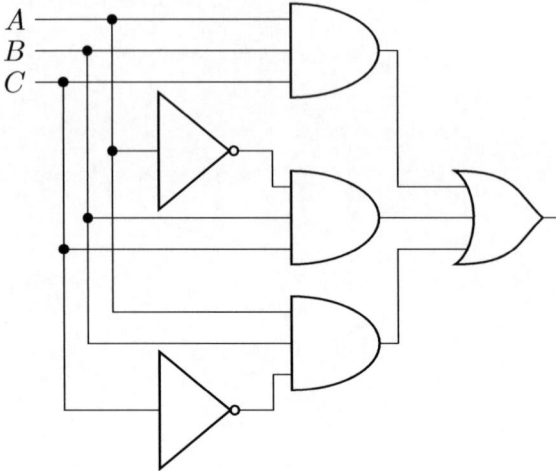

Exercise 1.37. Consider the following truth table with input bits A, B, and C:

A B C	Output
0 0 0	0
0 0 1	0
0 1 0	1
0 1 1	1
1 0 0	1
1 0 1	0
1 1 0	1
1 1 1	0

(a) Create a circuit consisting of NOT, AND, and OR gates that implements the truth table.
(b) Simplify your previous circuit using boolean algebra.

1.5 Reversible Logic Gates

1.5.1 Reversible Gates

A *reversible* gate, is a logic gate where, given the output(s) of the gate, we can always determine what the input(s) was (were). An example is the NOT gate:

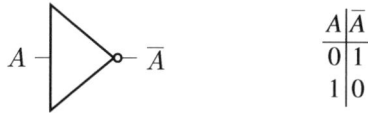

A	$\overline{A}$
0	1
1	0

From its truth table, the outputs are unique, so it is always possible to reverse the operation. That is, if we know that the output of the NOT gate is 1, we know that the input must have been 0, and if we know that the output is 0, we know that the input must have been 1. The gate is reversible because, given the output, we can always determine the input.

1.5.2 Irreversible Gates

An *irreversible* gate is the opposite of a reversible gate. Given the output(s) of the gate, it is not always possible to determine what the input(s) was (were). An example is the AND gate:

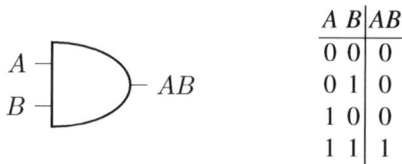

A	B	AB
0	0	0
0	1	0
1	0	0
1	1	1

From the truth table, if the output of the AND gate is 1, then we know with certainty that the inputs were both 1. If the output of the gate is 0, however, then it is impossible to know from this information alone which of the other three inputs (00, 01, and 10) were used. So in general, we are unable to determine the inputs to the AND gate from its output. Thus, it is irreversible.

Notice the AND gate has two input bits, which have four possible states (00, 01, 10, and 11), and one output bit, which has two possible states (0 and 1). Since there are fewer possibilities for the outputs than the inputs, the gate must be irreversible.

Conversely, if there are fewer input bits than output bits, the circuit is still irreversible because some of the outputs will be undetermined. For example, consider the following truth table with one input bit and two output bits:

A	B	C
0	0	1
1	1	0

The question, "If both outputs are 0, what was the input?" is undefined by the truth table, so its inverse is not completely specified.

Thus, for a logic gate to be reversible, it must have the same number of input bits and output bits. The converse is not true, however. Just because a logic gate has the same number of input bits and output bits does not necessarily mean it is reversible. For example, for the gates corresponding to the following truth tables, the gate on the left is reversible, but the gate on the right is irreversible:

A B	C D
0 0	0 1
0 1	1 0
1 0	1 1
1 1	0 0

Reversible

A B	C D
0 0	0 0
0 1	0 1
1 0	0 1
1 1	1 0

Irreversible

The gate on the left is reversible because, given the output, it is always possible to determine the input. The gate on the right is irreversible because given the output 01, one does not know if the input was 01 or 10.

Another way to contrast reversible and irreversible gates is whether information is lost. With a reversible gate, no information is lost since we can always recover the inputs from the outputs. With an irreversible gate, however, information is lost since, given an output, we generally do not know what the inputs were.

Exercise 1.38. Are the following gates reversible or irreversible? (a) OR. (b) XOR. (c) NAND. (d) NOR.

Exercise 1.39. Are the following gates reversible or irreversible?
(a) The half-adder from Section 1.3.2.
(b) A gate with two inputs (A and B) and two outputs (C and D), whose truth table is shown below:

A B	C D
0 0	0 0
0 1	1 1
1 0	1 0
1 1	0 1

Exercise 1.40. The *Fredkin gate* is depicted below:

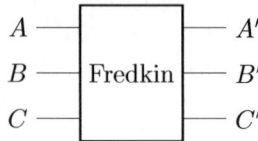

It takes three inputs A, B, and C, and has three outputs A', B', and C'. A is the control bit. If $A = 0$, then nothing happens to B and C. If $A = 1$, however, then B and C are swapped. The control bit is unchanged, so $A' = A$. Thus, the Fredkin gate is a controlled-SWAP gate.
(a) Write the truth table for the Fredkin gate.
(b) Based on the truth table, is the Fredkin gate reversible or irreversible? Why?

1.5.3 Toffoli Gate: A Reversible AND Gate

We have learned that the AND gate is irreversible, meaning we lose information when we use an AND gate because we generally cannot reconstruct the inputs from the outputs. It would be nice to have a reversible version of the AND gate, and in this section we introduce one called the *Toffoli gate*.

The Toffoli gate has three inputs A, B, and C. To be reversible, it needs to have three outputs, and they are A, B, and $AB \oplus C$:

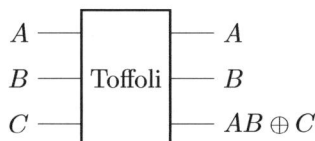

The Toffoli gate can be constructed using an AND gate and an XOR gate. We take the AND of A and B, and we take the XOR of AB with C to get $AB \oplus C$.

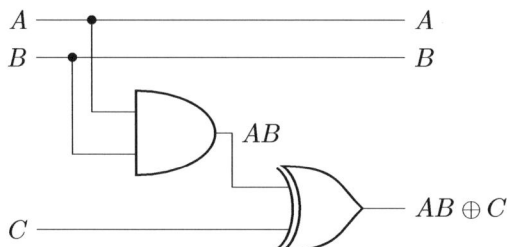

The truth table for the Toffoli gate is

A B C	A B $AB \oplus C$	
0 0 0	0 0	0
0 0 1	0 0	1
0 1 0	0 1	0
0 1 1	0 1	1
1 0 0	1 0	0
1 0 1	1 0	1
1 1 0	1 1	1
1 1 1	1 1	0

We see from the truth table that the outputs are unique, so the Toffoli gate is reversible. Notice when $C = 0$, the third output is the AND of A and B. This can also be seen using boolean algebra, since when $C = 0$, $AB \oplus C = AB \oplus 0 = AB$, which is the AND of A and B. Thus, the Toffoli gate is a reversible version of the AND gate.

From the above truth table, notice there are two rows where $A = 0$ and $B = 0$, and the third outputs of these two rows are opposite each other. Similarly, there are two rows where $A = 0$ and $B = 1$, and the third outputs are again opposite each other. This is true for every pair of rows with fixed A and B, and it ensures each output of the truth table is unique, so the circuit is reversible. This observation that each pair of rows has opposite third outputs can be proven using boolean algebra. From before, when $C = 0$, the third output is AB. When $C = 1$, the third output is $AB \oplus C = AB \oplus 1 = \overline{AB}$, so it is opposite AB. Furthermore, since $\overline{AB}$ is the NAND of A and B, and since NAND is universal, the Toffoli gate is also universal.

Also from the truth table, notice the third bit is flipped when A and B are both 1. For this reason, the Toffoli gate is also called the controlled-controlled-NOT gate or CCNOT gate. Whether the third bit is flipped is controlled by whether the first two bits are 1. That is, if $A = B = 1$, then the Toffoli gate flips C, and otherwise it does nothing.

Exercise 1.41. Consider the *anti-Toffoli gate*, which flips the third bit if the first two bits are both 0:

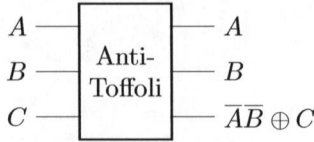

$$
\begin{array}{c}
A \longrightarrow \boxed{\begin{array}{c}\text{Anti-}\\\text{Toffoli}\end{array}} \longrightarrow A \\
B \qquad\qquad\qquad B \\
C \qquad\qquad\qquad \overline{AB} \oplus C
\end{array}
$$

(a) Write the truth table for the anti-Toffoli gate.
(b) In the above picture of the anti-Toffoli gate, $\overline{AB}$ appears in the third output. Which law from boolean algebra says that this is equal to $\overline{A} + \overline{B}$?
(c) When $C = 0$, is the third output the AND, OR, XOR, NAND, or NOR of A and B?
(d) When $C = 1$, is the third output the AND, OR, XOR, NAND, or NOR of A and B?
(e) Construct an anti-Toffoli gate using one Toffoli gate and four NOT gates.

1.5.4 Making Irreversible Gates Reversible

In the last section, we showed that the AND gate can be made reversible by XORing its output with a third input C. This procedure works in general, not just for AND gates. Say a gate has inputs A and B and one output $f(A, B)$, which is a *function* that outputs 0 or 1 depending on the inputs A and B:

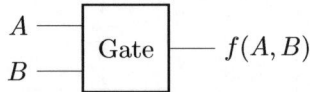

$$
\begin{array}{c}
A \longrightarrow \boxed{\text{Gate}} \longrightarrow f(A, B) \\
B \longrightarrow
\end{array}
$$

For example, for the AND gate, the function would map $f(0,0) = 0$, $f(0,1) = 0$, $f(1,0) = 0$, and $f(1,1) = 1$. Such a gate is irreversible because it has fewer outputs than inputs, but we can make it reversible by XORing its output with a third input C:

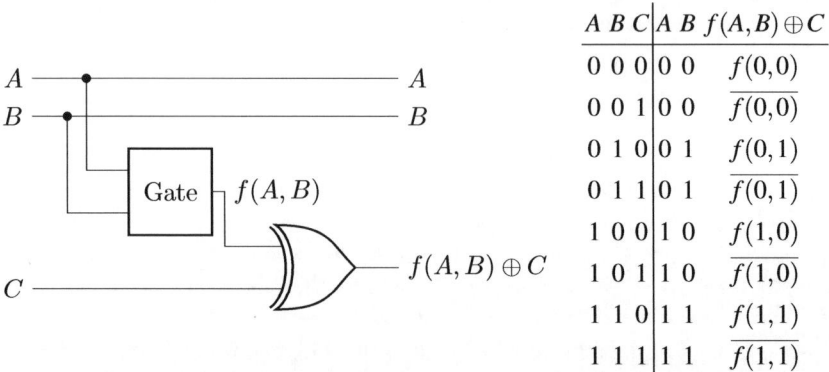

A	B	C	A	B	$f(A,B) \oplus C$
0	0	0	0	0	$f(0,0)$
0	0	1	0	0	$\overline{f(0,0)}$
0	1	0	0	1	$f(0,1)$
0	1	1	0	1	$\overline{f(0,1)}$
1	0	0	1	0	$f(1,0)$
1	0	1	1	0	$\overline{f(1,0)}$
1	1	0	1	1	$f(1,1)$
1	1	1	1	1	$\overline{f(1,1)}$

In the rightmost column of the truth table, we used $f(A,B) \oplus 0 = f(A,B)$ and $f(A,B) \oplus 1 = \overline{f(A,B)}$. So, this implements the original gate when $C = 0$. But, the overall circuit is reversible. In the output, every permutation of A and B shows up twice, once with $f(A,B)$ and once with $\overline{f(A,B)}$, ensuring that the outputs are unique.

We can generalize this technique several ways. First, the gate could be a function of any number of variables. For example, say we have a gate with three inputs A, B, C, and one output $f(A,B,C)$:

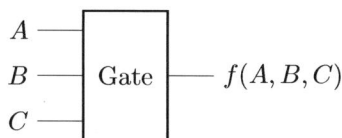

$$A \longrightarrow \boxed{\text{Gate}} \longrightarrow f(A,B,C)$$
$$B \longrightarrow$$
$$C \longrightarrow$$

This must be irreversible because there are fewer outputs than inputs. To make it reversible, we add a fourth input D that we XOR with $f(A,B,C)$:

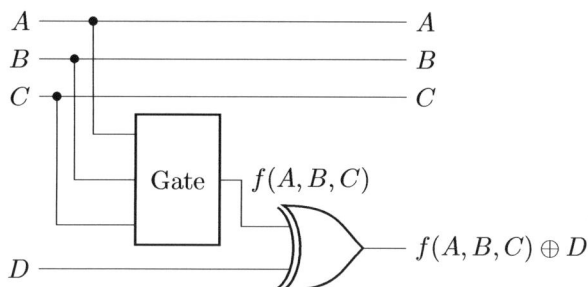

Now, when $D = 0$, the bottom wire outputs $f(A,B,C)$, and when $D = 1$, the bottom wire outputs $\overline{f(A,B,C)}$. The truth table for this is

A B C D	A B C	$D \oplus f(A,B,C)$
0 0 0 0	0 0 0	$f(0,0,0)$
0 0 0 1	0 0 0	$\overline{f(0,0,0)}$
0 0 1 0	0 0 1	$f(0,0,1)$
0 0 1 1	0 0 1	$\overline{f(0,0,1)}$
0 1 0 0	0 1 0	$f(0,1,0)$
0 1 0 1	0 1 0	$\overline{f(0,1,0)}$
0 1 1 0	0 1 1	$f(0,1,1)$
0 1 1 1	0 1 1	$\overline{f(0,1,1)}$
1 0 0 0	1 0 0	$f(1,0,0)$
1 0 0 1	1 0 0	$\overline{f(1,0,0)}$
1 0 1 0	1 0 1	$f(1,0,1)$
1 0 1 1	1 0 1	$\overline{f(1,0,1)}$
1 1 0 0	1 1 0	$f(1,1,0)$
1 1 0 1	1 1 0	$\overline{f(1,1,0)}$
1 1 1 0	1 1 1	$f(1,1,1)$
1 1 1 1	1 1 1	$\overline{f(1,1,1)}$

In the output, every permutation of A, B, and C shows up twice, once with $f(A,B,C)$ and $\overline{f(A,B,C)}$, ensuring that the outputs are unique. So, this circuit is reversible.

We can also generalize the technique to gates with multiple outputs. For example, say we have an irreversible gate with two inputs A and B and two outputs $f(A,B)$ and $g(A,B)$, which are functions of the inputs:

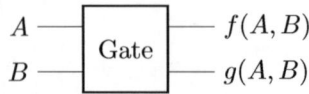

To make this reversible, follow the same procedure, but now we add two extra inputs and two XOR gates, one each for $f(A,B)$ and $g(A,B)$:

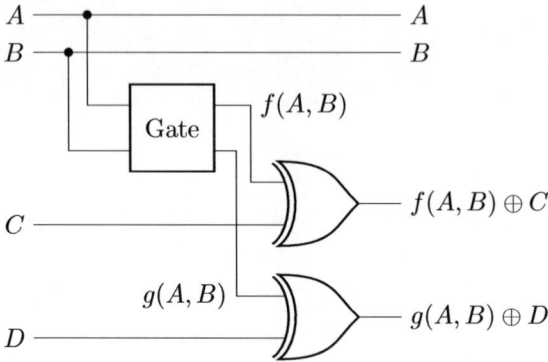

As before, for the third output, when $C = 0$, then $f(A,B) \oplus C = f(A,B) \oplus 0 = f(A,B)$, and when $C = 1$, then $f(A,B) \oplus C = f(A,B) \oplus 1 = \overline{f(A,B)}$. Similarly, the fourth output is $g(A,B)$ when $D = 0$ and $\overline{g(A,B)}$ when $D = 1$. So, the truth table of this circuit is

$A\ B\ C\ D$	$A\ B\ C \oplus f(A,B)$	$D \oplus g(A,B)$
$0\ 0\ 0\ 0$	$0\ 0$ $f(0,0)$	$g(0,0)$
$0\ 0\ 0\ 1$	$0\ 0$ $f(0,0)$	$\overline{g(0,0)}$
$0\ 0\ 1\ 0$	$0\ 0$ $\overline{f(0,0)}$	$g(0,0)$
$0\ 0\ 1\ 1$	$0\ 0$ $\overline{f(0,0)}$	$\overline{g(0,0)}$
$0\ 1\ 0\ 0$	$0\ 1$ $f(0,1)$	$g(0,1)$
$0\ 1\ 0\ 1$	$0\ 1$ $f(0,1)$	$\overline{g(0,1)}$
$0\ 1\ 1\ 0$	$0\ 1$ $\overline{f(0,1)}$	$g(0,1)$
$0\ 1\ 1\ 1$	$0\ 1$ $\overline{f(0,1)}$	$\overline{g(0,1)}$
$1\ 0\ 0\ 0$	$1\ 0$ $f(1,0)$	$g(1,0)$
$1\ 0\ 0\ 1$	$1\ 0$ $f(1,0)$	$\overline{g(1,0)}$
$1\ 0\ 1\ 0$	$1\ 0$ $\overline{f(1,0)}$	$g(1,0)$
$1\ 0\ 1\ 1$	$1\ 0$ $\overline{f(1,0)}$	$\overline{g(1,0)}$
$1\ 1\ 0\ 0$	$1\ 1$ $f(1,1)$	$g(1,1)$
$1\ 1\ 0\ 1$	$1\ 1$ $f(1,1)$	$\overline{g(1,1)}$
$1\ 1\ 1\ 0$	$1\ 1$ $\overline{f(1,1)}$	$g(1,1)$
$1\ 1\ 1\ 1$	$1\ 1$ $\overline{f(1,1)}$	$\overline{g(1,1)}$

In the output, every permutation of A and B shows up four times, once with $f(A,B)$ and $g(A,B)$, once with $f(A,B)$ and $\overline{g(A,B)}$, once with $\overline{f(A,B)}$ and $g(A,B)$, and once with $\overline{f(A,B)}$ and $\overline{g(A,B)}$, ensuring that the outputs are unique. So, this is reversible.

Exercise 1.42. Consider the following single-bit gates.
(a) The identity gate $f(A) = A$. Its truth table is

A	$f(A)$
0	0
1	1

Is this reversible or irreversible? If it is irreversible, turn it into a reversible circuit.
(b) The "always-1' gate $f(A) = 1$. Its truth table is

A	1
0	1
1	1

Is this reversible or irreversible? If it is irreversible, turn it into a reversible circuit.

Exercise 1.43. Write the truth table for XOR. Is it reversible or irreversible? If it is irreversible, turn it into a reversible circuit, and write the truth table of the reversible circuit.

Exercise 1.44. Consider the following two-bit gates, each with two outputs.
(a) The gate

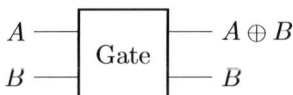

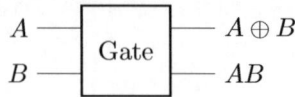

What is the truth table corresponding to this gate? Is it reversible or irreversible? If it is irreversible, turn it into a reversible circuit.

(b) The gate

$$A \longrightarrow \boxed{\text{Gate}} \longrightarrow A \oplus B$$
$$B \longrightarrow \phantom{\boxed{\text{Gate}}} \longrightarrow AB$$

What is the truth table corresponding to this gate? Is it reversible or irreversible? If it is irreversible, turn it into a reversible circuit.

Exercise 1.45. Consider the full adder from Section 1.3.3:

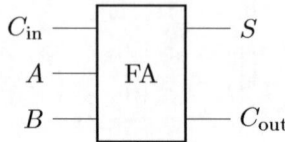

$$C_{\text{in}} \longrightarrow \boxed{\text{FA}} \longrightarrow S$$
$$A \longrightarrow \phantom{\boxed{\text{FA}}}$$
$$B \longrightarrow \phantom{\boxed{\text{FA}}} \longrightarrow C_{\text{out}}$$

Turn this into a reversible circuit.

1.6 Error Correction

1.6.1 Errors in Physical Devices

High energy particles like cosmic rays, neutrons produced in the earth's atmosphere, radiation from nuclear testing, and radiation from particle accelerators can strike computers, causing bits to flip from 0 to 1 and from 1 to 0. This is known as a *single event upset*.

Similarly, if we are transmitting data through the internet, then some bits may become corrupted. For example, photons traveling through a fiber optic cable can leak out due to imperfections in the cable. The sender may have sent a 1, but the receiver gets a 0.

Fortunately, as long as the number of errors is limited, there are schemes to detect and/or correct errors.

Exercise 1.46. Watch "The Universe is Hostile to Computers" by Veritasium on YouTube:

https://www.youtube.com/watch?v=AaZ_RSt0KP8

Answer the following questions and fill in the blanks.

(a) For the election in Belgium, Maria Vindevogel received 4096 extra votes because the thirteenth bit had flipped from 0 to 1, which added $2^{12} = 4096$ extra votes to her count. How many extra votes would she have received if the fourteenth bit had flipped instead?

(b) "In 1978, Intel reported some strange errors popping up in their 16 kilobit dynamic random access memory, or DRAM. Ones would _____ _____ to zeros with no apparent cause. The problem turned out to be the ceramic packaging the chip was encased in. With the demand for semiconductor packaging skyrocketing in the

1970's, a new manufacturing plant was constructed on the Green River in Colorado. Unfortunately, this site happened to be just downstream of an old uranium mill. _____
_____ made their way into the river and then into the ceramic packaging for Intel's microchips. Intel scientists investigating the problem found that even trace amounts of uranium and thorium in the ceramic was were sufficient to cause problems. In their DRAM, memory was stored as the _____ or _____ of electrons in a semiconductor well. The alpha particles emitted by uranium and thorium were energetic and ionizing enough to create electron-hole pairs in the silicon. If an alpha particle struck in just the right place, it could create a large number of free charge carriers, causing electrons to accumulate in the well, flipping a one to a zero. This is known as a _____
_____ _____."

(c) "The reason this problem was identified in the 1970s was because chip components had been _____ to the point where a single alpha particle could produce enough charge to flip a bit."

(d) "But the next year, he [Hess] conducted seven balloon flights up to an altitude of 5200 m. And here he discovered something remarkable. While there was an initial drop in radiation for the first several hundred meters, above one kilometer or so the level _____ with increasing altitude. At his his maximum height, the level of radiation was several times _____ than it was on the ground. The radiation appeared to be coming, not from the earth, but from the _____."

(e) "Victor Hess had discovered _____ _____, high energy radiation from space. But what were these rays exactly, and where were they coming from? Well, today we know they aren't electromagnetic rays, as many suspected, but _____. Around 90% are protons, 9% are helium nuclei, and 1% are heavier nuclei. Some of them are from the sun, but they have comparatively low energy. High energy cosmic rays moving very close to the speed of light come from exploding stars, supernovae, in our own galaxy and in others. And the highest energy particles are thought to come from _____ _____, including the super massive black holes at the centers of galaxies."

(f) "But primary cosmic rays like these don't make it down to earth's surface. Instead, they collide with air molecules around 25 kilometers above the ground and create new particles like pions. These collide and decay into other particles like neutrons, protons, muons, electrons, positrons, and photons, which in turn collide with other molecules in one long _____. So from a single primary cosmic ray comes a shower of particles streaming toward the earth. It is one of these particles that investigators suspect struck a _____ in a computer in Belgium, flipping the thirteenth bit from a zero to a one and giving Maria Vindevogel 4096 extra votes."

(g) "These days, there are a number of ways computer chips are made resilient in the face of bit flips, like _____ _____ _____ (or ECC) memory."

(h) "In 1996, IBM estimated that for each 256 megabytes of RAM, one bit flip occurs per _____. And the main culprit seems to be neutrons created in the shower of particles from _____."

(i) For a commercial airplane "At cruising altitude, this increases the chance of a single event upset by _____ _____ _____ times."

(j) "On one five day [space shuttle] mission, STS 48, there were _____ separate bit flips."

(k) "Above the atmosphere, cosmic rays are so energetic sometimes you can even see them." "Once in a while you have your eyes closed and you're not asleep yet, and if you wait a little while, you occasionally will see a _____ of light. And we think it is heavy particles or individual bursts of energy coming from radiation that are either going through the eyeball itself or going through the optic nerve. And the way that your body registers radiation going through it is amazingly enough by showing you a little flash in one of your eyes just to remind you that you are subject to the radiation of not only our sun, but _____ of the universe that is radiating at you."

1.6.2 Error Detection

The simplest way to detect errors is to repeat each bit multiple times so that multiple *physical* bits encode a single *logical* bit. This is called the *repetition code*.

For example, say we use two physical bits to encode one logical bit, i.e.,

00 encodes 0,

11 encodes 1.

So, if we want to send the letter "Q" in ASCII, which is represented by the seven-bit string 1010001, we would actually send

11 00 11 00 00 00 11.

If one of the physical bits is flipped, say due to a single event upset or transmission error, then instead of receiving 00 or 11, the recipient would receive

01   or   10.

If the recipient gets either of these pairs, they know that an error has occurred. This is an example of an *error-detecting code*. The recipient can then request that the message be resent.

The binary strings 00, 01, 10, and 11 are called *codewords*.

The *parity* of a bit string is whether the bit string has an even or odd number of 1's. The codewords 00 and 11 have even parity, while the codewords 01 an 10 have odd parity, so parity can be used to distinguish whether an error has occurred. Such indications of errors are called *error syndromes*.

Note parity can be computed using XOR, since $0 \oplus 0 = 1 \oplus 1 = 0$ indicates even parity, while $0 \oplus 1 = 1 \oplus 0 = 1$ indicates odd parity.

If more than one error occurs, then our encoding is unable to reliably detect the error. For example, if we transmit 00 and both bits get flipped to 11, then the recipient has no way of knowing that an error occurred. So, if we use the repetition code with two physical bits per logical bit, only one-bit errors can be detected.

Exercise 1.47. Another error-detecting scheme is to send a *parity bit*. For example, say I want to transmit to you the character "Q" in ASCII, which is encoded by seven bits 1010001. The parity of this bit string is odd, since there is an odd number of 1's in the string. (Alternatively, taking the XOR of all the bits yields 1.) I append this parity of 1 to the transmission, so I send you the eight bits 10100011.

Say the bits you actually receive are 11100011.

(a) Calculate the parity of the first seven bits you received.

(b) Does the parity you calculated in part (a) match the parity bit (the last bit)?

(c) Did an error occur in the transmission? Why or why not?

(d) Can this scheme reliably detect if more than one error occurred? Why or why not?

1.6.3 Error Correction

Besides being able to detect errors, it would be nice to also fix them. We call this error correction.

For example, if we use three bits for the repetition code, then

$$000 \text{ encodes } 0,$$
$$111 \text{ encodes } 1.$$

Now if a single bit gets flipped, the possible codewords are 001, 010, 100, 110, 101, and 011. We can correct the error by taking the majority vote:

$$001, 010, 100 \to 000,$$
$$110, 101, 011 \to 111.$$

This is an example of an *error-correcting code*.

This majority rule can also be implemented using parity checks as the error syndromes. Let us calculate the parity of the left two bits and the parity of the right two bits. Tabulating these for each possible codeword $b_2 b_1 b_0$:

Codeword	$b_2 \oplus b_1$	$b_1 \oplus b_0$
000	0	0
001	0	1
010	1	1
011	1	0
100	1	0
101	1	1
110	0	1
111	0	0

So if both parity bits are 0, the codeword is either 000 or 111, and there is no error. If the left parity bit is 0 and the right is 1, then the codeword is either 001 or 110, and the rightmost bit was flipped. If the left parity bit is 1 and the second is 0, then the codeword is either 011 or 100, and the left bit was flipped. Finally, if both parity bits are 1, then the codeword is 010 or 101, and the middle bit was flipped.

Note using parity checks allows us to detect and correct errors without needing to know the codeword. If we know that a bit flip occurred in the middle bit, we do not need to know if the codeword was 010 or 101. We can simply flip the middle bit to correct it, and proceed. This will be an important notion in quantum error correction, where determining the codeword can ruin the computation, so we must be able to correct errors without knowing the precise codeword.

Since this error-correcting code uses three physical bits to encode a logical bit, it is more likely that a bit will flip because there are more of them. If a single bit flips, it can be corrected. If two or all three bits flip, however, we cannot correct the error. We say an *uncorrectable error* has occurred. Using a little math, we can determine when error correction decreases the chance of an uncorrectable error because we can fix single bit flips, or when it increases the chance of an uncorrectable error because there are more bits to flip.

First, let p denote the probability of a single bit flipping. Without error correction, if the bit flips an uncorrectable error has occurred, so the probability of an uncorrectable occurring is p. Now with three physical bits representing one logical bit, single-bit errors can be corrected, so an uncorrectable error only occurs when two or three of the bits get flipped. The probability of two specific bits getting flipped while the third remains unflipped is $p^2(1-p)$, where p^2 comes from the two bits getting flipped, and $1-p$ comes from the unflipped third bit. Since there are three combinations for two of the three bits to be flipped (the two bits could be the first two bits, the last two bits, or the first and last bits), the probability of any two bits getting flipped is $3p^2(1-p)$. Another way to get the coefficient of 3 is using the *combination* "3 choose 2," where "n choose k" is

$$_nC_k = \frac{n!}{k!(n-k)!},$$

where the exclamation point denotes factorial, e.g., $5! = 5 \cdot 4 \cdot 3 \cdot 2 \cdot 1$ and $0! = 1$. Combinations are also called *binomial coefficients*.

Binomial coefficients can be calculated manually, perhaps with the help of a calculator. They can also be calculated using a *computer algebra system*, which is computer software that solves problems using algebraic manipulation and more. In this textbook, we will provide calculations in both Mathematica and SageMath, and you can choose whichever you prefer.

- *Mathematica.* Among physicists, a popular computer algebra system is Mathematica. It is proprietary, however, so it must be purchased, although many universities pay for a Mathematica subscription that allows their students to use it. The combination $_nC_k$ can be computing using Mathematica's `Binomial` function. For example, $_3C_2$ is:

```
Binomial[3,2]
```

  The output of this is 3, as expected.

- *SageMath.* Another popular computer algebra system is SageMath, often simply called Sage. It is based on the Python programming language. One of the main benefits of SageMath is that it is open-source, so anyone can download it from `sagemath.org` and install it for free. SageMath's `binomial` function can be used to compute the combination $_nC_k$. For example, $_3C_2$ is:

```
sage: binomial(3,2)
3
```

  We see that the answer is 3, as expected.

An uncorrectable error also occurs when all three bits get flipped, and the probability of that occurring is p^3. The coefficient of this is simply 1 because there is only 1 way to choose 3 bits out of 3. Alternatively, $_3C_3 = 1$. Adding together the probability of two bits flipping $[3p^2(1-p)]$ with the probability of three bits flipping

(p^3), the probability of an uncorrectable error occurring is

$$3p^2(1-p)+p^3.$$

As long as this is less than p, which is the probability that an error occurs without error correction, then it is favorable to do error correction. That is, it is favorable to do error correction when

$$3p^2(1-p)+p^3 < p.$$

We can solve this inequality using a computer algebra system. As promised, we will provide both Mathematica and SageMath code:

- *Mathematica.* Using Mathematica's Reduce function, the inequality can be solved using

```
Reduce[3 p^2(1-p) + p^3 < p, p]
```

  Executing this, the output is

$$0 < p < \frac{1}{2} \quad || \quad p > 1.$$

  In this result, the double bar $||$ means "or." So, there are two situations when the 3-bit repetition code is better than no error correction, when $0 < p < 1/2$ or when $p > 1$.
- *SageMath.* Using SageMath's solve function, the inequality can be solved using

```
sage: p = var('p')
sage: solve(3*p**2*(1-p) + p**3 < p, p)
[[p > 0, p < (1/2)], [p > 1]]
```

  So, there are two situations when the 3-bit repetition code is better than no error correction. The first is when $p > 0$ and $p < 1/2$. That is, when $0 < p < 1/2$. The second is when $p > 1$.

Thus, using either Mathematica or SageMath, the repetition code with three bits is better when the probability of a single bit flip is

$$0 < p < \frac{1}{2}, \quad p > 1.$$

Since p is a probability, it cannot be less than 0 or greater than 1. So, the 3-bit repetition code is better than no error correction when

$$p < \frac{1}{2}.$$

Thus, as long as the error probability is less than $1/2$, error correction is beneficial. For example, if $p = 0.1$, then $3p^2(1-p)+p^3 = 0.028$, so there is a smaller chance that an uncorrectable error occurs. If $p = 0.6$, then $3p^2(1-p)+p^3 = 0.648$, so an uncorrectable error is more likely to occur.

Exercise 1.48. Using the repetition code, you have a three-bit string that encodes a logical bit.
  (a) If the parity of the left two bits is odd, and the parity of the right two bits is also odd, has a single-bit error occurred? If yes, which bit was flipped (the left, middle, or right bit)?
  (b) If the parity of the left two bits is odd, but the parity of the right two bits is even, has a single-bit error occurred? If yes, which bit was flipped (the left, middle, or right bit)?
  (c) If the probability of a single bit flipping is $p = 0.2$, what is the probability that an uncorrectable error occurs with the 3-bit repetition code? In this case, does the 3-bit repetition code increase or decrease the probability of an uncorrectable error occurring?
  (d) If the probability of a single bit flipping is $p = 0.7$, what is the probability that an uncorrectable error occurs with the 3-bit repetition code? In this case, does the 3-bit repetition code increase or decrease the probability of an uncorrectable error occurring?

Exercise 1.49. Using the repetition code, you have a five-bit string that encodes a logical bit. This allows for the correction of two-bit errors, since three correct bits is the majority vote over the two incorrect bits. Say you receive a codeword $b_4 b_3 b_2 b_1 b_0$.
  (a) If $b_4 \oplus b_3 = 0$, $b_3 \oplus b_2 = 0$, $b_2 \oplus b_1 = 1$, and $b_1 \oplus b_0 = 1$, did an error occur? If an error has occurred, which bit(s) were flipped?
  (b) If $b_4 \oplus b_3 = 0$, $b_3 \oplus b_2 = 1$, $b_2 \oplus b_1 = 0$, and $b_1 \oplus b_0 = 1$, did an error occur? If an error has occurred, which bit(s) were flipped?
  (c) If the probability of a single bit flipping is p, what is the probability of an uncorrectable error occurring with this repetition code of 5 bits? Hint: One and two-bit flips can be corrected, so uncorrectable errors occur if three, four, or five bits are flipped. The probability of each occurring also depends on the number of combinations of bits flipping.
  (d) For what values of p is your result in part (c) less than p (the error rate without error correction)?
  (e) If $p = 0.1$, what is the probability that an uncorrectable error occurs with the 5-bit repetition code? In this case, does the 5-bit repetition code increase or decrease the probability of an uncorrectable error occurring?
  (f) For comparison, if $p = 0.1$, what is the probability that an uncorrectable error occurs with the 3-bit repetition code? How does it compare to the 5-bit code?

1.7 Computational Complexity

1.7.1 Asymptotic Notation

Say we want to add two 4-bit numbers using the ripple-carry adder from Section 1.3.4. This takes one half-adder, which has two logic gates, and three full-adders, which each have five logic gates, for a total of $2 + 3 \cdot 5 = 17$ logic gates. If we generalize this and add two n-bit numbers with a ripple-carry adder, it takes one half-adder and $(n - 1)$ full-adders, for a total of $2 + (n - 1)5 = 5n - 3$ logic gates. So, as the length n of the binary numbers increases, the number of logic gates $5n - 3$ scales linearly with n. This scaling can be expressed through *asymptotic notation*.

  Big-O notation is used to give an *upper bound* on the asymptotic behavior of a function. We write $5n - 3 = O(n^2)$ to mean that $5n - 3$ scales less than or equal to n^2 for large n. Mathematically, $f(n) = O(g(n))$ means there exists constants c and n_0 such that $f(n) \leq cg(n)$ for all values of n greater than n_0. Some other examples include $5n - 3 = O(n\log(n))$ and $5n - 3 = O(2^n)$. Since the scaling is "less than or equal to," we can also write $5n - 3 = O(n)$. Big-O is the most commonly used asymptotic notation, and it is useful for specifying the worst-case behavior of an algorithm. In our case, the number of logic gates needed to add two binary numbers of length n is no worse than linear, i.e., $O(n)$.

If we want the inequality to be strictly "less than," we use *little-o notation*. So we can write $5n - 3 = o(n^2)$, but $5n - 3 \neq o(n)$. Mathematically, $f(n) = o(g(n))$ means for all $c > 0$ there exists some n_0 (which may depend on c) such that $f(n) < cg(n)$ for all values of n greater than n_0.

Similarly, a *lower bound* on the asymptotic behavior of a function is denoted using *big-Omega notation*. We can write $5n - 3 = \Omega(\sqrt{n})$ to mean that $5n - 3$ scales greater than or equal to $\sqrt{n}$ for large n. Mathematically, $f(n) = \Omega(g(n))$ means there exists constants c and n_0 such that $f(n) \geq cg(n)$ for all values of n greater than n_0. We could also write $5n - 3 = \Omega(1)$ to mean that $5n - 3$ is lower bounded by a constant. Since the inequality is "greater than or equal to," we can also write $5n - 3 = \Omega(n)$.

As before, if we want the inequality to be strictly "greater than," we use a lowercase symbol, or *little-omega notation*. So, we can write $5n - 3 = \omega(\sqrt{n})$, but $5n - 3 \neq \omega(n)$. Mathematically, $f(n) = \omega(g(n))$ means for all $c > 0$ there exists some n_0 (which may depend on c) such that $f(n) > cg(n)$ for all values of n greater than n_0.

Finally, to specify that $5n - 3$ scales linearly with n, we use *big-Theta notation*. We write this as $5n - 3 = \Theta(n)$, and it means that $5n - 3$ is both upper bounded and lower bounded by n, asymptotically. That is, $5n - 3 = O(n)$ and $5n - 3 = \Omega(n)$. Combining the mathematical definitions of each, $f(n) = \Theta(g(n))$ means there exists constants c_1, c_2, and n_0 such that $c_1 g(n) \leq f(n) \leq c_2 g(n)$ for all values of n greater than n_0.

These asymptotic notations are summarized in Table 1.2.

Table 1.2: Summary of asymptotic notations. The mathematical symbol $\exists$ means "there exists," $\ni$ means "such that," and $\forall$ means "for all."

Notation	Description	Definition
$f(n) = O(g(n))$	f scales $\leq g$	$\exists c, n_0 \ni f(n) \leq cg(n) \ \forall n > n_0$
$f(n) = o(g(n))$	f scales $< g$	$\forall c > 0 \exists n_0 \ni f(n) < cg(n) \ \forall n > n_0$
$f(n) = \Omega(g(n))$	f scales $\geq g$	$\exists c, n_0 \ni f(n) \geq cg(n) \ \forall n > n_0$
$f(n) = \omega(g(n))$	f scales $> g$	$\forall c > 0 \exists n_0 \ni f(n) > cg(n) \ \forall n > n_0$
$f(n) = \Theta(g(n))$	f scales $= g$	$\exists c_1, c_2, n_0 \ni c_1 g(n) \leq f(n) \leq c_2 g(n) \ \forall n > n_0$

Exercise 1.50. Consider the following functions, one quadratic and another cubic:

$$f(n) = 5247n^2, \quad g(n) = 11n^3.$$

(a) Evaluate both functions when $n = 100$. Which is bigger, $f(100)$ or $g(100)$?

(b) Evaluate both functions when $n = 500$. Which is bigger, $f(500)$ or $g(500)$?
(c) At what value of n does $g(n)$ surpass $f(n)$?
(d) Label each of the following statements as true or false:

$$f(n) = O(g(n)) \qquad \text{true / false}$$
$$f(n) = o(g(n)) \qquad \text{true / false}$$
$$f(n) = \Theta(g(n)) \qquad \text{true / false}$$
$$f(n) = \Omega(g(n)) \qquad \text{true / false}$$
$$f(n) = \omega(g(n)) \qquad \text{true / false}$$

Exercise 1.51. Match each function to a possible asymptotic notation. Although each asymptotic notation can match multiple functions, each should only be used once.

(a) $3n^2 + 7n + 4$ (i) $o(\sqrt{n})$
(b) $\log n$ (ii) $\Omega(2^n)$
(c) $5e^n$ (iii) $\Theta(n^2)$
(d) $\pi\sqrt{n}$ (iv) $O(1)$
(e) π (v) $\omega(1)$

1.7.2 Complexity Classes

Since each logic gate takes some time to apply, we say an algorithm that utilizes, say, $O(n)$ logic gates, takes $O(n)$ *time*, ignoring the fact that some of the logic gates can be done in parallel.

In computer science, an algorithm is called *efficient* if it takes polynomial time or less. Polynomial time means the number of gates scales as a polynomial in n, such as the ripple-carry adder's $5n - 3$ gates, or algorithms that take n^2, n^3, or n^{1000} gates. Any other power function is also efficient, such as $n^{2.5}$, since this scales less than the polynomial n^3. Another example is $\sqrt{n} = n^{0.5}$, since this scales less than the polynomial n. Algorithms that takes constant time $O(1)$ or logarithmic time $O(\log(n))$ are faster than polynomial time, so they are also efficient. A loglinear runtime $O(n\log(n))$ is also efficient, since it grows faster than n but slower than n^2. On the other hand, an algorithm is *inefficient* if it takes more than polynomial time, called *superpolynomial time*. This includes algorithms that take *exponential time*, such as 2^n or $e^{n/1000}$. It also includes algorithms that take *subexponential time*, which are less than exponential time but greater than polynomial time, such as $2^{n^{1/3}}$.

Often, we call problems *easy* if their solutions are efficient, and problems *hard* if their solutions are inefficient. For example, adding numbers is easy because there is a polynomial-time algorithm for it. In practice, however, an easy problem whose algorithm takes n^{1000} time may be harder than a hard problem that takes $e^{n/1000}$ time because, for small problem sizes, the polynomial is bigger than the exponential. Despite this, distinguishing between easy and hard problems, or efficient and inefficient algorithms, in this manner is still useful.

Different problems are easier or harder than others, and we classify them using *complexity classes*, or classes of problems of some complexity or difficulty. Problems that can be solved efficiently (in polynomial time) by a classical computer are in the complexity class P, which stands for Polynomial-Time. Some problems in P include:

- Matchmaking in the "stable marriage problem." Given n men and n women who have ranked the other group in order of preference, marry the men with the women so that no two people would rather be with each other than with their spouses. The Gale-Shapley algorithm solves this in $O(n^2)$ time.
- Determining if a number is prime. Recall a *prime number* is a whole number greater than 1 whose only factors are 1 and itself, so 2, 3, 5, 7, 11, and 13 are all prime numbers, but 4 is not prime because it is equal to 2×2, and 6 is not prime because it is equal to 2×3. If the number to be tested has n digits, then the Agrawal–Kayal–Saxena (AKS) class of algorithms can determine if the number is prime in $O(n^6)$ time, ignoring factors $\log(n)$.
- Maximizing a linear function constrained by linear inequalities, also known as "linear programming." If there are n variables, algorithms exist that run in $O(n^3)$ and faster.

Another complexity class is the problems for which a solution can be quickly verified by a computer in polynomial time. This class is called NP (the N stands for a non-deterministic Turing machine—more on this later, and the P stands for polynomial), and it includes problems such as:

- Factoring, since it is easy to multiply the factors together to verify it equals the original number.
- Testing if two networks are equivalent, since it is easy to verify that two networks are equivalent if a map between the two is provided. This is known as the "graph isomorphism" problem.

Many problems of practical importance are in the class NP.

Certain problems within NP have a special property called *completeness*, and we call these problems NP-COMPLETE. If we can find an efficient solution to any NP-COMPLETE problem, then we can use it to find an efficient solution to *any* NP problem. That is, the overhead in applying the algorithm to other NP problems is at most polynomial, so an efficient solution to one NP-COMPLETE problem yields an efficient solution to all NP problems. Some NP-COMPLETE problems include:

- Solving $n \times n$ Sudoku puzzles.
- Finding the shortest possible tour that visits a list of cities exactly once and returns to its starting point, known as the "traveling salesman problem."
- Determining whether a tour that visits each location once and returns to its starting point exists, which is called the "Hamiltonian path problem."
- Determining whether a set of items can fit into certain boxes, known as the "bin packing problem."

A literal million dollar question is whether P and NP are equal. The Clay Mathematics Institute will pay one million U.S. dollars to whomever can prove whether the problems whose solutions are efficiently found are the same as the problems whose solutions are efficiently verified. It is known that all problems in P are *contained* within NP, since if one can efficiently solve a problem, one can also efficiently check proposed solutions by comparing them to the answer. But, it is unknown if NP contains any problems that are not in P. The general conjecture is that $P \neq NP$.

Another complexity class is PSPACE, which contains all the problems that can be solved by a computer using a polynomial amount of memory, without any limits on time. Generalizations of many games are in PSPACE, such as:

- Determining whether a winning strategy exists for the game of checkers generalised to an $n \times n$ board.
- Winning a generalized level of Super Mario Bros.

It is known that NP is contained in PSPACE because one has unlimited of time to check all possible answers. Although it seems like PSPACE should be a larger class of problems than NP, there is currently no proof. The general conjecture is that $NP \neq PSPACE$. It is even unknown if PSPACE is larger than P, but again the conjecture is that $P \neq PSPACE$.

To summarize, it is believed that $P \neq NP$ and $NP \neq PSPACE$ (and hence $PSPACE \neq P$), but none of these relations have been proved. These suspected relationships are summarized in Fig. 1.1.

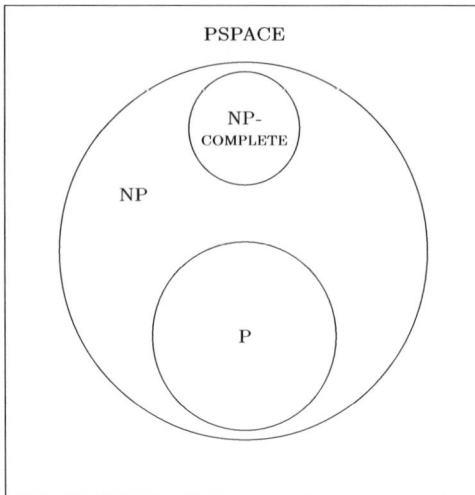

Fig. 1.1: The generally accepted relationships between the complexity classes NP, NP-COMPLETE, P, and PSPACE.

Exercise 1.52. Consider the following runtimes. Is each efficient or inefficient? (a) $\log^2(n)$ (b) n^3 (c) $n^5 \log^4(n)$ (d) $2^{\sqrt{n}}$ (e) $2^{n/2}$ (f) $n!$

Exercise 1.53. Visit `https://www.complexityzoo.net`. Look up the complexity class BPP.
 (a) What does BPP stand for?
 (b) BPP often identified as what?

Exercise 1.54. What is a problem in NP that is believed to not be in P?

Exercise 1.55. Visit the Clay Mathematics Institute website at `https://claymath.org` and find the Millenium Problems.
 (a) List the seven Millenium Prize Problems. Is each problem solved or unsolved?
 (b) Who first proposed the P vs NP problem? In what year?

Exercise 1.56. Visit the Wikipedia list of NP-COMPLETE problems at `https://en.wikiped ia.org/wiki/List_of_NP-complete_problems`. Describe three NP-COMPLETE problems.

1.8 Turing Machines

So far, we have examined circuit-based computers consisting of bits and logic gates. While circuit-based computers are very useful in practice, they are not always the best kind of computer to study mathematically. Other types of computers, or *models of computation*, exist and may be more convenient. In this section, we examine the *Turing machine*, which was introduced in 1936 and is still used today by computer scientists who study the abilities and limitations of computers.

1.8.1 Components

A Turing machine consists of four parts:

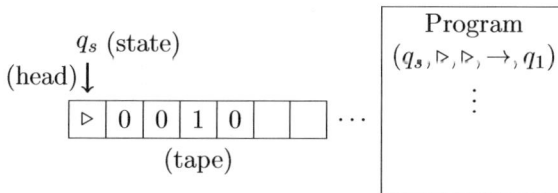

1. A *tape* divided into cells, each with a symbol from some finite alphabet. The left end of the tape is denoted by ▷, and the right end of the tape can extend as far as needed. In this textbook, the remaining cells can contain nothing (blank), 0, or 1.
2. A *head* that can read or write to the tape, and then move left one cell (←), right one cell (→), or stay put (•).

3. A *register* that stores the *state* of the Turing machine. Only a finite number of states are allowed. Two special states are required, a starting state q_s and a halting state q_h indicating that the program has finished.
4. A *list of instructions* or *program*. For each step, the Turing machine starts at the top of the list of instructions and goes down the list until it finds a line matching the current state of the machine and the current symbol on the tape. Then it write to the tape, moves according to the instruction, and updates the state of the machine.

While modern computers are not built like this, Turing machines can compute everything that a circuit-based computer can compute. But, they are easier to describe mathematically, so they allow computer scientists to study the power and limitations of computers. Before we discuss this, let us look at an example of how a Turing machine can compute something.

Exercise 1.57. Visit the Wikipedia page on Model of Computation at https://en.wikiped ia.org/wiki/Model_of_computation. Describe three models of computation besides the Turing model.

1.8.2 Incrementing Binary Numbers

Let us show how a Turing machine can increment (add 1 to) a binary number. First, consider incrementing 1011 by hand:

$$(\text{carry}) \, 0\,1\,1$$
$$1011$$
$$\underline{\text{``+''} \, 0001}$$
$$(\text{sum}) \quad 1100$$

From this process, we can deduce an algorithm for how to increment binary numbers. Starting at the rightmost column, when we add 1 to 1, we get 0, and we carry a 1 to the next column. Again, we add 1 to 1 and get 0, carrying 1 to the next column. Now we add 1 to 0, which yields 1, and nothing carries. Any remaining digits will be unchanged. Thus, to increment binary numbers, we can flip all 1's on the right to 0's, and when we reach the rightmost 0, we flip it to a 1.

This computation can be done using a Turing machine using the following program:

Current State	Current Tape	Write to Tape	Move	Update State
q_s	$\triangleright$	$\triangleright$	$\rightarrow$	q_1
q_1	0	0	$\rightarrow$	q_1
q_1	1	1	$\rightarrow$	q_1
q_1			$\leftarrow$	q_2
q_2	1	0	$\leftarrow$	q_2
q_2	0	1	$\bullet$	q_h

We will show that this correctly increments 1011 in a moment, but first let us give an overview of the program. The first line says that when the Turing machine starts, it should move right and change states to q_1. In the next three lines, the state is q_1, and the Turing machine keeps moving right until it reaches a blank cell, at which it moves left and changes to the state q_2. This moves the head all the way to the rightmost bit. Now in the state q_2, the last two lines say to flip any 1's to 0's, but the moment we reach a 0, we should flip it to a 1 and then halt.

Now, let us follow the program to increment 1011. The Turing machine begins in the state q_s with its head at the leftmost cell:

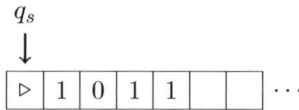

$$q_s$$
$$\downarrow$$

| $\triangleright$ | 1 | 0 | 1 | 1 | | | $\cdots$ |

The machine goes through its list of instructions from top to bottom, searching for the first instruction that matches its current state q_s with current tape symbol $\triangleright$. It finds the entry $(q_s, \triangleright, \triangleright, \rightarrow, q_1)$. So it writes $\triangleright$ to the tape (so it is unchanged), moves one cell right, and updates the state register to q_1:

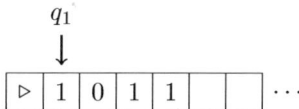

$$q_1$$
$$\downarrow$$

| $\triangleright$ | 1 | 0 | 1 | 1 | | | $\cdots$ |

The Turing machine again goes through its list of instructions from top to bottom, searching for the first instruction that matches its current state q_1 with current tape symbol 1. It finds the entry $(q_1, 1, 1, \rightarrow, q_1)$. So it writes 1 to the tape (so it is unchanged), moves one cell right, and sets the state register to q_1 (so it is unchanged):

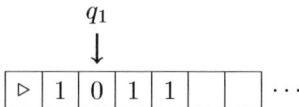

$$q_1$$
$$\downarrow$$

| $\triangleright$ | 1 | 0 | 1 | 1 | | | $\cdots$ |

Now the head reads 0 on the tape, so it searches its program from top to bottom, finding the instruction $(q_1, 0, 0, \rightarrow, q_1)$. Following this, it writes 0 to the tape (so it is unchanged), moves the head right, and sets the state to q_1 (so it is unchanged):

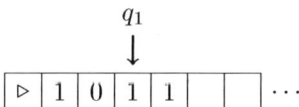

$$q_1$$
$$\downarrow$$

| $\triangleright$ | 1 | 0 | 1 | 1 | | | $\cdots$ |

Now the tape reads 1, so the machine follows the instruction $(q_1, 1, 1, \rightarrow, q_1)$. Following this, the head moves right again (while the tape and state are unchanged):

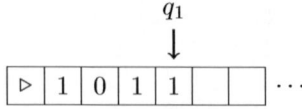

$$q_1$$
$$\downarrow$$

| ▷ | 1 | 0 | 1 | 1 | | | $\cdots$

The machine again follows the instruction $(q_1, 1, 1, \rightarrow, q_1)$, moving the head right:

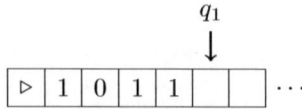

$$q_1$$
$$\downarrow$$

| ▷ | 1 | 0 | 1 | 1 | | | $\cdots$

Thus far, while the Turing machine was in the state q_1, the head moved to the right past all the bits. Now the head reads blank, so the Turing machine follows $(q_1, , , \leftarrow, q_2)$, writing a blank symbol (so it is unchanged), moving the head left, and updating the state to q_2:

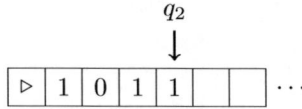

$$q_2$$
$$\downarrow$$

| ▷ | 1 | 0 | 1 | 1 | | | $\cdots$

The head is now at the rightmost bit, and the Turing machine follows $(q_2, 1, 0, \leftarrow, q_2)$, writing a 0 and moving left:

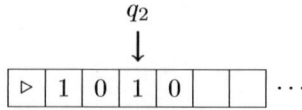

$$q_2$$
$$\downarrow$$

| ▷ | 1 | 0 | 1 | 0 | | | $\cdots$

The Turing machine follows $(q_2, 1, 0, \leftarrow, q_2)$ again, writing a 0 and moving left:

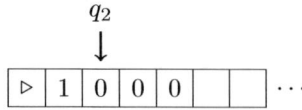

$$q_2$$
$$\downarrow$$

| ▷ | 1 | 0 | 0 | 0 | | | $\cdots$

Finally, the Turing machine follows $(q_2, 0, 1, \bullet, q_h)$, writing a 1 and halting:

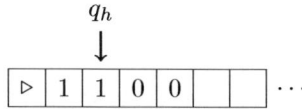

$$q_h$$
$$\downarrow$$

| ▷ | 1 | 1 | 0 | 0 | | | $\cdots$

So in the state q_2, the Turing machine moves to the left, flipping all 1's to 0's, until it sees the first 0, at which it flips it to a 1 and halts. As seen on the final tape, we have incremented 1011 to 1100, as expected.

Exercise 1.58. A Turing machine follows the program shown below:

Current State	Current Tape	Write to Tape	Move	Update State
q_s	▷	▷	→	q_1
q_1	0	0	→	q_2
q_1	1	1	→	q_1
q_2	0	0	→	q_2
q_2	1	1	→	q_2
q_1		0	•	q_h
q_2		1	•	q_h

(a) Apply this program to the tape shown to the right until it halts. What is the resulting tape?

q_s
↓
| ▷ | 0 | 0 | | | ···

(b) Apply this program to the tape shown to the right until it halts. What is the resulting tape?

q_s
↓
| ▷ | 0 | 1 | | | ···

(c) Apply this program to the tape shown to the right until it halts. What is the resulting tape?

q_s
↓
| ▷ | 1 | 0 | | | ···

(d) Apply this program to the tape shown to the right until it halts. What is the resulting tape?

q_s
↓
| ▷ | 1 | 1 | | | ···

(e) From your answers in parts (a) through (d), what does this Turing machine compute?

(f) What does the program do if the tape initially has more than two bits?

Exercise 1.59. Write a program for a Turing machine that calculates the parity of a bit string of arbitrary length. Assume the tape starts with the symbol ▷ and is followed by the bit string, which can be any length, followed by blanks. Write the parity as 0 or 1 (even or odd) to the blank after the bit string, and then halt.

1.8.3 Church-Turing Thesis

Turing machines are important for many reasons, but especially because of two long-held beliefs regarding computation:

- The *Church-Turing Thesis* says that everything that is computable can be computed with a Turing machine, although it could take a long time (e.g., exponential time).

  This correctly suggests that there are problems that cannot be computed. They are called *undecidable problems*, the most famous of which is the *halting problem* (see Exercise 1.60). Aside from such uncomputable problems, everything else can be computed, and it can be computed using a Turing machine.

- The *Strong Church-Turing Thesis* says that any model of computation, be it the circuit model or something else, can be simulated by a probabilistic Turing machine with at most polynomial overhead.
  A probabilistic Turing machine is a Turing machine where the state of the system can be set probabilistically, such as by the flip of a coin. The Strong Church-Turing Thesis says that a probabilistic Turing Machine can perform the same computations as any other kind of computer, and it only needs at most polynomially more steps than the other computer. This means an efficient algorithm on one kind of computer is also an efficient algorithm on a probabilistic Turing machine, since adding a polynomial overhead to a polynomial time algorithm is still a polynomial time algorithm. This is why defining efficient algorithms as those that run in polynomial time or faster is a useful notion.

Quantum computers would not violate the regular Church-Turing Thesis. That is, what is impossible to compute remains impossible. The hope, however, is that quantum computers can violate the Strong Church-Turing Thesis, that they will efficiently solve problems that are inefficient on classical computers.

While there is no proof of this hope, there is strong evidence. Here are three examples:

- Quantum computers can efficiently factor numbers using Shor's algorithm, which will be covered near the end of this book. Factoring is believed to be hard for classical computers, and the best known classical algorithm for factoring runs in subexponential time. Note factoring is in NP since it is easy to check if proposed factors are correct by multiplying them, but no algorithm has been found to put the problem in P. The believed difficulty of factoring is the basis for RSA, a widely used type of cryptography. RSA will be explained in Section 6.6.2. This would be a very useful application of quantum computers, but currently, quantum computers are too small to factor anything larger than $21 = 3 \times 7$.
- Determining the results of random quantum programs is called *random circuit sampling*. This is easy for quantum computers, but it is believed to be hard for classical computers. The best known classical algorithm takes exponential time. In 2019, scientists at Google and the University of California, Santa Barbara (UCSB) used a quantum processor to perform random circuit sampling. It took their quantum processor about three minutes and twenty seconds. In contrast, they argued that a typical classical computer would take approximately 10 000 years. Shortly after this result was published, IBM argued that Summit, the largest supercomputer in the world at the time, could theoretically perform the computation in 2.5 days rather than 10 000 years if it also used its massive amounts of hard drive disk storage. This approach could use roughly 72 petabytes of storage[3]. In practice, using an *entire* supercomputer for any amount of time is prohibitive, let alone for 2.5 days. This illustrates just how hard it is

---

[3] For the advanced reader, the experiment used 53 quantum bits. It takes 2^{53} numbers to write down the state of these quantum bits, and if each number uses 8 bytes, storing the entire quantum state would take $2^{53} \cdot 8 = 2^{56} = 72.058 \times 10^{15}$ bytes $= 72.058$ petabytes.

for classical computers, as we currently understand them, to perform random circuit sampling; either a ridiculous amount of time or a ridculous amount of storage is necessary to reproduce the results, as far as we know. Google/UCSB's result is the first demonstration of *quantum computational supremacy*, where a quantum computer performs a task that is out-of-reach of the known abilities of classical computers, without regard for whether the task is useful or not.

- Another example is called *boson sampling*. Bosons are a type of particle, and examples include photons (particles of light) that mediate the electromagnetic force, gluons that mediate the strong nuclear force, the $W^{\pm}$ and Z^0 bosons that mediate the weak force, and the Higgs boson that explains why particles have mass. By passing photons through half-silvered mirrors and reflecting them off mirrors, one gets a probability distribution for where the photons end up. This is a quantum process that is theoretically easy for a quantum device to perform. On the other hand, it is theoretically hard for a classical computer to compute. The best known classical algorithm takes exponential time. This boson sampling problem is in the complexity class #P (pronounced "sharp P"), and it is just as unlikely to be equal to P as NP is to equal P. A proof that P and #P are not equal, however, does not exist, just like a proof that P and NP are not equal does not exist. In 2020 and 2021, a series of experiments from the University of Science and Technology of China demonstrated boson sampling using photons. This is another example of quantum computational supremacy.

In each of the above examples, quantum computers are superpolynomially faster than the best known classical algorithms. This suggests that quantum computers can efficiently solve problems that are intractable for classical computers or (probabilistic) Turing machines, and so quantum computers may overturn the Strong Church-Turing Thesis. These are not proofs, however, because the difficulty for classical computers is not proven.

Despite this, there are other problems for which quantum computers do yield *provable* speedups over classical computers, but these speedups are polynomial at best. For example, quantum computers can search an unordered database in the square root of the amount of time a classical computer would take. These provable speedups do not violate the Strong Church-Turing Thesis since the thesis allows for polynomial overhead.

The complexity class of problems efficiently solved by a quantum computer is called BQP. It stands for Bounded-Error Quantum Polynomial-Time, and its suspected relationship to P, NP, NP-COMPLETE, and PSPACE is depicted in Fig. 1.2.

As we will see in this book, quantum computers can efficiently simulate classical computers, so they can efficiently solve everything that a classical computer can efficiently solve, which is precisely P, so P is definitely contained within in BQP. The question is how much bigger BQP is than P, if at all. A proof of this may be distant, however, as whether NP and PSPACE are bigger than P is still unsolved.

Exercise 1.60. The *halting problem* is to determine whether a computer program halts (finishes running) or runs forever (like an infinite loop). Turing proved in 1936 that an algorithm to solve this in general does not exist. For this problem, let us go through a sketch of a modern proof.

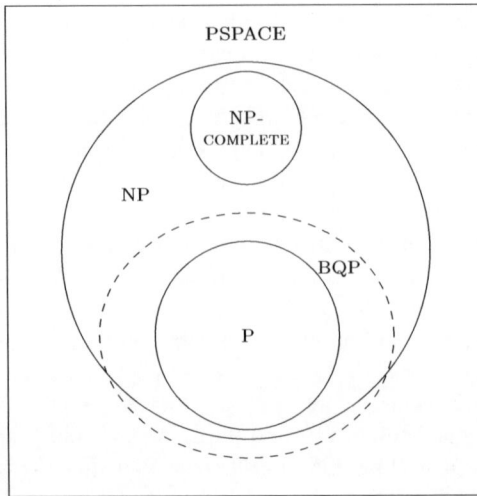

Fig. 1.2: The generally accepted relationships between the complexity classes BQP, NP, NP-COMPLETE, P, and PSPACE.

Say there exists a program H(P) that returns true if the program P halts and false otherwise. We will be proving that such a program cannot exist. In pseudocode, we can write H(P) as

```
program H(P):
  if P halts
    return true
  else:
    return false
end
```

Next, if H(P) exists, we can write a program Z(P) that does the opposite. Z(P) takes a program P and runs/loops forever if H(P) returns true, and it halts if H(P) returns false. In pseudocode,

```
program Z(P):
  if H(P) is true:
    run forever
  else:
    halt
end
```

(a) Say H says that some program P_1 halts, i.e., $H(P_1)$ returns true. Does $Z(P_1)$ halt or run forever?
(b) Say H says that some program P_2 runs forever, i.e., $H(P_2)$ returns false. Does $Z(P_2)$ halt or run forever?
Now consider what happens if we run Z(Z), i.e., program Z with its own code as input.
(c) If H(Z) returns true, does Z(Z) halt or run forever? Where is the contradiction?
(d) If H(Z) returns false, does Z(Z) halt or run forever? Where is the contradiction?
These contradictions mean that $H(P)$ cannot exist.

Exercise 1.61. Watch "The Halting Problem - An Impossible Problem to Solve" by Up and Atom on YouTube:

https://www.youtube.com/watch?v=t37GQgUPa6k

Answer the following questions and fill in the blanks.
(a) David Hilbert asked three questions...
   Is mathematics _____?
   Is mathematics _____?
   Is mathematics _____?
(b) Some more complicated programs can even have other _____ as inputs, and some can even have _____ as inputs.
(c) What is the Goldbach conjecture?
(d) If Hal says that Randy halts, what does Barrie do?
(e) If Hal says that Randy runs forever, what does Barrie do?
(f) If Hal says that Barrie halts, what does Barrie do? Is this a problem?
(g) If Hal says that Barrie runs forever, what does Barrie do? Is this a problem?
(h) In the same paper Turing also managed to answer Hilbert's third question, that no, mathematics is _____. There are some problems that we simply _____ _____.

Exercise 1.62. Visit the Wikipedia list of undecidable problems at

https://en.wikipedia.org/wiki/List_of_undecidable_problems

Describe three undecidable problems.

Exercise 1.63. Take a look at Google/UCSB's paper on quantum computational supremacy at

https://doi.org/10.1038/s41586-019-1666-5

From the abstract, fill in the blanks.
(a) "Our Sycamore processor takes about 200 seconds to sample one instance of a quantum circuit _____ _____ _____."
(b) "This dramatic increase in speed compared to _____ _____ classical algorithms is an experimental realization of _____ [computational] _____."

Exercise 1.64. Read the following excerpts from Scott Aaronson's article "The Limits of Quantum Computers" in Scientific American (March 2008):
(a) Page 65, box titled "The Good News." What would be the "killer app" for quantum computers?
(b) Page 66, box titled "What Classical Computers Can and Cannot Do." Fill in the blank: "NP-complete problems are the _____ of the NP problems."
(c) Page 67, box titled "Where Quantum Computers Fit In." Are quantum computers expected to solve some, most, or all problems in NP?

1.9 Summary

The smallest unit of classical information is the bit, which has two possible states, 0 or 1. Bits can be used to encode information, such as using ASCII. Bits are operated on by logic gates, including NOT, AND, OR, XOR, NAND, and NOR. Together, these gates can be used to perform any computation, and subsets of these gates are also universal, such as {NOT, AND, OR} and {NAND}. The mathematics that describes logic gates is called boolean algebra. Logic gates can be made reversible, and the Toffoli gate is a reversible version of the AND gate. In physical systems, errors sometimes occur, but as long as the error rates are sufficiently low, they can be corrected. Classical computers can efficiently solve some problems, while other problems take a superpolynomial amount of time. It is believed that quantum computers can efficiently solve some of the problems that are hard for classical computers.

Chapter 2
One Quantum Bit

By drawing parallels to classical computing from the previous chapter, we can introduce quantum information and computation in a natural way. Since we have not yet defined "quantum," just take it to mean a different set of rules, which we will bring up as they become relevant.

2.1 Qubit Touchdown: A Quantum Computing Board Game

Quantum physics has a reputation for being difficult and confusing, exacerbated by (incorrect) references to quantum mechanics in movies to justify their sci-fi plot elements. To help reduce this intimidation factor and ease the introduction of quantum computing, I made a board game called *Qubit Touchdown*. It is shown in Fig. 2.1, and it is available print-on-demand from The Game Crafter.[1]

Qubit Touchdown is a two player game. It consists of a game board, shown in Fig. 2.2a, an orange football token, a die with only zeros and ones on it, and fifty-two action cards, shown in Fig. 2.2b. To start the game, one player "kicks off" by rolling the binary die, and the football token starts at zero or one, depending on the outcome of the roll. Beginning with the other player, players take turns playing action cards, which move the football according to the lines and arrows on the game board. For example, at position 0, H moves the ball to position $+$; $\sqrt{X}$ moves the ball to $-i$; X and Y move the ball to 1; and Z, I, and S keep the ball at position 0. For the measurement card, if the football is at 0 or 1, nothing happens. Otherwise, one kicks off again by rolling the binary die. When a player scores a touchdown by moving the ball into their opponent's endzone, they roll the die to kick off again, and play continues with the other player. Whoever scores the most touchdowns, by the time all the action cards have been used, wins.

All of these game mechanics come from quantum computing.

---

[1] https://www.thegamecrafter.com/games/qubit-touchdown

Fig. 2.1: The complete Qubit Touchdown board game.

It is not necessary to play Qubit Touchdown in order to continue with this text-book.

Exercise 2.1. In Qubit Touchdown, say the ball is at position 0. Where would it move if you played (a) X, (b) Y, (c) Z, (d) H, (e) S, (f) $\sqrt{X}$, (g) I, (h) measurement?

Exercise 2.2. In Qubit Touchdown, say the ball is at position i. Where would it move if you played (a) X, (b) Y, (c) Z, (d) H, (e) S, (f) $\sqrt{X}$, (g) I, (h) measurement?

2.2 Superposition

2.2.1 Zero or One

A quantum bit, or *qubit*, is both similar to and different from a classical bit in some important ways. First, like a classical bit, a qubit can take two values, 0 or 1. Using *bra-ket notation* or *Dirac notation* from quantum physics, we write 0 and 1 enclosed between a vertical bar and an angle bracket called a *ket*:

$$|0\rangle, \quad |1\rangle.$$

Although it may seem strange to write a quantum 0 and a quantum 1 like this, it will be very useful later.

We can visualize these distinct states, $|0\rangle$ and $|1\rangle$, as the north and south poles of a sphere of radius 1 called the *Bloch sphere*:

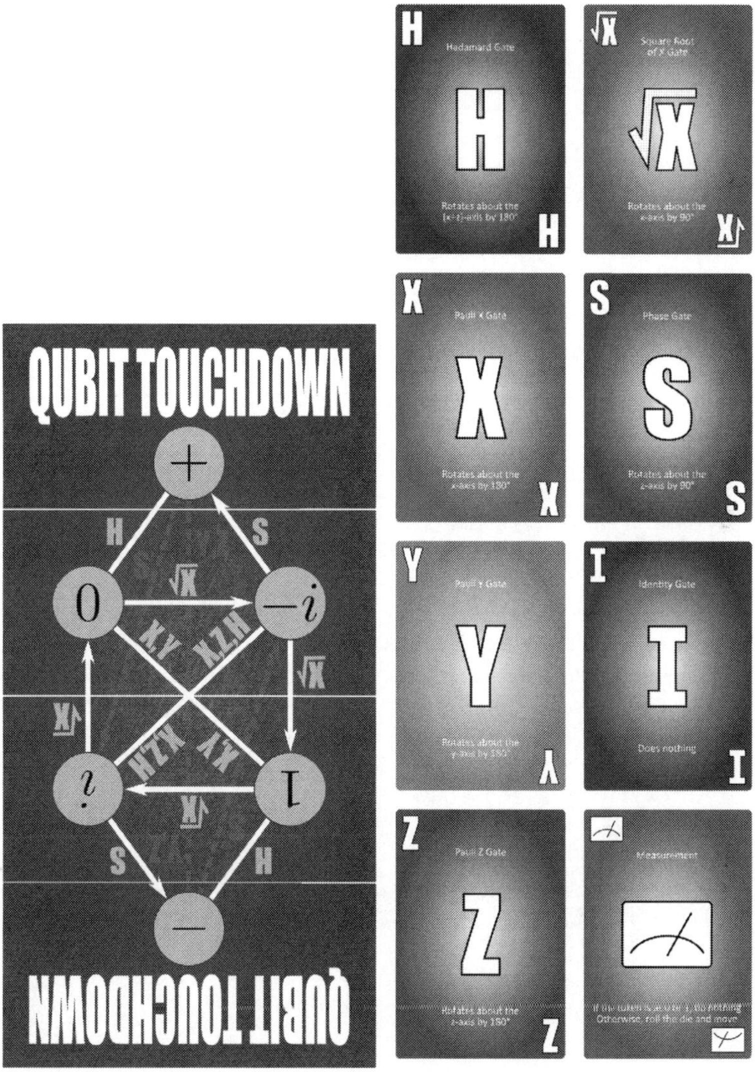

(a) (b)

Fig. 2.2: The Qubit Touchdown (a) game board and (b) action cards.

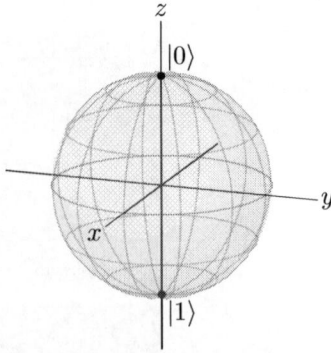

Following the standard physics convention, the x-axis comes out of the page, the y-axis points to the side, and z-axis is oriented up. Then, since the Bloch sphere has radius 1, $|0\rangle$ corresponds to the (x, y, z) point $(0, 0, 1)$, and $|1\rangle$ corresponds to $(0, 0, -1)$.

2.2.2 Superposition

If we had a classical bit, $|0\rangle$ and $|1\rangle$ would be the only two states. But, the laws of quantum mechanics allow the state of a qubit to be a combination of $|0\rangle$ *and* $|1\rangle$, called a *superposition* of $|0\rangle$ and $|1\rangle$. For example, here is a state that is equal parts $|0\rangle$ and $|1\rangle$:

$$\frac{1}{\sqrt{2}}\left(|0\rangle + |1\rangle\right).$$

In this state, the coefficient of $|0\rangle$ is $1/\sqrt{2}$, and the coefficient of $|1\rangle$ is also $1/\sqrt{2}$. So, it is equal parts $|0\rangle$ and $|1\rangle$. Given this, it should be on the equator of the Bloch sphere, which is halfway between the north and south poles:

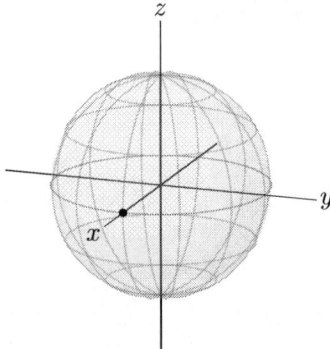

This state is at the (x, y, z) point $(1, 0, 0)$, where the Bloch sphere intersects the x-axis. Later, we will learn how to calculate these coordinates, but for now, we will focus on building geometric intuition.

There are many other states on the equator of the Bloch sphere, all of which are equal parts $|0\rangle$ and $|1\rangle$. We can reach them by changing the *relative phase* of $|0\rangle$ and $|1\rangle$. For example, if we instead use a negative sign, we get

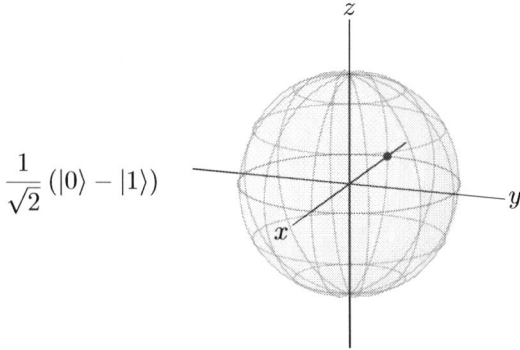

$$\frac{1}{\sqrt{2}}(|0\rangle - |1\rangle)$$

This state is at the point $(-1,0,0)$, on the $-x$-axis. To reach the y-axis at $(0,1,0)$, we instead use a phase of $i = \sqrt{-1}$:

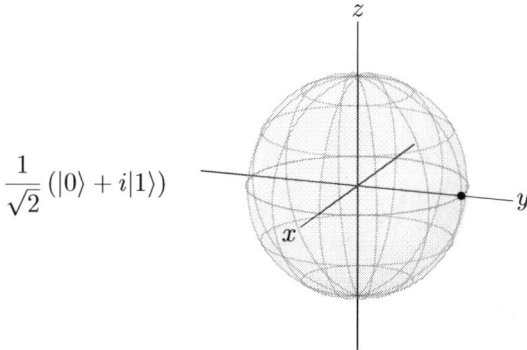

$$\frac{1}{\sqrt{2}}(|0\rangle + i|1\rangle)$$

We see that imaginary and complex numbers are used in quantum computing. In case it has been a while since you have used them, in the next section, we will review complex numbers in detail. Continuing, to reach the $-y$-axis at $(0,-1,0)$, we use a phase of $-i$:

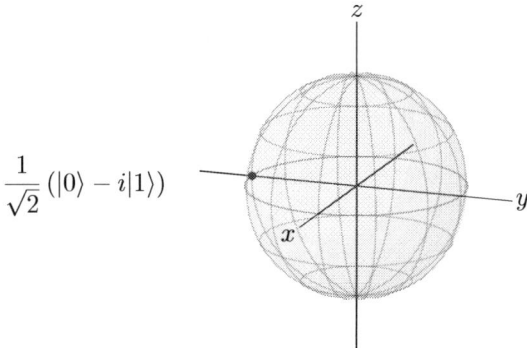

$$\frac{1}{\sqrt{2}}(|0\rangle - i|1\rangle)$$

These states appear frequently enough that they have names: "plus," "minus," "i,"
and "minus i":

$$|+\rangle = \frac{1}{\sqrt{2}}\left(|0\rangle + |1\rangle\right),$$
$$|-\rangle = \frac{1}{\sqrt{2}}\left(|0\rangle - |1\rangle\right),$$
$$|i\rangle = \frac{1}{\sqrt{2}}\left(|0\rangle + i|1\rangle\right),$$
$$|-i\rangle = \frac{1}{\sqrt{2}}\left(|0\rangle - i|1\rangle\right).$$

(2.1)

Drawing them together with $|0\rangle$ and $|1\rangle$ on the Bloch sphere, we get the following,
which also appears on the back of every action card in Qubit Touchdown:

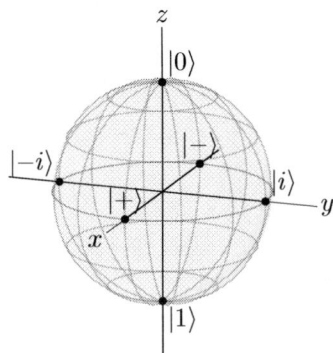

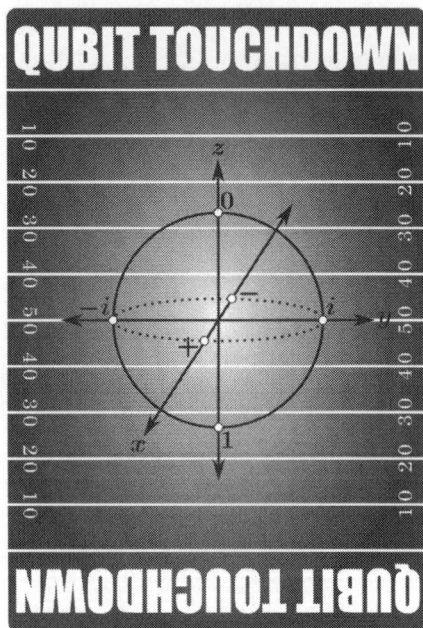

In Qubit Touchdown, these six states correspond to the six positions on the game
board in Fig. 2.2a. The football token corresponds to a qubit, so the ball moving
around the game board corresponds to a qubit changing between these states (more
on this later).

Of course, there are many other points on the equator of the Bloch sphere. We
can reach them using other complex phases, such as

$$\frac{1}{\sqrt{2}}\left(|0\rangle + e^{i\pi/6}|1\rangle\right)$$

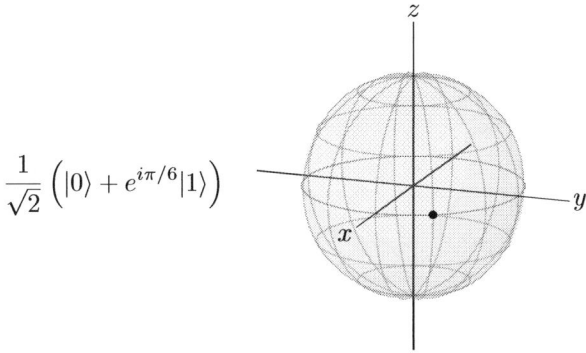

Superpositions are not restricted to the equator, either. They can favor $|0\rangle$ or $|1\rangle$ by being in the northern or southern hemisphere, such as

$$\frac{\sqrt{3}}{2}|0\rangle + \frac{1}{2}|1\rangle \qquad\qquad \frac{2}{3}|0\rangle + \frac{1-2i}{3}|1\rangle$$

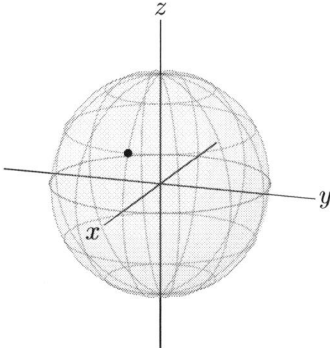

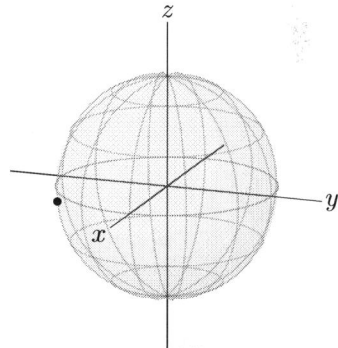

In fact,

A qubit can be *any* point on the Bloch sphere.

Again, we will later see how to calculate where a quantum state is on the Bloch sphere. Before we do that, however, we need to review complex numbers and discuss measuring qubits.

Exercise 2.3. Draw a Bloch sphere and label the following locations:
  (a) Where a qubit is exactly $|0\rangle$.
  (b) Where a qubit is exactly $|1\rangle$.
  (c) Where a qubit is half $|0\rangle$ and half $|1\rangle$.
  (d) Where a qubit is more $|0\rangle$ than $|1\rangle$.
  (e) Where a qubit is more $|1\rangle$ than $|0\rangle$.

2.2.3 Review of Complex Numbers

A complex number z is a number with a real part x plus i times an imaginary part y:

$$z = x + iy.$$

For example, $1 + i\sqrt{3}$ is a complex number. The parts are called *components*. We denote the real component of z as $\Re(z)$, and it just equals x:

$$\Re(z) = x.$$

Similarly, we denote the imaginary component as $\Im(z)$, and it just equals y:

$$\Im(z) = y.$$

For example, $\Re(1 + i\sqrt{3}) = 1$ and $\Im(1 + i\sqrt{3}) = \sqrt{3}$. Real numbers are complex numbers; their imaginary parts are just zero. Similarly, imaginary numbers are complex numbers; their real parts are just zero.

The above form $x + iy$ is called the *Cartesian form* or *rectangular form* of a complex number. In quantum computing, it is often useful to write a complex number as its length r times its complex phase $e^{i\theta}$:

$$z = re^{i\theta}.$$

This is called the *polar form* of a complex number, and any complex number can be written this way. To convert from the Cartesian form $x + iy$ to the polar form $re^{i\theta}$, we use the following equations, which we will prove in a moment:

$$r = \sqrt{x^2 + y^2}, \tag{2.2}$$

$$\theta = \tan^{-1}\left(\frac{y}{x}\right). \tag{2.3}$$

To convert from the polar form $re^{i\theta}$ to the Cartesian form $x + iy$, we use the following equations, which we will also prove in a moment:

$$x = r\cos\theta \tag{2.4}$$

$$y = r\sin\theta. \tag{2.5}$$

These relationships can be proved a couple different ways:

- Geometrically, complex number is a point on the complex plane, which has the real component as its x-axis and the imaginary component as its y-axis:

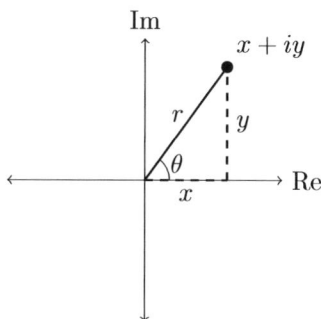

Its length is r, and the angle it makes counter-clockwise from the real axis is θ. Since x and y are the legs of a right triangle, and r is the hypotenuse, the Pythagorean theorem says that $x^2 + y^2 = r^2$. Taking the square root of each side, we get $r = \sqrt{x^2 + y^2}$, which proves Eq. (2.2).

Next, from the drawing, θ is an angle in a right triangle, and y is opposite of θ, x is adjacent, and r is the hypotenuse. We can relate these quantities using the trigonometric functions sine, cosine, and tangent.[2] First, using sine, we get $\sin\theta = y/r$. Multiplying both sides by r, we get $y = r\sin\theta$, which is Eq. (2.5). Next using cosine, we get $\cos\theta = x/r$. Multiplying both sides by r, we get $x = r\cos\theta$, which is Eq. (2.4). Finally, using tangent, we get $\tan\theta = y/x$. Taking the inverse tangent of both sides, we get $\theta = \tan^{-1}(y/x)$, which is Eq. (2.3).

- Algebraically, we can write a complex phase in Cartesian form using *Euler's formula*, which says says that

$$e^{i\theta} = \cos\theta + i\sin\theta. \tag{2.6}$$

If you have taken more advanced math than is required for this textbook, you may be familiar with Euler's formula and its proof. (It is typically seen during the second semester of calculus.) If not, no worries. You do not need to know where it comes from. It is simple enough to memorize now, which you should do, since it will show up again.

Now using Euler's formula, we can write the polar form of a complex number as

$$z = re^{i\theta} = r(\cos\theta + i\sin\theta) = \underbrace{r\cos\theta}_{x} + \underbrace{ir\sin\theta}_{y}.$$

Thus, the real part of z is $x = r\cos\theta$, which is Eq. (2.4), and the imaginary part is $y = r\sin\theta$, which is Eq. (2.5). If we take the sum of the squares of these components, we get

$$x^2 + y^2 = r^2\cos^2\theta + r^2\sin^2\theta = r^2\underbrace{(\cos^2\theta + \sin^2\theta)}_{1} = r^2.$$

---

[2] Many people remember the trigonometric functions using the mnemonic SOH-CAH-TOA, where sine is opposite over hypotenuse (SOH), cosine is adjacent over hypotenuse (CAH), and tangent is opposite over adjacent (TOA).

In the last equality, we used the *Pythagorean identity* $\sin^2\theta + \cos^2\theta = 1$ from trigonometry. Taking the square root of both sides, we get $r = \sqrt{x^2 + y^2}$, which proves Eq. (2.2). Next, if we divide $y = r\sin\theta$ by $x = r\cos\theta$, we get

$$\frac{y}{x} = \frac{\sin\theta}{\cos\theta} = \tan\theta.$$

Taking the inverse tangent of both sides, we get Eq. (2.3).

For example, say we have a complex number in Cartesian form, $z = 1 + i\sqrt{3}$. To convert this to polar form, we calculate its length $r = \sqrt{1^2 + \sqrt{3}^2} = \sqrt{1+3} = \sqrt{4} = 2$ and angle $\theta = \tan^{-1}(\sqrt{3}/1) = \pi/3$ radians or $60°$. The convention is to use radians, so putting these together, the polar form is $z = 2e^{i\pi/3}$.

There are a few more aspects of complex numbers that come up frequently in quantum computing, so let us review them now:

- The *complex conjugate* (or just *conjugate*) of a complex number is the complex number obtained by negating its imaginary part. That is, we replace i with $-i$. We denote the complex conjugate of z as z^*, so if $z = x + iy = re^{i\theta}$, then

$$z^* = x - iy = re^{-i\theta}.$$

From the previous example, $\left(1 + i\sqrt{3}\right)^* = 1 - i\sqrt{3}$ and $\left(2e^{i\pi/3}\right)^* = 2e^{-i\pi/3}$.
- The *norm* of a complex number z, which we denote $|z|$, is simply its length r:

$$|z| = r.$$

Then from the previous example, $|1 + i\sqrt{3}| = 2$, since its length r is 2.
- The *norm-square* of a complex number z, which we denote $|z|^2$, is simply the square of its norm, so it is r^2:

$$|z|^2 = r^2.$$

From the previous example, $|1 + i\sqrt{3}|^2 = 4$. One way to calculate the norm-square is multiplying a complex number by its conjugate:

$$|z|^2 = z^*z = zz^*. \tag{2.7}$$

We can prove that this works using either the Cartesian or polar form. In Cartesian form,

$$zz^* = (x + iy)(x - iy) = x^2 - ixy + ixy - i^2y^2 = x^2 + y^2 = r^2 = |z|^2,$$

where in the third step, we used $i^2 = \sqrt{-1}^2 = -1$. In polar form,

$$zz^* = re^{i\theta}re^{-i\theta} = r^2e^{i\theta - i\theta} = r^2e^0 = r^2 = |z|^2.$$

Finally, Eq. (2.7) gives us another way to find the norm of z, by taking the square root of z times its conjugate z^*:

$$|z| = \sqrt{|z|^2} = \sqrt{z^*z} = \sqrt{zz^*}.$$

Exercise 2.4. Consider the complex number $z = 1 + 2i$.
(a) Find $\Re(z)$.
(b) Find $\Im(z)$.
(c) Plot z as a point in the complex plane.
(d) Write z in polar form $re^{i\theta}$.
(e) Find z^*.
(f) Find $|z|$.
(g) Find $|z|^2$.

Exercise 2.5. Consider the complex number $z = -3 - i$.
(a) Find $\Re(z)$.
(b) Find $\Im(z)$.
(c) Plot z as a point in the complex plane.
(d) Write z in polar form $re^{i\theta}$. Hint: The angle should be between π and $3\pi/2$ (i.e., $180°$ and $270°$).
(e) Find z^*.
(f) Find $|z|$.
(g) Find $|z|^2$.

2.3 Measurement

2.3.1 Measurement in the Z-Basis

In a previous section, we had the following qubit, which was on the equator of the Bloch sphere:

$$\frac{1}{\sqrt{2}}\left(|0\rangle + e^{i\pi/6}|1\rangle\right)$$

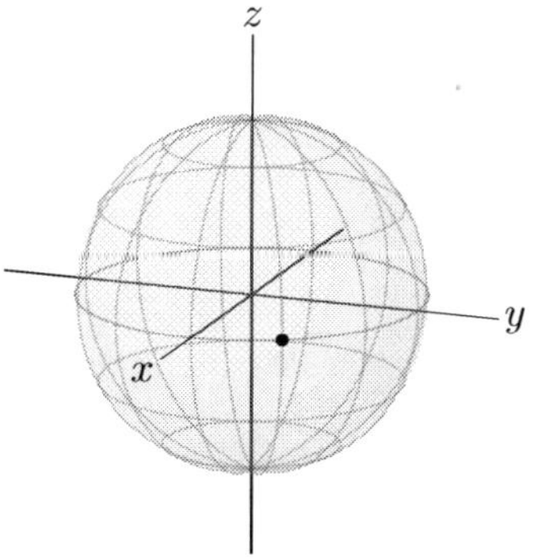

Although the laws of quantum mechanics permit this superposition of $|0\rangle$ and $|1\rangle$, it also demands that if we measure the qubit, such as at the end of a computation in order to read the result, we get a single, definite value. That is, we get $|0\rangle$ *or* $|1\rangle$, each with some probability, not a superposition of $|0\rangle$ *and* $|1\rangle$. Geometrically, this particular qubit lies on the equator, halfway between the north and south poles, so if we measure it, we get $|0\rangle$ with probability $1/2$ or $|1\rangle$ with probability $1/2$. To calculate these probabilities, we take the norm-square of the coefficient of $|0\rangle$ or $|1\rangle$. That is, the probability of getting $|0\rangle$ is

$$\left|\frac{1}{\sqrt{2}}\right|^2 = \frac{1}{2},$$

and the probability of getting $|1\rangle$ is

$$\left|\frac{e^{i\pi/6}}{\sqrt{2}}\right|^2 = \frac{e^{i\pi/6}}{\sqrt{2}} \frac{e^{-i\pi/6}}{\sqrt{2}} = \frac{e^0}{2} = \frac{1}{2}.$$

The coefficients are called *amplitudes*, so:

The probability is given by the norm-square of the amplitude.

Let us look at another example, which we also saw earlier:

$$\frac{2}{3}|0\rangle + \frac{1-2i}{3}|1\rangle$$

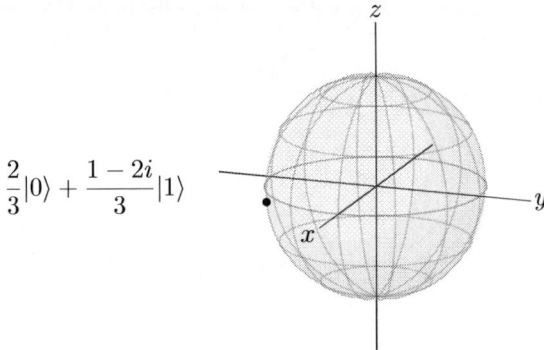

Geometrically, since the qubit is closer to the south pole, we expect that the probability of getting $|1\rangle$ is greater than the probability of getting $|0\rangle$. To get the exact probabilities, we calculate the norm-square of each amplitude:

$$\left|\frac{2}{3}\right|^2 = \frac{4}{9},$$

and

$$\left|\frac{1-2i}{3}\right|^2 = \frac{1-2i}{3}\frac{1+2i}{3} = \frac{1+2i-2i-4i^2}{9} = \frac{5}{9}.$$

So, if we measure the qubit, the probability of getting $|0\rangle$ is 4/9, and the probability of getting $|1\rangle$ is 5/9. As expected, the probability of getting $|1\rangle$ is greater than the probability of getting $|0\rangle$, and also note that the total probability is $4/9 + 5/9 = 1$, as it must.

Exercise 2.6. A qubit is in the state

$$\frac{1+i\sqrt{3}}{3}|0\rangle + \frac{2-i}{3}|1\rangle.$$

If you measure the qubit, what is the probability of getting
   (a) $|0\rangle$?
   (b) $|1\rangle$?

Say a qubit is superposition of $|0\rangle$ and $|1\rangle$. Say we measure it, and the outcome is $|0\rangle$. Now for something new: The qubit is no longer in a superposition of $|0\rangle$ and $|1\rangle$. It is now simply $|0\rangle$, and we know because we measured it. Measuring the qubit changed it. It forced it to take a stand. We say the state has *collapsed* to $|0\rangle$. If we measure the qubit again, we get $|0\rangle$ with probability 1. This aspect of measurement is important enough to box:

Measurement collapses the qubit.

In Qubit Touchdown, playing the measurement action card, or kicking off after a touchdown, corresponds to measuring the qubit. For the measurement action card, if the ball is at position 0 or 1, then nothing happens, just like measuring a qubit in state $|0\rangle$ or $|1\rangle$ returns the same state with probability 1. If the ball is at position i or $-i$, then the binary die is rolled, and the ball is moved to 0 or 1 with 50% probability each, just like measuring a qubit in the $|i\rangle$ or $|-i\rangle$ states collapses the state to $|0\rangle$ or $|1\rangle$ with 50% probability. Finally, after scoring a touchdown, the ball is either at the $+$ or $-$ positions in the endzones. Then, the binary die is rolled, moving the ball to 0 or 1 with 50% probability each. In the same way, when a qubit is in the $|+\rangle$ or $|-\rangle$ state, measuring it yields $|0\rangle$ or $|1\rangle$ with 50% probability each, and the state collapses to whichever state was measured.

Exercise 2.7. A qubit is in the state

$$\frac{2}{3}|0\rangle + \frac{1+2i}{3}|1\rangle.$$

Say you measure the qubit and get $|0\rangle$. If you measure the qubit a *second time*, what is the probability of getting
   (a) $|0\rangle$?
   (b) $|1\rangle$?

2.3.2 Normalization

We say a quantum state is *normalized* if its total probability is 1, as it should be. Sometimes, we must find an overall *normalization constant* to make this true. For example, a qubit is in the state

$$A\left(\sqrt{2}|0\rangle + i|1\rangle\right).$$

We normalize this state by finding the normalization constant A that ensures that the total probability is 1. So,

$$\begin{aligned} 1 &= (A\sqrt{2})(A\sqrt{2})^* + (Ai)(Ai)^* \\ &= 2|A|^2 + |A|^2 \\ &= 3|A|^2 \\ |A|^2 &= \frac{1}{3}. \end{aligned}$$

As we will prove later, the overall phase does not matter, so we might as well pick A to be real. Thus,

$$A = \frac{1}{\sqrt{3}},$$

and the normalized state is

$$\frac{1}{\sqrt{3}}\left(\sqrt{2}|0\rangle + i|1\rangle\right).$$

Exercise 2.8. A qubit is in the state

$$\frac{e^{i\pi/8}}{\sqrt{5}}|0\rangle + \beta|1\rangle.$$

What is a possible value of β?

Exercise 2.9. A qubit is in the state

$$A\left(2e^{i\pi/6}|0\rangle - 3|1\rangle\right).$$

(a) Normalize the state (i.e., find A).
(b) If you measure the qubit, what is the probability that you get $|0\rangle$?
(c) If you measure the qubit, what is the probability that you get $|1\rangle$?

2.3.3 Measurement in Other Bases

Even though we introduced $|0\rangle$ and $|1\rangle$ as the north and south poles, respectively, of the Bloch sphere, the Bloch sphere is not a planet, and it is not spinning. Then, any two opposite points could be taken as the north and south poles. For example, $|+\rangle$ and $|-\rangle$ could be the north and south poles, or $|i\rangle$ and $|-i\rangle$, or any opposite points. A set of distinct measurement outcomes is called a *basis*, and $\{|0\rangle, |1\rangle\}$ is called the *Z-basis* because they lie on the z-axis of the Bloch sphere. Similarly, $\{|+\rangle, |-\rangle\}$ is called the X-basis because they lie on the x-axis of the Bloch sphere, and $\{|i\rangle, |-i\rangle\}$ is called the Y-basis because they lie on the y-axis of the Bloch sphere. We can measure with respect to any of these bases, or with respect to any two states on opposite sides of the Bloch sphere.

For example, consider a qubit in the state

$$\frac{\sqrt{3}}{2}|0\rangle + \frac{1}{2}|1\rangle,$$

which appears on the Bloch sphere at an angle of $30°$ above the x-axis, as shown below:

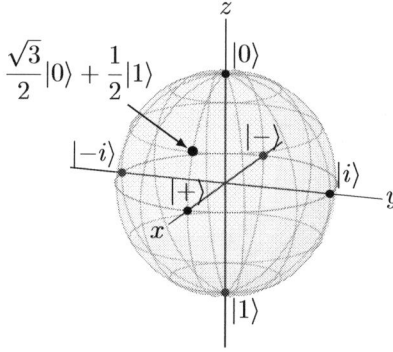

Let us measure this with respect to four different bases: the Z-basis $\{|0\rangle, |1\rangle\}$, the X-basis $\{|+\rangle, |-\rangle\}$, the Y-basis $\{|i\rangle, |-i\rangle\}$, and a fourth basis (below).

1. If we measure the qubit in the Z-basis $\{|0\rangle, |1\rangle\}$, then we get $|0\rangle$ with probability $3/4$ or $|1\rangle$ with probability $1/4$.

2. What if we measure in the X-basis $\{|+\rangle, |-\rangle\}$ instead? Geometrically, the probability of getting $|+\rangle$ should be much higher than the probability of getting $|-\rangle$ because the state is so much closer to $|+\rangle$ on the Bloch sphere. To calculate the probabilities precisely, we need to express the state in terms of $|+\rangle$ and $|-\rangle$ so that we can identify the amplitudes and then find their norm-squares. From the definitions of $|+\rangle$ and $|-\rangle$ in Eq. (2.1), we have

$$|0\rangle = \frac{1}{\sqrt{2}}(|+\rangle + |-\rangle), \quad |1\rangle = \frac{1}{\sqrt{2}}(|+\rangle - |-\rangle).$$

Substituting into the state of our qubit,

$$\frac{\sqrt{3}}{2}|0\rangle + \frac{1}{2}|1\rangle = \frac{\sqrt{3}}{2}\frac{1}{\sqrt{2}}(|+\rangle + |-\rangle) + \frac{1}{2}\frac{1}{\sqrt{2}}(|+\rangle - |-\rangle)$$

$$= \frac{\sqrt{3}+1}{2\sqrt{2}}|+\rangle + \frac{\sqrt{3}-1}{2\sqrt{2}}|-\rangle.$$

Now the amplitudes are easy to identify, and we can find the probabilities by taking their norm-squares. The probability of measuring $|+\rangle$ is

$$\left|\frac{\sqrt{3}+1}{2\sqrt{2}}\right|^2 = \frac{\sqrt{3}+2}{4} \approx 0.93,$$

and the probability of measuring $|-\rangle$ is

$$\left|\frac{\sqrt{3}-1}{2\sqrt{2}}\right|^2 = \frac{-\sqrt{3}+2}{4} \approx 0.07.$$

This is consistent with the Bloch sphere, since the state is much closer to $|+\rangle$ than it is to $|-\rangle$.

3. Now what if we measure in the $\{|i\rangle, |-i\rangle\}$ basis? Geometrically, the Bloch sphere reveals that the state is halfway between $|i\rangle$ and $|-i\rangle$, so we get one or the other with probability $1/2$ each. We can also calculate this by rewriting the state in terms of $|i\rangle$ and $|-i\rangle$ and then finding the norm-square of the amplitudes. From the definitions of $|i\rangle$ and $|-i\rangle$ in Eq. (2.1),

$$|0\rangle = \frac{1}{\sqrt{2}}(|i\rangle + |-i\rangle), \quad |1\rangle = \frac{-i}{\sqrt{2}}(|i\rangle - |-i\rangle).$$

Substituting,

$$\frac{\sqrt{3}}{2}|0\rangle + \frac{1}{2}|1\rangle = \frac{\sqrt{3}}{2}\frac{1}{\sqrt{2}}(|i\rangle + |-i\rangle) + \frac{1}{2}\frac{-i}{\sqrt{2}}(|i\rangle - |-i\rangle)$$

$$= \frac{\sqrt{3}-i}{2\sqrt{2}}|i\rangle + \frac{\sqrt{3}+i}{2\sqrt{2}}|-i\rangle.$$

So, the probability of getting $|i\rangle$ is

$$\left|\frac{\sqrt{3}-i}{2\sqrt{2}}\right|^2 = \frac{3+1}{8} = \frac{1}{2},$$

and the probability of getting $|-i\rangle$ is

$$\left|\frac{\sqrt{3}+i}{2\sqrt{2}}\right|^2 = \frac{3+1}{8} = \frac{1}{2},$$

as expected.

4. Consider the following two states, which we will call $|a\rangle$ and $|b\rangle$:

$$|a\rangle = \frac{\sqrt{3}}{2}|0\rangle + \frac{i}{2}|1\rangle,$$

$$|b\rangle = \frac{i}{2}|0\rangle + \frac{\sqrt{3}}{2}|1\rangle.$$

Here they are on the Bloch sphere:

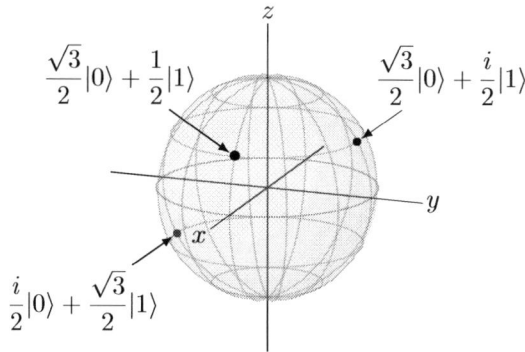

$|a\rangle$ is located 30° above the y-axis, and $|b\rangle$ is located 30° below the $-y$-axis. (You will prove this in Exercise 2.16.) Since they are located on opposite points of the Bloch sphere, they are a basis. Let us measure in this $\{|a\rangle, |b\rangle\}$ basis. Geometrically, the qubit is closer to $|a\rangle$, so we expect a higher probability of getting $|a\rangle$ than $|b\rangle$. To calculate the precise numbers, we first write $|0\rangle$ and $|1\rangle$ in terms of $|a\rangle$ and $|b\rangle$:

$$|0\rangle = \frac{\sqrt{3}}{2}|a\rangle - \frac{i}{2}|b\rangle, \quad |1\rangle = \frac{-i}{2}|a\rangle + \frac{\sqrt{3}}{2}|b\rangle.$$

Substituting, the state of our qubit is

$$\frac{\sqrt{3}}{2}|0\rangle + \frac{1}{2}|1\rangle = \frac{\sqrt{3}}{2}\left(\frac{\sqrt{3}}{2}|a\rangle - \frac{i}{2}|b\rangle\right) + \frac{1}{2}\left(\frac{-i}{2}|a\rangle + \frac{\sqrt{3}}{2}|b\rangle\right)$$

$$= \frac{3-i}{4}|a\rangle + \frac{\sqrt{3}(1-i)}{4}|b\rangle.$$

Taking the norm-square of each amplitude, the probability of getting $|a\rangle$ is

$$\left|\frac{3-i}{4}\right|^2 = \frac{9+1}{16} = \frac{5}{8},$$

and the probability of getting $|b\rangle$ is

$$\left|\frac{\sqrt{3}(1-i)}{4}\right|^2 = \frac{3}{8}.$$

Later, when we describe qubits in the mathematics of linear algebra, we will see another way to convert between bases.

Exercise 2.10. A qubit is in the state

$$\frac{1}{2}|0\rangle - \frac{\sqrt{3}}{2}|1\rangle.$$

(a) If you measure it in the Z-basis $\{|0\rangle, |1\rangle\}$, what states can you get and with what probabilities?
(b) Write the qubit's state in terms of $|+\rangle$ and $|-\rangle$.
(c) If you measure it in the basis $\{|+\rangle, |-\rangle\}$, what states can you get and with what probabilities?

Exercise 2.11. The following two states are opposite points on the Bloch sphere:

$$|a\rangle = \frac{\sqrt{3}}{2}|0\rangle + \frac{i}{2}|1\rangle,$$

$$|b\rangle = \frac{i}{2}|0\rangle + \frac{\sqrt{3}}{2}|1\rangle.$$

So, we can measure relative to them. Now consider a qubit in the state

$$\frac{1}{2}|0\rangle - \frac{\sqrt{3}}{2}|1\rangle.$$

(a) Write the qubit's state in terms of $|a\rangle$ and $|b\rangle$.
(b) If you measure the qubit in the basis $\{|a\rangle, |b\rangle\}$, what states can you get and with what probabilities?

2.3.4 Consecutive Measurements

We have already seen that measuring a qubit collapses the state to whatever was measured. This can lead to interesting statistics, even more so if we change the measurement basis. For example, consider the following three measurements:

1. Say we first measure the qubit in the Z-basis $\{|0\rangle, |1\rangle\}$. Then, the qubit collapses to $|0\rangle$ or $|1\rangle$.
2. Next, if we measure in the X-basis $\{|+\rangle, |-\rangle\}$, then since both $|0\rangle$ and $|1\rangle$ are halfway between $|+\rangle$ and $|-\rangle$, the qubit collapses to $|+\rangle$ or $|-\rangle$, each with probability $1/2$.
3. If we then measure in the Z-basis $\{|0\rangle, |1\rangle\}$, then since $|+\rangle$ and $|-\rangle$ are halfway between $|0\rangle$ and $|1\rangle$, the probability of each is $1/2$. We can continue alternating between these two measurement bases, each time having a 50:50 chance of getting each outcome.

Exercise 2.12. A qubit is in the state $|0\rangle$. If you measure it in the X-basis $\{|+\rangle, |-\rangle\}$ and then measure it again in the Z-basis $\{|0\rangle, |1\rangle\}$, what is the probability of getting
(a) $|0\rangle$?
(b) $|1\rangle$?

2.4 Bloch Sphere Mapping

We know that a qubit can be visualized as a point on the Bloch sphere. Now, let us explain how to determine where the point should be.

2.4.1 Global and Relative Phases

Say the qubit from the last section is multiplied by an overall, *global phase*:

$$e^{i\theta}\left(\frac{\sqrt{3}}{2}|0\rangle + \frac{1}{2}|1\rangle\right),$$

for some angle θ. If we measure this in the Z-basis, $\{|0\rangle, |1\rangle\}$ the probability of getting $|0\rangle$ is

$$\left|e^{i\theta}\frac{\sqrt{3}}{2}\right|^2 = \frac{3}{4},$$

and the probability of getting $|1\rangle$ is

$$\left|e^{i\theta}\frac{1}{2}\right|^2 = \frac{1}{4},$$

as they were without the global phase. So, the phase does not change anything.

If we instead measure in the X-basis $\{|+\rangle, |-\rangle\}$, then we can rewrite the state as

$$e^{i\theta}\left(\frac{\sqrt{3}+1}{2\sqrt{2}}|+\rangle + \frac{\sqrt{3}-1}{2\sqrt{2}}|-\rangle\right).$$

Then, the probability of getting $|+\rangle$ is

$$\left|e^{i\theta}\frac{\sqrt{3}+1}{2\sqrt{2}}\right|^2 = \frac{\sqrt{3}+2}{4} \approx 0.93,$$

and the probability of measuring $|-\rangle$ is

$$\left|e^{i\theta}\frac{\sqrt{3}-1}{2\sqrt{2}}\right|^2 = \frac{-\sqrt{3}+2}{4} \approx 0.07,$$

as they were before without the global phase. So again, the phase does not change anything.

This is true no matter what measurement basis we use, and it leads to the following result:

Global phases are physically irrelevant.

As such, global phases can be dropped/ignored. States that differ by a global phase are actually the same state; they correspond to the same point on the Bloch sphere.

Note that a *relative phase* is physically significant, such as

$$|+\rangle = \frac{1}{\sqrt{2}}(|0\rangle + |1\rangle)$$

vs

$$|i\rangle = \frac{1}{\sqrt{2}}(|0\rangle + i|1\rangle) = \frac{1}{\sqrt{2}}\left(|0\rangle + e^{i\pi/2}|1\rangle\right).$$

These correspond to different points on the Bloch sphere, and they can be distinguished by measurements in appropriate bases. Although measuring $|+\rangle$ and $|i\rangle$ in the Z-basis yields the same statistics, i.e., $|0\rangle$ with probability $1/2$ or $|1\rangle$ with probability $1/2$, measuring in the X-basis $\{|+\rangle, |-\rangle\}$ yields different results. Measuring $|+\rangle$ in the X-basis always yields $|+\rangle$, but measuring $|i\rangle$ in the X-basis yields $|+\rangle$ or $|-\rangle$ with a 50:50 probability.

Exercise 2.13. Is there a measurement that can distinguish the following pairs of states? If yes, give a measurement. If no, explain your reasoning.

(a) $|+\rangle = \frac{1}{\sqrt{2}}(|0\rangle + |1\rangle)$ and $e^{i\pi/8}|+\rangle = \frac{e^{i\pi/8}}{\sqrt{2}}(|0\rangle + |1\rangle)$.

(b) $|+\rangle = \frac{1}{\sqrt{2}}(|0\rangle + |1\rangle)$ and $|-\rangle = \frac{1}{\sqrt{2}}(|0\rangle - |1\rangle)$.

(c) $|0\rangle$ and $e^{i\pi/4}|0\rangle$.

2.4.2 Spherical Coordinates

A generic quantum state is typically called ψ (the Greek letter "psi," which is pronounced "sigh"), and since it is quantum, we write it as a ket $|\psi\rangle$. Now say we have a generic qubit $|\psi\rangle$ with some amplitudes α and β:

$$|\psi\rangle = \alpha|0\rangle + \beta|1\rangle,$$

where $|\alpha|^2 + |\beta|^2 = 1$ for normalization. Since the global phase does not matter, we can assume that α is real and positive, and β may be complex. To determine the location of this qubit on the Bloch sphere, we first *parameterize*, or write in terms of other parameters, α and β in terms of two angles θ and ϕ:

$$\alpha = \cos\left(\frac{\theta}{2}\right), \quad \beta = e^{i\phi}\sin\left(\frac{\theta}{2}\right).$$

With $0 \le \theta \le \pi$ and $0 \le \phi < 2\pi$, this captures all the properties we need: α is real and positive, β is complex, and the state is normalized. Substituting, we have rewritten the qubit's state as

$$|\psi\rangle = \cos\left(\frac{\theta}{2}\right)|0\rangle + e^{i\phi}\sin\left(\frac{\theta}{2}\right)|1\rangle. \tag{2.8}$$

Let us work through an example. Say a qubit is in the state

$$\frac{3+i\sqrt{3}}{4}|0\rangle - \frac{1}{2}|1\rangle.$$

We see that the amplitude of $|0\rangle$ is complex, but in Eq. (2.8), it needs to be real. To make it real, we first convert it to polar form. Since $(3+i\sqrt{3})/4 = (\sqrt{3}/2)e^{i\pi/6}$, the state is

$$\frac{\sqrt{3}}{2}e^{i\pi/6}|0\rangle - \frac{1}{2}|1\rangle.$$

Factoring, this becomes

$$e^{i\pi/6}\left(\frac{\sqrt{3}}{2}|0\rangle - e^{-i\pi/6}\frac{1}{2}|1\rangle\right) \equiv \frac{\sqrt{3}}{2}|0\rangle - e^{-i\pi/6}\frac{1}{2}|1\rangle,$$

where $\equiv$ denotes "equivalent to," and the states are equivalent because the global phase does not matter and can be dropped. Comparing this to the Bloch sphere parameterization in Eq. (2.8), we still need to change the minus sign to a plus sign. We can do this using $e^{i\pi} = -1$. Then, the state is

$$\frac{\sqrt{3}}{2}|0\rangle + e^{i\pi}e^{-i\pi/6}\frac{1}{2}|1\rangle = \frac{\sqrt{3}}{2}|0\rangle + e^{i5\pi/6}\frac{1}{2}|1\rangle.$$

Now it takes the form of Eq. (2.8), and we identify

$$\cos\left(\frac{\theta}{2}\right) = \frac{\sqrt{3}}{2}, \quad e^{i\phi} = e^{i5\pi/6}, \quad \sin\left(\frac{\theta}{2}\right) = \frac{1}{2}.$$

Solving the first or last equation for θ using the inverse cosine or inverse sine, and solving the second equation for ϕ, we get

$$\theta = \frac{\pi}{3}, \quad \phi = \frac{5\pi}{6}.$$

Thus, plugging into Eq. (2.8), the state of the qubit is equivalent to

$$\cos\left(\frac{\pi/3}{2}\right)|0\rangle + e^{i5\pi/6}\sin\left(\frac{\pi/3}{2}\right)|1\rangle.$$

Next, to map this qubit to a location on the Bloch sphere, we identify θ and ϕ as the following angles:

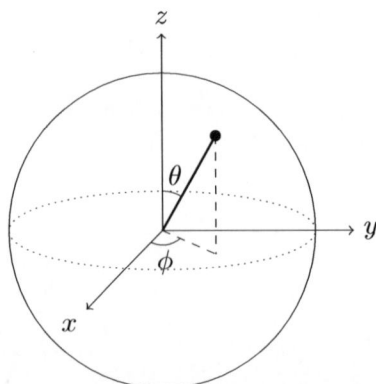

So, θ measures the angle down from the north pole, called the *polar angle*, and ϕ measures the angle across from the x-axis in the xy plane, called the *azimuthal angle*. If you have taken more advanced mathematics than is required for this book, these are precisely *spherical coordinates* with a radius of 1. Spherical coordinates are typically covered in the third semester of calculus, but everything you need for this textbook will be explained here.

Returning to our example, we had $\theta = \pi/3$ and $\phi = 5\pi/6$, so the state is located on the Bloch sphere at an angle of $\pi/3$ or $60°$ from the north pole, and $5\pi/6$ or $150°$ rotated to the side:

$$\frac{3+i\sqrt{3}}{4}|0\rangle - \frac{1}{2}|1\rangle$$

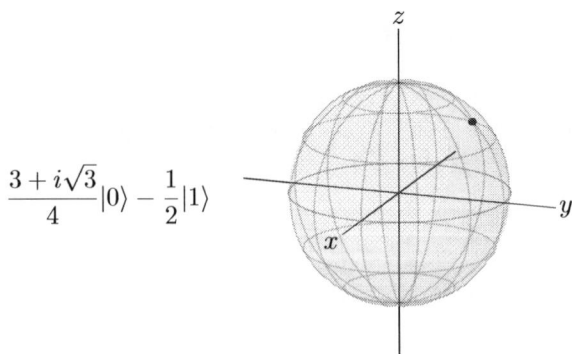

Exercise 2.14. A qubit is in the state

$$|i\rangle = \frac{1}{\sqrt{2}}(|0\rangle + i|1\rangle).$$

(a) Where on the Bloch sphere is this state? Give your answer in (θ, ϕ) coordinates.
(b) Sketch the point on the Bloch sphere.

Exercise 2.15. A qubit is in the state

$$\frac{1-i}{2\sqrt{2}}|0\rangle + \frac{\sqrt{3}}{2}|1\rangle.$$

(a) Where on the Bloch sphere is this state? Give your answer in (θ, ϕ) coordinates.

(b) Sketch the point on the Bloch sphere.

Exercise 2.16. Consider the following two states from Exercise 2.11:

$$|a\rangle = \frac{\sqrt{3}}{2}|0\rangle + \frac{i}{2}|1\rangle,$$

$$|b\rangle = \frac{i}{2}|0\rangle + \frac{\sqrt{3}}{2}|1\rangle.$$

Prove these are opposite points of the Bloch sphere by finding their points in spherical coordinates (θ_a, ϕ_a) and (θ_b, ϕ_b). Verify that $\theta_b = \pi - \theta_a$ and $\phi_b = \phi_a + \pi$, which means they lie on opposite points of the Bloch sphere.

2.4.3 Cartesian Coordinates

We can also determine the (x, y, z) coordinates, called *Cartesian coordinates*, of a point on the Bloch sphere. To see how to determine these from the spherical coordinates (θ, ϕ), let us first zoom in and focus on the polar angle θ:

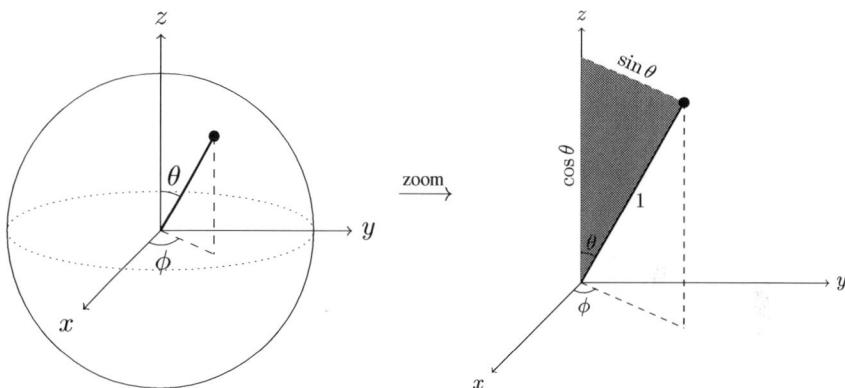

In this picture, we drew a dashed line from the point to the z-axis, perpendicular to it. This creates a right triangle, which we shaded gray. Since the radius of the Bloch sphere is 1, the hypotenuse of the gray triangle is 1, which we labeled in the picture. Then, since $\sin\theta$ is opposite over hypotenuse, and the hypotenuse is 1, we get that $\sin\theta$ is the opposite side, which we labeled in the picture. Similarly, since $\cos\theta$ is adjacent over hypotenuse, and the hypotenuse is 1, we get that $\cos\theta$ is the adjacent side, which we also labeled in the picture. This adjacent side gives the z-coordinate (height) of the point, i.e., $z = \cos\theta$.

To get the x and y coordinates, we look at the projection onto the xy-plane:

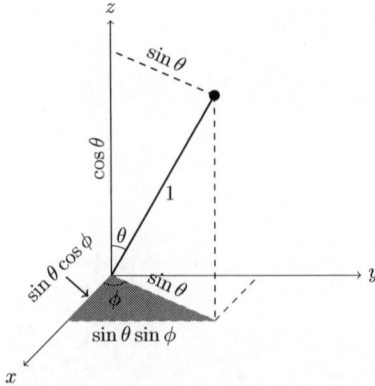

First, we copied $\sin \theta$ from the top dashed line to below, since they are opposite sides of a rectangle. This is the hypotenuse of the bottom gray triangle. Then, since $\sin \phi$ is opposite over hypotenuse, we get that the opposite side is equal to the hypotenuse times $\sin \phi$, or $\sin \theta \sin \phi$, which we labeled in the drawing. This corresponds to the y-coordinate (distance to the right) of the point, i.e., $y = \sin \theta \sin \phi$. Similarly, since $\cos \phi$ is adjacent over hypotenuse, we get that the adjacent side is equal to the hypotenuse times $\cos \phi$, or $\sin \theta \cos \phi$. This is labeled as the left side of the gray triangle in the drawing, and it corresponds to the x-coordinate (distance out of the page), i.e., $x = \sin \theta \cos \phi$. Combining these results with the z-coordinate, we can convert from spherical coordinates to Cartesian coordinates using the following formulas:

$$x = \sin \theta \cos \phi,$$
$$y = \sin \theta \sin \phi,$$
$$z = \cos \theta.$$

Continuing the previous example, we had $\theta = \pi/3$ and $\phi = 5\pi/6$, so the (x, y, z) coordinates are of the qubit are

$$x = \sin\left(\frac{\pi}{3}\right) \cos\left(\frac{5\pi}{6}\right) = \frac{\sqrt{3}}{2} \cdot \frac{-\sqrt{3}}{2} = -\frac{3}{4},$$
$$y = \sin\left(\frac{\pi}{3}\right) \sin\left(\frac{5\pi}{6}\right) = \frac{\sqrt{3}}{2} \cdot \frac{1}{2} = \frac{\sqrt{3}}{4},$$
$$z = \cos\left(\frac{\pi}{3}\right) = \frac{1}{2}.$$

So, the qubit corresponds to point $(-3/4, \sqrt{3}/4, 1/2)$ on the Bloch sphere.

Exercise 2.17. In Cartesian (x, y, z), coordinates, where on the Bloch sphere is the state from
(a) Exercise 2.14?
(b) Exercise 2.15?

2.5 Physical Qubits

Physically, any quantum system with two distinct states can be used as a qubit. While one is not expected to be familiar with quantum physics, some examples include:

- *Photons*, or quantum particles of light, have a property called *polarization*. A photon's polarization can be vertical or horizontal, or a superposition of both, and we can use this as a qubit.
- *Trapped ions.* An *ion* is an atom that has an overall charge (instead of being neutral) because it has gained or lost one or more electrons. Individual ions can be trapped in space using electric fields. Two energy levels of an ion can be used as a qubit.
- *Cold atoms.* Neutral atoms can be trapped at low temperatures using a *magneto-optical trap*, which uses magnetic fields and lasers to cool and trap the atoms. Another approach is using an *optical lattice* constructed by laser beams. Once trapped, two energy levels of an atom can be used as a qubit.
- *Nuclear magnetic resonance.* The nuclei of atoms and molecules have a quantum property called *spin*, which can be used as a qubit. Spins can be identified by their frequency of precession when subject to a strong magnetic field.
- *Quantum dots.* An electron can be bound to a small semiconductor device, similar to an electron bound to the nucleus of an atom. In these "artificial atoms," the spin of an electron, which can be "spin up" or "spin down," can be used as a qubit.
- *Defect qubits.* A diamond crystal may have a missing carbon atom, and if we replace a carbon atom next to this vacancy with a nitrogen atom, we get a "spin triplet" that can be used for quantum computing. This is called a *nitrogen-vacancy center* in diamond.
- *Superconductors.* In a superconducting circuit, charge flows with zero resistance. The magnetic flux across an inductor and the charge on a capacitor cause a harmonic potential energy with equally spaced, discrete energy levels. A *Josephson junction* is a thin insulating layer that is added, and it changes the potential energy so that the energy levels become unequally spaced. Then, the energy levels can be distinguished, and two of them can be used as a qubit.

Informationally, these systems contain the same amount of information: two distinct quantum states. So we simply use $|0\rangle$ and $|1\rangle$ for the rest of the discussion.

Exercise 2.18. A review of various ways to build a quantum computer is the article "Quantum Computers" by Ladd *et al.* (2010). The published version in *Nature* 464, 45–53 is available at https://dx.doi.org/10.1038/nature08812, but it may require a subscription. Search through the text and fill in the blanks:
  (a) Photons: "Realizing a qubit as the _____ state of a photon is appealing because photons are relatively free of the _____ that plagues other quantum systems."
  (b) Trapped ions: "Individual atomic ions can be confined in free space with nanometre precision using appropriate _____ _____ from nearby electrodes."
  (c) Cold atoms: "An array of cold neutral atoms may be confined in free space by a pattern of crossed _____ _____, forming an optical lattice."

(d) Nuclear magnetic resonance: "In a _____, nuclear Larmor frequencies vary from atom to atom [...] Irradiating the nuclei with resonant _____ pulses allows manipulation of nuclei of a distinct frequency, giving generic _____ gates."

(e) Quantum dots: "These 'artificial atoms' occur when a small semiconductor nanostructure, impurity or impurity complex binds one or more electrons or holes (empty valence-band states) into a localized potential with _____ _____ _____, which is analogous to an electron bound to an _____ _____."

(f) Doped solids: "_____ _____ may then be stored in either the donor electron, or in the state of the single ^{31}P nuclear spin, accessed via the electron-nuclear _____ coupling."

(g) Nitrogen-vacancy centers: "The _____ state of a nitrogen-vacancy centre may then be coherently manipulated with resonant _____ fields, and then detected in a few milliseconds via spin-dependent fluorescence in an _____ microscope."

(h) Superconductors: "There are three basic types of superconducting qubits—_____, _____ and _____."

Exercise 2.19. Visit https://en.wikipedia.org/wiki/List_of_companies_invo lved_in_quantum_computing_or_communication for a list of companies involved in quantum computing. For each of the following types of qubits, name a company that is using them.

(a) Photons
(b) Trapped ions
(c) Cold atoms
(d) Nuclear magnetic resonance (NMR)
(e) Quantum dots
(f) Defect qubits
(g) Superconductors

Exercise 2.20. Visit https://qubitzoo.org and pick your favorite qubit.

(a) What is the name of your qubit? (e.g., exchange-only qubit, not Steve.)
(b) What type of technology is your qubit?
(c) What is some motivation for building a qubit this way?

Exercise 2.21. Visit https://en.wikipedia.org/wiki/Qubit#Physical_impleme ntations and pick a qubit.

(a) What is the physical system or technology used for your qubit (physical support)?
(b) What is the name of your type of qubit?
(c) What physical property is used to store information (information support)?
(d) What state is typically used for $|0\rangle$?
(e) What state is typically used for $|1\rangle$?

2.6 Quantum Gates

2.6.1 Linear Maps

Quantum gates act on qubits, like logic gates act on bits. In this section, we will explore what quantum gates are.

A *quantum gate* transforms the state of a qubit into other states. As we will see later, we often use the capital letter U to denote a quantum gate. For example, consider a quantum gate that performs the following map:

$$U|0\rangle = \frac{\sqrt{2}-i}{2}|0\rangle - \frac{1}{2}|1\rangle,$$

$$U|1\rangle = \frac{1}{2}|0\rangle + \frac{\sqrt{2}+i}{2}|1\rangle.$$

A quantum gate must be *linear*, meaning we can distribute it across superpositions:

$$U(\alpha|0\rangle + \beta|1\rangle) = \alpha U|0\rangle + \beta U|1\rangle$$

$$= \alpha\left(\frac{\sqrt{2}-i}{2}|0\rangle - \frac{1}{2}|1\rangle\right) + \beta\left(\frac{1}{2}|0\rangle + \frac{\sqrt{2}+i}{2}|1\rangle\right)$$

$$= \left(\alpha\frac{\sqrt{2}-i}{2} + \beta\frac{1}{2}\right)|0\rangle + \left(-\alpha\frac{1}{2} + \beta\frac{\sqrt{2}+i}{2}\right)|1\rangle.$$

For this to be a valid quantum gate, the total probability must remain 1. Assuming the original state was normalized, i.e., $|\alpha|^2 + |\beta|^2 = 1$, we can calculate the total probability by summing the norm-square of each amplitude to see if it is still 1:

$$\left|\alpha\frac{\sqrt{2}-i}{2} + \beta\frac{1}{2}\right|^2 + \left|-\alpha\frac{1}{2} + \beta\frac{\sqrt{2}+i}{2}\right|^2$$

$$= \left(\alpha\frac{\sqrt{2}-i}{2} + \beta\frac{1}{2}\right)\left(\alpha^*\frac{\sqrt{2}+i}{2} + \beta^*\frac{1}{2}\right)$$

$$+ \left(-\alpha\frac{1}{2} + \beta\frac{\sqrt{2}+i}{2}\right)\left(-\alpha^*\frac{1}{2} + \beta^*\frac{\sqrt{2}-i}{2}\right)$$

$$= |\alpha|^2\frac{(\sqrt{2}-i)(\sqrt{2}+i)}{4} + \alpha\beta^*\frac{\sqrt{2}-i}{4} + \beta\alpha^*\frac{\sqrt{2}+i}{4} + |\beta|^2\frac{1}{4}$$

$$+ |\alpha|^2\frac{1}{4} - \alpha\beta^*\frac{\sqrt{2}-i}{4} - \beta\alpha^*\frac{\sqrt{2}+i}{4} + |\beta|^2\frac{(\sqrt{2}+i)(\sqrt{2}-i)}{4}$$

$$= |\alpha|^2\frac{3}{4} + |\beta|^2\frac{1}{4} + |\alpha|^2\frac{1}{4} + |\beta|^2\frac{3}{4}$$

$$= |\alpha|^2 + |\beta|^2$$

$$= 1.$$

So, U is a valid quantum gate. Then,

Quantum gates are linear maps that keep the total probability equal to 1.

In the next chapter, when we introduce linear algebra, we will learn that operators correspond to tables of numbers called matrices, and a valid quantum gate is a type of matrix called a unitary matrix. That is why quantum gates are often labeled U, for unitary.

Exercise 2.22. Consider a map U that transforms the Z-basis states as follows:

$$U|0\rangle = |0\rangle + |1\rangle,$$
$$U|1\rangle = |0\rangle - |1\rangle.$$

Say $|\psi\rangle = \alpha|0\rangle + \beta|1\rangle$ is a normalized quantum state, i.e., $|\alpha|^2 + |\beta|^2 = 1$.
(a) Calculate $U|\psi\rangle$.
(b) From your answer to (a), is U a valid quantum gate? Explain your reasoning.

Exercise 2.23. Consider a map U that transforms the Z-basis states as follows:

$$U|0\rangle = \frac{\sqrt{3}}{2}|0\rangle + \frac{\sqrt{3}+i}{4}|1\rangle,$$
$$U|1\rangle = \frac{\sqrt{3}+i}{4}|0\rangle - \frac{\sqrt{3}+3i}{4}|1\rangle.$$

Say $|\psi\rangle = \alpha|0\rangle + \beta|1\rangle$ is a normalized quantum state, i.e., $|\alpha|^2 + |\beta|^2 = 1$.
(a) Calculate $U|\psi\rangle$.
(b) From your answer to (a), is U a valid quantum gate? Explain your reasoning.

2.6.2 Classical Reversible Gates

Recall from Section 1.5 that a classical logic gate is reversible if its outputs are unique. For example, a gate with input A and output B with the following truth table is reversible, since it is always possible to determine the input from the output:

A	B
0	1
1	0

Thus, the gate does the following to a bit:

$$0 \to 1,$$
$$1 \to 0.$$

How would this gate act on a qubit? It would map the following:

$$\text{Gate}|0\rangle = |1\rangle,$$
$$\text{Gate}|1\rangle = |0\rangle.$$

Then, acting on a superposition $\alpha|0\rangle + \beta|1\rangle$, where $|\alpha|^2 + |\beta|^2 = 1$, it would do the following:

$$\text{Gate}\,(\alpha|0\rangle + \beta|1\rangle) = \alpha|1\rangle + \beta|0\rangle = \beta|0\rangle + \alpha|1\rangle.$$

We see that α and β simply got swapped. So, the final state is normalized, since

$$|\beta|^2 + |\alpha|^2 = |\alpha|^2 + |\beta|^2 = 1.$$

Thus, this classical reversible logic gate is also a valid quantum gate.

This is true in general. Any classical reversible logic gate simply permutes (shuffles) the amplitudes around. This chapter is just on a single qubit, but jumping ahead to Chapter 4 on multiple qubits, if there were more than two amplitudes, a classical reversible logic gate would just permute them, so the state stays normalized. Thus,

Classical reversible logic gates are valid quantum gates.

In contrast, irreversible gates are not valid quantum gates. For example, consider the irreversible gate with the following truth table:

A	B
0	0
1	0

This would act on the basis states of a qubit as:

$$\text{Gate}|0\rangle = |0\rangle,$$
$$\text{Gate}|1\rangle = |0\rangle.$$

Then, acting on a superposition,

$$\text{Gate}\,(\alpha|0\rangle + \beta|1\rangle) = \alpha|0\rangle + \beta|0\rangle = (\alpha + \beta)|0\rangle.$$

Now, the amplitudes are not permuted. Instead, they are combined. The total probability of this is

$$|\alpha + \beta|^2 = |\alpha|^2 + |\beta|^2 + \alpha^*\beta + \alpha\beta^* = 1 + \alpha^*\beta + \alpha\beta^* \neq 1,$$

so this is not a valid quantum gate.

Exercise 2.24. Consider each of the following classical logic gates with input A, output B, and truth table shown below. Is each gate a valid quantum gate? Why?

(a)

A	B
0	0
1	1

(b)

A	B
0	1
1	1

Exercise 2.25. Consider each of the following classical logic gates with inputs A and B, outputs C and D, and truth table shown below. Is each gate a valid quantum gate? Why?

(a)

A	B	C	D
0	0	0	1
0	1	1	1
1	0	0	0
1	1	1	0

(b)

A	B	C	D
0	0	0	0
0	1	0	0
1	0	1	0
1	1	1	1

2.6.3 Common One-Qubit Quantum Gates

Although any probability-preserving linear map is a valid quantum gate, let us list some important one-qubit gates that frequently appear in quantum computing:

- The *identity gate* turns $|0\rangle$ into $|0\rangle$ and $|1\rangle$ into $|1\rangle$, hence doing nothing:

$$I|0\rangle = |0\rangle,$$
$$I|1\rangle = |1\rangle.$$

This is a classical reversible gate (the identity gate), so it keeps states normalized and is a valid quantum gate.

In Qubit Touchdown, this corresponds to the Identity Gate action card, which does nothing to the football's position.

- The *Pauli X gate*, or *NOT gate*, turns $|0\rangle$ into $|1\rangle$, and $|1\rangle$ into $|0\rangle$:

$$X|0\rangle = |1\rangle,$$
$$X|1\rangle = |0\rangle.$$

This is a classical reversible gate (the NOT gate), so it keeps states normalized and is a valid quantum gate.

On the Bloch sphere, it can be shown that X is a rotation about the x-axis by $180°$:

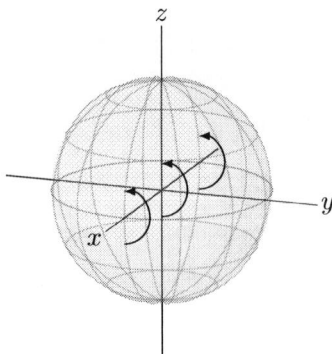

With this rotation in mind, we geometrically see that X causes $|0\rangle$ (the north pole) to rotate to $|1\rangle$ (the south pole), and vice versa. We also see that $|i\rangle$ and $|-i\rangle$ rotate to each other, whereas $|+\rangle$ and $|-\rangle$ are unchanged. Note, however, that mathematically $X|-\rangle = -|-\rangle \equiv |-\rangle$ since the global phase does not matter. If we apply the X gate twice, we rotate around the x-axis of the Bloch sphere by $360°$, which does nothing. Then, $X^2 = I$. We can use this fact to simplify consecutive applications of X. For example,

$$X^{1001} = X^{1000}X = \left(X^2\right)^{500}X = I^{500}X = X.$$

In Qubit Touchdown, the Pauli X Gate action card corresponds to the X gate.

- The *Pauli Y gate* turns $|0\rangle$ into $i|1\rangle$, and $|1\rangle$ into $-i|0\rangle$:

$$Y|0\rangle = i|1\rangle,$$
$$Y|1\rangle = -i|0\rangle.$$

This is not a classical gate at all because of the i and $-i$. Let us prove that it is a valid quantum gate by acting on a general superposition:

$$Y(\alpha|0\rangle + \beta|1\rangle) = \alpha\underbrace{Y|0\rangle}_{i|1\rangle} + \beta\underbrace{Y|1\rangle}_{-i|0\rangle} = i\alpha|1\rangle - i\beta|0\rangle = -i\beta|0\rangle + i\alpha|1\rangle.$$

The total probability of this is

$$|-i\beta|^2 + |i\alpha|^2 = (-i\beta)(i\beta^*) + (i\alpha)(-i\alpha^*) = |\beta|^2 + |\alpha|^2 = 1,$$

so it is a valid quantum gate.

On the Bloch sphere, it can be shown that Y is a rotation about the y-axis by $180°$:

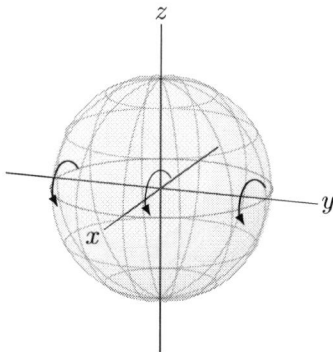

So, if we apply the Y gate twice, we rotate around the y-axis of the Bloch sphere by $360°$, which does nothing. Then, $Y^2 = I$. In Qubit Touchdown, the Pauli Y Gate action card corresponds to the Y gate.

- The *Pauli Z gate* keeps $|0\rangle$ as $|0\rangle$ and turns $|1\rangle$ into $-|1\rangle$:

$$Z|0\rangle = |0\rangle,$$
$$Z|1\rangle = -|1\rangle.$$

This is not a classical gate at all. In Exercise 2.28, you will show that this is a valid quantum gate.

On the Bloch sphere, it can be shown that Z is a rotation about the z-axis by $180°$:

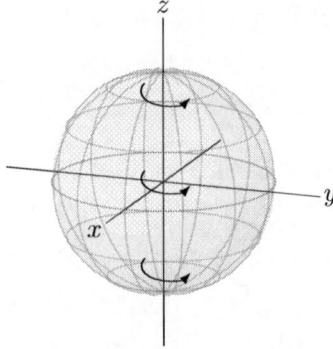

As before, $Z^2 = I$. In Qubit Touchdown, the Pauli Z Gate action card is the Z gate.

Exercise 2.26. Calculate $Z^{217} X^{101} Y^{50} (\alpha |0\rangle + \beta |1\rangle)$.

Exercise 2.27. Prove that
(a) $XZXZ(\alpha |0\rangle + \beta |1\rangle) = -(\alpha |0\rangle + \beta |1\rangle)$.
(b) $ZXZX(\alpha |0\rangle + \beta |1\rangle) = -(\alpha |0\rangle + \beta |1\rangle)$.
This will be used later in the textbook when we discuss Grover's algorithm.

- *Phase gate*, which is the square root of the Z gate (i.e., $S^2 = Z$):

$$S|0\rangle = |0\rangle,$$
$$S|1\rangle = i|1\rangle.$$

In Exercise 2.28, you will show that this is a valid quantum gate.
On the Bloch sphere, it can be shown that S is a rotation about the z-axis by $90°$:

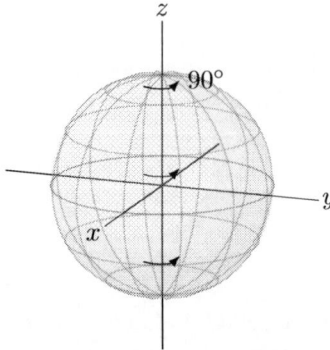

Now, S^2 rotates by $90°$ twice, so it is equivalent to rotating by $180°$. Then, $S^2 = Z$. We would need to apply S four times in order to return to the same point on the Bloch sphere, so $S^4 = I$. In Qubit Touchdown, the Phase Gate action card is the S gate.

- *T gate* (also called $\pi/8$ gate), which is the square root the S gate (i.e., $T^2 = S$), or fourth root of the Z gate:

$$T|0\rangle = |0\rangle,$$
$$T|1\rangle = e^{i\pi/4}|1\rangle.$$

In Exercise 2.28, you will show that this is a valid quantum gate.
On the Bloch sphere, T is a rotation about the z-axis by $45°$:

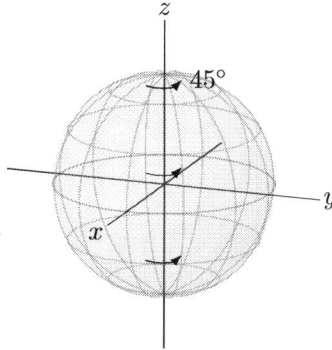

Then, it is obvious that $T^2 = S$ and $T^4 = Z$, since rotating by $45°$ twice is equivalent to rotating by $90°$, and rotating by $45°$ four times is equivalent to rotating by $180°$.

Exercise 2.28. Consider the gate $R_z(\theta)$, which rotates about the z-axis by angle θ:

$$R_z(\theta)|0\rangle = |0\rangle,$$
$$R_z(\theta)|1\rangle = e^{i\theta}|1\rangle.$$

The Z gate, S gate, and T gate are all specific instances of the R_z gate, with $Z = R_z(\pi)$, $S = R_z(\pi/2)$, and $T = R_z(\pi/4)$. Say $|\psi\rangle = \alpha|0\rangle + \beta|1\rangle$ is a normalized quantum state, i.e., $|\alpha|^2 + |\beta|^2 = 1$.
(a) Calculate $R_z(\theta)|\psi\rangle$.
(b) Show that the total probability of $R_z(\theta)|\psi\rangle$ is 1, so $R_z(\theta)$ is a valid quantum gate, and hence, Z, S, and T are all valid quantum gates.

- The *Hadamard gate* turns $|0\rangle$ into $|+\rangle$, and $|1\rangle$ into $|-\rangle$:

$$H|0\rangle = \frac{1}{\sqrt{2}}\left(|0\rangle + |1\rangle\right) = |+\rangle,$$

$$H|1\rangle = \frac{1}{\sqrt{2}}\left(|0\rangle - |1\rangle\right) = |-\rangle.$$

In Exercise 2.29, you will show that this is a valid quantum gate.
On the Bloch sphere, it can be shown that H is a rotation about the $x+z$-axis by $180°$:

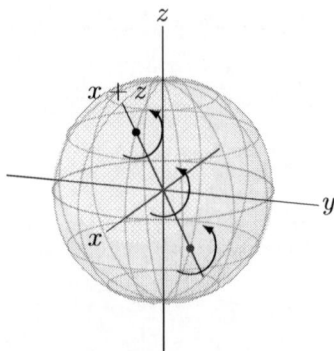

Then, H maps between $|0\rangle$ and $|+\rangle$, between $|1\rangle$ and $|-\rangle$, and between $|i\rangle$ and $|-i\rangle$. Let us also prove these algebraically. From the definition of the Hadamard gate, we already have $H|0\rangle = |+\rangle$ and $H|1\rangle = |-\rangle$. Going in the other direction,

$$
\begin{aligned}
H|+\rangle &= H\frac{1}{\sqrt{2}}\left(|0\rangle + |1\rangle\right) \\
&= \frac{1}{\sqrt{2}}\left(H|0\rangle + H|1\rangle\right) \\
&= \frac{1}{\sqrt{2}}\left[\frac{1}{\sqrt{2}}\left(|0\rangle + |1\rangle\right) + \frac{1}{\sqrt{2}}\left(|0\rangle - |1\rangle\right)\right] \\
&= |0\rangle,
\end{aligned}
$$

and similarly (Exercise 2.30),

$$
H|-\rangle = |1\rangle.
$$

We also have

$$
\begin{aligned}
H|i\rangle &= H\frac{1}{\sqrt{2}}\left(|0\rangle + i|1\rangle\right) \\
&= \frac{1}{\sqrt{2}}\left(H|0\rangle + iH|1\rangle\right) \\
&= \frac{1}{\sqrt{2}}\left[\frac{1}{\sqrt{2}}\left(|0\rangle + |1\rangle\right) + \frac{i}{\sqrt{2}}\left(|0\rangle - |1\rangle\right)\right] \\
&= \frac{1}{\sqrt{2}}\left(\frac{1+i}{\sqrt{2}}|0\rangle + \frac{1-i}{\sqrt{2}}|1\rangle\right) \\
&= \frac{1}{\sqrt{2}}\left(e^{i\pi/4}|0\rangle + e^{-i\pi/4}|1\rangle\right) \\
&= e^{i\pi/4}\frac{1}{\sqrt{2}}\left(|0\rangle + e^{-i\pi/2}|1\rangle\right) \\
&= e^{i\pi/4}\frac{1}{\sqrt{2}}\left(|0\rangle - i|1\rangle\right)
\end{aligned}
$$

$$= e^{i\pi/4}|-i\rangle$$
$$\equiv |-i\rangle.$$

Similarly (Exercise 2.30),

$$H|-i\rangle = e^{-i\pi/4}|i\rangle \equiv |i\rangle.$$

If we apply the H gate twice, we rotates by $360°$, which does nothing. So, $H^2 = I$.

In Qubit Touchdown, the Hadamard Gate action card is the Hadamard gate, which is why it moves the football between 0 and $+$, between 1 and $-$, and between i and $-i$.

Exercise 2.29. Say $|\psi\rangle = \alpha|0\rangle + \beta|1\rangle$ is a normalized quantum state, i.e., $|\alpha|^2 + |\beta|^2 = 1$.
(a) Calculate $H|\psi\rangle$.
(b) Show that the total probability of $H|\psi\rangle$ is 1, so H is a valid quantum gate.

Exercise 2.30. Work out the math to show that
(a) $H|-\rangle = |1\rangle$.
(b) $H|-i\rangle = e^{-i\pi/4}|i\rangle \equiv |i\rangle$.

We can combine these quantum gates to create all sorts of states. For example,

$$HSTH|0\rangle = HST\frac{1}{\sqrt{2}}(|0\rangle + |1\rangle)$$

$$= HS\frac{1}{\sqrt{2}}\left(|0\rangle + e^{i\pi/4}|1\rangle\right)$$

$$= H\frac{1}{\sqrt{2}}\left(|0\rangle + e^{i3\pi/4}|1\rangle\right)$$

$$= \frac{1}{\sqrt{2}}\left[\frac{1}{\sqrt{2}}(|0\rangle + |1\rangle) + e^{i3\pi/4}\frac{1}{\sqrt{2}}(|0\rangle - |1\rangle)\right]$$

$$= \frac{1}{2}\left[\left(1 + e^{i3\pi/4}\right)|0\rangle + \left(1 - e^{i3\pi/4}\right)|1\rangle\right], \tag{2.9}$$

where in the third line, we used $ie^{i\pi/4} = e^{i\pi/2}e^{i\pi/4} = e^{i3\pi/4}$ On the Bloch sphere, this state is in the southern hemisphere:

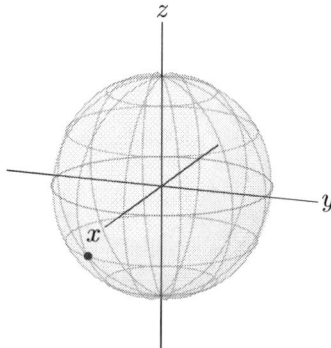

If we measure this qubit in the Z-basis $\{|0\rangle, |1\rangle\}$, the probability of getting $|0\rangle$ is

$$
\begin{aligned}
\left| \frac{1}{2} \left(1 + e^{i3\pi/4}\right) \right|^2 &= \frac{1}{2}\left(1 + e^{i3\pi/4}\right)\frac{1}{2}\left(1 + e^{-i3\pi/4}\right) \\
&= \frac{1}{4}\left(1 + e^{-i3\pi/4} + e^{i3\pi/4} + e^0\right) \\
&= \frac{1}{4}\left(2 + 2\cos\frac{3\pi}{4}\right) \\
&= \frac{1}{2}\left(1 - \frac{\sqrt{2}}{2}\right) \\
&\approx 0.146,
\end{aligned}
$$

where to go from the second to the third line, we used Euler's formula Eq. (2.6) so that $e^{i\theta} + e^{-i\theta} = 2\cos\theta$. Similarly, the probability of getting $|1\rangle$ is

$$
\left| \frac{1}{2}\left(1 - e^{i3\pi/4}\right) \right|^2 = \frac{1}{4}\left(2 - 2\cos\frac{3\pi}{4}\right) = \frac{1}{2}\left(1 + \frac{\sqrt{2}}{2}\right) \approx 0.854.
$$

As expected, since the state is in the southern hemisphere, there is a greater probability of getting $|1\rangle$ when measuring the qubit.

Exercise 2.31. Calculate $Y^{51} H^{99} T^{36} Z^{25} |0\rangle$.

Exercise 2.32. Prove that $HXH = Z$ by showing that $HXH|0\rangle$ and $Z|0\rangle$ result in the same state, and $HXH|1\rangle$ and $Z|1\rangle$ result in the same state. Such an equation is called a *circuit identity*.

Exercise 2.33. Answer the following:
(a) Calculate $HTHTH|0\rangle$.
(b) If you measure this in the Z-basis $\{|0\rangle, |1\rangle\}$, what is the probability that you get $|0\rangle$ and the probability that you get $|1\rangle$?

2.6.4 General One-Qubit Gates

You may have noticed that all the quantum gates from the last section were rotations by some angle around some axis. This is true in general:

One-qubit quantum gates are rotations on the Bloch sphere.

This is because rotations on the Bloch sphere satisfy the two properties that we require of quantum gates: they are linear maps, and they keep the total probability equal to 1. Proving that rotations are linear requires some math, which we sketch below. Rotations keep the total probability equal to 1 because a qubit is a point on the Bloch sphere, so if we rotate it, it remains a point on the Bloch sphere.

Mathematically, say we rotate by angle θ about some axis of rotation, which we can specify in terms of the x-, y-, and z-axes. We denote the direction of the x-axis by $\hat{x}$, the direction of the y-axis by $\hat{y}$, and the direction of the z-axis by $\hat{z}$. Then, we can denote the axis of rotation by $\hat{n}$, and

$$\hat{n} = n_x\hat{x} + n_y\hat{y} + n_z\hat{z}.$$

Note $\hat{n}$ is a *unit vector*, meaning it must has length 1, i.e., $n_x^2 + n_y^2 + n_z^2 = 1$.

For example, the Hadamard gate is a rotation by $\theta = 180° = \pi$ radians about the axis halfway between the x- and z-axes, and we can express this axis by

$$\hat{n} = \frac{1}{\sqrt{2}}\hat{x} + \frac{1}{\sqrt{2}}\hat{z},$$

Note $n_x^2 + n_y^2 + n_z^2 = 1/2 + 0 + 1/2 = 1$, as expected.

Now, we state as a fact (without proof) that a rotation by angle θ about axis $\hat{n} = (n_x, n_y, n_z)$ can be written in terms of I, X, Y, and Z:

$$U = e^{i\gamma}\left[\cos\left(\frac{\theta}{2}\right)I - i\sin\left(\frac{\theta}{2}\right)(n_xX + n_yY + n_zZ)\right], \tag{2.10}$$

where γ is a global phase that we can set to anything (or drop), since it does not have any physical relevance.

Returning to our example of the Hadamard gate, with $\theta = \pi$ and $\hat{n} = (1/\sqrt{2}, 0, 1/\sqrt{2})$, we have

$$U = e^{i\gamma}\left[\cos\left(\frac{\pi}{2}\right)I - i\sin\left(\frac{\pi}{2}\right)\left(\frac{1}{\sqrt{2}}X + 0Y + \frac{1}{\sqrt{2}}Z\right)\right]$$

$$= -ie^{i\gamma}\frac{1}{\sqrt{2}}(X + Z).$$

To show that U is the Hadamard gate, let us see how it acts on $|0\rangle$ and $|1\rangle$:

$$U|0\rangle - ie^{i\gamma}\frac{1}{\sqrt{2}}(X + Z)|0\rangle = -ie^{i\gamma}\frac{1}{\sqrt{2}}(X|0\rangle + Z|0\rangle)$$

$$= -ie^{i\gamma}\frac{1}{\sqrt{2}}(|1\rangle + |0\rangle) = -ie^{i\gamma}|+\rangle,$$

$$U|1\rangle = -ie^{i\gamma}\frac{1}{\sqrt{2}}(X + Z)|1\rangle = -ie^{i\gamma}\frac{1}{\sqrt{2}}(X|1\rangle + Z|1\rangle)$$

$$= -ie^{i\gamma}\frac{1}{\sqrt{2}}(|0\rangle - |1\rangle) = -ie^{i\gamma}|-\rangle.$$

We can drop the global phase of $-ie^{i\gamma}$, so $U|0\rangle = |+\rangle$ and $U|1\rangle = |-\rangle$, which is the Hadamard gate. Alternatively, we can choose $\gamma = \pi/2$, and then since $-i = e^{i3\pi/2}$, the global phase is $-ie^{i\gamma} = e^{i3\pi/2}e^{i\pi/2} = e^{i2\pi} = 1$.

We can also use Eq. (2.10) to prove that rotations are linear. Note U is a sum of I, X, Y, and Z with numbers as coefficients; we call this a *linear combination* of I, X, Y, and Z. Since each of these gates distribute over superpositions, U also distributes over superpositions, and so it is linear:

$$
\begin{aligned}
U(\alpha|0\rangle + \beta|1\rangle) &= e^{i\gamma}\left[\cos\left(\frac{\theta}{2}\right)I - i\sin\left(\frac{\theta}{2}\right)(n_xX + n_yY + n_zZ)\right](\alpha|0\rangle + \beta|1\rangle) \\
&= \alpha e^{i\gamma}\left[\cos\left(\frac{\theta}{2}\right)I - i\sin\left(\frac{\theta}{2}\right)(n_xX + n_yY + n_zZ)\right]|0\rangle \\
&\quad + \beta e^{i\gamma}\left[\cos\left(\frac{\theta}{2}\right)I - i\sin\left(\frac{\theta}{2}\right)(n_xX + n_yY + n_zZ)\right]|1\rangle \\
&= \alpha U|0\rangle + \beta U|1\rangle.
\end{aligned}
$$

Exercise 2.34. Consider a rotation by $45°$ about the z-axis.
(a) What is $\hat{n}$?
(b) Use Eq. (2.10) to express the rotation U is terms of I, X, Y, and Z.
(c) Find $U|0\rangle$.
(d) Find $U|1\rangle$.
(e) Show that U is the T gate, up to a global phase.

Exercise 2.35. Consider a rotation by $180°$ around the axis equidistant from the x-, y-, and z-axes. Below, the first picture shows the axis on the Bloch sphere. It may be a little difficult to visualize, however, so another description of it using a cube is shown below in the second picture. The cube has a corner at the origin and edges of length s along the x-, y-, and z-axes. Then, the axis of rotation goes through the origin and the point (s, s, s), and the axis of rotation is drawn as a thicker line.

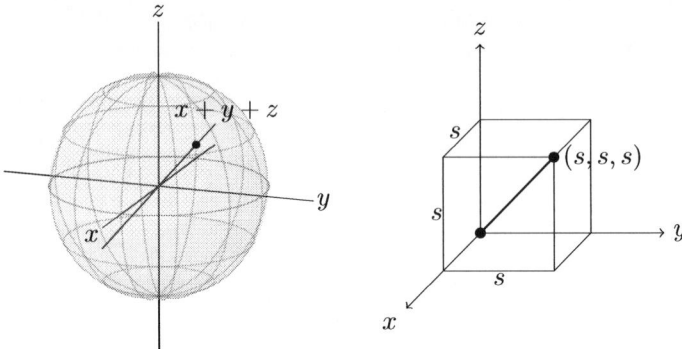

(a) Draw the Bloch sphere and show where $|0\rangle$ goes after applying the rotation. Do this without any calculations by visualizing the rotation on the Bloch sphere.
(b) Draw the Bloch sphere and show where $|1\rangle$ goes after applying the rotation. Do this without any calculations by visualizing the rotation on the Bloch sphere.
(c) What is $\hat{n}$? Hint: It should have equal components in the x-, y-, and z-axes, and it should be a unit vector.
(d) Use Eq. (2.10) to express the rotation U is terms of I, X, Y, and Z.
(e) Find $U|0\rangle$.
(f) Find $U|1\rangle$.

2.7 Quantum Circuits

2.7.1 Circuit Diagrams

Just like we can draw a classical circuit diagram consisting of bits and logic gates, we can draw *quantum circuit diagrams* consisting of qubits and quantum gates. For example, $HSTH|0\rangle$ is

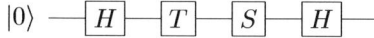

$$|0\rangle \quad \boxed{H}\!-\!\boxed{T}\!-\!\boxed{S}\!-\!\boxed{H}$$

The circuit is read left-to-right, just like a classical circuit diagram. So, we start with a single qubit in the $|0\rangle$ state and apply a Hadamard gate H to it, followed by a T gate, then a phase gate S, and finally another H gate. It is implied that we measure the qubit at the end of the circuit. We can also explicitly draw the measurement as a meter:

$$|0\rangle \quad \boxed{H}\!-\!\boxed{T}\!-\!\boxed{S}\!-\!\boxed{H}\!-\!\boxed{\angle}$$

2.7.2 Quirk

A great web-based tool for simulating quantum circuits is *Quirk* at `https://alga ssert.com/quirk`:

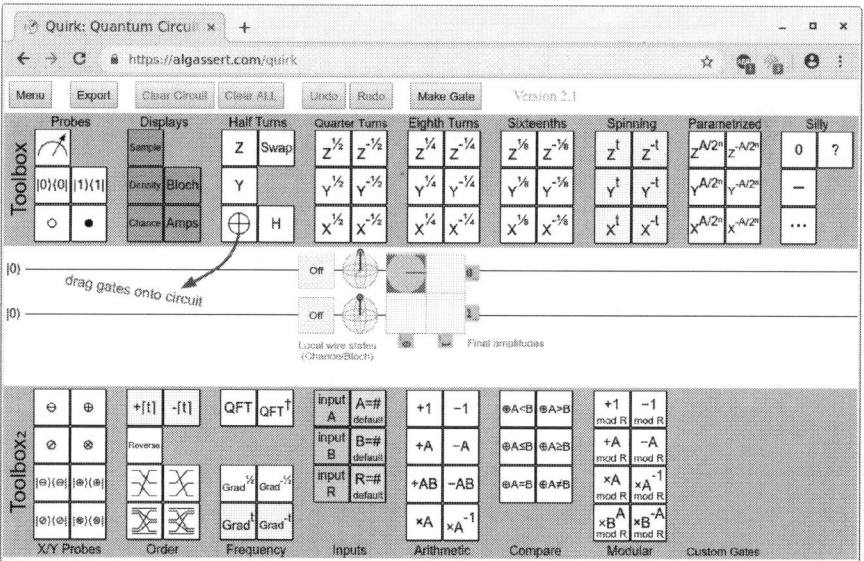

There are a variety of quantum gates that users can drag and drop onto the circuit, and users can also make custom gates. Each qubit is initially a $|0\rangle$, as shown below:

$$|0\rangle \text{————————————— Off }$$

The state of each qubit is visualized a couple ways. First, the probability that a measurement of the qubit yields $|1\rangle$ is zero, and this is labeled as "Off." Second, the Bloch sphere representation of the qubit is shown, and the state is a point at the north pole, as expected.

Now if we apply the X gate, Quirk shows the following:

$$|0\rangle \text{—⊕————————————— On }$$

Note Quirk uses $\oplus$ to denote a single X gate, whereas we use $\boxed{X}$ (later, we will also use $\oplus$ when the X gate is controlled by another qubit). Since $X|0\rangle = |1\rangle$, the probability of measuring $|1\rangle$ is 1. This is labeled as "On," and the Bloch sphere now shows the state at the south pole, as expected.

Now consider $H|0\rangle = |+\rangle$:

$$|0\rangle \text{—}\boxed{H}\text{————————————— 50.0\% }$$

In Quirk, it shows a 50% chance of being $|1\rangle$ when measured in the Z-basis, and it lies on the x-axis of the Bloch sphere, as expected.

Finally, let us simulate $HSTH|0\rangle$, which we earlier computed by hand to have a 0.146 probability of being $|0\rangle$ and a 0.854 probability of being $|1\rangle$. Simulating it in Quirk,

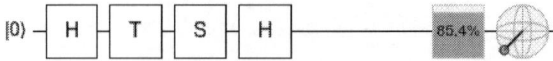

$$|0\rangle \text{—}\boxed{H}\text{—}\boxed{T}\text{—}\boxed{S}\text{—}\boxed{H}\text{———————— 85.4\% }$$

Quirk displays that the probability of measuring $|1\rangle$ is $85.4\% = 0.854$, in agreement with our previous calculations from Eq. (2.9).

Exercise 2.36. Answer the following about $HYTHX|0\rangle$.
(a) Draw $HYTHX|0\rangle$ as a quantum circuit.
(b) Using Quirk, sketch where $HYTHX|0\rangle$ appears on the Bloch sphere.
(c) Using Quirk, if you measure $HYTHX|0\rangle$ in the Z-basis, what is the probability that you get $|0\rangle$ and the probability that you get $|1\rangle$?

2.8 Summary

The smallest unit of quantum information is the qubit. Besides having two orthogonal states $|0\rangle$ and $|1\rangle$, a qubit can be a superposition of them with complex amplitudes. The norm-square of the amplitudes gives the probability of measuring the qubit as a 0 or 1, and depending on the outcome, the qubit collapses to $|0\rangle$ or $|1\rangle$. Qubits can also be measured in other bases. A qubit can be visualized on the Bloch sphere. Qubits are operated on by quantum gates, which are linear maps that keep the total probability equal to 1. A single-qubit gate is a rotation on the Bloch sphere. A quantum circuit is a drawing to depict what quantum gates act on a qubit, and an online simulator for quantum circuits is Quirk.

Chapter 3
Linear Algebra

So far, we have done quantum computing using elementary algebra and using the fact that quantum gates are linear, so they distribute across superpositions. This can be tedious, however, such as when calculating $HYTHX(\alpha|0\rangle + \beta|1\rangle)$. Fortunately, there is an easier way to do the math of quantum computing using *linear algebra*, where numbers are arranged in columns, rows, and tables (called matrices). Ultimately, linear algebra is a tool. Learning how to use a new tool may be difficult at first, but ultimately, it makes the job easier. We will show how linear algebra can be used for many of the calculations from the previous chapter.

We had a similar progression with classical computing. In Chapter 1, we could do all of classical computing using truth tables, including to show that $\overline{A}\overline{B}\overline{C} + \overline{A}\overline{B}C + A\overline{B}\overline{C} + AB\overline{C} = \overline{A} + B + A\overline{C}$. Boolean algebra makes such calculations easier, but it requires becoming proficient enough with the tool. Linear algebra is to quantum computing as boolean algebra is to classical computing.

3.1 Quantum States

3.1.1 Column Vectors

We write $|0\rangle$ and $|1\rangle$ as *column vectors*, which are vertical lists of numbers:

$$|0\rangle = \begin{pmatrix} 1 \\ 0 \end{pmatrix}, \quad |1\rangle = \begin{pmatrix} 0 \\ 1 \end{pmatrix}.$$

Our notation is to write vectors in large parenthesis, but some people use square brackets instead. These are called column vectors because they have a single column, and they have length 2 because they have two entries. Writing $|0\rangle$ and $|1\rangle$, this way, it is easy to write superpositions of them. A generic qubit with amplitudes α and β would be

$$|\psi\rangle = \alpha|0\rangle + \beta|1\rangle = \alpha\begin{pmatrix}1\\0\end{pmatrix} + \beta\begin{pmatrix}0\\1\end{pmatrix} = \begin{pmatrix}\alpha\\0\end{pmatrix} + \begin{pmatrix}0\\\beta\end{pmatrix}$$

$$= \begin{pmatrix}\alpha\\\beta\end{pmatrix}.$$

For example, $|i\rangle$ can be written as a column vector:

$$|i\rangle = \frac{1}{\sqrt{2}}|0\rangle + \frac{i}{\sqrt{2}}|1\rangle = \frac{1}{\sqrt{2}}\begin{pmatrix}1\\0\end{pmatrix} + \frac{i}{\sqrt{2}}\begin{pmatrix}0\\1\end{pmatrix} = \begin{pmatrix}1/\sqrt{2}\\0\end{pmatrix} + \begin{pmatrix}0\\i/\sqrt{2}\end{pmatrix}$$

$$= \begin{pmatrix}1/\sqrt{2}\\i/\sqrt{2}\end{pmatrix} = \frac{1}{\sqrt{2}}\begin{pmatrix}1\\i\end{pmatrix}.$$

Exercise 3.1. A qubit is in the following state:

$$\frac{1}{2}|0\rangle - \frac{\sqrt{3}}{2}|1\rangle.$$

Write this state as a column vector.

Exercise 3.2. A qubit is in the following state:

$$\begin{pmatrix}\sqrt{3}/2\\1/2\end{pmatrix}.$$

If you measure this qubit in the Z-basis $\{|0\rangle, |1\rangle\}$, what states can you get and with what probabilities?

3.1.2 Row Vectors

Next, the *transpose* of a column vector is obtained by rewriting it as a *row vector*, and it is denoted by ^{T} (a superscript letter T). So,

$$\begin{pmatrix}\alpha\\\beta\end{pmatrix}^{\mathsf{T}} = (\alpha\ \beta).$$

In quantum computing, we typically use the *conjugate transpose*, which is obtained by taking the complex conjugate of each component of the transpose. It is denoted by † (a dagger):

$$\begin{pmatrix}\alpha\\\beta\end{pmatrix}^{\dagger} = (\alpha^*\ \beta^*).$$

This is used so frequently in quantum mechanics that bra-ket notation has a special way of writing it: with an angle bracket and a vertical bar, called a *bra*:

$$\langle\psi| = (\alpha^*\ \beta^*).$$

Then, a bra is the conjugate transpose of a ket, and conversely, a ket is the conjugate transpose of a bra. Flipping between kets and bras is called "taking the dual", and the dual of a ket is its bra version, and the dual of a bra is its ket version. For example, the dual of $|i\rangle = \begin{pmatrix} 1/\sqrt{2} \\ i/\sqrt{2} \end{pmatrix}$ is

$$\langle i| = \begin{pmatrix} 1/\sqrt{2} & -i/\sqrt{2} \end{pmatrix}.$$

We can also take the conjugate transpose of $|0\rangle = \begin{pmatrix} 1 \\ 0 \end{pmatrix}$ and $|1\rangle = \begin{pmatrix} 0 \\ 1 \end{pmatrix}$ to get the Z-basis vectors as bras:

$$\langle 0| = \begin{pmatrix} 1 & 0 \end{pmatrix}, \quad \langle 1| = \begin{pmatrix} 0 & 1 \end{pmatrix}.$$

Then, $\langle \psi|$ can be written as

$$\langle \psi| = \begin{pmatrix} \alpha^* & \beta^* \end{pmatrix} = \begin{pmatrix} \alpha^* & 0 \end{pmatrix} + \begin{pmatrix} 0 & \beta^* \end{pmatrix} = \alpha^* \begin{pmatrix} 1 & 0 \end{pmatrix} + \beta^* \begin{pmatrix} 0 & 1 \end{pmatrix}$$
$$= \alpha^* \langle 0| + \beta^* \langle 1|.$$

Notice this has amplitudes α^* and β^*, so when we go from $|\psi\rangle$ to $\langle \psi|$, we need to take the complex conjugate of the amplitudes. For example, taking the dual of $|i\rangle = \frac{1}{\sqrt{2}}|0\rangle + \frac{i}{\sqrt{2}}|1\rangle$, we get

$$\langle i| = \frac{1}{\sqrt{2}} \langle 0| - \frac{i}{\sqrt{2}} \langle 1|.$$

To summarize, to go between kets and bras,

$$|\psi\rangle = \begin{pmatrix} \alpha \\ \beta \end{pmatrix} \quad \Longleftrightarrow \quad \langle \psi| = \begin{pmatrix} \alpha^* & \beta^* \end{pmatrix},$$
$$|\psi\rangle = \alpha|0\rangle + \beta|1\rangle \quad \Longleftrightarrow \quad \langle \psi| = \alpha^* \langle 0| + \beta^* \langle 1|.$$

Exercise 3.3. Consider the following two states $|a\rangle$ and $|b\rangle$:

$$|a\rangle = \frac{\sqrt{3}}{2}|0\rangle + \frac{1}{2}|1\rangle, \quad |b\rangle = \frac{2}{3}|0\rangle + \frac{1-2i}{3}|1\rangle.$$

Answer the following questions:
(a) What is $\langle a|$ in terms of $\langle 0|$ and $\langle 1|$?
(b) What is $\langle a|$ as a row vector?
(c) What is $\langle b|$ in terms of $\langle 0|$ and $\langle 1|$?
(d) What is $\langle b|$ as a row vector?

3.2 Inner Products

3.2.1 Inner Products Are Scalars

Say we have two states,

$$|\psi\rangle = \begin{pmatrix} \alpha \\ \beta \end{pmatrix}, \quad \text{and} \quad |\phi\rangle = \begin{pmatrix} \gamma \\ \delta \end{pmatrix}.$$

One way to multiply $|\psi\rangle$ and $|\phi\rangle$ is by taking their *inner product*, and it is defined as $\langle\psi|$ times $|\phi\rangle$:

$$\langle\psi||\phi\rangle = (\alpha^* \ \beta^*) \begin{pmatrix} \gamma \\ \delta \end{pmatrix}.$$

Typically, we combine the two vertical bars into one and write the inner product as

$$\langle\psi|\phi\rangle = (\alpha^* \ \beta^*) \begin{pmatrix} \gamma \\ \delta \end{pmatrix}.$$

We call $\langle\psi|\phi\rangle$ a *bra-ket* or *bracket*, and the word bracket is the origin of the terms bra and ket. To evaluate the inner product, from linear algebra, we multiply a row vector and a column vector by multiplying the first entry of each vector together, multiplying the second entry of each vector together, and adding them (i.e., taking their *dot product*):

$$\langle\psi|\phi\rangle = \alpha^*\gamma + \beta^*\delta.$$

Note the result is just a number, or *scalar*. So, an inner product is also called a *scalar product*.

The inner product of $|\phi\rangle$ and $|\psi\rangle$ is just the complex conjugate of the inner product of $|\psi\rangle$ and $|\phi\rangle$:

$$\langle\phi|\psi\rangle = \langle\psi|\phi\rangle^*.$$

To prove this, we can just do a simple calculation:

$$\langle\phi|\psi\rangle = (\gamma^* \ \delta^*) \begin{pmatrix} \alpha \\ \beta \end{pmatrix} = \gamma^*\alpha + \delta^*\beta = (\gamma\alpha^* + \delta\beta^*)^* = (\alpha^*\gamma + \beta^*\delta)^*$$
$$= \langle\psi|\phi\rangle^*.$$

Inner products have several uses, which we will see next and throughout this chapter.

Exercise 3.4. Consider

$$|a\rangle = \frac{3 + i\sqrt{3}}{4}|0\rangle + \frac{1}{2}|1\rangle,$$

$$|b\rangle = \frac{1}{4}|0\rangle + \frac{\sqrt{15}}{4}|1\rangle.$$

(a) Find $\langle a|b\rangle$.

(b) Find $\langle b|a\rangle$.

(c) What is the relationship between your answers to parts (a) and (b)?

3.2.2 Orthonormality

Several properties can be expressed using the inner product:

- First, let us take the inner product of $|\psi\rangle = \alpha|0\rangle + \beta|1\rangle$ with itself:

$$\langle\psi|\psi\rangle = \begin{pmatrix} \alpha^* & \beta^* \end{pmatrix}\begin{pmatrix} \alpha \\ \beta \end{pmatrix} = |\alpha|^2 + |\beta|^2 = 1.$$

So, $\langle\psi|\psi\rangle$ is just the total probability, and if $\langle\psi|\psi\rangle = 1$, the state $|\psi\rangle$ is normalized.

- Consider the inner product of the Z-basis states $|0\rangle$ and $|1\rangle$:

$$\langle 0|1\rangle = \begin{pmatrix} 1 & 0 \end{pmatrix}\begin{pmatrix} 0 \\ 1 \end{pmatrix} = 1\cdot 0 + 0\cdot 1 = 0 + 0 = 0.$$

Next, consider the inner product of the X-basis states $|+\rangle$ and $|-\rangle$:

$$\langle +|-\rangle = \frac{1}{\sqrt{2}}\begin{pmatrix} 1 & 1 \end{pmatrix}\frac{1}{\sqrt{2}}\begin{pmatrix} 1 \\ -1 \end{pmatrix} = \frac{1}{2}\begin{pmatrix} 1 & 1 \end{pmatrix}\begin{pmatrix} 1 \\ -1 \end{pmatrix} = \frac{1}{2}(1-1) = 0.$$

Finally, consider the inner product of the Y-basis states $|i\rangle$ and $|-i\rangle$:

$$\langle i|-i\rangle = \frac{1}{\sqrt{2}}\begin{pmatrix} 1 & -i \end{pmatrix}\frac{1}{\sqrt{2}}\begin{pmatrix} 1 \\ -i \end{pmatrix} = \frac{1}{2}\begin{pmatrix} 1 & -i \end{pmatrix}\begin{pmatrix} 1 \\ -i \end{pmatrix} = \frac{1}{2}(1+i^2) = 0,$$

where we used $i^2 = (\sqrt{-1})^2 = -1$.

In all of these, the outcome was zero. In fact, any two states on opposite sides of the Bloch sphere have zero inner product (Exercise 3.8). We say that states with zero inner product are *orthogonal*. Thus, orthogonal states are distinct measurement outcomes.

- These two properties, normalized and orthogonal, can be combined into a single word, *orthonormal*. So $|0\rangle$ and $|1\rangle$ are orthonormal because each state is individually normalized, and they are orthogonal to each other. Similarly, $|+\rangle$ and $|-\rangle$ are orthonormal, and $|i\rangle$ and $|-i\rangle$ are orthonormal.

Exercise 3.5. Consider a qubit in the following state

$$|\psi\rangle = A\left(2|0\rangle + 3i|1\rangle\right).$$

(a) Calculate $\langle\psi|\psi\rangle$.

(b) Find a value of A that normalizes $|\psi\rangle$.

Exercise 3.6. Determine if each pair of states is orthogonal or not.

(a) $|+\rangle$ and $|-\rangle$.
(b) $|0\rangle$ and $|+\rangle$.
(c) $\dfrac{1+\sqrt{3}i}{4}|0\rangle + \dfrac{\sqrt{2}-i}{2}|1\rangle$ and $\dfrac{\sqrt{2}+i}{2}|0\rangle + \dfrac{-1+\sqrt{3}i}{4}|1\rangle$.

Exercise 3.7. Consider

$$|a\rangle = \frac{3+i\sqrt{3}}{4}|0\rangle + \frac{1}{2}|1\rangle,$$

$$|b\rangle = \frac{1}{4}|0\rangle + x|1\rangle.$$

(a) Find x so that $|a\rangle$ and $|b\rangle$ are orthogonal.
(b) Find x so that $|b\rangle$ is normalized.
(c) For what values of x (if any) are $|a\rangle$ and $|b\rangle$ orthonormal?

Exercise 3.8. Say we have two qubits $|a\rangle$ and $|b\rangle$. We can parameterize them in spherical coordinates (θ, ϕ) on the Bloch sphere:

$$|a\rangle = \cos\left(\frac{\theta_a}{2}\right)|0\rangle + e^{i\phi_a}\sin\left(\frac{\theta_a}{2}\right)|1\rangle,$$

$$|b\rangle = \cos\left(\frac{\theta_b}{2}\right)|0\rangle + e^{i\phi_b}\sin\left(\frac{\theta_b}{2}\right)|1\rangle.$$

Now say $|a\rangle$ and $|b\rangle$ lie on opposite points of the Bloch sphere. This means $\theta_b = \pi - \theta_a$ and $\phi_b = \phi_a + \pi$. Show that $\langle a|b\rangle = 0$, i.e., they are orthogonal. Possibly useful trigonometric identities:

$$\sin(u \pm v) = \sin(u)\cos(v) \pm \cos(u)\sin(v),$$
$$\cos(u \pm v) = \cos(u)\cos(v) \mp \sin(u)\sin(v).$$

3.2.3 Projection, Measurement, and Change of Basis

Next, inner products can be used to find the amplitudes of quantum states, which can be norm-squared to yield measurement probabilities. The amplitudes can also be used to change the basis. As an example, consider a qubit in the following state:

$$|\psi\rangle = \frac{\sqrt{3}}{2}|0\rangle + \frac{1}{2}|1\rangle.$$

It appears on the Bloch sphere as shown below:

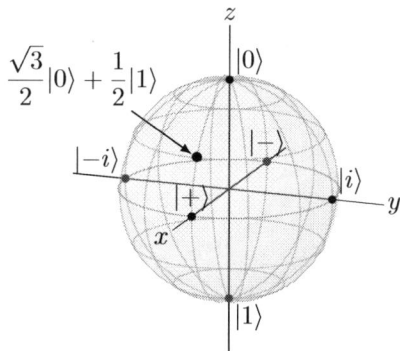

In Section 2.3.3, we measured this qubit in the Z-basis, X-basis, Y-basis, and a fourth basis. Let us see how to reproduce the results using inner products.

First, we want to find the possible measurement outcomes and their probabilities if we measure $|\psi\rangle$ in the $\{|0\rangle, |1\rangle\}$ basis. Although we can just "read off" the amplitudes of $|\psi\rangle$ with respect to $|0\rangle$ and $|1\rangle$ and take the norm-square of each to find the probabilities, we can also find the amplitudes using inner products and the orthonormality of $\{|0\rangle, |1\rangle\}$. For example, the amplitude of $|0\rangle$ is

$$\langle 0|\psi\rangle = \langle 0|\left(\frac{\sqrt{3}}{2}|0\rangle + \frac{1}{2}|1\rangle\right) = \frac{\sqrt{3}}{2}\underbrace{\langle 0|0\rangle}_{1} + \frac{1}{2}\underbrace{\langle 0|1\rangle}_{0} = \frac{\sqrt{3}}{2}.$$

When calculating this, the amplitude from $|1\rangle$ vanishes because $|0\rangle$ and $|1\rangle$ are orthogonal (i.e., $\langle 0|1\rangle = 0$). We get just the amplitude from $|0\rangle$ because $|0\rangle$ is normalized (i.e., $\langle 0|0\rangle = 1$). Similarly, the amplitude of $|1\rangle$ is

$$\langle 1|\psi\rangle = \langle 1|\left(\frac{\sqrt{3}}{2}|0\rangle + \frac{1}{2}|1\rangle\right) = \frac{\sqrt{3}}{2}\underbrace{\langle 1|0\rangle}_{0} + \frac{1}{2}\underbrace{\langle 1|1\rangle}_{1} = \frac{1}{2}.$$

Taking the norm-square of each of these, the possible measurement outcomes are $|0\rangle$ with probability $3/4$ and $|1\rangle$ with probability $1/4$. Since $\langle 0|\psi\rangle$ and $\langle 1|\psi\rangle$ are the amplitudes of $|0\rangle$ and $|1\rangle$, respectively, we can write the state of the qubit as

$$|\psi\rangle = \langle 0|\psi\rangle|0\rangle + \langle 1|\psi\rangle|1\rangle.$$

This technique is far more useful when we cannot just read off the amplitudes, such as when measuring in other bases. Let us measure in the X-basis $\{|+\rangle, |-\rangle\}$ now. The amplitude of $|+\rangle$ is

$$\langle +|\psi\rangle = \frac{1}{\sqrt{2}}(\langle 0| + \langle 1|)\left(\frac{\sqrt{3}}{2}|0\rangle + \frac{1}{2}|1\rangle\right)$$

$$= \frac{1}{\sqrt{2}} \left(\frac{\sqrt{3}}{2} \underbrace{\langle 0|0 \rangle}_{1} + \frac{1}{2} \underbrace{\langle 0|1 \rangle}_{0} + \frac{\sqrt{3}}{2} \underbrace{\langle 1|0 \rangle}_{0} + \frac{1}{2} \underbrace{\langle 1|1 \rangle}_{1} \right)$$

$$= \frac{1}{\sqrt{2}} \left(\frac{\sqrt{3}}{2} + \frac{1}{2} \right)$$

$$= \frac{\sqrt{3}+1}{2\sqrt{2}}.$$

This agrees with our calculation in Section 2.3.3. Similarly, the amplitude of $|-\rangle$ is $\langle -|\psi \rangle$, but now let us calculate it using linear algebra:

$$\langle -|\psi \rangle = \frac{1}{\sqrt{2}} (1 \ -1) \begin{pmatrix} \sqrt{3}/2 \\ 1/2 \end{pmatrix} = \frac{1}{\sqrt{2}} \left(\frac{\sqrt{3}}{2} - \frac{1}{2} \right) = \frac{\sqrt{3}-1}{2\sqrt{2}}.$$

Again, this agrees with Section 2.3.3. This approach is especially convenient because we can do the calculations using a computer algebra system that supports linear algebra, like Mathematica or SageMath:

- In Mathematica,

```
psi={{Sqrt[3]/2},{1/2}};
minus={{1/Sqrt[2]},{-1/Sqrt[2]}};
ConjugateTranspose[minus].psi
```

The first line defines a column vector named `psi` (for $|\psi\rangle$), and the second line defines a column vector named `minus` (for $|-\rangle$). To take their inner product, we take the conjugate transpose of `minus` (which is $\langle -|$) and perform a vector multiplication (denoted by the period) with `psi`. The result of this is

$$\frac{\sqrt{3}-1}{2\sqrt{2}},$$

as expected.
- In SageMath,

```
sage: psi = vector([sqrt(3)/2,1/2])
sage: minus = vector([1/sqrt(2),-1/sqrt(2)])
sage: minus.conjugate()*psi
1/4*sqrt(3)*sqrt(2)  -  1/4*sqrt(2)
```

The first line defines a vector `psi` (for $|\psi\rangle$), and the second line defines a vector `minus` (for $|-\rangle$). Note we do not need to specify whether it is a column vector or row vector in SageMath. It will automatically transpose the vector to whatever shape is needed. In the third line, we calculate `minus.conjugate()` (for $\langle -|$) and multiply it onto `psi` using an asterisks, yielding the fourth line as the answer. Let us simplify it:

$$(1/4)\sqrt{3}\sqrt{2} - (1/4)\sqrt{2} = \frac{\sqrt{3}\sqrt{2}}{4} - \frac{\sqrt{2}}{4} = \frac{\sqrt{3}-1}{2\sqrt{2}}.$$

This matches what we expected.

Since $\langle + | \psi \rangle$ and $\langle - | \psi \rangle$ are the amplitudes of $|+\rangle$ and $|-\rangle$, respectively, we can write the state of the qubit in the $\{|+\rangle, |-\rangle\}$ basis as

$$|\psi\rangle = \langle + | \psi \rangle | + \rangle + \langle - | \psi \rangle | - \rangle.$$

In Section 2.3.3, we also measured $|\psi\rangle$ in the Y-basis and in a fourth basis. These will be left as Exercise 3.9.

In general,

For an orthonormal basis $\{|a\rangle, |b\rangle\}$, the state of a qubit can be written as

$$|\psi\rangle = \alpha |a\rangle + \beta |b\rangle,$$

where $\alpha = \langle a | \psi \rangle$ and $\beta = \langle b | \psi \rangle$.

Finally, we end with some terminology. We have been saying that $\langle a | \psi \rangle$ is the amplitude of $|\psi\rangle$ in $|a\rangle$. We can also say that $\langle a | \psi \rangle$ is the amount of $|\psi\rangle$ that is in $|a\rangle$. Or, $\langle a | \psi \rangle$ is the amount that $|\psi\rangle$ and $|a\rangle$ *overlap*. In mathematical language, $\langle a | \psi \rangle$ is the *projection* of $|\psi\rangle$ onto $|a\rangle$.

Exercise 3.9. Consider a qubit in the following state

$$|\psi\rangle = \frac{\sqrt{3}}{2}|0\rangle + \frac{1}{2}|1\rangle.$$

Consider measuring this qubit in the Y-basis $\{|i\rangle, |-i\rangle\}$ and the orthonormal basis $\{|a\rangle, |b\rangle\}$, where

$$|a\rangle = \frac{\sqrt{3}}{2}|0\rangle + \frac{i}{2}|1\rangle,$$
$$|b\rangle = \frac{i}{2}|0\rangle + \frac{\sqrt{3}}{2}|1\rangle.$$

(a) Calculate $\langle i | \psi \rangle$.
(b) Calculate $\langle -i | \psi \rangle$.
(c) If you measure the qubit in the Y-basis, what states can you get and with what probabilities?
(d) Calculate $\langle a | \psi \rangle$.
(e) Calculate $\langle b | \psi \rangle$.
(f) If you measure the qubit in the $\{|a\rangle, |b\rangle\}$ basis, what states can you get and with what probabilities?

Hint: Your answers should agree with Section 2.3.3.

Exercise 3.10. Consider a qubit in the following state

$$|\psi\rangle = \frac{3 + i\sqrt{3}}{4}|0\rangle - \frac{1}{2}|1\rangle,$$

which lies on the Bloch sphere at $(\theta, \phi) = (\pi/3, 5\pi/6)$.

(a) If you measure it in the Z-basis $\{|0\rangle, |1\rangle\}$, what states can you get and with what probabilities?

(b) If you measure it in the X-basis $\{|+\rangle,|-\rangle\}$, what states can you get and with what probabilities?

(c) If you measure it in the Y-basis $\{|i\rangle,|-i\rangle\}$, what states can you get and with what probabilities?

Exercise 3.11. A qubit is in the state

$$|\psi\rangle = \frac{1}{\sqrt{6}}\begin{pmatrix} 1-2i \\ 1 \end{pmatrix}.$$

(a) Express this state in the $\{|+\rangle,|-\rangle\}$ basis.
(b) Express this state in the $\{|i\rangle,|-i\rangle\}$ basis.

3.3 Quantum Gates

3.3.1 Gates as Matrices

Recall a quantum gate U generally turns $|0\rangle$ and $|1\rangle$ into superpositions of $|0\rangle$ and $|1\rangle$:

$$U|0\rangle = a|0\rangle + b|1\rangle = \begin{pmatrix} a \\ b \end{pmatrix},$$

$$U|1\rangle = c|0\rangle + d|1\rangle = \begin{pmatrix} c \\ d \end{pmatrix}.$$

We can arrange the resulting amplitudes side-by-side, resulting in a *matrix*, which is a rectangular array/table of numbers:

$$U = \left(\begin{pmatrix} a \\ b \end{pmatrix} \begin{pmatrix} c \\ d \end{pmatrix} \right) = \begin{pmatrix} a & c \\ b & d \end{pmatrix}.$$

This is a 2×2 matrix because it has two rows and two columns. Plugging this matrix into $U|0\rangle$ and $U|1\rangle$, we get

$$U|0\rangle = \begin{pmatrix} a & c \\ b & d \end{pmatrix}\begin{pmatrix} 1 \\ 0 \end{pmatrix} = \begin{pmatrix} a \\ b \end{pmatrix},$$

$$U|1\rangle = \begin{pmatrix} a & c \\ b & d \end{pmatrix}\begin{pmatrix} 0 \\ 1 \end{pmatrix} = \begin{pmatrix} c \\ d \end{pmatrix}.$$

These correctly suggest that we can multiply a matrix and a vector in the following manner: To get the first (second) entry, we take the first (second) row of the matrix and multiply it component-by-component with the vector, then add the results:

$$\begin{pmatrix} a & c \\ b & d \end{pmatrix} \begin{pmatrix} 1 \\ 0 \end{pmatrix} = \begin{pmatrix} a \cdot 1 + c \cdot 0 \\ b \cdot 1 + d \cdot 0 \end{pmatrix} = \begin{pmatrix} a \\ b \end{pmatrix},$$

$$\begin{pmatrix} a & c \\ b & d \end{pmatrix} \begin{pmatrix} 0 \\ 1 \end{pmatrix} = \begin{pmatrix} a \cdot 0 + c \cdot 1 \\ b \cdot 0 + d \cdot 1 \end{pmatrix} = \begin{pmatrix} c \\ d \end{pmatrix}.$$

This is exactly the way matrices and vectors multiply in linear algebra.

Of course, U can also act on superpositions. If a qubit is in the state

$$|\psi\rangle = \alpha|0\rangle + \beta|1\rangle = \begin{pmatrix} \alpha \\ \beta \end{pmatrix},$$

then applying U transforms this to

$$\begin{aligned} U|\psi\rangle &= \alpha(a|0\rangle + b|1\rangle) + \beta(c|0\rangle + d|1\rangle) \\ &= (a\alpha + c\beta)|0\rangle + (b\alpha + d\beta)|1\rangle \\ &= \begin{pmatrix} a\alpha + c\beta \\ b\alpha + d\beta \end{pmatrix}. \end{aligned}$$

Let us show that the matrix representation of this yields the expected result:

$$U|\psi\rangle = \begin{pmatrix} a & c \\ b & d \end{pmatrix} \begin{pmatrix} \alpha \\ \beta \end{pmatrix} = \begin{pmatrix} a\alpha + c\beta \\ b\alpha + d\beta \end{pmatrix}.$$

This is exactly what we expect.

In the language of linear algebra, quantum gates are matrices. Of course, the matrix must ensure that the total probability remains 1, so in the previous example, we must have $|a\alpha + c\beta|^2 + |b\alpha + d\beta|^2 = 1$. This yields the following point:

Quantum gates are matrices that keep the total probability equal to 1.

For example, we previously showed in Section 2.6.1 that the following is a valid quantum gate because it keeps the total probability equal to 1:

$$U|0\rangle = \frac{\sqrt{2} - i}{2}|0\rangle - \frac{1}{2}|1\rangle = \begin{pmatrix} \frac{\sqrt{2}-i}{2} \\ -\frac{1}{2} \end{pmatrix},$$

$$U|1\rangle = \frac{1}{2}|0\rangle + \frac{\sqrt{2} + i}{2}|1\rangle = \begin{pmatrix} \frac{1}{2} \\ \frac{\sqrt{2}+i}{2} \end{pmatrix}.$$

Then, as a matrix,

$$U = \begin{pmatrix} \frac{\sqrt{2}-i}{2} & \frac{1}{2} \\ -\frac{1}{2} & \frac{\sqrt{2}+i}{2} \end{pmatrix}.$$

In Quirk, we can create this quantum gate by clicking the "Make Gate" button at the top of the page. A dialog box will pop up with different options, and we want to create a gate from a matrix:

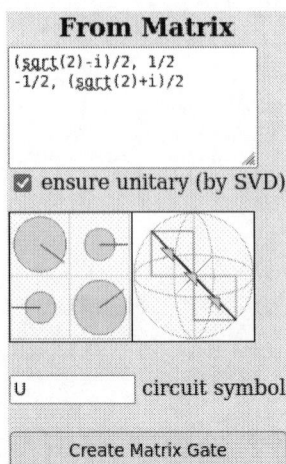

We enter the matrix, give it a name, and then click "Create Matrix Gate." Then, it will appear in the bottom-right toolbar under "Custom Gates:"

We can drag this onto the main circuit like any other gate. Here it is, along with a T and H gate:

From this, we see that $HTU|0\rangle$ has a 57.3% chance of collapsing to $|1\rangle$, and hence a 42.7% chance of collapsing to a $|0\rangle$.

Exercise 3.12. Consider an operator U performs the following mapping on the Z-basis states:

$$U|0\rangle = \frac{1}{\sqrt{2}}\begin{pmatrix} 1 \\ -i \end{pmatrix}, \quad U|1\rangle = \frac{1}{\sqrt{2}}\begin{pmatrix} -i \\ 1 \end{pmatrix}.$$

(a) What is U as a matrix?

(b) What is $U\begin{pmatrix} \alpha \\ \beta \end{pmatrix}$?

(c) From your answer to (b), is U a valid quantum gate? Explain your reasoning.

Exercise 3.13. A quantum gate U performs the following mapping on the Z-basis states:

$$U|0\rangle = \frac{1}{2\sqrt{3}}[(3+i)|0\rangle - (1+i)|1\rangle],$$

$$U|1\rangle = \frac{1}{2\sqrt{3}}[(1-i)|0\rangle + (3-i)|1\rangle].$$

(a) What is U as a matrix?
(b) Create U as a custom gate in Quirk. Using Quirk, if you measure $HUH|0\rangle$, what are the possible outcomes, and with what probabilities?

3.3.2 Common One-Qubit Gates as Matrices

Previously, we introduced several common one-qubit gates, including the identity gate I, Pauli X, Y, and Z gates, the phase gate S, the T gate, and the Hadamard gate H. Now, each of these can be represented as a matrix:

Gate	Action on Computational Basis	Matrix Representation
Identity	$I\|0\rangle = \|0\rangle$ $I\|1\rangle = \|1\rangle$	$I = \begin{pmatrix} 1 & 0 \\ 0 & 1 \end{pmatrix}$
Pauli X	$X\|0\rangle = \|1\rangle$ $X\|1\rangle = \|0\rangle$	$X = \begin{pmatrix} 0 & 1 \\ 1 & 0 \end{pmatrix}$
Pauli Y	$Y\|0\rangle = i\|1\rangle$ $Y\|1\rangle = -i\|0\rangle$	$Y = \begin{pmatrix} 0 & -i \\ i & 0 \end{pmatrix}$
Pauli Z	$Z\|0\rangle = \|0\rangle$ $Z\|1\rangle = -\|1\rangle$	$Z = \begin{pmatrix} 1 & 0 \\ 0 & -1 \end{pmatrix}$
Phase S	$S\|0\rangle = \|0\rangle$ $S\|1\rangle = i\|1\rangle$	$S = \begin{pmatrix} 1 & 0 \\ 0 & i \end{pmatrix}$
T	$T\|0\rangle = \|0\rangle$ $T\|1\rangle - e^{i\pi/4}\|1\rangle$	$T = \begin{pmatrix} 1 & 0 \\ 0 & e^{i\pi/4} \end{pmatrix}$
Hadamard H	$H\|0\rangle = \frac{1}{\sqrt{2}}(\|0\rangle + \|1\rangle)$ $H\|1\rangle = \frac{1}{\sqrt{2}}(\|0\rangle - \|1\rangle)$	$H = \frac{1}{\sqrt{2}} \begin{pmatrix} 1 & 1 \\ 1 & -1 \end{pmatrix}$

Of particular note is

$$I = \begin{pmatrix} 1 & 0 \\ 0 & 1 \end{pmatrix}.$$

This is called the 2×2 *identity matrix*. When it acts on a vector, it does nothing. For example,

$$\begin{pmatrix} 1 & 0 \\ 0 & 1 \end{pmatrix} \begin{pmatrix} \alpha \\ \beta \end{pmatrix} = \begin{pmatrix} 1\alpha + 0\beta \\ 0\alpha + 1\beta \end{pmatrix} = \begin{pmatrix} \alpha \\ \beta \end{pmatrix}.$$

The same is true of large matrices. An $N \times N$ matrix with 1's on the diagonal and 0's everywhere else is called the $N \times N$ identity matrix.

Exercise 3.14. Recall from Eq. (2.10) than a single-qubit gate is a rotation by some angle θ about some axis $\hat{n} = (n_x, n_y, n_z)$. Consider a quantum gate that rotates by 90° about the y-axis. Using Eq. (2.10) with $\gamma = 0$, what is this gate as a matrix?

3.3.3 Sequential Quantum Gates

Using linear algebra, we can compute the effect of a sequence of quantum gates. For example, we had previously shown in Eq. (2.9) that

$$HSTH|0\rangle = \frac{1}{2}\left[\left(1 + e^{i3\pi/4}\right)|0\rangle + \left(1 - e^{i3\pi/4}\right)|1\rangle\right].$$

Now, we can perform this same calculation using linear algebra by multiply each matrix onto the vector:

$$
\begin{aligned}
HSTH|0\rangle &= \frac{1}{\sqrt{2}}\begin{pmatrix} 1 & 1 \\ 1 & -1 \end{pmatrix}\begin{pmatrix} 1 & 0 \\ 0 & i \end{pmatrix}\begin{pmatrix} 1 & 0 \\ 0 & e^{i\pi/4} \end{pmatrix}\frac{1}{\sqrt{2}}\begin{pmatrix} 1 & 1 \\ 1 & -1 \end{pmatrix}\begin{pmatrix} 1 \\ 0 \end{pmatrix} \\
&= \frac{1}{2}\begin{pmatrix} 1 & 1 \\ 1 & -1 \end{pmatrix}\begin{pmatrix} 1 & 0 \\ 0 & i \end{pmatrix}\begin{pmatrix} 1 & 0 \\ 0 & e^{i\pi/4} \end{pmatrix}\begin{pmatrix} 1 \\ 1 \end{pmatrix} \\
&= \frac{1}{2}\begin{pmatrix} 1 & 1 \\ 1 & -1 \end{pmatrix}\begin{pmatrix} 1 & 0 \\ 0 & i \end{pmatrix}\begin{pmatrix} 1 \\ e^{i\pi/4} \end{pmatrix} \\
&= \frac{1}{2}\begin{pmatrix} 1 & 1 \\ 1 & -1 \end{pmatrix}\begin{pmatrix} 1 \\ e^{i3\pi/4} \end{pmatrix} \\
&= \frac{1}{2}\begin{pmatrix} 1 + e^{i3\pi/4} \\ 1 - e^{i3\pi/4} \end{pmatrix}.
\end{aligned}
$$

We can also compute this using any computing system that supports linear algebra, such as Mathematica or SageMath:

- In Mathematica,

```
zero = {{1}, {0}};
H = 1/Sqrt[2] {{1, 1}, {1, -1}};
S = {{1, 0}, {0, I}};
T = {{1, 0}, {0, E^(I Pi/4)}};
H.S.T.H.zero
```

The first line defines a column vector named zero, and the second, third, and fourth lines define the quantum gates as matrices. The fifth line multiplies them together. Note a period (.) must be used for matrix multiplication; an asterisk (*) denotes element-by-element multiplication. The output of this code is

$$\left\{\left\{\frac{1}{2} + \frac{1}{2}ie^{\frac{i\pi}{4}}\right\}, \left\{\frac{1}{2} - \frac{1}{2}ie^{\frac{i\pi}{4}}\right\}\right\},$$

which is precisely what we calculated by hand since $i = e^{i\pi/2}$, and so $ie^{i\pi/4} = e^{i\pi/2}e^{i\pi/4} = e^{i(\pi/2+\pi/4)} = e^{i3\pi/4}$.

- In SageMath,

```
sage: zero = vector([1,0]).column()
sage: H = 1/sqrt(2) * Matrix([[1,1],[1,-1]])
sage: S = Matrix([[1,0],[0,i]])
sage: T = Matrix([[1,0],[0,e^(i*pi/4)]])
sage: H*S*T*H*zero
[ (1/4*I - 1/4)*sqrt(2) + 1/2]
[-(1/4*I - 1/4)*sqrt(2) + 1/2]
```

The first line defines a column vector named zero, and the next three lines define the quantum gates as matrices. The fifth line multiplies them together, and the final two lines are the output, which is a column vector:

$$\begin{pmatrix} \left(\frac{i}{4}-\frac{1}{4}\right)\sqrt{2}+\frac{1}{2} \\ -\left(\frac{i}{4}-\frac{1}{4}\right)\sqrt{2}+\frac{1}{2} \end{pmatrix}.$$

Since $(i/4-1/4)\sqrt{2} = (i-1)/(2\sqrt{2})$ and $(i-1)/\sqrt{2} = e^{i3\pi/4}$, this becomes

$$\frac{1}{2}\begin{pmatrix} 1+e^{i3\pi/4} \\ 1-e^{i3\pi/4} \end{pmatrix},$$

which is exactly what we had before.

Exercise 3.15. In Section 3.3.1, we simulated the following circuit in Quirk:

where

$$U = \begin{pmatrix} \frac{\sqrt{2}-i}{2} & \frac{1}{2} \\ -\frac{1}{2} & \frac{\sqrt{2}+i}{2} \end{pmatrix}.$$

Calculate $HTU|0\rangle$.

3.3.4 Circuit Identities

In Exercise 2.32, we proved the circuit identity $HXH = Z$ by showing that $HXH|0\rangle$ and $Z|0\rangle$ result in the same state, and $HXH|1\rangle$ and $Z|1\rangle$ result in the same state. We can prove $HXH = Z$ another way using linear algebra:

$$\begin{aligned} HXH &= \frac{1}{\sqrt{2}}\begin{pmatrix} 1 & 1 \\ 1 & -1 \end{pmatrix}\begin{pmatrix} 0 & 1 \\ 1 & 0 \end{pmatrix}\frac{1}{\sqrt{2}}\begin{pmatrix} 1 & 1 \\ 1 & -1 \end{pmatrix} \\ &= \frac{1}{2}\begin{pmatrix} 1 & 1 \\ 1 & -1 \end{pmatrix}\begin{pmatrix} 0 & 1 \\ 1 & 0 \end{pmatrix}\begin{pmatrix} 1 & 1 \\ 1 & -1 \end{pmatrix}. \end{aligned}$$

To continue this calculation, let us multiply the two matrices on the right (X and H). The procedure is very similar to multiplying a matrix onto a column vector, except we now have two column vectors. So, we distribute the middle matrix across the two column vectors of the rightmost matrix.

$$HXH = \frac{1}{2} \begin{pmatrix} 1 & 1 \\ 1 & -1 \end{pmatrix} \left(\begin{pmatrix} 0 & 1 \\ 1 & 0 \end{pmatrix} \begin{pmatrix} 1 \\ 1 \end{pmatrix} \quad \begin{pmatrix} 0 & 1 \\ 1 & 0 \end{pmatrix} \begin{pmatrix} 1 \\ -1 \end{pmatrix} \right)$$

$$= \frac{1}{2} \begin{pmatrix} 1 & 1 \\ 1 & -1 \end{pmatrix} \left(\begin{pmatrix} 1 \\ 1 \end{pmatrix} \quad \begin{pmatrix} -1 \\ 1 \end{pmatrix} \right)$$

$$= \frac{1}{2} \begin{pmatrix} 1 & 1 \\ 1 & -1 \end{pmatrix} \begin{pmatrix} 1 & -1 \\ 1 & 1 \end{pmatrix}.$$

Now, we can multiply these two matrices by again distributing the left matrix so that it multiples both columns of the right vector:

$$HXH = \frac{1}{2} \left(\begin{pmatrix} 1 & 1 \\ 1 & -1 \end{pmatrix} \begin{pmatrix} 1 \\ 1 \end{pmatrix} \quad \begin{pmatrix} 1 & 1 \\ 1 & -1 \end{pmatrix} \begin{pmatrix} -1 \\ 1 \end{pmatrix} \right)$$

$$= \frac{1}{2} \left(\begin{pmatrix} 2 \\ 0 \end{pmatrix} \quad \begin{pmatrix} 0 \\ -2 \end{pmatrix} \right) = \frac{1}{2} \begin{pmatrix} 2 & 0 \\ 0 & -2 \end{pmatrix} = \begin{pmatrix} 1 & 0 \\ 0 & -1 \end{pmatrix}$$

$$= Z.$$

So, we have proved $HXH = Z$. We can also perform these calculations using a computer algebra system that supports linear algebra, such as Mathematica or Sage-Math:

- In Mathematica,

```
H = 1/Sqrt[2] {{1, 1}, {1, -1}};
X = {{0, 1}, {1, 0}};
H.X.H
```

  This defines the H and X gates as matrices and then multiplies them together, and the output is

$$\{\{1,0\},\{0,-1\}\}.$$

  This is precisely Z as a matrix.
- In SageMath,

```
sage: H = 1/sqrt(2) * Matrix([[1,1],[1,-1]])
sage: X = Matrix([[0,1],[1,0]])
sage: H*X*H
[ 1   0]
[ 0  -1]
```

  This defines the H and X gates as matrices and then multiplies them together, and the output is a 2×2 matrix, which is precisely Z.

Exercise 3.16. Prove that $XY = iZ$ two different ways:
(a) Show that $XY|0\rangle = iZ|0\rangle$ and $XY|1\rangle = iZ|1\rangle$.
(b) Multiply XY as matrices and show that it equals iZ.

3.3.5 Unitarity

Recall from Section 3.3.1 that if a quantum gate U transforms $|0\rangle$ and $|1\rangle$ as follows

$$U|0\rangle = a|0\rangle + b|1\rangle = \begin{pmatrix} a \\ b \end{pmatrix},$$

$$U|1\rangle = c|0\rangle + d|1\rangle = \begin{pmatrix} c \\ d \end{pmatrix},$$

then U can be written as a 2×2 matrix:

$$U = \begin{pmatrix} a & c \\ b & d \end{pmatrix}.$$

If we apply it to a state $|\psi\rangle = \alpha|0\rangle + \beta|1\rangle$, we get

$$U|\psi\rangle = \begin{pmatrix} a & c \\ b & d \end{pmatrix} \begin{pmatrix} \alpha \\ \beta \end{pmatrix} = \begin{pmatrix} a\alpha + c\beta \\ b\alpha + d\beta \end{pmatrix}.$$

We see that $U|\psi\rangle$ is a column vector, so we can also write it as a ket $|U\psi\rangle$:

$$U|\psi\rangle = |U\psi\rangle.$$

Now, consider the conjugate transpose of $|U\psi\rangle$:

$$\langle U\psi| = \begin{pmatrix} a^*\alpha^* + c^*\beta^* & b^*\alpha^* + d^*\beta^* \end{pmatrix} = \begin{pmatrix} \alpha^* & \beta^* \end{pmatrix} \begin{pmatrix} a^* & b^* \\ c^* & d^* \end{pmatrix}$$

$$- \begin{pmatrix} \alpha^* & \beta^* \end{pmatrix} \begin{pmatrix} a & c \\ b & d \end{pmatrix}^\dagger = \langle\psi|U^\dagger,$$

where the second equality comes from the convention for multiplying a row vector and a matrix, where the first column of the matrix is multiplied by the row vector according to the usual rule to yield the first entry, and the second column of the matrix is multiplied by the row vector according to the usual rule to yield the second entry. As another proof, a property of the (conjugate) transpose is that $(AB)^\dagger = B^\dagger A^\dagger$, and since $|\psi\rangle^\dagger = \langle\psi|$, we have

$$\langle U\psi| = (|U\psi\rangle)^\dagger = (U|\psi\rangle)^\dagger = |\psi\rangle^\dagger U^\dagger = \langle\psi|U^\dagger.$$

To summarize,

$$|U\psi\rangle = U|\psi\rangle,$$
$$\langle U\psi| = \langle\psi|U^\dagger. \tag{3.1}$$

Using this, we can come up with an easy way to determine whether a matrix keeps the total probability equal to 1. Consider a quantum gate (matrix) U. If it acts on $|\psi\rangle$, we have

$$U|\psi\rangle = |U\psi\rangle.$$

For U to be a quantum gate, this must be normalized. That is, the inner product of $|U\psi\rangle$ with itself must equal 1:

$$\langle U\psi|U\psi\rangle = 1$$
$$\langle\psi|U^\dagger U|\psi\rangle = \langle\psi|\psi\rangle$$
$$U^\dagger U = I.$$

A matrix that satisfies this property $U^\dagger U = I$ (and $UU^\dagger = I$) is called *unitary*. Thus,

Quantum gates are unitary matrices, and unitary matrices are quantum gates.

This is why we typically use U to denote a quantum gate. It stands for unitary. As an example application of this, is the following matrix a quantum gate?

$$U = \frac{1}{\sqrt{2}}\begin{pmatrix} 1 & i \\ -i & 1 \end{pmatrix}$$

We can just check whether it is unitary, so whether $U^\dagger U = I$ or not.

$$U^\dagger U = \frac{1}{\sqrt{2}}\begin{pmatrix} 1 & i \\ -i & 1 \end{pmatrix}\frac{1}{\sqrt{2}}\begin{pmatrix} 1 & i \\ -i & 1 \end{pmatrix} = \begin{pmatrix} 1 & i \\ -i & 1 \end{pmatrix} \neq I.$$

So no, it is not a quantum gate.

Exercise 3.17. Is

$$U = \frac{1}{\sqrt{2}}\begin{pmatrix} 1 & i \\ i & -1 \end{pmatrix}$$

a quantum gate? If so, what is $U|0\rangle$, and what is $U|1\rangle$?

Exercise 3.18. Is

$$U = \frac{1}{\sqrt{2}}\begin{pmatrix} 1 & 1 \\ i & -i \end{pmatrix}$$

a quantum gate? If so, what is $U|0\rangle$, and what is $U|1\rangle$?

3.3.6 Reversibility

A matrix M is *reversible* or *invertible* if there exists a matrix denoted M^{-1} such that

$$M^{-1}M = MM^{-1} = I.$$

So, if we multiply a vector by both a matrix and its inverse, nothing happens to the vector because this is equivalent to multiplying it by the identity matrix.

Now, since a quantum gate U must be unitary, it satisfies

$$U^\dagger U = UU^\dagger = I.$$

Then, the inverse of U is simply $U^\dagger$, i.e., $U^{-1} = U^\dagger$. So, a quantum gate is always reversible, and its inverse is its conjugate transpose:

A quantum gate U is always reversible, and its inverse is $U^\dagger$.

If we have a qubit and we applied a quantum gate U, we can undo the gate by applying $U^\dagger$:

$$U^\dagger U|\psi\rangle = I|\psi\rangle = |\psi\rangle.$$

Exercise 3.19. Consider the following quantum gate, written as a 2×2 matrix:

$$U = \begin{pmatrix} \frac{1+\sqrt{3}}{2\sqrt{2}} + i\frac{1-\sqrt{3}}{2\sqrt{6}} & \frac{1-\sqrt{3}}{2\sqrt{6}} + i\frac{1-\sqrt{3}}{2\sqrt{6}} \\ \frac{-1+\sqrt{3}}{2\sqrt{6}} + i\frac{1-\sqrt{3}}{2\sqrt{6}} & \frac{1+\sqrt{3}}{2\sqrt{2}} + i\frac{-1+\sqrt{3}}{2\sqrt{6}} \end{pmatrix}$$

(a) What is the inverse of U, written as a 2×2 matrix?
(b) A qubit is in the state

$$|\psi\rangle = \frac{\sqrt{3}}{2}|0\rangle + \frac{1}{2}|1\rangle.$$

What is $U^\dagger U|\psi\rangle$? Hint: You can answer this without any messy calculations.

3.4 Outer Products

3.4.1 Outer Products Are Matrices

Consider two states

$$|\psi\rangle = \alpha|0\rangle + \beta|1\rangle, \quad |\phi\rangle = \gamma|0\rangle + \delta|1\rangle.$$

Instead of multiplying $|\psi\rangle$ and $|\phi\rangle$ as an inner product $\langle\psi|\phi\rangle$, where the bra is on the left and the ket is on the right, another way to multiply them is by having the ket on the left and the bra on the right, which is called an *outer product*:

$$|\psi\rangle\langle\phi| = \begin{pmatrix} \alpha \\ \beta \end{pmatrix} \begin{pmatrix} \gamma^* & \delta^* \end{pmatrix}.$$

To multiply these vectors according to the rules of linear algebra, we multiply each row of $|\psi\rangle$ by each column of $|\phi\rangle$, resulting in

$$|\psi\rangle\langle\phi| = \left(\binom{\alpha}{\beta} \gamma^* \ \binom{\alpha}{\beta} \delta^* \right) = \left(\binom{\alpha\gamma^*}{\beta\gamma^*} \binom{\alpha\delta^*}{\beta\delta^*} \right) = \binom{\alpha\gamma^* \ \alpha\delta^*}{\beta\gamma^* \ \beta\delta^*}.$$

The result is a 2×2 matrix. So, whereas inner products result in scalars, outer products result in matrices, and we can add outer products together to construct various quantum gates.

For example, consider

$$U = |1\rangle\langle 0| + |0\rangle\langle 1|.$$

Let us find how this acts on $|\psi\rangle = \alpha|0\rangle + \beta|1\rangle$ and show that it is a valid quantum gate.

$$\begin{aligned}
U|\psi\rangle &= (|1\rangle\langle 0| + |0\rangle\langle 1|)(\alpha|0\rangle + \beta|1\rangle) \\
&= \alpha|1\rangle \underbrace{\langle 0|0\rangle}_{1} + \beta|1\rangle \underbrace{\langle 0|1\rangle}_{0} + \alpha|0\rangle \underbrace{\langle 1|0\rangle}_{0} + \beta|0\rangle \underbrace{\langle 1|1\rangle}_{1} \\
&= \alpha|1\rangle + \beta|0\rangle \\
&= \beta|0\rangle + \alpha|1\rangle.
\end{aligned}$$

The total probability of this is $|\beta|^2 + |\alpha|^2 = 1$, so this is a valid quantum gate. Applying U swapped $|0\rangle$ and $|1\rangle$, so it is just the X gate. As another approach, we can find U as a matrix:

$$U = |1\rangle\langle 0| + |0\rangle\langle 1| = \binom{0}{1}(1 \ 0) + \binom{1}{0}(0 \ 1) = \binom{0 \ 0}{1 \ 0} + \binom{0 \ 1}{0 \ 0} = \binom{0 \ 1}{1 \ 0}.$$

This is precisely the matrix for the X gate. To confirm that it is a valid quantum gate, we simply show that it is unitary, i.e., if $U^\dagger U = I$:

$$U^\dagger U = \binom{0 \ 1}{1 \ 0}\binom{0 \ 1}{1 \ 0} = \binom{1 \ 0}{0 \ 1} = I.$$

The outer product of $|\phi\rangle$ and $|\psi\rangle$ is just the conjugate transpose of the outer product of $|\psi\rangle$ and $|\phi\rangle$:

$$|\phi\rangle\langle\psi| = |\psi\rangle\langle\phi|^\dagger.$$

We can prove this through a simple calculation:

$$|\phi\rangle\langle\psi| = \binom{\gamma}{\delta}(\alpha^* \ \beta^*) = \binom{\gamma\alpha^* \ \gamma\beta^*}{\delta\alpha^* \ \delta\beta^*} = \binom{\alpha\gamma^* \ \alpha\delta^*}{\beta\gamma^* \ \beta\delta^*}^\dagger = |\psi\rangle\langle\phi|^\dagger.$$

In the above equtaion, one may use parenthesis to clarify that the entire outer product is conjugated and transposed, not just the bra, i.e., $|\phi\rangle\langle\psi| = (|\psi\rangle\langle\phi|)^\dagger$.

Exercise 3.20. Consider the following outer product

$$|i\rangle\langle-|.$$

(a) What is it as a matrix?
(b) Is this a valid quantum gate?

Exercise 3.21. Consider the following sum of outer products:

$$\frac{1}{\sqrt{2}}|0\rangle\langle0| + \frac{1}{\sqrt{2}}|0\rangle\langle1| + \frac{1}{\sqrt{2}}|1\rangle\langle0| - \frac{1}{\sqrt{2}}|1\rangle\langle1|.$$

(a) What is it as a matrix?
(b) Is this a valid quantum gate?

3.4.2 Completeness Relation

Recall from Section 3.2.3 that for any orthonormal basis $\{|a\rangle, |b\rangle\}$, the state of a qubit can be written as

$$|\psi\rangle = \alpha|a\rangle + \beta|b\rangle,$$

where $\alpha = \langle a|\psi\rangle$ and $\beta = \langle b|\psi\rangle$. Substituting these values,

$$|\psi\rangle = \underbrace{\langle a|\psi\rangle}_{\text{scalar}}|a\rangle + \underbrace{\langle b|\psi\rangle}_{\text{scalar}}|b\rangle.$$

As indicated above, the inner products are just scalars/numbers, so instead of multiply them onto the vectors $|a\rangle$ and $|b\rangle$ on the left, we can equivalently multiply them on the right:

$$|\psi\rangle = |a\rangle\underbrace{\langle a|\psi\rangle}_{\text{scalar}} + |b\rangle\underbrace{\langle b|\psi\rangle}_{\text{scalar}}.$$

Both of these terms are a ket times a bra times a ket. To make this more clear, we can write them as

$$|\psi\rangle = |a\rangle\langle a||\psi\rangle + |b\rangle\langle b||\psi\rangle.$$

Now, notice we have two outer products, $|a\rangle\langle a|$ and $|b\rangle\langle b|$. Since they are both multiplying $|\psi\rangle$, we can factor to get

$$|\psi\rangle = \big(|a\rangle\langle a| + |b\rangle\langle b|\big)|\psi\rangle.$$

For this to be true for all $|\psi\rangle$, we must have

$$|a\rangle\langle a| + |b\rangle\langle b| = I.$$

This is called the *completeness relation*, and it indicates the state of any qubit can be expressed in terms of $|a\rangle$ and $|b\rangle$, a property we call *completeness*. We say $\{|a\rangle, |b\rangle\}$ forms a *complete orthonormal basis*. All the bases we have discussed (any two states on opposite sides on the Bloch sphere) are complete.

Let us box this:

A complete orthonormal basis $\{|a\rangle, |b\rangle\}$ satisfies the completeness relation

$$|a\rangle\langle a| + |b\rangle\langle b| = I.$$

Exercise 3.22. Verify that $\{|+\rangle, |-\rangle\}$ is a complete orthonormal basis by showing that

$$|+\rangle\langle +| + |-\rangle\langle -| = I.$$

Exercise 3.23. Verify that $\{|0\rangle, |+\rangle\}$ is a *not* a complete orthonormal basis by showing that

$$|0\rangle\langle 0| + |+\rangle\langle +| \neq I.$$

3.5 Summary

The mathematical language of quantum computing is linear algebra. Quantum states are represented by column vectors called kets, and the conjugate transpose of a ket is a bra. Multiplying a bra and a ket is an inner product that yields the projection or amplitude of the states onto each other. A state whose inner product with itself is 1 is normalized, and states with zero inner product are orthogonal. Quantum gates are unitary matrices, which satisfy $U^\dagger U = I$. Unitary matrices are always reversible with $U^{-1} = U^\dagger$. Multiplying a ket and a bra is an outer product, which is a matrix. A complete orthonormal basis satisfies the completeness relation, meaning the sum of the outer products of each basis vector with itself equals the identity matrix.

Chapter 4
Multiple Quantum Bits

In Chapter 2, we explored the qubit, what happens when it is measured, and how quantum gates act on it. In Chapter 3, we upgraded our tools for working with a qubit by introducing linear algebra. Now, we are positioned to explore systems consisting of multiple qubits. Sometimes, these qubits are disjoint, but other times, the qubits are intertwined together. We will learn how quantum gates acting on multiqubit systems can be used to perform computations, namely adding binary numbers. This same addition problem was explored in Chapter 1 using classical computers, providing a comparison. Then, we will explore sets of universal quantum gates and how to correct for errors in quantum computers.

4.1 Entanglion: A Quantum Computing Board Game

4.1.1 Mechanics

IBM Research released an open-source board game called *Entanglion* to teach the fundamental ideas and mechanics of quantum computing. It is available at `https://entanglion.github.io`, and anyone can download and print the game board and pieces. The complete rules are available on the website, but let us summarize the most important parts here, since they reflect the rules of quantum computing.

Entanglion is a two-player collaborative game, and the goal is to collect, as a team, eight components to build a quantum computer that are scattered across different planets, while avoiding detection by the planetary defenses. There are three galaxies in the Entanglion universe: Centarious, Superious, and Entanglion, as shown in Fig. 4.1. Centarious has two planets, Zero and One, and Superious also has two planets, Plus and Minus. On the other hand, Entanglion has eight planets, each holding one of the components to build a quantum computer.

Each player has one spaceship, and one is red while the other is blue. Players determine the starting locations of their spaceships by rolling a die that only has 0

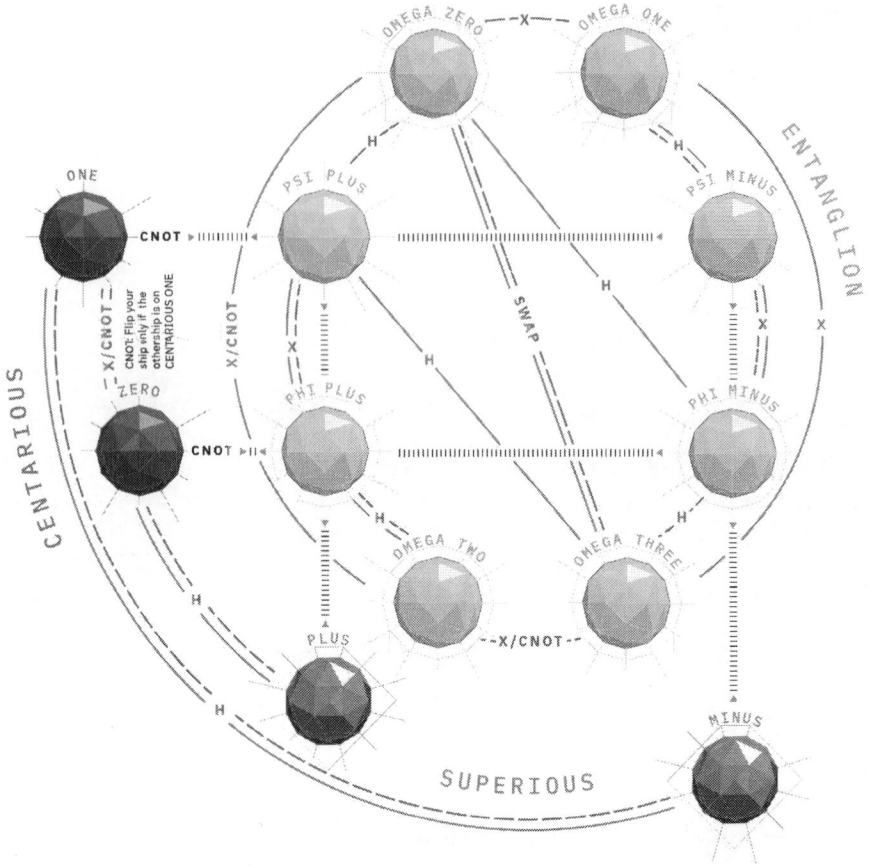

Fig. 4.1: The universe for the Entanglion board game. It consists of three galaxies: Centarious, Superious, and Entanglion. The two players' spaceships (red and blue) move across the board from planet to planet according to the labeled paths. Dashed paths correspond to the red player, and solid paths correspond to the blue player. Inside the Entanglion galaxy, both spaceships move together.

and 1 as the outcomes. This is called the Centarious die because the outcomes of 0 and 1 correspond to the planets Zero and One, both in the galaxy Centarious.

The players take turns moving their spaceships to different planets by playing engine cards H, X, CNOT, and SWAP. As shown in Fig. 4.1, different engine cards are used for transitions between different planets. In Centarious and Superious, players' spaceships can be on different planets. To move into the Entanglion galaxy, one player must be in Centarious, and the other player must be in Superious. Then the player in Centarious uses a CNOT engine card, and both spaceships move to the same planet in the Entanglion galaxy. This planet is where a horizontal line from the Centarious planet intersects with the vertical line from the Superious planet, as shown by the lines ▷ ||||||||| ◁ in Fig. 4.1. For example, if the red player is at One, and the blue player is at Plus, and the red player uses a CNOT engine card, then the red player moves horizontally from One to Psi Plus, and the blue player moves vertically from Plus to Psi Plus. Inside the Entanglion galaxy, the spaceships always move together as a pair, so they are always at the same planet.

Anytime the spaceships move to a planet in the Entanglion galaxy, or when a player attempts to retrieve a component to build a quantum computer, there is a chance they will be detected by the planetary defenses. The roll of an eight-sized die determines this, and if the spaceships are detected, both of them move to a random planet in Centarious determining by rolling the Centarious die.

The game also contains a shuffled deck of event cards, which are played whenever the spaceships are detected by planetary defenses, or after six engine cards have been played. The cards are named after important scientists who contributed to quantum physics and quantum computing, or after quantum effects. The mechanics of these cards do not precisely correlate with actual quantum computing, so we limit our discussion of them here.

Exercise 4.1. Refer to the Entanglion game board in Fig. 4.1.
 (a) When can a player use CNOT to move between planets Zero and One?
 (b) If the red player is at planet Zero and the blue player is at planet Minus, and the red player uses a CNOT engine card, where do the players move?
 (c) How can the players move between planets Psi Plus and Omega Three?

4.1.2 Connection to Quantum Computing

The rules of Entanglion reflect how quantum computers work. We will explore these connections in detail throughout this chapter, but here is a quick summary:

- The red and blue spaceships are qubits.
- The planets are various states that qubits can be in. Centarious contains the classical states $|0\rangle$ and $|1\rangle$, Superious contains the two superposition states $|+\rangle$ and $|-\rangle$, and Entanglion contains eight *entangled* states, where the states of the two qubits are intertwined, so the spaceships move together.
- The engine cards H, X, CNOT, and SWAP are quantum gates that are applied to the qubits. This transforms the qubits to different states, or moves the spaceships to different planets.
- Detection by planetary defenses corresponds to a measurement. Measuring a qubit yields a classical 0 or 1 with some probability, so the spaceships move to planet Zero or One according to a roll of the Centarious die.

Exercise 4.2. Read https://medium.com/qiskit/designing-a-quantum-computing-board-game-de4a450cad8c and answer the following questions:
 (a) How many major iterations of the board game were there?
 (b) The emphasis of the game was on _____ mastery.

(c) What win rates for AI players corresponded to an adequate level of challenge for human players?
(d) Entanglion is a play on what word?

4.2 States and Measurement

4.2.1 Tensor Product

When we have multiple qubits, we write their states as a *tensor product* $\otimes$. For example, two qubits, both in the $|0\rangle$ state, are written

$$|0\rangle \otimes |0\rangle,$$

and this is pronounced "zero tensor zero." Often, we compress the notation and leave out the tensor product in both writing and speech:

$$|0\rangle|0\rangle.$$

We frequently compress the notation further still:

$$|00\rangle.$$

With two qubits, the Z-basis is $\{|00\rangle, |01\rangle, |10\rangle, |11\rangle\}$. A general state is a superposition of these basis states:

$$c_0|00\rangle + c_1|01\rangle + c_2|10\rangle + c_3|11\rangle.$$

If we measure these two qubits in the Z-basis, we get $|00\rangle$ with probability $|c_0|^2$, $|01\rangle$ with probability $|c_1|^2$, $|10\rangle$ with probability $|c_2|^2$, or $|11\rangle$ with probability $|c_3|^2$. Thus, the total probability is $|c_0|^2 + |c_1|^2 + |c_2|^2 + |c_3|^2$, and it should equal 1.

With three qubits, there are eight Z-basis states $|000\rangle, |001\rangle, |010\rangle, |011\rangle, |100\rangle, |101\rangle, |110\rangle$, and $|111\rangle$. Sometimes, these binary strings are written as decimal numbers $|0\rangle, |1\rangle, \ldots, |7\rangle$. Inspired by this, let us call the right qubit the zeroth qubit, the middle qubit the first qubit, and the left qubit the second qubit, so a Z-basis state takes the form

$$|b_2 b_1 b_0\rangle.$$

Then, the decimal representation of this is

$$2^2 b_2 + 2^1 b_1 + 2^0 b_0.$$

In other words, we label qubits right-to-left, starting with zero. This convention, where the rightmost qubit is the zeroth qubit, is called *little endian*. Quirk and many quantum programming languages, including those in Chapter 5, also use little endian. In contrast, the opposite convention, where the leftmost qubit is the zeroth qubit, is called *big endian*. Of note, Nielsen and Chuang's standard advanced text-book uses the big endian convention. Disputes over which convention is "better" has raged classical computing for decades, and the same debates carry into quantum computing. The reality is that you should be able to use both, but for consistency, we use little endian throughout this textbook. Next, the general state of three qubits is a superposition of these basis vectors:

$$\sum_{j=0}^{7} c_j|j\rangle = c_0|0\rangle + c_1|1\rangle + \cdots + c_7|7\rangle,$$

and the probability of getting $|j\rangle$ when measuring in the Z-basis is $|c_j|^2$, so $\sum_j |c_j|^2 = 1$.

With n qubits, there are $N = 2^n$ Z-basis states, which we can label as n-bit strings or by the decimal numbers 0 through $N-1$. As an n-bit string,

$$|b_{N-1}\ldots b_1 b_0\rangle = |2^{N-1}b_{N-1} + \cdots + 2^1 b_1 + 2^0 b_0\rangle.$$

Of course, the general state of n-qubits is a superposition of these Z-basis states:

$$\sum_{j=0}^{N-1} c_j|j\rangle = c_0|0\rangle + c_1|1\rangle + \cdots + c_{N-1}|N-1\rangle.$$

This has N amplitudes c_0 through c_{N-1}. Thus, if we have just $n = 300$ qubits, then we must keep track of $N = 2^{300} \approx 2.04 \times 10^{90}$ amplitudes, which is more than the number of atoms in the visible universe (10^{78} to 10^{82}). This is evidence, but not a proof, that it is difficult for classical computers to simulate quantum computers. It is evidence because classical computers cannot keep track of this many amplitudes, but it is not a proof because it is unknown whether quantum computers need all these amplitudes. That is, if quantum computers can function with much fewer amplitudes (a polynomial number instead of an exponential number in n), a classical computer would be able to keep track of all of them. In terms of complexity classes, the exponential number of amplitudes in a general entangled state is evidence that P $\neq$ BQP.

We can also use powers to simplify the notation. If we have n qubits, each in the state $|0\rangle$, we can write the state as

$$|0\rangle^{\otimes n} = \underbrace{|0\rangle \otimes |0\rangle \otimes \cdots \otimes |0\rangle}_{n} = \underbrace{|0\rangle|0\rangle\ldots|0\rangle}_{n} = |\underbrace{00\ldots0}_{n}\rangle = |0^n\rangle.$$

With a single qubit, we could parameterize a state as

$$\cos\frac{\theta}{2}|0\rangle + e^{i\phi}\sin\frac{\theta}{2}|1\rangle,$$

with the coordinates (θ, ϕ) interpreted as a point on the Bloch sphere. With two qubits, however, we have four complex amplitudes c_0, c_1, c_2, c_3 (although one can be made real by factoring out an global phase), and unfortunately, this is too many parameters to represent in three-dimensions. There is no Bloch sphere representation for a general multi-qubit state.

The tensor product also works for bras, so

$$\langle 0| \otimes \langle 0| = \langle 0|\langle 0| = \langle 00|.$$

Then, the inner product of, say $\langle 01|$ and $|00\rangle$, is obtained by matching up qubits. For example,

$$\langle 01|00\rangle = \underbrace{\langle 0|0\rangle}_{1} \cdot \underbrace{\langle 1|0\rangle}_{0} = 0.$$

So $|01\rangle$ and $|00\rangle$ are orthogonal.

Exercise 4.3. Calculate the following inner products:
(a) $\langle 10|11\rangle$.
(b) $\langle +-|01\rangle$.
(c) $\langle 1+0|1-0\rangle$.

4.2.2 Kronecker Product

In linear algebra, the tensor product is simply the *Kronecker product*, which is obtained by multiplying each term of the first matrix/vector by the entire second matrix/vector. For example, with two qubits,

$$|00\rangle = |0\rangle|0\rangle = |0\rangle \otimes |0\rangle = \begin{pmatrix} 1 \\ 0 \end{pmatrix} \otimes \begin{pmatrix} 1 \\ 0 \end{pmatrix} = \begin{pmatrix} 1\begin{pmatrix} 1 \\ 0 \end{pmatrix} \\ 0\begin{pmatrix} 1 \\ 0 \end{pmatrix} \end{pmatrix} = \begin{pmatrix} 1 \\ 0 \\ 0 \\ 0 \end{pmatrix}.$$

$$|01\rangle = |0\rangle|1\rangle = |0\rangle \otimes |1\rangle = \begin{pmatrix} 1 \\ 0 \end{pmatrix} \otimes \begin{pmatrix} 0 \\ 1 \end{pmatrix} = \begin{pmatrix} 1\begin{pmatrix} 0 \\ 1 \end{pmatrix} \\ 0\begin{pmatrix} 0 \\ 1 \end{pmatrix} \end{pmatrix} = \begin{pmatrix} 0 \\ 1 \\ 0 \\ 0 \end{pmatrix}.$$

$$|10\rangle = |1\rangle|0\rangle = |1\rangle \otimes |0\rangle = \begin{pmatrix} 0 \\ 1 \end{pmatrix} \otimes \begin{pmatrix} 1 \\ 0 \end{pmatrix} = \begin{pmatrix} 0\begin{pmatrix} 1 \\ 0 \end{pmatrix} \\ 1\begin{pmatrix} 1 \\ 0 \end{pmatrix} \end{pmatrix} = \begin{pmatrix} 0 \\ 0 \\ 1 \\ 0 \end{pmatrix}.$$

$$|11\rangle = |1\rangle|1\rangle = |1\rangle \otimes |1\rangle = \begin{pmatrix} 0 \\ 1 \end{pmatrix} \otimes \begin{pmatrix} 0 \\ 1 \end{pmatrix} = \begin{pmatrix} 0\begin{pmatrix} 0 \\ 1 \end{pmatrix} \\ 1\begin{pmatrix} 0 \\ 1 \end{pmatrix} \end{pmatrix} = \begin{pmatrix} 0 \\ 0 \\ 0 \\ 1 \end{pmatrix}.$$

Then,

$$c_0|00\rangle + c_1|01\rangle + c_2|10\rangle + c_3|11\rangle = \begin{pmatrix} c_0 \\ c_1 \\ c_2 \\ c_3 \end{pmatrix}.$$

Similarly, with three qubits, its state can be written as a column vector with eight elements:

$$\sum_{j=0}^{7} c_j|j\rangle = c_0|0\rangle + c_1|1\rangle + \cdots + c_7|7\rangle = \begin{pmatrix} c_0 \\ c_1 \\ \vdots \\ c_7 \end{pmatrix}.$$

With n qubits, the vector has $N = 2^n$ elements:

$$|\psi\rangle = \sum_{j=0}^{N-1} c_j|j\rangle = c_0|0\rangle + c_1|1\rangle + \cdots + c_{N-1}|N-1\rangle = \begin{pmatrix} c_0 \\ c_1 \\ \vdots \\ c_{N-1} \end{pmatrix}.$$

With bras, the Kronecker product is still the tensor product. For example,

$$\langle 00| = \langle 0| \otimes \langle 0| = \begin{pmatrix} 1 & 0 \end{pmatrix} \otimes \begin{pmatrix} 1 & 0 \end{pmatrix} = \begin{pmatrix} 1\begin{pmatrix} 1 & 0 \end{pmatrix} & 0\begin{pmatrix} 1 & 0 \end{pmatrix} \end{pmatrix} = \begin{pmatrix} 1 & 0 & 0 & 0 \end{pmatrix}.$$

So, a general quantum state of n qubits, written as a bra, is

$$\langle \psi| = \sum_{j=0}^{N-1} c_j^*\langle j| = c_0^*\langle 0| + c_1^*\langle 1| + \cdots + c_{N-1}^*\langle N-1| = \begin{pmatrix} c_0^* & c_1^* & \cdots & c_{N-1}^* \end{pmatrix}.$$

Exercise 4.4. Verify that

$$|1\rangle \otimes |1\rangle \otimes |0\rangle = \begin{pmatrix} 0 \\ 0 \\ 0 \\ 0 \\ 0 \\ 0 \\ 1 \\ 0 \end{pmatrix}.$$

Exercise 4.5. Consider a two-qubit state

$$|\psi\rangle = \frac{1}{2}|00\rangle + \frac{i}{\sqrt{2}}|10\rangle + \frac{\sqrt{3}+i}{4}|11\rangle.$$

(a) What is $|\psi\rangle$ as a (column) vector?
(a) What is $\langle\psi|$ as a (row) vector?

Exercise 4.6. Show that $\{|00\rangle, |01\rangle, |10\rangle, |11\rangle\}$ is a complete orthonormal basis for the state of two qubits by showing that it satisfies the completeness relation

$$|00\rangle\langle 00| + |01\rangle\langle 01| + |10\rangle\langle 10| + |11\rangle\langle 11| = I,$$

where I is the 4×4 identity matrix:

$$I = \begin{pmatrix} 1 & 0 & 0 & 0 \\ 0 & 1 & 0 & 0 \\ 0 & 0 & 1 & 0 \\ 0 & 0 & 0 & 1 \end{pmatrix}.$$

4.2.3 Measuring Individual Qubits

Say we have two qubits in the state

$$\frac{1}{\sqrt{2}}|00\rangle + \frac{1}{2}|01\rangle + \frac{\sqrt{3}}{4}|10\rangle + \frac{1}{4}|11\rangle.$$

If we measure both qubits, we would get $|00\rangle$ with probability $1/2$, $|01\rangle$ with probability $1/4$, $|10\rangle$ with probability $3/16$, or $|11\rangle$ with probability $1/16$.

Now, instead of measuring both qubits, let us only measure the left qubit. This yields $|0\rangle$ or $|1\rangle$ with some probabilities, and the state collapses to some state, so the outcomes are

> $|0\rangle$ with some probability, and the state collapses to something,
>
> $|1\rangle$ with some probability, and the state collapses to something.

The probability of getting $|0\rangle$ when measuring the left qubit is given by the sum of the norm-squares of the amplitudes of $|00\rangle$ and $|01\rangle$, since those both have the left qubit as $|0\rangle$. That is, the probability of getting $|0\rangle$ is

$$\left|\frac{1}{\sqrt{2}}\right|^2 + \left|\frac{1}{2}\right|^2 = \frac{3}{4}.$$

Similarly, if the outcome is $|1\rangle$, then from the $|10\rangle$ and $|11\rangle$ states, the probability is

$$\left|\frac{\sqrt{3}}{4}\right|^2 + \left|\frac{1}{4}\right|^2 = \frac{1}{4}.$$

Then, the results of the measurement are:

> $|0\rangle$ with probability $\dfrac{3}{4}$, and the state collapses to something,
>
> $|1\rangle$ with probability $\dfrac{1}{4}$, and the state collapses to something.

Now for the states after measurement, if the outcome is $|0\rangle$, then the state collapses to the parts where the left qubit is $|0\rangle$, so it becomes

$$A\left(\frac{1}{\sqrt{2}}|00\rangle + \frac{1}{2}|01\rangle\right),$$

where A is a normalization constant. Similarly, if the outcome is $|1\rangle$, then the state collapses to the terms where the left qubit is $|1\rangle$, so it becomes

$$B\left(\frac{\sqrt{3}}{4}|10\rangle + \frac{1}{4}|11\rangle\right).$$

where B is a normalization constant. Normalizing these, we get $A = 2/\sqrt{3}$ and $B = 2$, so measuring the left qubit yields

$|0\rangle$ with probability $\frac{3}{4}$, and the state collapses to $\sqrt{\frac{2}{3}}|00\rangle + \frac{1}{\sqrt{3}}|01\rangle$,

$|1\rangle$ with probability $\frac{1}{4}$, and the state collapses to $\frac{\sqrt{3}}{2}|10\rangle + \frac{1}{2}|11\rangle$.

We can apply these ideas to any number of qubits. For example, if we have three qubits in the state

$$c_0|000\rangle + c_1|001\rangle + c_2|010\rangle + c_3|011\rangle + c_4|100\rangle + c_5|101\rangle + c_6|110\rangle + c_7|111\rangle,$$

and we measure the left and middle qubits, the possible outcomes are

$|00\rangle$ with probability $|c_0|^2 + |c_1|^2$, collapses to $\dfrac{c_0|000\rangle + c_1|001\rangle}{\sqrt{|c_0|^2 + |c_1|^2}}$,

$|01\rangle$ with probability $|c_2|^2 + |c_3|^2$, collapses to $\dfrac{c_2|010\rangle + c_3|011\rangle}{\sqrt{|c_2|^2 + |c_3|^2}}$,

$|10\rangle$ with probability $|c_4|^2 + |c_5|^2$, collapses to $\dfrac{c_4|100\rangle + c_5|101\rangle}{\sqrt{|c_4|^2 + |c_5|^2}}$,

$|11\rangle$ with probability $|c_6|^2 + |c_7|^2$, collapses to $\dfrac{c_6|110\rangle + c_7|111\rangle}{\sqrt{|c_6|^2 + |c_7|^2}}$.

Exercise 4.7. Two qubits are in the state

$$\frac{i}{\sqrt{10}}|00\rangle + \frac{1-2i}{\sqrt{10}}|01\rangle + \frac{e^{i\pi/100}}{\sqrt{10}}|10\rangle + \frac{\sqrt{3}}{\sqrt{10}}|11\rangle.$$

If we measure the qubits in the Z-basis $\{|00\rangle, |01\rangle, |10\rangle, |11\rangle\}$, what are the possible outcomes and with what probabilities?

Exercise 4.8. Normalize the following quantum state:

$$A\left(\frac{1}{2}|00\rangle + i|01\rangle + \sqrt{2}|10\rangle - |11\rangle\right).$$

4.2.4 Sequential Single-Qubit Measurements

We have answered the question of what happens when we measure just a single qubit or a subset of qubits. Now, let us take this a step further and consider what happens if we measure the qubits, one after another. For example, in the last section, we started with two qubits in the state

$$\frac{1}{\sqrt{2}}|00\rangle + \frac{1}{2}|01\rangle + \frac{\sqrt{3}}{4}|10\rangle + \frac{1}{4}|11\rangle.$$

If we first measure the left qubit, we get

$|0\rangle$ with probability $\frac{3}{4}$, and the state collapses to $\sqrt{\frac{2}{3}}|00\rangle + \frac{1}{\sqrt{3}}|01\rangle$,

$|1\rangle$ with probability $\frac{1}{4}$, and the state collapses to $\frac{\sqrt{3}}{2}|10\rangle + \frac{1}{2}|11\rangle$.

Now if we measure the right qubit after this, the possible outcomes for the sequence of measurements are $|00\rangle$, $|01\rangle$, $|10\rangle$, and $|11\rangle$. The probability of getting $|00\rangle$ is the probability of first getting $|0\rangle$ for the left qubit, which was $3/4$, times the probability of getting $|0\rangle$ for the right qubit, which is $2/3$ because the state collapsed after the first measurement. Multiplying these, the probability of getting $|00\rangle$ is $(3/4)(2/3) = 2/4 = 1/2$. We can perform this calculation for every possible outcome:

$$\text{Prob}(|00\rangle) = \text{Prob}(\text{first left } |0\rangle)\,\text{Prob}(\text{then right } |0\rangle) = \frac{3}{4}\frac{2}{3} = \frac{1}{2},$$
$$\text{Prob}(|01\rangle) = \text{Prob}(\text{first left } |0\rangle)\,\text{Prob}(\text{then right } |1\rangle) = \frac{3}{4}\frac{1}{3} = \frac{1}{4},$$
$$\text{Prob}(|10\rangle) = \text{Prob}(\text{first left } |1\rangle)\,\text{Prob}(\text{then right } |0\rangle) = \frac{1}{4}\frac{3}{4} = \frac{3}{16},$$
$$\text{Prob}(|11\rangle) = \text{Prob}(\text{first left } |1\rangle)\,\text{Prob}(\text{then right } |1\rangle) = \frac{1}{4}\frac{1}{4} = \frac{1}{16}.$$

Notice these outcomes and probabilities are exactly the same as if we had measured both qubits at the same time, as they should be. Measuring both qubits is the same as measuring one after another, assuming the state was not modified between the two measurements.

Exercise 4.9. Consider the two-qubit state

$$\frac{1}{4}|00\rangle + \frac{1}{2}|01\rangle + \frac{1}{\sqrt{2}}|10\rangle + \frac{\sqrt{3}}{4}|11\rangle.$$

If you measure only the left qubit, what are the resulting states, and with what probabilities?

Exercise 4.10. Consider the three-qubit state

$$\frac{1}{6}|000\rangle + \frac{1}{3\sqrt{2}}|001\rangle + \frac{1}{\sqrt{6}}|010\rangle + \frac{1}{2}|011\rangle + \frac{1}{6}|100\rangle + \frac{1}{3}|101\rangle + \frac{1}{6}|110\rangle + \frac{1}{\sqrt{3}}|111\rangle.$$

If you measure only the left and right qubits, but not the middle qubit, what are the resulting states, and with what probabilities?

4.3 Entanglement

4.3.1 Product States

Some quantum states can be factored into (the tensor product of) individual qubit states. For example,

$$\frac{1}{2}(|00\rangle - |01\rangle + |10\rangle - |11\rangle) = \underbrace{\frac{1}{\sqrt{2}}(|0\rangle + |1\rangle)}_{|+\rangle} \otimes \underbrace{\frac{1}{\sqrt{2}}(|0\rangle - |1\rangle)}_{|-\rangle}$$

$$= |+\rangle \otimes |-\rangle$$
$$= |+\rangle|-\rangle.$$

To confirm this to yourself, work it out in reverse order by multiplying out the states and showing that you get the original state. Such factorizable states are called *product states* or *simply separable states*. Each single-qubit state can be visualized on the Bloch sphere, so $|+\rangle|-\rangle$ would be two Bloch spheres, with the first at the x-axis, and the other at the $-x$-axis:

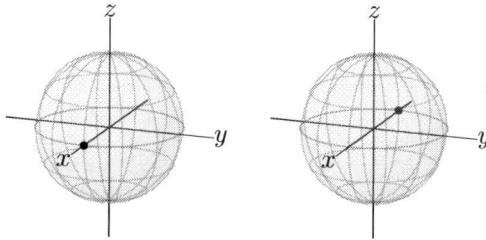

Let us work through an example of how to factor a state. Say two qubits are in the state

$$\frac{1}{2\sqrt{2}}\left(\sqrt{3}|00\rangle - \sqrt{3}|01\rangle + |10\rangle - |11\rangle\right).$$

We want to write this as the product of two single-qubit states,

$$|\psi_1\rangle|\psi_0\rangle,$$

where

$$|\psi_1\rangle = \alpha_1|0\rangle + \beta_1|1\rangle, \quad |\psi_0\rangle = \alpha_0|0\rangle + \beta_0|1\rangle.$$

Then,

$$|\psi_1\rangle|\psi_0\rangle = (\alpha_1|0\rangle + \beta_1|1\rangle)(\alpha_0|0\rangle + \beta_0|1\rangle)$$
$$= \alpha_1\alpha_0|00\rangle + \alpha_1\beta_0|01\rangle + \beta_1\alpha_0|10\rangle + \beta_1\beta_0|11\rangle.$$

Matching up the coefficients with our original state,

$$\alpha_1\alpha_0 = \frac{\sqrt{3}}{2\sqrt{2}}, \quad \alpha_1\beta_0 = \frac{-\sqrt{3}}{2\sqrt{2}}, \quad \beta_1\alpha_0 = \frac{1}{2\sqrt{2}}, \quad \beta_1\beta_0 = \frac{-1}{2\sqrt{2}}.$$

Using these equations, let us solve for the variables in terms of one of them. Starting with the first equation, we can solve for α_1 in terms of α_0:

$$\alpha_1 = \frac{\sqrt{3}}{2\sqrt{2}\alpha_0}.$$

Plugging this into the second equation, we can solve for β_0 in terms of α_0:

$$\beta_0 = -\alpha_0.$$

For the third equation, we can solve for β_1 in terms of α_0:

$$\beta_1 = \frac{1}{2\sqrt{2}\alpha_0}.$$

Finally, plugging in $\beta_1 = 1/2\sqrt{2}\alpha_0$ and $\beta_0 = -\alpha_0$ into the fourth equation, we get

$$\frac{-1}{2\sqrt{2}} = \frac{-1}{2\sqrt{2}},$$

which is a true statement, so it is satisfied, although it does not tell us anything new. So, we have solved for α_1, β_1, and β_0 in terms of α_0, and this is actually sufficient. Plugging into the product state,

$$|\psi_1\rangle|\psi_0\rangle = (\alpha_1|0\rangle + \beta_1|1\rangle)(\alpha_0|0\rangle + \beta_0|1\rangle)$$
$$= \left(\frac{\sqrt{3}}{2\sqrt{2}\alpha_0}|0\rangle + \frac{1}{2\sqrt{2}}\frac{1}{\alpha_0}|1\rangle\right)(\alpha_0|0\rangle - \alpha_0|1\rangle).$$

We see that α_0 cancels, yielding

$$|\psi_1\rangle|\psi_0\rangle = \left(\frac{\sqrt{3}}{2\sqrt{2}}|0\rangle + \frac{1}{2\sqrt{2}}|1\rangle\right)(|0\rangle - |1\rangle).$$

Moving the factor of $1/\sqrt{2}$ to the right qubit so that both qubits are normalized,

$$|\psi_1\rangle|\psi_0\rangle = \left(\frac{\sqrt{3}}{2}|0\rangle + \frac{1}{2}|1\rangle\right)\left(\frac{1}{\sqrt{2}}|0\rangle - \frac{1}{\sqrt{2}}|1\rangle\right).$$

Thus, the left qubit is in the state $\frac{\sqrt{3}}{2}|0\rangle + \frac{1}{2}|1\rangle$, and the right qubit is in the state $|-\rangle$. In general, a product state of n qubits can be written

$$(\alpha_{n-1}|0\rangle + \beta_{n-1}|1\rangle) \otimes \cdots \otimes (\alpha_1|0\rangle + \beta_1|1\rangle) \otimes (\alpha_0|0\rangle + \beta_0|1\rangle).$$

This only has $2n$ amplitudes, so a classical computer can efficiently store the amplitudes of product states. If quantum computers only used product states, they would be efficiently simulated by classical computers.

4.3.2 Entangled States

There exist quantum states that cannot be factored into product states. These are called *entangled states*. For example, with two qubits,

$$|\Phi^+\rangle = \frac{1}{\sqrt{2}}(|00\rangle + |11\rangle)$$

cannot be written as $|\psi_1\rangle|\psi_0\rangle$. As a proof, let us try writing it as a product state using the procedure from the last section:

$$\begin{aligned}|\psi_1\rangle|\psi_0\rangle &= (\alpha_1|0\rangle + \beta_1|1\rangle)(\alpha_0|0\rangle + \beta_0|1\rangle) \\ &= \alpha_1\alpha_0|00\rangle + \alpha_1\beta_0|01\rangle + \beta_1\alpha_0|10\rangle + \beta_1\beta_0|11\rangle.\end{aligned}$$

Matching the coefficients, we get

$$\alpha_1\alpha_0 = \frac{1}{\sqrt{2}}, \quad \alpha_1\beta_0 = 0, \quad \beta_1\alpha_0 = 0, \quad \beta_1\beta_0 = \frac{1}{\sqrt{2}}.$$

The second equation requires $\alpha_1 = 0$ or $\beta_0 = 0$. If $\alpha_1 = 0$, then the first equation gives $0 = 1/\sqrt{2}$, which is false. If $\beta_0 = 0$, then the fourth equation gives $0 = 1/\sqrt{2}$. Thus, there is no solution to these four equations, so $|\Phi^+\rangle$ cannot be written as a product state. It is an entangled state. This property that the state of the qubits are intertwined is called *entanglement*.

Since an entangled state cannot be factored, a general entangled state of n qubits would have $N = 2^n$ amplitudes c_0 through c_{N-1}:

$$|\psi\rangle = \sum_{j=0}^{N-1} c_j|j\rangle = c_0|0\rangle + c_1|1\rangle + \cdots + c_{N-1}|N-1\rangle = \begin{pmatrix} c_0 \\ c_1 \\ \vdots \\ c_{N-1} \end{pmatrix}.$$

In the Entanglion board game, the planets within the Entanglion galaxy correspond to two-qubit states that are entangled. Planet Phi Plus is precisely $|\Phi^+\rangle$.

We will discuss entanglement in more detail in Chapter 6.

Exercise 4.11. Are each of the following states a product state or entangled state? If it is a product state, give the factorization.

(a) $\frac{1}{\sqrt{2}} (|01\rangle + |10\rangle)$.

(b) $\frac{1}{\sqrt{2}} (|10\rangle + i|11\rangle)$.

Exercise 4.12. Are each of the following states a product state or entangled state? If it is a product state, give the factorization.

(a) $\frac{1}{4} \left(3|00\rangle - \sqrt{3}|01\rangle + \sqrt{3}|10\rangle - |11\rangle \right)$.

(b) $\frac{1}{\sqrt{3}}|0\rangle|+\rangle + \sqrt{\frac{2}{3}}|1\rangle|-\rangle$.

4.4 Quantum Gates

4.4.1 One-Qubit Quantum Gates

Say we have multiple qubits, and we want to apply a single-qubit gate (like I, X, Y, Z, S, T, or H) to just a single qubit. For example, say we have two qubits in the $|00\rangle = |0\rangle \otimes |0\rangle$ state, and we want to apply the Hadamard gate to the left qubit, but leave the right qubit alone (i.e., apply the identity gate to it). We write the gates using a tensor product, so we write

$$
\begin{aligned}
(H \otimes I)(|0\rangle \otimes |0\rangle) &= H|0\rangle \otimes I|0\rangle \\
&= |+\rangle \otimes |0\rangle \\
&= \frac{1}{\sqrt{2}} (|0\rangle + |1\rangle) \otimes |0\rangle \\
&= \frac{1}{\sqrt{2}} (|0\rangle \otimes |0\rangle + |1\rangle \otimes |0\rangle).
\end{aligned}
$$

Compressing the notation and also writing the result as a column vector,

$$
(H \otimes I)|00\rangle = \frac{1}{\sqrt{2}} (|00\rangle + |10\rangle) = \frac{1}{\sqrt{2}} \begin{pmatrix} 1 \\ 0 \\ 1 \\ 0 \end{pmatrix}.
$$

To draw as a quantum circuit, we use the convention that the rightmost qubit corresponds to the top row of the quantum circuit, and the leftmost qubit corresponds to the bottom row of the quantum circuit:

We follow this convention so that it matches Quirk, and in Chapter 5 the IBM Quantum Composer. Nielsen and Chuang follows the opposite convention, where the leftmost qubit corresponds to the top row of the quantum circuit.

We can find $H \otimes I$ as a matrix a couple different ways. First, we can find how $H \otimes I$ acts on each of the basis states $|00\rangle, |01\rangle, |10\rangle, |11\rangle$. We already found how it acts on $|00\rangle$ above. Continuing with the rest,

$$(H \otimes I)|01\rangle = \frac{1}{\sqrt{2}} (|01\rangle + |11\rangle) = \frac{1}{\sqrt{2}} \begin{pmatrix} 0 \\ 1 \\ 0 \\ 1 \end{pmatrix},$$

$$(H \otimes I)|10\rangle = \frac{1}{\sqrt{2}} (|00\rangle - |10\rangle) = \frac{1}{\sqrt{2}} \begin{pmatrix} 1 \\ 0 \\ -1 \\ 0 \end{pmatrix},$$

$$(H \otimes I)|11\rangle = \frac{1}{\sqrt{2}} (|01\rangle - |11\rangle) = \frac{1}{\sqrt{2}} \begin{pmatrix} 0 \\ 1 \\ 0 \\ -1 \end{pmatrix}.$$

As in Section 3.3.1, we can write $H \otimes I$ as a matrix by combining the column vectors for $(H \otimes I)|00\rangle, \ldots, (H \otimes I)|11\rangle$ as a 4×4 grid:

$$H \otimes I = \frac{1}{\sqrt{2}} \begin{pmatrix} 1 & 0 & 1 & 0 \\ 0 & 1 & 0 & 1 \\ 1 & 0 & -1 & 0 \\ 0 & 1 & 0 & -1 \end{pmatrix}.$$

The second way to find this matrix is by taking the Kronecker product of H and I:

$$H \otimes I = \frac{1}{\sqrt{2}} \begin{pmatrix} 1 & 1 \\ 1 & -1 \end{pmatrix} \otimes \begin{pmatrix} 1 & 0 \\ 0 & 1 \end{pmatrix} = \frac{1}{\sqrt{2}} \begin{pmatrix} 1 \cdot \begin{pmatrix} 1 & 0 \\ 0 & 1 \end{pmatrix} & 1 \cdot \begin{pmatrix} 1 & 0 \\ 0 & 1 \end{pmatrix} \\ 1 \cdot \begin{pmatrix} 1 & 0 \\ 0 & 1 \end{pmatrix} & 1 \cdot \begin{pmatrix} 1 & 0 \\ 0 & 1 \end{pmatrix} \end{pmatrix}$$

$$= \frac{1}{\sqrt{2}} \begin{pmatrix} 1 & 0 & 1 & 0 \\ 0 & 1 & 0 & 1 \\ 1 & 0 & -1 & 0 \\ 0 & 1 & 0 & -1 \end{pmatrix}.$$

This matches what we previously obtained. We can also find the Kronecker product using Mathematica or SageMath:

- In Mathematica,

```
H=1/Sqrt[2]*{{1,1},{1,-1}};
eye={{1,0},{0,1}};
KroneckerProduct[H,eye]
```

- In SageMath,

```
sage: H = 1/sqrt(2) * Matrix([[1,1],[1,-1]])
sage: eye = Matrix([[1,0],[0,1]])
sage: H.tensor_product(eye)
```

As another example, to act on the left qubit with H and the right qubit with X, we would write $H \otimes X$, so

$$(H \otimes X)|0\rangle|0\rangle = |+\rangle|1\rangle = \frac{1}{\sqrt{2}}(|01\rangle + |11\rangle).$$

As a quantum circuit, we would draw this as

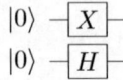

$$|0\rangle \;—\boxed{X}—$$
$$|0\rangle \;—\boxed{H}—$$

Simulating this in Quirk, we get

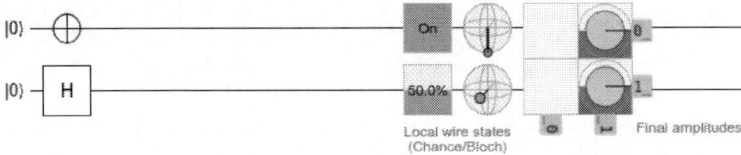

This is consistent with the state $|+\rangle|1\rangle$. Since the right/top qubit is $|1\rangle$, Quirk correctly shows that the probability of getting $|1\rangle$ when measuring it is 100% (On), and it correctly draws the state at the south pole of the Bloch sphere. Similarly, the left/bottom qubit is $|+\rangle$, and Quirk correctly shows that the probability of measuring it to be $|1\rangle$ is 50%, and it correctly draws the state at the x-axis of the Bloch sphere. In additional, Quirk also depicts the amplitudes on the real-imaginary plane, labeled "Final amplitudes." There are four boxes, and the top-left box depicts the amplitude of $|00\rangle$, which is zero, and the top-right box depicts the amplitude of $|01\rangle$, which is $1/\sqrt{2}$. Since this is real, it corresponds to a vector pointing along the real axis of the real-imaginary plane. The background is also half filled, indicating a probability of $|1/\sqrt{2}|^2 = 1/2$. Mousing over, we get

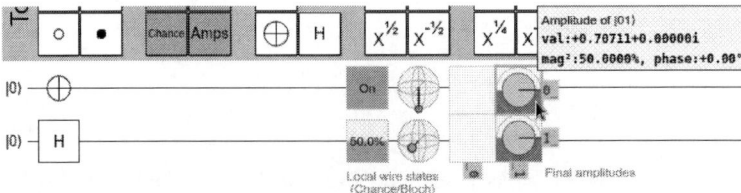

and the amplitude is also explicitly given as $0.70711 = 1/\sqrt{2}$, which has a phase or angle of $0°$ on the real-imaginary plane since it is purely real, and a norm-square magnitude of 50%. The bottom-left box depicts the amplitude of $|10\rangle$, which is zero, and finally the bottom-right box depicts the amplitude of $|11\rangle$, which is $1/\sqrt{2}$.

As a third example, if we have n qubits, and we want to apply H to all n qubits, we can write $H \otimes H \otimes \cdots \otimes H$ as $H^{\otimes n}$. For example,

$$H^{\otimes n}|0\rangle^{\otimes n} = |+\rangle^{\otimes n}.$$

Note one-qubit gates are unable to create entangled states because each qubit evolves independently of the others. To create entanglement, we need quantum gates that operate on multiple qubits at a time.

Exercise 4.13. In this problem, you will prove some of the game mechanics of Entanglion. Please refer to Fig. 4.1 for the game board. If the players are on planet Psi Plus, and either player uses an X engine card, they both move to planet Phi Plus, and vice versa. Similarly, if the players are on planet Psi Minus, and either player uses an X engine card, they both move to planet Phi Minus, and vice versa. These planets correspond to the following states:

$$\left|\Phi^+\right\rangle = \frac{1}{\sqrt{2}}\left(|00\rangle + |11\rangle\right),$$

$$\left|\Phi^-\right\rangle = \frac{1}{\sqrt{2}}\left(|00\rangle - |11\rangle\right),$$

$$\left|\Psi^+\right\rangle = \frac{1}{\sqrt{2}}\left(|01\rangle + |10\rangle\right),$$

$$\left|\Psi^-\right\rangle = \frac{1}{\sqrt{2}}\left(|01\rangle - |10\rangle\right).$$

(a) Show that when the X gate is applied to either qubit of $|\Psi^+\rangle$, the result is $|\Phi^+\rangle$, up to a global phase.
(b) Show that when the X gate is applied to either qubit of $|\Phi^+\rangle$, the result is $|\Psi^+\rangle$, up to a global phase.
(c) Show that when the X gate is applied to either qubit of $|\Psi^-\rangle$, the result is $|\Phi^-\rangle$, up to a global phase.
(d) Show that when the X gate is applied to either qubit of $|\Phi^-\rangle$, the result is $|\Psi^-\rangle$, up to a global phase.

Exercise 4.14. Answer the following questions.
(a) What is $H \otimes X$ as a 4×4 matrix?
(b) Consider

$$|\psi\rangle - \frac{1}{4}|00\rangle + \frac{1}{2}|01\rangle + \frac{1}{\sqrt{2}}|10\rangle + \frac{\sqrt{3}}{4}|11\rangle.$$

What is $(H \otimes X)|\psi\rangle$? Hint: You may use a computer.

4.4.2 Two-Qubit Quantum Gates

Quantum gates can also operate on two qubits at the same time. Some important examples include:

- The *CNOT gate* or *controlled-NOT gate* inverts the right qubit if the left qubit is 1:

$$CNOT|00\rangle = |00\rangle,$$
$$CNOT|01\rangle = |01\rangle,$$
$$CNOT|10\rangle = |11\rangle,$$
$$CNOT|11\rangle = |10\rangle.$$

The left qubit is called the *control qubit*, and the right qubit is called the *target qubit*. Note the control qubit is unchanged by CNOT, whereas the target qubit becomes the XOR (exclusive OR) of the inputs:

$$CNOT|a\rangle|b\rangle = |a\rangle|a \oplus b\rangle.$$

Thus, CNOT is a quantum XOR gate. Also, since the X gate is the NOT gate, the CNOT gate is also called the CX gate or *controlled-X gate*.

In Entanglion (see Fig. 4.1), the player who uses the CNOT engine card is the target qubit, and the other player is the control qubit. So, you can move between planets Zero and One by playing a CNOT engine card when the other player is at One.

Acting on a superposition,

$$
\begin{aligned}
CNOT\,(c_0|00\rangle &+ c_1|01\rangle + c_2|10\rangle + c_3|11\rangle) \\
&= c_0 CNOT|00\rangle + c_1 CNOT|01\rangle + c_2 CNOT|10\rangle + c_3 CNOT|11\rangle \\
&= c_0|00\rangle + c_1|01\rangle + c_2|11\rangle + c_3|10\rangle \\
&= c_0|00\rangle + c_1|01\rangle + c_3|10\rangle + c_2|11\rangle.
\end{aligned}
$$

So, the amplitudes of $|10\rangle$ and $|11\rangle$ are swapped.

As a matrix, the columns correspond to CNOT acting on $|00\rangle$, $|01\rangle$, $|10\rangle$, and $|11\rangle$:

$$
CNOT = \begin{pmatrix} 1 & 0 & 0 & 0 \\ 0 & 1 & 0 & 0 \\ 0 & 0 & 0 & 1 \\ 0 & 0 & 1 & 0 \end{pmatrix}.
$$

For example, acting on a general superposition,

$$
CNOT\,(c_0|00\rangle + c_1|01\rangle + c_2|10\rangle + c_3|11\rangle) = \begin{pmatrix} 1 & 0 & 0 & 0 \\ 0 & 1 & 0 & 0 \\ 0 & 0 & 0 & 1 \\ 0 & 0 & 1 & 0 \end{pmatrix} \begin{pmatrix} c_0 \\ c_1 \\ c_2 \\ c_3 \end{pmatrix} = \begin{pmatrix} c_0 \\ c_1 \\ c_3 \\ c_2 \end{pmatrix}.
$$

So, the amplitudes of $|10\rangle$ and $|11\rangle$ are swapped, as expected.

As a quantum circuit, CNOT spans two qubits or two lines:

The solid dot indicates control, and the $\oplus$ denotes the target, which is the XOR of the control and the target. Simulating this in Quirk, we drag an X gate onto the top line and a "Control" solid dot, which is in the top Toolbox under "Probes," onto the bottom line:

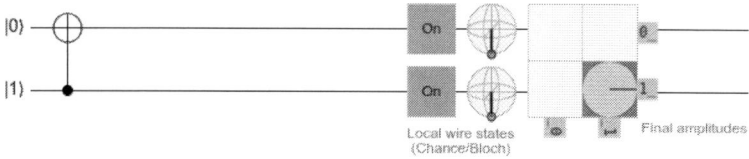

We also clicked on the initial state of the control qubit to change it to $|1\rangle$ (alternatively, we could leave the initial state as $|0\rangle$ and apply X to it, resulting in $|1\rangle$). This triggers the CNOT, changing the target from $|0\rangle$ to $|1\rangle$. The result is that both qubits are "On" with 100% probability. They are both at the south poles of their Bloch spheres, and the amplitude of $|11\rangle$ is 1.

To further clarify the control and target qubits, we may write CNOT with subscripts:

$\text{CNOT}_{ij} = \text{CNOT}$ with qubit i as the control and qubit j as the target.

Since we label the qubits from right-to-left starting with 0, we have been using

$$\text{CNOT} = \text{CNOT}_{10}.$$

If we instead want the control and target to be flipped, it would be CNOT_{01}, and we would draw the circuit as

To simulate this in Quirk, we just put the control on the zeroth qubit and the X gate on the first qubit:

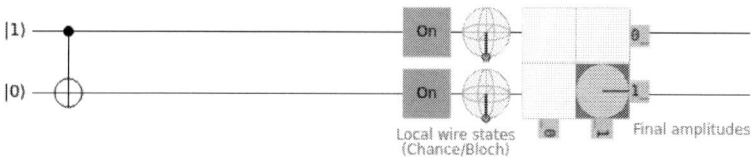

We set the control qubit to $|1\rangle$, and so the CNOT gate flipped the target to $|1\rangle$. Another way to flip the control and target qubits is to apply Hadamard gates to both sides of the CNOT:

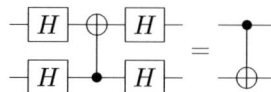

In other words,

$$(H \otimes H)\text{CNOT}(H \otimes H) = \text{CNOT}_{01}$$

We can prove this circuit identity using either elementary algebra or linear algebra. First, using elementary algebra, the right-hand-side of equation yields the following when applied to a superposition of the Z-basis states:

$$\text{CNOT}_{01} \left(c_0|00\rangle + c_1|01\rangle + c_2|10\rangle + c_3|11\rangle \right)$$
$$= c_0|00\rangle + c_1|11\rangle + c_2|10\rangle + c_3|01\rangle$$
$$= \left(c_0|00\rangle + c_3|01\rangle + c_2|10\rangle + c_1|11\rangle \right).$$

Let us show that the left-hand-side yields the same state:

$$c_0|00\rangle + c_1|01\rangle + c_2|10\rangle + c_3|11\rangle$$

$$\xrightarrow{H \otimes H} c_0|++\rangle + c_1|+-\rangle + c_2|-+\rangle + c_3|--\rangle$$

$$= \frac{c_0}{2} \left(|00\rangle + |01\rangle + |10\rangle + |11\rangle \right) + \frac{c_1}{2} \left(|00\rangle - |01\rangle + |10\rangle - |11\rangle \right)$$

$$+ \frac{c_2}{2} \left(|00\rangle + |01\rangle - |10\rangle - |11\rangle \right) + \frac{c_3}{2} \left(|00\rangle - |01\rangle - |10\rangle + |11\rangle \right)$$

$$= \frac{1}{2} \left(c_0 + c_1 + c_2 + c_3 \right) |00\rangle + \frac{1}{2} \left(c_0 - c_1 + c_2 - c_3 \right) |01\rangle$$

$$+ \frac{1}{2} \left(c_0 + c_1 - c_2 - c_3 \right) |10\rangle + \frac{1}{2} \left(c_0 - c_1 - c_2 + c_3 \right) |11\rangle$$

$$\xrightarrow{\text{CNOT}} \frac{1}{2} \left(c_0 + c_1 + c_2 + c_3 \right) |00\rangle + \frac{1}{2} \left(c_0 - c_1 + c_2 - c_3 \right) |01\rangle$$

$$+ \frac{1}{2} \left(c_0 + c_1 - c_2 - c_3 \right) |11\rangle + \frac{1}{2} \left(c_0 - c_1 - c_2 + c_3 \right) |10\rangle$$

$$= \frac{1}{2} \left(c_0 + c_1 + c_2 + c_3 \right) |00\rangle + \frac{1}{2} \left(c_0 - c_1 + c_2 - c_3 \right) |01\rangle$$

$$+ \frac{1}{2} \left(c_0 - c_1 - c_2 + c_3 \right) |10\rangle + \frac{1}{2} \left(c_0 + c_1 - c_2 - c_3 \right) |11\rangle$$

$$\xrightarrow{H \otimes H} \frac{1}{4} \left(c_0 + c_1 + c_2 + c_3 \right) |++\rangle + \frac{1}{4} \left(c_0 - c_1 + c_2 - c_3 \right) |+-\rangle$$

$$+ \frac{1}{4} \left(c_0 - c_1 - c_2 + c_3 \right) |-+\rangle + \frac{1}{4} \left(c_0 + c_1 - c_2 - c_3 \right) |--\rangle$$

$$= \frac{1}{4} \left(c_0 + c_1 + c_2 + c_3 \right) \left(|00\rangle + |01\rangle + |10\rangle + |11\rangle \right)$$

$$+ \frac{1}{4} \left(c_0 - c_1 + c_2 - c_3 \right) \left(|00\rangle - |01\rangle + |10\rangle - |11\rangle \right)$$

$$+ \frac{1}{4} \left(c_0 - c_1 - c_2 + c_3 \right) \left(|00\rangle + |01\rangle - |10\rangle - |11\rangle \right)$$

$$+ \frac{1}{4} \left(c_0 + c_1 - c_2 - c_3 \right) \left(|00\rangle - |01\rangle - |10\rangle + |11\rangle \right)$$

$$= c_0|00\rangle + c_3|01\rangle + c_2|10\rangle + c_1|11\rangle.$$

This is the same state, and so we have proved the circuit identity. It was rather tedious, however. Proving the circuit identity using linear algebra is easier. First, note that

$$\text{CNOT}_{01} = \begin{pmatrix} 1 & 0 & 0 & 0 \\ 0 & 0 & 0 & 1 \\ 0 & 0 & 1 & 0 \\ 0 & 1 & 0 & 0 \end{pmatrix},$$

since its columns show that $|00\rangle$ stays $|00\rangle$, $|01\rangle$ becomes $|11\rangle$, $|10\rangle$ stays $|10\rangle$, and $|11\rangle$ becomes $|01\rangle$. Now, let us show that $(H \otimes H)\text{CNOT}(H \otimes H)$ corresponds to the same matrix. First,

$$H \otimes H = \frac{1}{\sqrt{2}} \begin{pmatrix} 1 & 1 \\ 1 & -1 \end{pmatrix} \otimes \frac{1}{\sqrt{2}} \begin{pmatrix} 1 & 1 \\ 1 & -1 \end{pmatrix} = \frac{1}{2} \begin{pmatrix} 1 & 1 & 1 & 1 \\ 1 & -1 & 1 & -1 \\ 1 & 1 & -1 & -1 \\ 1 & -1 & -1 & 1 \end{pmatrix}.$$

Then,

$$(H \otimes H)\text{CNOT}(H \otimes H)$$

$$= \frac{1}{2} \begin{pmatrix} 1 & 1 & 1 & 1 \\ 1 & -1 & 1 & -1 \\ 1 & 1 & -1 & -1 \\ 1 & -1 & -1 & 1 \end{pmatrix} \begin{pmatrix} 1 & 0 & 0 & 0 \\ 0 & 1 & 0 & 0 \\ 0 & 0 & 0 & 1 \\ 0 & 0 & 1 & 0 \end{pmatrix} \frac{1}{2} \begin{pmatrix} 1 & 1 & 1 & 1 \\ 1 & -1 & 1 & -1 \\ 1 & 1 & -1 & -1 \\ 1 & -1 & -1 & 1 \end{pmatrix}$$

$$= \frac{1}{4} \begin{pmatrix} 1 & 1 & 1 & 1 \\ 1 & -1 & 1 & -1 \\ 1 & 1 & -1 & -1 \\ 1 & -1 & -1 & 1 \end{pmatrix} \begin{pmatrix} 1 & 1 & 1 & 1 \\ 1 & -1 & 1 & -1 \\ 1 & -1 & -1 & 1 \\ 1 & 1 & -1 & -1 \end{pmatrix}$$

$$= \frac{1}{4} \begin{pmatrix} 4 & 0 & 0 & 0 \\ 0 & 0 & 0 & 4 \\ 0 & 0 & 4 & 0 \\ 0 & 4 & 0 & 0 \end{pmatrix}$$

$$= \begin{pmatrix} 1 & 0 & 0 & 0 \\ 0 & 0 & 0 & 1 \\ 0 & 0 & 1 & 0 \\ 0 & 1 & 0 & 0 \end{pmatrix}.$$

This is precisely CNOT_{01}, and so we have proved the circuit identity using linear algebra. We also could have computed it using Mathematica or SageMath. Simulating the identity in Quirk,

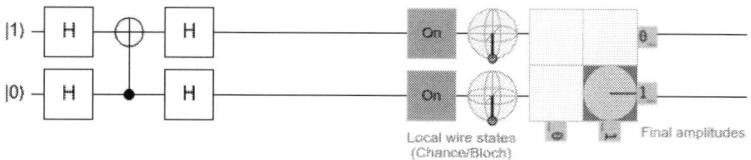

Local wire states
(Chance/Bloch)

Final amplitudes

Since the top qubit is initially $|1\rangle$, and it is now the control qubit, the bottom qubit gets flipped to $|1\rangle$. So, both qubits are "On."

The CNOT gate is important because it can produce entanglement. For example,

$$\text{CNOT}|+\rangle|0\rangle = \text{CNOT}\frac{1}{\sqrt{2}}(|00\rangle + |10\rangle) = \frac{1}{\sqrt{2}}(|00\rangle + |11\rangle) = |\Phi^+\rangle,$$

$$\text{CNOT}|-\rangle|0\rangle = \text{CNOT}\frac{1}{\sqrt{2}}(|00\rangle - |10\rangle) = \frac{1}{\sqrt{2}}(|00\rangle - |11\rangle) = |\Phi^-\rangle,$$

$$\text{CNOT}|+\rangle|1\rangle = \text{CNOT}\frac{1}{\sqrt{2}}(|01\rangle + |11\rangle) = \frac{1}{\sqrt{2}}(|01\rangle + |10\rangle) = |\Psi^+\rangle,$$

$$\text{CNOT}|-\rangle|1\rangle = \text{CNOT}\frac{1}{\sqrt{2}}(|01\rangle - |11\rangle) = \frac{1}{\sqrt{2}}(|01\rangle - |10\rangle) = |\Psi^-\rangle.$$

In Section 4.3.2, we proved that $|\Phi^+\rangle$ is entangled. It can be shown that the other three states, $|\Phi^-\rangle$, $|\Psi^+\rangle$, and $|\Psi^-\rangle$, are also entangled. So, in each of the above four calculations, we started with product states and ended up with entangled states. This demonstrates that CNOT can create entanglement. The four states, $|\Phi^+\rangle$, $|\Phi^-\rangle$, $|\Psi^+\rangle$, and $|\Psi^-\rangle$, are known as the *Bell states* or *EPR states* or *EPR pairs* (for Einstein, Podolsky, and Rosen). They form an orthonormal basis called the *Bell basis* (see Exercise 4.19), and they will be important in Chapter 6.

In Entanglion (see Fig. 4.1), the player who uses the CNOT engine card is the target qubit, and the other player is the control qubit. So, playing a CNOT engine card while at planet Zero, while your teammate is at planet Plus, causes both of you to move to planet Phi Plus. Similarly, the spaceships go from planets Zero and Minus to Phi Minus, One and Plus to Psi Plus, and One and Minus to Psi Minus.

Exercise 4.15. Prove the following circuit identities, such as by finding the matrix representation of each circuit.

(a) $\text{CNOT}(X \otimes I) = (X \otimes X)\text{CNOT}$.

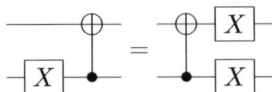

(b) $\text{CNOT}(I \otimes X) = (I \otimes X)\text{CNOT}$.

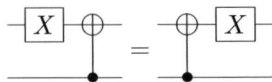

(c) $\text{CNOT}(Z \otimes I) = (Z \otimes I)\text{CNOT}$.

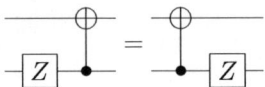

(d) $\text{CNOT}(I \otimes Z) = (Z \otimes Z)\text{CNOT}$.

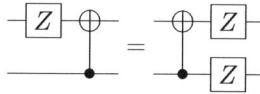

Exercise 4.16. Consider the following circuit, which consists of two CNOTs.

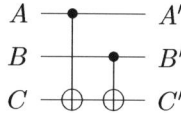

(a) What is the truth table for this circuit?

(b) How does it compare to the reversible circuit for XOR in Exercise 1.43?

Exercise 4.17. Recall CNOT flips the right qubit if the left qubit is 1. The *anti-controlled-NOT gate* flips the right qubit if the left qubit is 0. As a quantum circuit, the anti-control is drawn as an open dot instead of a solid dot. Prove that it can be obtained from an ordinary CNOT by applying an X gate to each side of the control:

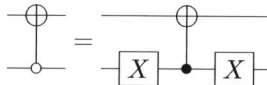

Exercise 4.18. If we apply CNOT in the Z-basis $\{|00\rangle, |01\rangle, |10\rangle, |11\rangle\}$, the left qubit acts as the control and the right qubit acts as the target. In this problem, we will prove that in the X-basis $\{|++\rangle, |+-\rangle, |-+\rangle, |--\rangle\}$, if the right qubit is $|-\rangle$, the left qubit gets flipped between $|+\rangle$ and $|-\rangle$, so the control and target are reversed. That is,

$$\text{CNOT}|+\rangle|+\rangle = |+\rangle|+\rangle,$$
$$\text{CNOT}|+\rangle|-\rangle = |-\rangle|-\rangle,$$
$$\text{CNOT}|-\rangle|+\rangle = |-\rangle|+\rangle,$$
$$\text{CNOT}|-\rangle|-\rangle = |+\rangle|-\rangle.$$

To prove these four equations, we start with the circuit identity from the main text:

$$(H \otimes H)\text{CNOT}(H \otimes H) = \text{CNOT}_{01}.$$

Then, we multiply on the left and on the right by $H \otimes H$:

$$(H \otimes H)(H \otimes H)\text{CNOT}(H \otimes H)(H \otimes H) = (H \otimes H)\text{CNOT}_{01}(H \otimes H).$$

Since $H^2 - I$, this becomes

$$(I \otimes I)\text{CNOT}(I \otimes I) = (H \otimes H)\text{CNOT}_{01}(H \otimes H).$$

Dropping the identity matrices,

$$\text{CNOT} = (H \otimes H)\text{CNOT}_{01}(H \otimes H).$$

Now it is straightforward to prove how CNOT acts in the X-basis. Beginning with $|++\rangle$,

$$\begin{aligned} \text{CNOT}|+\rangle|+\rangle &= (H \otimes H)\text{CNOT}_{01}(H \otimes H)|+\rangle|+\rangle \\ &= (H \otimes H)\text{CNOT}_{01}|0\rangle|0\rangle \\ &= (H \otimes H)|0\rangle|0\rangle \\ &= |+\rangle|+\rangle. \end{aligned}$$

Work out how CNOT acts on the remaining three basis states $|+-\rangle$, $|-+\rangle$, and $|--\rangle$.

Exercise 4.19. Prove that the Bell basis satisfies the completeness relation:

$$|\Phi^+\rangle\langle\Phi^+| + |\Phi^-\rangle\langle\Phi^-| + |\Psi^+\rangle\langle\Psi^+| + |\Psi^-\rangle\langle\Psi^-| = I,$$

where I is the 4×4 identity matrix.

- Just like CNOT, the *controlled-U* gate applies some quantum gate U to the right qubit if the left qubit is 1:

$$CU|00\rangle = |00\rangle,$$
$$CU|01\rangle = |01\rangle,$$
$$CU|10\rangle = |1\rangle \otimes U|0\rangle,$$
$$CU|11\rangle = |1\rangle \otimes U|1\rangle.$$

To get the matrix representation of CU, first say U acts on a single qubit as

$$U|0\rangle = a|0\rangle + b|1\rangle,$$
$$U|1\rangle = c|0\rangle + d|1\rangle.$$

So, U as a 2×2 matrix is

$$U = \begin{pmatrix} a & c \\ b & d \end{pmatrix}.$$

Then,

$$CU|00\rangle = |00\rangle,$$
$$CU|01\rangle = |01\rangle,$$
$$CU|10\rangle = |1\rangle \otimes (a|0\rangle + b|1\rangle) = a|10\rangle + b|11\rangle,$$
$$CU|11\rangle = |1\rangle \otimes (c|0\rangle + d|1\rangle) = c|10\rangle + d|11\rangle.$$

Representing each of these as column vectors and putting them together, CU as a 4×4 matrix is

$$CU = \begin{pmatrix} 1 & 0 & 0 & 0 \\ 0 & 1 & 0 & 0 \\ 0 & 0 & a & c \\ 0 & 0 & b & d \end{pmatrix}.$$

This agrees with

$$\text{CNOT} = CX = \begin{pmatrix} 1 & 0 & 0 & 0 \\ 0 & 1 & 0 & 0 \\ 0 & 0 & 0 & 1 \\ 0 & 0 & 1 & 0 \end{pmatrix}.$$

Some examples are controlled-Z and controlled-phase:

Exercise 4.20. What is the controlled-Z gate as a matrix?

- The *SWAP gate* simply swaps the two qubits:

$$
\begin{aligned}
\text{SWAP}|00\rangle &= |00\rangle, \\
\text{SWAP}|01\rangle &= |10\rangle, \\
\text{SWAP}|10\rangle &= |01\rangle, \\
\text{SWAP}|11\rangle &= |11\rangle.
\end{aligned}
$$

In other words,

$$
\text{SWAP}|a\rangle|b\rangle = |b\rangle|a\rangle.
$$

This gate cannot produce entanglement because, if the qubits are in a product state, swapping the factors results in a product state. Acting on a superposition,

$$
\begin{aligned}
\text{SWAP}&\left(c_0|00\rangle + c_1|01\rangle + c_2|10\rangle + c_3|11\rangle\right) \\
&= c_0\text{SWAP}|00\rangle + c_1\text{SWAP}|01\rangle + c_2\text{SWAP}|10\rangle + c_3\text{SWAP}|11\rangle \\
&= c_0|00\rangle + c_1|10\rangle + c_2|01\rangle + c_3|11\rangle \\
&= c_0|00\rangle + c_2|01\rangle + c_1|10\rangle + c_3|11\rangle.
\end{aligned}
$$

So, the amplitudes of $|01\rangle$ and $|10\rangle$ are swapped.

As a matrix, the columns correspond to SWAP acting on $|00\rangle$, $|01\rangle$, $|10\rangle$, and $|11\rangle$:

$$
\text{SWAP} = \begin{pmatrix} 1 & 0 & 0 & 0 \\ 0 & 0 & 1 & 0 \\ 0 & 1 & 0 & 0 \\ 0 & 0 & 0 & 1 \end{pmatrix}.
$$

For example, acting on a general superposition,

$$
\text{SWAP}\left(c_0|00\rangle + c_1|01\rangle + c_2|10\rangle + c_3|11\rangle\right) = \begin{pmatrix} 1 & 0 & 0 & 0 \\ 0 & 0 & 1 & 0 \\ 0 & 1 & 0 & 0 \\ 0 & 0 & 0 & 1 \end{pmatrix} \begin{pmatrix} c_0 \\ c_1 \\ c_2 \\ c_3 \end{pmatrix} = \begin{pmatrix} c_0 \\ c_2 \\ c_1 \\ c_3 \end{pmatrix}.
$$

So, the amplitudes of $|01\rangle$ and $|10\rangle$ are swapped, as expected.

As a quantum circuit, we can draw a SWAP gate using a vertical line with $\times$'s at each end, or by literally swapping the wires:

In Quirk, "Swap" is located in the top Toolbox under "Half Turns":

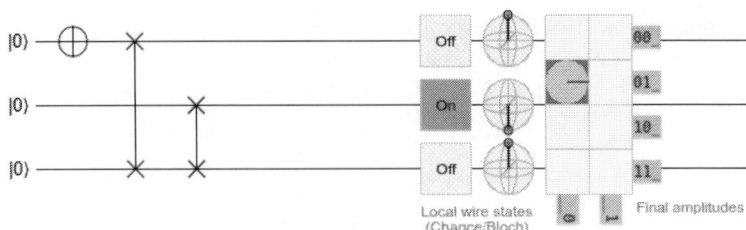

We also included an X gate so that the top qubit is a $|1\rangle$. This swaps with the bottom qubit, which then swaps with the middle qubit, so the result is that the middle qubit is $|1\rangle$.

A SWAP gate can also be created using three CNOT gates:

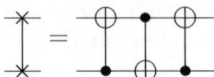

Or as an equation,

$$\text{SWAP} = (\text{CNOT})(\text{CNOT}_{01})(\text{CNOT}).$$

As a proof, we can work through what each CNOT does and show that the result is a SWAP:

$$|a\rangle|b\rangle \xrightarrow{\text{CNOT}} |a\rangle|a\oplus b\rangle \xrightarrow{\text{CNOT}_{01}} |a\oplus a\oplus b\rangle|a\oplus b\rangle = |(a\oplus a)\oplus b\rangle|a\oplus b\rangle$$

$$= |0\oplus b\rangle|a\oplus b\rangle = |b\rangle|a\oplus b\rangle \xrightarrow{\text{CNOT}} |b\rangle|a\oplus b\oplus b\rangle = |b\rangle|a\rangle.$$

As another proof, we can multiply the three CNOTs as matrices and show that we get the matrix of a SWAP:

$$\begin{pmatrix}1&0&0&0\\0&1&0&0\\0&0&0&1\\0&0&1&0\end{pmatrix}\begin{pmatrix}1&0&0&0\\0&0&0&1\\0&0&1&0\\0&1&0&0\end{pmatrix}\begin{pmatrix}1&0&0&0\\0&1&0&0\\0&0&0&1\\0&0&1&0\end{pmatrix} = \begin{pmatrix}1&0&0&0\\0&0&1&0\\0&1&0&0\\0&0&0&1\end{pmatrix} = \text{SWAP}.$$

Exercise 4.21. Entanglion contains four yellow planets besides the Bell States. Please see the game board at Fig. 4.1. They are labeled Omega Zero through Omega Three. These are not standard names, but they correspond to the quantum states

$$|\omega_0\rangle = \frac{1}{2}\left(|00\rangle - |01\rangle + |10\rangle + |11\rangle\right),$$

$$|\omega_1\rangle = \frac{1}{2}\left(-|00\rangle + |01\rangle + |10\rangle + |11\rangle\right),$$

$$|\omega_2\rangle = \frac{1}{2}\left(|00\rangle + |01\rangle + |10\rangle - |11\rangle\right),$$

$$|\omega_3\rangle = \frac{1}{2}\left(|00\rangle + |01\rangle - |10\rangle + |11\rangle\right).$$

The blue player corresponds to the left qubit, and the red player corresponds to the right qubit.

(a) Show that when the SWAP gate is applied to $|\omega_0\rangle$, we get $|\omega_3\rangle$.

(b) Show that when X is applied to the left qubit of $|\omega_1\rangle$, we get $|\omega_3\rangle$.

(c) Show that when CNOT_{01} is applied to $|\omega_2\rangle$, we get $|\omega_0\rangle$.

(d) Show that when $\text{CNOT} = \text{CNOT}_{10}$ is applied to $|\omega_3\rangle$, we get $|\omega_2\rangle$.

Exercise 4.22. The Mølmer-Sørensen (MS) gate is a two-qubit gate that can be naturally implemented on trapped ion quantum computers. It transforms Z-basis states by

$$|00\rangle \rightarrow \frac{1}{\sqrt{2}}\left(|00\rangle + i|11\rangle\right),$$

$$|01\rangle \rightarrow \frac{1}{\sqrt{2}}\left(|01\rangle - i|10\rangle\right),$$

$$|10\rangle \rightarrow \frac{1}{\sqrt{2}}\left(|10\rangle - i|01\rangle\right),$$

$$|11\rangle \rightarrow \frac{1}{\sqrt{2}}\left(|11\rangle + i|00\rangle\right).$$

(a) What is the MS gate as a matrix?

(b) Show that $\text{MS}^8 = I$. (You may use a computer.)

4.4.3 Toffoli Gate

A three-qubit gate that often appears in quantum computing is the Toffoli gate, or controlled-controlled-NOT gate, that we discussed in Section 1.5.3. Since it is reversible, it is a quantum gate, and it flips the right qubit if the left and middle qubits are 1:

$$\text{Toffoli}|000\rangle = |000\rangle,$$

$$\text{Toffoli}|001\rangle = |001\rangle,$$

$$\text{Toffoli}|010\rangle = |010\rangle,$$

$$\text{Toffoli}|011\rangle = |011\rangle,$$

$$\text{Toffoli}|100\rangle = |100\rangle,$$

$$\text{Toffoli}|101\rangle = |101\rangle,$$

$$\text{Toffoli}|110\rangle = |111\rangle,$$

$$\text{Toffoli}|111\rangle = |110\rangle.$$

Or

$$\text{Toffoli}|a\rangle|b\rangle|c\rangle = |a\rangle|b\rangle|ab \oplus c\rangle.$$

Recall from Section 1.5.3 that the Toffoli gate is universal for classical computing, and any efficient classical algorithm can be converted into an efficient algorithm only utilizing Toffoli gates. Since the Toffoli gate is a quantum gate, quantum computers can efficiently do everything a classical computer can efficiently do. In terms of complexity classes, P is contained within BQP.

As a matrix, the columns correspond to Toffoli acting on $|000\rangle, |001\rangle, \ldots, |111\rangle$:

$$\text{Toffoli} = \begin{pmatrix} 1 & 0 & 0 & 0 & 0 & 0 & 0 & 0 \\ 0 & 1 & 0 & 0 & 0 & 0 & 0 & 0 \\ 0 & 0 & 1 & 0 & 0 & 0 & 0 & 0 \\ 0 & 0 & 0 & 1 & 0 & 0 & 0 & 0 \\ 0 & 0 & 0 & 0 & 1 & 0 & 0 & 0 \\ 0 & 0 & 0 & 0 & 0 & 1 & 0 & 0 \\ 0 & 0 & 0 & 0 & 0 & 0 & 0 & 1 \\ 0 & 0 & 0 & 0 & 0 & 0 & 1 & 0 \end{pmatrix}.$$

In Section 1.5.3, we drew the Toffoli gate as a box. In quantum computing, we typically draw the Toffoli gate similarly to the CNOT gate, with solid dots indicating the control qubits and $\oplus$ indicating the target:

In Quirk, we simply drag two control dots onto the circuit, along with the X gate:

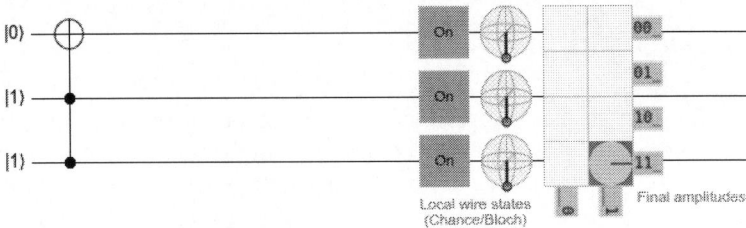

We made the bottom two qubits both in the $|1\rangle$ state, so the Toffoli gate flips the top qubit to $|1\rangle$.

Exercise 4.23. Show that the Toffoli gate can be constructed from the one-qubit gates Hadamard H, phase S, T, and $T^\dagger$, plus the two-qubit CNOT gate:

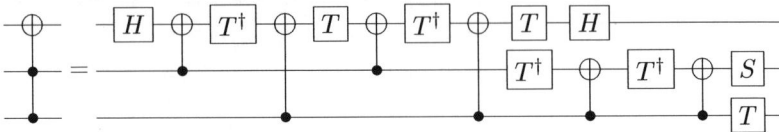

Just do the matrix multiplications on the computer.

Exercise 4.24. Consider the anti-Toffoli gate, which was introduced in Exercise 1.41. In quantum computing, it is typically drawn like the anti-CNOT gate from Exercise 4.17, with open dots indicating the anti-controls:

(a) How does the anti-Toffoli gate act on each basis state?
(b) What is the anti-Toffoli gate as a matrix?

4.4.4 No-Cloning Theorem

Classically, it is easy to copy or *clone* information by reading each bit and writing it somewhere. In quantum computing, cloning qubits is more complicated. Say we have a qubit in some superposition state. If we measure it in the Z-basis, we get $|0\rangle$ or $|1\rangle$ with some probability. So, we do not learn the original superposition state. Furthermore, the measurement collapses the state to $|0\rangle$ or $|1\rangle$, meaning we lost whatever superposition state we originally had.

To investigate this in greater detail, say we have a qubit in a known quantum state, such as $|+\rangle$. Since we know its state, we can produce additional copies of it:

$$|+\rangle|0\rangle \xrightarrow{I\otimes H} |+\rangle|+\rangle.$$

We went from having one copy to two. So, copying a known quantum state is no problem.

The issue is copying an unknown quantum state. Say we have a qubit in an unknown quantum state $|\psi\rangle = \alpha|0\rangle + \beta|1\rangle$, and we would like to make a copy of it:

$$|\psi\rangle|0\rangle \to |\psi\rangle|\psi\rangle.$$

Is there a quantum gate U that allows us to copy or clone a general unknown qubit? U would need to satisfy

$$U|\psi\rangle|0\rangle = |\psi\rangle|\psi\rangle.$$

Expressing this using linear algebra, we require

$$\begin{pmatrix} U_{11} & U_{12} & U_{13} & U_{14} \\ U_{21} & U_{22} & U_{23} & U_{24} \\ U_{31} & U_{32} & U_{33} & U_{34} \\ U_{41} & U_{42} & U_{43} & U_{44} \end{pmatrix} \begin{pmatrix} \alpha \\ \beta \end{pmatrix} \otimes \begin{pmatrix} 1 \\ 0 \end{pmatrix} = \begin{pmatrix} \alpha \\ \beta \end{pmatrix} \otimes \begin{pmatrix} \alpha \\ \beta \end{pmatrix}$$

$$\begin{pmatrix} U_{11} & U_{12} & U_{13} & U_{14} \\ U_{21} & U_{22} & U_{23} & U_{24} \\ U_{31} & U_{32} & U_{33} & U_{34} \\ U_{41} & U_{42} & U_{43} & U_{44} \end{pmatrix} \begin{pmatrix} \alpha \\ 0 \\ \beta \\ 0 \end{pmatrix} = \begin{pmatrix} \alpha^2 \\ \alpha\beta \\ \alpha\beta \\ \beta^2 \end{pmatrix}$$

$$\begin{pmatrix} U_{11}\alpha + U_{13}\beta \\ U_{21}\alpha + U_{23}\beta \\ U_{31}\alpha + U_{33}\beta \\ U_{41}\alpha + U_{43}\beta \end{pmatrix} = \begin{pmatrix} \alpha^2 \\ \alpha\beta \\ \alpha\beta \\ \beta^2 \end{pmatrix}$$

There are many possible solutions, such as

$$U_{11} = \alpha, \quad U_{13} = 0, \quad U_{21} = 0, \quad U_{23} = \alpha,$$
$$U_{31} = 0, \quad U_{33} = \alpha, \quad U_{41} = 0, \quad U_{43} = \beta,$$

but this requires knowing α and β, which we do not know. Any general solution requires knowing α and β, so there is no operator U that allows us to copy a general, unknown quantum state.

As another "proof," $U|\psi\rangle|0\rangle = |\psi\rangle|\psi\rangle$ is akin to going from ψ to ψ^2, and this is quadratic, not linear. The mathematics we are using is called linear algebra because matrices are linear. Vectors are transformed by linear transformations.

This result is called the *no-cloning theorem*. While classical information can be cloned, quantum information can not generally be cloned.

Using this theorem, some scientists have proposed quantum software that cannot be copied or pirated, and quantum money that cannot be copied or counterfeited, but that is beyond the scope of this textbook.

Exercise 4.25. Say there is a unitary U that is able to clone qubits in two known states $|\psi\rangle$ and $|\phi\rangle$. That is,

$$U|\psi\rangle|0\rangle = |\psi\rangle|\psi\rangle,$$
$$U|\phi\rangle|0\rangle = |\phi\rangle|\phi\rangle.$$

For example, an operator that can clone both $|0\rangle$ and $|1\rangle$ is CNOT, since $\text{CNOT}|00\rangle = |00\rangle$ and $\text{CNOT}|10\rangle = |11\rangle$. Taking the inner product of the previous two equations,

$$\langle\psi|\langle 0|U^\dagger U|\phi\rangle|0\rangle = ((\langle\psi|\langle\psi|)(|\phi\rangle|\phi\rangle))$$
$$((\langle\psi|\langle 0|)(|\phi\rangle|0\rangle)) = ((\langle\psi|\langle\psi|)(|\phi\rangle|\phi\rangle))$$
$$\langle\psi|\phi\rangle\langle 0|0\rangle = \langle\psi|\phi\rangle\langle\psi|\phi\rangle$$
$$\langle\psi|\phi\rangle = (\langle\psi|\phi\rangle)^2.$$

For $\langle\psi|\phi\rangle$ to be equal to its square, it must equal 0 or 1. Thus, $|\psi\rangle = |\phi\rangle$, or $|\psi\rangle$ and $|\phi\rangle$ are orthogonal. Thus, an operator can only clone states that are orthogonal.

Does there exist a quantum operator U that can clone both
(a) $|+\rangle$ and $|-\rangle$?
(b) $|i\rangle$ and $|-i\rangle$?
(c) $|0\rangle$ and $|+\rangle$?

4.5 Quantum Adders

In Section 1.3, after defining classical bits and logic gates, we demonstrated how to compute something: the sum of two binary numbers, each of length n. Now that we have defined qubits and quantum gates, let us also construct quantum circuits that add binary numbers. Before we do that, however, let us review the classical ripple-carry adder.

4.5.1 Classical Adder

First, to review, we can add two binary numbers as follows:

$$(\text{carry})\ 1\,1\,1\,0\,0$$
$$1011$$
$$\text{``+''}\ 1110$$
$$\overline{\phantom{\text{``+''}\ 1110}}$$
$$(\text{sum})\ 11001$$

Or, in terms of variables,

$$(\text{carry})\ c_4\,c_3\,c_2\,c_1\,c_0$$
$$a_3 a_2 a_1 a_0$$
$$\text{``+''}\ b_3 b_2 b_1 b_0$$
$$\overline{}$$
$$(\text{sum})\ s_4 s_3\,s_2\,s_1\,s_0$$

where the initial carry in is $c_0 = 0$. In general, if the binary numbers have length n, then the output has length $n + 1$.

Classically, we can add binary numbers using the ripple-carry adder from Section 1.3.5:

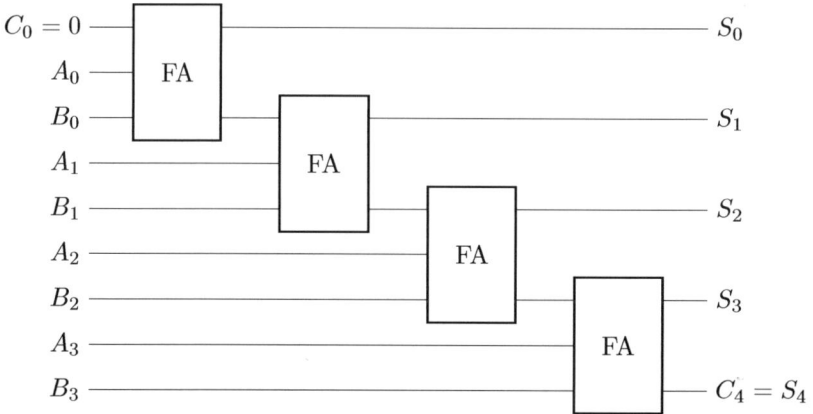

where FA denotes a full adder:

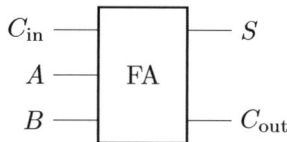

Each full adder has three inputs: a carry in C_{in} and two bits A and B. From these, it computes the sum $S = A \oplus B \oplus C_{\text{in}}$ and the carry out is $C_{\text{out}} = AB + C_{\text{in}}(A \oplus B)$.

4.5.2 *Making the Classical Adder a Quantum Gate*

This full adder is not reversible, since it does not have enough outputs to uniquely determine the inputs. So, it is not a quantum gate. There are several ways, however, to convert it to a quantum gate.

1. From Exercise 1.45, we can turn the full adder into a reversible circuit by taking the XOR of each of its outputs with and extra bit:

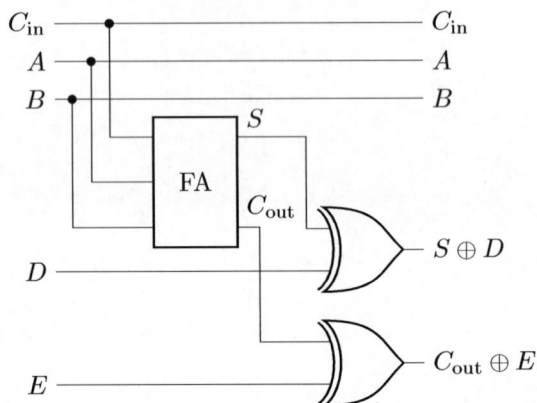

This entire circuit can be drawn as a single gate with five inputs and five outputs:

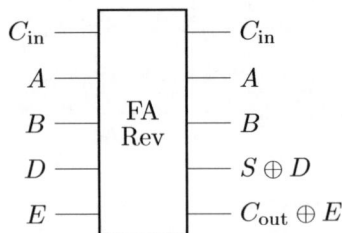

This gate is reversible, so it is a quantum gate. As we will discuss later in Section 4.6, it is always possible to break up a large quantum gate like this into the smaller gates we are familiar with, but it could take many smaller gates, and the best way to do this is an open area of research.

2. From Section 1.3.3, a full adder can be made from two XOR gates, two AND gates, and one OR gate:

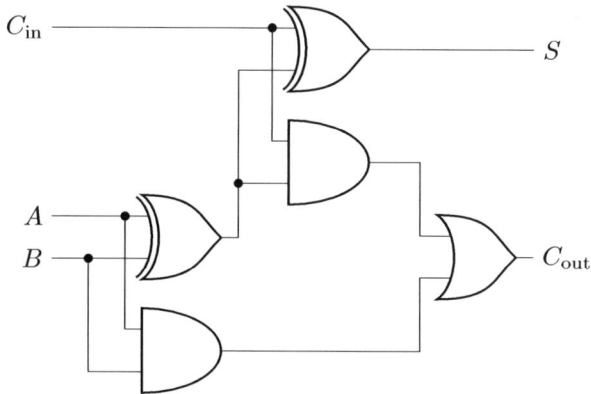

One approach is to replace all five of these logic gates with (more than five) NAND gates. Then, we can implement each NAND gate using a Toffoli gate, which is reversible and a quantum gate. While this works in principle, the procedure can be wasteful, leading to extra gates and qubits.

3. Adapting the previous method, instead of converting all the logic gates into NAND gates and then Toffoli gates, we convert each logic gate into a reversible/quantum gate more directly. The basic logic gates are NOT, AND, OR, XOR, NAND, and NOR. From Section 2.6.3, the X gate is simply the NOT gate. From Section 1.5.3, the Toffoli gate can implement AND and NAND by setting its third bit to 0 or 1, respectively. From Exercise 1.41, the anti-Toffoli gate can implement NOR and OR by setting its third bit to 0 or 1, respectively. From Exercise 4.16, two CNOT gates can be used to implement XOR. These results are summarized in the following table:

Classical	Reversible/Quantum
NOT $A \longrightarrow \overline{A}$	X-Gate $A -\boxed{X}- \overline{A}$
AND $\begin{matrix} A \\ B \end{matrix} \longrightarrow AB$	Toffoli $\begin{matrix} A \longrightarrow A \\ B \longrightarrow B \\ 0 \longrightarrow AB \end{matrix}$
OR $\begin{matrix} A \\ B \end{matrix} \longrightarrow A+B$	anti-Toffoli $\begin{matrix} A \longrightarrow A \\ B \longrightarrow B \\ 1 \longrightarrow A+B \end{matrix}$
XOR $\begin{matrix} A \\ B \end{matrix} \longrightarrow A \oplus B$	CNOTs $\begin{matrix} A \longrightarrow A \\ B \longrightarrow B \\ 0 \longrightarrow A \oplus B \end{matrix}$
NAND $\begin{matrix} A \\ B \end{matrix} \longrightarrow \overline{AB}$	Toffoli $\begin{matrix} A \longrightarrow A \\ B \longrightarrow B \\ 1 \longrightarrow \overline{AB} \end{matrix}$
NOR $\begin{matrix} A \\ B \end{matrix} \longrightarrow \overline{A+B}$	anti-Toffoli $\begin{matrix} A \longrightarrow A \\ B \longrightarrow B \\ 0 \longrightarrow \overline{A+B} \end{matrix}$

Replacing each gate in the full adder, we get the following circuit:

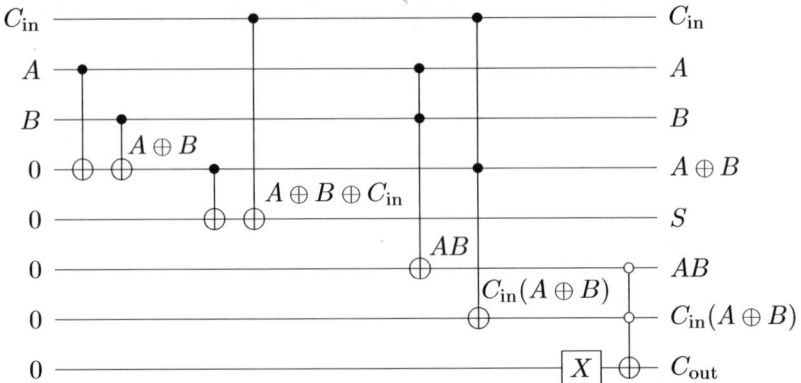

The first two CNOTs implement an XOR gate $(A \oplus B)$, and the next two CNOTs also implement an XOR gate, computing $A \oplus B \oplus C_{\text{in}} = S$. Next, the Toffoli gate implements an AND gate (AB), and another Toffoli gate implements another AND gate $[C_{\text{in}}(A \oplus B)]$. Finally, an X gate turns an extra bit from a 0 to a 1, and together with an anti-Toffoli gate, they implement an OR gate, yielding $AB + C_{\text{in}}(A \oplus B) = C_{\text{out}}$. Since these are all reversible gates, it is a quantum circuit.

Notice this method uses several extra bits. Besides the inputs (C_{in}, A, and B) and the outputs (S and C_{out}), three extra bits were used for intermediate calculations: $A \oplus B$, AB, and $C_{in}(A \oplus B)$. These extra bits are called *ancilla bits* or *ancillary bits*, and in quantum circuits, they should be cleaned up by turning them back into zeros. This is so they can be reused in later parts of a circuit and so that they do not cause unintended entanglement. One method for cleaning up ancillary bits is called *uncomputation*, where we apply in reverse order the inverses of the gates that were used to calculate the ancillas. Since the Toffoli and CNOT gates are their own inverses, the full adder becomes

Simulating in Quirk (see https://bit.ly/34BY6AD), we get

We see that with all three inputs C_{in}, A, and B set to 1, both the sum S and carry-out C_{out} are 1, as expected, and each of the three ancilla qubits correctly start and end in $|0\rangle$.

4. We can come up with a more clever implementation that uses fewer gates and bits. Let us do this over the next several sections.

4.5.3 Quantum Setup

Quantumly, we can encode the binary numbers in two *quantum registers* $|a\rangle$ and $|b\rangle$. One way to add them reversibly is to replace $|b\rangle$ with the sum:

$$|a\rangle|b\rangle \to |a\rangle|s\rangle,$$

where $s = a + b$. For example, using the quantum adder, $1011 + 1110 = 11001$, would be

$$|1011\rangle|01110\rangle \to |1011\rangle|11001\rangle.$$

By adding this way, it is always possible to determine the inputs: a is the left register, and b can be obtained by subtracting a from s. Since the sum can have length $n + 1$, this means our second register needs an extra qubit $|b_n\rangle$ that is initially $|0\rangle$:

$$|a\rangle = |a_{n-1}\rangle \ldots |a_1\rangle|a_0\rangle,$$
$$|b\rangle = |b_n = 0\rangle|b_{n-1}\rangle \ldots |b_1\rangle|b_0\rangle.$$

where $s = a + b$.

In the intermediate steps of the computation, the quantum adder also needs to keep track of carry bits, so we also have a quantum register of length n for the carry bits:

$$|c\rangle = |c_{n-1}\rangle \ldots |c_1\rangle|c_0\rangle.$$

Initially, this ancillary carry register contains all zeros, and at the end of our computation, we should restore them to all zeros. Putting these together, we want our quantum adder to map

$$|a\rangle|b\rangle|c\rangle \to |a\rangle|s\rangle|c\rangle.$$

4.5.4 Quantum Sum

Since $\mathrm{CNOT}|a\rangle|b\rangle = |a\rangle|a \oplus b\rangle$, we can implement the sum using two CNOTs:

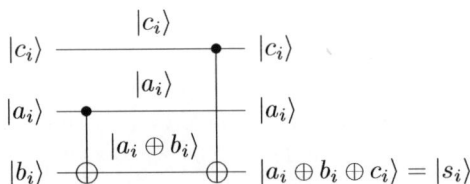

In the above circuit, the first CNOT turns $|b_i\rangle$ into $|a_i \oplus b_i\rangle$, and the second turns it into $|a_i \oplus b_i \oplus c_i\rangle$, which is $|s_i\rangle$: We can combine this into a single quantum gate:

$$
\begin{array}{c}
|c_i\rangle \quad\longrightarrow\quad |c_i\rangle \\[4pt]
|a_i\rangle \quad\boxed{S}\quad |a_i\rangle \\[4pt]
|b_i\rangle \quad\longrightarrow\quad |a_i \oplus b_i \oplus c_i\rangle = |s_i\rangle
\end{array}
$$

There are also several ways to create custom gates in Quirk. One way is to first create the sum by dragging and dropping controls and X gates:

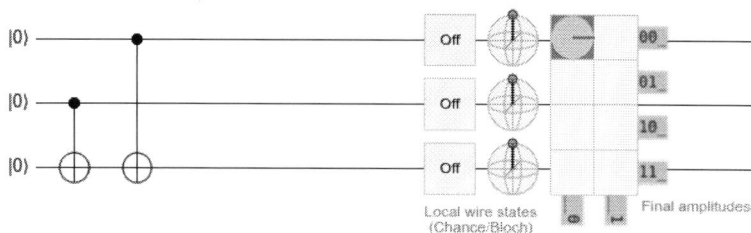

Next, we can click on the "Make Gate" button at the top of the page. A dialog box will pop up with different options, and we want to create a gate from the circuit we just drew:

We can either turn the whole circuit into a gate, or we can just select the first two columns (1:2). Let us also name the gate "S." If we click "Create Circuit Gate," we return to the main screen, and now our gate appears at the bottom right toolbar under "Custom Gates:"

Custom Gates

We can drag this onto the main circuit like any other gate:

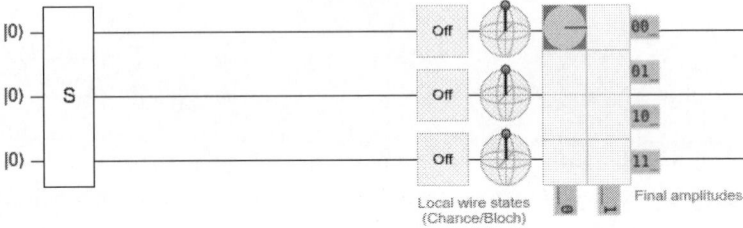

By changing the initial state of the qubits to $|1\rangle$, we can also test the circuit to verify that it adds correctly.

4.5.5 Quantum Carry

Recall from Exercise 1.30) that the OR gate that is used to calculate C_{out} can be replaced by an XOR gate. That is,

$$C_{\text{out}} = AB \oplus C_{\text{in}}(A \oplus B).$$

To implement this, recall the Toffoli gate is

$$\text{Toffoli}|a\rangle|b\rangle|c\rangle = |a\rangle|b\rangle|ab \oplus c\rangle.$$

This allows us to create the AND of A and B, XORed with C. Then, a quantum carry circuit is

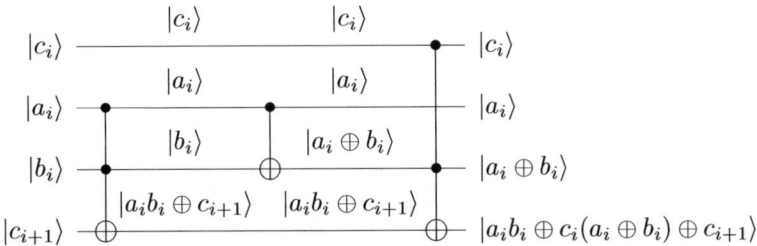

In the above circuit, when $c_{i+1} = 0$, this carry gate transforms it to $a_i b_i \oplus c_i(a_i \oplus b_i)$, which is precisely C_{out}. Combining all this into a single quantum gate,

$|c_i\rangle$ ——[ ]—— $|c_i\rangle$

$|a_i\rangle$ ——[C]—— $|a_i\rangle$

$|b_i\rangle$ ——[ ]—— $|a_i \oplus b_i\rangle$

$|c_{i+1}\rangle$ ——[ ]—— $|a_i b_i \oplus c_i(a_i \oplus b_i) \oplus c_{i+1}\rangle$

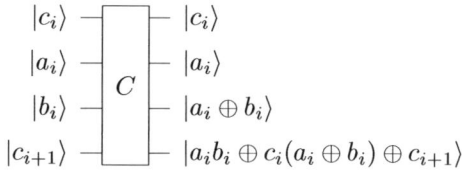

Note in the third row that $b_i \to a_i \oplus b_i$, so we will need to uncompute this later.

4.5.6 Quantum Ripple-Carry Adder

Now, let us construct a quantum adder that was proposed by Vedral, Barenco, and Ekert in 1996. We order the wires to alternate between c_i, a_i, and b_i:

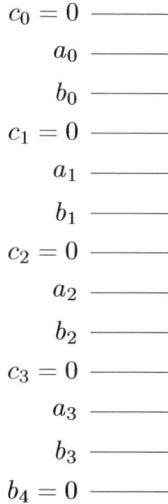

$$c_0 = 0 \ \text{———}$$
$$a_0 \ \text{———}$$
$$b_0 \ \text{———}$$
$$c_1 = 0 \ \text{———}$$
$$a_1 \ \text{———}$$
$$b_1 \ \text{———}$$
$$c_2 = 0 \ \text{———}$$
$$a_2 \ \text{———}$$
$$b_2 \ \text{———}$$
$$c_3 = 0 \ \text{———}$$
$$a_3 \ \text{———}$$
$$b_3 \ \text{———}$$
$$b_4 = 0 \ \text{———}$$

For the first operation, we can either calculate the sum s_0 using our sum circuit S, or we can calculate the carry c_1 using our carry circuit C. If we begin by calculating s_0, then we no longer have b_0, but we need b_0 to calculate the carry c_1. So, let us calculate the carry first:

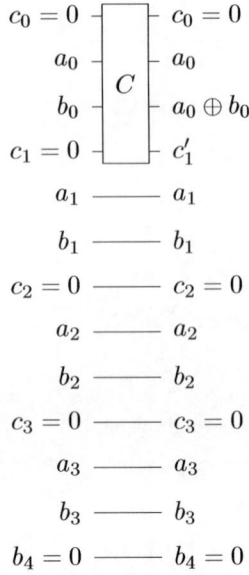

Now that we have c_1', we can either add it to a_1 and b_1, or we can calculate the carry c_2'. Again, if we add first, then we no longer have b_1 to calculate the carry. So, let us calculate the next carry, and repeating this argument, we calculate all the carries:

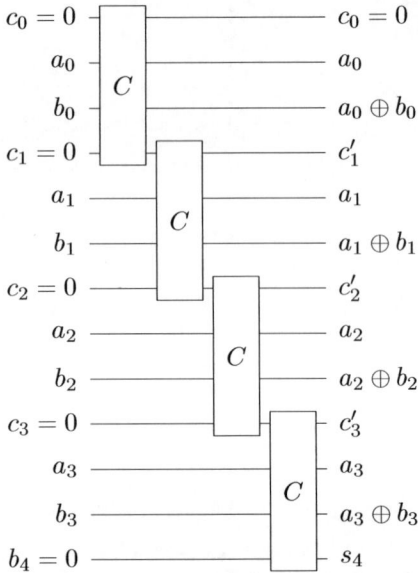

Note the last carry corresponds to the leftmost bit of the sum s_4. Now, to calculate s_3 using our sum circuit S, we need the inputs to be c_3', a_3, and b_3, but currently the third input is $a_3 \oplus b_3$. To make this third input simply b_3, we CNOT a_3 with it, resulting in $a_3 \oplus (a_3 \oplus b_3) = (a_3 \oplus a_3) \oplus b_3 = 0 \oplus b_3 = b_3$:

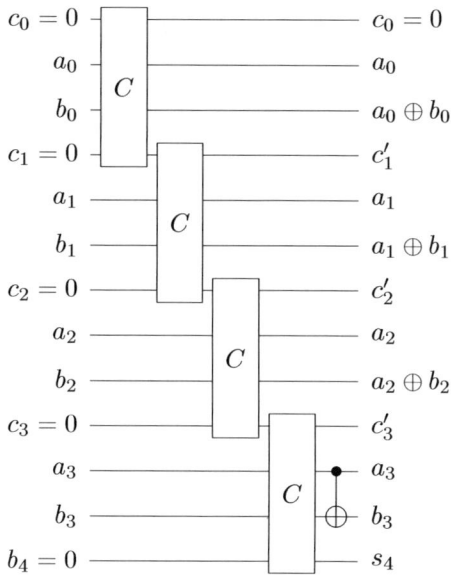

Now, we can use our sum circuit S to calculate b_3:

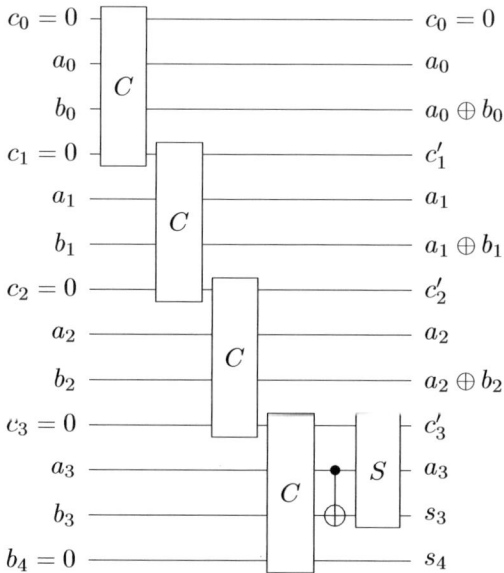

Next, we need to undo c'_3 so that we just have $c_3 = 0$. We can do this by inverting the carry gate:

Note since C is a quantum gate, it is unitary, so its inverse is equal to its conjugate transpose (i.e., $C^{-1} = C^{\dagger}$). Applying this,

This also converted $a_2 \oplus b_2$ back to b_2, so we can again use the sum circuit to find $s_2 = a_2 \oplus b_2 \oplus c_2'$:

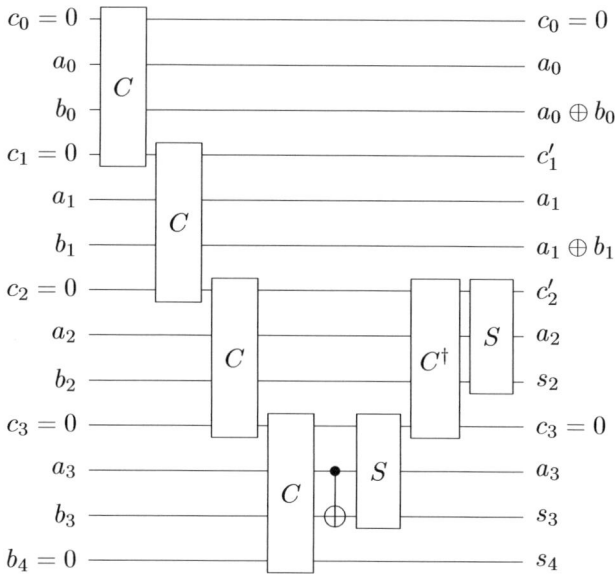

Repeating this process, we can apply $C^\dagger$ to convert c_2' back to $c_2 = 0$ and $a_1 \oplus b_1$ back to b_1, and then use the sum circuit to compute s_1, and so forth, resulting in the following complete circuit:

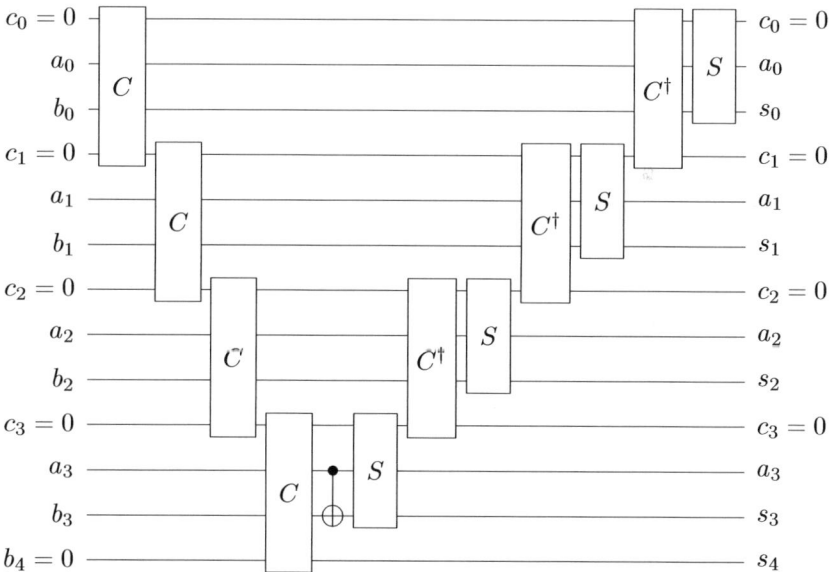

This is our quantum ripple-carry adder, and $|b\rangle$ has been replaced by $|s\rangle$ (while keeping $|a\rangle$ and $|c\rangle$ unchanged), as we wanted.

Note the qubits in this circuit have a different order. Rather than taking

$$|a\rangle|b\rangle|c\rangle \to |a\rangle|s\rangle|c\rangle,$$

our circuit takes

$$|b_4\rangle|b_3\rangle|a_3\rangle|c_3\rangle|b_2\rangle|a_2\rangle|c_2\rangle|b_1\rangle|a_1\rangle|c_1\rangle|b_0\rangle|a_0\rangle|c_0\rangle$$

to

$$|s_4\rangle|s_3\rangle|a_3\rangle|c_3\rangle|s_2\rangle|a_2\rangle|c_2\rangle|s_1\rangle|a_1\rangle|c_1\rangle|s_0\rangle|a_0\rangle|c_0\rangle.$$

Let us verify our quantum circuit in Quirk by adding $|a\rangle = |1011\rangle$ and $|b\rangle = |01110\rangle$, which should result in $|s\rangle = |11001\rangle$. With the qubit ordering from above, where all the carry qubits are $|0\rangle$ at the start and end of the computation, the quantum ripple-carry adder should take

$$|0110100110010\rangle \rightarrow |1110000010110\rangle.$$

You can view the circuit in Quirk by going to https://bit.ly/39NzEf9. It is also shown below:

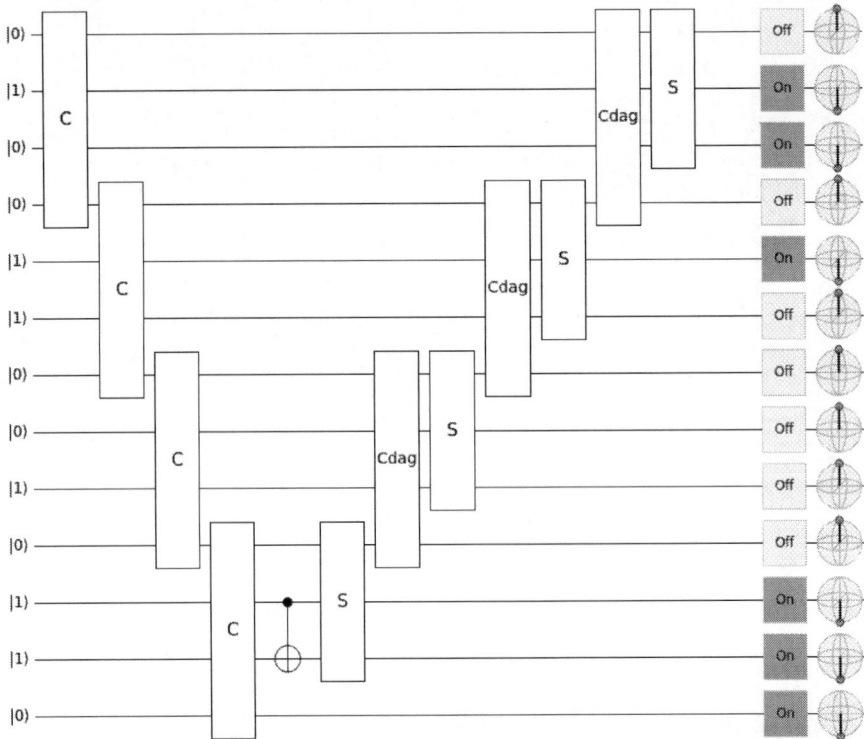

We see that with the input $|0110100110010\rangle$, the output is $|1110000010110\rangle$, as expected.

Exercise 4.26. Simulate the quantum ripple-carry adder in Quirk, and use it to add $1111 + 1011$.

Exercise 4.27. We can use an adder to subtract binary numbers by using the fact that

$$a - b = \overline{\overline{a} + b}.$$

In Quirk, modify your circuit from Exercise 4.26 to subtract $1111 - 1011$. Do this by adding X gates to each bit of the input a (this gives $\bar{a}$). Then, the adder computes $\bar{a} + b$. Then, add X gates to each bit of s, except for the extra bit s_4, since it is not needed and should stay 0. This gives $\overline{\bar{a} + b}$.

Exercise 4.28. While teaching a course on quantum computing in Fall 2018, one of my Creighton University students, Lorenzo Riva, proposed the following change to the quantum ripple-carry adder:

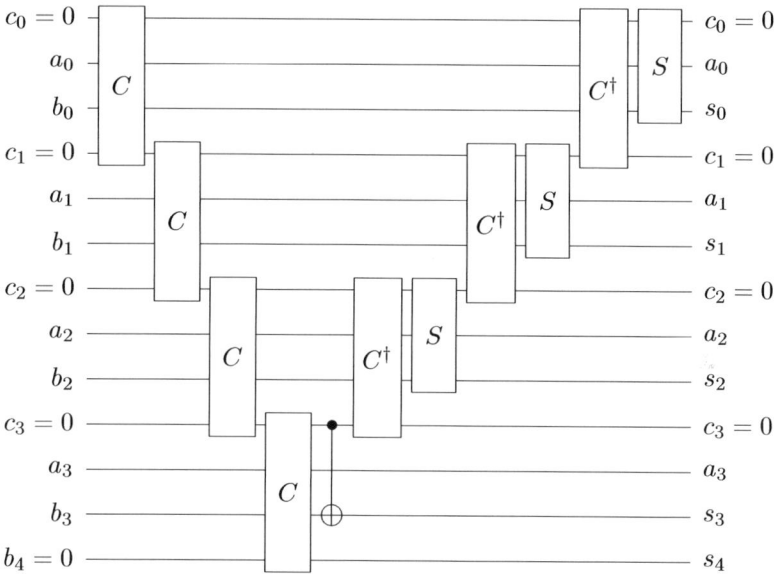

That is, the CNOT between a_3 and b_3, and the bottommost S (sum, not the $S = \sqrt{Z}$ gate), can be replaced by a single CNOT between c_3 and b_3.

(a) Explain why this simplification is correct.

(b) If each binary number has length n, how many Toffoli gates and how many CNOT gates does this circuit use?

Exercise 4.29. In this exercise, we will learn about another quantum adder that does not need carry bits. It is called *Draper's adder*, and it uses the "quantum Fourier transform," which will be discussed later in the textbook in Section 7.7.3.

First, let us define a single-qubit gate R_r that rotates about the z-axis of the Bloch sphere by angle $360°/2^r$. For example, $R_1 = Z$ is a rotation by $180°$, $R_2 = S$ is a rotation by $90°$, $R_3 = T$ is a rotation by $45°$, and R_4 is a rotation by $22.5°$. Rotations about axes can be created in Quirk using the "Make Gate" feature, e.g., R_4 is

From Rotation

z	axis
22.5	° angle
0	° global phase

| R4 | circuit symbol |

Create Rotation Gate

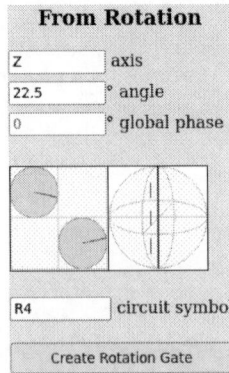

We also have the conjugate transpose (or inverse) of the rotation, which we denote $R_r^\dagger$, and it rotates about the z-axis by $-360°/2^r$. For example, $R_4^\dagger$ rotates by $-22.5°$, and since it is a negative angle, it rotates the "other way."

Draper's quantum adder transforms

$$|a\rangle|b\rangle \to |a+b\rangle|b\rangle,$$

and it does not use any carry qubits. Instead of using the ripple-carry adder, The circuit for the adder is a little long, so we break it up over three parts:

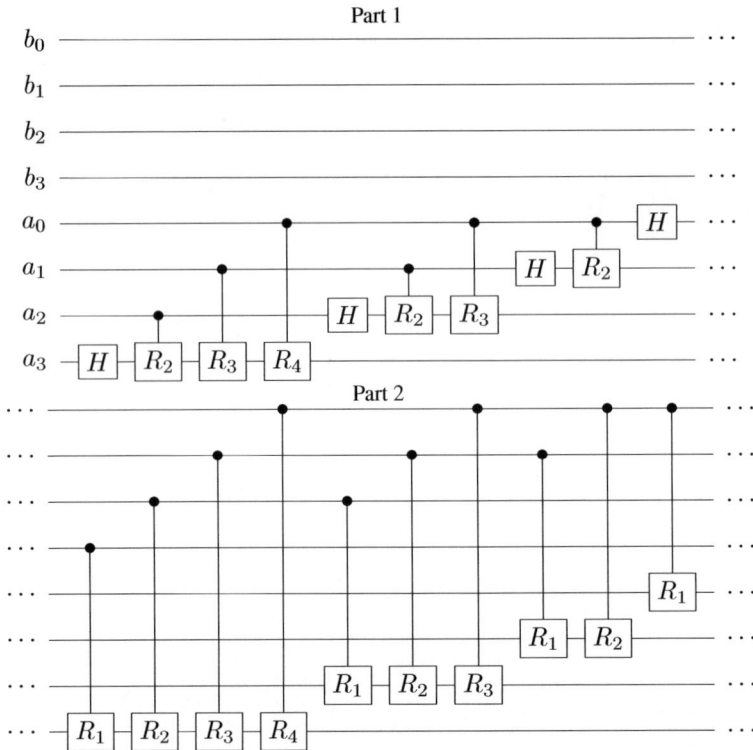

Part 1

Part 2

Part 3

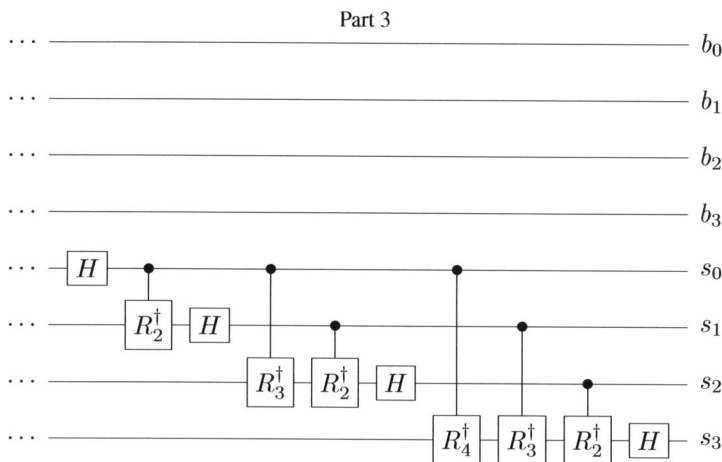

Implement Draper's adder in Quirk and use it to add $|a\rangle = |0111\rangle$ and $|b\rangle = |0011\rangle$.

4.5.7 Circuit Complexity

Generalizing this, adding two n-bit strings uses n carry gates C, $n-1$ inverses of the carry gate $C^\dagger$, n sum gates S, and an extra CNOT gate. Each C and $C^\dagger$ gate uses two Toffoli gates and one CNOT gate, and each S gate uses two CNOT gates. The total number of quantum gates to add two n-bit strings is summarized in the following table:

Gate	No. of Gates	Total No. of Toffolis	Total No. of CNOTs
C	n	$2n$	n
$C^\dagger$	$n-1$	$2(n-1)$	$n-1$
S	n	0	$2n$
Extra CNOT	1	0	1
		$4n-2$	$4n$

Altogether, the quantum ripple-carry adder uses $4n-2$ Toffoli gates and $4n$ CNOT gates, which is linear in n, i.e., $\Theta(n)$, so the algorithm is efficient.

Exercise 4.30. How many Toffoli gates and how many CNOT gates does the quantum ripple-carry adder need to add two (a) 4-bit strings, (b) 8-bit strings.

Exercise 4.31. To add two binary numbers of length 4, our quantum ripple-carry adder used 13 qubits. How many qubits does the quantum ripple-carry adder need to add two binary numbers of length n?

4.5.8 *Adding in Superposition*

Note our quantum ripple-carry adder is a quantum circuit, so it can also act on superpositions. For example, if $|a\rangle$ is an equal superposition of 6 and 3, i.e.,

$$|a\rangle = \frac{1}{\sqrt{2}}\left(|0110\rangle + |0011\rangle\right),$$

and if $|b\rangle$ is 11, then

$$|b\rangle = |01011\rangle,$$

then the quantum ripple-carry adder turns $|a\rangle|b\rangle$ into

$$\frac{1}{\sqrt{2}}\left(|0110\rangle|10001\rangle + |0011\rangle|01110\rangle\right).$$

It may appear as though we solved two addition problems at once, i.e., in "parallel," since both $6 + 11 = 17$ and $3 + 11 = 14$ appear in the answers as $|10001\rangle$ and $|01110\rangle$, respectively, but this is not the case. When we measure the result, we get one sum with probability $1/2$ or the other sum with probability $1/2$. In contrast, in parallel computing, two computers calculate both answers at the same time, so we get both sums at the end.

It is incorrect to think of a quantum computer as a massively parallel classical computer because we must measure and only get one result. In fact, this misunderstanding is so common that it might be best to avoid the term "parallel" altogether when describing quantum computing.

We have seen our first quantum algorithm: the ripple-carry adder. We will get to many more quantum algorithms in Chapter 7, but there are several other topics to cover first.

Exercise 4.32. Read "Quantum Computing: A Soccer Analogy" at

```
https://medium.com/@thomaswong_8663/quantum-computing-a-soccer-a
                    nalogy-1335644a1472
```

Answer the following questions and fill in the blanks.
 (a) Who is the author of the article, and what is their relationship with the author of this textbook?
 (b) "Analogously, the essence of quantum computing is to change the rules so that a computer can now use its "_____." That is, the rules of the game are changed from the laws of classical physics to the laws of _____ physics. As a result, a quantum computer can solve _____ problems faster by using its "hands." For other problems, using one's "feet" is better, so a quantum computer is _____ _____ for these problems."

4.6 Universal Quantum Gates

4.6.1 Definition

A set of quantum gates that allows us to approximate any quantum gate to any desired precision is called a *universal gate set*. Recall in Section 1.2.5 that we used the same term to describe a set of logic gates that can reproduce all classical gates. It is usually clear from the context. For example, if the Hadamard gate is involved, then we must be discussing quantum gates because there is no classical Hadamard gate. Or, we might describe a set as "universal for classical computing" or "universal for quantum computing."

Proving that a set of gates is universal is a more advanced topic, which we do not discuss in this textbook. Nielsen and Chuang is a good resource for additional details. Instead, we provide some intuition below.

4.6.2 Components of a Universal Gate Set

There are several components that we need for a set of quantum gates to be universal.

1. Superposition. We must be able to produce superpositions. For example the Hadamard gate can create superpositions, such as $H|0\rangle = |+\rangle$. Other gates are not. Z, S, and T only apply phases; they do not create superpositions of $|0\rangle$ and $|1\rangle$. Similarly, the X and CNOT gates only flip $|0\rangle$ and $|1\rangle$, so they cannot create superpositions. Y only applies phases and flips, so again superpositions cannot be created by it.

2. Entanglement. We must be able to entangle qubits. One-qubit gates, such as H, cannot do this since they only act on a single qubit. A gate must act on at least two qubits to produce entanglement. CNOT can produce entanglement since $\text{CNOT}|+\rangle|0\rangle = |\Phi^+\rangle$. Not all two qubit gates produce entanglement, however. The SWAP gate cannot generate entanglement since it only swaps two qubits.

3. Complex amplitudes. CNOT and H only contain real numbers, so they do not produce states with complex amplitudes.

Just because a set of gates contains these properties does not mean it is universal. For example, consider $\{\text{CNOT}, H, S\}$. Although this set satisfies all of the previous requirements (entanglement, superposition, and complex amplitudes), the *Gottesman-Knill theorem* says that a quantum circuit containing only these gates is efficiently simulated by a classical computer.

Introducing some terminology, the set of gates that can be constructed using, or *generated* by, $\{\text{CNOT}, H, S\}$ is called the *Clifford group*[1] Then, the set

---

[1] Mathematically, the Clifford group is the normalizer of the Pauli group, which is generated by the Pauli matrices.

$\{$CNOT$,H,S\}$ is called a *Clifford group generator*. Thus, a universal quantum gate set should generate more than the Clifford group:

4. Generate more than the Clifford group.

It is unknown if a set of quantum gates that generates superposition, entanglement, complex amplitudes, and more than the Clifford group must be universal. It may be that a set satisfies all four of these properties, but is still not universal.

Exercise 4.33. What property are each of the following gate sets lacking to be universal for quantum computing?
(a) $\{$Toffoli$,H,Z\}$.
(b) $\{H,X,Y,Z,S,T\}$.
(c) $\{$SWAP$,H,S,T\}$.

4.6.3 Examples of Universal Gate Sets

Some examples of universal gate sets are:

- $\{$CNOT$,$all single-qubit gates$\}$ is universal for quantum computing.[2]
- $\{$CNOT$,H,T\}$ is universal for quantum computing.[3] That is, although the Clifford group generator $\{$CNOT$,H,S\}$ is *not* universal for quantum computing, replacing S with T does yield a universal gate set. H and T are sufficient to approximate all one-qubit gates.
- $\{$CNOT$,R_{\pi/8},S\}$ is universal for quantum computing, where

$$R_{\pi/8} = \begin{pmatrix} \cos\left(\frac{\pi}{8}\right) & -\sin\left(\frac{\pi}{8}\right) \\ \sin\left(\frac{\pi}{8}\right) & \cos\left(\frac{\pi}{8}\right) \end{pmatrix}.$$

Although the Clifford group generator $\{$CNOT$,H,S\}$ is *not* universal for quantum computing, replacing H with $R_{\pi/8}$ does yield a universal gate set.
- $\{$Toffoli$,H,S\}$ is universal for quantum computing.[4] Although $\{$CNOT$,H,S\}$ is *not* universal for quantum computing, replacing CNOT with Toffoli does yield a universal gate set.
- H plus almost any two-qubit unitary.

Exercise 4.34. The Clifford group generator $\{$CNOT$,H,S\}$ is *not* universal for quantum computing. Give three ways to modify the it so that it is universal for quantum computing.

---

[2] A. Barenco, C. H. Bennett, R. Cleve, D. P. DiVincenzo, N. H. Margolus, P. W. Shor, T. Sleator, J. A. Smolin, and H. Weinfurter. Elementary gates for quantum computation. Phys. Rev. A 52, 3457 (1995).
[3] P. O. Boykin, T. Mor, M. Pulver, V. Roychowdhury, and F. Vatan. A new universal and fault-tolerant quantum basis. Information Processing Letters, 75, 101 (2000).
[4] A. Y. Kitaev. Quantum computations: Algorithms and error correction. RMS: Russian Mathematical Surveys 52, 1191 (1997).

4.6.4 Solovay-Kitaev Theorem

The *Solovay-Kitaev theorem* says that with any universal gate set, we can approximate a quantum gate on n qubits to precision ε using $\Theta(2^n \log^c(1/\varepsilon))$ gates for some constant c. The dependence on the number of qubits 2^n is what we might expect since an operator on n qubits is a matrix of $2^n \times 2^n$ entries. The dependence on the precision $\log^c(1/\varepsilon)$ is great! The precision ε is the "distance" (in some measurement or *metric*) that the approximate quantum gate is to the actual quantum gate, and we want it to be small. So $1/\varepsilon$ is big, but taking the logarithm of it makes it small. A logarithm to a constant power, such as $\log^c$, is a polynomial of a logarithm, so is also called *polylog*. This is also considered small. Thus, this dependence means our approximation quickly converges on the actual quantum gate.

4.6.5 Quantum Computing without Complex Numbers

Recall any complex number z has a real part x and an imaginary part y, i.e., $z = x + iy$. Since x and y are real numbers, this means we can express any complex number as two real numbers (x, y) and keep track of the fact that they play different roles. So in theory, we can formulate all of quantum computing just in terms of real numbers. Then, a universal set of quantum gates technically does not need to produce states with complex amplitudes. For example, the following sets are also universal for quantum computing:

- {Toffoli, any single-qubit gate that is basis-changing} is universal for quantum computing.[5] A gate is *basis-changing* if it changes the Z-basis $\{|0\rangle, |1\rangle\}$ to another basis. For example, H is basis-changing, since it changes between the Z-basis $\{|0\rangle, |1\rangle\}$ and the X-basis $\{|+\rangle, |-\rangle\}$, so {Toffoli, H} is universal for quantum computing. In contrast, Z is not basis-changing since $Z|0\rangle = |0\rangle$ and $Z|1\rangle = -|1\rangle \equiv |1\rangle$.
  As Dorit Aharonov said, "This is perhaps the simplest universal set of gates that one can hope for [...] It shows that one only needs to add the Hadamard gate to make a 'classical' set of gates quantum universal."[6]
- The controlled-Hadamard gate {CH} is universal for quantum computing.[7] In this gate, H is applied to the right qubit if the left qubit is 1. That is, it acts on Z-basis states as

---

[5] Y. Shi, Both Toffoli and controlled-NOT need little help to do universal quantum computation, arXiv:quant-ph/0205115 (2002).

[6] D. Aharonov, A Simple Proof that Toffoli and Hadamard are Quantum Universal, arXiv:quant-ph/0301040 (2003).

[7] D. J. Shepherd, T. Franz, and R. F. Werner, Universally Programmable Quantum Cellular Automaton, Phys. Rev. Lett. 97, 020502 (2006).

$$CH|00\rangle = |00\rangle,$$
$$CH|01\rangle = |01\rangle,$$
$$CH|10\rangle = |1+\rangle = \frac{1}{\sqrt{2}}\left(|10\rangle + |11\rangle\right),$$
$$CH|11\rangle = |1-\rangle = \frac{1}{\sqrt{2}}\left(|10\rangle - |11\rangle\right).$$

This can simulate both the Toffoli gate and the Hadamard gate, so from the previous bullet, it is universal.

- {CNOT, any single-qubit gate whose square is basis-changing} is universal for quantum computing.[8] An example of a single-qubit gate whose square is basis-changing is the following gate U:

$$U|0\rangle = \frac{\sqrt{3}}{2}|0\rangle + \frac{1}{2}|1\rangle,$$
$$U|1\rangle = \frac{-1}{2}|0\rangle + \frac{\sqrt{3}}{2}|1\rangle.$$

Next, if we apply U again, meaning twice to the Z-basis states, we get

$$U^2|0\rangle = U\left(\frac{\sqrt{3}}{2}|0\rangle + \frac{1}{2}|1\rangle\right) = \frac{1}{2}|0\rangle + \frac{\sqrt{3}}{2}|1\rangle,$$
$$U^2|1\rangle = U\left(\frac{-1}{2}|0\rangle + \frac{\sqrt{3}}{2}|1\rangle\right) = \frac{-\sqrt{3}}{2}|0\rangle + \frac{1}{2}|1\rangle.$$

This is an orthonormal basis, so U^2 is basis-changing. CNOT and U together form a universal set of quantum gates.

In contrast, the square of the Hadamard gate is not basis-changing because applying the Hadamard gate twice does nothing:

$$H^2|0\rangle = |0\rangle,$$
$$H^2|1\rangle = |1\rangle.$$

So, {CNOT, H} is *not* universal, whereas from the first bullet point, {Toffoli, H} is universal.

---

[8] Y. Shi (2002).

4.7 Quantum Error Correction

4.7.1 Decoherence

Recall a qubit can be represented by a point on the Bloch sphere:

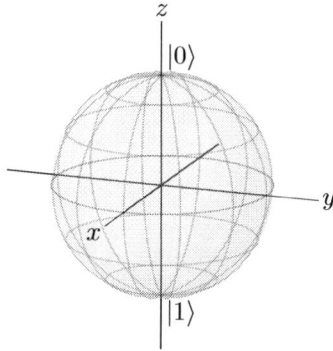

The north pole corresponds to $|0\rangle$ and the south pole corresponds to $|1\rangle$. For a classical bit, these would be the only possible states, and the only error is for the bit to completely flip between the north and south poles. For a qubit, however, every location on the Bloch sphere is a different state. For example, beginning at $|0\rangle$, instead of completely flipping to $|1\rangle$, a qubit could experience a partial *bit flip error*, where it only rotates a little toward $|1\rangle$:

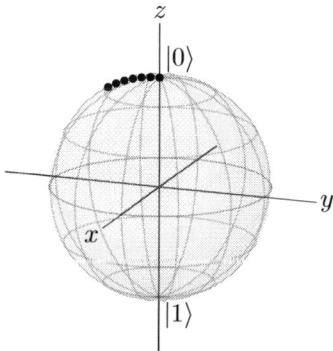

Since a full bit flip corresponds to the X gate, and the X gate is a rotation about the x-axis by $\pi = 180°$, a partial bit flip corresponds to rotating about the x-axis by some angle. So, in the above figure, the state is moving leftward, down the Bloch sphere, in the yz-plane. This small change is an error.

To further complicate matters, a qubit's state is not just its latitude up and down the Bloch sphere, but also its longitude around the Bloch sphere. For example, if a qubit initially in the $|+\rangle$ state gets bumped to the side, we get a different state:

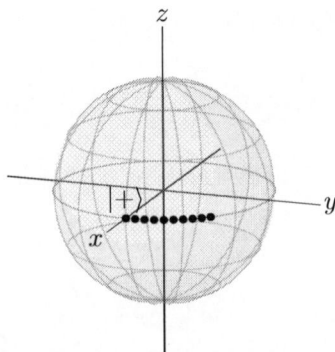

This is called a *phase flip error*, because rotations around the z-axis correspond changes in the relative phase. For example, $|+\rangle = (|0\rangle + |1\rangle)/\sqrt{2}$ and $|-\rangle = (|0\rangle - |1\rangle)/\sqrt{2}$ lie on opposite sides of the equator.

Since qubits are more sensitive to errors than classical bits, small interactions with the environment can move the qubit to a different location on the Bloch sphere. This process is called *decoherence*. In practice, decoherence is the biggest obstacle to building large-scale quantum computers, since it is very difficult to isolate a qubit from its environment while making it accessible for quantum gates and measurements.

Next, we will see how to correct for bit-flip errors and then phase-flip errors. Then, we will combine both types of error correction into what is known as the *Shor code*.

4.7.2 Bit-Flip Code

To make it possible to correct bit-flip errors, we use three physical qubits to encode each logical qubit:

$$|0_L\rangle = |000\rangle, \quad |1_L\rangle = |111\rangle,$$

where subscript L denotes a logical qubit. A logical qubit is, in general, a superposition of $|0_L\rangle$ and $|1_L\rangle$:

$$\alpha|0_L\rangle + \beta|1_L\rangle = \alpha|000\rangle + \beta|111\rangle.$$

A way to create this encoding is given in Exercise 4.35.

For the moment, let us first consider the case where a bit is completely flipped ($\varepsilon = 1$). For example, say the left qubit flips, so

$$\alpha|000\rangle + \beta|111\rangle \rightarrow \alpha|100\rangle + \beta|011\rangle$$
$$= \beta|011\rangle + \alpha|100\rangle.$$

We would like to detect this error and correct it. Classically, we could just measure the bits, see which one disagrees with the others, and then flip it back to correct it. Quantumly, however, if we measure the bits (or even just a single bit), the state collapses to $|100\rangle$ or $|011\rangle$, and we lose the superposition. So, instead of measuring the bits, we follow Section 1.6.3 and measure the parity of adjacent qubits. Recall that the parity of two bits, a and b, can be calculated using Exclusive OR. That is, $\text{parity}(a,b) = a \oplus b$. Also recall that $\text{CNOT}|a\rangle|b\rangle = |a\rangle|a \oplus b\rangle$. Then, we can use two CNOTs to calculate the parity of two qubits, putting the answer in an ancilla qubit:

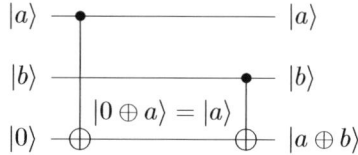

With three qubits, we can calculate the parities of adjacent qubits by doing this twice:

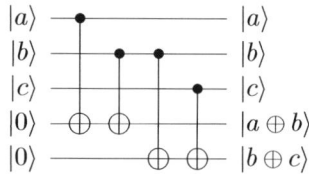

In this example, the parity of the left two qubits is 1, and the parity of the right two qubits is 0. This tells us that the left two qubits differ, and the right two qubits are the same. Then, we know the left qubit has flipped, and we inferred this without directly measuring and collapsing the state. This is called an *error syndrome*. To correct the error, we can simply apply $(X \otimes I \otimes I)$, which results in $\beta|111\rangle + \alpha|000\rangle = \alpha|000\rangle + \beta|111\rangle$, thus correcting the error.

Now, say there is a partial flip. In Section 2.6.4, it was stated that on the Bloch sphere, a rotation by angle θ about the axis $\hat{n} = (n_x, n_y, n_z)$ is given by Eq. (2.10):

$$e^{i\alpha} \left[\cos\left(\frac{\theta}{2}\right) I - i\sin\left(\frac{\theta}{2}\right) (n_x X + n_y Y + n_z Z) \right], \qquad \text{(2.10 revisited)}$$

where $e^{i\alpha}$ is a global phase, so α can be chosen as we please. Now, a partial bit flip corresponds to a rotation about the x-axis by some angle θ, so we have $\hat{n} = (1,0,0)$. We also choose $\alpha = \pi/2$. Then, the rotation corresponds to

$$i\cos\left(\frac{\theta}{2}\right) I + \sin\left(\frac{\theta}{2}\right) X.$$

Letting $\varepsilon = \sin(\theta/2)$, we get $\cos(\theta/2) = \sqrt{1 - \sin^2(\theta/2)} = \sqrt{1 - \varepsilon^2}$, so the rotation is

$$i\sqrt{1-\varepsilon^2}I + \varepsilon X = i\sqrt{1-\varepsilon^2}\begin{pmatrix}1 & 0\\ 0 & 1\end{pmatrix} + \varepsilon\begin{pmatrix}0 & 1\\ 1 & 0\end{pmatrix}$$

$$= \begin{pmatrix}i\sqrt{1-\varepsilon^2} & \varepsilon\\ \varepsilon & i\sqrt{1-\varepsilon^2}\end{pmatrix}.$$

Thus, the partial bit flip maps

$$|0\rangle \to i\sqrt{1-\varepsilon^2}|0\rangle + \varepsilon|1\rangle,$$
$$|1\rangle \to \varepsilon|0\rangle + i\sqrt{1-\varepsilon^2}|1\rangle.$$

When $\theta = \pi$, $\varepsilon = 1$, and we get $|0\rangle \to |1\rangle$ and $|1\rangle \to |0\rangle$, which is a complete bit flip, or the X gate.

For example, if the left qubit partially flips,

$$\alpha|000\rangle + \beta|111\rangle \to \alpha\left(i\sqrt{1-\varepsilon^2}|000\rangle + \varepsilon|100\rangle\right) + \beta\left(i\sqrt{1-\varepsilon^2}|111\rangle + \varepsilon|011\rangle\right)$$

$$= \alpha i\sqrt{1-\varepsilon^2}|000\rangle + \alpha\varepsilon|100\rangle + \beta i\sqrt{1-\varepsilon^2}|111\rangle + \beta\varepsilon|011\rangle$$

$$= \alpha i\sqrt{1-\varepsilon^2}|000\rangle + \beta\varepsilon|011\rangle + \alpha\varepsilon|100\rangle + \beta i\sqrt{1-\varepsilon^2}|111\rangle.$$

Now, we measure the parity of adjacent qubits. Labeling the qubits $|q_2 q_1 q_0\rangle$, we get the following possible outcomes with corresponding probabilities:

- parity$(q_2, q_1) = 0$ and parity$(q_1, q_0) = 0$ with probability

$$\left|\alpha i\sqrt{1-\varepsilon^2}\right|^2 + \left|\beta i\sqrt{1-\varepsilon^2}\right|^2 = |\alpha|^2(1-\varepsilon^2) + |\beta|^2(1-\varepsilon^2)$$

$$= \left(|\alpha|^2 + |\beta|^2\right)(1-\varepsilon^2)$$

$$= 1 - \varepsilon^2,$$

and the state collapses to

$$A\left(\alpha i\sqrt{1-\varepsilon^2}|000\rangle + \beta i\sqrt{1-\varepsilon^2}|111\rangle\right) = \alpha|000\rangle + \beta|111\rangle,$$

where $A = 1/i\sqrt{1-\varepsilon^2}$ is a normalization constant. We see that the resulting state is already corrected, so we do not need to do anything further to correct the error. That is, the measurement fixed the error.

- parity$(q_2, q_1) = 1$ and parity$(q_1, q_0) = 0$ with probability

$$|\beta\varepsilon|^2 + |\alpha\varepsilon|^2 = |\alpha|^2|\varepsilon|^2 + |\beta|^2|\varepsilon|^2$$

$$= \left(|\alpha|^2 + |\beta|^2\right)|\varepsilon|^2$$

$$= |\varepsilon|^2,$$

and the state collapses to

$$B\left(\beta\varepsilon|011\rangle + \alpha\varepsilon|100\rangle\right) = \beta|011\rangle + \alpha|100\rangle,$$

where $B = 1/\varepsilon$ is a normalization constant. To correct this state, we apply $(X \otimes I \otimes I)$ so that it becomes

$$\beta|111\rangle + \alpha|000\rangle = \alpha|000\rangle + \beta|111\rangle,$$

so we have corrected the error.

- parity$(q_2, q_1) = 0$ and parity$(q_1, q_0) = 1$ with probability 0.
- parity$(q_2, q_1) = 1$ and parity$(q_1, q_0) = 1$ with probability 0.

Finally, we need to reset the ancilla qubits to $|0\rangle$ so that we can reuse them, since we want to repeatedly do error correction to fix any errors that appear. We can do this by conditionally applying an X gate. If we measured a parity to be 0, we know that the ancilla qubit is $|0\rangle$, so we leave it alone. If we measured the parity to be 1, we know that the ancilla qubit is $|1\rangle$, and so we apply an X gate to it, turning it into a $|0\rangle$.

To summarize, when we have a partial bit flip, the measurement forces it to be corrected or to become a complete bit flip, which we can correct by applying an X gate. Here is the quantum circuit for this:

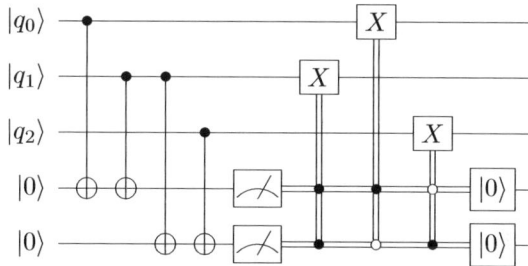

The first four columns are the CNOTs that calculate the parities of adjacent qubits. Then, we measure these parities, as shown by the meter symbols, which results in classical bits. We denote these classical bits/wires using double lines. We end with three X gates conditioned on these classical bits/parities. If both parities are 1, then q_1 flipped, so we apply an X gate to it to correct it. If parity$(q_2, q_1) = 0$ and parity$(q_1, q_0) = 1$, then q_0 flipped, so we apply an X gate to it to correct it. Finally, if parity$(q_2, q_1) = 1$ and parity$(q_1, q_0) = 0$, then q_2 flipped, so we apply an X gate to it to correct it. We end by resetting the ancillas to $|0\rangle$, indicated by the boxes with $|0\rangle$ in them. Simulating this in Quirk (see https://bit.ly/3jZ4zKQ),

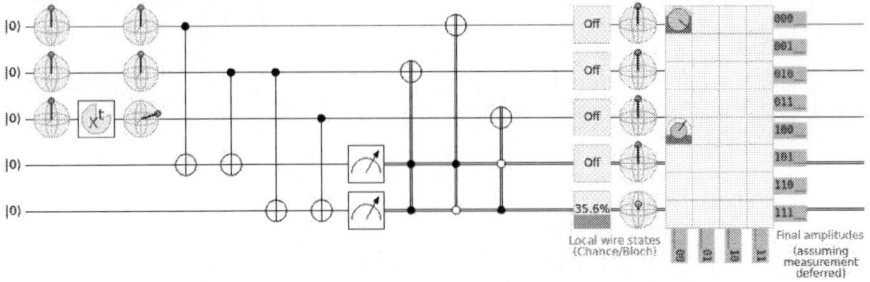

In this simulation, the logical qubit starts as $|0_L\rangle = |000\rangle$. In the first column of the circuit, we can visualize the states on Bloch spheres and confirm that we have $|000\rangle$. In the second column, we introduce a bit-flip error by applying a bit-flip X^t, with t varying from 0 to 360°, to q_2. In the third column, we again visualize the states on the Bloch sphere, confirming that $|q_2\rangle \neq |0\rangle$. Then, we have our error correction circuit, and at the very end of the circuit, the top three qubits are restored to $|000\rangle$, as expected. Note Quirk does not have a "reset" tool, so the ancillas have not yet been restored to $|0\rangle$. This would need to be done to repeat the circuit.

We can modify the above circuit using the *principle of deferred measurement*, which says,

> Intermediate measurements that are used to control operations can be moved after the operations, and the controls can be replaced by quantum controls.

Then, the previous quantum circuit to correct bit flips is equivalent to

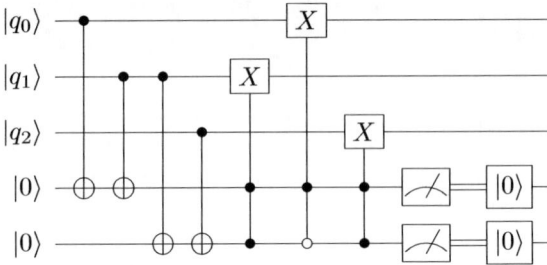

Phrased another way, we can collapse and then do the controlled operations, or we can do the controlled operations in superposition, and then collapse. Let us prove this for our previous example, where the qubits started in the state $\alpha|000\rangle + \beta|111\rangle$, but then the left qubit partially flips with amplitude ε. From earlier, if we include the ancilla qubits, the state after the first four CNOTs is

$$\alpha i\sqrt{1-\varepsilon^2}|00000\rangle + \beta\varepsilon|10011\rangle + \alpha\varepsilon|10100\rangle + \beta i\sqrt{1-\varepsilon^2}|00111\rangle.$$

Recall the qubits are ordered as $|\text{parity}(q_2,q_1)\rangle|\text{parity}(q_1,q_0)\rangle|q_2\rangle|q_1\rangle|q_0\rangle$. Now, if we apply the controlled- and anti-controlled-X gates to correct the answers, the state becomes

$$\alpha i \sqrt{1-\varepsilon^2}|00000\rangle + \beta\varepsilon|10111\rangle + \alpha\varepsilon|10000\rangle + \beta i \sqrt{1-\varepsilon^2}|00111\rangle$$

$$= i\sqrt{1-\varepsilon^2}|00\rangle\,(\alpha|000\rangle + \beta|111\rangle) + \varepsilon|10\rangle\,(\alpha|000\rangle + \beta|111\rangle)$$

$$= \left(i\sqrt{1-\varepsilon^2}|00\rangle + \varepsilon|10\rangle\right)(\alpha|000\rangle + \beta|111\rangle).$$

Measuring the ancilla qubits now, we get:

- parity$(q_2, q_1) = 0$ and parity$(q_1, q_0) = 0$ with probability $1 - \varepsilon^2$, and the state collapses to

$$|00\rangle\,(\alpha|000\rangle + \beta|111\rangle).$$

- parity$(q_2, q_1) = 1$ and parity$(q_1, q_0) = 0$ with probability ε^2, and the state collapses to

$$|10\rangle\,(\alpha|000\rangle + \beta|111\rangle).$$

This is the same result as before, where we first measured the ancilla qubits and then applied the controlled- and anti-controlled-X gates. Finally, if the second outcome occurs, we apply an X gate to the left ancilla to reset it to 0, yielding $|00\rangle\,(\alpha|000\rangle + \beta|111\rangle)$.

Simulating the circuit with deferred measurement in Quirk (see `https://bit.ly/3EyuBMK`),

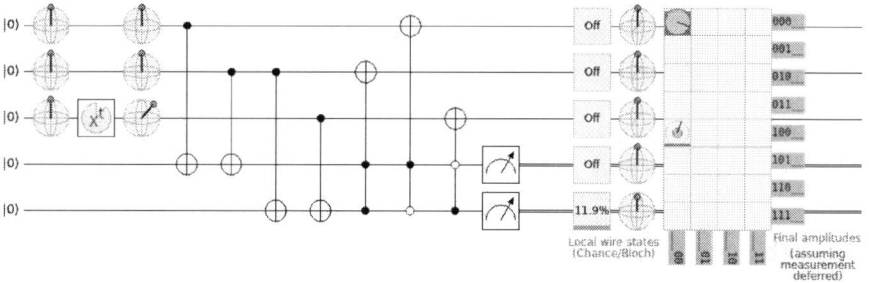

The top three qubits have been successfully corrected to $|000\rangle$. Again, we have not reset the ancilla qubits at the end of this circuit, which would be necessary to repeat the error correction scheme.

Exercise 4.35. In this exercise, we will work through encoding a qubit in the bit-flip code. Say we have a single qubit in the state

$$|\psi\rangle = \alpha|0\rangle + \beta|0\rangle.$$

We want to encode this using the bit-flip code. we add two more qubits to our system, all initially in $|0\rangle$, so our three qubits are in the state

$$|\psi 00\rangle = (\alpha|0\rangle + \beta|1\rangle)|00\rangle = \alpha|000\rangle + \beta|100\rangle.$$

Starting with this state, we apply the following quantum circuit:

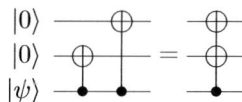

Show the final state, after the circuit, is

$$\alpha|000\rangle + \beta|111\rangle = \alpha|0_L\rangle + \beta|1_L\rangle.$$

Exercise 4.36. A logical qubit is in the state

$$|\psi\rangle = \frac{\sqrt{3}}{2}|0_L\rangle + \frac{1}{2}|1_L\rangle,$$

where we encode the logical qubit using three physical qubits:

$$|\psi\rangle = \frac{\sqrt{3}}{2}|000\rangle + \frac{1}{2}|111\rangle.$$

You suspect that a partial bit flip has occurred to one of the bits, so you measure the parity of adjacent qubits.

(a) If parity$(q_2, q_1) = 0$ and parity$(q_1, q_0) = 0$, what quantum gate(s) should you apply to fix the error, if any?

(b) If parity$(q_2, q_1) = 0$ and parity$(q_1, q_0) = 1$, what quantum gate(s) should you apply to fix the error, if any?

(c) If parity$(q_2, q_1) = 1$ and parity$(q_1, q_0) = 0$, what quantum gate(s) should you apply to fix the error, if any?

(d) If parity$(q_2, q_1) = 1$ and parity$(q_1, q_0) = 1$, what quantum gate(s) should you apply to fix the error, if any?

4.7.3 Phase-Flip Code

We can similarly correct phase-flip errors by using three physical qubits to encode each logical qubit, but instead of using three $|0\rangle$'s and $|1\rangle$'s, we use three $|+\rangle$'s and $|-\rangle$'s, i.e.,

$$|0_L\rangle = |+++\rangle, \quad |1_L\rangle = |---\rangle,$$

so a general superposition is

$$\alpha|0_L\rangle + \beta|1_L\rangle = \alpha|+++\rangle + \beta|---\rangle.$$

A way to create this encoding is given in Exercise 4.37. The reason why we use $|+\rangle$ and $|-\rangle$ is because a complete phase flip (the Z gate) switches between these states:

$$|+\rangle = \frac{1}{2}(|0\rangle + |1\rangle) \xrightarrow{Z} \frac{1}{2}(|0\rangle - |1\rangle) = |-\rangle,$$

$$|-\rangle = \frac{1}{2}(|0\rangle - |1\rangle) \xrightarrow{Z} \frac{1}{2}(|0\rangle + |1\rangle) = |+\rangle.$$

Say the left qubit experiences a complete phase flip:

$$\alpha|+++\rangle + \beta|---\rangle \rightarrow \alpha|-++\rangle + \beta|+--\rangle.$$

Then, we detect and correct this just like we did for the bit-flip error, except working in the X-basis. So, we measure the parity of consecutive qubits in the X-basis, which is 0 if the number of minuses is even and 1 if the number of minuses is odd. In Exercise 4.38 and Exercise 4.39, you will show that the parities can be calculated using

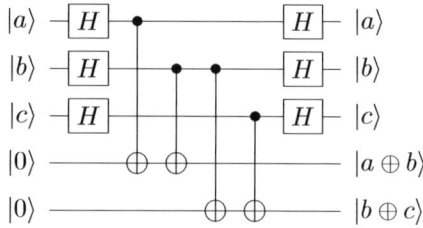

In our example where the left qubit experienced a phase flip, we get parity 1 for the left two qubits and parity 0 for the right two qubits, implying that the first qubit is flipped. So we apply $(Z \otimes I \otimes I)$, restoring $\alpha |+++\rangle + \beta|---\rangle$.

Now for partial phase flips, a partial phase flip corresponds to a rotation about the z-axis by some angle θ, so again using Eq. (2.10) with $\alpha = \pi/2$ and $\varepsilon = \sin(\theta/2)$, but now with $\hat{n} = (0,0,1)$, we get that the rotation is

$$i\sqrt{1-\varepsilon^2}I + \varepsilon Z = i\sqrt{1-\varepsilon^2}\begin{pmatrix} 1 & 0 \\ 0 & 1 \end{pmatrix} + \varepsilon \begin{pmatrix} 1 & 0 \\ 0 & -1 \end{pmatrix}$$

$$= \begin{pmatrix} i\sqrt{1-\varepsilon^2} + \varepsilon & 0 \\ 0 & i\sqrt{1-\varepsilon^2} - \varepsilon \end{pmatrix}.$$

Thus, the partial phase flip maps

$$|0\rangle \rightarrow \left(i\sqrt{1-\varepsilon^2} + \varepsilon\right)|0\rangle,$$

$$|1\rangle \rightarrow \left(i\sqrt{1-\varepsilon^2} - \varepsilon\right)|1\rangle.$$

Note when $\theta = \pi$, $\varepsilon = 1$, and we get $|0\rangle \rightarrow |0\rangle$ and $|1\rangle \rightarrow -|1\rangle$, which is a complete phase flip, or the Z gate. Let us see how a partial phase flip transforms $|+\rangle$ and $|-\rangle$:

$$|+\rangle = \frac{1}{\sqrt{2}}(|0\rangle + |1\rangle)$$

$$\rightarrow \frac{1}{\sqrt{2}}\left[\left(i\sqrt{1-\varepsilon^2} + \varepsilon\right)|0\rangle + \left(i\sqrt{1-\varepsilon^2} - \varepsilon\right)|1\rangle\right]$$

$$= i\sqrt{1-\varepsilon^2}\frac{1}{\sqrt{2}}(|0\rangle + |1\rangle) + \varepsilon\frac{1}{\sqrt{2}}(|0\rangle - |1\rangle)$$

$$= i\sqrt{1-\varepsilon^2}|+\rangle + \varepsilon|-\rangle,$$

$$|-\rangle = \frac{1}{\sqrt{2}}(|0\rangle - |1\rangle)$$

$$\rightarrow \frac{1}{\sqrt{2}}\left[\left(i\sqrt{1-\varepsilon^2} + \varepsilon\right)|0\rangle - \left(i\sqrt{1-\varepsilon^2} - \varepsilon\right)|1\rangle\right]$$

$$= \varepsilon \frac{1}{\sqrt{2}} (|0\rangle + |1\rangle) + i\sqrt{1-\varepsilon^2} \frac{1}{\sqrt{2}} (|0\rangle - |1\rangle)$$
$$= \varepsilon |+\rangle + i\sqrt{1-\varepsilon^2} |-\rangle.$$

Using this, if we have a logical qubit in the state

$$\alpha |0_L\rangle + \beta |1_L\rangle = \alpha |+++\rangle + \beta |---\rangle,$$

a partial phase flip on the left qubit transforms this to

$$\alpha \left(i\sqrt{1-\varepsilon^2} |+++\rangle + \varepsilon |-++\rangle \right) + \beta \left(\varepsilon |+--\rangle + i\sqrt{1-\varepsilon^2} |---\rangle \right)$$
$$= \alpha i\sqrt{1-\varepsilon^2} |+++\rangle + \alpha\varepsilon |-++\rangle + \beta\varepsilon |+--\rangle + \beta i\sqrt{1-\varepsilon^2} |---\rangle$$
$$= \alpha i\sqrt{1-\varepsilon^2} |+++\rangle + \beta\varepsilon |+--\rangle + \alpha\varepsilon |-++\rangle + \beta i\sqrt{1-\varepsilon^2} |---\rangle.$$

Now, we measure the parity of adjacent qubits in the X-basis (i.e., whether the number of $|-\rangle$'s are even or odd). We get:

- parity$(q_2, q_1) = 0$ and parity$(q_1, q_0) = 0$ with probability

$$\left| \alpha i\sqrt{1-\varepsilon^2} \right|^2 + \left| \beta i\sqrt{1-\varepsilon^2} \right|^2 = |\alpha|^2 (1-\varepsilon^2) + |\beta|^2 (1-\varepsilon^2)$$
$$= (|\alpha|^2 + |\beta|^2) (1-\varepsilon^2)$$
$$= 1 - \varepsilon^2,$$

and the state collapses to

$$A \left(\alpha i\sqrt{1-\varepsilon^2} |+++\rangle + \beta i\sqrt{1-\varepsilon^2} |---\rangle \right) = \alpha |+++\rangle + \beta |---\rangle,$$

where $A = 1/i\sqrt{1-\varepsilon^2}$ is a normalization constant. We see that the resulting state is already corrected, so we do not need to do anything further to correct the error. That is, the measurement fixed the error.

- parity$(q_2, q_1) = 1$ and parity$(q_1, q_0) = 0$ with probability

$$|\beta\varepsilon|^2 + |\alpha\varepsilon|^2 = |\alpha|^2 |\varepsilon|^2 + |\beta|^2 |\varepsilon|^2$$
$$= (|\alpha|^2 + |\beta|^2) |\varepsilon|^2$$
$$= |\varepsilon|^2,$$

and the state collapses to

$$B (\beta\varepsilon |+--\rangle + \alpha\varepsilon |-++\rangle) = \beta |+--\rangle + \alpha |-++\rangle,$$

where $B = 1/\varepsilon$ is a normalization constant. To correct this state, we apply $(Z \otimes I \otimes I)$ so that it becomes

$$\beta|---\rangle + \alpha|+++\rangle = \alpha|+++\rangle + \beta|---\rangle,$$

so we have corrected the error.

- parity$(q_2, q_1) = 0$ and parity$(q_1, q_0) = 1$ with probability 0.
- parity$(q_2, q_1) = 1$ and parity$(q_1, q_0) = 1$ with probability 0.

To summarize, when we have a partial phase flip, the measurement forces it to be corrected or to become a complete phase flip, which we can correct by applying a Z gate. The quantum circuit for this procedure is shown below:

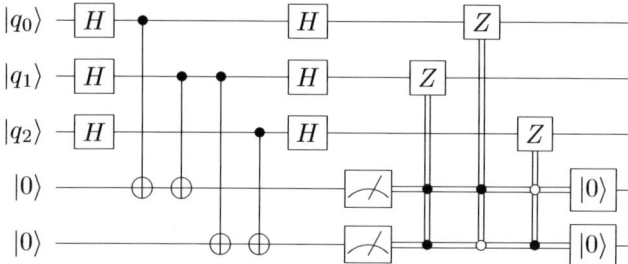

Simulating this in Quirk (https://bit.ly/3e7dNQR):

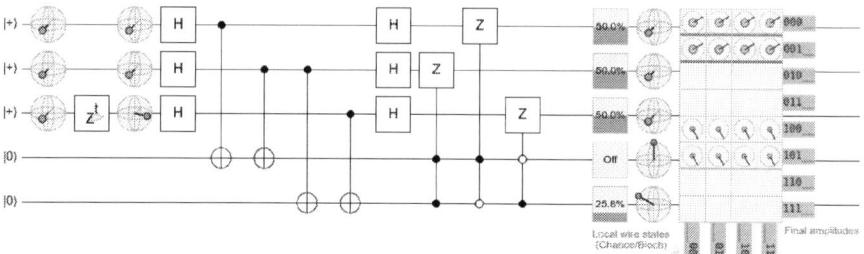

The top three qubits are $|0_L\rangle = |+++\rangle$, and the bottom two qubits will be used to calculate the parities. In the first column of the circuit, we can visualize the states on Bloch spheres and confirm that we have $|+++\rangle$. Next, we simulate an error by applying a phase-flip Z^t, with t varying from 0 to 360°, to the middle qubit. Now, another set of Bloch spheres confirms that the middle qubit has changed. We want to correct this so that we end up with $|+++\rangle$ again. The rest of our circuit is the same as the bit-flip circuit, except we apply Hadamard gates before and after it so that we work in the X-basis. In the output, we see that we have restored $|+++\rangle$. We can move the phase flip to any of the top three qubits, and our error-correcting circuit will restore the state to $|+++\rangle$. Note we also need to reset the ancilla qubits.

Exercise 4.37. In this exercise, we will work through an exercise for encoding a qubit in the phase-flip code. Say we have a single qubit in the state

$$|\psi\rangle = \alpha|0\rangle + \beta|0\rangle.$$

We want to encode this using the phase-flip code. we add two more qubits to our system, all initially in $|0\rangle$, so our three qubits are in the state

$$|\psi 00\rangle = (\alpha|0\rangle + \beta|1\rangle)|00\rangle = \alpha|000\rangle + \beta|100\rangle.$$

Starting with this state, we apply the following quantum circuit:

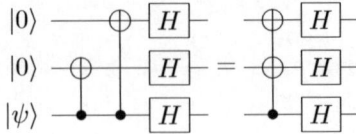

$$|0\rangle \quad |0\rangle \quad |\psi\rangle$$

Show the final state, after the circuit, is

$$\alpha|{+}{+}{+}\rangle + \beta|{-}{-}{-}\rangle = \alpha|0_L\rangle + \beta|1_L\rangle.$$

Exercise 4.38. Consider the following quantum circuit:

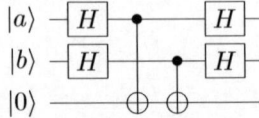

$$|a\rangle \quad |b\rangle \quad |0\rangle$$

Show that...
(a) If $|a\rangle = |+\rangle$ and $|b\rangle = |+\rangle$, find the resulting state at the end of the circuit.
(b) If $|a\rangle = |+\rangle$ and $|b\rangle = |-\rangle$, find the resulting state at the end of the circuit.
(c) If $|a\rangle = |-\rangle$ and $|b\rangle = |+\rangle$, find the resulting state at the end of the circuit.
(d) If $|a\rangle = |-\rangle$ and $|b\rangle = |-\rangle$, find the resulting state at the end of the circuit.
(e) Using your answers to the previous parts, explain why this circuit calculates the parity in the X-basis.

Exercise 4.39. Using two copies of the circuit from Exercise 4.38, we can calculate the parity of adjacent qubits in the X-basis using the following circuit:

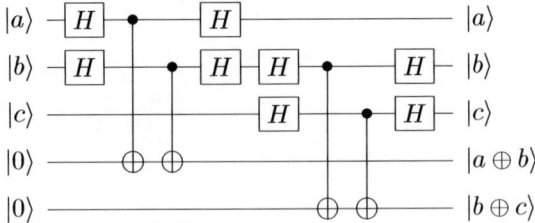

$$|a\rangle \quad |b\rangle \quad |c\rangle \quad |0\rangle \quad |0\rangle \;\to\; |a\rangle, |b\rangle, |c\rangle, |a \oplus b\rangle, |b \oplus c\rangle$$

Explain how this is equivalent to the circuit from the text.

Exercise 4.40. A logical qubit is in the state

$$\alpha|0_L\rangle + \beta|1_L\rangle,$$

where $|0_L\rangle$ and $|1_L\rangle$ are encoded using the phase-flip code:

$$|0_L\rangle = |{+}{+}{+}\rangle, \quad |1_L\rangle = |{-}{-}{-}\rangle.$$

That is, the physical qubits are in the state

$$\alpha|{+}{+}{+}\rangle + \beta|{-}{-}{-}\rangle.$$

Now, the left physical qubit suffers a slight phase flip, causing the state to become

$$\alpha\left(i\sqrt{1-\varepsilon^2}|{+}{+}{+}\rangle + \varepsilon|{-}{+}{+}\rangle\right) + \beta\left(i\sqrt{1-\varepsilon^2}|{-}{-}{-}\rangle + \varepsilon|{+}{-}{-}\rangle\right).$$

To detect/correct this, you measure the parity of the left two qubits and the parity of the right two qubits, both in the X-basis.

(a) What is the probability that both parities are even? If this probability is nonzero, say you get this outcome. What is the state after the measurement? What gate(s) should you apply to correct the error, if any?

(b) What is the probability that the parity of the left two qubits is odd and the parity of the right two qubits is even? If this probability is nonzero, say you get this outcome. What is the state after the measurement? What gate(s) should you apply to correct the error, if any?

(c) What is the probability that the parity of the left two qubits is even and the parity of the right two qubits is odd? If this probability is nonzero, say you get this outcome. What is the state after the measurement? What gate(s) should you apply to correct the error, if any?

(d) What is the probability that both parities are odd? If this probability is nonzero, say you get this outcome. What is the state after the measurement? What gate(s) should you apply to correct the error, if any?

4.7.4 Shor Code

We can combine the phase-flip code and bit-flip code to correct both kinds of errors. We begin with the phase-flip code, so we can correct phase-flip errors. That is,

$$|0_L\rangle = |+++\rangle$$
$$= \frac{1}{\sqrt{2}}(|0\rangle + |1\rangle)\frac{1}{\sqrt{2}}(|0\rangle + |1\rangle)\frac{1}{\sqrt{2}}(|0\rangle + |1\rangle)$$
$$= \frac{1}{2^{3/2}}(|0\rangle + |1\rangle)(|0\rangle + |1\rangle)(|0\rangle + |1\rangle).$$

Then, so we can correct bit-flip errors, we replace each of the three qubits with three qubits using the bit-flip encoding, i.e., $|0\rangle \rightarrow |000\rangle$ and $|1\rangle \rightarrow |111\rangle$, so that each logical qubit is encoded using nine physical qubits:

$$|0_L\rangle = \frac{1}{2^{3/2}}(|000\rangle + |111\rangle)(|000\rangle + |111\rangle)(|000\rangle + |111\rangle).$$

Similarly, we begin with $|1_L\rangle = |---\rangle$ and replace $|0\rangle \rightarrow |000\rangle$ and $|1\rangle \rightarrow |111\rangle$:

$$|1_L\rangle = \frac{1}{2^{3/2}}(|000\rangle - |111\rangle)(|000\rangle - |111\rangle)(|000\rangle - |111\rangle).$$

Then, the state of a general logical qubit is

$$\alpha|0_L\rangle + \beta|1_L\rangle = \frac{\alpha}{2^{3/2}}(|000\rangle + |111\rangle)(|000\rangle + |111\rangle)(|000\rangle + |111\rangle)$$
$$+ \frac{\beta}{2^{3/2}}(|000\rangle - |111\rangle)(|000\rangle - |111\rangle)(|000\rangle - |111\rangle).$$

This encoding is called the *Shor code*, and it is named after its inventor, Peter Shor, who proposed it in 1995 and, by doing so, invented quantum error correction. It uses nine physical qubits to encode one logical qubit. A way to create this encoding is given in Exercise 4.41.

Exercise 4.41. A qubit can be encoded using the Shor code by first encoding it in the three-qubit phase-flip code (Exercise 4.37) followed by encoding each of the three qubits using the three-qubit bit-flip code (Exercise 4.35), which results in nine qubits total. Applying these encodings one after another, a method called *concatenation*, yields the following circuit:

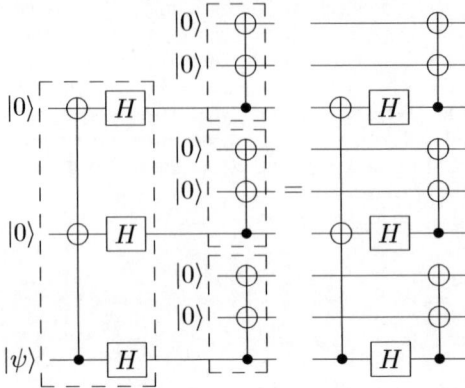

In the above circuit, the large dashed box to the left is the phase-flip encoding, which turns $|0\rangle \rightarrow |+++\rangle$ and $|1\rangle \rightarrow |---\rangle$. Then, the three dashed boxes in the middle are each the bit-flip encoding, which turns $|0\rangle \rightarrow |000\rangle$ and $|1\rangle \rightarrow |111\rangle$.

If the initial state of the circuit is $|\psi 00000000\rangle$, where $|\psi\rangle = \alpha|0\rangle + \beta|1\rangle$, show that:

(a) The state of the circuit after the first column (after the CNOT with two targets) is

$$\alpha|000\rangle|000\rangle|000\rangle + \beta|100\rangle|100\rangle|100\rangle.$$

(b) The state of the circuit after the second column (after the Hadamard gates) is

$$\frac{\alpha}{\sqrt{2}} (|000\rangle + |100\rangle) (|000\rangle + |100\rangle) (|000\rangle + |100\rangle)$$

$$+ \frac{\beta}{\sqrt{2}} (|000\rangle - |100\rangle) (|000\rangle - |100\rangle) (|000\rangle - |100\rangle).$$

(c) The final state of the circuit is

$$\frac{\alpha}{2^{3/2}} (|000\rangle + |111\rangle) (|000\rangle + |111\rangle) (|000\rangle + |111\rangle)$$

$$+ \frac{\beta}{2^{3/2}} (|000\rangle - |111\rangle) (|000\rangle - |111\rangle) (|000\rangle - |111\rangle).$$

This is precisely $\alpha|0_L\rangle + \beta|1_L\rangle$.

Let us see how to correct bit flips and phase flips using the Shor code, beginning with bit flips. First, remember that the qubits are ordered $q_8 q_7 \ldots q_0$. Say q_8 and q_3 both experience complete bit flips. Then, the state of the system is

$$\frac{\alpha}{2^{3/2}} (|100\rangle + |011\rangle) (|001\rangle + |110\rangle) (|000\rangle + |111\rangle)$$

$$+ \frac{\beta}{2^{3/2}} (|100\rangle - |011\rangle) (|001\rangle - |110\rangle) (|000\rangle - |111\rangle).$$

To detect this, we measure the parities of adjacent qubits within each triplet. In this example, we would get:

left triplet: $\text{parity}(q_8, q_7) = 1$, $\text{parity}(q_7, q_6) = 0$,

middle triplet: $\text{parity}(q_5, q_4) = 0$, $\text{parity}(q_4, q_3) = 1$,

right triplet: $\text{parity}(q_2, q_1) = 0$, $\text{parity}(q_1, q_0) = 0$.

This tells us that the eighth qubit and third qubit have flipped, so we can apply X gates to those two qubits to correct them. This also works with partial bit flips. Measuring the parities of adjacent qubits might collapse the state and correct the errors, or it might collapse the state into one with full bit flips, which we correct by applying X gates to the appropriate qubits.

Exercise 4.42. A logical qubit is encoded using nine physical qubits in the Shor code. In each triplet, you measure the parity of adjacent qubits and get the following results:

left triplet: $\text{parity}(q_8, q_7) = 0$, $\text{parity}(q_7, q_6) = 1$,

middle triplet: $\text{parity}(q_5, q_4) = 1$, $\text{parity}(q_4, q_3) = 0$,

right triplet: $\text{parity}(q_2, q_1) = 1$, $\text{parity}(q_1, q_0) = 1$.

Are there any bit flip errors? If so, which bits flipped, and what can you do to correct them?

Exercise 4.43. Bit flips can be corrected in the Shor code using the following quantum circuit:

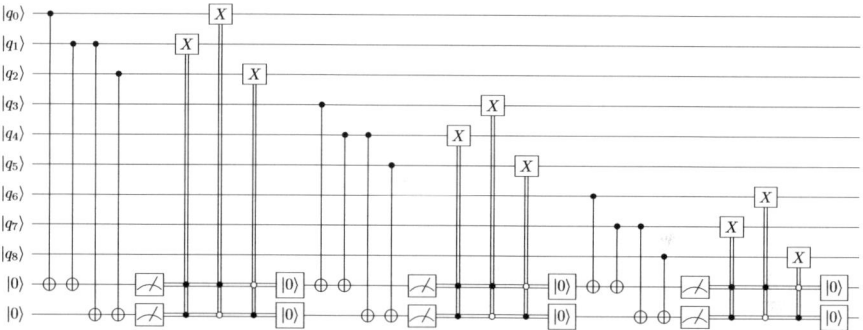

The first third of the circuit measures the parities of adjacent qubits in the top three qubits, correct any errors, and reset the ancillas. The middle third of the circuit calculates the parities of adjacent qubits in the next triplet, correcting any errors. Finally, it does the same for the last triplet of qubits.

Using Quirk, simulate this circuit by inserting it into the following circuit (see https://bit.ly/3D1kRKI):

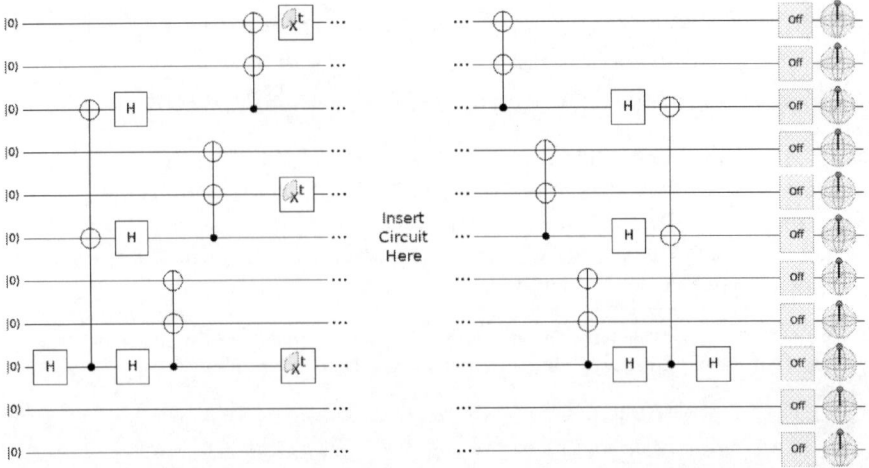

The first part of this circuit applies the Hadamard gate to $|q_8\rangle$, turning it into $|+\rangle$. Then, it uses the circuit in Exercise 4.41 to encode this in the Shor code. Then, the X^t gates applies a partial bit flip to one qubit in each triplet. In the middle section, you should add the previously given circuit. Although there is no reset feature in Quirk, you can use the *postselection* tool as a workaround. In Quirk, it is drawn as the outer product $|0\rangle\langle 0|$. It measures a qubit in the $\{|0\rangle, |1\rangle\}$ basis, and if the result is $|0\rangle$, the calculation continues. Otherwise, the simulation starts over. For our purposes, it has the effect of guaranteeing that the ancilla qubit is $|0\rangle$ before proceeding. A true "reset" feature would allow us to continue with the ancilla as $|0\rangle$ without the risk of restarting the simulation. In the last section of the circuit, we undo the Shor encoding and Hadamard gate so that all the qubits are $|0\rangle$ again. Verify that your circuit does this.

Next, let us see how the Shor code also allows us to correct phase flips. Say q_3 experiences a complete phase flip. Then, the state of the system is

$$\frac{\alpha}{2^{3/2}}\left(|000\rangle + |111\rangle\right)\left(|000\rangle - |111\rangle\right)\left(|000\rangle + |111\rangle\right)$$
$$+ \frac{\beta}{2^{3/2}}\left(|000\rangle - |111\rangle\right)\left(|000\rangle + |111\rangle\right)\left(|000\rangle - |111\rangle\right).$$

Then, we can measure the "phase parity" of adjacent triplets, i.e., whether the number of $(|000\rangle - |111\rangle)/\sqrt{2}$ triplets is even or odd. This is similar to the phase flip code, where we measured the parity in the X basis to determine if the number of $|-\rangle$'s was even or odd. How to measure this parity is shown in Exercise 4.44). In our example, we would get

$$\text{parity}(\text{triplet}_2, \text{triplet}_1) = 1, \quad \text{parity}(\text{triplet}_1, \text{triplet}_0) = 1.$$

This indicates that the middle triplet needs to be flipped, so we apply the Z gate to any one of the three qubits in that triplet. That is, we can apply the Z gate to either q_5, q_4, or q_3, correcting the error. Similarly, when there is a partial phase flip, if we measure all the phase parities and get zero, the state collapsed and corrected the error, and if there was a discrepancy in phase parities, we apply a Z gate to the appropriate triplet to correct it.

By alternating between correcting bit-flip errors and phase-flip errors, the Shor code corrects all quantum errors, assuming each triplet experiences at most one bit-flip error per correction cycle, and at most one triplet experiences a phase-flip error per correction cycle.

A quantum computer that accumulates errors slowly enough that errors can be corrected is called *fault tolerant*. Depending on the error correcting code that is used, the maximum correctable error rate can vary, and this is an area of active research. At the time of this writing, a fault tolerant quantum computer does not yet exist, and one could argue that building one is the "holy grail" of the field.

Exercise 4.44. Consider the following circuit, which computes the phase parity of adjacent triplets in the Shor code:

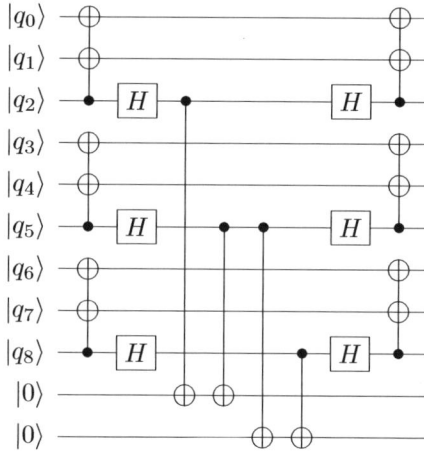

Comparing this circuit with Exercise 4.41, the first two layers of this circuit partially unencode the qubit. Then the middle four layers (the CNOTs) calculate the parity of adjacent triplets in two ancilla qubits. Then, the final two layers reencode the qubit. In this exercise, we will work through this for an example.

(a) A qubit $\alpha|0_L\rangle + \beta|1_L\rangle$ is encoded using the nine-qubit Shor code, but a physical qubit in the middle triplet experienced a phase flip, so the state of the nine qubits is

$$\frac{\alpha}{2^{3/2}} (|000\rangle + |111\rangle)(|000\rangle - |111\rangle)(|000\rangle + |111\rangle)$$

$$+ \frac{\beta}{2^{3/2}} (|000\rangle - |111\rangle)(|000\rangle + |111\rangle)(|000\rangle - |111\rangle).$$

Show that after the first two columns of the circuit (the CNOTs with two targets and the Hadamards), the state of the nine qubits is

$$\alpha|000100000\rangle + \beta|100000100\rangle.$$

(b) Show that after the middle layers of the circuit (CNOTs), the ancilla qubits now store the phase parities of adjacent triplets.

(c) Show that at the end of the circuit, the state of the nine qubits is again

$$\frac{\alpha}{2^{3/2}} \left(|000\rangle + |111\rangle \right) \left(|000\rangle - |111\rangle \right) \left(|000\rangle + |111\rangle \right)$$

$$+ \frac{\beta}{2^{3/2}} \left(|000\rangle - |111\rangle \right) \left(|000\rangle + |111\rangle \right) \left(|000\rangle - |111\rangle \right).$$

(d) From the parities in (b), what gate should be applied to fix the phase flip, and to which qubit?

Exercise 4.45. Construct a quantum circuit that corrects when a triplet experiences a phase flip error in the Shor code. To check your answer, simulate your circuit in Quirk by inserting it into the following circuit (see https://bit.ly/3kmbTAm):

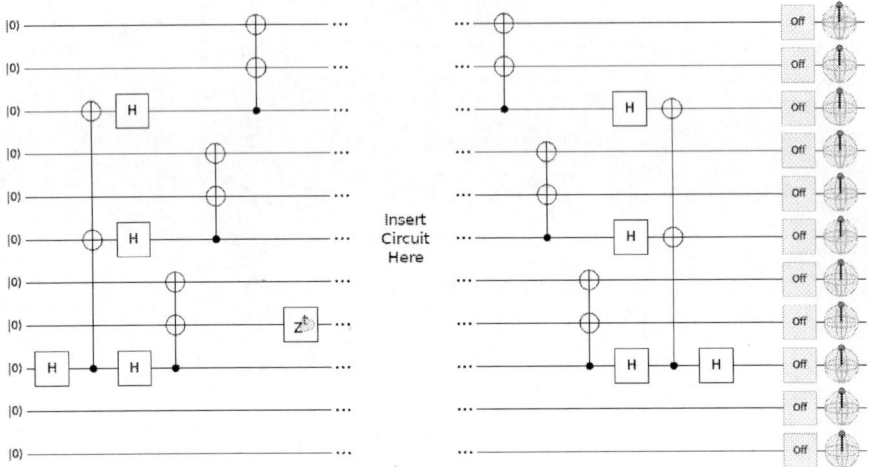

The first part of this circuit applies the Hadamard gate to $|q_8\rangle$, turning it into $|+\rangle$. Then, it uses the circuit in Exercise 4.41 to encode this in the Shor code. Then, the Z^t gates applies a partial bit flip to one triplet. In the middle section, you should add the previously given circuit. As described in Exercise 4.43, postselect on $|0\rangle$ as a workaround for resetting the ancilla qubits. In the last section of the circuit, we undo the Shor encoding and Hadamard gate so that all the qubits are $|0\rangle$ again. Verify that your circuit does this. Try moving the Z^t gate around to different triplets to ensure that the phase flip is corrected in all instances, as long as at most one triplet experiences a phase flip.

Exercise 4.46. You have a logical qubit encoded in nine physical qubits using the Shor code. Let us label the qubits $q_8 q_7 \ldots q_0$. They are grouped into three triplets $(\text{triplet}_2, \text{triplet}_1, \text{triplet}_0)$.
  (a) You begin by detecting bit flip errors. Within each triplet, you measure the parity of adjacent qubits in the Z-basis. Here are the results:

$$\begin{aligned} \text{left triplet:} &\quad \text{parity}(q_8, q_7) = 1, \;\; \text{parity}(q_7, q_6) = 1, \\ \text{middle triplet:} &\quad \text{parity}(q_5, q_4) = 0, \;\; \text{parity}(q_4, q_3) = 1, \\ \text{right triplet:} &\quad \text{parity}(q_2, q_1) = 1, \;\; \text{parity}(q_1, q_0) = 0. \end{aligned}$$

Are there any bit flip errors? If so, which bits flipped, and what can you do to correct them?
  (b) Next, you measure the parities of adjacent triplets in the H_3-basis. Here are the results:

$$\text{parity}(\text{triplet}_2, \text{triplet}_1) = 0, \quad \text{parity}(\text{triplet}_1, \text{triplet}_0) = 1.$$

Was there a phase flip error? If so, which triplet flipped, and what can you do to correct it?

4.8 Summary

The state of multiple qubits is written as as a tensor product. With n qubits, there are 2^n orthonormal basis states, and a general state is a superposition of these basis states. In a product state, measuring one qubit cannot affect the others, while in an entangled state, measuring one qubit can affect the other qubits. A quantum gate on n qubits is a $2^n \times 2^n$ unitary matrix. There are various ways to add binary numbers on a quantum computer. A universal set of quantum gates can approximate any quantum gate to any desired precision. Quantum bits can suffer from both bit-flip and phase-flip errors, but they can be corrected, so building a quantum computer "only" requires really good qubits, not perfect qubits.

Chapter 5
Quantum Programming

Quantum computing is currently emerging from the research lab onto the market-place. Many companies are building prototype quantum processors, and although these devices are not yet good enough for fault-tolerant quantum computation, they may still have uses. These rudimentary quantum processors are called *noisy intermediate-scale quantum* (NISQ) devices, where noisy means they suffer from too much decoherence to be fault-tolerant, and intermediate-scale means they have a moderate number of qubits, say roughly fifty to a few hundred. NISQ devices were used to demonstrate quantum computational supremacy, which we briefly discussed in Section 1.8.3.

Many companies have made their rudimentary quantum processors available for people to experiment with. In this chapter, we will learn how to program IBM's quantum computers over the internet. This is not an endorsement of their products or services, and other companies have similar tools for programming their own quantum devices, which you are encouraged to explore on your own. Rather, IBM has made several of their quantum processors freely available to the public, making them a prudent choice for a textbook. Furthermore, after learning one quantum programming toolkit, it will be easier to learn others, as there are many similarities across them.

5.1 IBM Quantum

5.1.1 Services

IBM was the first to make their quantum processors available over the internet (over the "cloud"), and their online platform is called IBM Quantum (formerly called IBM Quantum Experience). It can be accessed at `https://quantum-computing.ibm.c om`. Their smaller quantum processors are available to the public, and access to their larger, newer processors is available commercially. When we log in, we first see the Dashboard:

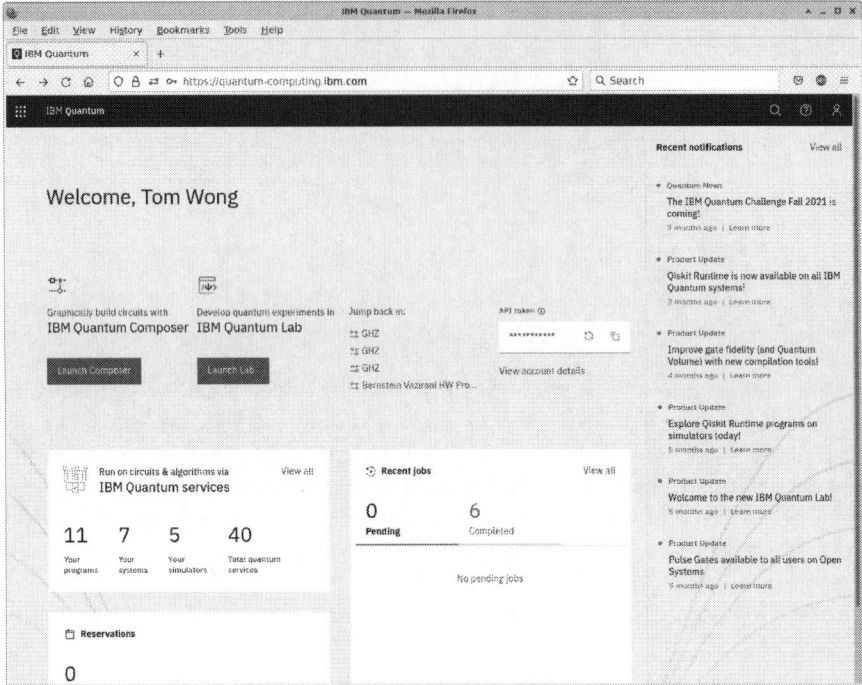

We can go to the Services page to view a list of quantum processors available to us. To get to the Services page, we can click on the menu icon in the top-left corner of the Dashboard, then click "Services:"

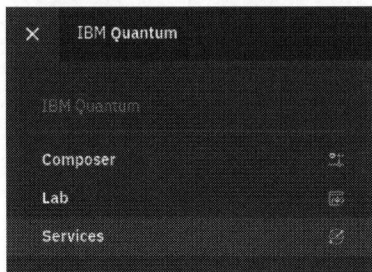

This brings us to the Services page:

On the Services page, we can click the "Systems" tab and then filter by "Your systems:"

This is the list of quantum processors that are available to us. If we click on a processor, such as ibmq_manila, we can see more information about it:

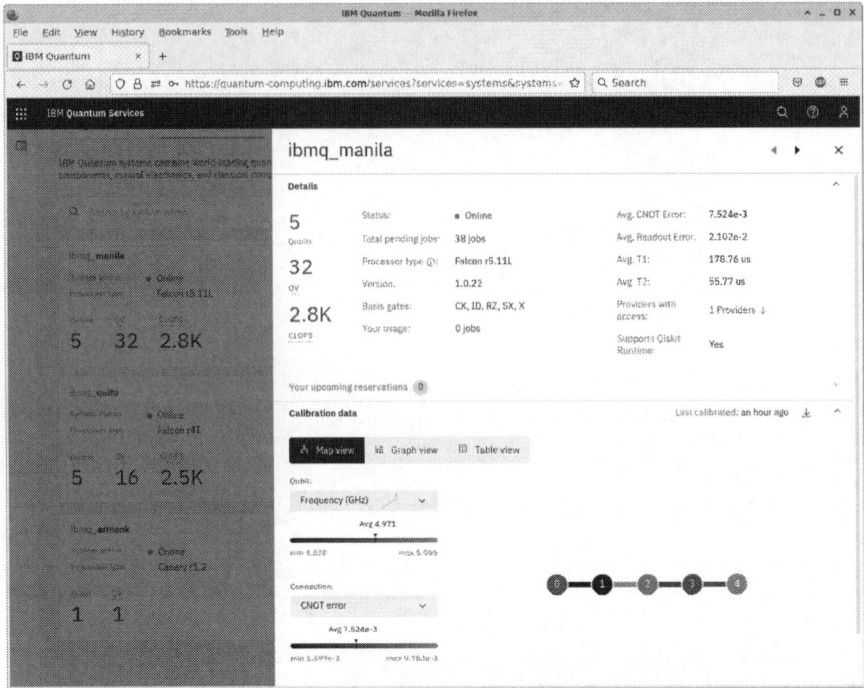

We see that this quantum processor has five qubits arranged in a line. This arrangement, or *topology*, can affect which quantum gates can be naturally applied. For
example, we can naturally apply CNOT between qubits 0 and 1. If we want to apply
CNOT between qubits 0 and 2, however, we would need to, for example, SWAP
qubits 2 and 1, apply CNOT between 0 and 1, then SWAP 1 back with 2.

5.1.2 Quantum Composer

The Quantum Composer (formerly called Circuit Composer) provides a drag-and-
drop interface for programming quantum circuits. To get to the Quantum Composer,
we can click on the menu icon in the top-left corner and then click "Composer:"

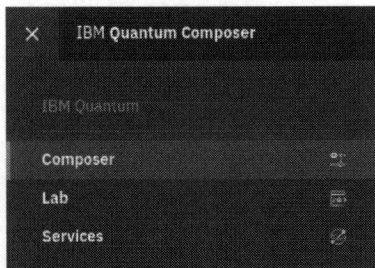

For example, let us program the following quantum circuit:

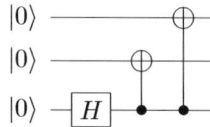

This circuit produces the following state:

$$|000\rangle \xrightarrow{H \otimes I \otimes I} \frac{1}{\sqrt{2}}\left(|000\rangle + |100\rangle\right)$$

$$\xrightarrow{\text{CNOT}_{21}} \frac{1}{\sqrt{2}}\left(|000\rangle + |110\rangle\right)$$

$$\xrightarrow{\text{CNOT}_{20}} \frac{1}{\sqrt{2}}\left(|000\rangle + |111\rangle\right).$$

This state is known as the Greenberger–Horne–Zeilinger state (GHZ state). It is an entangled state, and we will revisit it in the next chapter. If we measure it, we find that all the qubits are 0 with probability $1/2$ or all 1 with probability $1/2$.

Using the Quantum Composer, we can create this circuit by dragging a Hadamard gate and two CNOT gates onto the circuit:

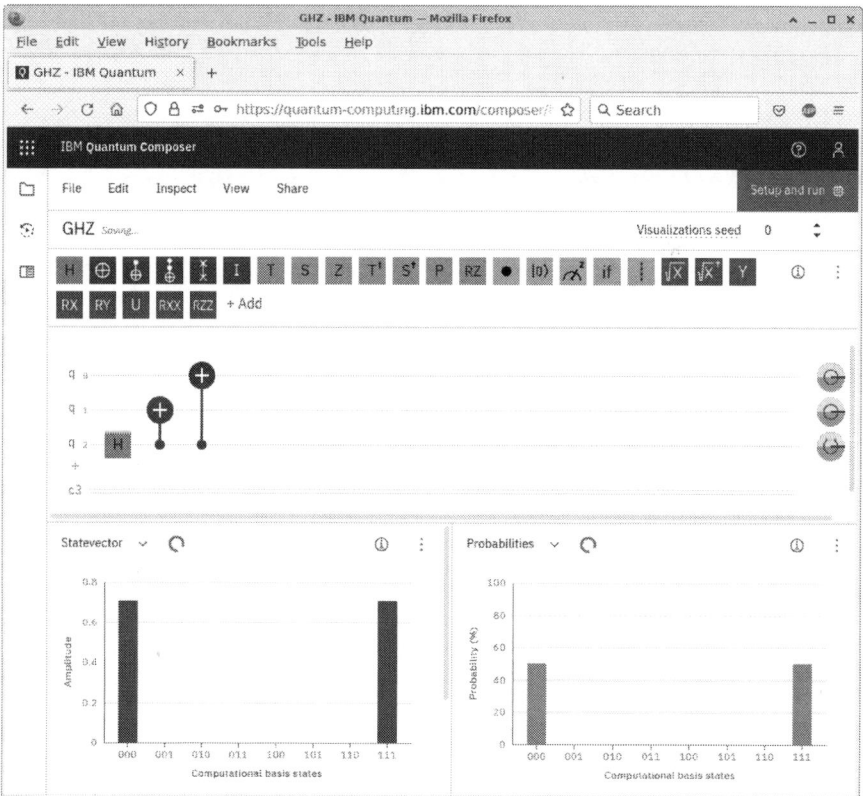

To change the control and target of CNOTs, we double-clicked on them and modified which qubit was the control and which was the target. For example, for $CNOT_{21}$, the control and target were set as shown below:

$\leftarrow$ Your circuit > cx

Qubits connections

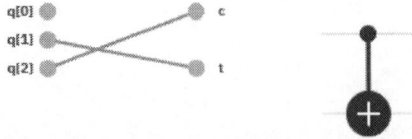

In the Quantum Composer, we also deleted some qubits so that there are only three. At the bottom of the webpage, the Quantum Composer automatically simulated the circuit, showing histograms indicating that the circuit yields $|000\rangle$ with probability 50% or $|111\rangle$ with probability 50%, as expected.

To run this on an actual quantum processor, we need to add at least one measurement. Let us measure all three qubits by adding measurement gates to the Quantum Composer:

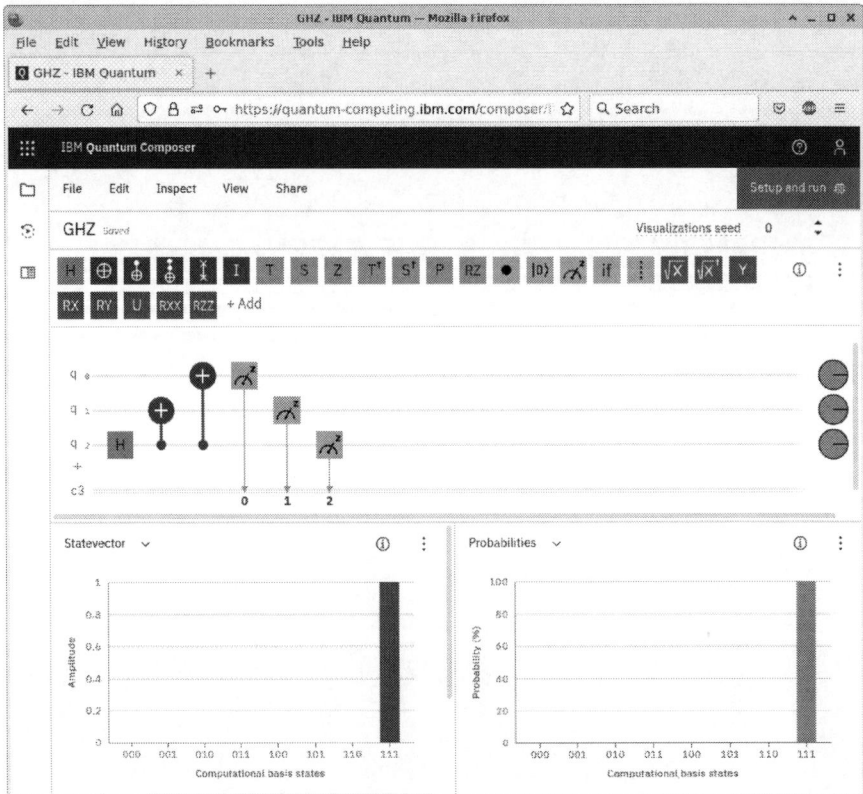

Now, the histograms at the bottom of the screen have changed. Instead of giving both $|000\rangle$ and $|111\rangle$, we only get one of them. This is because when measuring the qubits, we only get $|000\rangle$ or $|111\rangle$, not both. The Quantum Composer is choosing one of them using a pseudo-random number generator. At the top-right corner of the screen, we can change the "Visualization seed," which is a number that the pseudo-random number generator starts with to generate pseudo-random numbers.

5.1.3 Quantum Processor

We can run the quantum circuit on one of IBM's actual quantum processors. At the top of the Quantum Composer, there is a button that says "Setup and run." Clicking it shows the following menu:

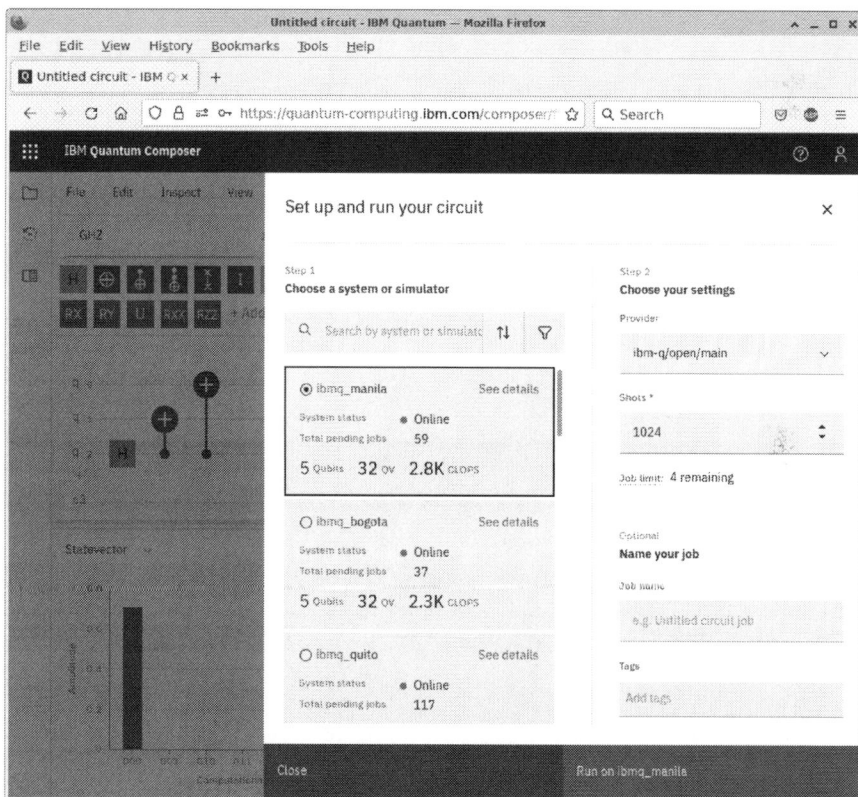

From this menu, we can select the quantum system on which to run the circuit. The number of shots defaults to 1024, meaning it will run our circuit 1024 times and return a histogram of the measurement outcomes. Ideally, we expect to get $|000\rangle$ 512 times and $|111\rangle$ 512 times. We also see our job limit. Each user is limited to having five jobs in the queue at a time. Clicking "Run on ibmq_xxx" adds our job to the queue. We can see its status by clicking the "Jobs" tab on the left side of the screen:

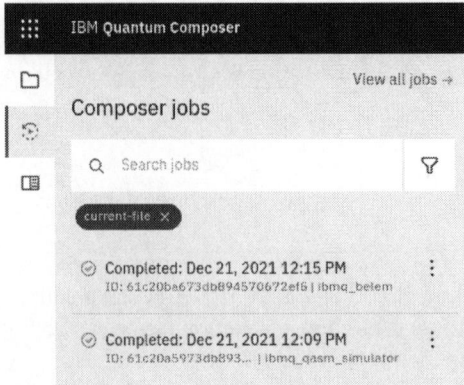

When it is done, we can click it to see the results. Here is what we got for the histogram:

Histogram

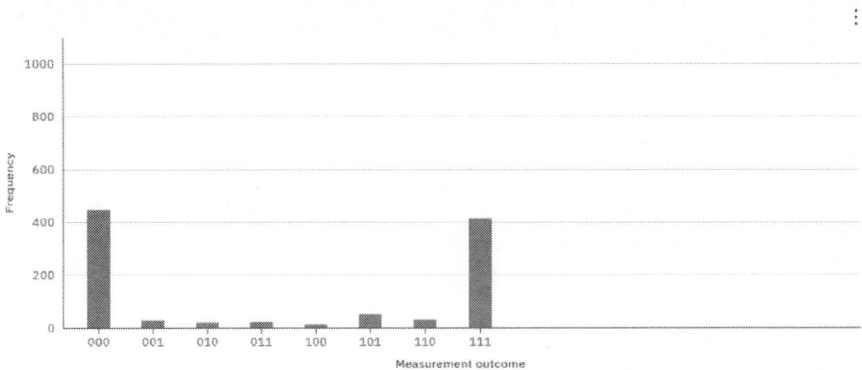

Theoretically, we expect 000 or 111, each half the time. Due to a limited number of shots and decoherence in the quantum processor, however, the results deviated from our expectations. The results page also shows the actual quantum circuit that was run, which is called the *transpiled* circuit:

Original circuit

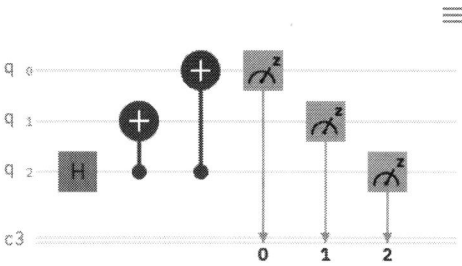

Transpiled circuit

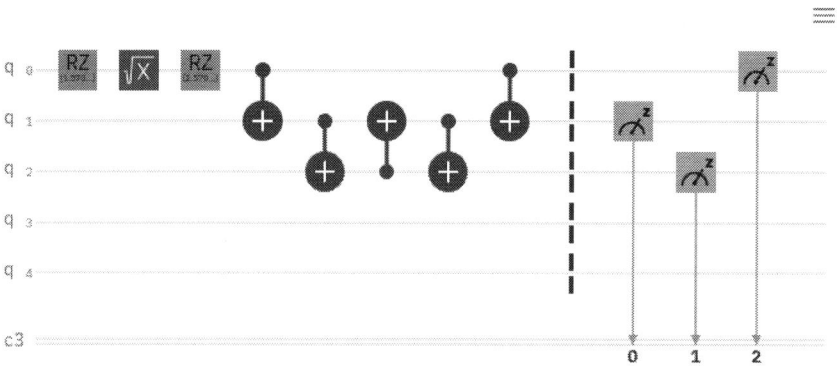

That is, it might not be possible to run our original quantum circuit on the device due to the topology or gate set available to the processor, so the software will transpile or convert our circuit to an equivalent one that can be physically run.

Exercise 5.1. Using the drag-and-drop Quantum Composer in IBM Quantum, run the following circuit on one of IBM's quantum processors:

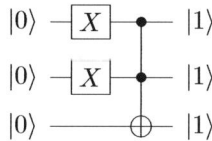

(a) Which processor did you use?
(b) Draw the topology of your processor (the arrangement of the qubits and their connections to each other).
(c) Draw the transpiled circuit.
(d) Draw the resulting histogram showing the probability of each measurement outcome.

5.1.4 Simulator

Sometimes, it can take a long time for a job to make it through the queue for an actual quantum processor. Or, the available quantum processors have too few qubits. In these cases, using a simulator rather than an actual quantum processor may be favorable. Let us try this for the previous circuit that creates the GHZ state. Clicking "Setup and run," let us run the circuit on ibm_qasm_simulator:

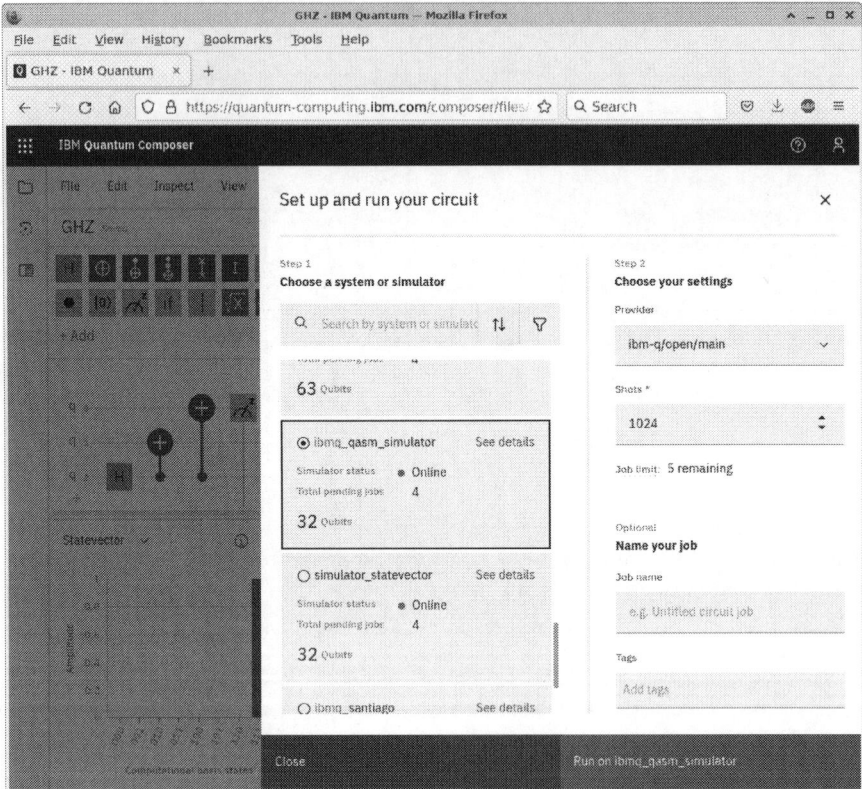

This results in the following histogram:

Histogram

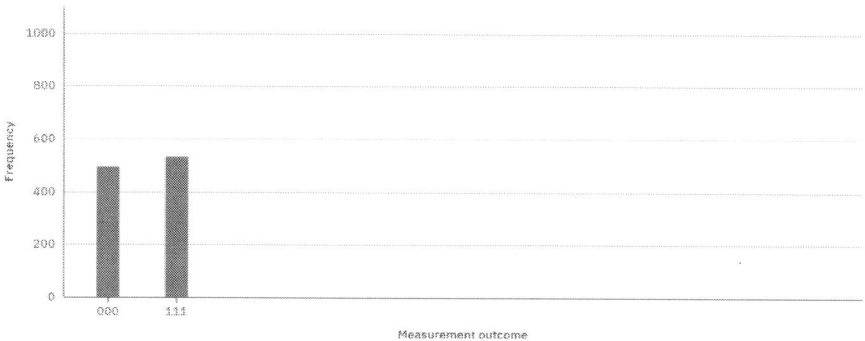

Out of the 1024 shots, the simulator measured $|000\rangle$ 493 times and $|111\rangle$ 531 times. Due to the limited number of shots and the use of a pseudo-random number generator to simulate the results, the results were not perfectly 50% each, but they are pretty close.

Exercise 5.2. Simulate the circuit from Exercise 5.1 using ibm_qasm_simulator. Draw the resulting histogram showing the probability of each measurement outcome.

5.2 Quantum Assembly Language

5.2.1 OpenQASM

Rather than dragging and dropping quantum gates to create a circuit, they can also be written using programming languages. We can describe quantum circuits using *OpenQASM*, where Open refers to the specification being open or freely available, and QASM (pronounced kazm) stands for quantum assembly language. Despite the name "assembly language," it is really more of a hardware description language like Verilog (see Section 1.3), where we defined registers and wires, listed logic gates with their inputs and outputs, and defined modules/functions. A document describing OpenQASM is available at https://arxiv.org/abs/1707.03429.
Here is an example of a simple OpenQASM program:

```
OPENQASM 2.0;

qreg q[3];
creg c[3];

U(pi,0,pi) q[0];
CX q[0], q[1];

measure q -> c;
```

The first line specifies that it is an OpenQASM program, version 2.0. Then we define a quantum register or array named q consisting of 3 qubits, $|q_2\rangle|q_1\rangle|q_0\rangle$. All of these qubits are initially $|0\rangle$, so q is initially $|000\rangle$. This is followed by a classical register named c consisting of 3 bits, also indexed $c_2c_1c_0$, and all these bits are initially 0. Next, we apply a one-qubit quantum gate U(pi,0,pi) to qubit q[0], where the one-qubit gate is parameterized as

$$U(\theta,\phi,\lambda) = \begin{pmatrix} e^{-i(\phi+\lambda)/2}\cos(\theta/2) & -e^{-i(\phi-\lambda)/2}\sin(\theta/2) \\ e^{i(\phi-\lambda)/2}\sin(\theta/2) & e^{i(\phi+\lambda)/2}\cos(\theta/2) \end{pmatrix}.$$

With appropriate choices for the angles, any one-qubit gate can be written this way, up to a global phase. Technically, this is a rotation about the z-axis of the Bloch sphere by λ, followed by a rotation about the y-axis by θ, followed by another rotation about the z-axis, but by ϕ. In this example, when $(\theta,\phi,\lambda) = (\pi,0,\pi)$, we get

$$U(\pi,0,\pi) = \begin{pmatrix} e^{-i\pi/2}\cos(\pi/2) & -e^{i\pi/2}\sin(\pi/2) \\ e^{-i\pi/2}\sin(\pi/2) & e^{i\pi/2}\cos(\pi/2) \end{pmatrix}$$

$$= \begin{pmatrix} 0 & -i \\ -i & 0 \end{pmatrix} = -i\begin{pmatrix} 0 & 1 \\ 1 & 0 \end{pmatrix} = -iX \equiv X,$$

where in the last step, $\equiv$ means "equivalent to" because the global phase of $-i$ can be dropped. So, this gate transforms q[0] from $|000\rangle$ to $-i|001\rangle$, but the global phase can be ignored, so it is just $|001\rangle$. Next, CNOT (cx) is applied with q[0] as the control and q[1] as the target, transforming the state from $|001\rangle$ to $|011\rangle$. Finally, q is measured, and the resulting bits are placed in the classical register c. So, c[2] = 0, c[1] = 1, and c[0] = 1.

$U(\theta,\phi,\lambda)$ and CX are the only two gates that OpenQASM has built-in because they form a universal gate set. That is, recall from Section 4.6 that the set {CNOT, all single-qubit gates} is universal for quantum computing. We can, however, define our own gates so that they are easier to use. Rewriting our previous code,

```
OPENQASM 2.0;

// Define the Pauli X gate.
gate x a
{
    U(pi,0,pi) a;
}

qreg q[3];
creg c[3];

x q[0];
CX q[0], q[1];

measure q -> c;
```

Comments are preceded by two slashes //, and names must start with a lowercase letter, so our gate is called x, not X.

5.2.2 Quantum Experience Standard Header

Rather than writing all one-qubit gates in the form $U(\theta, \phi, \lambda)$ or defining them ourselves, it would be convenient if commonly used quantum gates like X, Y, Z, H, and others were predefined. Thankfully, these and many of the gates used by IBM Quantum are defined in the library qelib1.inc, called the *IBM Quantum Experience standard header*, which we can include in OpenQASM. So our previous code can be written as

```
OPENQASM 2.0;
include "qelib1.inc";

qreg q[3];
creg c[3];

x q[0]
cx q[0], q[1];

measure q -> c;
```

Note CX has been replaced by cx, since we are now using CNOT defined in the Quantum Experience standard header instead of the CNOT that is native to Open-QASM.

Exercise 5.3. Recall OpenQASM parameterizes an arbitrary single-qubit gate as

$$U(\theta, \phi, \lambda) = \begin{pmatrix} e^{-i(\phi+\lambda)/2}\cos(\theta/2) & -e^{-i(\phi-\lambda)/2}\sin(\theta/2) \\ e^{i(\phi-\lambda)/2}\sin(\theta/2) & e^{i(\phi+\lambda)/2}\cos(\theta/2) \end{pmatrix}.$$

For convenience, let us define:

$$u_1(\lambda) = U(0,0,\lambda),$$
$$u_2(\phi,\lambda) = U(\pi/2,\phi,\lambda),$$
$$u_3(\theta,\phi,\lambda) = U(\theta,\phi,\lambda).$$

Now go to https://arxiv.org/abs/1707.03429 and download a PDF of the preprint that specifies OpenQASM. Go to Section 3.1 on the "Quantum Experience standard header." In terms of u_1, u_2, u_3, and CNOT (CX), what is
  (a) The H gate?
  (b) The $T^\dagger$ gate?
  (c) A rotation about the x-axis by angle θ?
  (d) The controlled-Z gate?
  (e) The Toffoli gate?

5.2.3 OpenQASM in IBM Quantum

Besides dragging and dropping quantum gates, IBM Quantum also supports programming using OpenQASM. From the previous circuit for the GHZ state, we can go to the menu and select "View" and then "Code Editor:"

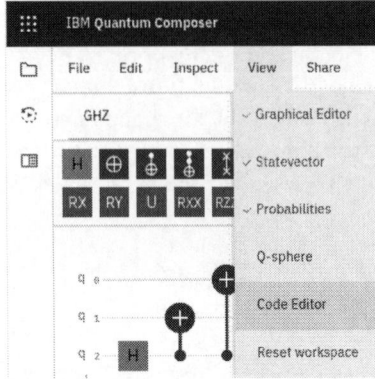

Then, the Code Editor will appear on the right side of the screen:

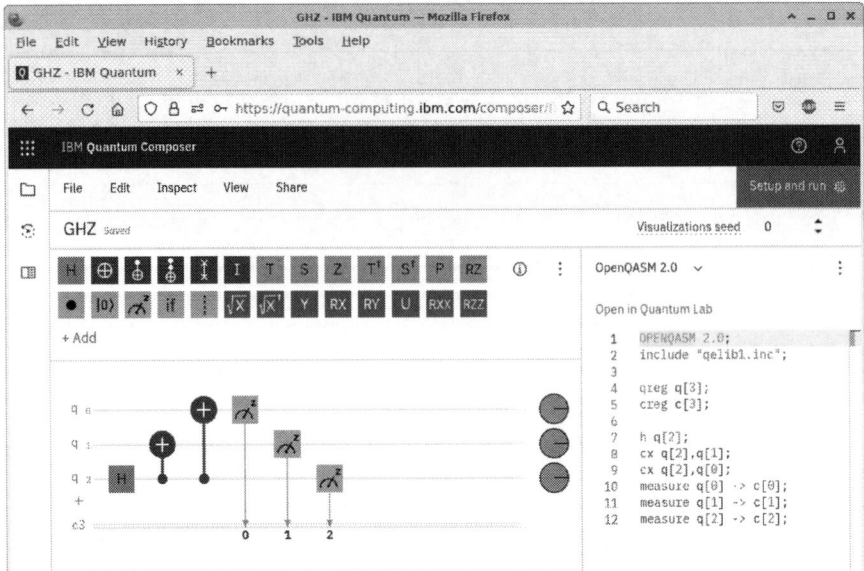

5.2.4 Quantum Adder

Now, let us write some OpenQASM code to add $1110 + 1011 = 11001$ using the quantum ripple-carry adder in Section 4.5.6 and simulate it in IBM Quantum Experience. We can define our own quantum gates to implement the sum S, carry C, and inverse carry $C^\dagger$. Note s is the S gate, so we cannot use it as an identifier/name.

```
OPENQASM 2.0;

// Include standard gates from IBM Quantum Experience.
include "qelib1.inc";

// Define the quantum sum gate.
gate sum cin, a, b
{
    cx a, b;
    cx cin, b;
}

// Define the quantum carry gate.
gate carry cin, a, b, cout
{
    ccx a, b, cout;
    cx a, b;
    ccx cin, b, cout;
}

// Define the inverse of the quantum carry gate.
gate carrydg cin, a, b, cout
{
    ccx cin, b, cout;
    cx a, b;
    ccx a, b, cout;
}

// Declare the quantum registers.
qreg c[4];
qreg a[4];
qreg b[5];

// Declare the classical registers.
creg bc[5];

// Set the input states by applying X gates.
x a[1];
x a[2];
x a[3]; // a = 1110
x b[0];
x b[1];
x b[3]; // b = 1011

// Add the numbers so that |a>|b> becomes |a>|a+b>.
carry c[0], a[0], b[0], c[1];
carry c[1], a[1], b[1], c[2];
carry c[2], a[2], b[2], c[3];
carry c[3], a[3], b[3], b[4];
cx a[3], b[3];
sum c[3], a[3], b[3];
```

```
carrydg c[2], a[2], b[2], c[3];
sum c[2], a[2], b[2];
carrydg c[1], a[1], b[1], c[2];
sum c[1], a[1], b[1];
carrydg c[0], a[0], b[0], c[1];
sum c[0], a[0], b[0];

// Measure the sum and put it in the classical register.
measure b -> bc;
```

In the Quantum Composer, if we click the button on the left to view the "Composer files," there is a button to upload an OpenQASM circuit:

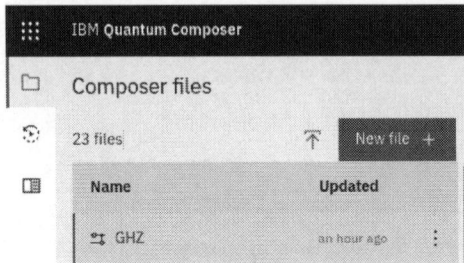

Uploading it, we get a new circuit:

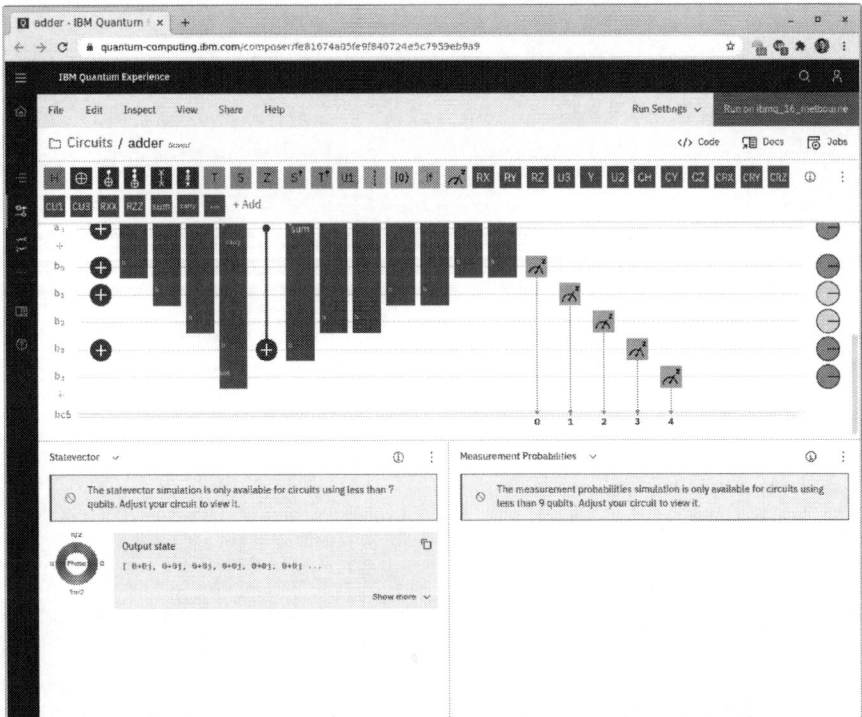

The circuit is too tall to include all of it in the above picture. Also, the histograms at the bottom of the circuit are not available because our circuit uses too many qubits. If we look at the Bloch spheres, however, at the end of the circuit, we see that $b_4b_3b_2b_1b_0 = 11001$, so the addition circuit works, as expected. We can also run the circuit on the ibm_qasm_simulator backend, which yields the following results:

Result

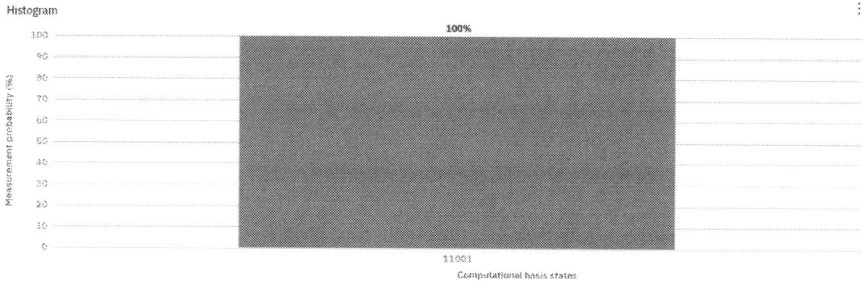

Again, the sum is 11001, as expected. Finally, we can run it on an actual quantum processor, yielding the following:

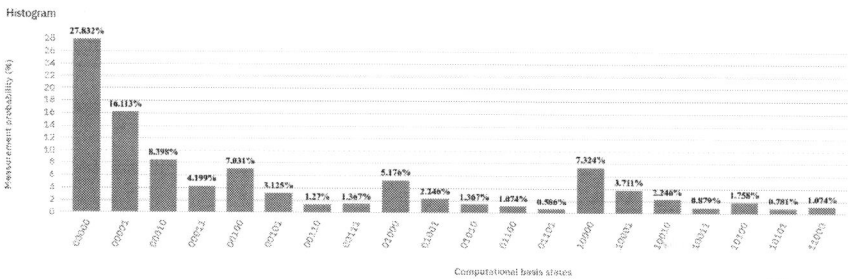

The histogram cannot fit all the results. If we click the three dots in the upper-right corner of the histogram, we can download the results as a CSV file. Here's what we get:

```
Computational basis states,Probabilities
00000,27.832
00001,16.113
00010,8.398
00011,4.199
00100,7.031
00101,3.125
00110,1.27
00111,1.367
01000,5.176
01001,2.246
01010,1.367
01011,0.391
01100,1.074
01101,0.586
01110,0.098
```

```
01111,0.293
10000,7.324
10001,3.711
10010,2.246
10011,0.879
10100,1.758
10101,0.781
10110,0.488
10111,0.293
11000,1.074
11001,0.488
11011,0.195
11100,0.098
11101,0.098
```

So, out of 1024 shots, the probability of getting the correct answer of 11001 is 0.488%, or less than half a percent. That is quite bad. To understand why, let us look at the transpiled circuit. It is so long that we split it across six images:

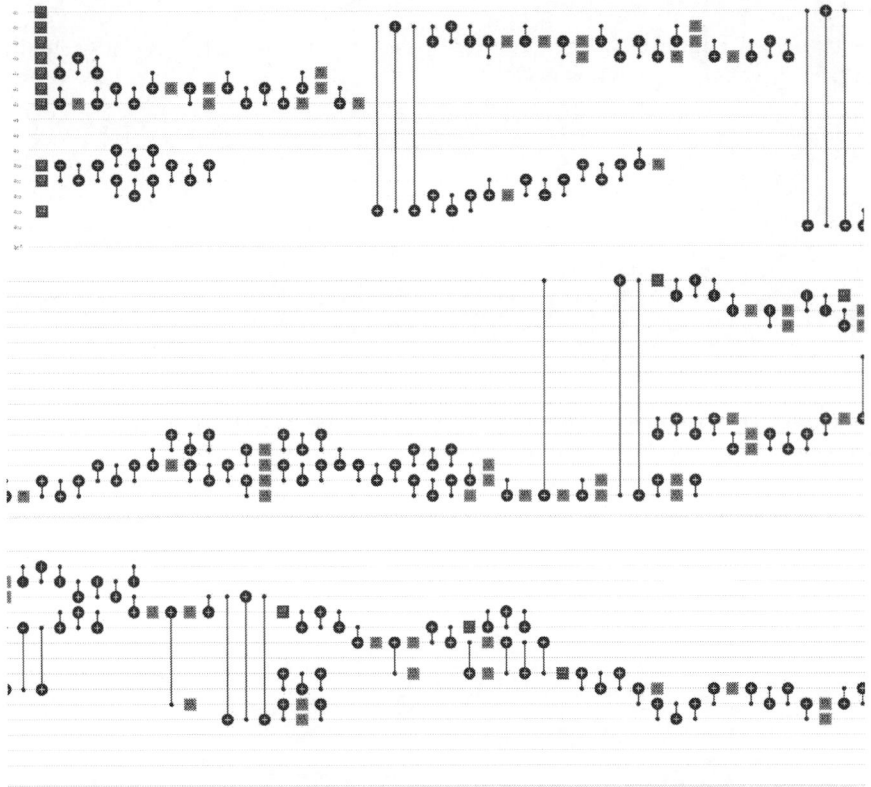

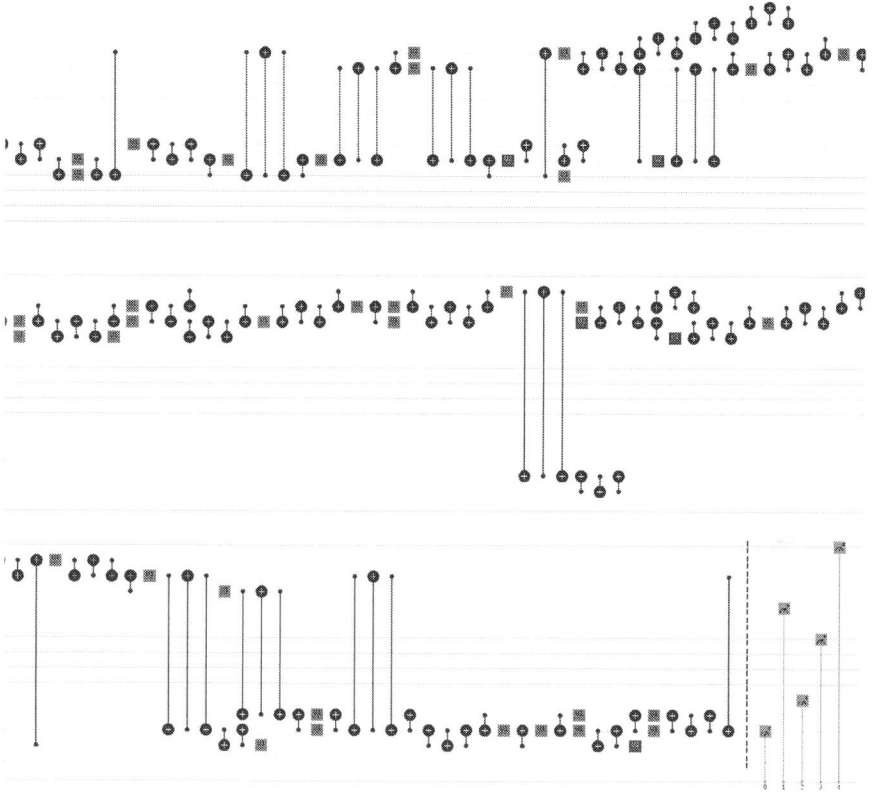

Since the transpiled circuit is so long, our qubits are noisy, and we do not yet have error correction, the errors just kept accumulating. It is unsurprising, then, that our histogram was so wrong.

Exercise 5.4. Consider the following quantum circuit:

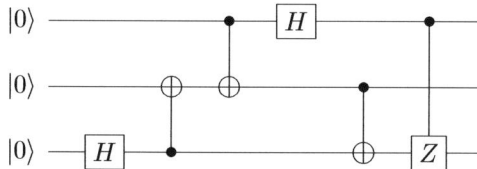

(a) Program this circuit using OpenQASM.
(b) Import your program into the Quantum Composer.
(c) Run your circuit on an actual quantum device. Which device did you choose, and what results did you get?

5.3 Qiskit

5.3.1 *Quantum Composer*

Besides the Quantum Composer and OpenQASM editor, IBM has provided another way to program their quantum processors. It is called *Qiskit*, where QIS stands for quantum information science, and kit refers to a software development kit (SDK). Qiskit is pronounced "kiz kit," although some variants exist, like, "quiz kit" and "kiss kit." Qiskit is not a programming language, but is rather a toolkit or package for the Python programming language. Qiskit is the most powerful way to program IBM's quantum computers because it provides more functionality than the other approaches, and it also allows users to use Python's vast network of packages and libraries. More information about Qiskit is available at `https://qiskit.org`.

You can use Qiskit inside IBM Quantum. To view a circuit as Qiskit code, in the Quantum Composer, just select "Qiskit" in the Code Editor. For the GHZ state, we get the following:

Here is the code again:

```
from qiskit import QuantumRegister, ClassicalRegister,
    ↪ QuantumCircuit
from numpy import pi

qreg_q = QuantumRegister(3, 'q')
creg_c = ClassicalRegister(3, 'c')
circuit = QuantumCircuit(qreg_q, creg_c)

circuit.h(qreg_q[2])
circuit.cx(qreg_q[2], qreg_q[1])
circuit.cx(qreg_q[2], qreg_q[0])
circuit.measure(qreg_q[0], creg_c[0])
circuit.measure(qreg_q[1], creg_c[1])
circuit.measure(qreg_q[2], creg_c[2])
```

The first line imports from the Qiskit package functions to define quantum registers, classical registers, and quantum circuits. In the second line, we import from the numpy package the number pi. Although it is not used in this circuit, it is used in many circuits, so it is included here for convenience.

In the next block of lines, the code defines a quantum register of length 3, labeled q, with the variable name qreg_q. Then, the three qubits would be qreg_q[0], qreg_q[1], and qreg_q[2]. Similarly, the next line defines a classical register of length 3, labeled c, with the variable name creg_c, so the bits are creg_c[0], creg_c[1], and creg_c[2]. After that, a quantum circuit is created containing the quantum and classical registers, and we name it circuit.

Finally, in the last block of 6 lines, we add a Hadamard gate to our quantum circuit, and it is applied to qubit qreg_q[2]. Then, we add a CNOT (CX) gate, with qreg_q[2] as the control and qreg_q[1] as the target. Then, we add another CNOT gate, again with qreg_q[2] as the control, but now with qreg_q[0] as the target. In the final three lines, we add measurements to the circuit, and the result of measuring qubit qreg_q[0] is placed in the classical bit creg_c[0], and so forth.

5.3.2 Quantum Lab

In the Quantum Composer, the Qiskit code is "read only," so it cannot be modified. To modify it, we click "Open in Quantum Lab." This opens a Jupyter notebook, where Python code can be executed and the results displayed in an interactive manner:

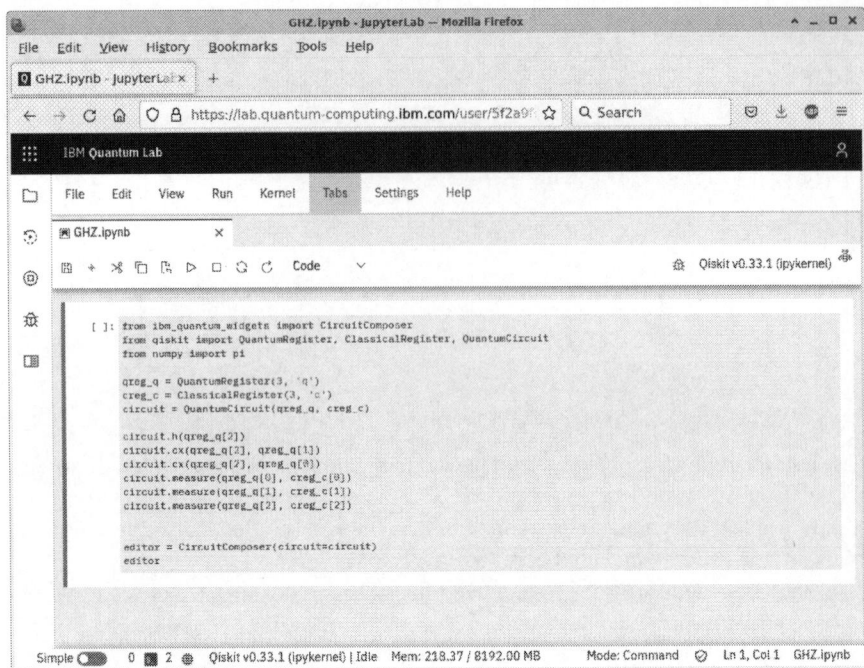

The first cell contains mostly the code from before, but now it starts and ends with some additional code:

```
from ibm_quantum_widgets import CircuitComposer

[same code as before]

editor = CircuitComposer(circuit=circuit)
editor
```

The first line loads a package that will allow us to view the Quantum Composer from within the Quantum Lab. The second-to-last line creates the Quantum Composer as an object named editor, and the last line displays the editor. We can run this cell by selecting the cell and clicking the ▷ Run button, or by pressing Shift+Enter on your keyboard. When we do, we get the following:

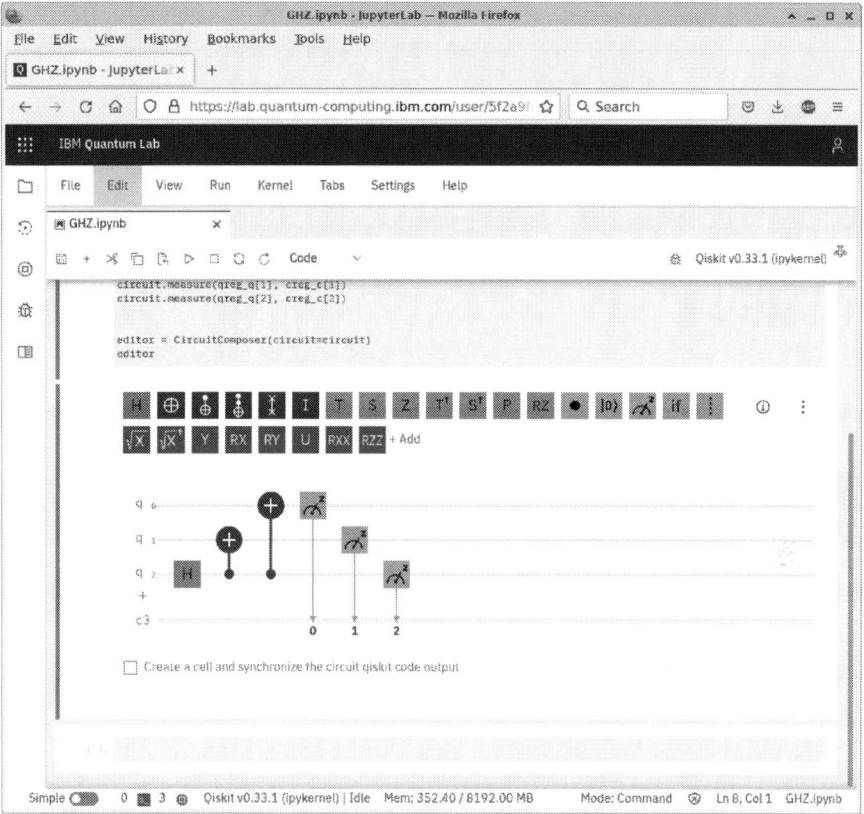

After running the cell, a second, empty cell appears below. We can put any Python code we would like. For example, we can draw the circuit without using the entire Quantum Composer using the `draw` function within `QuantumCircuit` to draw a picture of our quantum circuit:

```
QuantumCircuit.draw(circuit)
```

The output of this is

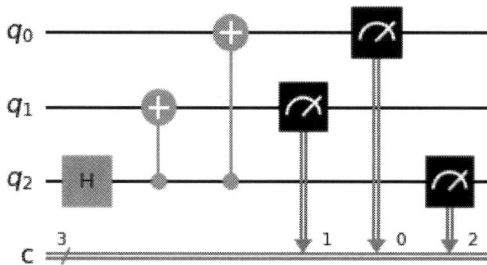

As another example, we can print the OpenQASM code for the quantum circuit:

```
print(circuit.qasm())
```

The output of this is

```
OPENQASM 2.0;
include "qelib1.inc";
qreg q[3];
creg c[3];
h q[2];
cx q[2],q[1];
cx q[2],q[0];
measure q[0] -> c[0];
measure q[1] -> c[1];
measure q[2] -> c[2];
```

5.3.3 Simulator

Now, let us simulate this quantum circuit. The simulators are contained in a Qiskit library called Aer, which we can import and then view the backends:

```
# Import the Qiskit Aer library
from qiskit import Aer

# View the Aer backends, which are all simulators.
Aer.backends()
```

The output of this is:

```
[AerSimulator('aer_simulator'),
 AerSimulator('aer_simulator_statevector'),
 AerSimulator('aer_simulator_density_matrix'),
 AerSimulator('aer_simulator_stabilizer'),
 AerSimulator('aer_simulator_matrix_product_state'),
 AerSimulator('aer_simulator_extended_stabilizer'),
 AerSimulator('aer_simulator_unitary'),
 AerSimulator('aer_simulator_superop'),
 QasmSimulator('qasm_simulator'),
 StatevectorSimulator('statevector_simulator'),
 UnitarySimulator('unitary_simulator'),
 PulseSimulator('pulse_simulator')]
```

Let us use qasm_simulator as the backend and execute the circuit on it:

```
# Choose the qasm_simulator backend.
backend = Aer.get_backend('qasm_simulator')

# Import the Qiskit execute function.
from qiskit import execute

# Execute the quantum circuit on the backend, creating a job.
job = execute(circuit, backend)
```

We can use the `job_monitor` function to see if the job is completed. It needs to be imported from Qiskit.

```
# Check the status of the job.
from qiskit.tools.monitor import job_monitor
job_monitor(job)
```

If the job has not yet run, the job monitor will periodically update itself. Once the job is done, we can get a count of the results and print them:

```
# Get a count of the results.
count = job.result().get_counts()

# Print the counts.
print(count)
```

The output of this is

```
{'000': 497, '111': 527}
```

We expect that each result should appear 512 times (half of 1024 shots), but just like flipping a coin 1024 times may not yield heads 512 times and tails 512 times, there is some deviation because of statistics, not because of errors. This is a simulation, not actual noisy quantum hardware.

We can also plot a histogram of the counts by importing the qiskit.visualizations package and calling the `plot_histogram` function:

```
# Import visualizations from Qiskit.
from qiskit.visualization import *

# Plot the count as a histogram.
plot_histogram(count)
```

This outputs the following image:

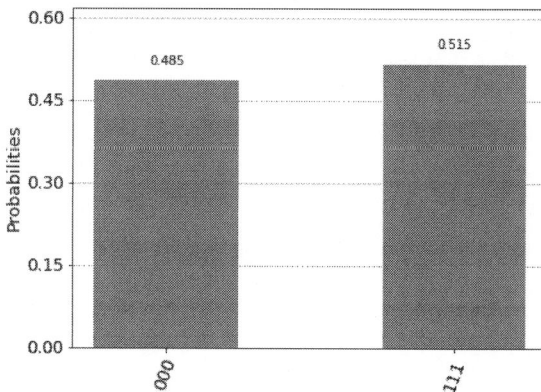

5.3.4 Quantum Processor

Now, let us run the quantum circuit on one of IBM's actual quantum processors. First, we need to load our IBM Quantum account to see what quantum processors are available to us:

```
# Import the Qiskit IBMQ library.
from qiskit import IBMQ

# Load our IBMQ account.
provider = IBMQ.load_account()

# List our backends.
provider.backends()
```

This prints the quantum processors that are available to us, which includes the public ones and any that we have paid access to. The output is

```
[<IBMQSimulator('ibmq_qasm_simulator') from IBMQ(hub='ibm-q',
    ↪ group='open', project='main')>,
 <IBMQBackend('ibmqx2') from IBMQ(hub='ibm-q', group='open',
    ↪ project='main')>,
 <IBMQBackend('ibmq_16_melbourne') from IBMQ(hub='ibm-q',
    ↪ group='open', project='main')>,
 <IBMQBackend('ibmq_vigo') from IBMQ(hub='ibm-q', group='open
    ↪ ', project='main')>,
 <IBMQBackend('ibmq_ourense') from IBMQ(hub='ibm-q', group='
    ↪ open', project='main')>,
 <IBMQBackend('ibmq_valencia') from IBMQ(hub='ibm-q', group='
    ↪ open', project='main')>,
 <IBMQBackend('ibmq_armonk') from IBMQ(hub='ibm-q', group='
    ↪ open', project='main')>,
 <IBMQBackend('ibmq_athens') from IBMQ(hub='ibm-q', group='
    ↪ open', project='main')>,
 <IBMQBackend('ibmq_santiago') from IBMQ(hub='ibm-q', group='
    ↪ open', project='main')>]
```

As before, let us pick a particular hardware backend and execute our circuit. We have previously imported the necessary functions and libraries, so we can just execute the commands:

```
# Choose a quantum processor as the backend.
backend = provider.get_backend('ibmq_athens')

# Execute the job.
job = execute(circuit, backend)
```

Again, we can use the job_monitor function to see if the job is completed. It is already imported, so we do not need to import it again:

```
job_monitor(job)
```

Once it has finished, we can get a count of the results, print them, and print a histogram:

```
count = job.result().get_counts()
print(count)
plot_histogram(count)
```

The output is

```
{'000': 499, '001': 7, '010': 8, '011': 13, '100': 1, '101':
    ↪ 22, '110': 17, '111': 457}
```

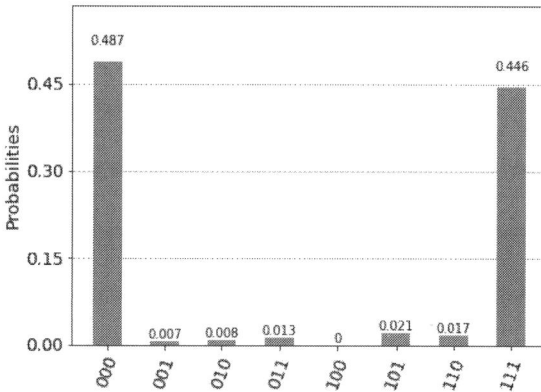

Most of the time, the result of the quantum circuit is 000 or 111, but due to decoherence, some other results are also obtained.

Exercise 5.5. In IBM Quantum, go to the Quantum Lab through the menu:

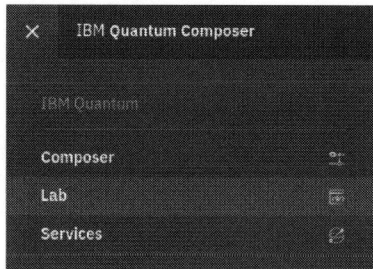

In the Quantum Lab, create a new Jupyter notebook for Qiskit (the arrow below indicates which button to click):

The notebook should be blank. Starting with this, import the necessary Qiskit libraries and functions and create the following quantum circuit:

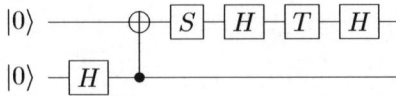

Note you should add measurements at the end of the circuit.
  (a) Simulate the circuit using qasm_simulator. What histogram of results do you get?
  (b) Run it on a sufficiently large quantum processor. Which processor did you choose? What histogram of results did you get?

5.4 Other Quantum Programming Languages

OpenQASM and Qiskit were both developed by IBM to work with their quantum devices. They are not the only options for quantum programming, however. Here are a few others, which you are free to explore on your own, and there are more beyond this list:

- Braket is Amazon's quantum computing platform, and they have their own Python software development kit for programming the devices on their platform.
- Cirq is Google's Python software library for programming their quantum computers.
- Microsoft developed a programming language called Q# (pronounced "Q-sharp") specifically for programming quantum computers.
- Quil is a quantum "instruction set architecture" made by Rigetti for programming its quantum computers. It is similar to OpenQASM. PyQuil is a library for programming Quil in Python.

5.5 Summary

Quantum computing is progressing from an academic research interest to a nascent industry, and the existence of this chapter on quantum programming is evidence of this. Actual quantum devices are being developed, and the tools described in this chapter provide an introduction for how to use them. We will continue using IBM Quantum for the rest of this textbook as we learn about more advanced protocols and algorithms.

Chapter 6
Entanglement and Quantum Protocols

In this chapter, we will explore entanglement in greater detail. We will see that if two qubits are entangled, measuring one affects the other, but there are limits to how quickly one can communicate using this behavior. We will see that if two people, Alice and Bob, share entangled qubits, they can exploit this entanglement to send information to each other using various protocols. With *superdense coding*, Alice can send one qubit to Bob, but Bob will be able to discern two classical bits worth of information. With *quantum teleportation*, Alice will be able to teleport the state of a qubit to Bob by only sending him classical information. We will also see a quantum protocol that does not use entanglement: *quantum key distribution*, where Alice and Bob will be able to agree on a secret *key* or code, and the laws of quantum mechanics prevent a third party from learning the key.

6.1 Measurements

In Section 4.3, we learned about product states, which can be factored into the tensor product of single-qubit states, and entangled states, which could not. For example,

$$\frac{1}{2}(|00\rangle - |01\rangle + |10\rangle - |11\rangle) = \underbrace{\frac{1}{\sqrt{2}}(|0\rangle + |1\rangle)}_{|+\rangle} \otimes \underbrace{\frac{1}{\sqrt{2}}(|0\rangle - |1\rangle)}_{|-\rangle}$$

$$= |+\rangle \otimes |-\rangle$$

$$= |+\rangle|-\rangle$$

is a product state, and

$$|\Phi^+\rangle = \frac{1}{\sqrt{2}}(|00\rangle + |11\rangle)$$

is an entangled state.

6.1.1 Product States

Now, if we measure a single qubit in a product state, it does not affect the other qubit. For example, if we measure the left qubit of $|+\rangle|-\rangle$, we get $|0\rangle$ or $|1\rangle$, each with probability $1/2$. Thus, the resulting states are $|0\rangle|-\rangle$ or $|1\rangle|-\rangle$. The right qubit remains $|-\rangle$, unaltered by the measurement of the left qubit. A product state has no entanglement.

6.1.2 Maximally Entangled States

If we measure a single qubit in an entangled state, it can affect the other qubits. For example, consider the entangled state $|\Phi^+\rangle = (|00\rangle + |11\rangle)/\sqrt{2}$. If we measure the left qubit, we get $|0\rangle$ or $|1\rangle$, each with probability $1/2$, and the state collapses to $|00\rangle$ or $|11\rangle$, respectively. So, if we measure the left qubit and get $|0\rangle$, we know that the right qubit is also in the state $|0\rangle$, and similarly, if we measures the left qubit and get $|1\rangle$, we know that the right qubit is also in the state $|1\rangle$.

This is another way to identify entanglement. A measurement of one qubit affects the other qubit.

In this example, $|\Phi^+\rangle$ has the maximum amount of entanglement, since measuring one qubit completely determines what the other qubit will be. That is, if we measure the left qubit and get $|0\rangle$, we know with certainty that a measurement of the second qubit will also yield $|0\rangle$. The same holds for $|1\rangle$. We say such entangled states are *maximally entangled*.

With two qubits, there are four maximally entangled states. They are the Bell states:

$$\left|\Phi^+\right\rangle = \frac{1}{\sqrt{2}}\left(|00\rangle + |11\rangle\right),$$

$$\left|\Phi^-\right\rangle = \frac{1}{\sqrt{2}}\left(|00\rangle - |11\rangle\right),$$

$$\left|\Psi^+\right\rangle = \frac{1}{\sqrt{2}}\left(|01\rangle + |10\rangle\right),$$

$$\left|\Psi^-\right\rangle = \frac{1}{\sqrt{2}}\left(|01\rangle - |10\rangle\right).$$

6.1.3 Partially Entangled States

Now, consider the following state of two qubits:

$$\frac{\sqrt{3}}{2\sqrt{2}}|00\rangle + \frac{\sqrt{3}}{2\sqrt{2}}|01\rangle + \frac{\sqrt{3}}{4}|10\rangle + \frac{1}{4}|11\rangle.$$

This state is entangled because it cannot be factored into the tensor product of single-qubit states (see Exercise 6.1). If we measure only the left qubit, we get

- 0 with probability $3/4$, and the state collapses to

$$\frac{1}{\sqrt{2}}\left(|00\rangle + |01\rangle\right) = |0\rangle\frac{1}{\sqrt{2}}\left(|0\rangle + |1\rangle\right).$$

- 1 with probability $1/4$, and the state collapses to

$$\frac{\sqrt{3}}{2}|10\rangle + \frac{1}{2}|11\rangle = |1\rangle\left(\frac{\sqrt{3}}{2}|0\rangle + \frac{1}{2}|1\rangle\right).$$

We see that measuring the left qubit does affect the right qubit because in one case, the right qubit collapses to $(|0\rangle + |1\rangle)/\sqrt{2}$, while in the other case, the right qubit collapses to $(\sqrt{3}|0\rangle + |1\rangle)/2$. So, there is entanglement. Next, if we measure the right qubit, we may get 0 or 1, with probabilities 50:50 or 0.75:0.25, depending on which state the qubit was in. So, even though measuring the left qubit affected the right qubit, it did not completely determine what a measurement of the right qubit would yield. Since we do not know exactly what the right qubit will be, the original state is not maximally entangled. We say it is *partially entangled*.

Various ways to quantify the amount of entanglement have been proposed, called *entanglement measures*. They all agree that product states have no entanglement, and they largely agree on which states are maximally entangled. They disagree on the degree to which partially entangled states are entangled. This is an area of active research and is beyond the scope of this textbook.

Exercise 6.1. Using the techniques from Section 4.3, show that

$$\frac{\sqrt{3}}{2\sqrt{2}}|00\rangle + \frac{\sqrt{3}}{2\sqrt{2}}|01\rangle + \frac{\sqrt{3}}{4}|10\rangle + \frac{1}{4}|11\rangle$$

cannot be factored into the tensor product of single-qubit states.

Exercise 6.2. Consider the following state of two qubits:

$$\frac{\sqrt{3}}{2\sqrt{2}}|00\rangle + \frac{1}{2\sqrt{2}}|01\rangle + \frac{1}{2\sqrt{2}}|10\rangle + \frac{\sqrt{3}}{2\sqrt{2}}|11\rangle$$

If you measure the left qubit, what outcomes can you get, what are the corresponding probabilities of those outcomes, and what does the state collapse to for each outcome? Is this state a product state, partially entangled state, or maximally entangled state?

Exercise 6.3. Consider the following state of two qubits:

$$\frac{1}{\sqrt{2}}\left(|01\rangle + |10\rangle\right).$$

If you measure the left qubit, what outcomes can you get, what are the corresponding probabilities of those outcomes, and what does the state collapse to for each outcome? Is this state a product state, partially entangled state, or maximally entangled state?

6.2 Bell Inequalities

6.2.1 EPR Paradox and Local Hidden Variables

In 1935, Einstein, Podolsky, and Rosen (EPR) published a paper where they took entangled measurements a step further. Einstein is famous for his Theory of Relativity, among other breakthroughs, and one idea that he pioneered was that the speed of light acted as a universal speed limit, that nothing can travel through space faster than light. This notion that no influence can propagate faster than light is called *locality*. The EPR paradox uses locality to question the meaning of quantum mechanics.

As a modern take on the EPR experiment, we take two qubits and prepare them in the $|\Phi^+\rangle$ state (such as by starting with $|00\rangle$, applying $H \otimes I$ to get $|+\rangle|0\rangle$, and then applying CNOT to get $|\Phi^+\rangle$). Now, we separate the two qubits so that two scientists, conventionally named Alice and Bob (A and B), each have one qubit:

$$\frac{1}{\sqrt{2}}\left(|00\rangle + |11\rangle\right)$$

Alice ●〜〜〜〜〜〜〜〜〜〜〜〜〜〜〜〜〜● Bob

Now, say Alice measures her qubit, and then Bob measures his qubit so quickly after Alice's measurement that any influence from Alice's qubit would have to travel faster than light in order to affect Bob's qubit. Alice and Bob can be sufficiently far apart to make this feasible.

According to the laws of quantum mechanics, whenever Alice measures $|0\rangle$, Bob should also measure $|0\rangle$, since the moment Alice measures $|0\rangle$, the state of the qubits is now $|00\rangle$. The same goes for $|1\rangle$ and $|1\rangle$. EPR proposed that for this to be true, either Alice's measurement was able to influence Bob's measurement faster than light, or the measurement outcomes were predetermined by some *hidden variable* that quantum mechanics did not account for, meaning quantum mechanics was incomplete. EPR's proposal became known as the *EPR paradox*.

EPR considered the former option absurd, and Einstein even called the faster-than-light collapse of the quantum state "spooky action-at-a-distance" to deride it. EPR advocated the latter option, that the measurement outcomes are determined before the measurement in a way that quantum mechanics does not account for. This belief is called *realism*, that the qubits have actual, real values before measurement.

Note EPR did not argue against quantum mechanics' correctness, just its completeness. That is, they did agree that whenever Alice measured $|0\rangle$, Bob would also measure $|0\rangle$, and the same goes for $|1\rangle$. But they argued that a local hidden variable theory must exist that explains these outcomes assuming locality, and this more complete theory would replace quantum mechanics.

The hardware necessary to do this experiment was not available at the time, and would not be for nearly fifty years in the early 1980's, long after Einstein's death in 1955. Even if scientists were able to do the experiment at the time, it would not have resolved the paradox. If scientists did the experiment and Alice and Bob's qubits agreed as predicted by quantum mechanics, it would show that quantum mechanics was correct, but we would still not know if it meant that Alice's qubit could influence Bob's qubit faster than light, or if there is a hidden variable not accounted for by quantum mechanics that determines the measurement outcomes. If scientists did the experiment and Alice and Bob's qubits disagreed from the predictions of quantum mechanics, then it would mean that quantum mechanics was simply wrong, not incomplete.

Almost thirty years into the EPR paradox, however, an important result was found that would allow scientists to determine which was right, quantum mechanics or local realism.

Exercise 6.4. Watch "Misconceptions About the Universe" by Veritasium at `https://www.yo utube.com/watch?v=XBr4GkRnY04`. Fill in the blanks:
  (a) "There was a time when the universe was expanding so rapidly that parts of it were moving apart from each other faster than the speed of light. That time is _____ _____."
  (b) "Relativity says nothing can move through _____ faster than light, but that doesn't stop _____ itself from expanding however it likes."

6.2.2 Bell Inequalities and the CHSH Inequality

In 1964, John Stewart Bell proved an important result that would further distinguish quantum mechanics from the local hidden variable theories that EPR, and others, proposed. Bell calculated the measurement statistics of quantum mechanics for a general problem. Then, he calculated the measurement statistics of *any* local hidden variable theory and showed that they must obey an inequality. The amazing result is that the quantum mechanical statistics disobeyed or violated the inequality, giving a way to experimentally determine whether nature followed quantum mechanics or a local hidden variable theory. If the experiment agreed with quantum mechanics, then nature is not described by any local hidden variable theory, and if the experiment agreed with the inequality, the quantum mechanics is not simply incomplete, it is wrong, because it made an incorrect prediction. An experiment that tests this is called a *Bell test*.

The general result that Bell proved is beyond the scope of this textbook, but we will focus on a particular Bell inequality proposed by Clauser, Horne, Shimony, and Holt (CHSH). In this experiment, Alice and Bob each have one qubit in the $|\Phi^+\rangle$ state:

$$\frac{1}{\sqrt{2}}(|00\rangle + |11\rangle)$$

Alice •∼∼∼∼∼∼∼∼∼∼∼∼∼∼∼∼∼∼∼∼∼• Bob

Alice will either measure her qubit in the Z-basis $A = \{|0\rangle, |1\rangle\}$ or the X-basis $A' = \{|+\rangle, |-\rangle\}$. Of course, measuring A is just a typical measurement. Measuring in the X-basis can be done by first applying H, which turns $|+\rangle$ to $|0\rangle$ and $|-\rangle$ to $|1\rangle$, and then measuring in the Z-basis:

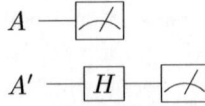

Bob will measure his qubit in one of two bases. The first is

$$B = \left\{ \frac{1}{\sqrt{4+2\sqrt{2}}} \left[(1+\sqrt{2})|0\rangle + |1\rangle \right], \frac{1}{\sqrt{4-2\sqrt{2}}} \left[(1-\sqrt{2})|0\rangle + |1\rangle \right] \right\},$$

and they appear on the Bloch sphere on the $x+z$-axis:

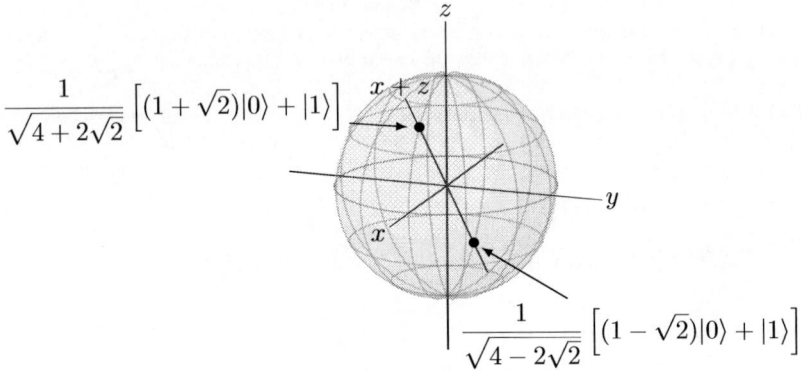

The other basis for Bob is

$$B' = \left\{ \frac{1}{\sqrt{4+2\sqrt{2}}} \left[(-1-\sqrt{2})|0\rangle + |1\rangle \right], \frac{1}{\sqrt{4-2\sqrt{2}}} \left[(-1+\sqrt{2})|0\rangle + |1\rangle \right] \right\},$$

and they appear on the Bloch sphere on the $-x+z$-axis:

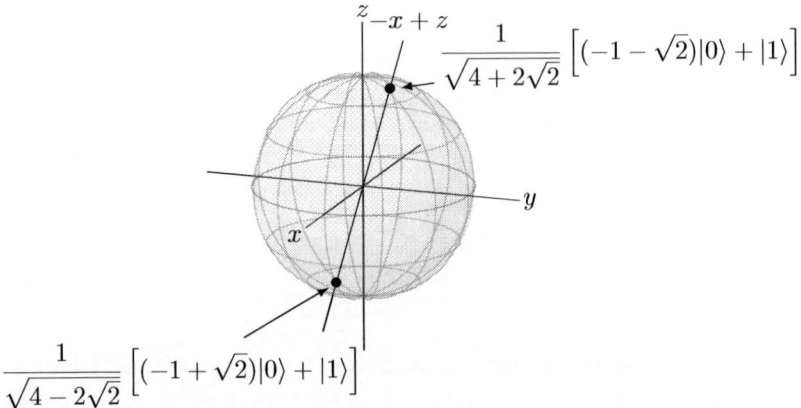

To measure in these bases, we apply the following gates, and then measure in the Z-basis:

$$B \; —\boxed{S}—\boxed{H}—\boxed{T}—\boxed{H}—\measuredangle$$

$$B' \; —\boxed{S}—\boxed{H}—\boxed{T^\dagger}—\boxed{H}—\measuredangle$$

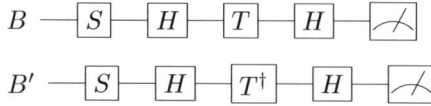

These circuits convert the basis states to $|0\rangle$ and $|1\rangle$, and then we measure in the Z-basis (see Exercise 6.5).

Exercise 6.5. Consider Bob's two measurement bases, B and B':

$$B = \left\{ \frac{1}{\sqrt{4+2\sqrt{2}}} \left[(1+\sqrt{2})|0\rangle + |1\rangle \right], \; \frac{1}{\sqrt{4-2\sqrt{2}}} \left[(1-\sqrt{2})|0\rangle + |1\rangle \right] \right\}.$$

$$B' = \left\{ \frac{1}{\sqrt{4+2\sqrt{2}}} \left[(-1-\sqrt{2})|0\rangle + |1\rangle \right], \; \frac{1}{\sqrt{4-2\sqrt{2}}} \left[(-1+\sqrt{2})|0\rangle + |1\rangle \right] \right\},$$

(a) Show that the following quantum circuit converts the basis states of B to $|0\rangle$ and $|1\rangle$, up to a global phase.

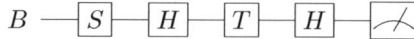

$$B \; —\boxed{S}—\boxed{H}—\boxed{T}—\boxed{H}—\measuredangle$$

(b) Show that the following quantum circuit converts the basis states of B' to $|0\rangle$ and $|1\rangle$, up to a global phase.

$$B' \; —\boxed{S}—\boxed{H}—\boxed{T^\dagger}—\boxed{H}—\measuredangle$$

You can do these calculations by hand if you would like, but I recommend using a computer algebra system.

So, there are four combinations of bases, AB, AB', $A'B$, and $A'B'$. For each of these four bases, Alice and Bob run the experiment many times, and they get some probability distribution for them both getting 0, getting 0 and 1, getting 1 and 0, and both getting 1:

$$P_{00}, \quad P_{01}, \quad P_{10}, \quad P_{11}.$$

Now Alice and Bob interpret their measurement results as $+1$ and -1. So, if Alice measures $|0\rangle$, she records it as $+1$, and when she gets $|1\rangle$, she records it as -1. Bob does the same thing. If we multiply their measurement results, then $|00\rangle$ would be $(1)(1) = 1$, $|01\rangle$ would be $(1)(-1) = -1$, $|10\rangle$ would be $(-1)(1) = -1$, and $|11\rangle$ would be $(-1)(-1) = 1$. Then, the average outcome are these values multiplied by their probabilites, added together:

$$E(A,B) = (1)P_{00} + (-1)P_{01} + (-1)P_{10} + (1)P_{11}$$
$$= P_{00} - P_{01} - P_{10} + P_{11}.$$

This is called the *quantum correlation*, and it is simply the average or expected value of the product of their measurement results. Finally, consider the following quantity that comes from adding/subtracting the quantum correlations for the four measurement bases:

$$S = E(A,B) + E(A,B') + E(A',B) - E(A',B').$$

The *CHSH inequality* is a Bell inequality that says for any local hidden variable theory,

$$|S| \leq 2.$$

The derivation of this is beyond the scope of this textbook. We can calculate, however, what quantum mechanics predicts S should be. First, if Alice measures in the Z-basis A and Bob measures in the basis B, then the circuit we apply is

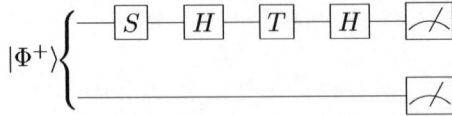

Then, the state at the end of the circuit, before the measurements, is

$$(I \otimes H)(I \otimes T)(I \otimes H)(I \otimes S)|\Phi^+\rangle.$$

We could calculate this by hand, but Mathematica or SageMath might be easier:

- Using Mathematica,

```
PhiPlus = {{1/Sqrt[2]}, {0}, {0}, {1/Sqrt[2]}};
H = 1/Sqrt[2] {{1, 1}, {1, -1}};
S = {{1, 0}, {0, E^(I Pi/2)}};
T = {{1, 0}, {0, E^(I Pi/4)}};
Eye = IdentityMatrix[2];
KroneckerProduct[Eye, H] . KroneckerProduct[Eye, T] .
 KroneckerProduct[Eye, H] . KroneckerProduct[Eye, S] .
     ↪ PhiPlus
```

The output is

$$\frac{1+e^{i\pi/4}}{2\sqrt{2}}|00\rangle + \frac{1-e^{i\pi/4}}{2\sqrt{2}}|01\rangle + i\frac{1-e^{i\pi/4}}{2\sqrt{2}}|10\rangle + i\frac{1+e^{i\pi/4}}{2\sqrt{2}}|11\rangle.$$

- Using SageMath,

```
sage: PhiPlus = vector([1/sqrt(2), 0, 0, 1/sqrt(2)]).column()
sage: H = 1/sqrt(2) * Matrix([[1,1],[1,-1]])
sage: S = Matrix([[1,0],[0,e^(i*pi/2)]])
sage: T = Matrix([[1,0],[0,e^(i*pi/4)]])
sage: Eye = Matrix([[1,0],[0,1]])
sage: Eye.tensor_product(H) * Eye.tensor_product(T) * Eye.
     ↪ tensor_product(H)
....: * Eye.tensor_product(S) * PhiPlus
[   -1/8*sqrt(2)*(-(I + 1)*sqrt(2) - 2)]
[    -1/8*sqrt(2)*((I + 1)*sqrt(2) - 2)]
[ -1/8*sqrt(2)*((I - 1)*sqrt(2) - 2*I)]
[-1/8*sqrt(2)*(-(I - 1)*sqrt(2) - 2*I)]
```

Since $(1+i)/\sqrt{2} = e^{i\pi/4}$, the output simplifies to

$$\frac{1+e^{i\pi/4}}{2\sqrt{2}}|00\rangle + \frac{1-e^{i\pi/4}}{2\sqrt{2}}|01\rangle + i\frac{1-e^{i\pi/4}}{2\sqrt{2}}|10\rangle + i\frac{1+e^{i\pi/4}}{2\sqrt{2}}|11\rangle.$$

Then, the probability of getting each state is

$$P_{00} = \left| \frac{1 + e^{i\pi/4}}{2\sqrt{2}} \right|^2 = \frac{2 + \sqrt{2}}{8},$$

$$P_{01} = \left| \frac{1 - e^{i\pi/4}}{2\sqrt{2}} \right|^2 = \frac{2 - \sqrt{2}}{8},$$

$$P_{10} = \left| i\frac{1 - e^{i\pi/4}}{2\sqrt{2}} \right|^2 = \frac{2 - \sqrt{2}}{8},$$

$$P_{11} = \left| i\frac{1 + e^{i\pi/4}}{2\sqrt{2}} \right|^2 = \frac{2 + \sqrt{2}}{8}.$$

Then, the quantum correlation is

$$\begin{aligned}
E(A,B) &= P_{00} - P_{01} - P_{10} + P_{11} \\
&= \frac{2 + \sqrt{2}}{8} - \frac{2 - \sqrt{2}}{8} - \frac{2 - \sqrt{2}}{8} + \frac{2 + \sqrt{2}}{8} \\
&= \frac{4\sqrt{2}}{8} = \frac{1}{\sqrt{2}}.
\end{aligned}$$

Similarly, if we calculate the quantum correlation for the other measurement bases, we would get

$$E(A,B') = \frac{1}{\sqrt{2}}, \quad E(A',B) = \frac{1}{\sqrt{2}}, \quad E(A',B') = \frac{-1}{\sqrt{2}}.$$

Note the negative sign for $E(A',B')$.

Exercise 6.6. Alice and Bob share an entangled pair of qubits in the $|\Phi^+\rangle = \frac{1}{\sqrt{2}}(|00\rangle + |11\rangle)$ state. If Alice measures her qubit in the X-basis $A' = \{|+\rangle, |-\rangle\}$ and Bob measures his qubit in the basis

$$B' = \left\{ \frac{1}{\sqrt{4 + 2\sqrt{2}}} \left[(-1 - \sqrt{2})|0\rangle + |1\rangle \right], \frac{1}{\sqrt{4 - 2\sqrt{2}}} \left[(-1 + \sqrt{2})|0\rangle + |1\rangle \right] \right\},$$

find
(a) P_{00}.
(b) P_{01}.
(c) P_{10}.
(d) P_{11}.
(e) $E(A',B') = P_{00} - P_{01} - P_{10} + P_{11}$.
You can do these calculations by hand if you would like, but I recommend using a computer algebra system that supports linear algebra.

Then,

$$S = E(A,B) + E(A,B') + E(A',B) - E(A',B') = \frac{4}{\sqrt{2}} = 2\sqrt{2} \approx 2.83.$$

Thus, we see that quantum mechanics violates the CHSH inequality, since quantum mechanics predicts $S = 2.83$, while any local hidden variable theory predicts $|S| < 2$. Now, the true value of S is a matter of experiment. If we get a value of S greater than 2, then local hidden variable theories are wrong. If we get a value less that 2, then quantum mechanics is not only incomplete, but wrong because it made an incorrect prediction.

Tsirelson proved that the value for S that we just calculated is the maximum amount that S can be using quantum mechanics, i.e.,

$$|S| \leq 2\sqrt{2}.$$

This inequality is known as *Tsirelson's inequality*, and it is the maximum amount that the CHSH inequality can be violated by quantum mechanics.

6.2.3 Quantum Processor Experiment

Since we have access to IBM's quantum processors, let us try running the CHSH experiment to see if we get a value of $|S|$ less than or greater than 2.

We need to run four experiments, one for each of the measurement bases AB, AB', $A'B$, and $A'B'$. Beginning with AB:

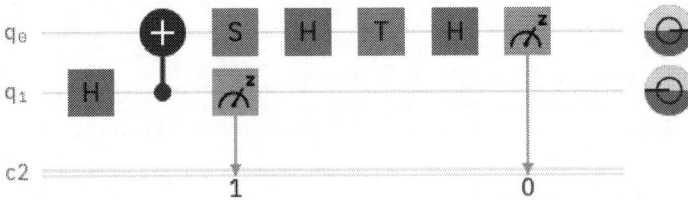

In this circuit, we have two qubits that are initially $|00\rangle$. We apply $H \otimes I$ to get $|+0\rangle$ and then CNOT to get $|\Phi^+\rangle$. Now Alice measures in the Z-basis A, and Bob measures in the B basis. We are not interested in the simulation because the simulation is simply following the laws of quantum mechanics, and we want to test if quantum mechanics is actually correct experimentally or not. Running this on ibmq_athens, we get the following results:

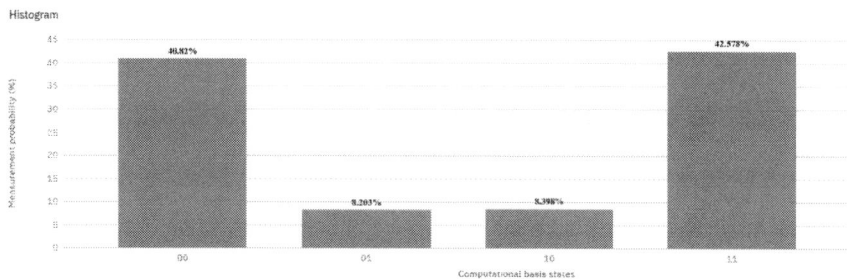

Note you also ran this circuit on a quantum processor in Exercise 5.5.

Next, for AB', Alice again measures in the Z-basis, but now Bob measures in the B' basis:

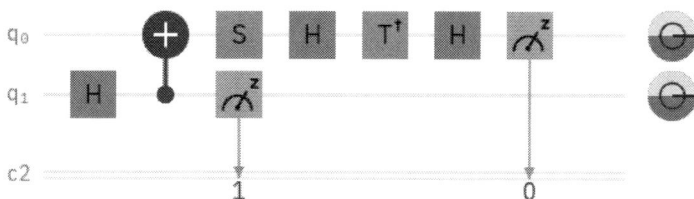

Executing this on ibmq_athens,

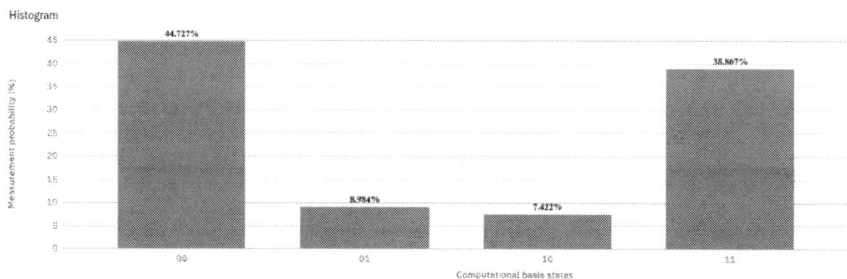

Third, for $A'B$, Alice now measures in the X-basis, and Bob measures in the B basis:

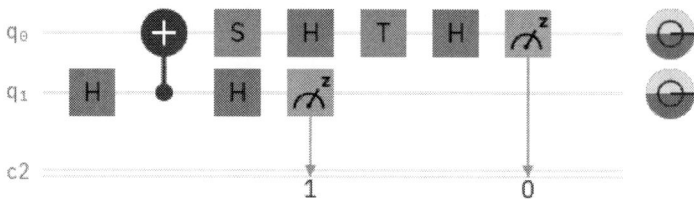

Executing this on ibmq_athens,

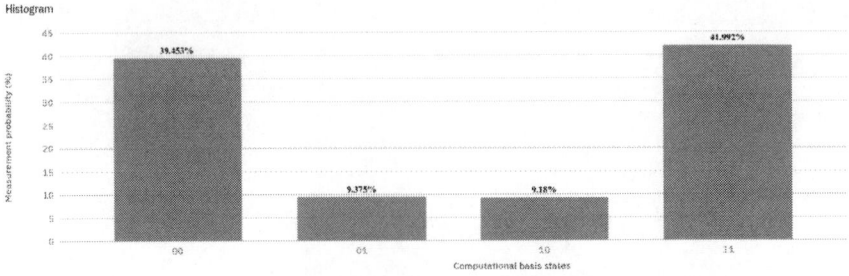

Finally, for $A'B'$, Alice measures in the X-basis, and Bob measures in the B' basis:

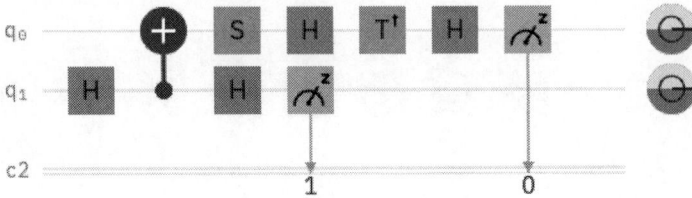

Executing this on ibmq_athens,

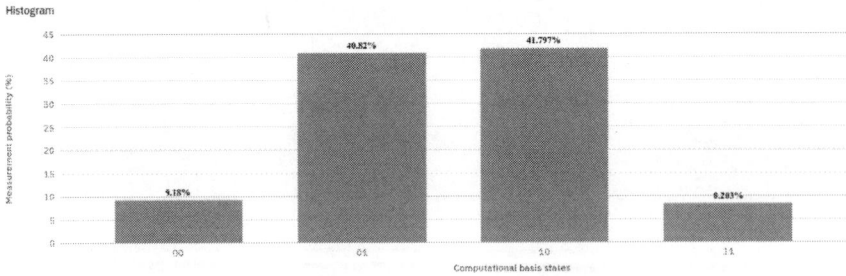

Let us put all these probabilities in a table:

Basis	P_{00}	P_{01}	P_{10}	P_{11}	E
AB	0.40820	0.08203	0.08398	0.42578	0.66797
AB'	0.44727	0.08984	0.07422	0.38867	0.67188
$A'B$	0.39453	0.09375	0.09180	0.41992	0.62890
$A'B'$	0.09180	0.40820	0.41797	0.08203	-0.65234

Then, our quantity of interest is

$$S = E(A,B) + E(A,B') + E(A',B) - E(A',B')$$
$$= 0.66797 + 0.67188 + 0.62890 - (-0.65234)$$
$$= 2.62109.$$

Since this is greater than 2, quantum mechanics is right. Nature is not described by a local hidden variable theory.

6.2.4 Other Experiments

Our previous experiment using a quantum processor is not very precise, however. We do not know how much time occurred between the measurements of the two qubits, so we have not guaranteed that we measured them so closely that an influence would need to travel faster than light. Far more precise experiments, not using quantum processors, were performed in the early 1980's by Alain Aspect and others (see Exercise 6.7), and Alice and Bob's qubits were sufficiently far apart that the collapse of one would need to travel faster than light to affect Bob's qubit. They showed that the Bell inequalities were indeed violated, meaning the universe is not locally realistic (i.e., not described by local hidden variable theories). Since then, even more experiments have been done that have closed various "loopholes" that skeptics have raised (see Exercise 6.8).

Exercise 6.7. Go to `https://doi.org/10.1103/PhysRevLett.49.91` and download the PDF.
  (a) From the abstract, the scientists measured pairs of what?
  (b) From Eq. (2), Bell's inequalities say that for "realistic local theories," the quantity S must be between what two values?
  (c) From Eq. (6), quantum mechanics predicts what value of S for the experiment?
  (d) From Eq. (4), what value of S did they actually measure?
  (e) Did their measured value for S in (d) agree or disagree with Bell's inequalitiy for realistic local theories in (b)?

Exercise 6.8. Go to `https://doi.org/10.1038/nature15759`, which is a paper on the first "loophole-free" Bell test. From the abstract, answer the following questions.
  (a) The scientists used the spins of what particle to perform their Bell test?
  (b) What is a loophole that their experiment closed/addressed?
  (c) How far apart were their spins?
  (d) Which Bell inequality did they test, and what bound on S does it place?
  (e) What observed value of S did they measure?
  (f) What p-value did they obtain? That is, what is the probability that a local hidden variable theory could produce the data they observed?

6.2.5 No-Signaling Principle

From the above experiments, the collapse of an entangled state occurs faster than light. While this seems to violate a fundamental tenant of physics, that nothing can travel through space faster than light, it does not permit information to be transmitted faster than light. So, while the universe permits "spooky action at a distance," it does not permit "spooky communication at a distance."

Say Alice and Bob share seven maximally entangled pairs of qubits, with each pair in the state $|\Phi^+\rangle$. Alice is on Earth, and Bob travels to another galaxy with his qubits.

$$\frac{1}{\sqrt{2}}(|00\rangle + |11\rangle)$$

$$\frac{1}{\sqrt{2}}(|00\rangle + |11\rangle)$$

$$\frac{1}{\sqrt{2}}(|00\rangle + |11\rangle)$$

$$\frac{1}{\sqrt{2}}(|00\rangle + |11\rangle)$$

Alice   Bob

$$\frac{1}{\sqrt{2}}(|00\rangle + |11\rangle)$$

$$\frac{1}{\sqrt{2}}(|00\rangle + |11\rangle)$$

$$\frac{1}{\sqrt{2}}(|00\rangle + |11\rangle)$$

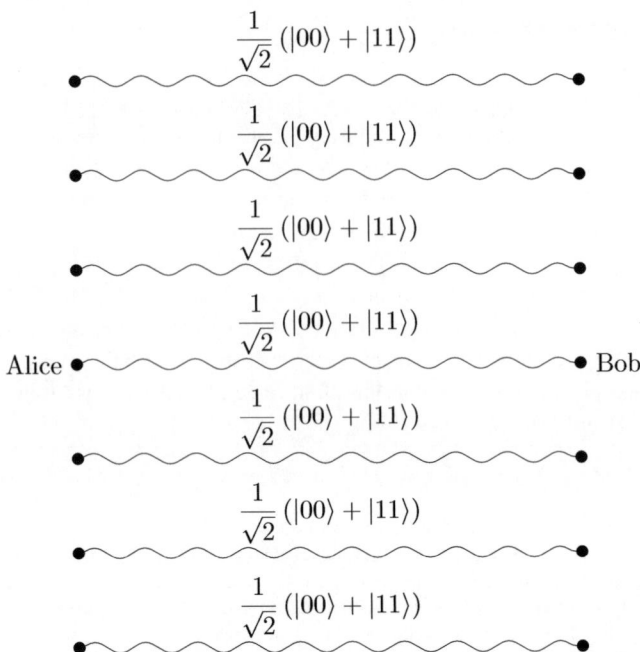

Alice wants to send the ASCII letter "Q" (i.e., the bit string 1010001) to Bob. Classically, Alice would need to physically send the bits, such as via radio waves transmitted through space, or by writing a letter and sending it on a spaceship. Either way, her message (the letter "Q") cannot travel faster than light. But quantumly, can they use their entangled qubits to communicate faster than light?

What might Alice try doing? If she measures each of her seven qubits, she gets $|0\rangle$ or $|1\rangle$ for each qubit, and Bob's qubits would match hers. But since she gets each value with probability $1/2$, Alice and Bob get matching random strings, not 1010001 that encodes the letter Q.

In hopes of getting something less random, suppose Alice measures a qubit in the Z-basis $\{|0\rangle, |1\rangle\}$ to try to communicate 0, and in the X-basis $\{|+\rangle, |-\rangle\}$ to try to communicate 1. So to send 1010001, Alice would measure her first qubit in the X-basis, her second qubit in the Z-basis, her third qubit in the X-basis, her fourth through sixth qubits in the Z-basis, and her seventh qubit in the X-basis. When she measures in the Z-basis, she gets $|0\rangle$ or $|1\rangle$, each with probability $1/2$. If she measures in the X-basis, then we can show that (see Exercise 6.9):

$$|\Phi^+\rangle = \frac{1}{\sqrt{2}}(|++\rangle + |--\rangle),$$

and so she gets $|+\rangle$ or $|-\rangle$, each with probability $1/2$. Bob's qubits match Alice's exactly. To determine the message, Bob needs to determine which basis the qubits were measured in. But there is no way for him to do that. If he measures in the same basis as Alice, he gets the same result as Alice. But if he measures in the wrong basis (X when Alice used Z, or Z when Alice used X), he gets an answer with probability

1/2. Either way, he does not know if the answer he got was correct or random unless he calls Alice on the phone and asks her, which is a classical communication bound by the speed of light.

In fact, no matter what Alice and Bob try, they cannot use entanglement to communicate faster than light. This is called the *no-signaling principle*, and it is a statement of *no faster-than-light communication* or *no superluminal communication*.

Exercise 6.9. Show that $|\Phi^+\rangle = \frac{1}{\sqrt{2}}(|00\rangle + |11\rangle)$, in the X-basis, is

$$\frac{1}{\sqrt{2}}(|++\rangle + |--\rangle).$$

6.2.6 Other Theories

The Bell tests show that nature is not locally realistic. Whether locality is wrong, realism is wrong, or both, however, is still a matter of debate.

Our explanation of quantum computing and quantum mechanics, that quantum states are superpositions and measurement collapses the state, is known as the *Copenhagen interpretation*. It was formulated by Niels Bohr and Werner Heisenberg, two of the "fathers" of quantum mechanics, in the 1920's, and is named after Copenhagen, Denmark because that is where they worked. It is the most popular interpretation of quantum mechanics. Following this interpretation, the EPR paradox would be resolved by the understanding that quantum states are superpositions and do not take "real" values until measurement, and the collapse occurs instantaneously, although information cannot be communicated faster than light.

It is not the only interpretation, however, and others explain the EPR paradox differently:

- Some physicists theorize that entangled particles are connected through *wormholes* or *Einstein-Rosen bridges*. Then, the collapse of entangled states does not occur faster than light because these bridges provide shortcuts across spacetime.
- In *pilot wave theory* or *de Broglie-Bohm theory* or *Bohmian mechanics*, an actual, real particle interacts with a wave that guides it, and the wave evolves by the laws of quantum mechanics. This maintains realism but abandons locality. From the Bell tests, our universe is not described by a local hidden variable theory, but that does not exclude the possibility that nature obeys a non-local hidden variable theory. Pilot wave theory is a non-local hidden variable theory.
- In the *many-worlds interpretation*, quantum states do not collapse. Rather, when a measurement is made, parallel universes are created, one where each possible outcome occurred. Both outcomes are equally real in each universe. This is local and realistic.

Exercise 6.10. Watch "Quantum Entanglement and the Great Bohr-Einstein Debate" by PBS Space Time at https://www.youtube.com/watch?v=tatGLU2EUOA. Fill in the blanks.

(a) "This notion that the universe exists independent of the mind of the observer is called _____ in physics."

(b) "Niels Bohr insisted that it was meaningless to assign reality to the universe in the absence of observation; in the intervals between measurements, quantum systems truly exist as a fuzzy mixture of all possible properties, what we call a _____ of states."

(c) "Albert Einstein insisted on an objective reality, a reality independent of our observation of it. He insisted that the wave function, and by extension quantum mechanics, is _____. There must exist what we call _____ _____ that reflect a more physical underlying reality."

(d) "[EPR] proposed a quantum scenario that showed in order to abandon the assumption of realism, you also had to abandon a concept almost as sacred—_____. _____ is the idea that each bit of the universe only acts on its immediate surroundings. This is fundamental to Einstein's relativity, which tells us that the chain of cause and effect can't propagate any faster than the _____ _____ _____."

(e) "Quantum mechanics requires that we describe the particle pair with a single combined wave function that encompasses all possible states of both particles. We call such particles an _____ _____. Now, according to the Copenhagen interpretation, any measurement of one particle automatically collapses the entire entangled wave function and so affects the results of measurements of the other particle. That's an influence that could theoretically be transmitted _____ across any distance, and even back in time, violating locality and possibly violating causality. Einstein *et al.* thought this was very silly. They thought that every special point in the universe must be real and physical and defined by knowable quantities, _____ _____ _____ that could affect each other no faster than the speed of light."

(f) "Measurement _____ the alignment of the measured particle."

(g) "Scenario one, if Einstein was right, imagine the response of each particle to all possible spin measurements is encoded in each particle at the moment of their creation as _____ _____ local to each particle. _____ we do later to one particle will then effect the other. When we later measure the spins of both particles, there will be a correlation in the results because the particles were once connected. But there'll be _____ _____ due to our choice of measurement axis."

(h) "Scenario two—Bohr was right. What if between creating and measurement, the electron and positron only exist as a wave function of all possible states. In that case, measurement of one particle spin should cause the entire wave function to collapse, to take on _____ _____. Both particles should then manifest opposite spins along whichever axis we choose for one of the particles. That should lead to a correlation between our choice of measurement axis for the first particle and the spin of direction then measured for the second. This is exactly the _____ _____ at a distance that made Einstein so uncomfortable."

(i) "John Steward Bell figured out a set of observable results, the so-called _____ _____, that we expect to see in the case that Einstein was right and quantum mechanics needs local hidden variables. But if an entanglement experiment violates the Bell inequalities, then local realism is also violated."

(j) "But in the early '80s, French physicist Alain Aspect succeeded. Instead of looking at the entangled spins of an electron-positron pair, he used photon pairs with entangled polarizations. [...] And Aspect showed that there was a correlation between the choice of polarization measurement axis for one photon and the final polarization direction of its entangled partner. The Bell inequalities were _____. The experiment was even set up so that the influence had to travel between the photons at _____ _____ the speed of light."

(k) "It's now been thoroughly confirmed that the Bell inequalities are violated, suggesting that the wave function cannot have _____ _____ _____."

(l) "The results of these entanglement experiments do seem to violate local realism. But that may mean a violation of _____, or just of _____."

(m) "Non-locality requires that entangled particles affect each other instantaneously. That sounds blasphemous to anyone who accepts Einstein's theory of relativity. However, non-locality and relativity can actually be perfectly _____. Relativity requires that causality is preserved, so no faster than light _____ flow. But none of these entanglement experiments allow any real information to be transmitted between particles. It's only possible to see the influence between the entangled partners after measurements have been made and those measurements are compared."

(n) "The _____ interpretation remains consistent with all quantum observations."

6.3 Monogamy of Entanglement

6.3.1 Classical Correlations

Classical correlations can be shared among multiple parties. For example, say there are three people, Alice, Bob, and Charlie, and they each have a bit. Say Alice and Bob's bits are perfectly correlated: if Alice's bit is 0, then Bob's bit is also 0, and if Alice's bit is 1, then Bob's bit is also 1:

Alice	Bob
0	0
1	1

Classically, it is possible for Charlie's bit to be perfectly correlated with Alice's bit as well:

Alice	Bob	Charlie
0	0	0
1	1	1

This satisfies two properties. First, if we remove Charlie, we retain perfect correlation between Alice and Bob. Second, if we remove Bob, Alice and Charlie have the same correlation as Alice did with Bob. Put another way, if we swap Bob and Charlie, we get the same distribution. Together, Alice is perfectly correlated with both Bob and Charlie.

6.3.2 Quantum Entanglement

Is this possible for quantum entanglement? That is, if Alice, Bob, and Charlie have qubits, is it possible for them to satisfy the two properties above? Say Alice and Bob's qubits are in the maximally entangled state

$$|\Phi^+\rangle = \frac{1}{\sqrt{2}}(|0\rangle \otimes |0\rangle + |1\rangle \otimes |1\rangle).$$

We want to add Charlie's qubit $|\psi_c\rangle$ so that if we remove him, Alice and Bob's qubits are still in the $|\Phi^+\rangle$ state. Then the three-qubit state must look like

$$\frac{1}{\sqrt{2}}(|0\rangle \otimes |0\rangle + |1\rangle \otimes |1\rangle) \otimes |\psi_c\rangle.$$

But now the second property is not satisfied—swapping Bob and Charlie yields a different state. Alice is not entangled with them to the same degree. In fact, Alice is maximally entangled with Bob, but she is not entangled at all with Charlie!

From this result, we say that entanglement is *monogamous*, like a monogamous relationship between people is exclusive. Two people perfectly "entangled" with each other (Alice and Bob) are not entangled at all with a third party (Charlie).

Finally, note if Alice and Bob are partially entangled, then it is possible for there to be some entanglement with Charlie. A proper treatment of this involves expressing quantum states, not as kets or vectors, but as *density matrices*, which also allow probabilistic mixtures of kets, but that is beyond the scope of this textbook.

Exercise 6.11. The Greenberger–Horne–Zeilinger state (GHZ state) is an entangled state of three-qubits. It is:

$$\frac{1}{\sqrt{2}}(|000\rangle + |111\rangle).$$

(a) Verify that the GHZ state is produced by the following quantum circuit:

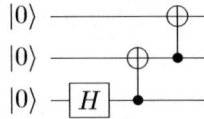

(b) If we measure the left qubit, what are the possible resulting states and with what probabilities?
(c) Are the resulting states after the measurement entangled?

Exercise 6.12. The W state is an entangled state of three qubits. It is:

$$|W\rangle = \frac{1}{\sqrt{3}}(|001\rangle + |010\rangle + |100\rangle).$$

(a) Verify that the W state is produced by the following quantum circuit:

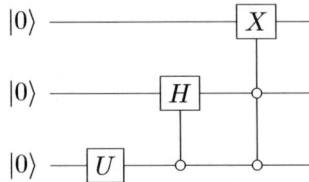

where

$$U = \begin{pmatrix} \sqrt{\frac{2}{3}} & -\frac{1}{\sqrt{3}} \\ \frac{1}{\sqrt{3}} & \sqrt{\frac{2}{3}} \end{pmatrix}.$$

Also, as a reminder, the hollow circle is anti-control. So the second gate applies the Hadamard gate to the middle qubit if the bottom qubit is 0.

(b) If we measure the left qubit, what are the possible resulting states and with what probabilities?
(c) Are the resulting states after the measurement entangled?

6.4 Superdense Coding

6.4.1 The Problem

Alice wants to send classical information to Bob, say one of four possible restaurant options: American, Chinese, Italian, or Mexican. She can either send her preference using classical bits or qubits, and we will see that if Alice and Bob share entanglement, Alice only needs to send half the number of qubits as she would bits.

6.4.2 Classical Solution

Classically, Alice would have to send two bits to Bob, since two bits have four possible states 00, 01, 10, or 11. One bit would not suffice, since it only has two states 0 or 1.

6.4.3 Quantum Solution

Quantumly, Alice can send just one qubit, but it needs to be entangled with a second qubit that Bob already has. Say Alice and Bob share a pair of entangled qubits in the $|\Phi^+\rangle$ state:

$$\frac{1}{\sqrt{2}}\left(|00\rangle + |11\rangle\right)$$

Alice $\bullet\!\!\!\sim\!\!\!\sim\!\!\!\sim\!\!\!\sim\!\!\!\sim\!\!\!\sim\!\!\!\sim\!\!\!\sim\!\!\!\sim\!\!\!\sim\!\!\!\sim\!\!\!\sim\!\!\!\bullet$ Bob

Depending on which of the four options Alice wants to communicate to Bob, she can apply quantum gates to her qubit, then send her one qubit to Bob so that Bob ends up with both qubits:

- If Alice wants to send 00, she does nothing to her qubit, and sends it to Bob so that he has both qubits.
- If Alice wants to send 01, she applies the X gate to her qubit, which transforms $|\Phi^+\rangle$ to

$$|\Psi^+\rangle = \frac{1}{\sqrt{2}}\left(|10\rangle + |01\rangle\right).$$

Then she sends her qubit to Bob, so that he has both qubits.

- If Alice wants to send 10, she applies the Z gate to her qubit, which transforms $|\Phi^+\rangle$ to

$$|\Phi^-\rangle = \frac{1}{\sqrt{2}}\left(|00\rangle - |11\rangle\right).$$

Then she sends her qubit to Bob, so that he has both qubits.

- Finally, if Alice wants to send 11, she applies both X and Z to her qubit. Applying X transforms $|\Phi^+\rangle$ to $|\Psi^+\rangle$, and appling Z transforms $|\Psi^+\rangle$ to

$$|\Psi^-\rangle = \frac{1}{\sqrt{2}}(|01\rangle - |10\rangle).$$

Then Alice sends her qubit to Bob, so that he has both qubits.

Now Bob has both qubits, and they are in one of four states:

$$|\Phi^+\rangle = \frac{1}{\sqrt{2}}(|00\rangle + |11\rangle),$$

$$|\Psi^+\rangle = \frac{1}{\sqrt{2}}(|01\rangle + |10\rangle),$$

$$|\Phi^-\rangle = \frac{1}{\sqrt{2}}(|00\rangle - |11\rangle),$$

$$|\Psi^-\rangle = \frac{1}{\sqrt{2}}(|01\rangle - |10\rangle).$$

Since these four states are orthonormal, they form a measurement basis called the *Bell basis*. Bob can measure the two qubits this Bell basis to distinguish them, thus determining what Alice wanted to send. This is called a *Bell measurement*.

Another way to understand the Bell measurement is to apply CNOT and then $H \otimes I$, then measuring in the Z-basis. That is,

$$|\Phi^+\rangle \xrightarrow{CNOT} \frac{1}{\sqrt{2}}(|00\rangle + |10\rangle) = |+\rangle|0\rangle \xrightarrow{H\otimes I} = |00\rangle,$$

$$|\Psi^+\rangle \xrightarrow{CNOT} \frac{1}{\sqrt{2}}(|01\rangle + |11\rangle) = |+\rangle|1\rangle \xrightarrow{H\otimes I} = |01\rangle,$$

$$|\Phi^-\rangle \xrightarrow{CNOT} \frac{1}{\sqrt{2}}(|00\rangle - |10\rangle) = |-\rangle|0\rangle \xrightarrow{H\otimes I} = |10\rangle,$$

$$|\Psi^-\rangle \xrightarrow{CNOT} \frac{1}{\sqrt{2}}(|01\rangle - |11\rangle) = |-\rangle|1\rangle \xrightarrow{H\otimes I} = |11\rangle.$$

Computationally, this protocol still requires two qubits, as it must because *Holevo's theorem* says that n qubits can only store n bits of classical information. Yet as a communication protocol, it only requires one qubit to be sent.

Generalizing this, if Alice and Bob share n pairs of entangled qubits (so there are $2n$ qubits total), then Alice can measure each of her n qubits or not depending on what she wants to send, then send them to Bob.

Exercise 6.13. Verify that $|\Phi^+\rangle$, $|\Psi^+\rangle$, $|\Phi^-\rangle$, and $|\Psi^-\rangle$ are orthonormal to each other. That is, calculate $\langle \Phi^+|\Phi^-\rangle$, etc.

Exercise 6.14. Say Alice wants to send one of sixteen possible states to Bob.
 (a) How many classical bits would Alice need to send to Bob?
 (b) How many qubits would Alice need to send to Bob if they share entanglement?

(c) How many qubits total would it take, counting both Alice's and Bob's qubits?

Exercise 6.15. Consider the following quantum circuit that implements superdense coding.

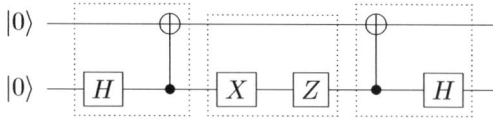

The bottom qubit is Alice's, and the top qubit is Bob's. In the first dotted square, Alice and Bob create the maximally entangled state $|\Phi^+\rangle$ by applying $H \otimes I$ and $CNOT$. Bob then goes away on a trip. Alice wants to send Bob a message, so in the second dotted square, she applies X followed by Z to her qubit. Then, she sends her qubit to Bob. Bob now has both qubits. To read Alice's message, in the third square, he applies CNOT followed by $H \otimes I$, and then measures in the Z-basis.

(a) What result should Bob get for his measurement?
(b) Run the circuit on an actual quantum processor using IBM Quantum. Which processor did you use? What histogram of results do you get?
(c) How would you modify the circuit so that Alice sends $|01\rangle$ to Bob?

6.5 Quantum Teleportation

6.5.1 The Problem

In the previous section on superdense coding, we used qubits to send classical information. In this section, we consider the opposite. We can only send bits, but we want to send quantum information. In particular, Alice would like to send a qubit's unknown state $|\psi\rangle = \alpha|0\rangle + \beta|1\rangle$ to Bob.

6.5.2 Classical Solution

Since Alice does not know the state $|\psi\rangle$, she cannot describe it to Bob. If she measures the qubit, she will collapse it to $|0\rangle$ or $|1\rangle$, and she will not know the original superposition $\alpha|0\rangle + \beta|1\rangle$. So, in general, Alice cannot tell Bob the state $|\psi\rangle$.

If Alice had many qubits, each in the state $|\psi\rangle$, then she could measure each one, possibly in different bases, to get a sense of what $|\psi\rangle$ might be. This is called *quantum state tomography*. The more qubits Alice has in the state $|\psi\rangle$, the more accurately she can determine $|\psi\rangle$, and then she can tell Bob her best guess of the state. In the problem we are trying to solve, however, Alice only has one qubit in the state $|\psi\rangle$, and from the no-cloning theorem, she cannot make extra copies.

Even if she did know the state, the amplitudes are in general complex numbers that can take rational or irrational values, and the irrational values would take an infinite number of bits to express. So, Alice would need to send Bob many bits to describe the state of the qubit. Next, we will see how entanglement can be used so that Alice can get Bob the state $|\psi\rangle$ by only telling him two bits.

6.5.3 *Quantum Solution*

If Alice and Bob already share entanglement, they can use it to teleport the quantum state. Say they share a pair of entangled qubits in the state $|\Phi^+\rangle$. Alice has one of these qubits, plus the one she wants to send $|\psi\rangle$. Bob has the other entangled qubit.

$$|\psi\rangle = \alpha|0\rangle + \beta|1\rangle \qquad\qquad \frac{1}{\sqrt{2}}\left(|00\rangle + |11\rangle\right)$$

Alice $\bullet\!\!\sim\!\!\sim\!\!\sim\!\!\sim\!\!\sim\!\!\sim\!\!\sim\!\!\sim\!\!\sim\!\!\sim\!\!\sim\!\!\sim\!\!\sim\!\!\sim\!\!\sim\!\!\bullet$ Bob

Altogether, the three qubits are in the state

$$
\begin{aligned}
|\psi\rangle|\Phi^+\rangle &= \alpha|0\rangle|\Phi^+\rangle + \beta|1\rangle|\Phi^+\rangle \\
&= \alpha|0\rangle\frac{1}{\sqrt{2}}\left(|00\rangle + |11\rangle\right) + \beta|1\rangle\frac{1}{\sqrt{2}}\left(|00\rangle + |11\rangle\right) \\
&= \frac{1}{\sqrt{2}}\left[\alpha\left(|000\rangle + |011\rangle\right) + \beta\left(|100\rangle + |111\rangle\right)\right].
\end{aligned}
$$

The left two qubits belong to Alice, and the right qubit belongs to Bob. First, Alice applies a CNOT gate to her two qubits, resulting in the state

$$\frac{1}{\sqrt{2}}\left[\alpha\left(|000\rangle + |011\rangle\right) + \beta\left(|110\rangle + |101\rangle\right)\right].$$

Next, she applies a Hadamard gate to her left qubit, yielding

$$
\begin{aligned}
&\frac{1}{\sqrt{2}}\left[\alpha\left(|{+}00\rangle + |{+}11\rangle\right) + \beta\left(|{-}10\rangle + |{-}01\rangle\right)\right] \\
&= \frac{1}{2}\left[\alpha\left(|0\rangle + |1\rangle\right)\left(|00\rangle + |11\rangle\right) + \beta\left(|0\rangle - |1\rangle\right)\left(|10\rangle + |01\rangle\right)\right] \\
&= \frac{1}{2}\Big[|00\rangle\left(\alpha|0\rangle + \beta|1\rangle\right) + |01\rangle\left(\beta|0\rangle + \alpha|1\rangle\right) \\
&\qquad + |10\rangle\left(\alpha|0\rangle - \beta|1\rangle\right) + |11\rangle\left(-\beta|0\rangle + \alpha|1\rangle\right)\Big].
\end{aligned}
$$

Then, Alice measures her two qubits. She gets 00, 01, 10, 11, each with probability $1/4$. So after the measurement, the possible states are

$$
\begin{aligned}
&|00\rangle\left(\alpha|0\rangle + \beta|1\rangle\right), \\
&|01\rangle\left(\beta|0\rangle + \alpha|1\rangle\right), \\
&|10\rangle\left(\alpha|0\rangle - \beta|1\rangle\right), \\
&|11\rangle\left(-\beta|0\rangle + \alpha|1\rangle\right).
\end{aligned}
$$

Now Alice tells Bob the results of her measurement, which are two classical bits. This is a classical communication. Bob uses this information to possibly apply quantum gates to his qubit.

- If Alice's measurement was 00, Bob does nothing because his qubit is now in the state $|\psi\rangle$ that Alice wanted to send him.
- If Alice's measurement was 01, then Bob applies an X gate to his qubit, transforming it into $|\psi\rangle$.
- If Alice's measurement was 10, then Bob applies a Z gate to his qubit, transforming it into $|\psi\rangle$.
- Finally, if Alice's qubit was 11, then Bob applies an X gate followed by a Z gate, transforming it into $|\psi\rangle$.

So Bob's qubit is now in the state $|\psi\rangle$, achieving the goal of transferring the state of Alice's qubit to Bob's qubit. This is called *quantum teleportation*. Note that Alice's qubit was not physically transferred to Bob, only information about what state it was in. In the process, Alice had to measure her qubit, destroying the quantum information. This is necessary because of the no-cloning theorem. Furthermore, even though the state of Bob's qubit changed instantly when Alice measured her qubits and collapsed the state, this information was not useful until Alice told Bob the result of her measurement, which is a classical communication bounded by the speed of light. So, quantum teleportation cannot be performed faster than light, which is consistent with the no-signaling principle.

Quantum teleportation is implemented by the following circuit:

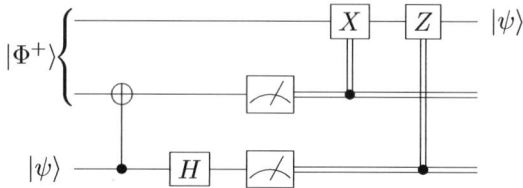

The top qubit is Bob's, and the bottom two qubits are Alice's. The bottom qubit starts in the unknown state $|\psi\rangle$, which Alice wants to teleport to Bob, and the top two qubits start in the entangled state $|\Phi^+\rangle$. Alice applies a CNOT to her qubits followed by H on her bottom qubit. Then she measures her qubits, getting 00, 01, 10, or 11. If her right qubit was 1, Bob applies X, and if her left qubit was 1, Bob applies Z. These are controlled-X and controlled-Z gates. This completes the teleportation, and Bob's qubit ends up in the state $|\psi\rangle$.

Using the principle of deferred measurement (introduced on page 194), we can move the measurements after the controls and replace the classical controls with quantum ones:

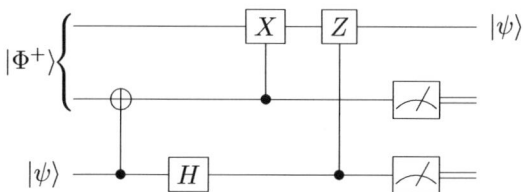

Simulating this in Quirk at `https.//bit.ly/3pn1hCj`,

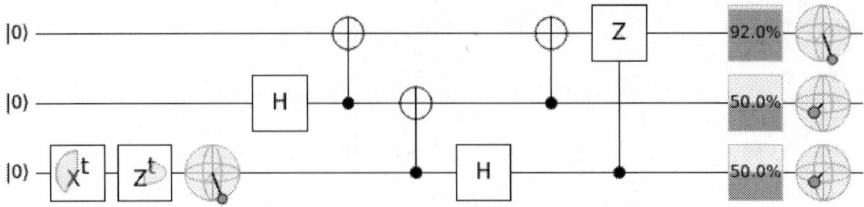

This begins with X^t and Z^t, which put the bottom qubit in some state $|\psi\rangle$ depicted on the Bloch sphere. Then, we have the teleportation circuit, and at the end, the three Bloch spheres show that the top qubit is in the state $|\psi\rangle$, while the bottom qubit is no longer in this state.

Exercise 6.16. Alice wants to teleport a qubit in an unknown state $|\psi\rangle = \alpha|0\rangle + \beta|1\rangle$ to Bob. Instead of sharing two entangled qubits in the $|\Phi^+\rangle$ state, they share two entangled qubits in the $|\Psi^+\rangle$ state:

$$|\psi\rangle = \alpha|0\rangle + \beta|1\rangle \qquad\qquad \frac{1}{\sqrt{2}}(|01\rangle + |10\rangle)$$

Alice •∿∿∿∿∿∿∿∿∿∿∿∿∿∿∿∿∿∿∿∿∿∿• Bob

Altogether, the initial state of the system is

$$|\psi\rangle|\Psi^+\rangle = (\alpha|0\rangle + \beta|1\rangle)\frac{1}{\sqrt{2}}(|01\rangle + |10\rangle)$$
$$= \frac{1}{\sqrt{2}}(\alpha|001\rangle + \alpha|010\rangle + \beta|101\rangle + \beta|110\rangle).$$

So, the left two qubits are Alice's, and the right qubit is Bob's.

(a) Show that if Alice applies CNOT to her two qubits, followed by H to her left qubit, the state of the system becomes

$$\frac{1}{2}\left[|00\rangle(\beta|0\rangle + \alpha|1\rangle) + |01\rangle(\alpha|0\rangle + \beta|1\rangle)\right.$$
$$\left. + |10\rangle(-\beta|0\rangle + \alpha|1\rangle) + |11\rangle(\alpha|0\rangle - \beta|1\rangle)\right].$$

(b) Next, Alice measures both of her qubits. What values can she get, with what probabilities, and what does the state collapse to in each case?

(c) Finally, Alice tells Bob the results of her measurement. For each possible result, what should Bob do to his qubit so that it is $\alpha|0\rangle + \beta|1\rangle$, the state that Alice wanted to teleport to him?

Exercise 6.17. Alice wants to teleport a qubit in an unknown state $|\psi\rangle = \alpha|0\rangle + \beta|1\rangle$ to Bob. Instead of sharing two entangled qubits in a Bell state, they share three entangled qubits in the GHZ state:

$$|GHZ\rangle = \frac{1}{\sqrt{2}}(|000\rangle + |111\rangle).$$

The left two qubits are with Alice, and the right qubit is with Bob.

$$|\psi\rangle = \alpha|0\rangle + \beta|1\rangle \qquad\qquad \frac{1}{\sqrt{2}}(|000\rangle + |111\rangle)$$

Alice •∿∿∿∿∿∿∿∿∿∿∿∿∿∿∿∿∿∿∿∿∿∿➤• Bob

Altogether, the initial state of the system is

$$|\psi\rangle|GHZ\rangle = (\alpha|0\rangle + \beta|1\rangle)\frac{1}{\sqrt{2}}(|000\rangle + |111\rangle)$$

$$= \frac{1}{\sqrt{2}}(\alpha|0000\rangle + \alpha|0111\rangle + \beta|1000\rangle + \beta|1111\rangle).$$

So, the left three qubits are Alice's, and the right qubit is Bob's.

(a) Show that if Alice applies $CNOT_{21}$ (recall the qubits are numbered right-to-left starting with zero), followed by $CNOT_{32}$, followed by $H \otimes I \otimes I \otimes I$, the state of the system becomes

$$\frac{1}{2}\big[|000\rangle(\alpha|0\rangle + \beta|1\rangle) + |010\rangle(\beta|0\rangle + \alpha|1\rangle)$$

$$+ |100\rangle(\alpha|0\rangle - \beta|1\rangle) + |110\rangle(-\beta|0\rangle + \alpha|1\rangle)\big].$$

(b) Next, Alice measures all three of her qubits. What values can she get, with what probabilities, and what does the state collapse to in each case?

(c) Finally, Alice tells Bob the results of her measurement. For each possible result, what should Bob do to his qubit so that it is $\alpha|0\rangle + \beta|1\rangle$, the state that Alice wanted to teleport to him?

Exercise 6.18. Alice wants to teleport a qubit in an unknown state $|\psi\rangle = \alpha|0\rangle + \beta|1\rangle$ to Charlie, and Bob is helping her. They share three entangled qubits in the GHZ state:

$$|GHZ\rangle = \frac{1}{\sqrt{2}}(|000\rangle + |111\rangle).$$

The left qubit is Alice's, the middle qubit is Bob's, and the right qubit is Charlie's.

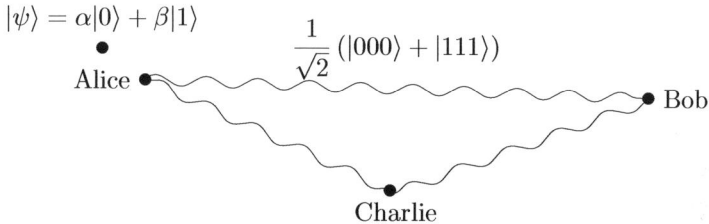

Altogether, the initial state of the system is

$$|\psi\rangle|GHZ\rangle = (\alpha|0\rangle + \beta|1\rangle)\frac{1}{\sqrt{2}}(|000\rangle + |111\rangle)$$

$$= \frac{1}{\sqrt{2}}(\alpha|0000\rangle + \alpha|0111\rangle + \beta|1000\rangle + \beta|1111\rangle).$$

So, the left two qubits are Alice's, the second-to-right qubit is Bob's, and the right qubit is Charlie's.

(a) Show that if Alice applies CNOT to her qubits (so the far left qubit is the control and the second-to-left qubit is the target) and then the Hadamard gate to her left qubit, the state of the system becomes

$$\frac{1}{2}\big[|00\rangle(\alpha|00\rangle + \beta|11\rangle) + |01\rangle(\beta|00\rangle + \alpha|11\rangle)$$

$$+ |10\rangle(\alpha|00\rangle - \beta|11\rangle) + |11\rangle(-\beta|00\rangle + \alpha|11\rangle)\big].$$

(b) Next, Alice measures her two qubits and makes the results known. What values can she get, with what probabilities, and what does the state collapse to in each case?

(c) After Alice has completed the above, Bob applies the Hadamard gate to his qubit. Show that the state of the system after Bob does this is the following four states, depending on the result of Alice's measurement:

$$\frac{1}{\sqrt{2}}|00\rangle\left[|0\rangle\left(\alpha|0\rangle+\beta|1\rangle\right)+|1\rangle\left(\alpha|0\rangle-\beta|1\rangle\right)\right],$$

$$\frac{1}{\sqrt{2}}|01\rangle\left[|0\rangle\left(\beta|0\rangle+\alpha|1\rangle\right)+|1\rangle\left(\beta|0\rangle-\alpha|1\rangle\right)\right],$$

$$\frac{1}{\sqrt{2}}|10\rangle\left[|0\rangle\left(\alpha|0\rangle+\beta|1\rangle\right)+|1\rangle\left(\alpha|0\rangle-\beta|1\rangle\right)\right],$$

$$\frac{1}{\sqrt{2}}|11\rangle\left[|0\rangle\left(-\beta|0\rangle+\alpha|1\rangle\right)+|1\rangle\left(-\beta|0\rangle-\alpha|1\rangle\right)\right].$$

(d) Then, Bob measures his qubit and makes his result known. For each of the above states, what does the state collapse to? For each possible outcome, what quantum gate(s) should Charlie apply to his qubit so that it is $\alpha|0\rangle+\beta|1\rangle$, the state that Alice wanted to teleport to him?

6.6 Quantum Key Distribution

6.6.1 Encryption

Alice and Bob would like to send private messages to each other over the internet. This means others can see the bits they send, but the meaning should be hidden from everyone except Alice and Bob.

To do this, Alice and Bob need to have a secret *key* or code that only they know. Using this secret key, they can *encrypt* their messages to each other.

For example, say Alice and Bob share a secret key of fourteen random bits that only they know:

$$\text{key} = 11010110011011.$$

Alice wants to send "Hi" to Bob, which in ASCII is 1001000 1101001. This is called the *plaintext.* If she sends these bits, everyone will know that the message is "Hi." So instead, she takes the XOR of each bit of the message with each bit of the secret key, yielding the *ciphertext*

$$
\begin{aligned}
\text{plaintext} &= 1001000\ 1101001 \\
\oplus \qquad \text{key} &= 1101011\ 0011011 \\
\hline
\text{ciphertext} &= 0100011\ 1110010
\end{aligned}
$$

Now Alice sends this ciphertext to Bob over the internet. If someone intercepts it along the way, like *Eve* the eavesdropper, then she will not be able to determine the original plaintext since she does not have the secret key. Now Bob has the ciphertext, and he takes the XOR of it with the secret key, which he knows:

$$\text{ciphertext} = 0100011\ 1110010$$
$$\oplus \qquad \text{key} = 1101011\ 0011011$$
$$\overline{\text{plaintext} = 1001000\ 1101001}$$

Bob decodes the plaintext as "Hi," receiving the message.

This scheme is called a *one-time pad*, and it assumes that the secret key is only used once and is random. If the secret key is used more than once, then Eve might be able to discern the key, and if it is not random, Eve might be able to guess the pattern. But as long as these assumptions are satisfied, it is *information-theoretically secure*, meaning it is secure from a mathematical standpoint, but perhaps not secure from someone breaking into Bob's office and stealing the secret key.

Due to this information-theoretic security, the one-time pad is used for the most critical of communications, such as the Moscow–Washington hotline that allows direct, secure communication between Russia and the United States. This hotline was developed during the Cold War, and is still used today. Since the secret keys cannot just be sent over the internet for all to see, they have to be delivered in-person to each country's embassy.

For those who need strong security, but not at the level of a one-time pad, the Advanced Encryption Standard (AES) can be used. The secret key can be shorter than the message, and the ciphertext is created through a series of substitutions, shifts, and mixes. Nevertheless, a secret key must be established.

Exercise 6.19. You are Bob, and you and Alice are communicating using a one-time pad. You receive from Alice the ciphertext

1101010 1010011 0000011 0010010 1101001 1011001 1001100,

and you know the secret key

0101001 0111011 1100010 1100000 0000101 0110000 0101001.

What is the plaintext binary string, and what does it encode in ASCII?

6.6.2 Classical Solution: Public Key Cryptography

A classical way to send a secret message, such as to establish a secret key, is the *RSA cryptosystem*, which is an acronym for its inventors Rivest, Shamir, and Adleman.[1] It is an example of a *public-key cryptosystem*, where each user reveals some public information while still maintaining some private (secret) information.

Say Alice wants to send a message to Bob. To do this securely, Bob prepares some public and private information. The public information allows anyone to send him encrypted messages. The private information allows Bob, and only Bob, to

---

[1] Actually, RSA was invented a few years earlier by Clifford Cocks, a mathematician working for a British intelligence agency, but his work was classified and not revealed until decades later.

decrypt the message. To do this, Bob begins by choosing two distinct prime numbers p and q, with some conditions that are beyond the scope of this textbook. A *prime number* is any whole number greater than 1 whose only factors are 1 and itself. Prime numbers can be listed using Mathematica or SageMath:

- In Mathematica, the first ten prime numbers can be listed using

```
Table[Prime[i], {i, 10}]
```

  The output is
  $$\{2,3,5,7,11,13,17,19,23,29\}.$$

- In SageMath, the prime numbers less than 30 can be listed using

```
sage: list(primes(30))
[2, 3, 5, 7, 11, 13, 17, 19, 23, 29]
```

We can also use Mathematica or SageMath to check if a number is prime.

- In Mathematica, we can check if a number is prime using the `PrimeQ` function, where the "Q" stands for "query" meaning to ask. With this function, we are asking if a particular number is prime. For example, consider

```
PrimeQ[2003]
```

  The output of this is True, so 2003 is a prime number. As another example, consider

```
PrimeQ[2005]
```

  The output of this is False, so 2005 is not a prime number.
- In SageMath, we can check if a number is prime using the `is_prime` function. For example,

```
sage: is_prime(2003)
True
sage: is_prime(2005)
False
```

For example, say Bob chooses $p = 17$ and $q = 41$. Bob keeps these two numbers a secret, but he does reveal their product. That is, bob computes $n = pq = 17 \cdot 41 = 697$ and makes the number 697 known to Alice and the world. This product n is one of Bob's two public keys, and he publishes it so that Alice can use it to send him a secret message. The length of n in bits is called the *key length*, and at the time of this writing, the recommended key length of RSA is 2048-bits. For example, 697 in binary is 1010111001, so we are using a key length of 10, which is much too short in practice.

Bob then computes the product $\phi = (p-1)(q-1)$. Continuing our example, Bob computes $\phi = 16 \cdot 40 = 640$. Using this, he then finds some integer e between 1 and ϕ that is *relatively prime* or *coprime* to ϕ, meaning the greatest common divisor of e and ϕ is 1, which we write as $\gcd(e, \phi) = 1$. Put another way, e and ϕ share no common factors except 1. Note there is a fast method called *Euclid's algorithm* from 300 BC/BCE for calculating the greatest common divisor of two integers, and the number of steps is at most five times the number of digits of the smaller integer. See Exercise 6.20 for a description of the algorithm. We can use Euclid's algorithm to find an e such that $\gcd(e, \phi) = 1$, or we can just use Mathematica or SageMath:

- In Mathematica, we can list all the numbers between 2 and 639, inclusive, that are relatively prime to 640 using the following:

```
Table[If[GCD[i, 640] == 1, i, Nothing], {i, 2, 639}]
```

The output of this is

$\{3,7,9,11,13,17,19,21,23,27,29,31,33,37,39,41,43,47,49,51,53,57,59,$
$61,63,67,69,71,73,77,79,81,83,87,89,91,93,97,99,101,103,107,109,$
$111,113,117,119,121,123,127,129,131,133,137,139,141,143,147,149,$
$151,153,157,159,161,163,167,169,171,173,177,179,181,183,187,189,$
$191,193,197,199,201,203,207,209,211,213,217,219,221,223,227,229,$
$231,233,237,239,241,243,247,249,251,253,257,259,261,263,267,269,$
$271,273,277,279,281,283,287,289,291,293,297,299,301,303,307,309,$
$311,313,317,319,321,323,327,329,331,333,337,339,341,343,347,349,$
$351,353,357,359,361,363,367,369,371,373,377,379,381,383,387,389,$
$391,393,397,399,401,403,407,409,411,413,417,419,421,423,427,429,$
$431,433,437,439,441,443,447,449,451,453,457,459,461,463,467,469,$
$471,473,477,479,481,483,487,489,491,493,497,499,501,503,507,509,$
$511,513,517,519,521,523,527,529,531,533,537,539,541,543,547,549,$
$551,553,557,559,561,563,567,569,571,573,577,579,581,583,587,589,$
$591,593,597,599,601,603,607,609,611,613,617,619,621,623,627,629,$
$631,633,637,639\}$

- In SageMath, we can list all the numbers less than 640 that are relatively prime to 640 using the coprime_integers function:

```
sage: phi = 640
sage: phi.coprime_integers(phi)
[1, 3, 7, 9, 11, 13, 17, 19, 21, 23, 27, 29, 31, 33, 37, 39,
41, 43, 47, 49, 51, 53, 57, 59, 61, 63, 67, 69, 71, 73, 77,
79, 81, 83, 87, 89, 91, 93, 97, 99, 101, 103, 107, 109, 111,
113, 117, 119, 121, 123, 127, 129, 131, 133, 137, 139, 141,
143, 147, 149, 151, 153, 157, 159, 161, 163, 167, 169, 171,
173, 177, 179, 181, 183, 187, 189, 191, 193, 197, 199, 201,
203, 207, 209, 211, 213, 217, 219, 221, 223, 227, 229, 231,
233, 237, 239, 241, 243, 247, 249, 251, 253, 257, 259, 261,
263, 267, 269, 271, 273, 277, 279, 281, 283, 287, 289, 291,
293, 297, 299, 301, 303, 307, 309, 311, 313, 317, 319, 321,
323, 327, 329, 331, 333, 337, 339, 341, 343, 347, 349, 351,
353, 357, 359, 361, 363, 367, 369, 371, 373, 377, 379, 301,
383, 387, 389, 391, 393, 397, 399, 401, 403, 407, 409, 411,
```

```
413,  417,  419,  421,  423,  427,  429,  431,  433,  437,  439,  441,
443,  447,  449,  451,  453,  457,  459,  461,  463,  467,  469,  471,
473,  477,  479,  481,  483,  487,  489,  491,  493,  497,  499,  501,
503,  507,  509,  511,  513,  517,  519,  521,  523,  527,  529,  531,
533,  537,  539,  541,  543,  547,  549,  551,  553,  557,  559,  561,
563,  567,  569,  571,  573,  577,  579,  581,  583,  587,  589,  591,
593,  597,  599,  601,  603,  607,  609,  611,  613,  617,  619,  621,
623,  627,  629,  631,  633,  637,  639]
```

Note we require $e > 1$, so we should ignore the first entry.

Bob can choose any of these numbers. Say he chooses $e = 3$. This number e is Bob's second public key, and he publishes it. It is called e because later, Alice will use it as an exponent.

Finally, Bob computes $d = e^{-1}$ mod ϕ, where mod refers to the *modulus* or remainder when dividing by ϕ.[2] For example, the 12-hour clock is *modulo* 12, since $7 + 8 = 15 = 3$ mod 12. Continuing our example, we can compute d using Mathematica or SageMath:

- In Mathematica, the inverse of a number modulo some other number can be found using

```
ModularInverse[3,640]
```

  The output is 427.
- In SageMath, the inverse of a number modulo some other number can be found using

```
sage: e = 3
sage: phi = 640
sage: e.inverse_mod(phi)
427
```

So, Bob computed $d = 3^{-1}$ mod $640 = 427$. Since d is the inverse of e modulo ϕ, if we multiply e and d modulo ϕ, we should get 1, i.e., $ed = 1$ mod ϕ. The number d is Bob's private key. It will allow him to decrypt messages sent to him, so he keeps it a secret. No one else knows d because even though Bob published e, one also needs to know ϕ in order to calculate d. Bob may now throw away p and q, but keeping it does allow him to decrypt a little faster using the *Chinese remainder theorem*, but that is beyond the scope of this book.

Alice wants to send Bob a plaintext message that is encoded as a number M, such that $0 < M < n$. She finds Bob's public keys n and e and computes the ciphertext $C = M^e$ mod n, and then she sends C to Bob. For example, Alice wants to send $M = 104$ to Bob, which in binary is 1101000. She can compute the ciphertext using Mathematica or SageMath:

- In Mathematica,

```
PowerMod[104,3,697]
```

---

[2] From number theory, the inverse of e mod ϕ exists precisely because e was chosen to be relatively prime to ϕ.

The output is 603.
- In SageMath,

```
sage: power_mod(104,3,697)
603
```

Thus, $C = 104^3 \bmod 697 = 603$, and alice sends the number 603 to Bob.

When Bob receives the ciphertext C, he computes $C^d \bmod n = (M^e)^d \bmod n = M^{ed} \bmod n = M^1 \bmod n = M$, receiving the message.[3] Continuing our example, Bob computes $603^{427} \bmod 697$. Computing this in Mathematica or SageMath,

- In Mathematica,

```
PowerMod[603,427,697]
```

The output is 104.
- In SageMath,

```
sage: power_mod(603,427,697)
104
```

So, $603^{427} \bmod 697 = 104$, which is the message.

The sequence of steps in this example is summarized below:

Alice	Bob
	Chooses primes $p = 17$, $q = 41$.
	Calculates $n = pq = 697$.
	Publishes n.
	Computes $\phi = 16 \cdot 40 = 640$.
	Chooses $e = 3$ since $\gcd(3, 640) = 1$.
	Publishes e.
	Computes $d = 3^{-1} \bmod 640 = 427$.
Chooses message $M = 104$.	
Computes $C = 104^3 \bmod 697 = 603$.	
Alice Sends to C to Bob.	
	Computes $603^{427} \bmod 697 = 104 = M$.

Decryption is hard for an eavesdropper, Eve, to do, because she does not know the secret key d. She only knows Bob's public keys, n and e. To find the secret key $d = e^{-1} \bmod \phi$, she needs to know $\phi = (p-1)(q-1)$, but this requires knowing p and q, which involves factoring n. There is no known efficient, classical algorithm for factoring large numbers, although a quantum computer can efficiently factor numbers using Shor's algorithm, which is the culminating algorithm in this textbook. As described in Section 1.7.2 on complexity classes, this is evidence, but not proof, that BQP is larger than P.

---

[3] The plaintext and ciphertext are modulo n, but the exponents are modulo ϕ. It can be proved using Fermat's Little Theorem that with these moduli, $M^{ed} \bmod n = M \bmod n$, but the proof is beyond the scope of this textbook.

Exercise 6.20. Euclid's algorithm is a method for finding the greatest common divisor of two integers by converting the problem into finding the greatest common divisor of successively smaller and smaller pairs of integers until we get one that is easy to find.

For example, say we want to find $\gcd(1122, 422)$. We begin by dividing the larger number by the smaller number. That is, $1122/442$ is 2 with a remainder of 238, which we can write as

$$1122 = 2 \cdot 442 + 238.$$

The claim is that the greatest common divisor of the dividend 1122 and divisor 442 is equal to the greatest common divisor of the divisor 442 and the remainder 238, i.e., $\gcd(1122, 442) = \gcd(442, 238)$. This is because they have the same common divisors, including their greatest common divisor.[4]

Using this fact, let us instead find $\gcd(442, 238)$. Dividing these numbers, $442/238$ is 1 with a remainder of 204, so we can write:

$$442 = 1 \cdot 238 + 204.$$

Using the same fact from before, the greatest common divisor of the dividend and divisor is equal to the greatest common divisor of the divisor and remainder, i.e., $\gcd(442, 238) = \gcd(238, 204)$.

So, we instead find $\gcd(238, 204)$. Again, we divide these numbers. Since $238/204$ is 1 with a remainder of 34, we write,

$$238 = 1 \cdot 204 + 34.$$

Again using the fact, $\gcd(238, 204) = \gcd(204, 34)$.

Now, we instead find $\gcd(204, 34)$. Dividing, $204/34$ is 6 with no remainder, so

$$204 = 6 \cdot 34 + 0.$$

We again use the fact, $\gcd(204, 34) = \gcd(34, 0)$.

Finally, we have $\gcd(34, 0) = 34$. This is because 34 is the largest integer that divides both 34 and 0 with no remainder. Since this is also the greatest common divisor of our original question, we have

$$\gcd(1122, 442) = 34.$$

(a) Use Euclid's algorithm to find $\gcd(51, 57)$.
(b) Use Euclid's algorithm to find $\gcd(34, 39)$.

Exercise 6.21. You are Bob, and you and Alice are communicating using RSA cryptography. You picked two prime numbers $p = 59$ and $q = 127$. Find
(a) Your public key n.
(b) A valid public key e.
(c) Your private key given your choice in part (b).

Exercise 6.22. You are Alice, and you and Bob are communicating using RSA cryptography. Bob has secret keys $n = 2\,035\,153$ and $e = 5$. You want to send him a message $M = 1\,234\,567$ using RSA. What ciphertext C do you send him?

Exercise 6.23. You are Bob, and you and Alice are communicating using RSA cryptography. Alice sends you some ciphertext $C = 1\,873\,198$. Your public keys are $n = 2\,035\,153$ and $e = 5$, and your secret key is $d = 1\,219\,277$. What is the plaintext message (number) that Alice sent?

---

[4] As a proof, let us show that any divisor of 1122 and 422 is also a divisor of their remainder 238, and any divisor of 422 and 238 is also a divisor of 1122. First, say d is a common divisor of 1122 and 422. Then, d is is also a divisor of $1122 - 2 \cdot 442$, since division is distributive. Since $238 = 1122 - 2 \cdot 442$, d is also a divisor of 238. Going the other direction, say e is a common divisor of 422 and 238. Then, e is also a divisor of $2 \cdot 442 + 238$, since division is distributive. Since $2 \cdot 442 + 238 = 1122$, e is also a divisor of 1122. So, $\gcd(1122, 442) = \gcd(442, 238)$.

Exercise 6.24. In 1991, the RSA Factoring Challenge was created to encourage research into factoring by giving values of n of increasing sizes and offering prize money for people who factored them. Visit

https://en.wikipedia.org/wiki/RSA_Factoring_Challenge

to learn more about the challenge.
  (a) How many bits long is the first RSA number, and when was it factored?
  (b) What is the largest RSA number that has been factored? How many bits does it have? When was it factored?
  (c) If the RSA Factoring Challenge were still active, how much prize money would you earn for factoring a 2048-bit long value of n?

6.6.3 Quantum Solution: BB84

A quantum method for establishing a shared secret key was introduced by Bennett and Brassard in 1984, and it is called the BB84 protocol. It is an example of *quantum key distribution* (QKD). Even though it does not use entanglement, it is a quantum protocol, so it is included in this chapter. There do exist other protocols for QKD that do utilize entanglement, such as E91, which is named after Ekert who discovered it in 1991, but they are beyond the scope of this textbook.

In BB84, Alice begins with a bunch of random bits, and for each bit, she randomly chooses either the Z-basis $\{|0\rangle, |1\rangle\}$ or the X-basis $\{|+\rangle, |-\rangle\}$. For example,

Alice's Bits	0 1 0 1 1 0 1 1 1
Alice's Bases	Z Z X Z X X X Z Z

If the bit she wants to send is a 0, and she picked the Z-basis, then she sends Bob $|0\rangle$, and if she picked the X-basis, then she sends Bob $|+\rangle$. If Alice instead wants to send the bit 1, and she picked the Z-basis, then she sends Bob $|1\rangle$, and if she picked the X-basis, then she sends Bob $|-\rangle$. Continuing the example,

Alice's Bits	0	1	0	1	1	0	1	1	1
Alice's Bases	Z	Z	X	Z	X	X	X	Z	Z
Alice Sends	$|0\rangle$	$|1\rangle$	$|+\rangle$	$|1\rangle$	$|-\rangle$	$|+\rangle$	$|-\rangle$	$|1\rangle$	$|1\rangle$

Bob receives the qubits, and he randomly measures each one in either the Z-basis or X-basis. If the basis he picked was the same as Alice's, then he will get the same result as Alice. If he picked the opposite basis, however, then he will get each possible result with probability $1/2$. For example, if Alice sends $|0\rangle$ and Bob measures in the Z-basis, he is certain to get $|0\rangle$. But if he measures in the X-basis, he gets $|+\rangle$ with probability $1/2$ or $|-\rangle$ with probability $1/2$. He interprets $|0\rangle$ and $|+\rangle$ as 0, and $|1\rangle$ and $|-\rangle$ as 1. Continuing the example,

Alice's Bits	0	1	0	1	1	0	1	1	1
Alice's Bases	Z	Z	X	Z	X	X	X	Z	Z
Alice Sends	$|0\rangle$	$|1\rangle$	$|+\rangle$	$|1\rangle$	$|-\rangle$	$|+\rangle$	$|-\rangle$	$|1\rangle$	$|1\rangle$
Bob's Bases	Z	X	X	Z	Z	X	Z	X	Z
Bob's Measurement	$|0\rangle$	$|-\rangle$	$|+\rangle$	$|1\rangle$	$|0\rangle$	$|+\rangle$	$|1\rangle$	$|+\rangle$	$|1\rangle$
Bob's Bits	0	1	0	1	0	0	1	0	1

Now Alice and Bob call each other and openly (publicly) share what basis they used for each measurement. If they used the same basis, then they know that their measurement outcomes should agree, and they have a shared secret bit. If they used different bases, then their measurement outcomes might agree or disagree, and they discard these bits. Continuing the example.

Alice's Bits	0	1	0	1	1	0	1	1	1
Alice's Bases	Z	Z	X	Z	X	X	X	Z	Z
Alice Sends	$|0\rangle$	$|1\rangle$	$|+\rangle$	$|1\rangle$	$|-\rangle$	$|+\rangle$	$|-\rangle$	$|1\rangle$	$|1\rangle$
Bob's Bases	Z	X	X	Z	Z	X	Z	X	Z
Bob's Measurement	$|0\rangle$	$|-\rangle$	$|+\rangle$	$|1\rangle$	$|0\rangle$	$|+\rangle$	$|1\rangle$	$|+\rangle$	$|1\rangle$
Bob's Bits	0	1	0	1	0	0	1	0	1

Public Discussion of Basis					
Shared Secret Key	0	0 1	0		1

So, their shared secret key is 00101.

To ensure Eve did not measure the qubits along the way, Alice and Bob can reveal a fraction of their shared secret key and make sure they agree. For example, if Alice and Bob want 256 bits in their shared secret key, they can generate 306 bits using BB84, reveal 50 of them to ensure there was no eavesdropper, and then use the remaining 256 for their shared secret key.

If Alice and Bob reveal 50 bits of their shared secret key, what is the probability they will catch Eve, if Eve is measuring every qubit along the way? To answer this, let us start with revealing one bit. Say Alice and Bob are revealing a bit where they both used the Z-basis, and say Alice sent a qubit in the state $|0\rangle$. Then, Alice will reveal that her bit is 0, while Bob could reveal that his bit is 0 or 1, and we determine the probabilities of these outcomes using the following diagram:

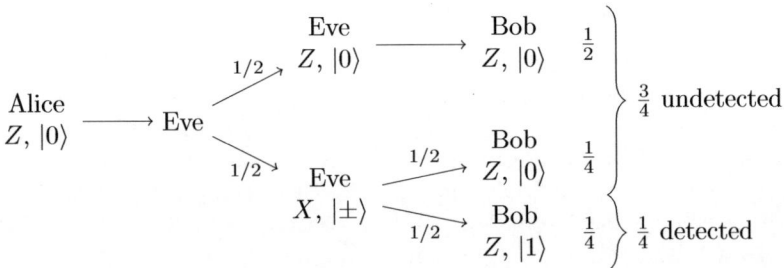

On the left side of the diagram, Alice is using the Z-basis, and she sends a qubit in the $|0\rangle$ state. In the middle of the diagram, Eve intercepted the qubit and measured it in either the Z-basis or the X-basis, each with probability $1/2$. If Eve measured in the Z-basis, she got $|0\rangle$, and then forwarded the qubit to Bob. Bob measured the qubit in the Z-basis, so he also got $|0\rangle$. This is the top row of the above diagram. In this scenario, which occurs with probability $1/2$, Alice and Bob both reveal that they got the bit 0, and Eve's eavesdropping was undetected. Now, if Eve measured in the X-basis instead, then she collapsed the state to $|+\rangle$ or $|-\rangle$ and forwarded it to Bob. In the above figure, this is the bottom row. Bob then measured the qubit in the Z-basis, getting $|0\rangle$ with probability $1/2$ or $|1\rangle$ with probability $1/2$. Overall, each of these outcomes occur with probability $1/4$. If Bob got $|0\rangle$, Eve is undetected, but if he got $|1\rangle$, Alice and Bob will realize there was an eavesdropper when they reveal their results. Overall, Eve has a probability of $3/4$ of being undetected and a probability of $1/4$ of being detected, as indicated by the curly brace in the above figure, when Alice and Bob reveal this bit of their shared secret key. In other words, there is a probability of $3/4$ that Alice and Bob both have 0 as their bits, and probability $1/4$ that Alice has 0 and Bob has 1.

If Alice and Bob share n bits of their shared secret key, the probability that Eve is undetected for all n bits is $(3/4)^n$. Then, the probability that Eve is detected is one minus this, or

$$\text{Probability Alice and Bob detect Eve} = 1 - \left(\frac{3}{4}\right)^n.$$

Thus, if Alice and Bob share 50 bits of their shared secret key, the probability that they detect Eve is $1 - (3/4)^{50} = 0.99999943$, which is very close to certainty.

In order to use BB84 in practice, we need the ability to send qubits to each other through a network. This is called a *quantum network*, and building a quantum network is an area of active research.

Exercise 6.25. You are Alice, and you and Bob are establishing a secret key using BB84. You have the following random bits and random bases. What qubits do you send to Bob?

Alice's Bits	1 0 0 1 0 0 0 1 1
Alice's Bases	X X Z Z Z X X X X
Alice Sends	? ? ? ? ? ? ? ? ?

Exercise 6.26. You are Bob, and you and Alice are establishing a secret key using BB84. You choose the following random bases to measure each qubit in, and you got the following results.

Bob's Bases	X X Z X Z Z X X Z
Bob's Measurement	$\|+\rangle$ $\|-\rangle$ $\|0\rangle$ $\|-\rangle$ $\|0\rangle$ $\|1\rangle$ $\|1\rangle$ $\|+\rangle$ $\|1\rangle$
Bob's Bits	0 1 0 1 0 1 1 0 1

Next, you call Alice and learn that she used the following bases:

Alice's Bases	Z Z Z Z Z X X Z Z

What is your shared secret key?

Exercise 6.27. Alice and Bob want to catch a possible eavesdropper with a probability of 99%. How many bits of their shared secret key should they reveal?

6.7 Summary

Entanglement is a feature of quantum states that does not exist with classical bits. Entangled qubits can influence each other faster than the speed of light, but this influence cannot be used to communicate faster than light. Entanglement is monogamous, meaning if two qubits are maximally entangled, they cannot be entangled at all with a third qubit. Using superdense coding, entanglement does allow Alice to send Bob $2n$ bits of information by only physically sending him n qubits. Entanglement also allows the state of a qubit to be teleported with the aid of classical communication. Finally, the BB84 quantum key distribution protocol does not use entanglement, but it illustrates how a shared secret key can be established between Alice and Bob, and the security is guaranteed by the laws of physics.

Chapter 7
Quantum Algorithms

In Chapters 1 and 4, we saw a classical algorithm and a quantum algorithm for adding two binary numbers, each of length n. The classical ripple-carry adder in Section 1.3.4 used $5n - 3$ logic gates, whereas from Section 4.5.7, the quantum ripple-carry adder used $4n - 2$ Toffoli gates and $4n$ CNOT gates, for a total of $8n - 2$ gates. Thus, the quantum algorithm uses more gates than the classical algorithm. Furthermore, if we decompose the Toffoli gates into one- and two-qubit gates, the number of quantum gates would be even greater. This is a disappointing result. We want quantum computers to be faster (i.e., use fewer gates) than classical computers. In this chapter, we consider quantum algorithms that are actually better than their classical counterparts.

7.1 Circuit vs Query Complexity

7.1.1 Circuit Complexity

The most precise way to quantify the complexity of a quantum circuit is to count the least number of quantum gates required to implement it, relative to some universal set of quantum gates. This is called its *circuit complexity*. For example, if we permit only one- and two-qubit quantum gates, then recall from Exercise 4.23 that the Toffoli gate can be decomposed into

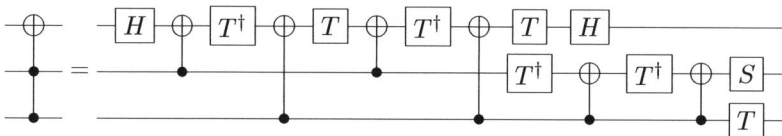

This has sixteen one- and two-qubit gates, but it is not the circuit complexity of the Toffoli gate. In the top row, the last T and H gates can be combined into a single one-qubit gate, reducing the number of one- and two-qubit gates to fifteen. Yet this

is still not the circuit complexity. A circuit that uses even fewer one- and two-qubit gates is

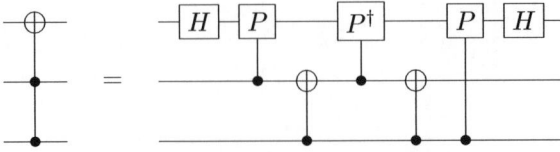

where P is some one-qubit gate. This only uses seven one- and two-qubit gates. It is an active area of research to determine whether Toffoli can be simplified further. If only CNOT and one-qubit gates are permitted, however, it has been proved that Toffoli requires at least six CNOT gates (plus one-qubit gates). Suffice it to say that circuit complexity is generally hard to find.

In terms of circuit complexity, an *efficient* quantum algorithm is one with a polynomial circuit complexity. For example, the quantum adder is efficient since its $4n - 2$ Toffoli gates can each be decomposed into seven one- and two-qubit gates. Adding the $4n$ CNOT gates, this results in $7(4n - 2) + 4n = 32n - 14$ one- and two-qubit gates, which is polynomial (linear) in n.

It is also difficult to find the circuit complexity of classical circuits. It can be hard to determine if a logic circuit has been fully simplified, and it depends on what gates are allowed. For example, should the final circuit only consist of AND, OR, and NOT, or can it also include XOR? Should it only consist of NAND gates? Are three-bit logic gates allowed, or only one- and two-bit gates?

7.1.2 Query Complexity

Since circuit complexity can be hard to find, we often turn to *query complexity* instead. The query complexity of a problem is the number of calls to a function, or *queries* to an *oracle* or *black box* needed to solve the problem. We give an input to the function or oracle or black box, and it returns an output, without us knowing its inner workings. Hence, it is opaque or black. It is significantly easier to find the query complexity of a problem, or when that is not possible, mathematically prove upper or lower bounds on it.

For example, a problem we will explore later this chapter is brute-force searching. Say we are searching a database of 100 items for one particular item, and we have an oracle that tells us whether an item is the correct one or not. We can query, "Oracle, is item number 1 correct?" If the oracle replies, "Yes," we have found our item. If the oracle replies "No," we can inquire about another item: "Oracle, is item number 2 correct?" We can continue in this manner until the oracle says "Yes." Mathematically, the oracle is just a function $f(x)$ that outputs 0 (no) or 1 (yes). So, evaluating $f(1)$ is inquiring whether item number 1 is correct. If $f(1) = 1$, we have found the correct item, but if $f(1) = 0$, we can inquire about another item, like $f(2)$, and so on. The query complexity is the number of times we need to evaluate $f(x)$

in order to find the item. As we will see later in Section 7.6, if the database has N entries, a classical computer takes $O(N)$ queries, but a quantum computer only takes $O(\sqrt{N})$ queries using Grover's algorithm. We call such an improvement or speedup in the number of oracle queries an *oracle separation*.

The first part of this chapter will cover quantum algorithms with oracle separations, meaning they take fewer queries than classical computers to solve problems. These algorithms are generally easier to understand. Then, the second part of this chapter will cover quantum algorithms with better circuit complexities, which are generally more advanced. Before we start looking at oracular problems, i.e., problems with an oracle, let us discuss next how an oracle $f(x)$ acts in a quantum computer.

7.1.3 Quantum Oracles

An oracle is simply a *boolean function*, meaning a function that acts on bits. Then, it can be defined using a truth table, and it can be constructed using logic gates. For it to be a quantum oracle, however, it needs to be reversible. Fortunately, from Section 1.5.4, we can turn it into a reversible circuit by XORing its output with an extra bit. For example, if the function is $f(x)$, the reversible circuit is

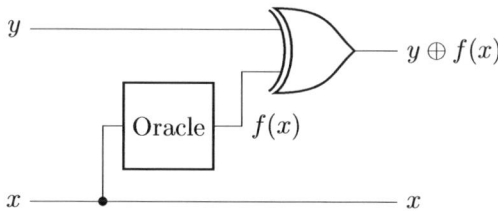

Since this entire circuit is reversible, it is a quantum gate. Let us call the gate U_f to emphasize that it is unitary. We can draw it as

That is, the quantum oracle U_f acts as

$$|x\rangle|y\rangle \xrightarrow{U_f} |x\rangle|y \oplus f(x)\rangle.$$

Note we can find $f(0)$ and $f(1)$ by setting $y = 0$. That is,

$$|0\rangle|0\rangle \xrightarrow{U_f} |0\rangle|0 \oplus f(0)\rangle = |0\rangle|f(0)\rangle,$$
$$|1\rangle|0\rangle \xrightarrow{U_f} |1\rangle|0 \oplus f(1)\rangle = |1\rangle|f(1)\rangle.$$

The extra qubit $|y\rangle$ is called an *answer qubit* or *target qubit*, and $|x\rangle$ is called the *input qubit*.

Exercise 7.1. Consider a classical oracle $f(x) = \bar{x}$, where x is a bit, and $\bar{x}$ is the NOT of x. We want to turn this into a quantum oracle U_f that acts according to

$$|x\rangle|y\rangle \xrightarrow{U_f} |x\rangle|y \oplus f(x)\rangle.$$

Answer the following questions about this operator:
(a) What is the truth table of the quantum oracle?

x	y	x	$y \oplus f(x)$
0	0	?	?
0	1	?	?
1	0	?	?
1	1	?	?

(b) Is the operation reversible?
(c) What is the quantum oracle as a 4×4 matrix?
(d) Verify that the matrix is unitary.

Exercise 7.2. Go to `https://bit.ly/3m3Zcei`. By following this link, you should have access to a custom gate called U_f.

Custom Gates

This is the oracle. It acts on two qubits according to

$$|y\rangle \quad \boxed{} \quad |y \oplus f(x)\rangle$$
$$|x\rangle \quad \boxed{U_f} \quad |x\rangle$$

(a) Using Quirk, query the oracle with appropriate inputs to find $f(0)$.
(b) Using Quirk, query the oracle with appropriate inputs to find $f(1)$.

7.1.4 Phase Oracle

If we query a quantum oracle the standard way described above, the input qubit $|x\rangle$ is unchanged while the answer qubit $|y\rangle$ becomes $|y \oplus f(x)\rangle$. There is a way to query the quantum oracle, however, that causes the answer qubit $|y\rangle$ to be unchanged while multiplying $|x\rangle$ by a phase. It works by setting $|y\rangle = |-\rangle$, which can be done by initializing the answer qubit to $|0\rangle$, applying X to turn it into $|1\rangle$, and then applying H to turn it into $|-\rangle$. That is, writing both the input and answer qubits,

$$|x\rangle|0\rangle \xrightarrow{I \otimes X} |x\rangle|1\rangle \xrightarrow{I \otimes H} |x\rangle|-\rangle.$$

Note it is possible to prepare the answer qubit $|y\rangle$ in the state $|-\rangle$ because the state of a qubit can be a superposition of $|0\rangle$ and $|1\rangle$; with a classical answer bit, this would be impossible. Now, let us expand $|x\rangle|-\rangle$ and see what happens when we query the oracle:

$$|x\rangle|-\rangle = |x\rangle \frac{1}{\sqrt{2}} (|0\rangle - |1\rangle)$$

$$= \frac{1}{\sqrt{2}} (|x\rangle|0\rangle - |x\rangle|1\rangle)$$

$$\xrightarrow{U_f} \frac{1}{\sqrt{2}} (|x\rangle|0 \oplus f(x)\rangle - |x\rangle|1 \oplus f(x)\rangle)$$

$$= \begin{cases} \frac{1}{\sqrt{2}} (|x\rangle|0\rangle - |x\rangle|1\rangle), & f(x) = 0 \\ \frac{1}{\sqrt{2}} (|x\rangle|1\rangle - |x\rangle|0\rangle), & f(x) = 1 \end{cases}$$

$$= \begin{cases} |x\rangle|-\rangle, & f(x) = 0 \\ -|x\rangle|-\rangle, & f(x) = 1 \end{cases}$$

$$= (-1)^{f(x)} |x\rangle|-\rangle.$$

We can interpret this as the answer qubit staying in the $|-\rangle$ state while the input qubit goes from $|x\rangle$ to $(-1)^{f(x)}|x\rangle$. That is, the input qubit acquires a phase. This is called *phase kickback*. Often, we drop the answer qubit, since it stays in the $|-\rangle$ state, and only write the input qubit:

$$|x\rangle \xrightarrow{U_f} (-1)^{f(x)} |x\rangle.$$

This is called a *phase oracle*, where the qubit $|x\rangle$ is multiplied by a phase $(-1)^{f(x)}$. The phase oracle will be very useful for the oracular problems we will cover.

Exercise 7.3. Quantum oracles are quantum gates, so they act across superpositions. Consider an input qubit in the superposition state

$$\frac{\sqrt{3}}{2}|0\rangle + \frac{1}{2}|1\rangle,$$

and an answer qubit in the state $|-\rangle$. Show that the quantum oracle acts by

$$\left(\frac{\sqrt{3}}{2}|0\rangle + \frac{1}{2}|1\rangle \right)|-\rangle \xrightarrow{U_f} \left(\frac{\sqrt{3}}{2}(-1)^{f(0)}|0\rangle + \frac{1}{2}(-1)^{f(1)}|1\rangle \right)|-\rangle.$$

Exercise 7.4. We saw that when the answer qubit is in the state $|-\rangle$, we get phase kickback. Let us explore what happens if the answer qubit is in the state $|+\rangle$. Suppose an input qubit and answer qubit are in the state $|x\rangle|+\rangle$, where x is a bit. If we apply the quantum oracle U_f to this, which maps $|x\rangle|y\rangle$ to $|x\rangle|y \oplus f(x)\rangle$, what do we get if
(a) $f(x) = 0$?
(b) $f(x) = 1$?
(c) How do your answers in parts (a) and (b) compare to the initial state $|x\rangle|+\rangle$?

7.2 Parity

7.2.1 The Problem

For the first algorithm, we have two unknown bits b_0 and b_1, and we want to find the parity of the two bits. That is, we want to find $b_0 \oplus b_1$, or equivalently, whether the number of 1's is even or odd. To do this, we are given an oracle $f(x) = b_x$ that takes as input an index $x \in \{0, 1\}$ and returns the corresponding bit. That is,

$$f(0) = b_0, \quad f(1) = b_1.$$

We will show that to find the parity of b_0 and b_1, we must query this oracle twice classically, but only once quantumly.

7.2.2 Classical Solution

Classically, we need to know both bits in order to find $b_0 \otimes b_1$. So, we need to query the oracle twice, once to find b_0 and again to find b_1:

$$b_0 = f(0), \quad b_1 = f(1).$$

Then we take the XOR of b_0 and b_1 to find the parity. Thus, the classical query complexity is 2.

7.2.3 Quantum Solution: Deutsch's Algorithm

Quantumly, it only takes 1 query using *Deutsch's algorithm*. It uses one input qubit and one answer qubit, and the algorithm is shown in the following quantum circuit:

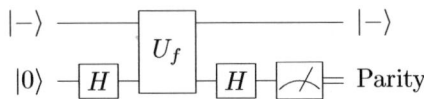

Let us work through each step of the circuit. Ignoring the answer qubit, we first apply the Hadamard gate to the input qubit:

$$|0\rangle \xrightarrow{H} \frac{1}{\sqrt{2}} (|0\rangle + |1\rangle).$$

Next, we query the oracle, which acts as a phase oracle because the answer qubit is $|-\rangle$. From Exercise 7.3, we get

$$\frac{1}{\sqrt{2}} \left[(-1)^{f(0)} |0\rangle + (-1)^{f(1)} |1\rangle \right].$$

To show why this is helpful, let us rewrite this. First, we substitute $f(0) = b_0$ and $f(1) = b_1$:

$$\frac{1}{\sqrt{2}} \left[(-1)^{b_0} |0\rangle + (-1)^{b_1} |1\rangle \right].$$

Then, we factor out $(-1)^{b_0}$.

$$(-1)^{b_0} \frac{1}{\sqrt{2}} \left[|0\rangle + (-1)^{b_1 - b_0} |1\rangle \right].$$

Now, depending on whether b_0 and b_1 are equal, this is

$$\begin{cases} (-1)^{b_0} \frac{1}{\sqrt{2}} (|0\rangle + |1\rangle), & b_0 = b_1 \\ (-1)^{b_0} \frac{1}{\sqrt{2}} (|0\rangle - |1\rangle), & b_0 \neq b_1 \end{cases}.$$

These are just $|+\rangle$ and $|-\rangle$, each with a phase:

$$\begin{cases} (-1)^{b_0} |+\rangle, & b_0 = b_1 \\ (-1)^{b_0} |-\rangle, & b_0 \neq b_1 \end{cases}.$$

So, if b_0 and b_1 are equal, we have $|+\rangle$ with an overall phase, and if b_0 and b_1 are unequal, we have $|-\rangle$ with an overall phase. We can distinguish these by measuring in the X-basis $\{|+\rangle, |-\rangle\}$. Or, we can apply the Hadamard gate again and then measure in the Z-basis $\{|0\rangle, |1\rangle\}$. Applying the Hadamard gate, we get

$$\begin{cases} (-1)^{b_0} |0\rangle, & b_0 = b_1 \\ (-1)^{b_0} |1\rangle, & b_0 \neq b_1 \end{cases}.$$

If we measure this, we either get $|0\rangle$ or $|1\rangle$, since the overall phase of $(-1)^{b_0}$ does not matter. If we get $|0\rangle$, we know that $b_0 = b_1$, and so the parity of the bits is 0 (even). On the other hand, if we get $|1\rangle$, we know that $b_0 \neq b_1$, and so the parity of the bits is 1 (odd). Thus, depending on whether we get $|0\rangle$ or $|1\rangle$, we know whether the parity of the two bits is 0 or 1, and we determined this with just one query to the oracle. Thus, the quantum query complexity is 1, which is an improvement over the classical query complexity of 2. While the improvement in query complexity from 2 to 1 may be small, it is our first concrete example of a quantum computer outperforming a classical computer.

Note in Deutsch's algorithm, we never learned the values of b_0 and b_1 themselves, which would require two oracle queries. Instead, we only learned whether they are equal or opposite, which corresponds to even or odd parity, respectively.

Exercise 7.5. There are two unknown bits b_0 and b_1, and you want to find the parity of the two bits by querying an oracle. Go to https://bit.ly/2ILe3cF. By following this link, you should have access to a custom gate called U_f. This is the oracle, and it acts on two qubits by

For this problem, the function $f(x)$ returns bit x, so $f(x) = b_x$.

(a) In Quirk, use Deutsch's algorithm to find the parity of b_0 and b_1 using just one query to U_f. Note you will need to prepare the answer qubit so that it is in the minus state.

(b) In Quirk, query U_f in such a way as to find b_0.

(c) In Quirk, query U_f in such a way as to find b_1.

(d) Since you now know b_0 and b_1 from parts (b) and (c), find their parity. Verify that it agrees with your result from part (a).

(e) In the worst case, how many queries does it take to solve the problem classically?

Exercise 7.6. There are two unknown bits b_0 and b_1, and you want to find the parity of the two bits by querying an oracle. Go to https://ibm.co/3GxSWTT. By following this link, you should have access to a custom gate called U_f:

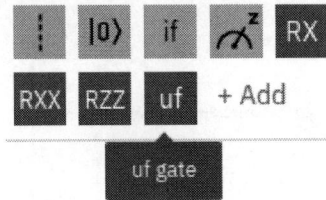

This is the oracle, and it acts on two qubits by

For this problem, the function $f(x)$ returns bit x, so $f(x) = b_x$.

(a) Program Deutsch's algorithm in IBM Quantum, and use the quantum simulator to find the parity of b_0 and b_1.

(b) Run the circuit on an actual quantum processor using IBM Quantum. Which processor did you use, and what histogram of results do you get?

Exercise 7.7. Say you are trying to use Deutsch's algorithm, but you neglect the last Hadamard gate. That is, you apply

$$|0\rangle \xrightarrow{H} |+\rangle \xrightarrow{U_f} \frac{1}{\sqrt{2}}\left[(-1)^{f(0)}|0\rangle + (-1)^{f(1)}|1\rangle\right].$$

If you measure the system now, what possible states do you get, and with what probabilities?

7.2.4 Generalization to Additional Bits

What if we have n bits $b_0, b_1, \ldots, b_{n-1}$, and we want to find their parity? Classically, we need to know all n bits, so it takes n queries. Quantumly, we can use Deutsch's algorithm to find the parity of pairs of bits:

$$\underbrace{b_0, b_1}_{\text{parity}}, \underbrace{b_2, b_3}_{\text{parity}}, \ldots \underbrace{b_{n-2}, b_{n-1}}_{\text{parity}}.$$

This takes $n/2$ queries. Then we can take the XOR of all these parities to get the parity of all the bits. This takes no additional queries. So, the quantum query complexity is $n/2$, which is half classical query complexity. Note both the classical and quantum runtimes are $O(n)$, however, so there is no improvement in their asymptotic scaling.

Exercise 7.8. You have eight bits, and using Deutsch's algorithm, you have found the parities of pairs of bits, shown below:

$$\underbrace{b_0, b_1}_{1}, \underbrace{b_2, b_3}_{1}, \underbrace{b_4, b_5}_{0}, \underbrace{b_6, b_7}_{1}.$$

(a) What is the parity of all eight bits?
(b) How many queries to the oracle did it take to find the parity of all eight bits?
(c) In the worst case, how many queries does it take to solve the problem classically?

Exercise 7.9. You have nine bits, and using Deutsch's algorithm, you have found the parities of the first four pairs of bits. Then you queried the oracle for the last bit, revealing whether it's a 1 or a 0. This is shown below:

$$\underbrace{b_0, b_1}_{0}, \underbrace{b_2, b_3}_{1}, \underbrace{b_4, b_5}_{0}, \underbrace{b_6, b_7}_{0}, \underbrace{b_8}_{1}.$$

(a) What is the parity of all nine bits?
(b) How many queries to the oracle did it take to find the parity of all nine bits?
(c) In the worst case, how many queries does it take to solve the problem classically?

7.3 Constant vs Balanced Functions

7.3.1 The Problem

In this problem, we have a function $f(x)$ that takes as input a binary number $x = x_{n-1} \ldots x_1 x_0$ of length n and outputs 0 or 1. Mathematically, we can write this as $f : \{0,1\}^n \to \{0,1\}$, where $\{0,1\}^n$ denotes bit strings of length n. We additionally have the promise that f is constant (always outputs 0 or always outputs 1) or *balanced* (outputs 0 half the time, and outputs 1 half the time), and the problem is to determine which we have. Put another way, f outputs 1 none of the time, all of the time, or half of the time, and the task is to determine if it is none or all of the time (constant) or half of the time (balanced).

For example, the following function on binary strings of length 3 (i.e., on 3 bits) is balanced since it outputs 0 half the time and 1 the other half of the time:

x_2	x_1	x_0	$f(x)$
0	0	0	0
0	0	1	0
0	1	0	1
0	1	1	1
1	0	0	0
1	0	1	1
1	1	0	1
1	1	1	0

Note $n = 1$ is Deutsch's algorithm since the input is a single bit, and if the function is constant, the parity is 0 or even, and if the function is balanced, the parity is 1 or odd. So the Deutsch-Jozsa algorithm can be seen as a generalization of Deutsch's algorithm.

7.3.2 Classical Solution

Classically, to determine with certainty whether f is constant or balanced, we need to query half the inputs, plus one, in the worst case scenario. That is, if we query half the inputs and get zero each time, then we still do not know if just half the outputs are zero, or if all the outputs are zero. Querying one more input resolves this. Since there are 2^n possible inputs (binary strings of length n), the classical query complexity is $2^{n-1} + 1$. Note this scales exponentially in n, i.e., it is $O(2^n)$.

In practice, however, one may accept a classical algorithm that guesses the correct answer most of the time. For example, say we query f with $c = 10$ different random inputs, and we get $f = 0$ each time. Then, we can guess that f is constant with some degree of certainty. As we will show next, the probability that our guess is wrong can be made smaller than any constant using some suitable constant value for c. Then, such a randomized algorithm can solve the problem with just c queries, which is $O(1)$.

To show this, say we classically query f for c different random inputs. If we get the same output every time, we guess that f is constant, and if we get a mix of 0's and 1's, we guess that f is balanced. Let us calculate the probability that these guesses are incorrect. First, if f is constant, we will get the same output for all c of our inputs, and we will correctly guess that f is constant, so there is no error in this case. If f is balanced and the c outputs are any mix of 0's and 1's, we will correctly guess that f is balanced, so there is no error in this case, either. If f is balanced and all c of our outputs are the same, however, we will incorrectly guess that f is constant, which is an error. Let us find the probability of this error. Say all c of our outputs are 0, but f is actually balanced. To get the first 0, there are $2^n/2 = 2^{n-1}$ outputs that are 0 out of a total of 2^n outputs, so the probability of getting a 0 is $2^{n-1}/2^n$. For the second 0, there are $2^{n-1} - 1$ outputs remaining that are 0 out of a total of $2^n - 1$ outputs remaining, so the probability of getting a second 0 is $(2^{n-1} - 1)/(2^n - 1)$. Continuing this reasoning, the probability of getting c zeros is

$$\frac{2^{n-1}}{2^n} \frac{2^{n-1}-1}{2^n-1} \frac{2^{n-1}-2}{2^n-2} \cdots \frac{2^{n-1}-(c-1)}{2^n-(c-1)}$$
$$\approx \frac{2^{n-1}}{2^n} \frac{2^{n-1}}{2^n} \frac{2^{n-1}}{2^n} \cdots \frac{2^{n-1}}{2^n}$$
$$= \frac{1}{2} \frac{1}{2} \frac{1}{2} \cdots \frac{1}{2} = \frac{1}{2^c},$$

where in the second line, we have approximated the expression for large n. Similarly, the probability of all c queries yielding 1 even though f is balanced is also $1/2^c$. Together, the total probability of incorrectly guessing that f is constant when it is actually balanced is

$$\frac{1}{2^c} + \frac{1}{2^c} = \frac{1}{2^{c-1}}.$$

This does not depend on n. So, we can bound the error by checking an appropriate number of inputs. For example, if we want the probability of error to be less than 1%, we only need to query f for $c = 8$ different inputs, and this is a constant number of queries regardless of n. Thus, this randomized algorithm takes $O(1)$ queries of f.

From Exercise 1.53, problems that are efficiently solved with bounded error by such randomized algorithms are contained in the complexity class *bounded-error probabilistic polynomial time* (BPP). It is believed that $P = BPP$, but it is not proven. Since we gave an efficient randomized algorithm for determining whether f is constant or balanced, this problem is in BPP.

To review, for a classical computer to determine with certainty whether f is constant or balanced, it needs $2^{n-1} + 1$ queries to f in the worst case, which is $O(2^n)$. For a probabilistic classical computer to guess the answer with bounded error, it only needs a constant number of queries to f, which is $O(1)$.

Exercise 7.10. When determining if an oracle f is constant or balanced,
  (a) What is the probability of an error if you evaluate f for $c = 7$ different inputs?
  (b) What is the probability of an error if you evaluate f for $c = 8$ different inputs?
  (c) How many times should f be evaluated to reduce the error probability to less than 0.1%?

7.3.3 Quantum Solution: Deutsch-Jozsa Algorithm

A quantum computer using the *Deutsch-Jozsa algorithm* can determine with certainty whether f is constant or balanced using just 1 query to f. This is an exponential speedup over the exact classical algorithm, but no speedup over the bounded-error probabilistic classical algorithm.

The Deutsch-Jozsa algorithm is very similar to Deutsch's algorithm, but we now have n qubits (plus an answer qubit, which we ignore by using a phase oracle). These n qubits are initially each in the $|0\rangle$ state, and we apply Hadamards to put them in a superposition of all n-bit strings. Then, we query the oracle on this superposition.

Finally, we apply Hadamards to all the qubits to create a state that we measure, and whose measurement outcome allows us to distinguish whether the function is constant or balanced. Including the answer qubit, the Deutsch-Jozsa algorithm as a quantum circuit is

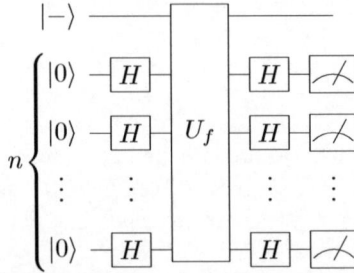

Let us work out the math to show why this determines whether f is constant or balanced. Ignoring the answer qubit, we begin with n qubits, all in the $|0\rangle$ state. First applying the Hadamard gate to each of these n qubits, we get

$$|0\rangle^{\otimes n} \xrightarrow{H^{\otimes n}} |+\rangle^{\otimes n}$$

$$= \frac{1}{\sqrt{2^n}} (|0\rangle + |1\rangle)^{\otimes n}$$

$$= \frac{1}{\sqrt{2^n}} \sum_{x \in \{0,1\}^n} |x\rangle. \qquad (7.1)$$

So, applying Hadamards to the all zero state creates a uniform superposition over all binary strings. Next, we query the phase oracle:

$$\frac{1}{\sqrt{2^n}} \sum_{x \in \{0,1\}^n} |x\rangle \xrightarrow{U_f} \frac{1}{\sqrt{2^n}} \sum_{x \in \{0,1\}^n} (-1)^{f(x)} |x\rangle.$$

Finally, we again apply the Hadamard gate to each of the n qubits:

$$\frac{1}{\sqrt{2^n}} \sum_{x \in \{0,1\}^n} (-1)^{f(x)} |x\rangle \xrightarrow{H^{\otimes n}} \frac{1}{\sqrt{2^n}} \sum_{x \in \{0,1\}^n} (-1)^{f(x)} H^{\otimes n} |x\rangle. \qquad (7.2)$$

This is the final state of the algorithm before the measurement, and to interpret this, let us focus on just one $H^{\otimes n}|x\rangle$, where $|x\rangle$ is a single n-bit string:

$$H^{\otimes n}|x\rangle = H^{\otimes n}|x_{n-1} \ldots x_1 x_0\rangle$$

$$= H|x_{n-1}\rangle \ldots H|x_1\rangle H|x_0\rangle.$$

Depending on whether x_i is 0 or 1, $H|x_i\rangle$ is either $|+\rangle$ or $|-\rangle$. To account for the difference in sign between $|+\rangle$ and $|-\rangle$, we can write $H|x_i\rangle$ as

$$H|x_i\rangle = \frac{1}{\sqrt{2}} \left[|0\rangle + (-1)^{x_i} |1\rangle \right].$$

This way, when $x_i = 0$, $(-1)^{x_i} = 1$, and the result is $|+\rangle$, and when $x_i = 1$, $(-1)^{x_i} = -1$, and the result is $|-\rangle$. Writing each $H|x_i\rangle$ like this, we get

$$H|x_0\rangle H|x_1\rangle \ldots H|x_{n-1}\rangle$$
$$= \frac{1}{\sqrt{2}}\left[|0\rangle + (-1)^{x_{n-1}}|1\rangle\right] \ldots \frac{1}{\sqrt{2}}\left[|0\rangle + (-1)^{x_1}|1\rangle\right]\frac{1}{\sqrt{2}}\left[|0\rangle + (-1)^{x_0}|1\rangle\right].$$

Multiplying out the terms, this becomes

$$\frac{1}{\sqrt{2^n}}\Big[|0\ldots000\rangle + (-1)^{x_0}|0\ldots001\rangle + (-1)^{x_1}|0\ldots010\rangle$$
$$+ (-1)^{x_1}(-1)^{x_0}|0\ldots011\rangle + (-1)^{x_2}|0\ldots100\rangle + (-1)^{x_2}(-1)^{x_0}|0\ldots101\rangle$$
$$+ (-1)^{x_2}(-1)^{x_1}|0\ldots110\rangle + (-1)^{x_2}(-1)^{x_1}(-1)^{x_0}|0\ldots111\rangle + \ldots\Big].$$

Writing $(-1)^{x_1}(-1)^{x_0}$ as $(-1)^{x_1+x_0}$, and similarly elsewhere, we get

$$\frac{1}{\sqrt{2^n}}\Big[|0\ldots000\rangle + (-1)^{x_0}|0\ldots001\rangle + (-1)^{x_1}|0\ldots010\rangle$$
$$+ (-1)^{x_1+x_0}|0\ldots011\rangle + (-1)^{x_2}|0\ldots100\rangle + (-1)^{x_2+x_0}|0\ldots101\rangle$$
$$+ (-1)^{x_2+x_1}|0\ldots110\rangle + (-1)^{x_2+x_1+x_0}|0\ldots111\rangle + \ldots\Big].$$

This is a sum over all n-bit strings $|z\rangle = |z_{n-1}\ldots z_1 z_0\rangle$, so it becomes

$$\frac{1}{\sqrt{2^n}}\sum_{z\in\{0,1\}^n}(-1)^{\sum_{i:z_i=1}x_i}|z\rangle.$$

For the negative sign, the power is the sum of the values of x_i such that $z_i = 1$. We can also write this sum using the *dot product* $x \cdot z$,

$$x \cdot z = x_{n-1}z_{n-1} + \cdots + x_1 z_1 + x_0 z_0.$$

In this dot product, the only x_i's that survive are those where $z_i = 1$. Using this notation, we get

$$H^{\otimes n}|x\rangle = \frac{1}{\sqrt{2^n}}\sum_{z\in\{0,1\}^n}(-1)^{x\cdot z}|z\rangle. \tag{7.3}$$

Plugging this into Eq. (7.2), the final state of the algorithm before measurement is

$$\frac{1}{\sqrt{2^n}}\sum_{x\in\{0,1\}^n}(-1)^{f(x)}H^{\otimes n}|x\rangle = \frac{1}{\sqrt{2^n}}\sum_{x\in\{0,1\}^n}(-1)^{f(x)}\frac{1}{\sqrt{2^n}}\sum_{z\in\{0,1\}^n}(-1)^{x\cdot z}|z\rangle$$
$$= \sum_{z\in\{0,1\}^n}\left(\frac{1}{2^n}\sum_{x\in\{0,1\}^n}(-1)^{f(x)+x\cdot z}\right)|z\rangle. \tag{7.4}$$

To see how measuring this state lets us determine whether the function is constant or balanced, let us calculate the probability of getting all zeros $|0\ldots00\rangle$. The amplitude of $|0\ldots00\rangle$ (right before measurement) is

$$\frac{1}{2^n}\sum_{x\in\{0,1\}^n}(-1)^{f(x)}.$$

This amplitude depends on whether $f(x)$ is constant or balanced:

- If $f(x)$ is constant, then $f(x)$ always outputs the same value, so $f(x)=f(0\ldots00)$ for all x, and the amplitude is

$$\frac{1}{2^n}\sum_{x\in\{0,1\}^n}(-1)^{f(0\ldots00)}=\frac{1}{2^n}(-1)^{f(0\ldots00)}2^n=(-1)^{f(0\ldots00)}.$$

  Taking the norm-square of this, if $f(x)$ is constant, the probability of measuring $|0\ldots00\rangle$ is 1.
- If $f(x)$ is balanced, then $(-1)^{f(x)}$ is 1 half the time and -1 the other half the time, so the amplitude is 0. Hence, if $f(x)$ is balanced, the probability of measuring $|0\ldots00\rangle$ is 0, so we are guaranteed to get something other than $|0\ldots00\rangle$ when we measure.

Thus, to determine if f is constant or balanced, we measure the n qubits, and if we get $|0\ldots00\rangle$, the function is constant, and if we get anything else, the function is balanced.

Exercise 7.11. Apply $H\otimes H\otimes H$ to $|000\rangle$, and show that the resulting state is a uniform superposition of all binary strings of length 3. If you measure the qubits, what possible outcomes can you get, and with what probabilities?

Exercise 7.12. There is a function on three bits $f(b_2,b_1,b_0)$, with the promise that the function is constant or balanced. You want to determine which by querying an oracle. Go to https://bit.ly/38P0Nig. By following this link, you should have access to a custom gate called U_f. This is the oracle, and it acts on four qubits by

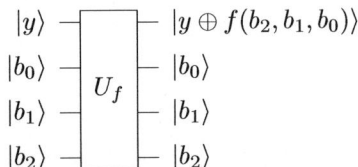

$$\begin{array}{ll}|y\rangle & |y\oplus f(b_2,b_1,b_0)\rangle\\ |b_0\rangle & |b_0\rangle\\ |b_1\rangle\quad U_f & |b_1\rangle\\ |b_2\rangle & |b_2\rangle\end{array}$$

(a) In Quirk, use the Deutsch-Jozsa algorithm to determine whether $f(x)$ is constant or balanced using just one query to U_f. Note you will need to prepare the answer qubit so that it is in the minus state.
(b) In Quirk, query U_f in various ways to determine $f(b_2,b_1,b_0)$:

b_2 b_1 b_0	$f(b_2,b_1,b_0)$
0 0 0	?
0 0 1	?
0 1 0	?
0 1 1	?
1 0 0	?
1 0 1	?
1 1 0	?
1 1 1	?

(c) Since you now know $f(b_2,b_1,b_0)$ completely from part (b), verify that it agrees with your result from part (a).

(d) In the worst case, how many queries does it take to solve the problem classically?

Exercise 7.13. There is a function on three bits $f(b_2,b_1,b_0)$, with the promise that the function is constant or balanced. You want to determine which by querying an oracle. Go to https://ibm.co/3EWbltg. By following this link, you should have access to a custom gate called U_f. This is the oracle, and it acts on four qubits by

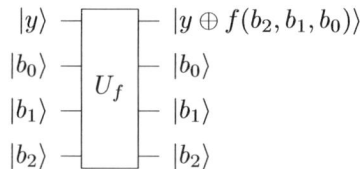

$$
\begin{array}{ll}
|y\rangle & |y \oplus f(b_2,b_1,b_0)\rangle \\
|b_0\rangle & |b_0\rangle \\
\quad\quad U_f & \\
|b_1\rangle & |b_1\rangle \\
|b_2\rangle & |b_2\rangle
\end{array}
$$

(a) Program the Deutsch-Jozsa algorithm in IBM Quantum, and use the quantum simulator to determine if $f(b_0,b_1,b_2)$ is constant or balanced.

(b) Run the circuit on an actual quantum processor using IBM Quantum. Which processor did you use, and what histogram of results do you get?

7.4 Secret Dot Product String

7.4.1 The Problem

Deutsch's algorithm and the Deutsch-Jozsa algorithm both followed the same steps: apply Hadamard gate(s), query the oracle, apply Hadamard gate(s) again, and then measure. Since this worked so well, are there any other problems that can be solved by this procedure?

The answer is yes. There is another problem that a quantum computer can solve using this procedure, and it is finding a secret n-bit string by querying an oracle that takes the dot product of the string with the input. That is, we again have a function f that takes as input a binary string of length n and outputs 0 or 1, so $f : \{0,1\}^n \to \{0,1\}$. But now the promise is that $f(x) = s \cdot x$, where s is some n-bit string $s_{n-1}\ldots s_1 s_0$, and the dot product of s and x is the sum of the products of their elements, i.e.,

$$s \cdot x = s_{n-1}x_{n-1} + \cdots + s_1 x_1 + s_0 x_0.$$

The problem is to find s, which means finding $s_{n-1}\ldots s_1 s_0$.

7.4.2 Classical Solution

Since we need to determine all n bits of s, the classical solution requires n queries, one to learn each bit of s. For example, if $n = 4$, then

$$
\begin{aligned}
f(0001) &= s_3(0) + s_2(0) + s_1(0) + s_0(1) = s_0, \\
f(0010) &= s_3(0) + s_2(0) + s_1(1) + s_0(0) = s_1, \\
f(0100) &= s_3(0) + s_2(1) + s_1(0) + s_0(0) = s_2, \\
f(1000) &= s_3(1) + s_2(0) + s_1(0) + s_0(0) = s_3.
\end{aligned}
$$

It is known that a bounded-error probabilistic algorithm must also take at least n queries to f, but the details are beyond the scope of this textbook.

7.4.3 Quantum Solution: Bernstein-Vazirani Algorithm

Quantumly, we only need one query using the *Bernstein-Vazirani algorithm*, which is a polynomial speedup over classical computers. It follows the exact same steps as the Deutsch-Jozsa algorithm, where we apply Hadamards, query the oracle, and then apply Hadamards again, so as a quantum circuit, it is

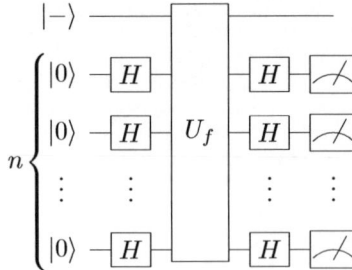

Let us work out the math to show that this works. Ignoring the answer qubit, from Eq. (7.4), the state of the n qubits before measurement is

$$
\sum_{z \in \{0,1\}^n} \left(\frac{1}{2^n} \sum_{x \in \{0,1\}^n} (-1)^{f(x) + x \cdot z} \right) |z\rangle.
$$

For the problem of the secret dot product string, $f(x) = s \cdot x$. Plugging this in, we get

$$
\sum_{z \in \{0,1\}^n} \left(\frac{1}{2^n} \sum_{x \in \{0,1\}^n} (-1)^{(s+z) \cdot x} \right) |z\rangle.
$$

where $s + z$ denotes bitwise addition (no carry), also known as bitwise XOR. That is, $(s + z)_i = s_i \oplus z_i$. Now we measure this, and to determine the possible measurement outcomes, let us consider the amplitude of getting $|s\rangle$. When $z = s$, $s + z$ is a bit string of all zeros. Then the amplitude of $|s\rangle$ is

$$\frac{1}{2^n}\sum_x(-1)^0 = \frac{1}{2^n}\sum_x 1 = \frac{1}{2^n}2^n = 1.$$

Thus, normalization implies that the amplitude of all other states is 0, so the final state of the qubits is

$$|s\rangle.$$

Measuring this is certain to yield $|s\rangle$, and we have determined s with just one query to the oracle.

This is a polynomial speedup over the $O(n)$ queries needed by a classical computer. The above speedup holds for bounded error, so it yields an oracle separation between the complexity classes P and BQP. However, the problem is efficient for both classical and quantum computers. The next algorithm, Simon's algorithm, gives the first "true" exponential speedup, where the problem is inefficient for a classical computer, but efficient for a quantum computer, in the number of oracle queries.

Exercise 7.14. There is a function on six bits $f(b_5,b_4,b_3,b_2,b_1,b_0) = s_5b_5 + \cdots + s_1b_1 + s_0b_0$. Find $s = s_5 \ldots s_1 s_0$ by querying an oracle. Go to https://bit.ly/31YCBZu. By following this link, you should have access to a custom gate called U_f. This is the oracle, and it acts on seven qubits by

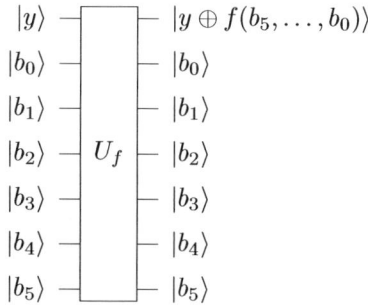

$$
\begin{array}{ll}
|y\rangle & |y \oplus f(b_5,\ldots,b_0)\rangle \\
|b_0\rangle & |b_0\rangle \\
|b_1\rangle & |b_1\rangle \\
|b_2\rangle \quad U_f & |b_2\rangle \\
|b_3\rangle & |b_3\rangle \\
|b_4\rangle & |b_4\rangle \\
|b_5\rangle & |b_5\rangle
\end{array}
$$

(a) In Quirk, use the Bernstein-Vazirani algorithm to determine s using just one query to U_f. Note you will need to prepare the answer qubit so that it is in the minus state.
(b) In Quirk, query U_f in various ways to determine each bit of s. Verify that it agrees with your result from part (a).
(c) In the worst case, how many queries does it take to solve the problem classically?

Exercise 7.15. There is a function on four bits $f(x_3,x_2,x_1,x_0) = s_3x_3 + s_2x_2 + s_1x_1 + s_0x_0$. Find $s = s_3s_2s_1s_0$ by querying an oracle. Go to https://ibm.co/3INITfq. By following this link, you should have access to a custom gate called U_f. This is the oracle, and it acts on five qubits by

$$|y\rangle \quad \boxed{} \quad |y \oplus f(x_3, \ldots, x_0)\rangle$$
$$|x_0\rangle \quad \quad |x_0\rangle$$
$$|x_1\rangle \quad U_f \quad |x_1\rangle$$
$$|x_2\rangle \quad \quad |x_2\rangle$$
$$|x_3\rangle \quad \boxed{} \quad |x_3\rangle$$

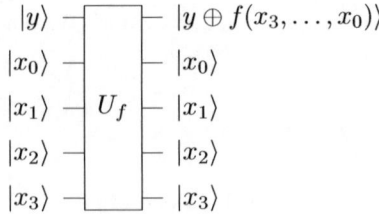

(a) Program the Bernstein-Vazirani algorithm in IBM Quantum, and use the quantum simulator to find $s = s_3 s_2 s_1 s_0$.

(b) Run the circuit on an actual quantum processor using IBM Quantum. Which processor did you use, and what histogram of results do you get?

Exercise 7.16. In the Bernstein-Vazirani algorithm, recall the final state of the qubits (before measurement) is

$$\frac{1}{2^n} \sum_{z \in \{0,1\}^n} \left(\sum_{x \in \{0,1\}^n} (-1)^{(s+z)\cdot x} \right) |z\rangle.$$

Say $n = 3$ and consider $z \neq s$ such that $s + z = 001$ (using bitwise addition). Show that the amplitude of this choice of $|z\rangle$ is zero by filling in the following table, and then computing the sum of the last column.

x	$(s+z)\cdot x$	$(-1)^{(s+z)\cdot x}$
000	?	?
001	?	?
010	?	?
011	?	?
100	?	?
101	?	?
110	?	?
111	?	?
$\sum_x (-1)^{(s+z)\cdot x}$:		?

7.4.4 Recursive Problem

The problem of finding a hidden dot product string can be made recursive, meaning we embed the problem in a bigger instance of the problem, which is embedded in a bigger instance of the problem, and so forth. The details are beyond the scope of this textbook, but if we have k levels, then a classical computer takes $\Omega(n^k)$ queries to solve the problem (recall from Section 1.7.1 that big-Ω is a lower bound, so a classical computer takes at least this many queries). In contrast, a quantum computer using a recursive version of the Bernstein-Vazirani algorithm, however, can solve this problem with 2^k queries. If we have $k = \log_2(n)$ levels, then the classical algorithm takes $\Omega(n^{\log n})$ queries, which is bigger than any polynomial. We call this *superpolynomial*. The quantum computer, however, only takes n queries, which is linear and efficient. Thus, the recursive version of the hidden dot product string problem shows that a quantum computer can yield a superpolynomial speedup in queries. This speedup, however, is less than exponential. Next, we will see a problem with an exponential speedup.

7.5 Secret XOR Mask

7.5.1 The Problem

In this problem, the oracle takes as input an n-bit string $x = x_{n-1} \ldots x_1 x_0$ and outputs an n-bit string $f(x) = f_{n-1} \ldots f_1 f_0$. That is, $f : \{0,1\}^n \to \{0,1\}^n$. We are promised that

$$f(x) = f(y)$$

if and only if the two inputs x and y are related by

$$x = y \oplus s, \quad \text{and} \quad y = x \oplus s$$

for some "secret" n-bit string $s = s_{n-1} \ldots s_1 s_0 \neq 0 \ldots 00$, where $\oplus$ denotes the bitwise XOR. That is, $f(x) = f(y)$ if and only if

$$x_i = y_i \oplus s_i, \quad \text{and} \quad y_i = x_i \oplus s_i.$$

The goal is to find the secret n-bit string $s = s_{n-1} \ldots s_1 s_0$. The secret bit string is called a *mask*, and since it is used to XOR the inputs, it is called an *XOR mask*. The problem is to find the secret XOR mask $s = s_{n-1} \ldots s_1 s_0$.

For example, say $n = 3$ and $s = 110$. Then, for each value of x, $x \oplus s$ is shown in the following table:

x	$x \oplus s$
000	110
001	111
010	100
011	101
100	010
101	011
110	000
111	001

Notice these come in pairs. That is, 000 and 110 are a pair, 001 and 111 are a pair, 010 and 100 are a pair, and 011 and 101 are a pair. This is because if $y = x \oplus s$, then it is automatically true that $x = y \oplus s$. As a proof, we start with

$$y = x \oplus s.$$

Next, if we XOR both sides with s, we get

$$y \oplus s = x \oplus s \oplus s.$$

Since $s \oplus s = 0$, this is

$$y \oplus s = x \oplus 0.$$

Thus,

$$y \oplus s = x,$$

or reversing the two sides, $x = y \oplus s$. Now, from the promise about the oracle, for each pair x and y, $f(x)$ and $f(y)$ must be the same. For example, here are two possible truth tables for $f(x)$, satisfying that $f(x) = f(y)$ if and only if $y = x \oplus s$:

x	$f(x)$
000	011
001	101
010	001
011	000
100	001
101	000
110	011
111	101

x	$f(x)$
000	110
001	001
010	111
011	000
100	111
101	000
110	110
111	001

Notice that in both examples, $f(000) = f(110)$, $f(001) = f(111)$, $f(010) = f(100)$, and $f(011) = f(101)$. Also note there are 1680 different possible truth tables for $f(x)$. This is because we have four pairs that we need to assign outputs to, and there are $2^3 = 8$ different outputs. For the first pair, we have 8 choices of outputs. For the second pair, we have 7 choices of outputs. For the third pair, we have 6 choices of outputs. And for the fourth pair, we have 5 choices of outputs. Altogether, we have $8 \cdot 7 \cdot 6 \cdot 5 = 1680$ possible permutations.

Exercise 7.17. Say $n = 3$ and $s = 010$.
 (a) Find the pairs of n-bit strings x and y such that $y = x \oplus s$.
 (b) Give a possible truth table for $f(x)$ that satisfies the promise that $f(x) = f(y)$ if and only if $y = x \oplus s$.

7.5.2 Classical Solution

Classically, we can find the secret XOR mask s by finding a *collision*, meaning a pair x and y such that f maps them to the same string, i.e., $f(x) = f(y)$. From the promise about f, this implies that $x = y \oplus s$ and $y = x \oplus s$, and we can take the XOR of x and y to find s:

$$x \oplus y = x \oplus (x \oplus s) = \underbrace{(x \oplus x)}_{0} \oplus s = s.$$

One approach is to trying the inputs one-by-one until we find a collision. In the worst case, we could try half of the inputs without yet seeing a collision. We are guaranteed, however, that trying one more input will yield a collision, so the query complexity with this approach is $O(2^{n-1} + 1)$.

We can do better, however. If we query f with *random* inputs. This prevents f from being designed to be as worse as possible as previously described, where half the inputs, plus 1, must be queried to find a collision. Now, say we have queried

f a total of k times, so we have k values of f. The probability of there being a collision in these k values of f is given by the number of pairs of values, which is the combination $_kC_2 = k(k-1)/2 = O(k^2)$. Since this grows quadratically with the number of queries, one expects to query f roughly $\sqrt{2^n} = 2^{n/2}$ times in order to find a collision. Although this is an improvement, it is still exponential in n.

Exercise 7.18. We have an oracle $f : \{0,1\}^n \to \{0,1\}^n$ with a secret XOR mask s. Say $n = 4$. Querying the oracle with some various inputs, we find that $f(1011) = 0010$ and $f(0111) = 0010$. What is s?

Exercise 7.19. The task of finding a collision is closely related to a famous problem called the *birthday problem*, which is to find the probability that in a room of n people, at least two of them share the same birthday. We ignore leap years, so there are 365 days in a year. We also assume that people's birthdays are randomly distributed. In reality, this is not true, as some birthdays are more common than others, but this only makes a shared birthday more likely.

To solve this problem, we find the probability that the n people do *not* share any birthdays. Then, the probability that at least two people share the same birthday is 1 minus this. To calculate the probability that no one shares a birthday, we add people to the room one-by-one. The first person in the room does not share a birthday with anyone else because there is no one else. The second person in the room has 364 possible birthdays so as to not share a birthday with the first person, and the probability of this is 364/365. The third person in the room has 363 possible birthdays so as to not share a birthday with the first two people, and the probability of this is 363/365. The fourth person has 362 possible birthdays to avoid sharing, which has a probability of 362/365. Continuing this, the probability of no one sharing a birthday is

$$\frac{364}{365}\frac{363}{365}\frac{362}{365}\cdots\frac{365-(n-1)}{365}.$$

Multiplying this by 365/365, we get

$$\frac{365}{365}\frac{364}{365}\frac{363}{365}\frac{362}{365}\cdots\frac{365-(n-1)}{365} = \frac{365\cdot364\cdot363\cdot362\cdot\ldots\cdot(365-(n-1))}{365^n}.$$

Thus, the probability that at least two people share the same birthday is

$$1 - \frac{365\cdot364\cdot363\cdot362\cdot\ldots\cdot(365-(n-1))}{365^n}.$$

This can be calculated using a computer algebra system. For example, with $n = 23$ people,

- Using Mathematica,

```
n=23;
1 - Product[i/365., {i, 365-(n-1), 365}]
```

The Product function multiplies $(365-(n-1))/365$ up through 365/365, and the output of 1 minus this product is 0.507297.
- Using SageMath,

```
sage: n=23
sage: 1 - prod(i/365. for i in ((365-(n-1))..365))
0.507297234323986
```

The prod function multiplies $(365-(n-1))/365$ up through 365/365.

So, there is over a 50% chance that at least two people share the same birthday. This may be higher than one might expect, so some call the birthday problem the *birthday paradox*.

(a) With $n = 30$, what is the probability that at least two of them share the same birthday?
(b) With $n = 40$, what is the probability that at least two of them share the same birthday?
(c) With $n = 50$, what is the probability that at least two of them share the same birthday?
(d) With $n = 60$, what is the probability that at least two of them share the same birthday?

7.5.3 Quantum Solution: Simon's Algorithm

Simon's algorithm follows the pattern we have seen so far: apply Hadamards, query the oracle, and apply Hadamards again. But now we have n input qubits and n answer qubits, and we start each of the answer qubits in the $|0\rangle$ state (so we are using the regular quantum oracle, not the phase oracle). For the oracle, it maps

$$|x\rangle|y\rangle \xrightarrow{U_f} |x\rangle|y \oplus f(x)\rangle,$$

where

$$|x\rangle = |x_{n-1}\ldots x_1 x_0\rangle,$$
$$|y\rangle = |y_{n-1}\ldots y_1 y_0\rangle,$$
$$|y \oplus f(x)\rangle = |y_{n-1} \oplus f_{n-1},\ldots,y_1 \oplus f_1, y_0 \oplus f(x_0)\rangle.$$

Another difference with Simon's algorithm is that we will measure all the qubits, not just the input qubits.

The quantum circuit for Simon's algorithm is

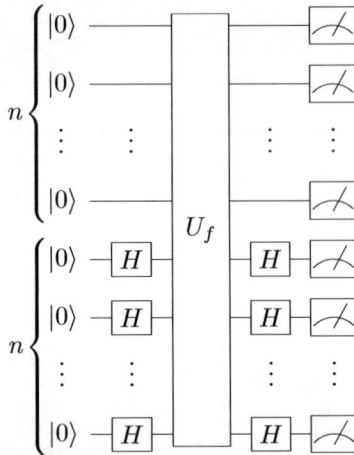

Let us work through the math of what this does. Initially, we have two n-qubit registers, one for the input qubits, and another for the answer qubits.

$$|0\ldots00\rangle|0\ldots00\rangle.$$

Now, we apply the Hadamard gate to each of the input qubits, resulting in

$$|+\cdots++\rangle|0\ldots00\rangle.$$

Multiplying out the $|+\rangle$ states, we get a uniform superposition over n-bit strings:

$$\frac{1}{\sqrt{2^n}}\sum_{x\in\{0,1\}^n}|x\rangle|0\ldots00\rangle.$$

Next, querying the oracle, we get

$$\frac{1}{\sqrt{2^n}}\sum_{x\in\{0,1\}^n}|x\rangle|f(x)\rangle.$$

Now, we again apply the Hadamard gate to each of the input qubits, resulting in

$$\frac{1}{\sqrt{2^n}}\sum_{x\in\{0,1\}^n}H^{\otimes n}|x\rangle|f(x)\rangle.$$

From Eq. (7.3), $H^{\otimes n}|x\rangle$ is a uniform superposition of bit strings $|z\rangle$ multiplied by a phase of $(-1)^{x\cdot z}$, so we get

$$\frac{1}{\sqrt{2^n}}\sum_{x\in\{0,1\}^n}\frac{1}{\sqrt{2^n}}\sum_{z\in\{0,1\}^n}(-1)^{x\cdot z}|z\rangle|f(x)\rangle.$$

Now, let us measure the answer qubits. We will get one particular value of $f(x)$. Let us call the value f'. There are two values of x for which $f(x) = f'$. Let us call them x' and x''. That is, $f(x') = f(x'') = f'$. So, x' and x'' are a pair of inputs for which there is a collision. Then, the state will collapse to these two values of x:

$$\frac{1}{\sqrt{2}}\frac{1}{\sqrt{2^n}}\sum_{z\in\{0,1\}^n}\left[(-1)^{x'\cdot z}+(-1)^{x''\cdot z}\right]|z\rangle|f'\rangle.$$

Note the first coefficient went from $1/\sqrt{2^n}$ to $1/\sqrt{2}$ because the number of possible outcomes for x went from 2^n (all possible bit strings) to 2 ($|x'\rangle$ and $|x''\rangle$). Combining the coefficients,

$$\frac{1}{\sqrt{2^{n+1}}}\sum_{z\in\{0,1\}^n}\left[(-1)^{x'\cdot z}+(-1)^{x''\cdot z}\right]|z\rangle|f'\rangle.$$

Next, we measure the input qubits. To determine the possible results, note that $(-1)^{x'\cdot z} = \pm 1$ and $(-1)^{x''\cdot z} = \pm 1$ depending on what x' and x'' are. Then, their sum is either ± 2 or 0:

$$(-1)^{x'\cdot z}+(-1)^{x''\cdot z} = \begin{cases} \pm 2, & x'\cdot z = x''\cdot z \bmod 2, \\ 0, & x'\cdot z \neq x''\cdot z \bmod 2. \end{cases}$$

Thus, when measuring the input qubits, we only get a value of $|z\rangle$ where

$$x' \cdot z = x'' \cdot z \text{ mod } 2.$$

Adding $x'' \cdot z$ to both sides, we get

$$x' \cdot z + x'' \cdot z = x'' \cdot z + x'' \cdot z \text{ mod } 2.$$

The right-hand side of this equation is 0 because if we add any bit to itself modulo 2, we get 0. Thus,

$$x' \cdot z + x'' \cdot z = 0 \text{ mod } 2.$$

Factoring the left-hand side,

$$(x' + x'') \cdot z = 0 \text{ mod } 2.$$

Since x' and x'' are a pair of inputs for which there is a collision, $x' \oplus x'' = s$. Then, we have

$$s \cdot z = 0 \text{ mod } 2.$$

Thus, when measuring the input qubits, we get a value of $|z\rangle = |z_{n-1} \ldots z_1 z_0\rangle$ such that its dot product with s is 0 mod 2. Writing out the dot product,

$$s_{n-1} z_{n-1} + \cdots + s_1 z_1 + s_0 z_0 = 0 \text{ mod } 2. \tag{7.5}$$

This is an equation containing all n of our unknowns, the s_i's.

If we repeat this process, we will get a $|z\rangle = |z_{n-1} \ldots z_1 z_0\rangle$ that satisfies Eq. (7.5) and is likely different from the first because there are an exponential number of them. To see this, the probability of measuring any such $|z\rangle$ is

$$\left| \frac{\pm 2}{\sqrt{2^{n+1}}} \right|^2 = \frac{4}{2^{n+1}} = \frac{1}{2^{n-1}}.$$

Or, put another way, there are 2^{n-1} possible $|z\rangle$'s whose dot product with s is zero, and we have the same probability of getting each one.

Repeating the quantum algorithm $O(n)$ times, we can get n different $|z\rangle$'s, each satisfying Eq. (7.5). Together, they are a system of n equations and n unknowns, which we can solve for the s_i's. Thus, we can find s with $O(n)$ queries to the oracle, and this was the first exponential oracle separation between classical and quantum computers.

Exercise 7.20. You are using Simon's algorithm to find an $n = 3$ bit string $s = s_2 s_1 s_0$. You run the quantum circuit three times, and you get the following values for $|z\rangle$, such that $s \cdot z = 0$ mod 2:

$$|001\rangle, |110\rangle, |111\rangle,$$

What is s?

Exercise 7.21. You are using Simon's algorithm to find an $n = 8$ bit string $s = s_7 s_6 s_5 s_4 s_3 s_2 s_1 s_0$.
  (a) How many different values of $|z\rangle$ are there, such that $s \cdot z = 0$ mod 2?

(b) If you run the quantum circuit three times, what is the probability that all three values of $|z\rangle$ are different?

7.5.4 Summary

We have examined several quantum algorithms that all follow the same procedure: apply Hadamards, query the oracle, and apply Hadamards again. The following table summarizes the problems, query complexities, and asymptotic quantum speedups:

Problem	Classical Queries	Quantum Algorithm	Quantum Queries	Asymptotic Speedup
n-bit Parity	n	Deutsch	$n/2$	None
Constant vs Balanced	Exact: $2^{n-1}+1$ Bounded: $O(1)$	Deutsch-Jozsa	1	Exponential None
Dot Product String	n	Bernstein-Vazirani	1	Polynomial
Recursive Dot Product String	$\Omega(n^{\log_2 n})$	Recursive Bernstein-Vazirani	n	Superpolynomial
XOR Mask	$O(2^{n/2})$	Simon	$O(n)$	Exponential

We started with the parity problem. The quantum algorithm does offer an improvement in that it takes half as many queries, but asymptotically, both the classical and quantum algorithms are $O(n)$, so there is no speedup in that sense. Then, we looked at determining whether the oracle is constant or balanced. Although the quantum algorithm yields an exponential improvement over the exact classical algorithm, it is no improvement over the bounded algorithm that is often acceptable in practice. For a true asymptotic speedup, the problem of finding a secret dot product string is solved by a quantum computer using polynomially fewer queries, and a recursive version of the problem is solved with superpolynomially fewer queries. Finally, finding a secret XOR mask takes exponentially fewer queries on a quantum computer, which shows that for oracular problems, quantum computers can yield an exponential speedup.

7.6 Brute-Force Searching

7.6.1 The Problem

Before moving on to problems where we can calculate the circuit complexity, let us discuss one more oracular problem where we count the number of oracle queries.

It is the problem of *brute-force searching*. We again have a function f that takes as input a binary string of length n and outputs 0 or 1, so $f : \{0,1\}^n \to \{0,1\}$. This function, however, only outputs 1 for one input, so it outputs 0 for all other inputs. The problem is to find this one special input, which we will call w (for winner).

A common motivation for this problem is searching a telephone book, which is a list of people in alphabetical order along with each person's telephone number:[1]

Name	Phone Number
Alice	314-1592
Bob	271-8281
Charlie	105-4571
Dave	885-4187
Eve	125-6637
Frank	299-7924
Grace	729-7352
⋮	⋮
Zoe	200-2319

Given a name, it is easy to find the corresponding phone number, since the names are sorted in alphabetical order. For example, we can start in the middle of the list and determine if the person we are looking for is in the first half or the last half of the phone book. Say it is the first half. Then we can look at the middle entry of this half of the phone book and determine if the person we are looking for is in the first quarter or second quarter of the list. Repeating this, we reduce the number entries by one-half each time until we find the entry we are looking for. This process is called *binary search*, and if the number of entries is N, it takes at most $\log_2 N$ steps.

The inverse problem, however, is harder to do. Given a phone number, say 299-7924, finding the name it corresponds to is harder since the numbers are unsorted. In fact, we might need to look though every phone number until we find a match. This inverse problem is the brute-force searching problem that we want to solve, and a classical computer needs $O(N)$ queries to solve it. This problem is also phrased as searching an unordered database, and it is also called unstructured searching. In terms of a function, we have $f(\text{name}) = \text{number}$, and we want to find the name. So, this is also the problem of inverting a function, i.e., of starting with an output and trying to find the input.

It is possible to have a function or oracle that recognizes the correct answer, even if it does not know what the correct answer is. For example, it is generally hard to factor numbers (see Section 6.6.2 on RSA cryptography), but it is easy to verify if the product of numbers equals the number we are trying to factor. Recall from Section 1.7.2 that the problems whose possible solutions are easy to check comprise the complexity class NP. So, brute-force searching includes trying to solve problems in NP by checking each input to see which output is correct.

---

[1] These phone numbers are inspired by the mathematical constants π and e, and the physical constants $\hbar$, ε_0, μ_0, c, α, and g_s.

7.6.2 Classical Solution

Classically, we must query all $N = 2^n$ possible bit strings in the worst case. Or on average, we must query half the bit strings, or $N/2$, since it is equally likely that the winner is the first input as the last. Either way, the classical runtime is $O(N)$.

7.6.3 Quantum Solution: Grover's Algorithm

A quantum computer can solve the brute-force searching problem using only $O(\sqrt{N})$ queries using *Grover's algorithm*. Ignoring the answer qubit, the algorithm begins with the qubits all in the $|+\rangle$ state. Let us call this starting state $|s\rangle$. From Eq. (7.1), this is a uniform superposition over all n-bit strings:

$$|s\rangle = |+\rangle^{\otimes n} = \frac{1}{\sqrt{N}} \sum_{x \in \{0,1\}^n} |x\rangle,$$

where $N = 2^n$. We can create this initial state by applying Hadamard gates to the all-zeros state, i.e., $|+\rangle^{\otimes n} = H^{\otimes n}|0\rangle^{\otimes n}$. Since the initial state is a uniform superposition over all n-bit strings, it includes the binary string $|w\rangle$ we are trying to find, and all the other ones:

$$\begin{aligned}
|s\rangle &= \frac{1}{\sqrt{N}} \left(|w\rangle + \sum_{i \neq w} |i\rangle \right) \\
&= \frac{1}{\sqrt{N}}|w\rangle + \frac{1}{\sqrt{N}} \sum_{i \neq w} |i\rangle \\
&= \frac{1}{\sqrt{N}}|w\rangle + \sqrt{\frac{N-1}{N}} \underbrace{\frac{1}{\sqrt{N-1}} \sum_{i \neq w} |i\rangle}_{|r\rangle} \\
&= \frac{1}{\sqrt{N}}|w\rangle + \sqrt{\frac{N-1}{N}}|r\rangle \\
&= \sin\theta|w\rangle + \cos\theta|r\rangle,
\end{aligned}$$

where $|r\rangle$ is defined as the uniform superposition over all n-bit strings that are not $|w\rangle$, and θ is defined such that

$$\sin\theta = \frac{1}{\sqrt{N}}, \quad \cos\theta = \sqrt{\frac{N-1}{N}}.$$

Drawing the initial state in a coordinate plane with $|r\rangle$ and $|w\rangle$ as the x- and y-axes, we get

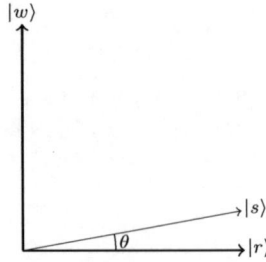

Next, we query the phase oracle U_f. Since $f(x) = 1$ only when $x = w$, the state becomes

$$U_f|s\rangle = (-1)^1 \sin\theta|w\rangle + (-1)^0 \cos\theta|r\rangle$$
$$= -\sin\theta|w\rangle + \cos\theta|r\rangle.$$

Thus, the amplitude of $|w\rangle$ is inverted. Drawn in the coordinate plane, this is equivalent to a reflection through $|w\rangle$:

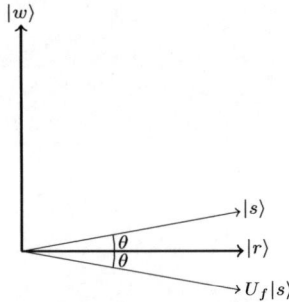

Next, we apply a quantum gate R_s that reflects about $|s\rangle$ (more on how to do this, and how to interpret it, later). Drawn in the rw-plane,

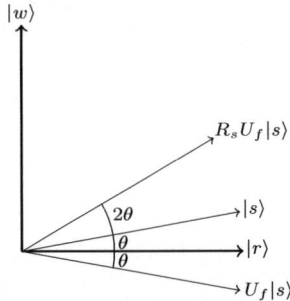

We see that the net effect of these two reflections is a rotation by 2θ. If we apply U_f and R_s again, we rotate by 2θ again:

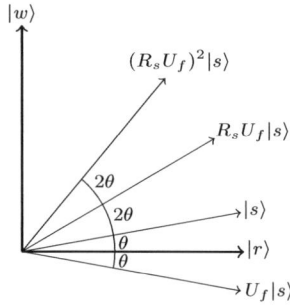

In this manner, we keep rotating by 2θ by applying U_f and R_s until the final state is close to $|w\rangle$. Say this takes a total of t rotations. Then, since the angle between $|r\rangle$ and $|w\rangle$ is $90°$, or $\pi/2$ radians,

$$\theta + t(2\theta) = \frac{\pi}{2}$$

$$t(2\theta) = \frac{\pi}{2} - \theta$$

$$t = \frac{\pi}{4\theta} - \frac{1}{2}.$$

Assuming N is large,

$$\theta = \sin^{-1}\left(\frac{1}{\sqrt{N}}\right) \approx \frac{1}{\sqrt{N}},$$

and so

$$t \approx \frac{\pi}{4}\sqrt{N} - \frac{1}{2} \approx \frac{\pi}{4}\sqrt{N}.$$

Thus, the number of queries is $O(\sqrt{N})$, which is a quadratic speedup over the classical computer's $O(N)$.

The angle of the final state may not be exactly $\pi/2$, so the success probability may not be exactly 1. This is not an issue, however, for a couple of reasons. First, for large N, the angle θ is small. So, the final state may only miss $|w\rangle$ by a small amount. Second, there are ways to adjust this algorithm so that the last step rotates by a different angle, causing the final state to be exactly aligned with $|w\rangle$. This is beyond the scope of this textbook.

Including the answer qubit, as a quantum circuit, Grover's algorithm is

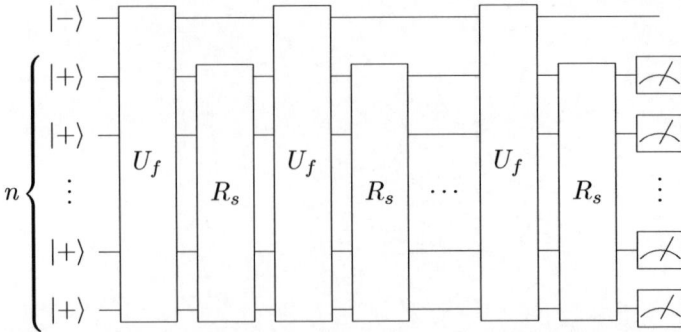

Exercise 7.22. Prove that when $N = 4$ ($n = 2$), the final state of Grover's algorithm is exactly $|w\rangle$.

Exercise 7.23. Answer the following questions about Grover's algorithm:
  (a) When the n qubits are in their initial state (all $|+\rangle$ states), if you measure the qubits, what is the probability that you get $|w\rangle$? Express your answer in terms of $N = 2^n$.
  (b) Say you apply just one step of Grover's algorithm (one query U_f and one reflection R_s). If you measure the qubits after this one step, what is the probability that you get $|w\rangle$? Express your answer in terms of $N = 2^n$. Hint: In the rw-plane, the amplitude of the state in $|w\rangle$ is the sine of the angle between the state and $|r\rangle$.

Exercise 7.24. Go to https://bit.ly/3qoOErN. By following this link, you should have access to the custom gates U_f and R_s. U_f is the oracle, and it acts on five qubits by

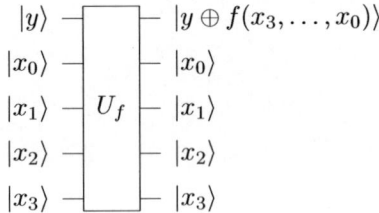

R_s acts on four qubits, and it reflects about $|s\rangle$.
  (a) What is n?
  (b) What is N?
  (c) For this problem, how many queries does Grover's algorithm take?
  (d) Using Quirk, implement Grover's algorithm and find $|w\rangle$.
  (e) Using Quirk, query U_f in various ways to fill out the following table:

x	$f(x)$
0000	?
0001	?
0010	?
0011	?
0100	?
0101	?
0110	?
0111	?
1000	?
1001	?
1010	?
1011	?
1100	?
1101	?
1110	?
1111	?

Do your results agree with your answer to part (d)?

7.6.4 Reflection About Uniform State

Now, let us explore the reflection about $|s\rangle$, which we denoted R_s. Since we want $|s\rangle$ to be unchanged, but states perpendicular to $|s\rangle$ to be reflected (i.e., take on a minus sign), we can write R_s as

$$R_s = 2|s\rangle\langle s| - I.$$

Recall from Section 3.4 that the outer product $|s\rangle\langle s|$ is a matrix, and I is the identity matrix that acts on n qubits, so it is $N \times N$ in size. Let us show that this keeps $|s\rangle$ the same, but flips any state $|s^\perp\rangle$ that is orthogonal to $|s\rangle$, as we expect a reflection about $|s\rangle$ to do:

$$R_s|s\rangle = 2|s\rangle \underbrace{\langle s|s\rangle}_{1} - |s\rangle = 2|s\rangle - |s\rangle = |s\rangle,$$

$$R_s|s^\perp\rangle = 2|s\rangle \underbrace{\langle s|s^\perp\rangle}_{0} - |s^\perp\rangle = -|s^\perp\rangle.$$

To write R_s in terms of elementary gates, which also proves that it is a valid quantum gate, recall

$$|s\rangle = |+\rangle^{\otimes n} = H^{\otimes n}|0^{\otimes n}\rangle = H|0\rangle \dots H|0\rangle.$$

Then, taking the dual using Eq. (3.1),

$$\langle s| = \langle 0|H^\dagger \dots \langle 0|H^\dagger = \langle 0|H \dots \langle 0|H = \langle 0^{\otimes n}|H^{\otimes n},$$

where we used the fact that $H^\dagger = H$. Plugging these into R_s,

$$R_s = 2H^{\otimes n}|0^n\rangle\langle 0^n|H^{\otimes n} - I.$$

We can also write the n-qubit identity matrix as

$$I = I \otimes \cdots \otimes I = HH \otimes \cdots \otimes HH = (H \otimes \cdots \otimes H)(H \otimes \cdots \otimes H) = H^{\otimes n}H^{\otimes n}.$$

Plugging this into R_s, we get

$$\begin{aligned}
R_s &= 2\left(H^{\otimes n}|0^n\rangle\right)\left(\langle 0^n|H^{\otimes n}\right) - H^{\otimes n}H^{\otimes n} \\
&= H^{\otimes n}\underbrace{\left(2|0^n\rangle\langle 0^n| - I\right)}_{R_0}H^{\otimes n} \\
&= H^{\otimes n}R_0 H^{\otimes n},
\end{aligned}$$

where we have defined another operator

$$R_0 = 2|0^n\rangle\langle 0^n| - I.$$

We will discuss R_0 in a moment, but the point is that R_s is equal to R_0 surrounded by Hadamards on both sides:

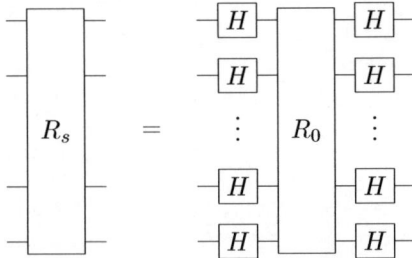

Now for R_0, let us calculate how it acts on the all 0's state $|0^n\rangle$ and how it acts any other state $|a\rangle$:

$$R_0|s\rangle = 2|0^n\rangle\underbrace{\langle 0^n|0^n\rangle}_{1} - |0^n\rangle = 2|0^n\rangle - |0^n\rangle = |0^n\rangle,$$

$$R_0|a\rangle = 2|0^n\rangle\underbrace{\langle 0^n|a\rangle}_{0} - |a\rangle = -|a\rangle.$$

Thus, R_0 is a reflection about the all zeros state $|0^n\rangle$. To create a circuit for R_0, recall $Z|0\rangle = |0\rangle$ and $Z|1\rangle = -|1\rangle$. Then the following circuit flips the sign of the all ones state $|1\ldots 1\rangle$ only:

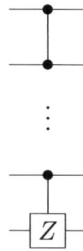

If we multiply this on both sides by X gates, the resulting circuit will flip the sign of the all zeros state $|0\dots0\rangle$ only:

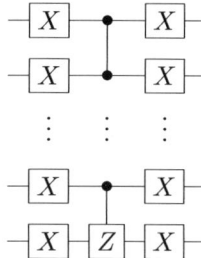

But, we want the all zeros state to be unchanged, while all other states are flipped. Using Exercise 2.27, we use $ZXZX$ to flip the sign of the top qubit, which flips the sign of the entire state.

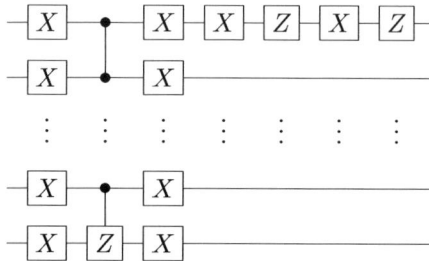

Using $X^2 = I$, R_0 is

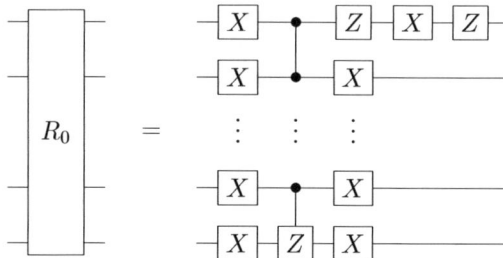

So, we have a quantum circuit for R_0. By "sandwiching" this between Hadamard gates, we get R_s. Then, we can implement Grover's algorithm.

Exercise 7.25. Go to `https://bit.ly/3pZacec`. By following this link, you should have access to the custom gate U_f. This is the oracle, and it acts on six qubits in the usual way.
  (a) What is n?
  (b) What is N?
  (c) For this problem, many queries does Grover's algorithm take?
  (d) Using Quirk, create a custom gate for R_0.
  (e) Using Quirk, create a custom gate for R_s.
  (f) Using Quirk, implement Grover's algorithm and find $|w\rangle$.

7.6.5 Optimality

It is proven that a quantum computer cannot solve the brute-force problem faster than $O(\sqrt{N})$, so Grover's algorithm is optimal, the best that a quantum computer can do. Then, if it takes a classical computer an exponential number of queries to solve a problem in NP, a quantum computer also takes an exponential number of queries (albeit a smaller exponential). This is because the square root of an exponential is still an exponential, e.g., $\sqrt{2^n} = 2^{n/2}$. Thus, quantum computers cannot brute-force solve NP problems by simply checking all the answers in superposition. If quantum computers can solve NP problems efficiently, they would have to exploit some other structure of the problems besides the fact that their potential solutions are efficiently checkable. All evidence, however, suggests that quantum computers cannot solve NP problems.

7.7 Discrete Fourier Transform

7.7.1 Application: Analyzing Music

We have finished exploring oracular algorithms. For the rest of this chapter, we will explore problems where quantum computers have a better gate complexity than classical computers, meaning the number of elementary gates/steps is less.

In this section, we will explore a method of analyzing data that has wide applications in science, engineering, and technology: the discrete Fourier transform. To introduce it, let us look at a specific application: analyzing music and sound.

Sound is vibration. The pluck of a guitar string, flutter of our vocal chords, or pulse of a speaker causes air molecules to vibrate. These vibrations reverberate through subsequent air molecules, eventually reaching our ears. A diagram of an ear is shown below:

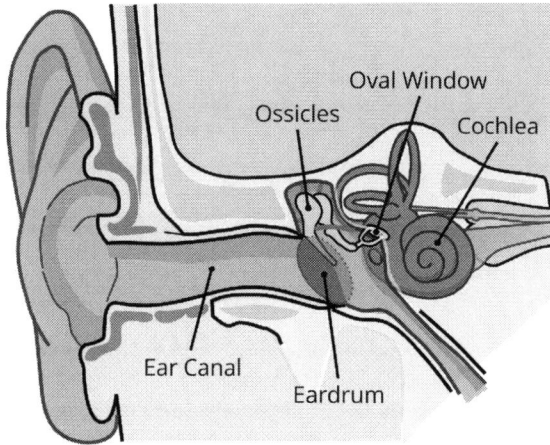

Image credit: Adapted from https://commons.wikimedia.org/wiki/File:
Anatomy_of_the_Human_Ear_blank.svg

The air in the ear canal carries these vibrations to the eardrum, a stretchy membrane, causing it to vibrate. The vibrations continue through three bones, the smallest in the human body, called ossicles. The third ossicle rests on the oval window, another stretchy membrane, and the vibrations transmit through it into the cochlea, a spiral-shaped hollow bone. Inside the cochlea are tiny hair receptors that convert the vibrations into nerve signals that are sent to the brain's hearing center and interpreted as sound.[2]

The following *waveform* shows the vibrations of a piano playing a C major chord (made of middle C and the E and G notes above it) for one second:

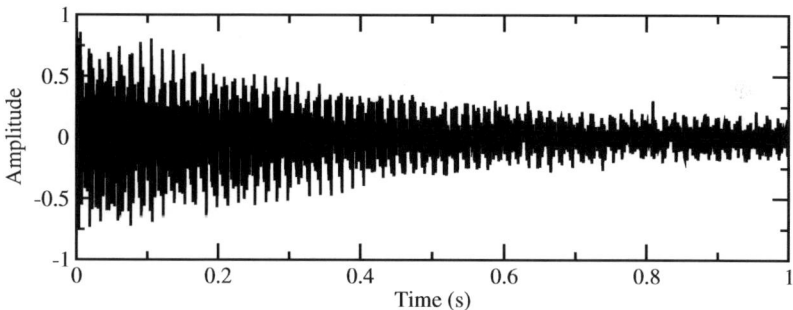

The details of the vibrations are hard to see, so let us zoom in to the first 0.05 seconds:

---

[2] In the 2013 Academy Award winning film *Gravity*, many of the scenes are silent because there is no air in space to transmit sound.

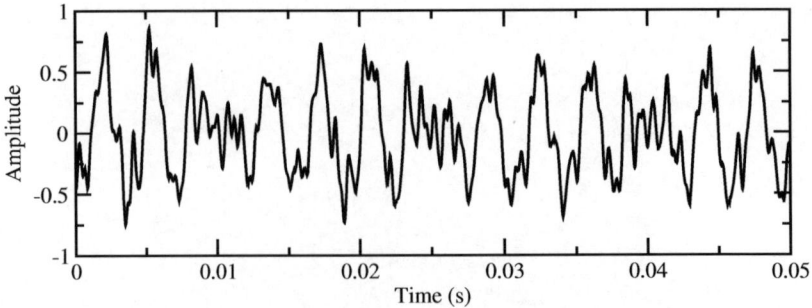

You can download a WAV file of the one-second piano tune at https://tinyur
l.com/2p86zew6. The WAV file, and the previous waveforms, consists of 44100
points for the one second of sound, and we say that the sound was *sampled* at a rate
of 44100 Hertz (Hz), or 44100 points per second. Since the first plot is one second
long, it has 44100 points, and since the second plot is 0.05 seconds long, it contains
2205 points. The 44100 points can be downloaded from https://tinyurl.com/
jsavt7ez, and they begin and end with the following (x, y) coordinates:

```
0.00000,-0.46933
0.00002,-0.46011
0.00005,-0.44931
0.00007,-0.41455
0.00009,-0.38632
0.00011,-0.34164
0.00014,-0.28851
    . . .
0.99993,0.12177
0.99995,0.12454
0.99998,0.13571
```

Now, say we want to find the frequencies that make up the previous C chord, which
correspond to the pitches or notes that make up the sound. If we let the number of samples be $N = 44100$ and label the previous amplitudes $a_0 = -0.46933$,
$a_1 = -0.46011$, ..., $a_{N-1} = 0.13571$, then the *discrete Fourier transform* of the
waveform is a sequence of N points $\phi_0, \phi_1, \ldots, \phi_{N-1}$ defined to be

$$\phi_k = \frac{1}{\sqrt{N}} \sum_{j=0}^{N-1} a_j e^{2\pi i jk/N}. \tag{7.6}$$

For example,

$$\phi_0 = \frac{1}{\sqrt{44100}} \left(-0.46933 e^{2\pi i(0)(0)/44100} - 0.46011 e^{2\pi i(1)(0)/44100} + \ldots \right.$$

$$\left. + 0.13571 e^{2\pi i(44099)(0)/44100} \right) = -0.0973861,$$

$$\phi_1 = \frac{1}{\sqrt{44100}} \left(-0.46933 e^{2\pi i(0)(1)/44100} - 0.46011 e^{2\pi i(1)(1)/44100} + \ldots \right.$$

$$+ 0.13571e^{2\pi i(44099)(1)/44100}\Big) = -0.118737 + 0.136405i,$$

$$\phi_2 = \frac{1}{\sqrt{44100}}\Big(-0.46933e^{2\pi i(0)(2)/44100} - 0.46011e^{2\pi i(1)(2)/44100} + \ldots$$

$$+ 0.13571e^{2\pi i(44099)(2)/44100}\Big) = -0.106039 + 0.0597867i,$$

$$\vdots$$

$$\phi_{44098} = \frac{1}{\sqrt{44100}}\Big(-0.46933e^{2\pi i(0)(44098)/44100} - 0.46011e^{2\pi i(1)(44098)/44100} + \ldots$$

$$+ 0.13571e^{2\pi i(44099)(44098)/44100}\Big) = -0.106039 - 0.0597867i$$

$$\phi_{44099} = \frac{1}{\sqrt{44100}}\Big(-0.46933e^{2\pi i(0)(44099)/44100} - 0.46011e^{2\pi i(1)(44099)/44100} + \ldots$$

$$+ 0.13571e^{2\pi i(44099)(44099)/44100}\Big) = -0.118737 - 0.136405i.$$

Calculating these by hand would be incredibly tedious, as each ϕ_k contains 44100 terms in its sum. In the next subsection, we will discuss how to calculate these using a computer algebra system. For now, let us continue interpreting these numbers. Notice ϕ_1 is the complex conjugate of ϕ_{44099}. Similarly, ϕ_2 is the complex conjugate of ϕ_{44098}, and so forth, through $\phi_{22051} = \phi_{22049}^*$. That is, $\phi_k = \phi_{N-k}^*$ for $k = 1, 2, \ldots, N/2 - 1$, so ϕ_0 and $\phi_{N/2}$ are unique. In general, the ϕ_k's are complex numbers. Let us take the norm of each of them. We get

$$|\phi_0| = 0.097386$$
$$|\phi_1| = 0.180844$$
$$|\phi_2| = 0.121732$$

$$\vdots$$

$$|\phi_{44098}| = 0.121732$$
$$|\phi_{44099}| = 0.180844.$$

Due to the symmetry of the discrete Fourier transform, $|\phi_1| = |\phi_{44099}|$, $|\phi_2| = |\phi_{44098}|$, etc. Plotting k on the x-axis and $|\phi_k|$ on the y-axis with $k = 0, 1, \ldots, 22050$, we get the *frequency spectrum* of the waveform:

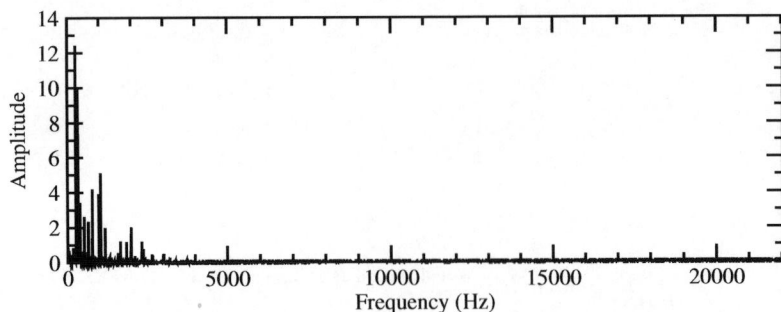

This is hard to read, so let us zoom into the first 1000 points of the x-axis:

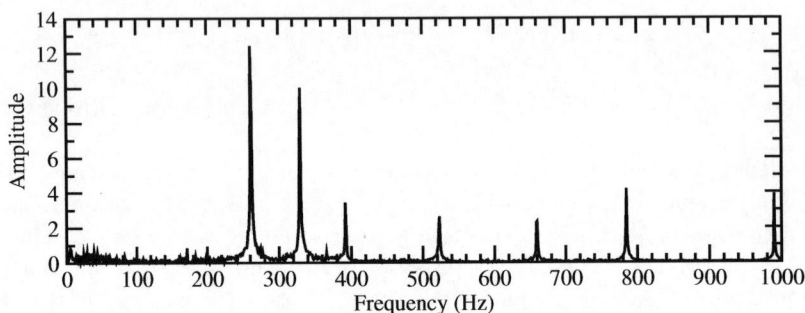

Here, the x-axis corresponds to the frequency, which is measured in Hertz (Hz) and corresponds to the pitch, so a higher frequency is a higher pitch note. The y-axis corresponds to the strength of note, so there are several frequencies that are stronger than the rest. The biggest is around 262 Hz. This corresponds to Middle C on the piano, which has a frequency of 261.6256 Hz. There is another large spike around 330 Hz, and this corresponds to the E key on the piano above Middle C, and this has a frequency of 329.6276 Hz. Beyond that, there is another spike at 392 Hz, and this corresponds to the next G key on the piano, which has a frequency of 391.9954 Hz. These three piano keys were pressed in order to create the music, so they contribute strongly to the sound. Note the other prominent frequencies are *resonances* of these three fundamental frequencies, and they occur at integer multiples of the aforementioned frequencies. For example, the spike at 522 Hz is twice Middle C's 262 Hz, the spike at 660 Hz is twice the E key's 330 Hz, the spike at 784 Hz is roughly three times Middle C's 262 Hz and twice the G key's 392 Hz, and the spike at 990 Hz is three times the E key's 330 Hz.

Exercise 7.26. Consider a sequence of four points

$$a_0 = 0.841,$$
$$a_1 = 0.909,$$
$$a_2 = 0.141,$$
$$a_3 = -0.757.$$

Calculate the discrete Fourier transform of this (i.e., ϕ_0, ϕ_1, and ϕ_2) using Eq. (7.6). You may use a calculator, but not a computer algebra system.

Exercise 7.27. Visit `https://en.wikipedia.org/wiki/Piano_key_frequencies`
and answer the following questions:
  (a) What is the scientific name for the E key above Middle C, which has a frequency of 329.6276
  Hz?
  (b) What is the frequency of the A_4 key?

7.7.2 Classical Solution: Fast Fourier Transform

Calculating just one ϕ_k using Eq. (7.6) requires adding together N terms. Since there
are N different ϕ_k's, altogether, this is a total of N^2 terms. Although this $O(N^2)$ runtime is efficient in the language of computational complexity, since it is a polynomial
in N, in practice, it can be quite slow because of the large number of points that a
long audio recording can contain.

Another way to interpret Eq. (7.6) is as a matrix-vector multiplication. To write
it more cleanly, let us define $\omega = e^{2\pi i/N}$. Then, Eq. (7.6) becomes

$$\phi_k = \frac{1}{\sqrt{N}} \sum_{j=0}^{N-1} a_j \omega^{jk}.$$

For example,

$$\phi_0 = \frac{1}{\sqrt{N}}\left(a_0 + a_1 + a_2 + \cdots + a_{N-1}\right),$$

$$\phi_1 = \frac{1}{\sqrt{N}}\left(a_0 + a_1\omega + a_2\omega^2 + \cdots + a_{N-1}\omega^{N-1}\right),$$

$$\phi_2 = \frac{1}{\sqrt{N}}\left(a_0 + a_1\omega^2 + a_2\omega^4 + \cdots + a_{N-1}\omega^{2(N-1)}\right),$$

$$\vdots$$

$$\phi_{N-1} = \frac{1}{\sqrt{N}}\left(a_0 + a_1\omega^{N-1} + a_2\omega^{2(N-1)} + \cdots + a_{N-1}\omega^{(N-1)^2}\right).$$

These equations can be written as

$$\begin{pmatrix} \phi_0 \\ \phi_1 \\ \phi_2 \\ \vdots \\ \phi_{N-1} \end{pmatrix} = \begin{pmatrix} 1 & 1 & 1 & \cdots & 1 \\ 1 & \omega & \omega^2 & \cdots & \omega^{N-1} \\ 1 & \omega^2 & \omega^4 & \cdots & \omega^{2(N-1)} \\ \vdots & \vdots & \vdots & \ddots & \vdots \\ 1 & \omega^{N-1} & \omega^{2(N-1)} & \cdots & \omega^{(N-1)^2} \end{pmatrix} \begin{pmatrix} a_0 \\ a_1 \\ a_2 \\ \vdots \\ a_{N-1} \end{pmatrix}. \qquad (7.7)$$

Thus, the discrete Fourier transform can be interpreted as a matrix that acts on a
vector of amplitudes. Although this is useful conceptually, it is just as slow as using

Eq. (7.6) directly, since we must calculate all N^2 terms of the matrix, and then do the matrix-vector multiplication.

Fortunately, faster classical algorithms for the discrete Fourier transform exist that only take $O(N \log N)$ steps. These are called *fast Fourier transform* (FFT) algorithms. The precise workings of these algorithms are beyond the scope of this textbook, but they are used by computer algebra systems like Mathematica and SageMath.

First, download the waveform from `https://tinyurl.com/jsavt7ez`. It is a `csv` file, which stands for comma-separated values. Its contents are the 44100 (x, y) points of the waveform:

```
0.00000,-0.46933
0.00002,-0.46011
0.00005,-0.44931
0.00007,-0.41455
0.00009,-0.38632
0.00011,-0.34164
0.00014,-0.28851
      . . .
0.99993,0.12177
0.99995,0.12454
0.99998,0.13571
```

Say the filename is `waveform.csv`.

- Place `waveform.csv` in the same folder as the Mathematica notebook. Then, we can import these points into Mathematica using

```
wave = Import["waveform.csv"];
```

In the variable `wave`, the first column of numbers is the time of each sample, and the second column is the amplitude. We can just get the amplitudes using `wave[[;;,2]]`, and we can take the discrete Fourier transform of these amplitudes using the `Fourier` command:

```
ft = Fourier[wave[[;;,2]]];
```

Finally, we can plot the first 1000 points of the frequency spectrum using the following command:

```
ListPlot[Transpose[{Table[i, {i, 0, 999}], Abs[ft
   ↪ [[1;;1000]]]}],
 PlotRange -> All, Joined -> True]
```

Above, `Table[i, {i, 0, 999}]` creates a list of numbers $0, 1, \ldots, 999$, and it serves as the x-axis of the frequency spectrum. Then, `ft[[1;;1000]]` lists the first 1000 points of the discrete Fourier transform, and `Abs` takes their absolute values, and this is the y-axis of the frequency spectrum. We combine these into a list that contains all the x-coordinates followed by all the y-coordinates, and then we take the transpose to obtain a list of (x, y) coordinates, which we then plot using `ListPlot`. The parameter `PlotRange -> All` ensures that we can see the full y-axis, and `Joined -> True` joins the points of the scatter plot.

- Place `waveform.csv` in the same folder as the SageMath instance. In Sage-Math, we import the points using

```
sage: import csv
sage: file = open("waveform.csv","r")
sage: wave = list(csv.reader(file, quoting=csv.
    ↪ QUOTE_NONNUMERIC))
```

The variable `wave` contains the (time, amplitude) coordinates of the waveform. To calculate the discrete Fourier transform, we only want the amplitudes. To get them, we create an empty array called `amps` of size 44100 using the `FFT` command, and then we go through `wave` and copy its amplitudes to the variable `amp`:

```
sage: amps = FFT(44100)
sage: for j in range(44100):
....:      amps[j] = wave[j][1]
```

Next, we calculate the discrete Fourier transform using the `forward_transform` function. Note this does not include the overall factor of $1/\sqrt{N}$ in Eq. (7.6), so we will need to include it later.

```
sage: amps.forward_transform()
```

Now, we want to plot the first 1000 points of the frequency spectrum. To do this, we create an empty list of 1000 (x,y) coordinates. The x coordinates are just the frequencies $0,1,\ldots,999$, and the y-coordinates are $|\phi_k|^2$, which we divide by $\sqrt{N}$ because the `forward_transform` function did not include $1/\sqrt{N}$.

```
sage: freq = [[0,0] for k in range(1000)]
sage: for j in range(1000):
....:      freq[j][0] = j
....:      freq[j][1] = abs(vector(amps[j])) / sqrt(44100)
```

Finally, we plot the frequency spectrum:

```
sage: list_plot(freq, plotjoined=true)
Launched png viewer for Graphics object consisting of 1
    ↪ graphics primitive
```

The graph should pop up.

Exercise 7.28. A one-second recording of a piano playing a triad (a three-note chord), sampled at 44100 Hz, is available at https://tinyurl.com/43yzv7s3, and the waveform can be downloaded at https://tinyurl.com/hebe2tj9. Using a computer algebra system, answer the following.
  (a) Plot the first 1000 points of the frequency spectrum of the waveform.
  (b) Determine the frequencies of the three keys that make up the chord. You can estimate them off the plot.
  (c) Visit https://en.wikipedia.org/wiki/Piano_key_frequencies. Using your answers to part (b), what are the scientific names of the three keys?

7.7.3 Quantum Solution: Quantum Fourier Transform

In the last section, we showed in Eq. (7.7) that the discrete Fourier transform can be written as a matrix-vector multiplication. It turns out that the $N \times N$ matrix is unitary, so it is a valid quantum gate, which we call the *quantum Fourier transform* (QFT). Later, we will show how to implement this using single-qubit and two-qubit quantum gates, which proves that the QFT is unitary. Alternatively, Exercise 7.29 outlines the proof that $\text{QFT}^\dagger \text{QFT} = I$. Then, if

$$|\psi\rangle = \begin{pmatrix} a_0 \\ a_1 \\ a_2 \\ \vdots \\ a_{N-1} \end{pmatrix} = a_0|0\rangle + \cdots + a_{N-1}|N-1\rangle$$

is a normalized quantum state, then applying the QFT yields another normalized quantum state

$$|\phi\rangle = \begin{pmatrix} \phi_0 \\ \phi_1 \\ \phi_2 \\ \vdots \\ \phi_{N-1} \end{pmatrix} = \phi_0|0\rangle + \cdots + \phi_{N-1}|N-1\rangle.$$

We call $|\phi\rangle$ the quantum Fourier transform of $|\psi\rangle$. Put another way, using Eq. (7.6), the QFT transforms the state

$$|\psi\rangle = \sum_{j=0}^{N-1} a_j|j\rangle \longrightarrow |\phi\rangle = \sum_{k=0}^{N-1} \phi_k|k\rangle = \frac{1}{\sqrt{N}} \sum_{k=0}^{N-1}\sum_{j=0}^{N-1} a_j e^{2\pi i jk/N}|k\rangle.$$

Examining the above equation, the QFT transforms basis states from

$$|j\rangle \longrightarrow \frac{1}{\sqrt{N}} \sum_{k=0}^{N-1} e^{2\pi i jk/N}|k\rangle. \tag{7.8}$$

The QFT is a large quantum gate acting on n qubits, whose general state has $N = 2^n$ amplitudes. We want to implement it, however, using single-qubit and two-qubit gates. From Section 4.6, the Solovay-Kitaev theorem says we can decompose a n-qubit gate into a universal gate set up to precision ε using $\Theta(2^n \log^c(1/\varepsilon))$ gates, for some constant c. Or, since $N = 2^n$, this is $\Theta(N \log^c(1/\varepsilon))$. Compared to the classical fast Fourier transform algorithms, which run in $O(N \log N)$ time, the quantum implementation could be a little better or worse by logarithmic factors, depending on the constant c. This is not the kind of speedup we desire.

Fortunately, there is a more clever way to implement the QFT using single-qubit and two-qubit gates, and it only takes $O(\log^2 N)$ of them, which is an exponential speedup in circuit complexity over the classical fast Fourier transform algorithms.

To construct this implementation, we express j as an n-bit binary number:

$$j = j_{n-1}j_{n-2}\ldots j_1 j_0$$
$$= j_{n-1}2^{n-1} + j_{n-2}2^{n-2} + \cdots + j_1 2 + j_0.$$

Then, j/N can be represented using a binary point, which is like a decimal point, but in base 2:

$$\frac{j}{N} = \frac{j_{n-1}2^{n-1} + j_{n-2}2^{n-2} + \cdots + j_1 2 + j_0}{2^n}$$
$$= \frac{j_{n-1}}{2} + \frac{j_{n-2}}{2^2} + \cdots + \frac{j_1}{2^{n-1}} + \frac{j_0}{2^n}$$
$$= 0.j_{n-1}j_{n-2}\ldots j_1 j_0.$$

Similarly, we can express k as an n-bit binary number:

$$k = k_{n-1}k_{n-2}\ldots k_1 k_0$$
$$= k_{n-1}2^{n-1} + k_{n-2}2^{n-2} + \cdots + k_1 2 + k_0.$$

Using these, the exponential in Eq. (7.8) is

$$e^{2\pi i jk/N} = e^{2\pi i (j/N)k}$$
$$= e^{2\pi i (0.j_{n-1}j_{n-2}\cdots j_1 j_0)(k_{n-1}2^{n-1}+k_{n-2}2^{n-2}+\cdots+k_1 2+k_0)}$$
$$= e^{2\pi i (0.j_{n-1}j_{n-2}\cdots j_1 j_0)k_{n-1}2^{n-1}} e^{2\pi i (0.j_{n-1}j_{n-2}\cdots j_1 j_0)k_{n-2}2^{n-2}} \cdots$$
$$\times\, e^{2\pi i (0.j_{n-1}j_{n-2}\cdots j_1 j_0)k_1 2} e^{2\pi i (0.j_{n-1}j_{n-2}\cdots j_1 j_0)k_0}$$
$$= e^{2\pi i (j_{n-1}j_{n-2}\cdots j_1 \cdot j_0)k_{n-1}} e^{2\pi i (j_{n-1}j_{n-2}\cdots j_2 \cdot j_1 j_0)k_{n-2}} \cdots$$
$$\times\, e^{2\pi i (j_{n-1}\cdot j_{n-2}\cdots j_1 j_0)k_1} e^{2\pi i (0.j_{n-1}j_{n-2}\cdots j_1 j_0)k_0}.$$

We can drop all the bits left of the binary point. To see why, take for example the first exponential in the previous line:

$$e^{2\pi i (j_{n-1}j_{n-2}\cdots j_1 \cdot j_0)k_{n-1}} = e^{2\pi i (j_{n-1}2^{n-2}+j_{n-2}2^{n-3}\ldots j_1 + j_0/2)k_{n-1}}$$
$$= \underbrace{e^{2\pi i j_{n-1}2^{n-2}k_{n-1}}}_{1} \underbrace{e^{2\pi i j_{n-2}2^{n-3}k_{n-1}}}_{1} \cdots \underbrace{e^{2\pi i j_1 k_{n-1}}}_{1} e^{2\pi i j_0/2 k_{n-1}}$$
$$= e^{2\pi i 0.j_0 k_{n-1}}.$$

The exponentials are 1 because they are either $e^0 = 1$ or $e^{2\pi i m} = 1$ for some positive integer m. Dropping all the bits left of the binary point, we have

$$e^{2\pi i jk/N} = e^{2\pi i (0.j_0)k_{n-1}} e^{2\pi i (0.j_1 j_0)k_{n-2}} \cdots$$
$$\times\, e^{2\pi i (0.j_{n-2}\cdots j_1 j_0)k_1} e^{2\pi i (0.j_{n-1}j_{n-2}\cdots j_1 j_0)k_0}.$$

Plugging this into Eq. (7.8), we get

$$
|j\rangle \rightarrow \frac{1}{\sqrt{N}} \sum_{k=0}^{N-1} e^{2\pi i jk/N} |k\rangle
$$

$$
= \frac{1}{\sqrt{N}} \sum_{k=0}^{N-1} e^{2\pi i (0.j_0)k_{n-1}} e^{2\pi i (0.j_1 j_0)k_{n-2}} \cdots
$$

$$
\times e^{2\pi i (0.j_{n-2}\cdots j_1 j_0)k_1} e^{2\pi i (0.j_{n-1}j_{n-2}\cdots j_1 j_0)k_0} |k\rangle.
$$

Since we are summing over all n-bit binary numbers k, each bit $k_{n-1}, k_{n-2}, \ldots, k_0$ sums through 0 and 1, so this becomes

$$
\frac{1}{\sqrt{N}} \sum_{k_{n-1}=0}^{1} \cdots \sum_{k_0=0}^{1} e^{2\pi i (0.j_0)k_{n-1}} e^{2\pi i (0.j_1 j_0)k_{n-2}} \cdots
$$

$$
\times e^{2\pi i (0.j_{n-2}\cdots j_1 j_0)k_1} e^{2\pi i (0.j_{n-1}j_{n-2}\cdots j_1 j_0)k_0} |k_{n-1}\ldots k_0\rangle.
$$

Since $|k_{n-1}\ldots k_0\rangle$ is shorthand for $|k_{n-1}\rangle \ldots |k_0\rangle$, we can move the terms to get

$$
\frac{1}{\sqrt{N}} \sum_{k_{n-1}=0}^{1} \cdots \sum_{k_0=0}^{1} e^{2\pi i (0.j_0)k_{n-1}} |k_{n-1}\rangle e^{2\pi i (0.j_1 j_0)k_{n-2}} |k_{n-2}\rangle \cdots
$$

$$
\times e^{2\pi i (0.j_{n-2}\cdots j_1 j_0)k_1} |k_1\rangle e^{2\pi i (0.j_{n-1}j_{n-2}\cdots j_1 j_0)k_0} |k_0\rangle.
$$

Moving the summations,

$$
\frac{1}{\sqrt{N}} \sum_{k_{n-1}=0}^{1} e^{2\pi i (0.j_0)k_{n-1}} |k_{n-1}\rangle \sum_{k_{n-2}=0}^{1} e^{2\pi i (0.j_1 j_0)k_{n-2}} |k_{n-2}\rangle \cdots
$$

$$
\times \sum_{k_1=0}^{1} e^{2\pi i (0.j_{n-2}\cdots j_1 j_0)k_1} |k_1\rangle \sum_{k_0=0}^{1} e^{2\pi i (0.j_{n-1}j_{n-2}\cdots j_1 j_0)k_0} |k_0\rangle.
$$

Since $e^0 = 1$, if we evaluate the sums, we get

$$
\frac{1}{\sqrt{N}} \left(|0\rangle + e^{2\pi i (0.j_0)} |1\rangle \right) \left(|0\rangle + e^{2\pi i (0.j_1 j_0)} |1\rangle \right) \cdots
$$

$$
\times \left(|0\rangle + e^{2\pi i (0.j_{n-2}\cdots j_1 j_0)} |1\rangle \right) \left(|0\rangle + e^{2\pi i (0.j_{n-1}j_{n-2}\cdots j_1 j_0)} |1\rangle \right).
$$

Finally, since $\sqrt{N} = \sqrt{2^n} = (\sqrt{2})^n$, we get the product state

$$
\frac{1}{\sqrt{2}} \left(|0\rangle + e^{2\pi i (0.j_0)} |1\rangle \right) \frac{1}{\sqrt{2}} \left(|0\rangle + e^{2\pi i (0.j_1 j_0)} |1\rangle \right) \cdots \tag{7.9}
$$

$$
\times \frac{1}{\sqrt{2}} \left(|0\rangle + e^{2\pi i (0.j_{n-2}\cdots j_1 j_0)} |1\rangle \right) \frac{1}{\sqrt{2}} \left(|0\rangle + e^{2\pi i (0.j_{n-1}j_{n-2}\cdots j_1 j_0)} |1\rangle \right).
$$

This is another way of stating the definition of the QFT, but in binary. If we can create a quantum circuit that converts $|j\rangle = |j_{n-1} \ldots j_0\rangle$ to Eq. (7.9), we will have a quantum circuit for the QFT.

Let us now prove that we can create a circuit for the QFT using Hadamard gates and controlled rotations. Consider the rightmost term of Eq. (7.9). To begin constructing it, we apply the Hadamard gate to $|j_{n-1}\rangle$:

$$H|j_{n-1}\rangle = \frac{1}{\sqrt{2}}\left(|0\rangle + (-1)^{j_{n-1}}|1\rangle\right) = \frac{1}{\sqrt{2}}\left(|0\rangle + (e^{i\pi})^{j_{n-1}}|1\rangle\right)$$

$$= \frac{1}{\sqrt{2}}\left(|0\rangle + e^{2\pi i j_{n-1}/2}|1\rangle\right) = \frac{1}{\sqrt{2}}\left(|0\rangle + e^{2\pi i(0.j_{n-1})}|1\rangle\right).$$

Next, consider a single-qubit gate that rotates about the z-axis of the Bloch sphere by $2\pi/2^r$ radians, which we call R_r. It acts on basis states by

$$R_r|0\rangle = |0\rangle,$$
$$R_r|1\rangle = e^{2\pi i/2^r}|1\rangle,$$

and its matrix representation is

$$R_r = \begin{pmatrix} 1 & 0 \\ 0 & e^{2\pi i/2^r} \end{pmatrix}.$$

After the previous Hadamard matrix, we apply R_2 to qubit $n-1$, controlled by qubit $n-2$. That is, for the state of qubit $n-1$, the amplitude of $|1\rangle$ is multiplied by $e^{2\pi i/2^2}$ if $j_{n-2} = 1$, and nothing happens otherwise. That is, the state of the $(n-1)$th qubit goes from

$$\frac{1}{\sqrt{2}}\left(|0\rangle + e^{2\pi i(0.j_{n-1})}|1\rangle\right) \rightarrow \frac{1}{\sqrt{2}}\left(|0\rangle + e^{2\pi i(0.j_{n-1})}(e^{2\pi i/2^2})^{j_{n-2}}|1\rangle\right)$$

$$= \frac{1}{\sqrt{2}}\left(|0\rangle + e^{2\pi i(0.j_{n-1})}e^{2\pi i(0.0j_{n-2})}|1\rangle\right)$$

$$- \frac{1}{\sqrt{2}}\left(|0\rangle + e^{2\pi i(0.j_{n-1}j_{n-2})}|1\rangle\right).$$

Similarly, we can apply R_3 to $n-1$, controlled by qubit $n-3$. Then, the state of qubit $n-1$ would be

$$\frac{1}{\sqrt{2}}\left(|0\rangle + e^{2\pi i(0.j_{n-1}j_{n-2}j_{n-3})}|1\rangle\right).$$

Continuing this through R_n, controlled by qubit 0, the state of qubit $n-1$ is

$$\frac{1}{\sqrt{2}}\left(|0\rangle + e^{2\pi i(0.j_{n-1}j_{n-2}j_{n-3}\cdots j_0)}|1\rangle\right).$$

This is the rightmost factor of Eq. (7.9). Similarly, we can apply Hadamard and controlled-R_r gates to the other qubits to construct the other factors, resulting in the following quantum circuit:

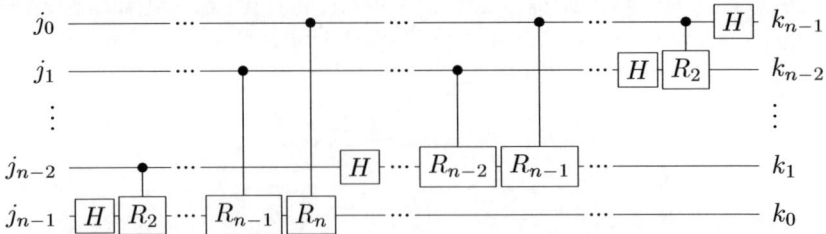

Note the order of the outputs is reversed, so we need to reverse the order, such as by using SWAP gates

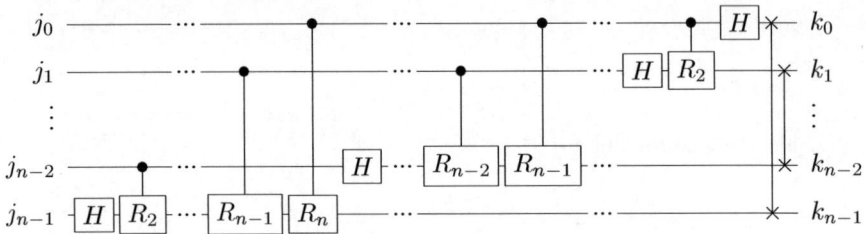

This is our quantum circuit for the QFT. For example, with $n = 4$ qubits,

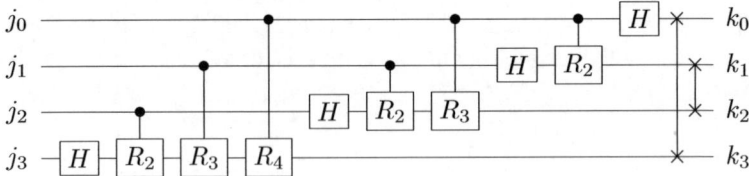

Let us add up the total number of gates in the QFT circuit with n qubits, beginning with the Hadamard and controlled-R_r gates. The bottom row of the circuit uses n gates, the row above it uses $n - 1$ gates, and so fourth, until we get to one gate at the top row. So, the total number of Hadamard and controlled-R_r gates is

$$n + (n-1) + (n-2) + \cdots + 3 + 2 + 1 = \frac{n(n+1)}{2}.$$

The first equality can be obtained by pairing up terms from the outside in. That is, the first term n and the last term 1 add up to $n + 1$. Similarly, the second term $(n-1)$ and the second-to-last term 2 add up to $n + 1$. Next, the third term $(n-2)$ and the third-to-last term 3 add up to $n + 1$. Altogether, there are $n/2$ pairs, so they total $(n/2)(n+1) = n(n+1)/2$. There are also $n/2$ swap gates to reverse the order of the outputs. Altogether, the total number of single-qubit and two-qubit gates is

$$\frac{n(n+1)}{2} + \frac{n}{2} = O(n^2) = O(\log^2 N).$$

This runtime of $O(\log^2 N)$ is an exponential speedup over the classical fast Fourier transform algorithms, which run in $O(N \log N)$ time. This speedup, however, comes with a major caveat. With the classical algorithm, we get all the terms of the discrete Fourier transform. In contrast, with the QFT, we get a quantum state whose amplitudes correspond to the discrete Fourier transform, and we cannot access these amplitudes all at once. We can only measure the qubits, which yields a bit string with a probability given by the norm-square of the amplitude. Thus, obtaining actual speedups using the QFT requires clever application of it, and in the next section, we will see an example called phase estimation.

Exercise 7.29. The quantum Fourier transform was given as a $N \times N$ matrix in Eq. (7.7). In this problem, we will show that the matrix is unitary, so it is a valid quantum gate. Let $M = \text{QFT}^\dagger \text{QFT}$ and let M_{rs} denote the element of matrix M at row r and column s. We want to prove that $M_{rs} = 1$ when $r = s$ and $M_{rs} = 0$ when $r \neq s$, so M is equal to the identity matrix.

(a) Show that

$$M_{rs} = \frac{1}{N} \sum_{k=0}^{N-1} \omega^{-kr} \omega^{ks} = \frac{1}{N} \sum_{k=0}^{N-1} \omega^{k(s-r)}.$$

(b) Show that $M_{rs} = 1$ when $r = s$.
(c) Show that $M_{rs} = 0$ when $r \neq s$. Hint: When $r \neq s$, M_{rs} is a geometric series. You may need to look up the geometric series formula from Algebra II. Also note that $\omega^{mN} = e^{2\pi i m} = 1$ for integer m.

Exercise 7.30. In this exercise, we will use Quirk to simulate the quantum Fourier transform on six qubits. Go to https://bit.ly/3DNKSxl to access the following quantum circuit:

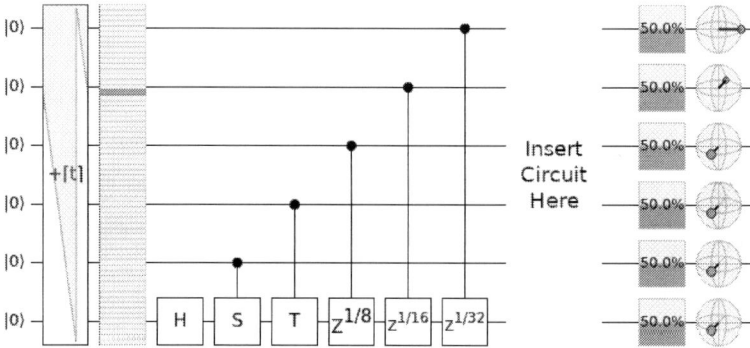

The first part of the QFT circuit, which calculates the Fourier transform of the bottom qubit, has been done for you. Note the Z gate is a rotation about the x-axis by π radians, so we have the following relations:

$$R_2 = Z^{1/2} = S, \quad R_3 = Z^{1/4} = T, \quad R_4 = Z^{1/8}, \quad R_5 = Z^{1/16}, \quad R_6 = Z^{1/32}.$$

In Quirk, fill in the remainder of the QFT circuit.

Exercise 7.31. Using the IBM Quantum Lab, use the following code to create a quantum circuit for the QFT:

```
# Number of qubits.
n = 4
```

```
# Create a quantum circuit.
qc = QuantumCircuit(n)

# Iterate through each target qubit from (n-1) to 0.
for target in range(n-1,-1,-1):
    # Apply the Hadamard gate.
    qc.h(target)

    # Iterate through the control qubits from (target-1) to 0.
    for control in range(target-1,-1,-1):
        # Calculate "r," the rotation by 2*pi/2**r.
        r = target - control + 1

        # Apply the controlled phase/rotation.
        qc.cp(2*np.pi/2**r, control, target)

# Swap qubits.
for qubit in range(n//2):
    qc.swap(qubit, n - qubit - 1)

# Draw the circuit.
qc.draw()
```

What circuit is shown? Why is it equivalent to the QFT circuit shown in the textbook?

7.7.4 Inverse Quantum Fourier Transform

The *inverse quantum Fourier transform* (IQFT) undoes the QFT. Since the QFT performs the mapping in Eq. (7.8), the IQFT does the reverse:

$$\frac{1}{\sqrt{N}} \sum_{k=0}^{N-1} e^{2\pi i jk/N} |k\rangle \longrightarrow |j\rangle. \qquad (7.10)$$

As a quantum circuit, the IQFT can be performed by reversing the order of the gates the QFT and replacing them with their inverses:

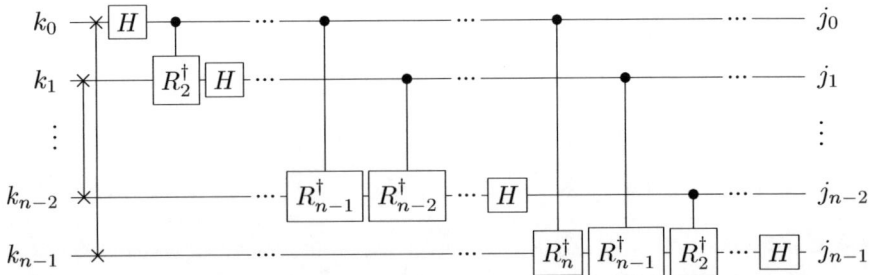

Since quantum gates are unitary, the inverses are their conjugate transposes. Note $\text{SWAP}^{\dagger} = \text{SWAP}$, $H^{\dagger} = H$, and $R_r^{\dagger}$ is a rotation about the z-axis of the Bloch sphere by $-2\pi/2^r$ radians. The IQFT has the same gate complexity as the QFT, which is $O(n^2)$.

Exercise 7.32. Go to `https://bit.ly/3kUXfQN` to access the following quantum circuit:

Insert the IQFT circuit in the space provided, and verify that it cancels out the QFT gate that is already present, so the qubits are unchanged. Use single-qubit gates and controls to construct the circuit, not the QFT† gate that comes with Quirk. Also, note $R_4^\dagger = Z^{-1/8}$, and this can be made with the "Formula Z Rotation" in Quirk, which has a label $Z^{f(t)}$.

Exercise 7.33. Modify the code in Exercise 7.31 so that it creates a circuit for the IQFT.

7.8 Phase / Eigenvalue Estimation

7.8.1 The Problem

We learned in Chapter 3 that a quantum gate can be represented by a unitary matrix, and a quantum state can be represented by a vector. For example, we can use linear algebra to see how the X gate transforms the state $(\sqrt{3}/2)|0\rangle + (1/2)|1\rangle$:

$$X\left(\frac{\sqrt{3}}{2}|0\rangle + \frac{1}{2}|1\rangle\right) = \begin{pmatrix} 0 & 1 \\ 1 & 0 \end{pmatrix}\begin{pmatrix} \sqrt{3}/2 \\ 1/2 \end{pmatrix} = \begin{pmatrix} 1/2 \\ \sqrt{3}/2 \end{pmatrix} = \frac{1}{2}|0\rangle + \frac{\sqrt{3}}{2}|1\rangle.$$

Most of the time, when the X gate is applied to a vector, we get a different vector as the result. There are some special vectors, however, called *eigenvectors*, where applying the X gate results in the exact same vector, multiplied by a number called an *eigenvalue*. For example, $|+\rangle$ is an eigenvector of the X gate, since if we apply the X gate to it, we get $|+\rangle$ multiplied by 1, so its eigenvalue is 1:

$$X|+\rangle = \begin{pmatrix} 0 & 1 \\ 1 & 0 \end{pmatrix}\begin{pmatrix} 1/\sqrt{2} \\ 1/\sqrt{2} \end{pmatrix} = \begin{pmatrix} 1/\sqrt{2} \\ 1/\sqrt{2} \end{pmatrix} = |+\rangle.$$

Similarly, $|-\rangle$ is an eigenvector of the X gate with eigenvalue -1, meaning when we apply the X gate to it, we get $|-\rangle$ multiplied by -1:

$$X|-\rangle = \begin{pmatrix} 0 & 1 \\ 1 & 0 \end{pmatrix}\begin{pmatrix} 1/\sqrt{2} \\ -1/\sqrt{2} \end{pmatrix} = \begin{pmatrix} -1/\sqrt{2} \\ 1/\sqrt{2} \end{pmatrix} = -\begin{pmatrix} 1/\sqrt{2} \\ -1/\sqrt{2} \end{pmatrix} = -|-\rangle.$$

When the eigenvector is the state of a quantum system, it is often called an *eigenstate*. So, $|+\rangle$ and $|-\rangle$ are eigenstates of the X gate.

Although the eigenvectors and eigenvalues of a matrix are very important in many areas of science, technology, and engineering, including quantum mechanics and quantum computing, the details of their importance are beyond the scope of this introductory textbook. How to find eigenvectors and eigenvalues of a matrix are also beyond the scope of this textbook. Instead, we will focus on a specific problem:

> Given a *unitary* matrix U and one of its eigenvectors $|v\rangle$, find or estimate its eigenvalue.

From linear algebra, it is known that the eigenvalues of a unitary matrix must have the form $e^{i\theta}$ for some real number θ. For this reason, this problem is called *phase estimation*, since finding the eigenvalue is equivalent to finding the phase θ.

Exercise 7.34. Consider the Hadamard gate,

$$H = \frac{1}{\sqrt{2}} \begin{pmatrix} 1 & 1 \\ 1 & -1 \end{pmatrix}.$$

(a) Verify that $\begin{pmatrix} 1+\sqrt{2} \\ 1 \end{pmatrix}$ is an eigenvector of the Hadamard gate with eigenvalue 1.

(b) Verify that $\begin{pmatrix} 1-\sqrt{2} \\ 1 \end{pmatrix}$ is an eigenvector of the Hadamard gate with eigenvalue -1.

Exercise 7.35. Consider the following unitary matrix

$$U = \frac{1}{\sqrt{2}} \begin{pmatrix} 1 & 0 & 1 & 0 \\ 0 & e^{i\pi/4} & 0 & e^{i\pi/4} \\ 1 & 0 & -1 & 0 \\ 0 & e^{i\pi/4} & 0 & -e^{i\pi/4} \end{pmatrix}.$$

Verify that $\begin{pmatrix} 0 \\ 1 \\ 0 \\ \sqrt{2}-1 \end{pmatrix}$ is an eigenvector of U with eigenvalue $e^{i\pi/4}$.

7.8.2 Classical Solution

Since we are promised that $|v\rangle$ is an eigenvector of U, and its eigenvalue takes the form $e^{i\theta}$, then we know that multiplying $|v\rangle$ by U will result in $|v\rangle$ multiplied by $e^{i\theta}$, i.e.,

$$U|v\rangle = e^{i\theta}|v\rangle.$$

If $|v\rangle$ is an N-dimensional vector and U is an $N \times N$ matrix, we can write out this equation as

$$\begin{pmatrix} U_{11} & U_{12} & \cdots & U_{1N} \\ U_{21} & U_{22} & \cdots & U_{2N} \\ \vdots & \vdots & \ddots & \vdots \\ U_{N1} & U_{N2} & \cdots & U_{NN} \end{pmatrix} \begin{pmatrix} v_1 \\ v_2 \\ \vdots \\ v_N \end{pmatrix} = e^{i\theta} \begin{pmatrix} v_1 \\ v_2 \\ \vdots \\ v_N \end{pmatrix}.$$

Multiplying out the left-hand side,

$$\begin{pmatrix} U_{11}v_1 + U_{12}v_2 + \cdots + U_{1N}v_N \\ U_{21}v_1 + U_{22}v_2 + \cdots + U_{2N}v_N \\ \vdots \\ U_{N1}v_1 + U_{N2}v_2 + \cdots + U_{NN}v_N \end{pmatrix} = e^{i\theta} \begin{pmatrix} v_1 \\ v_2 \\ \vdots \\ v_N \end{pmatrix}.$$

We can use any row to find $e^{i\theta}$. For example, using the first row,

$$U_{11}v_1 + U_{12}v_2 + \cdots + U_{1N}v_N = e^{i\theta}v_1.$$

Thus the eigenvalue is

$$e^{i\theta} = \frac{U_{11}v_1 + U_{12}v_2 + \cdots + U_{1N}v_N}{v_1}.$$

This takes N multiplications, $N - 1$ additions, and one division, for a total of $2N = O(N)$ elementary arithmetic operations.

7.8.3 Quantum Solution

Say the unitary matrix U is an n-qubit quantum gate, so U is an $N \times N$ matrix, where $N = 2^n$. We assume that we have n qubits whose state is the eigenstate $|v\rangle$:

$$\underbrace{|v\rangle}_{n \text{ qubits}}.$$

To estimate the phase of its corresponding eigenvalue to m bits of precision, we also have m additional qubits, all initially in the $|0\rangle$ state:

$$\underbrace{|0\ldots000\rangle}_{m \text{ qubits}} \underbrace{|v\rangle}_{n \text{ qubits}}.$$

So, the total number of qubits in our circuit is $m + n$. Let us refer to these groupings as the "eigenvalue register" and the "eigenstate register," since the m qubits will eventually contain an m-bit approximation of the phase of the eigenvalue, and the n qubits are in the eigenstate $|v\rangle$. To estimate the phase of the eigenvalue, we apply the following quantum circuit:

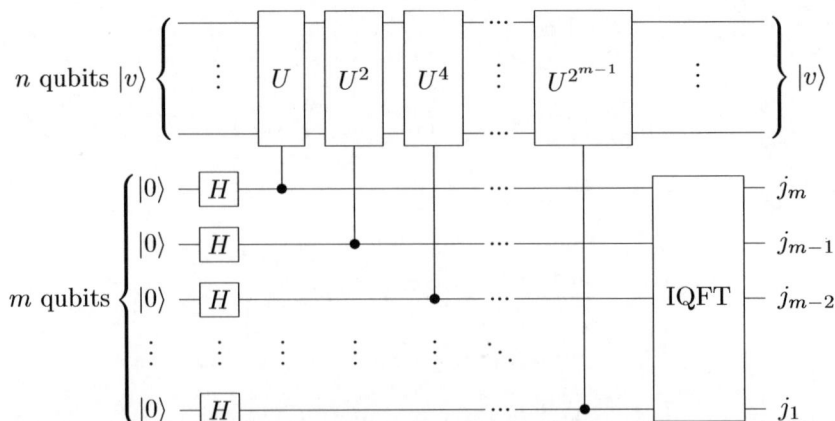

Let us go through each step of this circuit to see how it works. First, we apply the Hadamard gate to each qubit of the eigenvalue register, and we get

$$|++\cdots+\rangle|v\rangle = \frac{1}{\sqrt{2}}(|0\rangle+|1\rangle)\frac{1}{\sqrt{2}}(|0\rangle+|1\rangle)\ldots\frac{1}{\sqrt{2}}(|0\rangle+|1\rangle)|v\rangle$$
$$= \frac{1}{\sqrt{2^m}}(|0\rangle+|1\rangle)(|0\rangle+|1\rangle)\ldots(|0\rangle+|1\rangle)|v\rangle.$$

Next, we apply a controlled-U gate, where the rightmost qubit of the eigenvalue register is the control, and the eigenstate register is the target. Since $U|v\rangle = e^{i\theta}|v\rangle$, this causes the state to acquire a phase of $e^{i\theta}$ when the control qubit is $|1\rangle$:

$$\frac{1}{\sqrt{2^m}}(|0\rangle+|1\rangle)\ldots(|0\rangle+|1\rangle)(|0\rangle+|1\rangle)\left(|0\rangle+e^{i\theta}|1\rangle\right)|v\rangle.$$

Then, we apply the controlled-U^2 gate, which cause the second-to-rightmost qubit of the eigenvalue register to acquire a phase of $e^{i\theta}$ twice, which is a phase of $e^{2i\theta}$, when the control qubit is $|1\rangle$:

$$\frac{1}{\sqrt{2^m}}(|0\rangle+|1\rangle)\ldots(|0\rangle+|1\rangle)\left(|0\rangle+e^{2i\theta}|1\rangle\right)\left(|0\rangle+e^{i\theta}|1\rangle\right)|v\rangle.$$

Then, we apply the controlled-U^4 gate, which applies a phase of $e^{4i\theta}$:

$$\frac{1}{\sqrt{2^m}}(|0\rangle+|1\rangle)\ldots\left(|0\rangle+e^{4i\theta}|1\rangle\right)\left(|0\rangle+e^{2i\theta}|1\rangle\right)\left(|0\rangle+e^{i\theta}|1\rangle\right)|v\rangle.$$

Continuing with the controlled gates, we eventually apply controlled-$U^{2^{m-1}}$, where the phase is $e^{2^{m-1}i\theta}$:

$$\frac{1}{\sqrt{2^m}}\left(|0\rangle+e^{2^{m-1}i\theta}|1\rangle\right)\ldots\left(|0\rangle+e^{4i\theta}|1\rangle\right)\left(|0\rangle+e^{2i\theta}|1\rangle\right)\left(|0\rangle+e^{i\theta}|1\rangle\right)|v\rangle.$$

Now, let us change the variables using $\theta = 2\pi j$, so if we can find j, we simply multiply it by 2π to find θ. Substituting, the previous state becomes

$$\frac{1}{\sqrt{2^m}} \left(|0\rangle + e^{2\pi i 2^{m-1} j}|1\rangle \right) \cdots \left(|0\rangle + e^{2\pi i 4j}|1\rangle \right) \left(|0\rangle + e^{2\pi i 2j}|1\rangle \right) \left(|0\rangle + e^{2\pi i j}|1\rangle \right) |v\rangle.$$

Since $0 \le \theta < 2\pi$, we have $0 \le j < 1$. Expressing j as an m-bit binary number $0.j_1 j_2 \ldots j_m$, which is a number less than 1, the state becomes

$$\frac{1}{\sqrt{2^m}} \left(|0\rangle + e^{2\pi i (j_1 j_2 \cdots j_{m-1} \cdot j_m)}|1\rangle \right) \cdots \left(|0\rangle + e^{2\pi i (j_1 j_2 \cdot j_3 \cdots j_m)}|1\rangle \right)$$
$$\times \left(|0\rangle + e^{2\pi i (j_1 \cdot j_2 \cdots j_m)}|1\rangle \right) \left(|0\rangle + e^{2\pi i (0.j_1 \cdots j_m)}|1\rangle \right) |v\rangle.$$

From Section 7.7.3, we can ignore the bits to the left of the binary point because they contribute multiples of $e^{2\pi i} = 1$, so the state is equivalent to

$$\frac{1}{\sqrt{2^m}} \left(|0\rangle + e^{2\pi i (0.j_m)}|1\rangle \right) \cdots \left(|0\rangle + e^{2\pi i (0.j_3 \cdots j_m)}|1\rangle \right)$$
$$\times \left(|0\rangle + e^{2\pi i (0.j_2 \cdots j_m)}|1\rangle \right) \left(|0\rangle + e^{2\pi i (0.j_1 \cdots j_m)}|1\rangle \right) |v\rangle.$$

Comparing this to Eq. (7.9), this is precisely the QFT of $|j_1 j_2 \ldots j_m\rangle$, so we can find $|j_1 j_2 \ldots j_m\rangle$ by taking the IQFT of the eigenvalue register, resulting in:

$$|j_1 j_2 \ldots j_m\rangle |v\rangle.$$

This completes the quantum circuit for phase estimation. After measuring these qubits and obtaining $j_1, j_2, \ldots, j_m$, we do a little *postprocessing*. We calculate

$$j = 0.j_1 j_2 \ldots j_m$$
$$= \frac{j_1}{2} + \frac{j_2}{4} + \cdots + \frac{j_m}{2^m}.$$

Then, the phase of the eigenvalue is $\theta = 2\pi j$, and the eigenvalue is $e^{i\theta}$.

To estimate the eigenvalue to m bits of precision, we need m Hadamard gates, m controlled-U^p operations, and an IQFT on m qubits that takes $O(m^2)$ gates. Altogether, the number of gates is $O(m^2)$. The classical method takes $O(N) = O(2^n)$ elementary arithmetic operations, so depending on the number of bits of precision m, the quantum method can be faster, although it assumes we can create $|v\rangle$ and do controlled-U^p operations.

Exercise 7.36. Go to https://tinyurl.com/fdtm5fas to access the following quantum circuit:

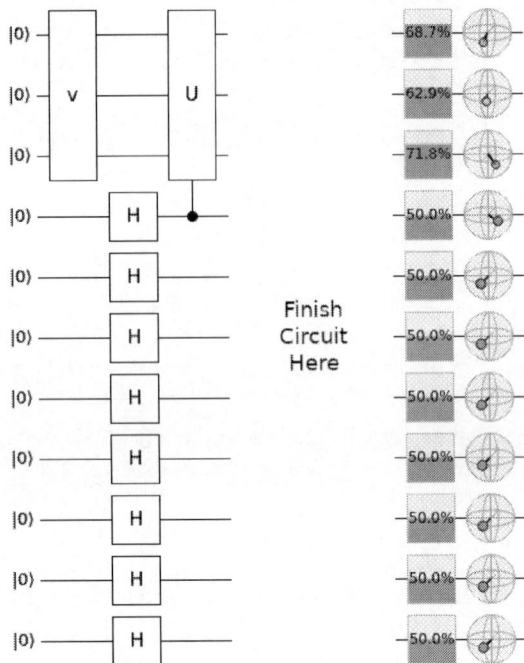

There are two custom three-qubit gates, v and U. The v gate turns $|000\rangle$ into $|v\rangle$, which is an eigenstate of U whose eigenvalue we want to estimate to $m = 8$ bits. The beginning of the phase estimation circuit has been started for you.

(a) Using two copies of U, use Quirk's "Make Gate" "From Circuit" to create the gate U^2. Then using two copies of U^2, make U^4. Continuing, make $U^8, U^{16}, U^{32}, U^{64}$, and U^{128}.

(b) Fill in the rest of the phase estimation circuit. Hint: Use Quirk's IQFT function, which is called QFT†, rather than constructing it from scratch.

(c) What is $j = 0.j_1 j_2 \ldots j_7$ as a binary number?

(d) What is j as a decimal number?

(e) What is θ, the phase of the eigenvalue $e^{i\theta}$?

(f) What is the eigenvalue $e^{i\theta}$.

(g) Explain why your value for $e^{i\theta}$ is only an estimate, and the actual value may be slightly different.

7.8.4 Multiple Eigenstates

Say we have two eigenstates of U, which we call $|v_1\rangle$ and $|v_2\rangle$, with corresponding eigenvalues $e^{2\pi i j_1}$ and $e^{2\pi i j_2}$. Say we are using the previous phase estimation algorithm but prepare the eigenstate register in the following superposition of $|v_1\rangle$ and $|v_2\rangle$:

$$\frac{\sqrt{3}}{2}|v_1\rangle + \frac{1}{2}|v_2\rangle.$$

We also have the m qubits that each start in the $|0\rangle$ state, so the initial state of the phase estimation circuit is

$$|0\ldots000\rangle\left(\frac{\sqrt{3}}{2}|v_1\rangle + \frac{1}{2}|v_2\rangle\right) = \frac{\sqrt{3}}{2}|0\ldots000\rangle|v_1\rangle + \frac{1}{2}|0\ldots000\rangle|v_2\rangle.$$

Following the same calculation as the previous section, the final state of the phase estimation circuit is

$$\frac{\sqrt{3}}{2}|j_1 j_2 \ldots j_m\rangle|v_1\rangle + \frac{1}{2}|j_1' j_2' \ldots j_m'\rangle|v_2\rangle,$$

where $0.j_1 j_2 \ldots j_m$ is an m-bit approximation of j_1 and $0.j_1' j_2' \ldots j_m'$ is an m-bit approximation of j_2. Then, when we measure the qubits at the end of the circuit, we get an approximation of j_1 with probability $3/4$ or an approximation of j_2 with probability $1/4$.

Exercise 7.37. Consider three eigenstates of U, $|v_1\rangle$, $|v_2\rangle$, and $|v_3\rangle$, with corresponding eigenvalues $e^{2\pi i j_1}$, $e^{2\pi i j_2}$, and $e^{2\pi i j_3}$. If we use the phase estimation algorithm but prepare the eigenstate register in the following state,

$$\frac{\sqrt{3}}{2\sqrt{2}}|v_1\rangle + \frac{1}{\sqrt{2}}|v_2\rangle + \frac{1}{2\sqrt{2}}|v_3\rangle,$$

what is the probability that we get an approximation to j_1, j_2, and j_3?

7.9 Period of Modular Exponentiation

7.9.1 The Problem

Recall from Section 6.6.2 that "mod" refers to modulus, or the remainder when dividing. For example, $15 = 3 \bmod 12$ because 15 divided by 12 has a remainder of 3. This is also how a twelve-hour clock works, as 15 o'clock corresponds to 3 o'clock.

Modular exponentiation is taking powers of a number modulo some other number. For example, consider powers of 2 taken modulo 7:

$$2^0 \bmod 7 = 1 \bmod 7,$$
$$2^1 \bmod 7 = 2 \bmod 7,$$
$$2^2 \bmod 7 = 4 \bmod 7,$$
$$2^3 \bmod 7 = 8 \bmod 7 = 1 \bmod 7,$$
$$2^4 \bmod 7 = 16 \bmod 7 = 2 \bmod 7,$$
$$2^5 \bmod 7 = 32 \bmod 7 = 4 \bmod 7,$$
$$2^6 \bmod 7 = 64 \bmod 7 = 1 \bmod 7,$$
$$2^7 \bmod 7 = 128 \bmod 7 = 2 \bmod 7,$$
$$2^8 \bmod 7 = 256 \bmod 7 = 4 \bmod 7,$$

$$2^9 \bmod 7 = 512 \bmod 7 = 1 \bmod 7,$$

$$\vdots$$

Notice the results are $1, 2, 4, \ldots$ repeated. The *period* or *order* r of the modular exponential is the length of the repeating sequence, so in this example, $r = 3$. Next, let us consider another example: powers of 3 taken modulo 10:

$$3^0 \bmod 10 = 1 \bmod 10,$$

$$3^1 \bmod 10 = 3 \bmod 10,$$

$$3^2 \bmod 10 = 9 \bmod 10,$$

$$3^3 \bmod 10 = 27 \bmod 10 = 7 \bmod 10,$$

$$3^4 \bmod 10 = 81 \bmod 10 = 1 \bmod 10,$$

$$3^5 \bmod 10 = 243 \bmod 10 = 3 \bmod 10,$$

$$3^6 \bmod 10 = 729 \bmod 10 = 9 \bmod 10,$$

$$3^7 \bmod 10 = 2187 \bmod 10 = 7 \bmod 10,$$

$$3^8 \bmod 10 = 6561 \bmod 10 = 1 \bmod 10,$$

$$\vdots$$

Now, the pattern is $1, 3, 9, 7$ repeated, and the period is $r = 4$. In both of these examples, the repeated sequences started with a 1. This is always true because $a^0 = 1$ for any positive integer a. Furthermore, the modular exponential $a^x \bmod N$ always follows a repeated pattern as long as a and N are relatively prime (i.e., their greatest common divisor is 1, so they share no common factors except 1). This fact comes from a branch of mathematics called *number theory*.

Since the repeated sequence always starts with 1, another way to define the period is as the smallest positive exponent r such that $a^r \bmod N = 1 \bmod N$. For example, with $2^x \bmod 7$, $r = 3$ was the smallest positive exponent to yield $1 \bmod 7$, so it takes $r = 3$ terms for the pattern to repeat to 1. For the second example, $r = 4$ is the smallest exponent such that $3^x \bmod 10 = 1 \bmod N$. More generally, since the numbers repeat every r powers, $a^{x+r} \bmod N = a^x \bmod N$.

The problem is to find the period of modular exponentials. Since this is a mouthful, we often just call this problem *period finding* or *order finding*. Note the period r must be less than N, and so the challenge is to find the period for large N.

Exercise 7.38. Consider the modular exponential $4^x \bmod 5$.
(a) Confirm that 4 and 5 are relatively prime.
(b) Calculate enough terms of $4^x \bmod 5$, where $x = 0, 1, 2, \ldots$, to see a pattern.
(c) What is the sequence that is repeated?
(d) What is the period?

Exercise 7.39. Consider the modular exponential $4^x \bmod 13$.
(a) Confirm that 4 and 13 are relatively prime.

(b) Calculate enough terms of 4^x mod 13, where $x = 0, 1, 2, \ldots$, to see a pattern.

(c) What is the sequence that is repeated?

(d) What is the period?

7.9.2 Classical Solution

Finding a single modular exponent is fast using the *repeated squaring* method. For example, say we want to find

$$91^{43} \bmod 131.$$

We do *not* want to calculate 91^{43}, as this is a very big number. Instead, we want to calculate it in pieces, taking it modulo 131 as we go. To do this, we express the exponent in binary:

$$43 = 101011_2$$
$$= 1 \cdot 2^5 + 0 \cdot 2^4 + 1 \cdot 2^3 + 0 \cdot 2^2 + 1 \cdot 2^1 + 1 \cdot 2^0$$
$$= 1 \cdot 32 + 0 \cdot 16 + 1 \cdot 8 + 0 \cdot 4 + 1 \cdot 2 + 1 \cdot 1.$$

So, we want to calculate

$$91^{43} \bmod 131 = 91^{1 \cdot 32 + 0 \cdot 16 + 1 \cdot 8 + 0 \cdot 4 + 1 \cdot 2 + 1 \cdot 1} \bmod 131$$
$$= 91^{1 \cdot 32} 91^{0 \cdot 16} 91^{1 \cdot 8} 91^{0 \cdot 4} 91^{1 \cdot 2} 91^{1 \cdot 1} \bmod 131$$
$$= \left(91^{32}\right)^1 \left(91^{16}\right)^0 \left(91^8\right)^1 \left(91^4\right)^0 \left(91^2\right)^1 \left(91^1\right)^1 \bmod 131 \quad (7.11)$$

This consists of square powers of 91 modulo 131, and we can calculate them by starting with 91^1, then squaring it to get 91^2, then squaring it to get 91^4, then squaring it to get 91^8, and so forth:

$91^1 \bmod 131 = 91 \bmod 131,$

$91^2 \bmod 131 = 8281 \bmod 131 = 28 \bmod 131,$

$91^4 \bmod 131 = (92^2)^2 \bmod 131 = 28^2 \bmod 131 = 784 \bmod 131 = 129 \bmod 131,$

$91^8 \bmod 131 = (92^4)^2 \bmod 131 = 129^2 \bmod 131 = 16641 \bmod 131 = 4 \bmod 131,$

$91^{16} \bmod 131 = (92^8)^2 \bmod 131 = 4^2 \bmod 131 = 16 \bmod 131,$

$91^{32} \bmod 131 = (92^{16})^2 \bmod 131 = 16^2 \bmod 131 = 256 \bmod 131 = 125 \bmod 131.$

By repeatedly squaring, we were able to calculate these using relatively small numbers. Plugging these into Eq. (7.11), we get

$$91^{43} \bmod 131 = (125)^1 (16)^0 (4)^1 (129)^0 (28)^1 (91)^1 \bmod 131$$
$$= 125 \cdot 4 \cdot 28 \cdot 91 \bmod 131$$
$$= 1\,274\,000 \bmod 131$$

$$= 25 \bmod 131.$$

In this case, multiplying $125 \cdot 4 \cdot 28 \cdot 91$ is small enough to be done on an ordinary calculator, but if it were not, it could also be multiplied progressively, e.g.,

$$\begin{aligned}
125 \cdot 4 \cdot 28 \cdot 91 \bmod 131 &= 125(4(28 \cdot 91)) \bmod 131 \\
&= 125(4(2548)) \bmod 131 \\
&= 125(4(59)) \bmod 131 \\
&= 125(236) \bmod 131 \\
&= 125(105) \bmod 131 \\
&= 13125 \bmod 131 \\
&= 25 \bmod 131.
\end{aligned}$$

To go from the second line to the third, we used $2548 \bmod 131 = 59 \bmod 131$. Thus, $91^{43} \bmod 131 = 25 \bmod 131$, and we were able to calculate this using relatively small numbers, as opposed to trying to calculate 91^{43} from the start.

Repeated squaring and other similar methods for calculating modular exponentials have been implemented in computer algebra systems like Mathematica and SageMath:

- In Mathematica, $91^{43} \bmod 131$ can be computed using:

```
PowerMod[91,43,131]
```

   The output is 25, as expected.
- In SageMath, $91^{43} \bmod 131$ can be computed using:

```
sage: power_mod(91,43,131)
25
```

   Alternatively, since SageMath is based on Python, we can use Python's built-in `pow()` function:

```
sage: pow(91,43,131)
25
```

For the computational complexity of the repeated squaring method, say we are calculating $a^x \bmod N$, where x is an n-bit binary number. Then, we start with a and square it $n-1$ times, modulo N. Once we have these, we may have to multiply them together, which following the progressive approach above takes up to $n-1$ multiplications, modulo N. Together, this is $(n-1)+(n-1) = 2(n-1) = O(n)$ decimal arithmetic operations modulo N. We may be interested in the number of bit operations, however, rather than decimal operations. Recall from elementary school that you can multiply two d-digit numbers by multiplying $O(d^2)$ pairs of digits. For example, to multiply 123 and 456,

$$
\begin{array}{r}
123 \\
\times\ 456 \\
\hline
738 \\
6150 \\
+\ 49200 \\
\hline
56088
\end{array}
$$

That is, we multiplied each digit of 123 by 6, then multiplied each digit of 123 by 5, and then multiplied each digit of 123 by 4, doing the carries along the way. Altogether, we multiplied 9 pairs of numbers. Then, we added 9 digits together, ignoring the zeros that we padded on the right. So, the total number of operations on digits is $9 + 9 = d^2 + d^2 = 2d^2 = O(d^2)$. Similarly, to multiply two n-bit strings, this method takes $O(n^2)$ multiplications of pairs of bits and additions. For example, to multiply 101 and 110,

$$
\begin{array}{r}
101 \\
\times\ 110 \\
\hline
000 \\
1010 \\
+\ 10100 \\
\hline
11110
\end{array}
$$

Converting to decimal, $101 = 5$, $110 = 6$, and $11110 = 30$, so we get $5 \times 6 = 30$, as expected. Now, the repeated squares method takes $O(n)$ multiplications/squares, and we just saw that each of these takes $O(n^2)$ binary multiplications/additions, and so the total number of elementary binary arithmetic operations for modular exponentiation is $O(n^3)$, which is still a polynomial and is hence efficient.

Although calculating a single modular exponential using the previous repeated squares method is fast, finding the period is slow because, when N is large, we may need to calculate many individual modular exponentials before a pattern forms. There is no known efficient algorithm for period finding.

Computer algebra systems often have functions for finding the period of modular exponentials. Although they are slow for large N, they are fast for small values.

- In Mathematica, the `MultiplicativeOrder` function can be used to find the period of $a^x \bmod N$. For example, the order of $3^x \bmod 10$ is

```
MultiplicativeOrder[3, 10]
```

  The output is 4, as expected.
- In SageMath, the `multiplicative_order()` function within a modulus object can be used to find the period of $a^x \bmod N$. For example, the order of $3^x \bmod 10$ is

```
sage: Mod(3,10).multiplicative_order()
4
```

Exercise 7.40. Use the repeated squares algorithm to calculate 91^{53} mod 131. Hint: Many of the numbers were calculated for you in the text. Check your answer using a computer algebra system.

Exercise 7.41. Use the repeated squares algorithm to calculate 87^{38} mod 197. Check your answer using a computer algebra system.

7.9.3 Quantum Solution

A quantum computer can efficiently find the period of a^x mod N by utilizing a quantum gate U that performs *modular multiplication*, which multiplies a number y by a mod N, so it maps

$$U|y\rangle = |ay \bmod N\rangle.$$

Since we are working modulo N, y is a number between 0 and $N-1$. If N can be written using n bits, then $|y\rangle$ would require n qubits. By repeatedly applying U to $|1\rangle$, we get a to some power:

$$U^0|1\rangle = |1 \bmod N\rangle = |a^0 \bmod N\rangle,$$
$$U^1|1\rangle = |a \bmod N\rangle = |a^1 \bmod N\rangle,$$
$$U^2|1\rangle = |a^2 \bmod N\rangle,$$
$$U^3|1\rangle = |a^3 \bmod N\rangle,$$
$$\vdots$$
$$U^r|1\rangle = |a^r \bmod N\rangle = |a^0 \bmod N\rangle.$$

This is exactly the modular exponential a^x mod N because exponentiation is repeated multiplication. The last term is a^r mod $N = a^0$ mod $N = 1$ mod N because r is the order of a^x mod N, and the sequence repeats itself.

Now, consider a superposition of $|a^0 \bmod N\rangle$, $|a^1 \bmod N\rangle$, ..., $|a^{r-1} \bmod N\rangle$ with respective coefficients $e^{-2\pi i s(0)/r}$, $e^{-2\pi i s(1)/r}$, ..., $e^{-2\pi i s(r-1)/r}$, where s is an integer taking values $0, 1, \ldots, r-1$:

$$|v_s\rangle = \frac{1}{\sqrt{r}}\left(e^{-2\pi i s(0)/r}|a^0 \bmod N\rangle + e^{-2\pi i s(1)/r}|a^1 \bmod N\rangle + \ldots\right.$$
$$\left. + e^{-2\pi i s(r-2)/r}|a^{r-2} \bmod N\rangle + e^{-2\pi i s(r-1)/r}|a^{r-1} \bmod N\rangle\right)$$
$$= \frac{1}{\sqrt{r}}\sum_{k=0}^{r-1}e^{-2\pi i s k/r}|a^k \bmod N\rangle.$$

Let us show that $|v_s\rangle$ is an eigenvector of U with eigenvalue $e^{2\pi i s/r}$:

$$U|v_s\rangle = \frac{1}{\sqrt{r}} \sum_{k=0}^{r-1} e^{-2\pi i s k/r} U |a^k \bmod N\rangle$$

$$= \frac{1}{\sqrt{r}} \left(e^{-2\pi i s(0)/r} U |a^0 \bmod N\rangle + e^{-2\pi i s(1)/r} U |a^1 \bmod N\rangle + \ldots \right.$$

$$\left. + e^{-2\pi i s(r-2)/r} U |a^{r-2} \bmod N\rangle + e^{-2\pi i s(r-1)/r} U |a^{r-1} \bmod N\rangle \right)$$

$$= \frac{1}{\sqrt{r}} \left(e^{-2\pi i s(0)/r} |a^1 \bmod N\rangle + e^{-2\pi i s(1)/r} |a^2 \bmod N\rangle + \ldots \right.$$

$$\left. + e^{-2\pi i s(r-2)/r} |a^{r-1} \bmod N\rangle + e^{-2\pi i s(r-1)/r} \underbrace{|a^r \bmod N\rangle}_{|a^0 \bmod N\rangle} \right)$$

$$= \frac{1}{\sqrt{r}} \left(e^{-2\pi i s(r-1)/r} |a^0 \bmod N\rangle + e^{-2\pi i s(0)/r} |a^1 \bmod N\rangle \right.$$

$$\left. + e^{-2\pi i s(1)/r} |a^2 \bmod N\rangle + \cdots + e^{-2\pi i s(r-2)/r} |a^{r-1} \bmod N\rangle \right).$$

Multiplying by $1 = e^0 = e^{2\pi i s/r - 2\pi i s/r} = e^{2\pi i s/r} e^{-2\pi i s/r}$, this becomes

$$U|v_s\rangle = e^{2\pi i s/r} \frac{1}{\sqrt{r}} \left(e^{-2\pi i s(r)/r} |a^0 \bmod N\rangle + e^{-2\pi i s(1)/r} |a^1 \bmod N\rangle \right.$$

$$\left. + e^{-2\pi i s(2)/r} |a^2 \bmod N\rangle + \cdots + e^{-2\pi i s(r-1)/r} |a^{r-1} \bmod N\rangle \right).$$

Note the first coefficient $e^{-2\pi i s(r)/r} = e^{-2\pi i s} = 1$ since s is an integer, and since $e^{-2\pi i s(0)/r} = 1$, the is equation can be written as

$$U|v_s\rangle = e^{2\pi i s/r} \frac{1}{\sqrt{r}} \left(e^{-2\pi i s(0)/r} |a^0 \bmod N\rangle + e^{-2\pi i s(1)/r} |a^1 \bmod N\rangle \right.$$

$$\left. + e^{-2\pi i s(2)/r} |a^2 \bmod N\rangle + \cdots + e^{-2\pi i s(r-1)/r} |a^{r-1} \bmod N\rangle \right)$$

$$= e^{2\pi i s/r} |v_s\rangle.$$

Thus, $|v_s\rangle$ is an eigenvector of U with eigenvalue $e^{2\pi i s/r}$.

Since $|v_s\rangle$ is an eigenvector of U, we can use the phase estimation algorithm from Section 7.8 to estimate its eigenvalue $e^{2\pi i s/r}$. That is, we can find s/r for some s, which will allow us to find r, the period of the modular exponential, hence solving the problem. To do this, however, we need to work out three more items:

1. How to construct the controlled-U gates for the phase estimation algorithm.
2. How to construct the eigenvector $|v_s\rangle$ for the phase estimation algorithm.
3. How to take the result of the phase estimation, which is an m-bit estimate for s/r, and find r.

Let us address each of these now.

For the first item, we need controlled-U, controlled-U^2, controlled-U^4, through controlled-$U^{2^{m-1}}$. We choose to approximate the eigenvalue to $m = O(n)$ bits. Writing the control qubit as $|z\rangle$ and the target qubits as $|y\rangle$, the operation of CU^{2^j} is:

$$CU^{2^j}|z\rangle|y\rangle = |z\rangle \left| a^{z2^j} y \bmod N \right\rangle.$$

This way, when $z = 0$, the target remains unchanged as y, and when $z = 1$, the target is multiplied by a^{2^j} and taken mod N. From Section 7.9.2, repeated squaring is a fast classical method for computing $a^x \bmod N$ that takes $O(n^2)$, and we can convert this into a reversible circuit and hence a quantum gate. In Section 4.5.2, we discussed methods for this by converting a classical adder into a quantum adder. The process would be similar, but we would need to discuss how to square integers and take the modulo using a classical computer first, so to avoid the lengthy discussion, the details are beyond the scope of this textbook. Also, the best way to do this is also an open research question.

For the second item, we need to prepare an eigenvector of U. A trick is, instead of preparing a single eigenvector of U, we prepare the following equal superposition of them:

$$\frac{1}{\sqrt{r}} \sum_{s=0}^{r-1} |v_s\rangle.$$

In a moment, we will see that this superposition is easy to construct. First, the broader picture is that we will use this superposition in the phase estimation algorithm. Since the eigenvalue of $|v_s\rangle$ is $e^{2\pi i s/r}$, the phase estimation will yield an m-bit approximation to s/r for one $s = 0, 1, \ldots, r-1$, where each value of s has a probability of $1/r$.

Now, let us show that the equal superposition is easy to construct. Plugging in the definition of $|v_s\rangle$, the equal superposition becomes

$$\frac{1}{\sqrt{r}} \sum_{s=0}^{r-1} |v_s\rangle = \frac{1}{\sqrt{r}} \sum_{s=0}^{r-1} \frac{1}{\sqrt{r}} \sum_{k=0}^{r-1} e^{-2\pi i s k/r} \left| a^k \bmod N \right\rangle$$

$$= \frac{1}{r} \sum_{k=0}^{r-1} \underbrace{\left(\sum_{s=0}^{r-1} e^{-2\pi i s k/r} \right)}_{\substack{r \text{ when } k=0, \\ 0 \text{ otherwise.}}} \left| a^k \bmod N \right\rangle.$$

Let us show why the term in parenthesis is r when $k = 0$ and why it is 0 when $k \neq 0$. First, when $k = 0$, the term in parenthesis is

$$\sum_{s=0}^{r-1} e^{-2\pi i s k/r} = \sum_{s=0}^{r-1} e^0 = \sum_{s=0}^{r-1} 1 = r.$$

Next, when $k \neq 0$, let us define $\omega = e^{-2\pi i k}$. Then, the term in parenthesis is

$$\sum_{s=0}^{r-1} e^{-2\pi i s k/r} = \sum_{s=0}^{r-1} \omega^s = 1 + \omega + \omega^2 + \cdots + \omega^{r-1}.$$

This is a geometric series. We could look up the formula from Algebra II, but let us quickly derive it. Let us call the series S:

$$S = 1 + \omega + \cdots + \omega^{r-1}.$$

If we multiply S by ω, we get

$$\omega S = \omega + \omega^2 + \cdots + \omega^r.$$

Subtracting these series,

$$S - \omega S = \left(1 + \omega + \cdots + \omega^{r-1}\right) - \left(\omega + \omega^2 + \cdots + \omega^r\right)$$
$$= 1 - \omega^r.$$

The left-hand side is $(1 - \omega)S$, so this becomes

$$(1 - \omega)S = 1 - \omega^r.$$

Dividing, we get a formula for the geometric series S:

$$S = \frac{1 - \omega^r}{1 - \omega}.$$

Using this formula, let us plug in for ω:

$$S = \frac{1 - e^{-2\pi i s k}}{1 - e^{-2\pi i s k/r}} = \frac{1 - 1}{1 - e^{-2\pi i s k/r}} = 0,$$

where in the numerator, we noted that e to any multiple of 2π is equivalent to $e^0 = 1$. Thus, we have proved that the term in parenthesis from several lines ago is 0 when $k \neq 0$. Thus, the equal superposition that we were considering is equal to

$$\frac{1}{\sqrt{r}} \sum_{s=0}^{r-1} |v_s\rangle = \frac{1}{r} r |a^0 \bmod N\rangle = |1 \bmod N\rangle.$$

Thus, the equal superposition of the eigenstates $|v_s\rangle$ is precisely equal to $|1 \bmod N\rangle$, which is easily prepared by starting all the qubits as $|00...00\rangle$ and then applying an X gate to the rightmost qubit to yield $|00...01\rangle = |1 \bmod N\rangle$. Then, from Section 7.8.4, if we use the phase estimation algorithm, we get an approximation to the phase of one $|v_s\rangle$, with $s \in \{0, \ldots, r-1\}$, with probability $1/r$. That is, since $|v_s\rangle$ is an eigenstate of U with eigenvalue $e^{2\pi i s/r}$, the phase estimation yields $0.j_1 j_2 \ldots j_m$, which is an m-bit approximation to $j = s/r$.

For example, let us implement this in Quirk to find the order of $3^x \bmod 7$. See
https://bit.ly/3otwt4n:

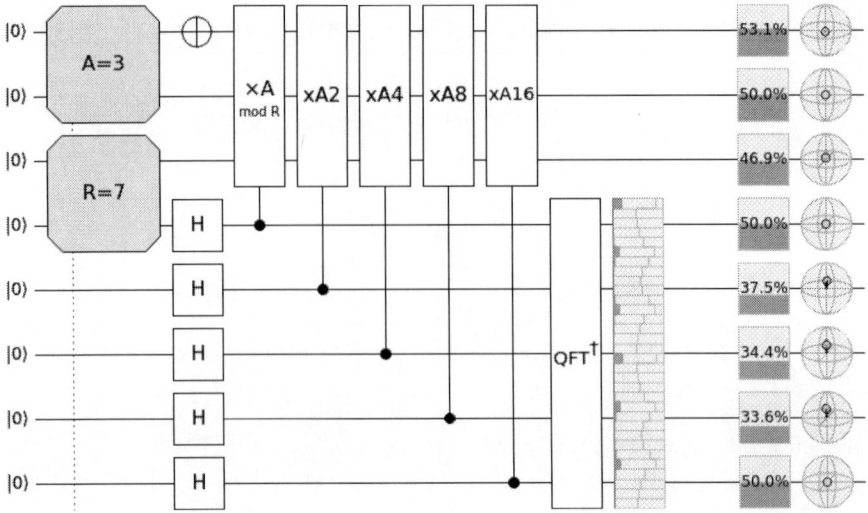

Quirk has a built-in modular multiplication gate under the "Modular" toolbox. It is labeled $\begin{smallmatrix} \times A \\ \mod R \end{smallmatrix}$. To use this, we need to specify the values of A and R. We can do this using a tool under the "Inputs" toolbox, and the tools look like $\begin{smallmatrix} A=\# \\ \text{default} \end{smallmatrix}$ and $\begin{smallmatrix} R=\# \\ \text{default} \end{smallmatrix}$. On the above circuit, they look like large gray squares with squared off corners. Next, gates that multiply by modular powers of A can be created using the "Make Gate" feature, i.e., $\times A^2$ is two copies of $\times A$, and $\times A^4$ is two copies of $\times A^2$, etc. The output of the quantum circuit can be hard to read, so we added a "Chance" display that we resized across all five qubits of the eigenvalue register. By hovering the mouse cursor over the Chance display, we can see the probability of various outcomes for the eigenvalue register:

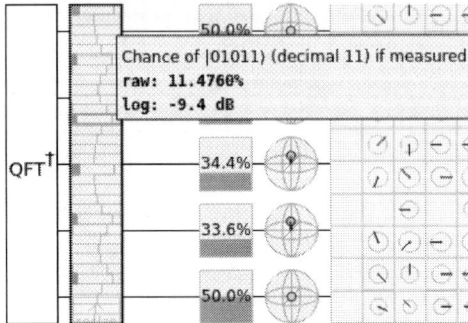

Here are the most likely outcomes for the eigenvalue register:

Probability	Binary Approx. of s/r	Decimal Approx. of s/r
16.7963%	$\lvert 00000\rangle$	0
11.4759%	$\lvert 00101\rangle$	0.1562
11.4760%	$\lvert 01011\rangle$	0.3438
16.7963%	$\lvert 10000\rangle$	0.5
11.4759%	$\lvert 10101\rangle$	0.6562
11.4760%	$\lvert 11011\rangle$	0.8438

These are the likely values for our approximation of s/r. For example, we have an 11.4759% chance of measuring the eigenvalue register to be $\lvert 00101\rangle$, so 0.00101 is a binary approximation of s/r. Converting this to decimal, we get that s/r is approximately 0.1562.

Now for the third item, how do we take an approximation to s/r, like 0.1562 from above, and find s and r? We use a method called *continued fractions*. A continued fraction has the form

$$a_0 + \cfrac{1}{a_1 + \cfrac{1}{a_2 + \cfrac{1}{\ddots + \cfrac{1}{a_\ell}}}}$$

for some non-negative integer ℓ. For example, from the table above, consider the number 0.1562. To express this as a continued fraction, we begin by expressing 0.1562 as $1562/10000$, which we express as a mixed number, i.e., a whole number 0 and fractional part $1562/10000$:

$$0.1562 = \frac{1562}{10000} = 0 + \frac{1562}{10000}.$$

Next, we invert the fractional part to get

$$0 + \frac{1}{\frac{10000}{1562}}.$$

Then, we express $10000/1562$ as a mixed number, resulting in

$$0 + \cfrac{1}{6 + \cfrac{628}{1562}}.$$

Again, we invert the fractional part and then express it as a mixed number:

$$0 + \cfrac{1}{6 + \cfrac{1}{\cfrac{1562}{628}}} = 0 + \cfrac{1}{6 + \cfrac{1}{2 + \cfrac{306}{628}}}.$$

Continuing this, we eventually arrive at

$$0.1562 = 0 + \cfrac{1}{6 + \cfrac{1}{2 + \cfrac{1}{2 + \cfrac{1}{19 + \cfrac{1}{8}}}}}.$$

By listing all the whole numbers, plus the very last denominator, we can write the continued fraction as $[a_0, a_1, \ldots, a_5] = [0, 6, 2, 2, 19, 8]$.

A computer algebra system can quickly write a number as a continued fraction:

- In Mathematica, we can convert 0.1562 to a continued fraction using the ContinuedFraction function:

```
ContinuedFraction[1562/10000]
```

The output of this is

$$\{0, 6, 2, 2, 19, 8\}.$$

- Using SageMath, we can use the continued_fraction function to convert 0.1562 into a continued fraction:

```
sage: continued_fraction(0.1562)
[0; 6, 2, 2, 19, 8]
```

The reason why we care about continued fractions is they allow us to find rational approximations to numbers by truncating the continued fraction. These are called *convergents*. For example, for 0.1562, the convergents are:

0th convergent $= [0] = 0,$

1st convergent $= [0, 6] = 0 + \dfrac{1}{6} = \dfrac{1}{6},$

2nd convergent $= [0, 6, 2] = 0 + \cfrac{1}{6 + \cfrac{1}{2}} = \dfrac{2}{13},$

3rd convergent $= [0, 6, 2, 2] = 0 + \cfrac{1}{6 + \cfrac{1}{2 + \cfrac{1}{2}}} = \dfrac{5}{32},$

$$\text{4rd convergent} = [0,6,2,2,19] = 0 + \cfrac{1}{6 + \cfrac{1}{2 + \cfrac{1}{2 + \cfrac{1}{19}}}} = \frac{97}{621},$$

$$\text{5th convergent} = [0,6,2,2,19,8] = 0 + \cfrac{1}{6 + \cfrac{1}{2 + \cfrac{1}{2 + \cfrac{1}{19 + \cfrac{1}{8}}}}} = \frac{781}{5000}.$$

In this example, the 5th convergent contains all the terms of the continued fraction, and so the 5th convergent is exactly $0.1562 = 781/5000 = 1562/10000$. We can also calculate the convergents using a computer algebra system:

- In Mathematica, we can find a convergent using the FromContinuedFraction function:

```
FromContinuedFraction[{0}]
FromContinuedFraction[{0, 6}]
FromContinuedFraction[{0, 6, 2}]
FromContinuedFraction[{0, 6, 2, 2}]
FromContinuedFraction[{0, 6, 2, 2, 19}]
FromContinuedFraction[{0, 6, 2, 2, 19, 8}]
```

This outputs the following numbers:

$$0, \frac{1}{6}, \frac{2}{13}, \frac{5}{32}, \frac{97}{621}, \frac{781}{5000}.$$

- Using SageMath, we can find a convergent using the value() function within a continued fraction object:

```
sage: continued_fraction([0]).value()
0
sage: continued_fraction([0, 6]).value()
1/6
sage: continued_fraction([0, 6, 2]).value()
2/13
sage: continued_fraction([0, 6, 2, 2]).value()
5/32
sage: continued_fraction([0, 6, 2, 2, 19]).value()
97/621
sage: continued_fraction([0, 6, 2, 2, 19, 8]).value()
781/5000
```

The higher the convergent, the better the approximation to 0.1562.

For our period finding problem, 0.1562 is a guess for s/r, where r is the period of the modular exponential $a^x \bmod N$, and s is an integer between 0 and $r - 1$. Note

r must be less than N. Then, looking at the convergents, the best approximation to s/r such that $r < N = 7$ is $1/6$. Thus, using the convergents of continued fractions, we were able to guess that $s = 1$ and $r = 6$. To check whether our guess is correct, we can calculate $3^r \bmod 7$ and see if we get $1 \bmod 7$:

$$3^6 \bmod 7 = 1 \bmod 7.$$

Thus, with this measurement result, we successfully found the period $r = 6$. Note it is known that the continued fraction algorithm yields a guess for s and r in $O(n^3)$ steps, if s and r are n-bit numbers.

From the previous table of significant measurement outcomes of the Quirk circuit for phase estimation, some other likely estimates for s/r are $0, 0.3438, 0.5, 0.6562$, and 0.8438. For 0, we get $s = 0$ and no guess for r, so if we get this value, we need to run the quantum circuit again in hopes for a better outcome. For the other values, we can use the continued fraction algorithm and get the following guesses for s and r:

Probability	Binary Approx. of s/r	Decimal Approx. of s/r	Guess of s/r	$3^r \bmod 7$
16.7963%	$\lvert 00000\rangle$	0	N/A	N/A
11.4759%	$\lvert 00101\rangle$	0.1562	1/6	1
11.4760%	$\lvert 01011\rangle$	0.3438	1/3	6
16.7963%	$\lvert 10000\rangle$	0.5	1/2	2
11.4759%	$\lvert 10101\rangle$	0.6562	2/3	6
11.4760%	$\lvert 11011\rangle$	0.8438	5/6	1

For example, for 0.3438, the continued fraction algorithm yields $s = 1$ and $r = 3$. Checking if this guess for the period is correct, we calculate $3^r \bmod 7 = 3^3 \bmod 7 = 6 \bmod 7 \neq 1 \bmod 7$, so 3 is not the period. Then, we run the quantum circuit again, hoping to get a better guess for r. The guess for s and r, and the value of $3^r \bmod 7$ for each guess for r, is shown in the above table (see Exercise 7.42). The number of times we may have to repeat the quantum circuit is small enough that it does not affect the overall runtime of the algorithm, although a proof of this fact is beyond the scope of this textbook (see Nielsen and Chuang for it).

Speaking of the overall runtime, let us find the circuit complexity assuming $m = O(n)$. The quantum algorithm takes one X gate to prepare the eigenvector register in the state $\lvert 00\ldots 01\rangle$, m Hadamard gates, and m controlled-U^{power} gates, and an IQFT on m qubits. Each of the m controlled-U^{power} gates takes $O(n^2)$ gates for a total of $O(mn^2) = O(n^3)$ gates. The IQFT takes $O(m^2) = O(n^2)$ gates. Finally, the continued fraction algorithm takes $O(n^3)$ gates. Thus, the circuit complexity of the quantum period algorithm is $O(n^3)$, which is a polynomial in n, so it is efficient.

Exercise 7.42. In the text, we considered the example of $2^x \bmod 7$, and we found several approximations to s/r. For each of the approximations $0.3438, 0.5, 0.6562$, and 0.8438, do the following:
  (a) Express the decimal as a continued fraction.
  (b) Find the convergents of the continued fraction.
  (c) What is the fractional guess for s/r, and hence, what are the guesses s and r?
  (d) Calculate $2^r \bmod 7$.

(e) Is this guess for r the period or not?

Exercise 7.43. Modify the Quirk circuit from the text to find the period of $2^x \bmod 7$. List the most likely outcomes for the 5-bit approximation of s/r, and in each case, find what r would be and calculate $2^r \bmod 7$ to see if it is the correct period. What is the period?

Exercise 7.44. Use Quirk to simulate the quantum circuit to find the period of $2^x \bmod 15$. Since $N = 15$, you will need $n = 4$ qubits for the eigenvector register. You can use Quirk's built-in modular multiplication gate and use it to make gates with higher powers. For the eigenvalue register, use $m = 8$ qubits. List the most likely outcomes for the m-bit approximation of s/r, and in each case, find what r would be and calculate $2^r \bmod 15$ to see if it is the correct period. What is the period?

7.10 Factoring

7.10.1 The Problem

Say we are given a number N that is the product of two prime numbers p and q. The goal is to factor N, i.e., to find its factors p and q. In Section 6.6.2, we learned that the believed difficulty of this factoring problem for classical computers is the basis of RSA cryptography.

7.10.2 Classical Solution

The best known classical algorithm for factoring is the *number field sieve*. How it works is beyond the scope of this textbook, but to factor an n-bit number, its runtime is roughly $e^{n^{1/3}}$, which is subexponential. It grows faster than polynomial, so factoring is inefficient for classical computers, but it is also not exponential because of the natural logarithms.

7.10.3 Quantum Solution: Shor's Algorithm

An efficient quantum algorithm for factoring was invented by Peter Shor in 1994. (This is the same Peter Shor who invented the Shor code from Section 4.7.4 in 1995.) This means quantum computers, if they can be built at scale, can break RSA cryptography from Section 6.6.2. Historically, this greatly increased the amount of money for research in quantum computing and is one of the reasons why quantum computing has developed into the field it is today. The subexponential speedup over the best known classical algorithm is evidence against the Strong Church-Turing Thesis from Section 1.8.3, meaning a probabilistic Turing machine may not be able to efficiently compute everything that is efficiently computable.

To factor $N = pq$, Shor's algorithm consists of the following three steps:

1. Pick any number $1 < a < N$. Calculate the $\gcd(a,N)$ to determine if we were extraordinarily lucky and picked a multiple of p or q. If the gcd is not 1, then the gcd is a nontrivial common factor of a and N, and so we have found one of the factors of N. Let us call it $p = \gcd(a,N)$. Then, $q = N/p$, and we are done factoring. If $\gcd(a,N) = 1$, we continue to the next step.

2. Find the period r of $a^x \bmod N$. Note this is believed to be hard for classical computers, but it is efficient for quantum computers using the period finding algorithm from the previous section. Make sure the period r is even; if it is odd, go back to step 1 and pick a different a. Also, calculate $a^{r/2} \bmod N$ and make sure it does not equal $N - 1$; if it equals $N - 1$, go back to step 1 and pick a different a. It is known that there is at least a 50% chance of picking a "good" a that meets both criteria, so we will not have to try too many times. The proof of this is beyond the scope of this textbook, but Theorem 5.3 of Nielsen and Chuang has more details.

3. Since we calculated the period r in the previous step, we know that $a^r = 1 \bmod N$. Subtracting 1 from both sides, this means

$$a^r - 1 = 0 \bmod N.$$

This says $a^r - 1$ divided by N has a remainder of 0, so $a^r - 1$ is a multiple of N. Let us call the multiple k, so

$$a^r - 1 = kN.$$

Also substituting $N = pq$, we get

$$a^r - 1 = kpq.$$

Now, factoring the left-hand side, we get

$$(a^{r/2} - 1)(a^{r/2} + 1) = kpq.$$

From Step 2, we know that r is even. So, $a^{r/2}$ is an integer, and $a^{r/2} \pm 1$ are also integers. Now, for the product of $a^{r/2} - 1$ and $a^{r/2} + 1$ to equal kpq, at least one of the terms $a^{r/2} - 1$ or $a^{r/2} + 1$ must contain p and/or q as a factor. That is, for some integers c and d such that $cd = k$, we have three possibilities for $a^{r/2} - 1$ and $a^{r/2} + 1$:

1. $\underbrace{(a^{r/2} - 1)}_{c}\underbrace{(a^{r/2} + 1)}_{dpq} = kpq,$

2. $\underbrace{(a^{r/2} - 1)}_{cp}\underbrace{(a^{r/2} + 1)}_{dq} = kpq,$

3. $\underbrace{(a^{r/2} - 1)}_{cpq}\underbrace{(a^{r/2} + 1)}_{d} = kpq.$

Let us show that the first and third cases are impossible by showing that $a^{r/2} - 1$ and $a^{r/2} + 1$ are not multiples of N. That is, we want to show that $(a^{r/2} - 1) \bmod N \neq 0 \bmod N$ and $(a^{r/2} + 1) \bmod N \neq 0 \bmod N$, so neither has N as a factor.

Let us start with $(a^{r/2} - 1) \bmod N = 0 \bmod N$ and show that this equation is not true. If we add 1 to both sides, we get $a^{r/2} = 1 \bmod N$. We know that r is the period of $a^x \bmod N$, however, which means r is the smallest value of x such that $a^x = 1 \bmod N$. Thus, it cannot be that $a^{r/2} = 1 \bmod N$, otherwise $r/2$ would be a smaller value of x such that $a^x = 1 \bmod N$. Therefore, the equation $(a^{r/2} - 1) \bmod N = 0 \bmod N$ is incorrect, and it must be that $(a^{r/2} - 1) \bmod N \neq 0 \bmod N$, so $(a^{r/2} - 1)$ does not have N as one of its factors.

Next, let us show that $(a^{r/2} + 1) \bmod N = 0 \bmod N$ is not true. If we subtract 1 from both sides, we get $a^{r/2} \bmod N = -1 \bmod N$. Recall that the modulus works in a "cyclical" fashion. For example, with a 12-hour clock, 15 o'clock corresponds to 3 o'clock. Similarly, -1 o'clock corresponds to 11 o'clock. Thus, our modular equation becomes $a^{r/2} \bmod N = N - 1 \bmod N$. This is not true, however, because in Step 2, we made sure that $a^{r/2} \bmod N \neq N - 1 \bmod N$. Thus, $a^{r/2} + 1$ also does not have N as one of its factors.

Thus, only the second case is possible:

$$\underbrace{(a^{r/2} - 1)}_{cp} \underbrace{(a^{r/2} + 1)}_{dq} = kpq.$$

This means $a^{r/2} - 1$ and $a^{r/2} + 1$ each share a nontrivial factor with $N = pq$, and we can obtain them using the greatest common divisor:

$$p = \gcd(a^{r/2} - 1, N),$$
$$q = \gcd(a^{r/2} + 1, N).$$

Thus, we have factored N.

As an example, say we want to factor $N = 15$. We begin Shor's algorithm by picking a value for a that is greater than 1 but less than $N = 15$:

1. Say we pick $a = 6$. We calculate $\gcd(a, N) = \gcd(6, 15) = 3$. This means that 3 is a factor of both a and N. Thus, we have found one of the factors of N. Let us call it $p = 3$. The other factor is $q = N/p = 15/3 = 5$. So, we have factored $N = 15$ into $pq = 3 \cdot 5$, and we are done.

Let us work out what might happen if we did not have such a lucky pick for a.

1. Say we pick $a = 2$. We calculate $\gcd(a, N) = \gcd(2, 15) = 1$, so we continue to Step 2.
2. We find the period of $a^x \bmod N = 2^x \bmod 15$. This was Exercise 7.44, and we used the quantum period finding algorithm to determine $r = 4$. This period is even, and we confirm that $a^{r/2} + 1 = 5 \bmod 15 \neq 14 \bmod 15$.
3. Calculate the factors.

$$p = \gcd(a^{r/2} - 1, N) = \gcd(2^2 - 1, 15) = \gcd(3, 15) = 3,$$
$$q = \gcd(a^{r/2} + 1, N) = \gcd(2^2 + 1, 15) = \gcd(5, 15) = 5.$$

Thus, the factors of $N = 15$ are $p = 3$ and $q = 5$.

The bottleneck for Shor's algorithm is Step 2, finding the period of the modular exponential. It is efficient on a quantum computer, but there is no known polynomial-time algorithm for a classical computer.

Although quantum computers would break RSA cryptography, their creation does not necessarily mean the end of digital privacy. Already, efforts are underway to choose a new public-key cryptography standard that is resistant to quantum computers. *Post-quantum cryptography* refers to such classical cryptographic algorithms that are resistant to attacks from future quantum computers. Besides this, there is also quantum key distribution protocols, such as BB84 that was covered in Section 6.6.3, that are secure from quantum computers. They require a quantum network, however, to be used.

Exercise 7.45. Use Shor's algorithm to factor $N = 35$.
  (a) Pick a value of a such that $\gcd(a, N) = 1$ so that we can continue with the remaining steps of the algorithm.
  (b) What is the period of $a^x \bmod N$? For the sake of this problem, just find the period classically since the numbers are small. Make sure the period r is even and $a^{r/2} \neq N - 1 \bmod N$. If not, go back and pick a different value for a.
  (c) Calculate the factors $p = \gcd(a^{r/2} - 1, N)$ and $q = \gcd(a^{r/2} + 1, N)$.

Exercise 7.46. Use Shor's algorithm to factor $N = 209$. Say we pick $a = 22$.
  (a) Show that $\gcd(a, N) \neq 1$.
  (b) What are the factors of N?

7.11 Summary

For many algorithms in classical and quantum computing, it is easier to find the query complexity of the algorithms, which is the number of calls to a function. Quantum computers can provide provable exponential speedups in query complexity, and we saw an example for the problem of finding a secret XOR mask. Quantum computers also provide a quadratic speedup for the general problem of brute-force searching. The most accurate way to quantify the complexity of an algorithm, however, is counting the number of elementary gates, but this circuit complexity can differ depending on what gates are permitted, and even then it is difficult to know if a circuit can be simplified further. Despite this, quantum computers are known to provide speedups in circuit complexity for several problems, such as discrete Fourier transforms, estimating the phases of eigenvalues of unitary matrices, finding the period of modular exponents, and factoring. Factoring, in particular, is very relevant to the real-world, as it underpins RSA cryptography, and the quantum speedup is subexponential over the best known classical algorithms.

Chapter 8
Next Steps

Congratulations on finishing *Introduction to Classical and Quantum Computing*! As you have seen, although this an introductory textbook with only minimal prerequisites, the material did not stay at an elementary or conceptual level. Instead, we learned the mathematics needed to understand quantum computing more deeply. You have learned a lot, and I am proud of you.

In this short chapter, we will explore some possible careers in quantum computing. They range from technical jobs where the ideas you learned in this textbook will be used regularly, to supporting roles where a general familiarity with quantum computing is helpful, but not required. For those who want to continue learning the technical details, we discuss possible next steps.

8.1 Careers in Quantum Computing

Quantum computing, long confined to the halls of academic research, is now an emerging industry. As such, there are many companies involved in quantum computing, and they could be grouped into various types:

1. *Traditional technology companies.* Many well established computer companies have noted that quantum computing may be the future of computer technology, and they want to be leaders in the field. As such, they are investing heavily in building quantum hardware and/or developing quantum software expertise.
2. *Technology startup companies.* Since quantum computing is a relatively new technological field, there is still plenty of room for new companies with new ideas. As a result, startups have also entered the nascent quantum computing industry. Some specialize in hardware, others specialize in software, while others are attempting both.
3. *Companies that use computing technology.* Banks, car companies, airplane manufacturers, and accounting firms are all examples of companies that have been hiring experts in quantum computing. They are not interested in building quantum computers themselves, but they want to know how future quantum

computers can be used for each of their businesses. If they wait for fault-tolerant quantum computers to be built before investigating their uses, they will be left behind by competitors.

These companies are desperately trying to hire qualified individuals. Some of the jobs are quantumly technical, such as building quantum computers and developing quantum algorithms. Other jobs are classically technical. For example, web programmers and software engineers were needed to create the IBM Quantum Experience website, and these jobs require little or no prior experience with quantum computing. As another example, electrical engineers with experience with radio-frequency devices can easily pivot to helping to build superconducting qubits, where radio frequency interactions are very important. Still, other jobs are non-technical. Companies need accountants, marketers, experts in human resources, business administrators, and more who may not need any knowledge of quantum computing at all, although a general understanding may be useful. All this is to say that if you want a job related to quantum computing but do not have the quantum skills, yet, there are job opportunities that utilize non-quantum skills.

More universities are also hiring professors in quantum computing, recognizing the growth of the field. In 2017, the Division of Quantum Information was formed in the American Physical Society, placing it alongside well-established areas of physics like astrophysics, condensed matter physics, and particles and fields.

While many students are aware of industrial and academic jobs, often, students have little exposure to government careers. To ignore government jobs, however, is to ignore a large sector of the quantum computing ecosystem. For example, the U.S. Department of Defense is the largest employer of scientists and engineers in the United States, and many of these are civilian jobs in research laboratories. Increasingly, government laboratories are hiring people to investigate how quantum computers affect the missions of their organizations. Besides technical roles, experts in quantum computing are also needed for program management, policy, and advising roles to help the government prioritize quantum computing research and workforce development. Government jobs typically come with good non-salary benefits, including retirement pensions and work-life balance. There are also many jobs at national laboratories. Although national laboratories are funded by the government, they are managed by contractors, so employees at national laboratories are typically employees of the contractors and are not government employees. But, many of their jobs are similar in that they can be mission-focused.

If you want a quantumly technical job, you will likely want to study quantum computing, mathematics, and physics beyond this introductory textbook, and some suggestions for possible next steps are next.

8.2 Technical Next Steps

As stated in the preface and throughout this textbook, Nielsen and Chuang's textbook, *Quantum Computation and Quantum Information* is the standard advanced textbook and will dive deeply into many of the results that were out of the scope of this introductory textbook, such as proving the Solovay-Kitaev theorem about universal sets of quantum gates, and calculating the probability that the quantum phase estimation algorithm will yield the wrong answer. There are plenty of resources on the internet as well, including lecture notes from professors, video lectures, and tutorials.

A major concept that one should learn is the *mixed state*. In this entire textbook, the state of a qubit was $|0\rangle$, $|1\rangle$, or some superposition of $|0\rangle$ and $|1\rangle$. For all of these, the state can be known with certainty, even though the measurement outcome may be probabilistic. These states were visualized as points on the Bloch sphere, and they are called *pure states*. In contrast, if we are not sure if a qubit is in one pure state or another pure state, then the state itself and not just its outcome is probabilistic. These are called mixed states, and they can be visualized as a point *inside* the Bloch sphere, so in this context, it is actually a *Bloch ball*, which also contains the inside and not just the surface. While a pure state was written using vectors (with "kets" being column vectors and "bras" being row vectors), a mixed state is written using a matrix called a *density matrix*. Some of the topics that we covered in this textbook should actually be done in terms of mixed states, namely quantum error correction, the no-signaling principle, and aspects of entanglement. Again, Nielsen and Chuang go into detail about all this.

If you are a student, you may wonder what courses or majors to consider. Physics, computer science, mathematics, and engineering are all fine. If you are interested in quantum hardware, experimental physics or electrical engineering are good choices. If you are interested in the theoretical side of quantum computing and quantum algorithms, then theoretical physics, computer science, and mathematics are good choices. Personally, I work on quantum algorithms. My PhD was in theoretical physics, but my PhD advisor was a mathematician. Then, I did two postdoctoral research fellowships in computer science before landing a tenure-track job as a physics professor. So, my own story is a good illustration of the interplay between physics, mathematics, and computer science.

For students, a great way to learn quantum computing is to do research with a professor. Look around at your university to see if any professors work on quantum computing, and do not be afraid to look outside of your department. Remember my story, that I was a physics student who was advised by a math professor. If there are no professors at your university who work on quantum computing, see if any professors are interested in learning about quantum computing, and if you can do an independent study with them, where you read Nielsen and Chuang or some other educational resource and teach the professor what you have been learning. This way, if you apply for graduate school, there is a professor who can write you a letter of recommendation and explain that you have been self-learning quantum computing and even teaching them. Another way to gain research experience is to apply for summer internships and research fellowships. Many quantum computing companies, as well as government and national labs, host students for summer research. There is also the Research Experiences for Undergraduates (REU) program, and some of the universities may have quantum computing research projects for students.

Some people make broad statements like, "You don't need to know *so and so* to do quantum computing." For example, a common critique among some computer scientists is that you do not need to know Schrödinger's equation, the fundamental physics equation of quantum mechanics, to do quantum computing. In some sense, that is true, as this is literally the first time I have mentioned Schrödinger's equation in this textbook. But, that is because this textbook builds up to quantum circuits and algorithms. There are many other aspects of quantum computing where knowing Schrödinger's equation is necessary, such as for physical quantum hardware, for analog quantum algorithms like continuous-time quantum walks, and for many optimization algorithms like those based on quantum annealing or the quantum approximate optimization algorithm (QAOA). You may want to learn Schrödinger's equation yourself, depending on what aspects of quantum computing you wish to pursue. If you major in physics, you will certainly come across it in a Modern Physics course and in a Quantum Mechanics course. I bring this up to say there is no one right path to be come a quantum information scientist. If you want to take a traditional physics approach through Schrödinger's equation, that is fine. If you want to take an alternative approach, that is also fine. Just because your path does not look like someone else's does not mean it is the wrong path for you.

8.3 Questions

I regret that I do not have the capacity to respond to individual questions, nor do I have the expertise to answer most questions beyond my specific research area. So, if you have any questions, I suggest submitting them to the Quantum Computing Stack Exchange at

$$\texttt{https://quantumcomputing.stackexchange.com}$$

Many members of our community volunteer their expertise on the website to help others, including those who are newer to the field.

8.4 Parting Words

As we end our journey together, I again want to celebrate your completion of this textbook. You did it! I hope you will consider quantum computing as a potential career. If you do become a quantum information scientist, please let me know. I would be delighted to hear that I played a role in your journey. Also, I wrote this textbook for my students, that it might help them in their learning. By completing this textbook, you have, in some way, also become one of my students, and so this textbook is also dedicated to you.

Answers to Exercises

Exercises of Chapter 1

1.1 (a) $2^4 = 16$. (b) $2^5 = 32$.

1.2 (a) $6^4 = 1296$. (b) $6^5 = 7776$.

1.3 1.

1.4 (a) 5 coins. (b) 2 dice.

1.5 (a) 23. (b) 202.

1.6 (a) 101010. (b) 111101111.

1.7 (a) 15228. (b) 11111111. (c) FA = 250, 10 = 16, E4 = 228.

1.8

Binary (Two's Complement)	Decimal (Base 10)
000	0
001	1
010	2
011	3
100	-4
101	-3
110	-2
111	-1

1.9 Answer varies. See Table 1.1.

1.10 Quantum.

1.11 (a)   (b) NAND.

A B	Output
0 0	1
0 1	1
1 0	1
1 1	0

.

1.12 (a)   (b) NOR.

A B	Output
0 0	1
0 1	0
1 0	0
1 1	0

.

1.13 (a) On. (b). On. (c). On. (d) Off. (e) NAND.

1.14 (a) Off. (b). On. (c) On. (d) On. (e) OR.

1.15 (a) On. (b). Off. (c) Off. (d) Off. (e) NOR.

1.16 (a) Off. (b). On. (c) Off. (d) XOR.

1.17 (a) Answer varies. One example is the Intel 8086, introduced in 1978, which had 29,000 transistors.
(b) Answer varies. One example is the Apple M1, introduced in 2020, which had 16,000,000,000 transistors.

1.18 (a)   (b) 0. (c) 1.

A B	Output	
0 0	0	0
0 0	1	1
0 1	0	1
0 1	1	0
1 0	0	1
1 0	1	0
1 1	0	0
1 1	1	1

.

1.19

A B C	Output
0 0 0	1
0 0 1	1
0 1 0	0
0 1 1	1
1 0 0	0
1 0 1	1
1 1 0	0
1 1 1	1

.

1.20 (a) $2^{2^1} = 2^2 = 4$. (b) $2^{2^2} = 2^4 = 16$. (c) $2^{2^3} = 2^8 = 256$. (d) $2^{2^4} = 2^{16} = 65536$. (e) 2^{2^n}.

1.21 Answer varies. One answer is:

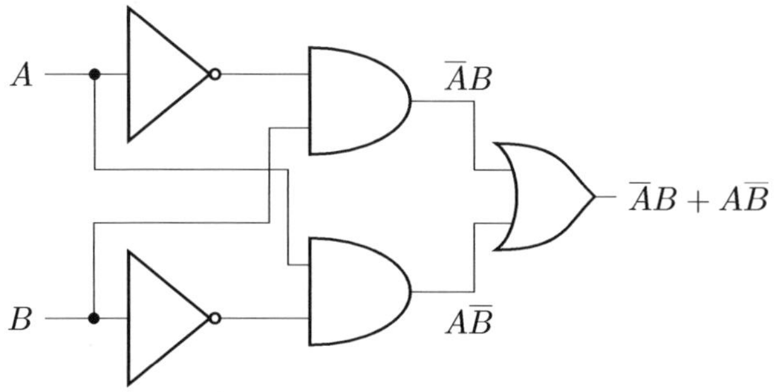

1.22 Answer varies. One answer is $\overline{A}\overline{B}C + \overline{A}B\overline{C} + A\overline{B}C + ABC$:

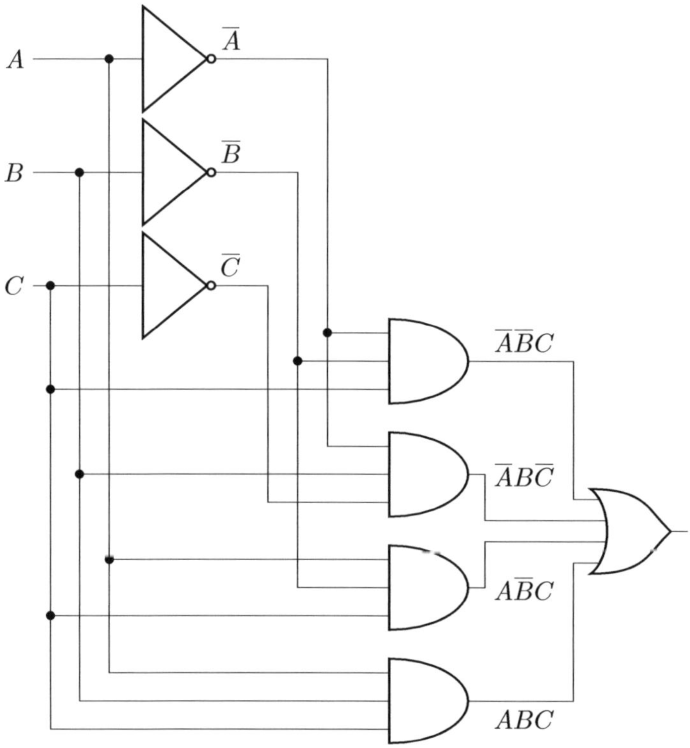

1.23 Answer varies. One answer is $\overline{A}B\overline{C} + A\overline{B}C = \overline{\overline{\overline{A}B\overline{C}}\,\overline{A\overline{B}C}}$:

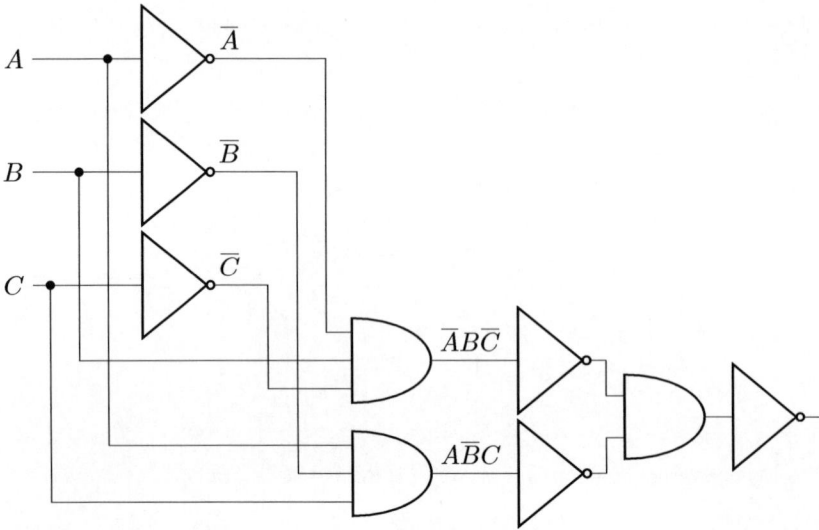

1.24 In the text, the OR gate was implemented using three NOT gates and one AND gate. Each NOT gate can be implemented using a single NAND gate, and the AND gate can be implemented by one NAND gate and one NOT gate. The last two NOT gates cancel out, however, yielding the following:

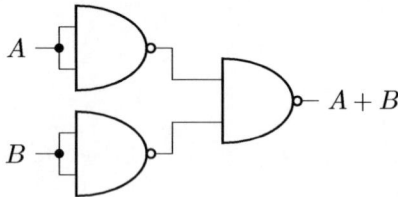

1.25 Start with $\{\text{NOT}, \text{AND}, \text{OR}\}$:

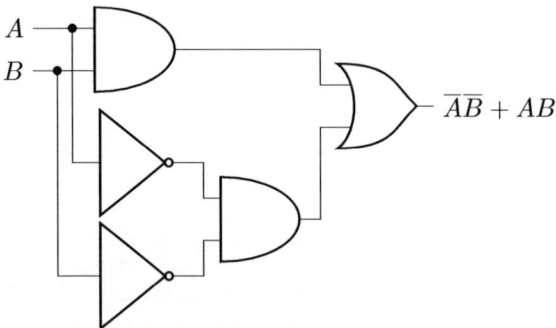

Then replace the gates with NANDs:

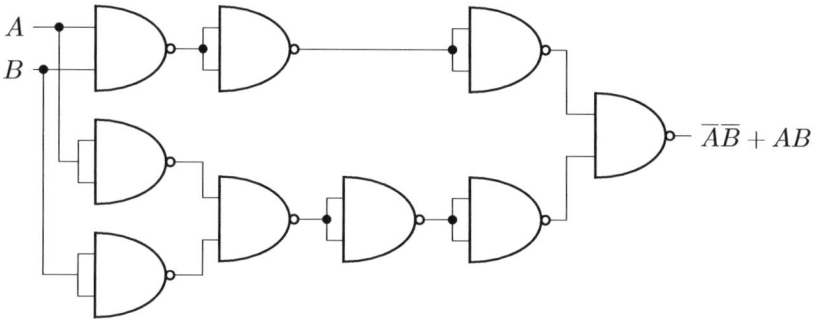

1.26

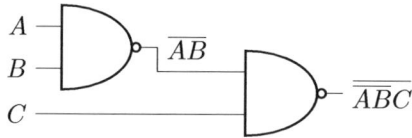

1.27

A B	$\bar{A}$ $\bar{B}$	$\bar{A}+\bar{B}$	$\overline{\bar{A}+\bar{B}}$
0 0	1 1	1	0
0 1	1 0	1	0
1 0	0 1	1	0
1 1	0 0	0	1

1.28 (a)

A	Output
0	1
1	0

(b)

A B	Output
0 0	0
0 1	1
1 0	1
1 1	1

1.29 The outputs are all 1. Makes sense because $B+\bar{B}=1$, and $A+1=1$.

1.30 Changing the OR to an XOR does not change the logic, so the truth table stays the same.

1.31 10000 or 16.

1.32 11100110.

1.33 10100 or 20.

1.34 $A+B$.

1.35 $A+\bar{B}+C$.

1.36 $ABC+\bar{A}BC+AB\bar{C}=B(A+C)$.

1.37 (a) $\bar{A}B\bar{C}+\bar{A}BC+A\bar{B}\bar{C}+AB\bar{C}$. (b) $\bar{A}B+A\bar{C}$.

1.38 (a) Irreversible. (b) Irreversible. (c) Irreversible. (d) Irreversible.

1.39 (a) Irreversible. (b) Reversible.

1.40 (a)   (b) Reversible since the outputs are unique.

A B C	A' B' C'
0 0 0	0 0 0
0 0 1	0 0 1
0 1 0	0 1 0
0 1 1	0 1 1 .
1 0 0	1 0 0
1 0 1	1 1 0
1 1 0	1 0 1
1 1 1	1 1 1

1.41 (a)   (b) De Morgan's Law. (c) NOR. (d) OR. (e) Start with

A B C	A B	$\overline{A}\,\overline{B} \oplus C$
0 0 0	0 0	1
0 0 1	0 0	0
0 1 0	0 1	0
0 1 1	0 1	1
1 0 0	1 0	0
1 0 1	1 0	1
1 1 0	1 1	0
1 1 1	1 1	1

a Toffoli gate and add a NOT gate before the first two inputs and after the first two outputs.

1.42 (a) Reversible. (b) Irreversible. A reversible version is:

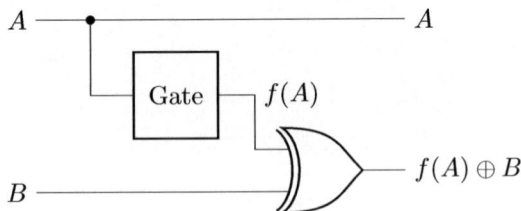

1.43 The truth table is

A B	$A \oplus B$
0 0	0
0 1	1 .
1 0	1
1 1	0

It is irreversible. A reversible version is:

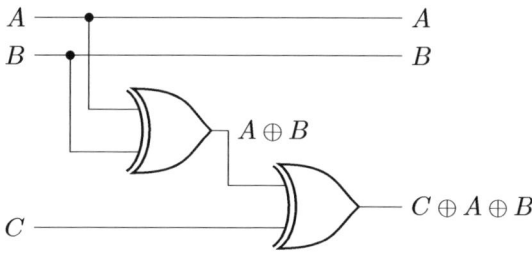

A B C	A B	A⊕B⊕C
0 0 0	0 0	0
0 0 1	0 0	1
0 1 0	0 1	1
0 1 1	0 1	0
1 0 0	1 0	1
1 0 1	1 0	0
1 1 0	1 1	0
1 1 1	1 1	1

1.44 (a) The truth table is   It is reversible.

A B	A⊕B	B
0 0	0	0
0 1	1	1
1 0	1	0
1 1	0	1

(b) The truth table is

A B	A⊕B	AB
0 0	0	0
0 1	1	0
1 0	1	0
1 1	0	1

It is irreversible. A reversible version is

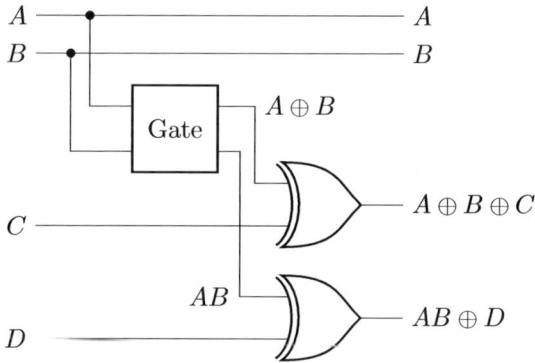

1.45

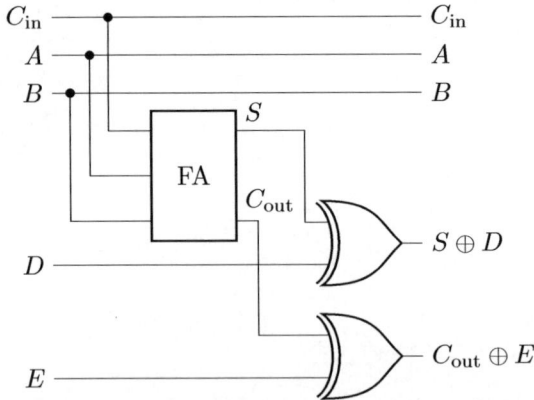

1.46 (a) $2^{13} = 8192$. (b) spontaneously flip, Radioactive atoms, presence, absense, single event upset. (c) miniaturized. (d) increased, greater, sky (e) cosmic rays, particles, black holes. (f) cascade, transistor. (g) error correction code. (h) month, cosmic rays. (i) 10 to 30. (j) 161. (k) flash, every star.

1.47 (a) Even. (b) No. (c) Yes. The parity of the first seven bits doesn't match the parity bit. (d) No. If two bits flipped, the parity would be unchanged.

1.48 (a) Yes, the middle bit has flipped. (b) Yes, the left bit has flipped. (c) 0.1040. Decrease, since $0.1040 < 0.2$. (d) 0.7840. Increase, since $0.78404 > 0.7$.

1.49 (a) Yes, b_1 was flipped. (b) Yes, b_2 and b_1 were flipped. (c) $10p^3(1-p)^2 + 5p^4(1-p) + p^5$. (d) $p < 1/2$. (e) 0.00856, decreases. (f) For 3-bit code, the probability of an uncorrectable error is 0.028, which is more likely than the 5-bit code's 0.00856.

1.50 (a) $f(100)$. (b) $g(500)$. (c) They are equal when $n = 477$, after which $g(n)$ is greater than $f(n)$. (d) true, true, false, false, false.

1.51 Possibilities are (a) iii or v, (b) i or v, (c) ii or v, (d) v, (e) i or iv. Thus, the only correct answer is (a) iii, (b) i, (c) ii, (d) v, (e) iv.

1.52 (a) Efficient. (b) Efficient. (c) Efficient. (d) Inefficient. (e) Inefficient. (f) Inefficient.

1.53 (a) Bounded-Error Probabilistic Polynomial-Time. (b) "As the class of feasible problems for a computer with access to a genuine random-number source."

1.54 Many possible answers, including factoring, graph isomorphism, $n \times n$ Sudoku, traveling salesman, Hamiltonian path, and bin packing.

1.55 (a) Yang–Mills and Mass Gap, Riemann Hypothesis, P vs NP Problem, Navier–Stokes Equation, Hodge Conjecture, Poincaré Conjecture, and Birch and Swinnerton-Dyer Conjecture. Only the Poincaré Conjecture is solved. (b) Stephen Cook and Leonid Levin in 1971.

1.56 Answers vary.

1.57 Answers vary.

1.58 (a) ▷ 0 0 1. (b) ▷ 0 1 1. (c) ▷ 1 0 1. (d) ▷ 1 1 0. (e) NAND. (f) Calculates the NAND of all the bits.

1.59 Answers may vary. Here is one:

Current State	Current Tape	Write to Tape	Move	Update State
q_s	▷	▷	→	q_1
q_1	0	0	→	q_1
q_1	1	1	→	q_2
q_2	0	0	→	q_2
q_2	1	1	→	q_1
q_1		0	•	q_h
q_2		1	•	q_h

1.60 (a) Run forever. (b) Halt. (c) By returning true, H is saying that Z halts. But then Z responds to this by running forever. Z can't both halt and run forever. That's a contradiction. (d) By returning false, H is saying that Z runs forever. But then Z responds to this by halting. Z can't both run forever and halt. That's a contradiction.

1.61 (a) complete, consistent, decidable. (b) programs, themselves. (c) Can every even number greater than 2 be written as the sum of two primes? (d) Runs forever. (e) Halts. (f) Runs forever. Yes, it's a contradiction. (g) Runs forever. Yes, it's a contradiction. (h) undecidable, can't solve.

1.62 Answers vary.

1.63 (a) a million times. (b) all known, quantum supremacy.

1.64 (a) Simulating quantum physics. (b) Hardest. (c) Some.

Exercises of Chapter 2

2.1 (a) 1. (b) 1. (c) 0. (d) +. (e) 0. (f) $-i$. (g) 0. (h) 0.

2.2 (a) $-i$. (b) i. (c) $-i$. (d) $-i$. (e) $-$. (f) 0. (g) i. (h) 0 or 1 depending on die roll.

2.3 (a) The north pole. (b) The south pole. (c) The equator. (d) The northern hemisphere. (e) The southern hemisphere.

2.4 (a) 1. (b) 2. (c)

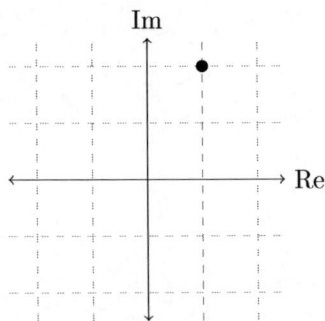

(d) $\sqrt{5}e^{i\tan^{-1}(2)} = \sqrt{5}e^{i(1.107)} = \sqrt{5}e^{i63.4°}$. (e) $1-2i$ or $\sqrt{5}e^{-i(1.107)}$. (f) $\sqrt{5}$. (g) 5.

2.5 (a) -3. (b) -1. (c)

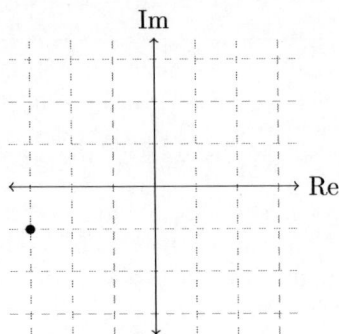

(d) $\sqrt{10}e^{i(\tan^{-1}(1/3)+\pi)} = \sqrt{10}e^{i(0.32+\pi)} = \sqrt{10}e^{i3.46}$ or $\sqrt{10}e^{i(18.4°+180°)} = \sqrt{10}e^{i198.4°}$. (e) $-3+i$ or $\sqrt{10}e^{-i3.46}$. (f) $\sqrt{10}$. (g) 10.

2.6 (a) 4/9. (b) 5/9.

2.7 (a) 1. (b) 0.

2.8 $2/\sqrt{5}e^{i\theta}$ for any real θ.

2.9 (a) $A = e^{i\theta}/\sqrt{13}$ for any real θ. (b) 4/13. (c) 9/13.

2.10 (a) $|0\rangle$ with probability 1/4 or $|1\rangle$ with probability 3/4. (b) $\dfrac{1-\sqrt{3}}{2\sqrt{2}}|+\rangle + \dfrac{1+\sqrt{3}}{2\sqrt{2}}|-\rangle$. (c) $|+\rangle$ with probability $(2-\sqrt{3})/4 \approx 0.07$ or $|-\rangle$ with probability $(2+\sqrt{3})/4 \approx 0.93$.

2.11 (a) $\dfrac{\sqrt{3}(1+i)}{4}|a\rangle - \dfrac{3+i}{4}|b\rangle$. (b) $|a\rangle$ with probability 3/8 or $|b\rangle$ with probability 5/8.

2.12 (a) 1/2. (b) 1/2.

2.13 (a) No, they differ by a global phase, which is irrelevant. They are the same quantum state. (b) Yes. Measuring in the X-basis distinguishes them. (c) No, they differ by a global phase, which is irrelevant. They are the same quantum state.

2.14 (a) $(\theta, \phi) = (90°, 90°) = (\pi/2, \pi/2)$. (b)

$$\frac{1}{\sqrt{2}}(|0\rangle + i|1\rangle)$$

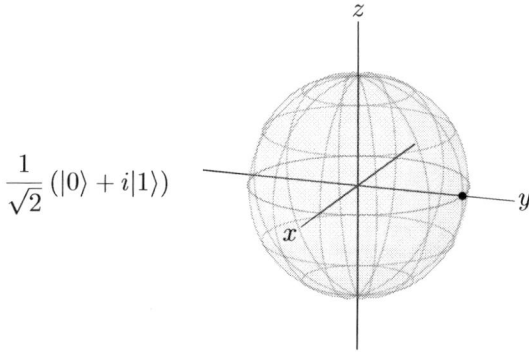

2.15 (a) $(\theta, \phi) = (120°, 45°) = (2\pi/3, \pi/4)$. (b)

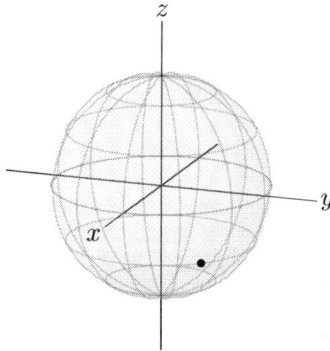

2.16 $(\theta_a, \phi_a) = (\pi/3, \pi/2)$ and $(\theta_b, \phi_b) = (2\pi/3, 3\pi/2)$, so $\theta_b = \pi - \theta_a$ and $\phi_b = \phi_a + \pi$.

2.17 (a) $(x, y, z) = (0, 1, 0)$. (b) $(x, y, z) = (\sqrt{3}/2\sqrt{2}, \sqrt{3}/2\sqrt{2}, -1/2)$.

2.18 (a) polarization, decoherence. (b) electric fields. (c) laser beams. (d) molecule, radio-frequency, one-qubit. (e) discrete energy levels, atomic nucleus. (f) Quantum information, hyperfine. (g) spin, microwave, optical. (h) charge, flux, phase.

2.19 Answers vary.

2.20 Answers vary.

2.21 Answers vary. One is the Josephson junction is used to create a superconducting flux qubit, which uses currect as its qubit. Clockwise current corresponds to $|0\rangle$, and counterclockwise current corresponds to $|1\rangle$.

2.22 (a) $(\alpha + \beta)|0\rangle + (\alpha - \beta)|1\rangle$. (b) No, the total probability is 2, which is not possible.

2.23 (a) $\left(\frac{\sqrt{3}}{2}\alpha + \frac{\sqrt{3}+i}{4}\beta\right)|0\rangle + \left(\frac{\sqrt{3}+i}{4}\alpha + \frac{-\sqrt{3}-3i}{4}\beta\right)|1\rangle$. (b) Yes, the total probability is 1.

2.24 (a) Yes, reversible. (b) No, not reversible.

2.25 (a) Yes, reversible. (b) No, not reversible.

2.26 $ZX(\alpha|0\rangle + \beta|1\rangle) = Z(\beta|0\rangle + \alpha|1\rangle) = \beta|0\rangle - \alpha|1\rangle$

2.27 (a) $XZXZ|0\rangle = -|0\rangle$, $XZXZ|1\rangle = -|1\rangle$. (b) $ZXZX|0\rangle = -|0\rangle$, $ZXZX|1\rangle = -|1\rangle$.

2.28 (a) $\alpha|0\rangle + \beta e^{i\theta}|1\rangle$. (b) $|\alpha|^2 + |\beta e^{i\theta}|^2 = |\alpha|^2 + |\beta|^2 = 1$.

2.29 (a) $\frac{\alpha+\beta}{\sqrt{2}}|0\rangle + \frac{\alpha-\beta}{\sqrt{2}}|1\rangle$. (b) $\left|\frac{\alpha+\beta}{\sqrt{2}}\right|^2 + \left|\frac{\alpha-\beta}{\sqrt{2}}\right|^2 = |\alpha|^2 + |\beta|^2 = 1$.

2.30 Answers vary.

2.31 $YH|0\rangle = Y|+\rangle = -i|-\rangle$.

2.32 $HXH|0\rangle = Z|0\rangle = |0\rangle$ and $HXH|1\rangle = Z|1\rangle = -|1\rangle$.

2.33 (a) $\frac{1}{2\sqrt{2}}\left[(1-i+2e^{i\pi/4})|0\rangle + (1+i)|1\rangle\right]$ or $\frac{1}{2\sqrt{2}}\left[\left(1+\sqrt{2}-(1-\sqrt{2})i\right)|0\rangle + (1+i)|1\rangle\right]$. (b) 3/4 and 1/4.

2.34 (a) $(0,0,1)$. (b) $e^{i\gamma}\left[\cos\left(\frac{\pi}{8}\right)I - i\sin\left(\frac{\pi}{8}\right)Z\right]$. (c) $e^{i\gamma}e^{-i\pi/8}|0\rangle$. (d) $e^{i\gamma}e^{i\pi/8}|1\rangle$. (e) If $\gamma = \pi/8$, get $U|0\rangle = |0\rangle$ and $U|1\rangle = e^{i\pi/4}|1\rangle$, which is the T gate.

2.35 (a)   (b)

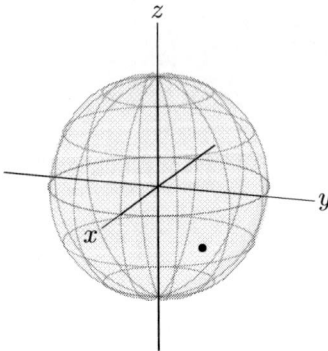
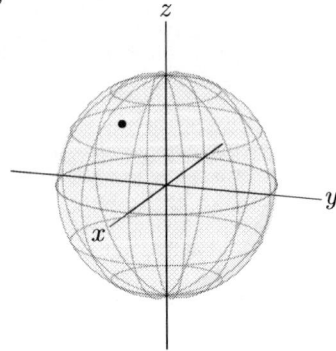

(c) $(1/\sqrt{3}, 1/\sqrt{3}, 1/\sqrt{3})$. (d) $-ie^{i\gamma}\frac{1}{\sqrt{3}}(X+Y+Z)$. (e) $-ie^{i\gamma}\frac{1}{\sqrt{3}}\left[|0\rangle + (1+i)|1\rangle\right]$. (f) $-ie^{i\gamma}\frac{1}{\sqrt{3}}\left[(1-i)|0\rangle - |1\rangle\right]$.

2.36 (a,b)

(c) 85.4% probability of getting $|0\rangle$, and 14.6% probability of getting $|1\rangle$.

Exercises of Chapter 3

3.1 $\begin{pmatrix} \frac{1}{2} \\ -\frac{\sqrt{3}}{2} \end{pmatrix}$.

3.2 $|0\rangle$ with probability $3/4$ and $|1\rangle$ with probability $1/4$.

3.3 (a) $\frac{\sqrt{3}}{2}\langle 0| + \frac{1}{2}\langle 1|$. (b) $\left(\frac{\sqrt{3}}{2} \ \frac{1}{2} \right)$. (c) $\frac{2}{3}\langle 0| + \frac{1+2i}{3}\langle 1|$. (d) $\left(\frac{2}{3} \ \frac{1+2i}{3} \right)$.

3.4 (a) $(3 + 2\sqrt{15} - i\sqrt{3})/16$. (b) $(3 + 2\sqrt{15} + i\sqrt{3})/16$. (c) Complex conjugates.

3.5 (a) $13|A|^2$. (b) $A = 1/\sqrt{13}$.

3.6 (a) $\langle +|-\rangle = \begin{pmatrix} 1 & 0 \end{pmatrix} \begin{pmatrix} 0 \\ 1 \end{pmatrix} = 0$, so orthogonal.

(b) $\langle 0|+\rangle = 1/\sqrt{2} \neq 0$, so not orthogonal.
(c) The inner product is 0, so orthogonal.

3.7 (a) $x = (-3 + i\sqrt{3})/8$. (b) $x = e^{i\theta}\sqrt{15}/4$. (c) none.

3.8

$$\begin{aligned} \langle a|b\rangle &= \cos(\theta_a/2)\cos(\theta_b/2) + e^{i(\theta_b - \theta_a)}\sin(\theta_a/2)\sin(\theta_b/2) \\ &= \cos(\theta_a/2)\cos(\theta_b/2) - \sin(\theta_a/2)\sin(\theta_b/2) \\ &= \cos((\theta_a + \theta_b)/2) = \cos(\pi/2) = 0. \end{aligned}$$

3.9 (a) $(\sqrt{3} - i)/2\sqrt{2}$. (b) $(\sqrt{3} + i)/2\sqrt{2}$. (c) $|i\rangle$ with probability $1/2$, $|-i\rangle$ with probability $1/2$. (d) $(3 - i)/4$. (e) $\sqrt{3}(1 - i)/4$. (f) $|a\rangle$ with probability $5/8$, $|b\rangle$ with probability $3/8$.

3.10 (a) $|0\rangle$ with probability $3/4$ and $|1\rangle$ with probability $1/4$. (b) $|+\rangle$ with probability $1/8$ and $|-\rangle$ with probability $7/8$. (c) $|i\rangle$ with probability $(4 + \sqrt{3})/8 \approx 0.717$, $|-i\rangle$ with probability $(4 - \sqrt{3})/8 = 0.283$.

3.11 (a) $\frac{1-i}{\sqrt{3}}|+\rangle - \frac{i}{\sqrt{3}}|-\rangle$. (b) $\frac{1-3i}{2\sqrt{3}}|i\rangle + \frac{1-i}{2\sqrt{3}}|-i\rangle$.

3.12 (a) $U = \frac{1}{\sqrt{2}}\begin{pmatrix} 1 & -i \\ -i & 1 \end{pmatrix}$. (b) $\frac{1}{\sqrt{2}}\begin{pmatrix} \alpha - i\beta \\ -i\alpha + \beta \end{pmatrix}$. (c) Yes, the total probability is
$\left|\frac{\alpha - i\beta}{\sqrt{2}}\right|^2 + \left|\frac{-i\alpha + \beta}{\sqrt{2}}\right|^2 = 1$.

3.13 (a) $U = \frac{1}{2\sqrt{3}}\begin{pmatrix} 3+i & 1-i \\ -(1+i) & 3-i \end{pmatrix}$. (b) See `https://bit.ly/3qR5HnR`. $|0\rangle$ with probability 83.3%, $|1\rangle$ with probability 16.7%.

3.14 $\frac{1}{\sqrt{2}}\begin{pmatrix} 1 & -1 \\ 1 & 1 \end{pmatrix}$.

3.15

$$HTU|0\rangle = \frac{1}{\sqrt{2}} \begin{pmatrix} 1 & 1 \\ 1 & -1 \end{pmatrix} \begin{pmatrix} 1 & 0 \\ 0 & e^{i\pi/4} \end{pmatrix} \frac{1}{2} \begin{pmatrix} \sqrt{2}-i & 1 \\ -1 & \sqrt{2}+i \end{pmatrix} \begin{pmatrix} 1 \\ 0 \end{pmatrix}$$

$$= \frac{1}{2\sqrt{2}} \begin{pmatrix} \sqrt{2}-i-e^{i\pi/4} \\ \sqrt{2}-i+e^{i\pi/4} \end{pmatrix}.$$

3.16 (a) $XY|0\rangle = i|0\rangle$, $iZ|0\rangle = i|0\rangle$. $XY|1\rangle = -i|1\rangle$, $iZ|1\rangle = -i|1\rangle$. (b)

$$XY = \begin{pmatrix} 1 & 0 \\ 0 & 1 \end{pmatrix} \begin{pmatrix} 0 & -i \\ i & 0 \end{pmatrix} = \begin{pmatrix} i & 0 \\ 0 & -i \end{pmatrix}, \quad iZ = i \begin{pmatrix} 1 & 0 \\ 0 & -1 \end{pmatrix} = \begin{pmatrix} i & 0 \\ 0 & -i \end{pmatrix}.$$

3.17 $U^\dagger U = \begin{pmatrix} 1 & i \\ -i & 1 \end{pmatrix} \neq I$, so no.

3.18 $U^\dagger U = I$, so yes. $U|0\rangle = |i\rangle$, and $U|1\rangle = |-i\rangle$.

3.19 (a)

$$U^{-1} = U^\dagger = \begin{pmatrix} \frac{1+\sqrt{3}}{2\sqrt{2}} - i\frac{1-\sqrt{3}}{2\sqrt{6}} & \frac{-1+\sqrt{3}}{2\sqrt{6}} - i\frac{1-\sqrt{3}}{2\sqrt{6}} \\ \frac{1-\sqrt{3}}{2\sqrt{6}} - i\frac{1-\sqrt{3}}{2\sqrt{6}} & \frac{1+\sqrt{3}}{2\sqrt{2}} - i\frac{-1+\sqrt{3}}{2\sqrt{6}} \end{pmatrix}$$

(b) $|\psi\rangle = \frac{\sqrt{3}}{2}|0\rangle + \frac{1}{2}|1\rangle$.

3.20 (a) $\frac{1}{2} \begin{pmatrix} 1 & -1 \\ i & -i \end{pmatrix}$. (b) No, not unitary.

3.21 (a) $\frac{1}{\sqrt{2}} \begin{pmatrix} 1 & 1 \\ 1 & -1 \end{pmatrix}$. (b) Yes, it is unitary.

3.22

$$\frac{1}{\sqrt{2}} \begin{pmatrix} 1 \\ 1 \end{pmatrix} \frac{1}{\sqrt{2}} (1\ 1) + \frac{1}{\sqrt{2}} \begin{pmatrix} 1 \\ -1 \end{pmatrix} \frac{1}{\sqrt{2}} (1\ -1) = \begin{pmatrix} 1 & 0 \\ 0 & 1 \end{pmatrix}.$$

3.23

$$\begin{pmatrix} 1 \\ 0 \end{pmatrix} (1\ 0) + \frac{1}{\sqrt{2}} \begin{pmatrix} 1 \\ 1 \end{pmatrix} \frac{1}{\sqrt{2}} (1\ 1) = \frac{1}{2} \begin{pmatrix} 3 & 1 \\ 1 & 1 \end{pmatrix}.$$

Exercises of Chapter 4

4.1 (a) When the other player is on ONE. (b) To planet Phi Minus. (c) When the blue player uses an H engine card.

4.2 (a) 5. (b) Conceptual. (c) 50-60%. (d) Entanglement.

4.3 (a) 0. (b) $-1/2$. (c) 0.

4.4 $|1\rangle \otimes |1\rangle \otimes |0\rangle = \begin{pmatrix} 0 \\ 1 \end{pmatrix} \otimes \begin{pmatrix} 0 \\ 1 \end{pmatrix} \otimes \begin{pmatrix} 1 \\ 0 \end{pmatrix}.$

4.5 (a) $|\psi\rangle = \begin{pmatrix} 1/2 \\ 0 \\ i/\sqrt{2} \\ (\sqrt{3}+i)/4 \end{pmatrix}$. (b) $\langle\psi| = \left(1/2 \ \ 0 \ -i/\sqrt{2} \ \ (\sqrt{3}-i)/4\right)$.

4.6

$$\begin{pmatrix} 1 \\ 0 \\ 0 \\ 0 \end{pmatrix}(1\ 0\ 0\ 0) + \begin{pmatrix} 0 \\ 1 \\ 0 \\ 0 \end{pmatrix}(0\ 1\ 0\ 0) + \begin{pmatrix} 0 \\ 0 \\ 1 \\ 0 \end{pmatrix}(0\ 0\ 1\ 0) + \begin{pmatrix} 0 \\ 0 \\ 0 \\ 1 \end{pmatrix}(0\ 0\ 0\ 1)$$

$$= \begin{pmatrix} 1\ 0\ 0\ 0 \\ 0\ 1\ 0\ 0 \\ 0\ 0\ 1\ 0 \\ 0\ 0\ 0\ 1 \end{pmatrix}.$$

4.7 $|00\rangle$ with probability $1/10$, $|01\rangle$ with probability $1/2$, $|10\rangle$ with probability $1/10$, or $|11\rangle$ with probability $3/10$.

4.8 $A = 2/\sqrt{17}$.

4.9 $\frac{1}{\sqrt{5}}|00\rangle + \frac{2}{\sqrt{5}}|01\rangle$ with probability $5/16$ or $\frac{2\sqrt{2}}{\sqrt{11}}|10\rangle + \sqrt{\frac{3}{11}}|11\rangle$ with probability $11/16$.

4.10 $(|000\rangle + \sqrt{6}|010\rangle)/\sqrt{7}$ with probability $7/36$, $(\sqrt{2}|001\rangle + 3|011\rangle)/\sqrt{11}$ with probability $11/36$, $(|100\rangle + |110\rangle)/\sqrt{2}$ with probability $1/18$, or $(|101\rangle + \sqrt{3}|111\rangle)/2$ with probability $4/9$.

4.11 (a) Entangled state. (b) Product state. $|1\rangle \otimes \frac{1}{\sqrt{2}}(|0\rangle + i|1\rangle) = |1\rangle \otimes |i\rangle$.

4.12 (a) Product state. $\left(\frac{\sqrt{3}}{2}|0\rangle + \frac{1}{2}|1\rangle\right) \otimes \left(\frac{\sqrt{3}}{2}|0\rangle - \frac{1}{2}|1\rangle\right)$. (b) Entangled state.

4.13 (a) $(X \otimes I)|\Psi^+\rangle = (I \otimes X)|\Psi^+\rangle = |\Phi^+\rangle$.
(b) $(X \otimes I)|\Phi^+\rangle = (I \otimes X)|\Phi^+\rangle = |\Psi^+\rangle$.
(c) $(X \otimes I)|\Psi^-\rangle = -|\Phi^-\rangle \equiv |\Phi^-\rangle$, $(I \otimes X)|\Psi^-\rangle = |\Phi^-\rangle$.
(d) $(X \otimes I)|\Phi^-\rangle = -|\Psi^-\rangle \equiv |\Phi^-\rangle$, $(I \otimes X)|\Phi^-\rangle = |\Psi^-\rangle$.

4.14 (a) $\frac{1}{\sqrt{2}}\begin{pmatrix} 0\ 1\ 0\ \ 1 \\ 1\ 0\ 1\ \ 0 \\ 0\ 1\ 0\ -1 \\ 1\ 0\ -1\ 0 \end{pmatrix}$. (b) $\frac{2+\sqrt{3}}{4\sqrt{2}}|00\rangle + \frac{4+\sqrt{2}}{8}|01\rangle + \frac{2-\sqrt{3}}{4\sqrt{2}} + \frac{\sqrt{2}-4}{8}|11\rangle$.

4.15 (a) $\begin{pmatrix} 0\ 0\ 1\ 0 \\ 0\ 0\ 0\ 1 \\ 0\ 1\ 0\ 0 \\ 1\ 0\ 0\ 0 \end{pmatrix}$. (b) $\begin{pmatrix} 0\ 1\ 0\ 0 \\ 1\ 0\ 0\ 0 \\ 0\ 0\ 1\ 0 \\ 0\ 0\ 0\ 1 \end{pmatrix}$. (c) $\begin{pmatrix} 1\ 0\ 0\ \ 0 \\ 0\ 1\ 0\ \ 0 \\ 0\ 0\ 0\ -1 \\ 0\ 0\ -1\ 0 \end{pmatrix}$. (d) $\begin{pmatrix} 1\ \ 0\ \ 0\ \ 0 \\ 0\ -1\ 0\ \ 0 \\ 0\ \ 0\ 0\ -1 \\ 0\ \ 0\ 1\ \ 0 \end{pmatrix}$.

4.16 (a)   (b) It is the same.

A B C	A′ B′ C′
0 0 0	0 0 0
0 0 1	0 0 1
0 1 0	0 1 1
0 1 1	0 1 0 .
1 0 0	1 0 1
1 0 1	1 0 0
1 1 0	1 1 0
1 1 1	1 1 1

4.17 As matrices, both circuits are equal to $\begin{pmatrix} 0 & 1 & 0 & 0 \\ 1 & 0 & 0 & 0 \\ 0 & 0 & 1 & 0 \\ 0 & 0 & 0 & 1 \end{pmatrix}$.

4.18 $\text{CNOT}|+\rangle|-\rangle = |-\rangle|-\rangle$, $\text{CNOT}|-\rangle|+\rangle = |-\rangle|+\rangle$, $\text{CNOT}|-\rangle|-\rangle = |+\rangle|-\rangle$.

4.19

$$\frac{1}{\sqrt{2}}\begin{pmatrix} 1 \\ 0 \\ 0 \\ 1 \end{pmatrix}\frac{1}{\sqrt{2}}(1\ 0\ 0\ 1) + \frac{1}{\sqrt{2}}\begin{pmatrix} 1 \\ 0 \\ 0 \\ -1 \end{pmatrix}\frac{1}{\sqrt{2}}(1\ 0\ 0\ -1) + \frac{1}{\sqrt{2}}\begin{pmatrix} 0 \\ 1 \\ 1 \\ 0 \end{pmatrix}\frac{1}{\sqrt{2}}(0\ 1\ 1\ 0)$$

$$+ \frac{1}{\sqrt{2}}\begin{pmatrix} 0 \\ 1 \\ -1 \\ 0 \end{pmatrix}\frac{1}{\sqrt{2}}(0\ 1\ -1\ 0) = \begin{pmatrix} 1 & 0 & 0 & 0 \\ 0 & 1 & 0 & 0 \\ 0 & 0 & 1 & 0 \\ 0 & 0 & 0 & 1 \end{pmatrix}.$$

4.20 $\text{CZ} = \begin{pmatrix} 1 & 0 & 0 & 0 \\ 0 & 1 & 0 & 0 \\ 0 & 0 & 1 & 0 \\ 0 & 0 & 0 & -1 \end{pmatrix}$.

4.21 (a) $\text{SWAP}|\omega_0\rangle = |\omega_3\rangle$. (b) $(X \otimes I)|\omega_1\rangle = |\omega_3\rangle$. (c) $\text{CNOT}_{01}|\omega_2\rangle = |\omega_0\rangle$. (d) $\text{CNOT}|\omega_3\rangle = |\omega_2\rangle$.

4.22 (a) $\text{MS} = \frac{1}{\sqrt{2}}\begin{pmatrix} 1 & 0 & 0 & i \\ 0 & 1 & -i & 0 \\ 0 & -i & 1 & 0 \\ i & 0 & 0 & 1 \end{pmatrix}$. (b) $\text{MS}^8 = I$.

4.23
$$
\begin{pmatrix}
1 & 0 & 0 & 0 & 0 & 0 & 0 & 0 \\
0 & 1 & 0 & 0 & 0 & 0 & 0 & 0 \\
0 & 0 & 1 & 0 & 0 & 0 & 0 & 0 \\
0 & 0 & 0 & 1 & 0 & 0 & 0 & 0 \\
0 & 0 & 0 & 0 & 1 & 0 & 0 & 0 \\
0 & 0 & 0 & 0 & 0 & 1 & 0 & 0 \\
0 & 0 & 0 & 0 & 0 & 0 & 0 & 1 \\
0 & 0 & 0 & 0 & 0 & 0 & 1 & 0
\end{pmatrix}.
$$

4.24 (a) $|000\rangle \to |001\rangle$, $|001\rangle \to |000\rangle$, and everything else stays the same.

(b)
$$
\begin{pmatrix}
0 & 1 & 0 & 0 & 0 & 0 & 0 & 0 \\
1 & 0 & 0 & 0 & 0 & 0 & 0 & 0 \\
0 & 0 & 1 & 0 & 0 & 0 & 0 & 0 \\
0 & 0 & 0 & 1 & 0 & 0 & 0 & 0 \\
0 & 0 & 0 & 0 & 1 & 0 & 0 & 0 \\
0 & 0 & 0 & 0 & 0 & 1 & 0 & 0 \\
0 & 0 & 0 & 0 & 0 & 0 & 1 & 0 \\
0 & 0 & 0 & 0 & 0 & 0 & 0 & 1
\end{pmatrix}.
$$

4.25 (a) Yes, since they are orthogonal. (b) Yes, since they are orthogonal. (c) No, since they are not orthogonal.

4.26 See `https://bit.ly/30LBtIi`:

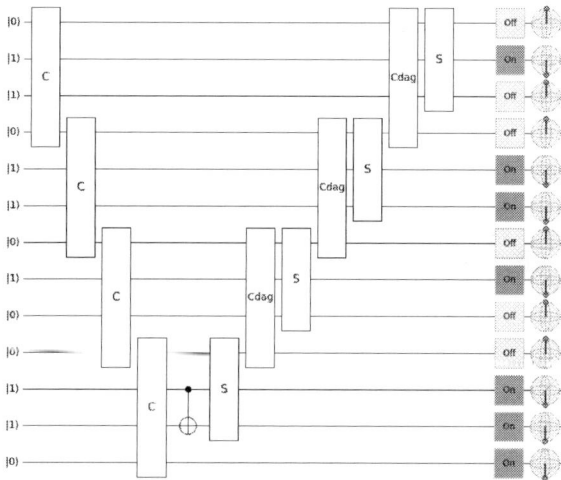

4.27 See `https://bit.ly/30BByOi`:

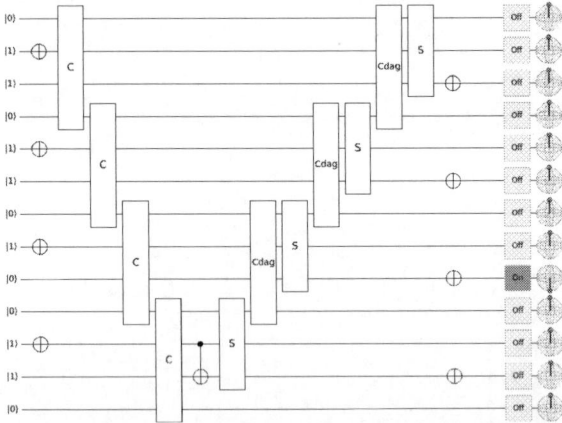

4.28 (a) After all the carries, but before the CNOT, the bottom four qubits are c_3', a_3, $a_3 \oplus b_3$, and s_4. Taking the CNOT of c_3' and $a_3 \oplus b_3$ changes the target to $s_3 = a_3 \oplus b_3 \oplus c_3'$.

(b) The number of C gates is n, and the number of $C^\dagger$ gates is $(n-1)$. Both C and $C^\dagger$ each have two Toffoli gates, so there is a total of $2n + 2(n-1) = 4n - 2$ Toffoli gates. The C and $C^\dagger$ gates each have one CNOT gate, and the $n-1$ S gates each have two CNOT gates, plus the extra CNOT, for a total of $n + (n-1) + 2(n-1) + 1 = 4n - 2$ CNOT gates.

4.29 The final state should be $|s\rangle|b\rangle = |1010\rangle|0011\rangle$. The circuit can be viewed in Quirk at `https://bit.ly/3omgh1U`, and a picture is below:

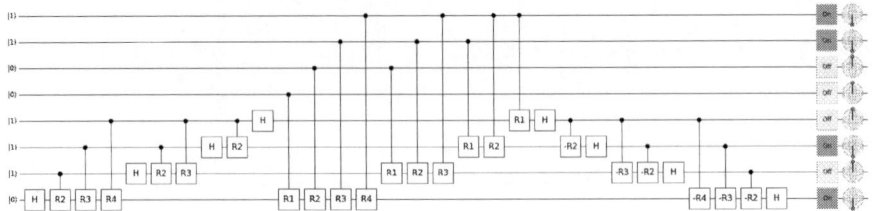

4.30 (a) 14 Toffoli gates and 16 CNOT gates. (b) 30 Toffoli gates and 32 CNOT gates.

4.31 $3n + 1$.

4.32 (a) Tom Wong, the author of the textbook. (b) hands, quantum, some, no faster.

4.33 (a) Missing complex amplitudes.

(b) Cannot generate entanglement (no 2-qubit gates).

(c) Cannot generate entanglement. SWAP is 2-qubit, but cannot generate entanglement.

4.34 Possible answers are replacing CNOT with Toffoli, H with $R_{\pi/8}$, or S with T.

4.35

$$|\psi 00\rangle = \alpha|000\rangle + \beta|100\rangle \xrightarrow{\text{CNOT}_{2,1}} \alpha|000\rangle + \beta|110\rangle \xrightarrow{\text{CNOT}_{2,0}} \alpha|000\rangle + \beta|111\rangle.$$

4.36 (a) Nothing. (b) Apply X to the rightmost qubit. (c) Apply X to the leftmost qubit. (d) Apply X to the middle qubit.

4.37

$$|\psi 00\rangle = \alpha|000\rangle + \beta|100\rangle \xrightarrow{\text{CNOT}_{2,1}} \alpha|000\rangle + \beta|110\rangle \xrightarrow{\text{CNOT}_{2,0}} \alpha|000\rangle + \beta|111\rangle$$
$$\xrightarrow{H^{\otimes 3}} \alpha|+++\rangle + \beta|---\rangle.$$

4.38 (a) $|0++\rangle$. (b) $|1-+\rangle$. (c) $|1+-\rangle$. (d) $|0--\rangle$. (e) It outputs 0 when there is an even number of $|-\rangle$'s, and outputs 1 when there is an odd number of $|-\rangle$'s.

4.39 In the top row, the Hadamard gate can be moved to the end of the circuit. In the next row, $H^2 = I$, so we can remove the Hadamard gates in the middle. In the next row, we can move the Hadamard gate to the beginning of the circuit.

4.40 (a) Probability $1 - \varepsilon^2$, and the resulting state is $\alpha|+++\rangle + \beta|---\rangle$, so there is no error to correct.
(b) Probability ε^2, and the resulting state is $\alpha|-++\rangle - \beta|+--\rangle$, so we apply $Z \otimes I \otimes I$ to get $\alpha|+++\rangle - \beta|---\rangle$, then $X \otimes I \otimes I$ to get $\alpha|+++\rangle + \beta|---\rangle$.
(c) Probability zero.
(d) Probability zero.

4.41 (a)

$$|\psi 00000000\rangle = \alpha|000000000\rangle + \beta|100000000\rangle$$
$$\xrightarrow{\text{CNOT}_{8;5,2}} \alpha|000000000\rangle + \beta|100100100\rangle$$

(b)

$$\xrightarrow{H_8,H_5,H_2} \alpha|+\rangle|00\rangle|+\rangle|00\rangle|+\rangle|00\rangle + \beta|-\rangle|00\rangle|-\rangle|00\rangle|-\rangle|00\rangle$$
$$= \alpha \frac{1}{\sqrt{2}}(|0\rangle + |1\rangle)|00\rangle \frac{1}{\sqrt{2}}(|0\rangle + |1\rangle)|00\rangle \frac{1}{\sqrt{2}}(|0\rangle + |1\rangle)|00\rangle$$
$$+ \beta \frac{1}{\sqrt{2}}(|000\rangle - |100\rangle) \frac{1}{\sqrt{2}}(|000\rangle - |100\rangle) \frac{1}{\sqrt{2}}(|000\rangle - |100\rangle)$$
$$= \frac{\alpha}{\sqrt{2}}(|000\rangle + |100\rangle)(|000\rangle + |100\rangle)(|000\rangle + |100\rangle)$$
$$+ \frac{\beta}{\sqrt{2}}(|000\rangle - |100\rangle)(|000\rangle - |100\rangle)(|000\rangle - |100\rangle)$$

(c)

$$\xrightarrow{\text{CNOTs}} \frac{\alpha}{\sqrt{2}}\left(|000\rangle + |111\rangle\right)\left(|000\rangle + |111\rangle\right)\left(|000\rangle + |111\rangle\right)$$

$$+ \frac{\beta}{\sqrt{2}}\left(|000\rangle - |111\rangle\right)\left(|000\rangle - |111\rangle\right)\left(|000\rangle - |111\rangle\right)$$

$$= \alpha|0_L\rangle + \beta|1_L\rangle.$$

4.42 Qubits q_6, q_5, and q_1 flipped. Correct by applying an X gate to each one.

4.43 See https://bit.ly/3wvdGrI:

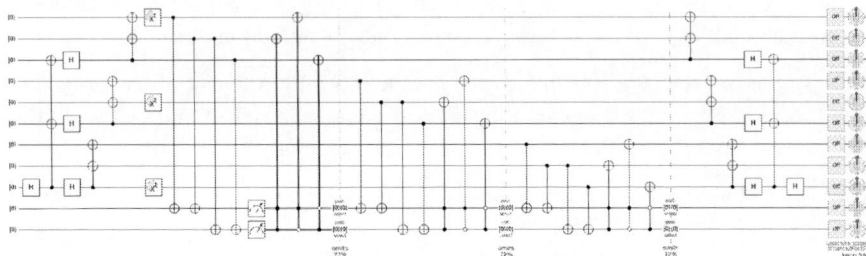

4.44 Answers vary.

4.45 See https://bit.ly/309WJXu:

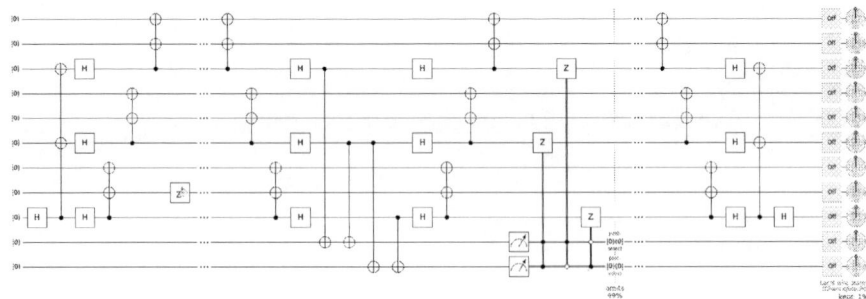

4.46 (a) Qubits $|q_7\rangle$, $|q_3\rangle$, and $|q_1\rangle$ flipped. Fix by applying the X gate to each one. (b) Triplet$_0$ has a phase flip. Fix by applying a Z gate to any one of $|q_2\rangle$, $|q_1\rangle$, or $|q_0\rangle$.

Exercises of Chapter 5

5.1 Answers vary.

5.2 All 1024 times, the output should be 111.

5.3 (a) $U_2(0, \pi)$. (b) $U_1(-\pi/4)$. (c) $U_3(\theta, -\pi/2, \pi/2)$.

(d)

```
gate cz a,b
{
    h b;
    cx a,b;
    h b;
}
```

(e)

```
gate ccx a,b,c
{
    h c;
    cx b,c;
    tdg c;
    cx a,c;
    t c;
    cx b,c;
    tdg c;
    cx a,c;
    t b;
    t c;
    h c;
    cx a,b;
    t a;
    tdg b;
    cx a,b;
}
```

5.4 (a)

```
OPENQASM 2.0;
include "qelib1.inc";

qreg q[3];
creg c[3];

h q[2];
cx q[2], q[1];
cx q[0], q[1];
h q[0];
cx q[1], q[2];
cz q[0], q[2];

measure q -> c;
```

(b)

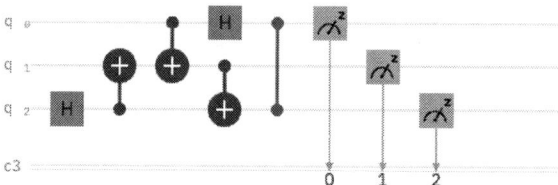

(c) $|000\rangle$, $|001\rangle$, $|010\rangle$, or $|011\rangle$, each with probability $1/4$.

5.5 Answers vary.

Exercises of Chapter 6

6.1 Answers vary.

6.2 $|0\rangle$ with probability $1/2$, and the state collapses to $\frac{\sqrt{3}}{2}|00\rangle + \frac{1}{2}|01\rangle = |0\rangle\left(\frac{\sqrt{3}}{2}|0\rangle + \frac{1}{2}|1\rangle\right)$. $|1\rangle$ with probability $1/2$, and the state collapses to $\frac{1}{2}|10\rangle + \frac{\sqrt{3}}{2}|11\rangle = |1\rangle\left(\frac{1}{2}|0\rangle + \frac{\sqrt{3}}{2}|1\rangle\right)$. Partially entangled.

6.3 $|0\rangle$ with probability $1/2$, and the state collapses to $|01\rangle$. $|1\rangle$ with probability $1/2$, and the state collapses to $|10\rangle$. Maximally entangled.

6.4 (a) right now. (b) space, space.

6.5 (a)

$$HTHS\frac{1}{\sqrt{4+2\sqrt{2}}}\left[(1+\sqrt{2})|0\rangle + |1\rangle\right] = \frac{1+\sqrt{2}+i}{\sqrt{4+2\sqrt{2}}}|0\rangle = e^{i\theta}|0\rangle,$$

$$\text{where } \theta = \tan^{-1}\left(\frac{1}{1+\sqrt{2}}\right),$$

$$HTHS\frac{1}{\sqrt{4-2\sqrt{2}}}\left[(1-\sqrt{2})|0\rangle + |1\rangle\right] = \frac{1-\sqrt{2}+i}{\sqrt{4-2\sqrt{2}}}|1\rangle = e^{i\theta}|1\rangle,$$

$$\text{where } \theta = \pi - \tan^{-1}\left(1+\sqrt{2}\right).$$

(b)

$$HT^{\dagger}HS\frac{1}{\sqrt{4+2\sqrt{2}}}\left[(-1-\sqrt{2})|0\rangle + |1\rangle\right] = \frac{-1-\sqrt{2}+i}{\sqrt{4+2\sqrt{2}}}|0\rangle = e^{i\theta}|0\rangle,$$

$$\text{where } \theta = \pi + \tan^{-1}\left(1-\sqrt{2}\right),$$

$$HT^{\dagger}HS\frac{1}{\sqrt{4-2\sqrt{2}}}\left[(-1+\sqrt{2})|0\rangle + |1\rangle\right] = \frac{-1+\sqrt{2}+i}{\sqrt{4-2\sqrt{2}}}|1\rangle = e^{i\theta}|1\rangle,$$

$$\text{where } \theta = \tan^{-1}\left(1+\sqrt{2}\right).$$

6.6 (a) $\frac{2-\sqrt{2}}{8}$. (b) $\frac{2+\sqrt{2}}{8}$. (c) $\frac{2+\sqrt{2}}{8}$. (d) $\frac{2-\sqrt{2}}{8}$. (e) $\frac{-1}{\sqrt{2}}$.

6.7 (a) photons. (b) $-2 \le S \le 2$. (c) $S = 2.70 \pm 0.05$. (d) $S = 2.697 \pm 0.015$. (e) disagree.

6.8 (a) electron. (b) detection loophole. (c) 1.3 kilometers. (d) CHSH-Bell inequality, $S \le 2$. (e) 2.42 ± 0.20. (f) 0.039.

6.9 $\frac{1}{\sqrt{2}}(|++\rangle + |--\rangle)$.

6.10 (a) realism. (b) superposition. (c) incomplete, hidden variables. (d) locality, Locality, speed of light. (e) entangled pair, instantly, local hidden variables (f) forces (g) hidden variables, Nothing, no correlation (h) defined values, spooky action (i) Bell inequalities, (j) violated, faster than (k) local hidden variables (l) realism, locality (m) consistent, information (n) Copenhagen

6.11 (b) $|000\rangle$ or $|111\rangle$, each with probability $1/2$.
(c) No. $|000\rangle$ and $|111\rangle$ are product states.

6.12 (b) $\frac{1}{\sqrt{2}}(|001\rangle + |010\rangle)$ with probability $2/3$ or $|100\rangle$ with probability $1/3$.
(c) $\frac{1}{\sqrt{2}}(|001\rangle + |010\rangle) = |0\rangle|\Psi^+\rangle$, so there is entanglement between the right two qubits. $|100\rangle$ is not entangled.

6.13 $\langle\Phi^+|\Phi^+\rangle = 1$, $\langle\Phi^+|\Psi^+\rangle = 0$, $\langle\Phi^+|\Phi^-\rangle = 0$, $\langle\Phi^+|\Psi^-\rangle = 0$, $\langle\Psi^+|\Psi^+\rangle = 1$, $\langle\Psi^+|\Phi^-\rangle = 0$, $\langle\Psi^+|\Psi^-\rangle = 0$, $\langle\Phi^-|\Phi^-\rangle = 1$, $\langle\Phi^-|\Psi^-\rangle = 0$, $\langle\Psi^-|\Psi^-\rangle = 1$.

6.14 (a) 4. (b) 2. (c) 4.

6.15 (a) $|11\rangle$. (b) Answers vary. (c) In the middle section, instead of applying X and Z, Alice simply applies X.

6.16 (b)

$|00\rangle$ with probability $1/4$, collapses to $|00\rangle\,(\beta|0\rangle + \alpha|1\rangle)$,
$|01\rangle$ with probability $1/4$, collapses to $|01\rangle\,(\alpha|0\rangle + \beta|1\rangle)$,
$|10\rangle$ with probability $1/4$, collapses to $|10\rangle\,(-\beta|0\rangle + \alpha|1\rangle)$,
$|11\rangle$ with probability $1/4$, collapses to $|11\rangle\,(\alpha|0\rangle - \beta|1\rangle)$.

(c)

$|00\rangle\,(\beta|0\rangle + \alpha|1\rangle)$, X gate
$|01\rangle\,(\alpha|0\rangle + \beta|1\rangle)$, nothing
$|10\rangle\,(-\beta|0\rangle + \alpha|1\rangle)$, X then Z gates
$|11\rangle\,(\alpha|0\rangle - \beta|1\rangle)$. Z gate.

6.17 (b)

$|000\rangle$ with probability $1/4$, collapses to $|000\rangle\,(\alpha|0\rangle + \beta|1\rangle)$,
$|010\rangle$ with probability $1/4$, collapses to $|010\rangle\,(\beta|0\rangle + \alpha|1\rangle)$,
$|100\rangle$ with probability $1/4$, collapses to $|100\rangle\,(\alpha|0\rangle - \beta|1\rangle)$,
$|110\rangle$ with probability $1/4$, collapses to $|110\rangle\,(-\beta|0\rangle + \alpha|1\rangle)$.

(c)

$|000\rangle\,(\alpha|0\rangle + \beta|1\rangle)$, nothing
$|010\rangle\,(\beta|0\rangle + \alpha|1\rangle)$, X gate

$|100\rangle\,(\alpha|0\rangle-\beta|1\rangle)$, Z gate

$|110\rangle\,(-\beta|0\rangle+\alpha|1\rangle)$, X then Z gates.

6.18 (b)

$|00\rangle$ with probability $1/4$, collapses to $|00\rangle\,(\alpha|00\rangle+\beta|11\rangle)$,

$|01\rangle$ with probability $1/4$, collapses to $|01\rangle\,(\beta|00\rangle+\alpha|11\rangle)$,

$|10\rangle$ with probability $1/4$, collapses to $|10\rangle\,(\alpha|00\rangle-\beta|11\rangle)$,

$|11\rangle$ with probability $1/4$, collapses to $|11\rangle\,(-\beta|00\rangle+\alpha|11\rangle)$.

(d)

$|000\rangle\,(\alpha|0\rangle+\beta|1\rangle)$, nothing

$|001\rangle\,(\alpha|0\rangle-\beta|1\rangle)$, Z gate

$|010\rangle\,(\beta|0\rangle+\alpha|1\rangle)$, X gate

$|011\rangle\,(\beta|0\rangle-\alpha|1\rangle)$, Z then X

$|100\rangle\,(\alpha|0\rangle+\beta|1\rangle)$, nothing

$|101\rangle\,(\alpha|0\rangle-\beta|1\rangle)$, Z gate

$|110\rangle\,(-\beta|0\rangle+\alpha|1\rangle)$, X then Z gates

$|111\rangle\,(-\beta|0\rangle-\alpha|1\rangle)$, Z then X then Z gates.

6.19 1000011 1101000 1100001 1110010 1101100 1101001 1100101 = Charlie.

6.20 (a) 3. (b) 1.

6.21 (a) 7493. (b) Any e satisfying $\gcd(e,7308)=1$. (c) $d=e^{-1} \bmod 7308$.

6.22 1 679 734.

6.23 1 501 096.

6.24 (a) 330 bits, 1991. (b) As of this writing, RSA 250, 829 bits, 2020. (c) $200,000.

6.25 $|-\rangle,|+\rangle,|0\rangle,|1\rangle,|0\rangle,|+\rangle,|+\rangle,|-\rangle,|-\rangle$.

6.26 0011.

6.27 $\log_{0.75}(0.01)=16$.

Exercises of Chapter 7

7.1 (a)

x y	x $y \oplus f(x)$
0 0	0 1
0 1	0 0
1 0	1 0
1 1	1 1

(b) Yes, since the outputs are unique. (c)

$$U_f = \begin{pmatrix} 0 & 1 & 0 & 0 \\ 1 & 0 & 0 & 0 \\ 0 & 0 & 1 & 0 \\ 0 & 0 & 0 & 1 \end{pmatrix}.$$

(d) $U_f^\dagger U_f = I$.

7.2 (a) $f(0) = 1$:

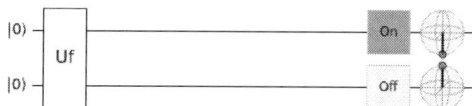

(b) $f(1) = 0$:

7.3 $\left(\frac{\sqrt{3}}{2}|0\rangle + \frac{1}{2}|1\rangle \right)|-\rangle \;=\; \frac{\sqrt{3}}{2\sqrt{2}}\left(|0\rangle|0\rangle - |0\rangle|1\rangle\right) \;+\; \frac{1}{2\sqrt{2}}\left(|1\rangle|0\rangle - |1\rangle|1\rangle\right)$

$\xrightarrow{U_f} \frac{\sqrt{3}}{2\sqrt{2}}\left(|0\rangle|0 \oplus f(0)\rangle - |0\rangle|1 \oplus f(0)\rangle\right) \;+\; \frac{1}{2\sqrt{2}}\left(|1\rangle|0 \oplus f(1)\rangle - |1\rangle|1 \oplus f(1)\rangle\right)$

$= \frac{\sqrt{3}}{2}(-1)^{f(0)}|0\rangle|-\rangle + \frac{1}{2}(-1)^{f(1)}|1\rangle|-\rangle = \left(\frac{\sqrt{3}}{2}(-1)^{f(0)}|0\rangle + \frac{1}{2}(-1)^{f(1)}|1\rangle \right)|-\rangle.$

7.4 (a) $|x\rangle|+\rangle$. (b) $|x\rangle|+\rangle$. (c) They are equal to the initial state, so the oracle does nothing to $|x\rangle|+\rangle$.

7.5 (a) The parity is 0 or even. See https://bit.ly/3s9rmsa:

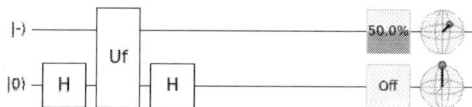

(b) $b_0 = 1$. (c) $b_1 = 1$. (d) $b_0 \oplus b_1 = 0$. (e) 2.

7.6 (a) The parity is 1 or odd.

(b) Answers vary.

7.7 $|0\rangle$ with probability $1/2$ or $|1\rangle$ with probability $1/2$.

7.8 (a) 1 or odd. (b) Four queries. (c) 8.

7.9 (a) 0 or even. (b) Five queries. (c) 9.

7.10 (a) 0.015625. (b) 0.0078125. (c) $c = 11$.

7.11 $(H \otimes H \otimes H)|000\rangle = |+++\rangle = (|000\rangle + |001\rangle + |010\rangle + |011\rangle + |100\rangle + |101\rangle + |110\rangle + |111\rangle)/2^{3/2}$. Get one of the basis states $|000\rangle$, $|001\rangle$, $|010\rangle$, $|011\rangle$, $|100\rangle$, $|101\rangle$, $|110\rangle$, or $|111\rangle$, each with probability $1/8$.

7.12 (a) See `https://bit.ly/3nwbFFS`:

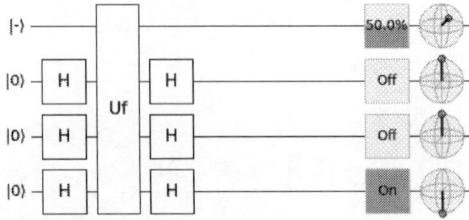

This yields $|100\rangle$, so the function is balanced.
(b)   (c) Balanced. (d) 5.

b_2	b_1	b_0	$f(b_0,b_1,b_2)$
0	0	0	0
0	0	1	0
0	1	0	0
0	1	1	0
1	0	0	1
1	0	1	1
1	1	0	1
1	1	1	1

7.13 (a) See `https://ibm.co/3yykVjK`:

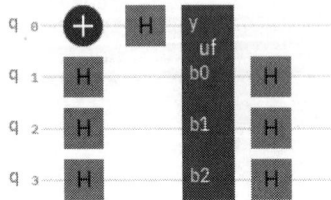

This yields $|000\rangle$, so the function is constant. (b) Answers vary.

7.14 (a) See `https://bit.ly/3m30FS6`:

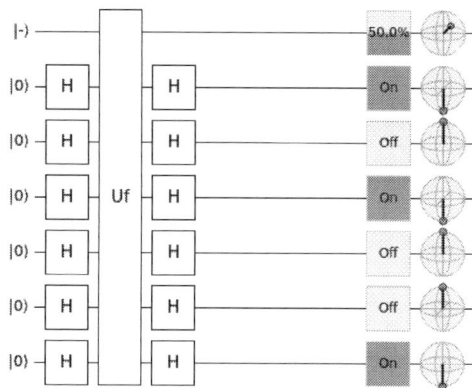

$s = 100101$. (b) Set $|y\rangle = |0\rangle$. Then, $|y \oplus f(b_5,\ldots,b_0)\rangle = |f(b_5,\ldots,b_0)\rangle$. Get $s_0 = f(000001) = 1, s_1 = f(000010) = 0, s_2 = f(000100) = 1, s_3 = f(001000) = 0, s_4 = f(010000) = 0, s_5 = f(100000) = 1$. (c) 6.

7.15 (a) See `https://ibm.co/3m0WPZB`:

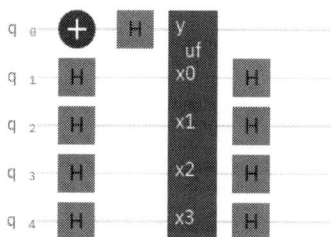

$s = 1101$. (b) Answers vary.

7.16

x	$(s+y) \cdot x$	$(-1)^{(s+y)\cdot x}$
000	0	1
001	1	-1
010	0	1
011	1	-1
100	0	1
101	1	-1
110	0	1
111	1	-1
$\sum_x (-1)^{(s+y)\cdot x}$:		0

7.17 (a) The x, y pairs are 000 and 010, 001 and 011, 100 and 110, and 101 and 111.
(b) There are many different possible truth tables for $f(x)$ that satisfies $f(x) = f(y)$. One is:

x	y
000	100
001	101
010	100
011	101
100	011
101	000
110	011
111	000

7.18 $s = 1100$.

7.19 (a) 0.706316. (b) 0.891232. (c) 0.970374. (d) 0.994123.

7.20 $s = 110$.

7.21 (a) 128. (b) $8001/8192 = 0.977$.

7.22 Geometrically, the initial angle is $\theta = \sin^{-1}(1/\sqrt{N}) = \sin^{-1}(1/2) = \pi/6$. Applying $R_s U_f$ to this adds 2θ to this, resulting in $3\theta = \pi/2$, which is perfectly aligned with $|w\rangle$.

7.23 (a) $1/N$. (b) $9/N - 24/N^2 + 16/N^3$.

7.24 (a) 4. (b) 16. (c) 3. (d) See https://bit.ly/3E3WnzZ:

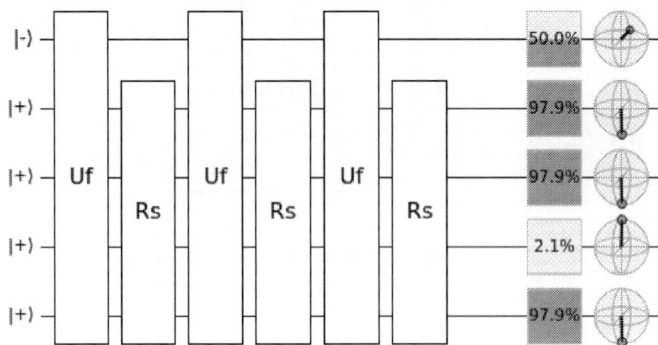

$w = 1011$.

(e)

x	$f(x)$
0000	0
0001	0
0010	0
0011	0
0100	0
0101	0
0110	0
0111	0
1000	0
1001	0
1010	0
1011	1
1100	0
1101	0
1110	0
1111	0

7.25 (a) 5. (b) 32. (c) 4. (d,e,f) See `https://bit.ly/3q4ExrK`

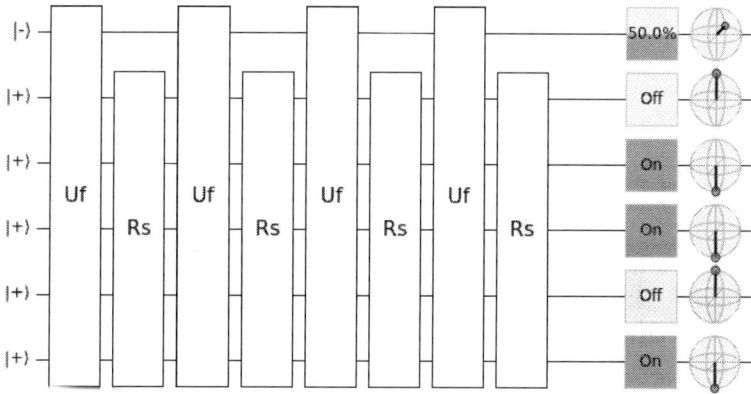

$w = 10110$.

7.26 $\phi_0 = 0.567, \phi_1 = 0.35 + 0.833i, \phi_2 = 0.415, \phi_3 = 0.35 - 0.833i$.

7.27 (a) G_4. (b) 440 Hz.

7.28 (a)

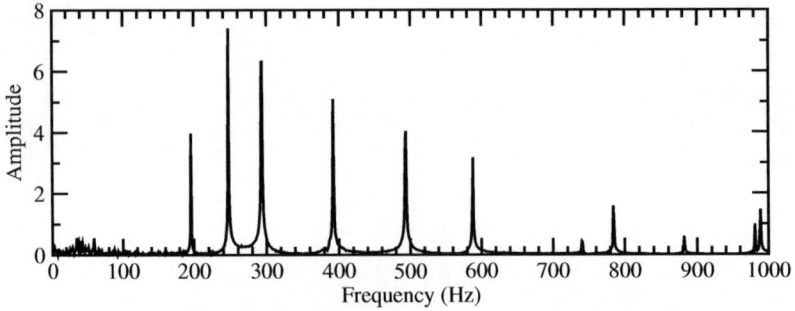

(b) 196 Hz, 247 Hz, 294 Hz. (c) G_3, B_3, D_4.

7.29 (a) M_{rs} is row r of $\text{QFT}^\dagger$ multiplied component-by-component with column s of QFT, then added together. $(\omega^p)^* = \omega^{-p}$, so $\text{QFT}^\dagger$ is the same matrix as QFT, except with negative powers. Then, ignoring the overall factor of $1/\sqrt{N}$, the rth row of $\text{QFT}^\dagger$ has terms $\omega^{-0r} = 1$, ω^{-1r}, ω^{-2r}, ..., $\omega^{-(N-1)r}$. Similarly, the sth column of QFT has terms $\omega^{0s} = 1$, ω^{-1s}, ω^{-2s}, ..., $\omega^{-(N-1)s}$, again ignoring the overall factor of $1/\sqrt{N}$. Thus,

$$M_{rs} = \frac{1}{N}\left(\omega^{-0r}\omega^{0s} + \omega^{-1r}\omega^{1s} + \omega^{-2r}\omega^{2s} + \cdots + \omega^{-(N-1)r}\omega^{(N-1)s}\right)$$

$$= \frac{1}{N}\sum_{k=0}^{N-1}\omega^{-kr}\omega^{ks} = \frac{1}{N}\sum_{k=0}^{N-1}\omega^{k(s-r)}.$$

(b) If $r = s$,

$$M_{rs} = \frac{1}{N}\sum_{k=0}^{N-1}\omega^0 = \frac{1}{N}\sum_{k=0}^{N-1}1 = \frac{1}{N}\underbrace{(1 + \cdots + 1)}_{N \text{ times}} = \frac{1}{N}N = 1.$$

(c) If $r \neq s$, then $c = s - r$ is a nonzero integer, and M is a geometric series with common ratio ω^c, i.e.,

$$M = \sum_{k=0}^{N-1}(\omega^c)^k = \frac{1}{N}\left[1 + \omega^c + (\omega^c)^2 + (\omega^c)^3 + \cdots + (\omega^c)^{N-1}\right].$$

Using the closed-form formula for a geometric series,

$$M = \frac{1}{N}\frac{1-\omega^{Nc}}{1-\omega^c} = \frac{1}{\sqrt{N}}\frac{1-(e^{2\pi i/N})^{Nc}}{1-\omega^c} = \frac{1}{\sqrt{N}}\frac{1-e^{2\pi ic}}{1-\omega^c} = \frac{1}{\sqrt{N}}\frac{1-1}{1-\omega^c} = 0.$$

7.30 See https://bit.ly/2ZgKfxr.

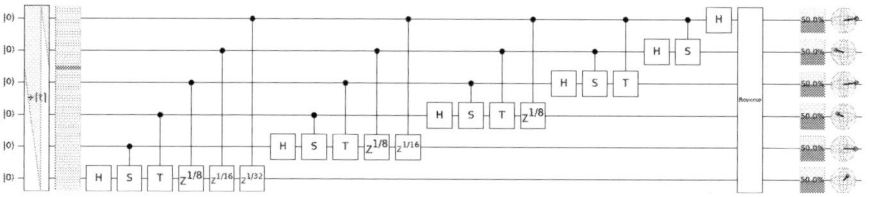

7.31

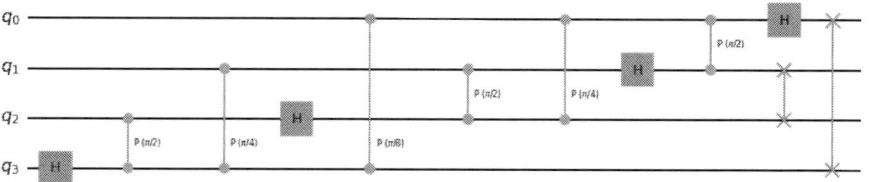

The Hadamard gate on q_2 can be swapped with the $P(\pi/8)$ gate, so the circuit is equivalent to the textbook's.

7.32 See https://bit.ly/3nJIPoB:

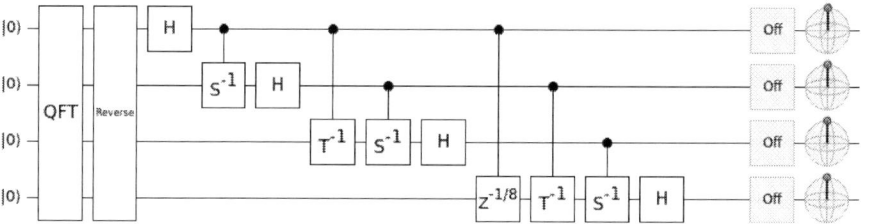

7.33

```python
# Number of qubits.
n = 4

# Create a quantum circuit.
qc = QuantumCircuit(n)

# Swap qubits.
for qubit in range(n//2):
    qc.swap(qubit, n - qubit - 1)

# Iterate through each target qubit from 0 to (n-1).
for target in range(n):
    # Iterate through the control qubits from 0 to (target-1).
    for control in range(target):
        # Calculate "r," the rotation by -2*pi/2**r.
        r = target - control + 1

        # Apply the controlled phase/rotation.
        qc.cp(-2*np.pi/2**r, control, target)

    # Apply the Hadamard gate.
```

```
    qc.h(target)

# Draw the circuit.
qc.draw()
```

7.34 (a) $H\begin{pmatrix} 1+\sqrt{2} \\ 1 \end{pmatrix} = \begin{pmatrix} 1+\sqrt{2} \\ 1 \end{pmatrix}$. (b) $H\begin{pmatrix} 1+\sqrt{2} \\ 1 \end{pmatrix} = -\begin{pmatrix} 1+\sqrt{2} \\ 1 \end{pmatrix}$.

7.35 $U\begin{pmatrix} \dfrac{2+i}{\sqrt{2}+1} \\ 1 \\ 1 \end{pmatrix} = e^{i\pi/4}\begin{pmatrix} \dfrac{2+i}{\sqrt{2}+1} \\ 1 \\ 1 \end{pmatrix}$.

7.36 (a,b) See https://tinyurl.com/emcnnxfk:

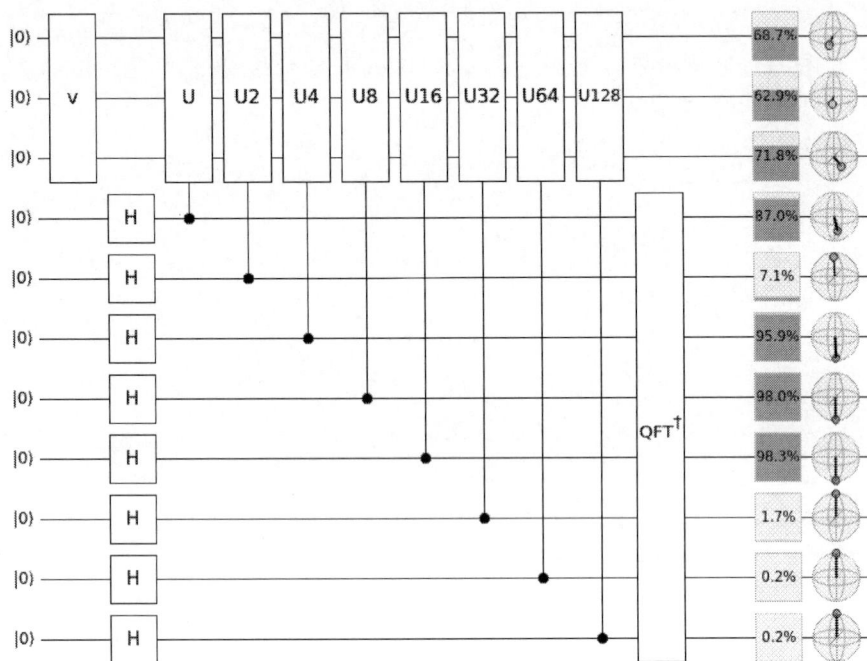

(c) 0.00011101. (d) 0.1133. (e) 0.7118. (f) $e^{0.7118i} = 0.7572 + 0.6532i$. (g) We only estimated j to eight binary places, and the actual value may need more bits.

7.37 $3/8, 1/2, 1/8$.

7.38 (a) $\gcd(4,5) = 1$. (b) 1, 4, 1, 4. (c) 1, 4. (d) 2.

7.39 (a) $\gcd(4,13) = 1$. (b) 1, 4, 3, 12, 9, 10, 1, 4, 3, 12, 9, 10. (c) 1, 4, 3, 12, 9, 10. (d) 6.

7.40 49 mod 131.

7.41 33 mod 197.

7.42 (a) $0.3438 = [0, 2, 1, 9, 1, 18, 1, 1, 1, 2]$. (b) Its convergents are 0, 1/2, 1/3, 10/29, 11/32, 208/605, 219/637, 427/1242, 646/1879, 1719/5000. (c) Best s/r is 1/3, so $s = 1$ and $r = 3$. (d) 3^3 mod 7 = 6 mod 7. (e) Not the period.

(a) $0.5 = [0, 1]$. (b) Its convergents are 0, 1/2. (c) Best s/r is 1/2, so $s = 1$ and $r = 2$. (d) 3^2 mod 7 = 2 mod 7. (e) Not the period.

(a) $0.6562 = [0, 1, 1, 1, 9, 1, 18, 1, 1, 1, 2]$. (b) Its convergents are 0, 1, 1/2, 2/3, 19/29, 21/32, 397/605, 418/637, 815/1242, 1233/1879, 3281/5000. (c) Best s/r is 2/3, so $s = 2$ and $r = 3$. (d) 3^3 mod 7 = 6 mod 7. (e) Not the period.

(a) $0.8438 = [0, 1, 5, 2, 2, 19, 8]$. (b) Its convergents are 0, 1, 5/6, 11/13, 27/32, 524/621, 4219/5000. (c) Best s/r is 5/6, so $s = 5$ and $r = 6$. (d) 3^6 mod 71 mod 7. (e) The period.

7.43 See `https://bit.ly/31E6M8h`:

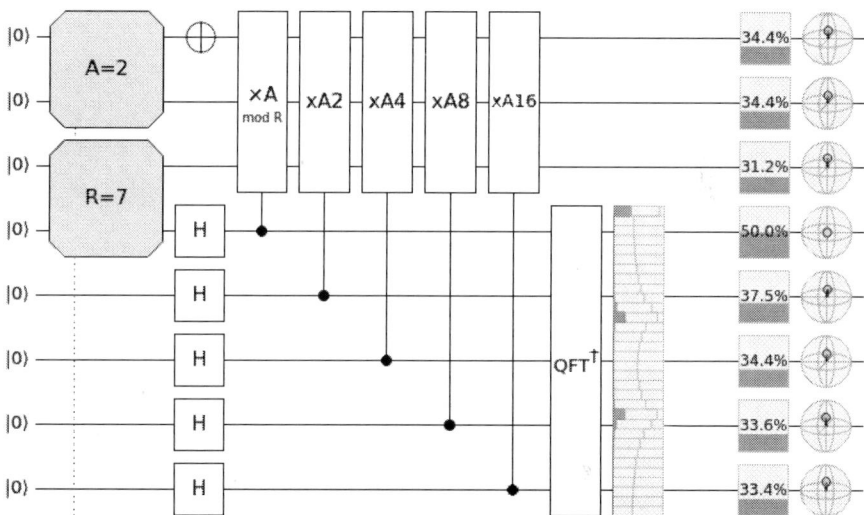

Probability	Binary Approx. of s/r	Decimal Approx. of s/r	Guess of s/r	7^r mod 13
33.3974%	$|00000\rangle$	0	N/A	N/A
5.7377%	$|01010\rangle$	0.3125	1/3	1
22.8399%	$|01011\rangle$	0.3438	1/3	1
22.8399%	$|10101\rangle$	0.6562	2/3	1
5.7377%	$|10110\rangle$	0.6875	2/3	1

The period is $r = 3$.

7.44 See `https://bit.ly/3y1rmLX`:

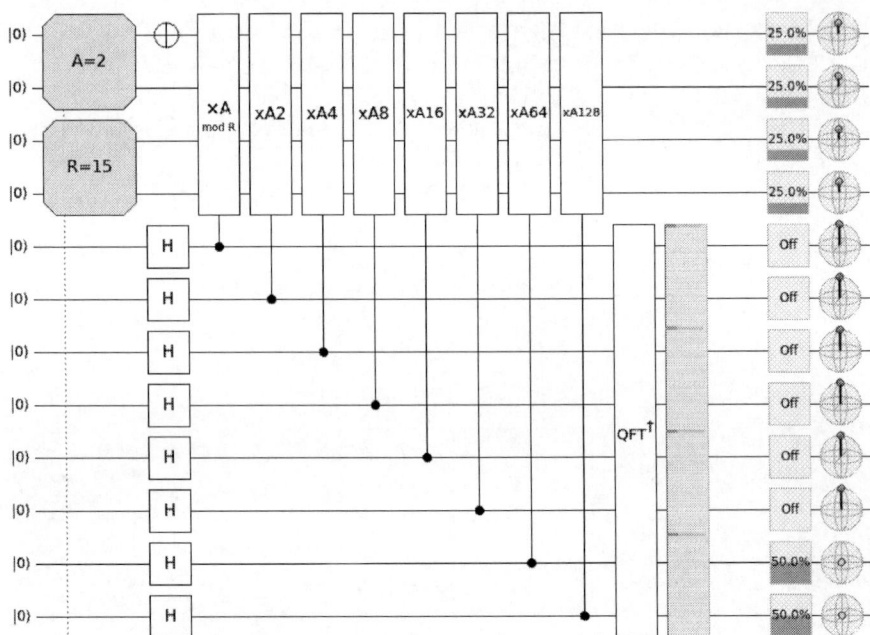

Probability	Binary Approx. of s/r	Decimal Approx. of s/r	Guess of s/r	2^r mod 15
25%	$|00000000\rangle$	0	N/A	N/A
25%	$|01000000\rangle$	0.25	1/4	1
25%	$|10000000\rangle$	0.5	1/2	4
25%	$|11000000\rangle$	0.75	3/4	1

The period is $r = 4$.

7.45 Answers vary.

7.46 (a) $\gcd(22, 209) = 11$. (b) $p = 11$, $q = 209/11 = 19$.

Index

Printed in Great Britain
by Amazon

d4b11836-7483-4497-b393-c41210419a53R01